A-Z of
Stoke City

A-Z of Stoke City

Tony Matthews

The Breedon Books
Publishing Company
Derby

First published in Great Britain by
The Breedon Books Publishing Company Limited
44 Friar Gate, Derby, DE1 1DA.
1997

© Tony Matthews 1997

All Rights Reserved. No part of this publication may be reproduced, stored in a retrieval system, or transmitted in any form, or by any means, electronic, mechanical, photocopying, recording or otherwise without the prior permission in writing of the Copyright holders, nor be otherwise circulated in any form or binding or cover other than in which it is published and without a similar condition being imposed on the subsequent publisher.

ISBN 1 85983 100 1

Printed and bound by Butler & Tanner, Frome, Somerset.
Jacket printed by Lawrence Allen Ltd, Weston-super-Mare, Somerset.
Colour film by RPS Ltd of Leicester.

Contents

A	Abandoned Games — Ancell	8-20
B	Bacos — Butler	20-48
C	Caernarven — Curtis	48-67
D	Da Costa — Dyson	67-77
E	Eardley — Eyres	77-81
F	Family Connections — Fursland	82-95
G	Gadsden — Gynn	95-105
H	Hackett — Hyslop	105-120
I	Ilkeston — Isle of Man	120-123
J	Jackson — Jump	124-128
K	Kamara — Knott	128-134
L	Lacey — Luton	134-142
M	McAlindon — Myatt	142-166
N	Naughton — Nyamah	166-170
O	O'Callaghan — Oxford	170-174
P	Page — Pugh	175-190
Q	Queens Park — Queens Park Rangers	190
R	Raisbeck — Russell	190-198
S	Sale — Swindon	198-224
T	Talbot — Twemlow	224-234
U	UEFA — Usherwood	234
V	Vernon — Viollet	235-237
W	Waddington — Wycombe	237-254
Y	Yates — Youth Cup	254-255
Z	Zenith Data	255

Acknowledgements

I would like to thank the following people for their contribution (knowingly or unknowingly) towards the compilation of the book A-Z of Stoke City : loyal Potters supporters Michael Bailey, Stephen Barnett, Reg Bennett, Julian Boodell, Maureen Bradburn, Ian Dale, Robert Edwards, David Eyre, Tony Johnson, Graham Lowe, Roger Martin, Wade Martin, Wilf Martin, Barry Pointon, Bob Shenton, Les Skeels, David Slack, Phil Snape, Tony Southall and Peter Wyatt; ex-Stoke City players George Berry, the late Eddie Clamp, Terry Conroy, Alan Dodd, Sir Stanley Matthews, Jimmy O'Neill, John Ritchie, Eric Skeels and Denis Smith; Mike Potts (Secretary of Stoke City FC); Tony Tams (Marketing Services Manager; Stoke City FC); Paul Bradbury (the Stoke City club photographer); my wife Margaret Matthews; Alan Smith (formerly of Lion Press); fellow statisticians Jim Creasy, Mike Davage, Doug Lamming, Colin Mackenzie, and Ray Spiller; those respected members of the AFS whose 'Complete Records' and 'Who's Whos' to which I have I continually referred.

Introduction

TO CELEBRATE the end of an era – 119 years of playing football at The Victoria Ground – I felt the time was right to elaborate on Stoke City's history and compile a detailed A-Z of the club. Included in this book is a complete 'Who's Who' – biographies of 800-or-so players who have served the Potters in a major League or Cup game down the years.

Stoke's playing record against every senior club they have met is given in full detail.

There is a list of all the players who have gained full and intermediate honours on the international scene while with the club; sections on abandoned matches, admission charges, age (the youngest and oldest players at the club); appearances, casualties, club colours, cricketing-footballers, family links, firsts, gate receipts, goalscoring, hat-tricks, long service, managers and coaches, nicknames, overseas players, overseas tours, partnerships, sendings-off and transfers.

Stoke's exploits in the FA Cup, League Cup and European competitions are covered in depth, as well as coverage of the club's seasons in the Birmingham and District League, Southern League and in Wartime football, plus reserve team information and Stoke's ventures in the FA Youth Cup.

There is a history of The Victoria Ground and details of Stoke City's new headquarters, The Britannia Stadium.

With over 200 pictures added to the text, this A-Z is much more than a history book – it is a complete encyclopaedia of one of Britain's oldest football clubs, formed in 1868 and still going strong.

Whilst every care has been taken in the preparation of this book, invariably there will be an occasional error or omission contained somewhere in the text and therefore the compiler asks that if any are found, he would be pleased to receive such information through the publishers.

Tony Matthews
Summer 1997

ABANDONED GAMES

Over the years Stoke have been very fortunate not to have had more games abandoned than the ones listed below. Result of the rearranged game in brackets with Stoke's score given first in each case.

Football League

23 Nov	1889	v Notts Co	(h) 2-2	– 68 mins (1-1)
18 Nov	1893	v Sheffield W	(a) 1-3	– 70 mins (1-4)
9 Mar	1895	v West Brom A	(h) 1-2	– 70 mins (1-1)
6 Apr	1895	v Sheffield W	(a) 0-0	– 72 mins (4-2)
25 Jan	1896	v Burnley	(a) 0-4	– 70 mins (0-2)
7 Jan	1899	v Burnley	(a) 1-2	– 60 mins (1-1)
24 Dec	1904	v Small Heath	(h) 0-0	– 18 mins (1-0)
25 Nov	1922	v Blackburn R	(a) 1-0	– 86 mins (5-1)
15 Mar	1947	v Aston Villa	(a) 2-2	– 57 mins (1-0)
2 Jan	1954	v West Ham U	(a) 1-4	– 84 mins (2-2)
3 Dec	1960	v Liverpool	(h) 0-0	– 45 mins (3-1)
22 Dec	1962	v Swansea T	(h) 0-0	– 41 mins (2-0)

Southern League

2 Dec	1911	v QPR	(h) 0-2	–88 mins (result allowed to stand)

FA Cup

11 Jan	1913	v Reading	(h) 2-1	– 25 mins (2-2)
11 Jan	1930	v Doncaster R	(a) 3-2	– 76 mins (0-1)
6 Jan	1979	v Oldham A	(h) 2-0	– 45 mins (0-1)

Friendly/Other Matches

1883	v West Brom A	(h) 1-1	– 80 mins
1883	v Burslem Port Vale	(a) 0-3	– 26 mins
1886	v Nottingham F	(a) 0-2	– 60 mins (as a draw)
1983	v Qatar	(a) 1-0	– abandoned second-half

● The Stoke-Sheffield Wednesday game in April 1895 was abandoned after the referee had been hit by a clod of earth thrown by a spectator.

● On 25 November 1922, Stoke's train, en route to Blackburn, was delayed due to a hold-up further down the line. Two taxis were summoned to transfer the players to the ground, but one of them with six members inside, broke down. The match at Ewood Park finally started 32 minutes late and was abandoned due to bad light with just four minutes remaining with Stoke a goal in front. To make matters worse, Rovers won the rearranged game 5-1 and Stoke were fined £25 for being late for the initial match.

● The vital North Staffordshire District League game between Stoke and Port Vale on 3 April 1910, was abandoned after 81 minutes when the home supporters invaded the pitch and tried to throw the visiting goalkeeper and former Stoke player Dicky Roose into the River Trent. Vale were leading 2-0 at the time and this score was allowed to stand.

Amazingly, this game between Stoke and Everton at The Victoria Ground in the early 1980s went the full distance. Robbie James and Peter Reid can just be seen through the blizzard.

● The Leeds United-Stoke City FA Cup-tie in season 1962-63 was postponed 12 times before it finally went ahead.

ABERDARE ATHLETIC

Stoke's playing record against the Welsh club is:
Southern League

Venue	P	W	D	L	F	A
Home	3	3	0	0	8	3
Away	3	3	0	0	10	4
Totals	6	6	0	0	18	7

These six games were played between 1910 and 1914. Stoke recorded two 4-2 away wins and a 4-1 home victory, the latter in season 1913-14 when Billy Herbert scored a hat-trick.

Players with both clubs: Percy Brooke, Jim Martin, Sam Spencer and Billy Tompkinson.

ABERTILLERY

Stoke's playing record against Abertillery is:
Southern League

Venue	P	W	D	L	F	A
Home	1	1	0	0	3	0
Away	1	0	0	1	0	1
Totals	2	1	0	1	3	1

These two games took place in season 1913-14. A crowd numbering 8,000 saw the game at Stoke and there were 3,500 fans present for the fixture in Wales.

Former Stoke inside-forward Amos Baddeley was player-manager of Abertillery for a short time before World War One.

ACCRINGTON

Stoke's full playing record against the Lancashire club who were also founder members of the Football League in 1888, is:

Venue	P	W	D	L	F	A
Home	4	2	1	1	4	8
Away	4	0	0	4	3	12
Totals	8	2	1	5	7	20

FA Cup

Venue	P	W	D	L	F	A
Away	1	0	0	1	1	2

When Stoke beat Accrington 7-1 at home in March 1890, Bob Ramsey became the first Potter to score a hat-trick in a League game and he did so in front of 2,500 fans.

Accrington's best League win over Stoke is 5-2 at Peel Park in December 1892.

The FA Cup meeting was a 1st qualifying round tie which took place in January 1893 before 4,000 spectators.

ACCRINGTON STANLEY

Football League

Venue	P	W	D	L	F	A
Home	1	1	0	0	1	0
Away	1	1	0	0	1	0
Totals	2	2	0	0	2	0

Both these games were played in Stoke City's Third Division North championship-winning campaign of 1926-27. A crowd of 5,803 saw Dick Johnson score at Peel Park early in December and 8,440 fans cheered Johnny Eyres' 49th-minute winning goal at The Victoria Ground in late April. This latter victory clinched the title for the Potters.

Players with both clubs: Percy Brooke, Ernie Cull, Sam Davis, Frank Hesham, Jack Howshall and Edgar Powell.

ADAM, James

A Glaswegian, born on 13 May 1931, Adam played his early football as an amateur with Blantyre Celtic and Aldershot. He turned professional with the latter club in 1950 and two years later moved to Spennymoor United. Following spells with Berwick Rangers and Hibernian, he returned to League football with Luton Town in 1953. After six seasons and 137 League outings for the Hatters he was transferred to Aston Villa (1959). Stoke secured his services for £5,000 in July 1961 and in two years at The Victoria Ground, this fast and elusive winger, who could occupy both flanks, hit seven goals in 24 appearances. He left Stoke in July 1962 to join Falkirk.

ADAMS, Elijah

Longton-born centre-forward (now deceased) Adams had just two senior outings for Stoke, both in March 1911. He joined the club from Kidsgrove as a 22-year-old earlier that season and left The Victoria Ground for Burslem Port Vale.

ADAMS, Michael Richard

Micky Adams

Born in Sheffield on 8 November 1961, hard working midfielder Adams played in well over 500 games as a professional before taking over as player-manager at Craven Cottage in 1995. Adams started off his professional career with Gillingham in November 1979. He then joined Coventry City for £75,000 (July 1983) and went on to play for Leeds United (signed for £110,000 in January 1987), Southampton (bought for £250,000 in March 1989), Stoke City (from March to July 1994), scoring three goals in his 10 League outings for the Potters, and Fulham. Adams won England youth honours as a teenager and in 1997 guided the Cottagers to promotion from the Third Division.

ADAMS, Neil James

An orthodox outside-right (or wide midfielder in present-day terms) Adams was born in Stoke on 23 November 1965 and began his career at The Victoria Ground in 1983, turning professional two years later (July 1985). He scored four goals in 39 first-team games for the Potters before moving to Everton for £150,000 in July 1986. With the Merseysiders he won a First Division championship medal (1987) and from Goodison Park he went to Oldham Athletic (initially on loan, signing permanently in June 1989 for £100,000). In February 1994, almost three years after helping the Latics win the Second Division title, he was transferred to Norwich City for £250,000. An England Under-21 international (one cap), Adams passed the milestone of 350 club appearances during 1996-97.

ADMISSION PRICES

Before the commencement of League Football in 1888-89, the general charge for admission to a Stoke home game varied from 1d (½p) and 6d (3p). The 6d charge remained as a minimum entrance fee until after World War One (1919) when it was increased to one shilling (5p). For the next 23 years that shilling admission price remained in force, but for the 1942-43 wartime season it went up to 1s 3d (7p).

From then on increases on the minimum entrance fee and the highest admittance charge, have both been gradual.

Here is a guide to the dearest adult entrance prices to The Victoria Ground over the last 40 years.

Seasons	Terraces	Seats
1955-56	2s 0d (10p)	4s 6d (23p)
1960-61	2s 6d (13p)	5s 0d (25p)
1963-64	3s 0d (15p)	6s 0d (30p)
1964-65	3s 6d (18p)	7s 5d (38p)
1965-66	4s 0d (20p)	8s 6d (43p)
1967-68	5s 0d (25p)	10s 0d (50p)
1970-71	9s 0d (45p)	15s 0d (75p)
1972-73	10s 0d (50p)	17s 6d (87p)
1974-75	60p	£1.00
1978-79	£1.00	£1.50
1979-80	£1.30	£2.30
1980-81	£1.50	£2.50
1981-82	£2.00	£3.00
1984-85	£2.50	£5.00
1987-88	£3.00	£6.00
1989-90	£4.00	£7.00
1990-91	£4.50	£7.50
1992-93	£6.00	£9.00
1995-96	£8.00	£12.00
1996-97	£9.00	£13.00

A Family Ticket was introduced during the mid-1990s.

● For season 1997-98 when Stoke moved to their new all-seater Britannia Stadium, the cheapest seat for an adult was £11, the dearest £16.

Season Tickets

An 1880s ground season ticket to watch Stoke cost the supporter 3s (15p) – in those days a club used to play between 15 and 20 home matches per season.

When League Football arrived in 1888-89, the average price for a season ticket was 5s (25p).

At the turn of the century (1900-01) the price had risen to 10s (50p) and in the first season after World War One (1919-20) a season ticket at The Victoria Ground was priced at 15s (75p).

Over the next 20 years or so the overall price rose slowly – in 1930 supporters paid 30s a time (£1.50); in 1934 it had risen to £2 per season ticket and just before League Football was suspended in 1939 the cost had climbed to three guineas (£3.15p).

Immediately after World War Two, the admission charge had reached £4 a time; it was £5 ten years later (in 1956) and in 1960 the average price of a season ticket was £8.

Between 1961 and 1974 season ticket prices went up slowly – from £9 to £10 to £12 to £15 to £18 – and for the 1974-75 campaign fans at The Victoria Ground were paying £20 (in the Boothen Stand) plus an extra £6 for five cup matches and £17 (plus £5) in the Butler Street Stand.

In 1979-80, the price for an adult of a Stoke City season ticket (in the main stand) was around the £60 mark (this was the norm up and down the country for the majority of First Division clubs). And since then the general cost of a season ticket has risen steadily, from £50 (terraces) and £100 (seats) in 1984-85, from £60/£120 in 1987-88, from £84/£147 in 1989-90, from £126/£198 in 1992-93, from £147/£200 in 1994-95 to a high of £273 for the 1996-97 campaign (the last at The Victoria Ground). Obviously prices fluctuated, depending on where the supporter to chose to watch his football.

● On moving to their new ground (The Britannia Stadium) in the summer of 1997, the dearest adult season ticket (without concession) was priced at £368. The cheapest was listed at £187.

Complimentary Tickets

For Football League matches, the visiting club can normally claim a total of 37 complimentary tickets – 25 for use by the players, manager and coach – and 12 for the directors. There is no set limit on how many complimentary tickets the home club can issue.

All-Ticket Games

In 1996-97, any all-ticket matches at The Victoria Ground, would have a 23,000 limit put on them by the local Police in conjunction with the club itself (for safety reasons).

Up until the 1950s there were no all-ticket matches at Stoke – the first game made all-ticket is believed to have been the Stoke City-Blackburn Rovers FA Cup-tie on 27 January 1962 when the gate was set at 50,000.

Since then only a few have had the all-ticket tag placed on them, although from time to time, there have been all-ticket arrangements made for visiting supporters.

AGE

Youngest players

Here is a list of the top 12 young players who have appeared in senior games for Stoke City since 1946-47:

Player	Debut age	Debut date
Peter Bullock	16 years, 153 days	April 1958
Gerry Bridgwood	16 years, 194 days	April 1961
Lee Fowler	16 years, 247 days	April 1988
Stanley Bevans	16 years, 349 days	March 1951
Mark Devlin	17 years, 15 days	February 1991
John Woodward	17 years, 42 days	February 1965
Steve Farrell	17 years, 47 days	April 1990
Steve Parkin	17 years, 120 days	March 1983

Paul Ware   17 years, 176 days   May 1988
Bill Asprey   17 years, 180 days   March 1954

● Stuart Roberts is the youngest goalkeeper ever to play for Stoke City, aged 17 years 258 days in December 1984 v Ipswich Town. Bob Dixon, John Farmer, Paul Reece and Roy John were all 18.

● Tony Ford, a Stoke City player for three years, 1986-89, holds the record for being the youngest League debutant for Grimsby Town.

● Garth Crooks is the youngest player ever to score a League hat-trick for Stoke. He was 20 years and eight days old when he netted three times at home against Blackburn Rovers in March 1978.

● Lee Chapman was aged 20 years, 345 days, when he netted a League hat-trick for Stoke against Norwich City in November 1980.

● Peter Shilton was the youngest ever FA Cup Final goalkeeper when he lined up for Leicester City against Manchester City in April 1969 at the age of 19 years, seven months.

● Paul Allen, who was with Stoke in the mid-1990s, is the youngest player to appear in an FA Cup Final this century – lining up for West Ham against Arsenal in 1980, aged 17 years 256 days.

● Another future Potters star, Howard Kendall, was 17 years 345 days old when he played for Preston against West Ham in the 1964 FA Cup Final.

Oldest players
This is a list of the top ten oldest players who have appeared in League games for Stoke City since 1946-47:

Player	Age	Date of game
Stan Matthews	50 years, 5 days	February 1965
Norman Wilkinson	41 years, 275 days	March 1952
Mick Mills	38 years, 289 days	October 1987
Frank Bowyer	38 years, 13 days	April 1960
John McCue	37 years, 217 days	March 1960
George Eastham	37 years, 6 days	September 1973
Mickey Thomas	36 years, 308 days	May 1991
Jock Kirton	36 years, 253 days	November 1952
Bill Robertson	36 years, 241 days	November 1959
Dave Watson	36 years, 200 days	April 1983

● In season 1934-35 full-back Bob McGrory played in all 42 First Division matches for Stoke City at the age of 43. This is a League record for most appearances made by a player over the age of 40 in a full season.

● Goalkeeper Jack Robertson (born March 1870) was 39 years, six months old when he joined Stoke in September 1909. He played his last game for the club in February 1911, at the age of 40 years, 11 months.

● Norman Wilkinson, another goalkeeper, was aged 42 when he left The Victoria Ground in July 1952 to join Oswestry Town.

● Stanley Matthews' last game for Stoke at the age of 50, was in the First Division against Fulham at The Victoria Ground in 1965.

● Matthews also holds the club record for being the oldest Stoke player to appear in a major Cup-tie. He was 49 years, two weeks old when he lined up against Swansea Town in the FA Cup competition in February 1964. He netted in the 2-2 draw against the Welsh club, and thus became the oldest player ever to score a goal for Stoke City.

● By coincidence, one of the oldest players ever to appear in a League or Cup match against Stoke is the same Stanley Matthews, who lined up for Blackpool against the Potters in a First Division match at Bloomfield Road in April 1953, at the age of 38 years, two months and two weeks.

● Tom Brittleton was 41 years, four months old when he joined Stoke in 1920. He played his last game for the club in April 1925, aged 46.

● Goalkeepers Bruce Grobbelaar and Peter Fox were both over 35 years of age when they played for Stoke City.

● George Eastham, at the age of 35 years, 161 days, was the oldest recipient of a League Cup winners' medal when he helped Stoke win the trophy in 1972.

● Ex-Stokie Stanley Matthews was 38 years of age when he won an FA Cup winners' medal with Blackpool in 1953 and another former Potters player, George Baddeley, was almost aged 38 when he played for West Brom in the 1912 FA Cup Final.

ALDERSHOT

Stoke's playing record against the Shots is:
FA Cup

Venue	P	W	D	L	F	A
Home	1	0	1	0	0	0
Away	2	1	1	0	3	0
Totals	3	1	2	0	3	0

Stoke never played Aldershot in League Football. The three meetings between the clubs were all in the FA Cup in 1960-61 when Stoke went through to round five by winning a 2nd replay 3-0 at neutral Molineux after two goalless draws. Dennis Wilshaw (2) and Bill Asprey scored those three goals in that vital third meeting.

Players with both clubs: Jimmy Adam, George Berry, Joe Buller, Ernie Cull, Phil Heath, Dave Puckett, Mark Stein, Brian Talbot and Arthur Tutin.

ALLEN, Anthony

Born shortly after the outbreak of World War Two in Stoke (27 November 1939) Allen, with his distinctive blond hair, was a splendid left-back, sure-footed with a fine tackle and temperament. He appeared in 473 games for Stoke City during the 1950s and '60s, helping the team win the Second Division championship in 1962-63 and reach the League Cup final the following year against Leicester City. Capped three times by England, he left The Victoria Ground for Bury in 1970, moving for a fee of £10,000. Later he went to South Africa to play for Hellenic FC returning to live and work in the Potteries in the 1980s as well as

assisting Stafford Rangers. Allen had a record run of 121 consecutive League appearances between March 1960 and March 1963.

ALLEN, Paul Kevin

Member of the famous footballing family, unlike most of his relatives Paul Allen was a midfielder who began his League career with West Ham in 1979. He made almost 200 appearances for the Hammers and followed up with more than 370 outings for Tottenham Hotspur who paid £400,000 for his services in 1985. He remained at White Hart Lane until 1993 when he joined Southampton for £550,000. He was on loan at both Luton and Stoke City during the 1994-95 season and scored once in 19 appearances for the Potters. In October 1995 Allen moved from The Dell to Swindon Town and in January 1997 he switched to Bristol City on a free transfer. Capped three times by England at Under-21 level, he won an FA Cup winners' medal with West Ham in 1980 at the age of 17 years, 256 days (the youngest such winner this century) and he collected a second FA Cup winners' medal with Spurs in 1991, later adding a Second Division championship medal to his collection with Swindon in 1995. In 1996-97 Allen passed the personal milestone of 675 appearances at League and Cup level.

ALLINSON, Ian J.R.

A winger or inside-forward, Allinson played in 11 League games for Stoke during the opening months of the 1987-88 season. Born in Hitchin in 1957, he made over 300 appearances for Colchester United and almost 100 for Arsenal before moving to the Potteries from Highbury. He remained with Stoke for just four months before moving to Luton Town for £15,000 and then back again to Colchester. In later years he became player-manager of Baldock Town and also

Ian Allinson

served with Stevenage Borough. He gained a Full Members' Cup runners up medal with Luton in 1988.

ALMOND, Henry John

Almond helped form Stoke (City) Football Club in 1868. Born in London on the 17 April 1850, the son of William Almond of Westminster, Almond junior played a useful game of soccer for his house team, Gownboys, at Charterhouse School between April 1863 and May 1868 and for the School first XI in season 1867-68. During his last year at Charterhouse, he assisted in the formation of the Stoke (City) club. Surprisingly, soon after leaving his educational studies, and skippering Stoke in their first few games (he scored the first ever Stoke goal incidentally against E.W.May's 15, Almond completely forgot about football (soccer) and became a very successful Civil Engineer, going abroad to work in Costa Rica for the Venezuela-based La Guayra and Caracus Railway Company. He died in 1910, aged 60.

ALMOND, John

Reserve outside-left who joined Stoke from his home-town club, Prescot Cables in 1935 and left the club for Tranmere Rovers for £250 after just three League outings for Potters (one goal scored). Born in Prescot in 1915, he played regularly for Shrewsbury Town for two seasons (1937-39) and guested for Crewe Alexandra during World War Two.

AMATEURS

In the club's early years each and every player was an amateur. Stoke eventually turned professional in 1885 – seven years after its formation.

Among the well-known amateur footballers who have been associated with Stoke City are defender John Ewart Beswick (two spells with the club between 1921 and 1926), Corinthian Willie Ferns (1890s), defender Sam Ashworth (early 1900s), forward Fred Hargreaves (scorer of 11 goals in 14 games in 1908-09), goalkeeper Horace Bailey, full-back Herbert Smith and outside-left Harold Hardman, who were all capped at amateur and full international levels by England as well as winning Olympic gold medals in 1908, and forward Len Hales, who also played for Crewe Alexandra and represented England against Germany in an unofficial international in season 1901-02.

Goalkeeper Harry Gregg was capped by Northern Ireland as an amateur along with inside-forward Sammy Smyth, and both players served Stoke City after having turned professional and won full caps for their country. Scotsman David Herd, too, won caps at both levels as did Dr Leigh Richmond Roose (the famous Welsh international) and 'Dai' Jones.

Liverpool-born centre-forward Harry Connor was the last amateur to play senior football for Stoke City FC, doing so in 1953.

ANDERSON, John H.

Diminutive Scottish inside-forward, born in Renfrewshire on 11 January 1937, who scored twice in 24 League games for Stoke City between 1957 and 1961. Spotted playing for Johnstone Burgh, Anderson had good ball skills, but never quite fulfilled the promise he had displayed north of the border. After National Service, he left The Victoria Ground on a free transfer for non-League side Bangor City.

ANDRADE, Jose Manuel Zay

A six-foot striker, born in Portugal in June 1970, Andrade was on loan to Stoke from Academica Coimbra from late March to early May 1995, appearing in four League games and scoring one goal. He sadly broke a leg in his last game (at Swindon) and returned to Portugal during the summer of 1995.

ANDREW, Ronald E.H.

Andrew was a dogged but natural centre-half (or right-back) who scored twice in 129 League and Cup appearances for Stoke between 1957 and 1963. Born in Ellesmere Port in 1936, he joined staff at The Victoria Ground from Ellesmere Port Town in May 1954 (initially as reserve to Ken Thomson) and left the Potters for rivals Port Vale 10 years later. He retired from competitive football in 1955.

ANGLO-ITALIAN CUP

Stoke City have played a total of 23 games in the Anglo-Italian Cup competition, the details of which are as follows:

Season 1970-71

v AS Roma	(home)	draw	2-2
v Verona	(home)	won	2-0
v AS Roma	(away)	won	1-0
v Verona	(away)	draw	1-1

Season 1971-72

v Cantanzaro	(away)	won	3-0
v AS Roma	(away)	lost	0-2
v Cantanzaro	(home)	won	2-0
v AS Roma	(home)	lost	1-2

Season 1993-94

v Wolves	(away)	draw	3-3
v Birmingham C	(home)	won	2-0
v Cosenza	(home)	won	2-1
v Fiorentina	(home)	draw	0-0
v Padova	(away)	lost	0-3
v Pescara	(away)	lost	1-2

Season 1994-95

v Cesena	(away)	won	2-0
v Ancona	(home)	draw	1-1
v Udinese	(away)	won	3-1
v Piacenza	(home)	won	4-0
v Notts County	(away)	draw	0-0
v Notts County	(home)	draw	0-0*

County won 3-2 on penalties

Season 1995-96

v Foggia	(away)	draw	1-1
v Salernitana	(home)	draw	2-2
v Brescia	(home)	draw	1-1

● John Ritchie scored that dramatic winning goal in the Olympic Stadium against AS Roma in the 1970-71 tournament when Stoke finished third in the English Group.

● Martin Carruthers netted twice in Stoke's 4-0 win over Piacenza in November 1994 and in that same season, Stoke reached the English Area Final, only to lose on penalties (at The Victoria Ground) to Notts County, after playing out two goalless draws.

● In season 1995-96 Stoke were scheduled to play a fourth game away to Reggiana, but heavy rain caused the postponement of the contest with neither side receiving any points.

Stoke's full record in the competition is:

Venue	P	W	D	L	F	A
Home	12	5	6	1	19	9
Away	11	4	4	3	15	13
Totals	23	9	10	4	34	22

ANGLO-SCOTTISH CUP

Stoke participated in this short-lived competition in seasons 1970-71 and 1971-72. The results of the six games played are as follows:

Season 1970-71

v Motherwell	(away)	lost	0-1
v Motherwell	(home)	won	2-1*

Motherwell won 4-3 on penalties after the scores had finished level over two legs.

Season 1971-72

v Motherwell	(away)	won	1-0
v Motherwell	(home)	won	4-1
v Derby County	(away)	lost	2-3
v Derby County	(home)	draw	2-2

Stoke's full record in the competition is:

Venue	P	W	D	L	F	A
Home	3	2	1	0	8	4
Away	3	1	0	2	3	4
Totals	6	3	1	2	11	8

● John Ritchie scored twice in that 4-1 win over Motherwell in September 1971 and almost 45,000 supporters witnessed the two games with Derby County in October/November 1971 with 23,461 attending the fixture at The Victoria Ground.

ANTONIO, George (née George Rowlands)

Antonio was a talented inside-forward and later wing-half, who was originally named Rowlands. He gave Stoke City excellent service for 10 years, being one of the few players to represent the club before, during and after World War Two. Born in Whitchurch in November 1914, and brought up by an Italian family, Antonio played for Oswestry Technical College and Oswestry Town before moving to The Victoria Ground for just £200 in 1936, Stoke manager Bob McGrory just pipping Bolton Wanderers for his signature. He went on to score 15 goals in 98 League and FA Cup appearances for the Potters before transferring to Derby County for £5,000 in 1946. After leaving The Baseball Ground he had good spells with Doncaster Rovers (34 League outings) and Mansfield Town (67 League games) and during the hostilities he guested for nine other clubs, namely Aldershot, Ipswich Town, Leeds United, Leyton Orient, Norwich City, Nottingham Forest, Notts County, Wrexham and York City. After retiring in the early 1950s, Antonio returned to his native Shropshire to run a sports outfitters business, combining his work with two spells as player-manager/coach at Wellington Town (now Telford United); two at Oswestry Town (in a similar role) as well as assisting both Stafford Rangers and Berriew. In his prime, Antonio was selected to play for Wales, but before he could pull on the famous red jersey, it was discovered that he had been born a mile or so 'over the border' on the English side and therefore missed out on an international cap.

APPEARANCES

Here are lists of Stoke's top ten appearance-makers in League, FA Cup, League Cup and wartime competitions.

Football League

507	Eric Skeels
502	John McCue
479	Bob McGrory
417	Tony Allen
409	Peter Fox
407	Denis Smith
398	Frank Bowyer
391	Frank Mountford
388	Alan Bloor
388	Harry Davies

FA Cup

44	Eric Skeels

40	John McCue
38	Alan Bloor
38	Frank Bowyer
37	Stan Matthews
34	Frank Mountford
32	Bob McGrory
32	Jackie Marsh
30	Tony Allen
30	Jock Kirton

League Cup

40	Peter Dobing
38	John Ritchie
38	Eric Skeels
37	Alan Bloor
35	Jackie Marsh
34	Denis Smith
32	Peter Fox
29	Jimmy Greenhoff
29	Mike Pejic
26	Tony Allen
26	Terry Conroy

Wartime

260	Tommy Sale
213	Harry Brigham
186	Neil Franklin
183	Frank Mountford
162	Frank Bowyer
155	Bobby Liddle
135	Billy Herbert
133	Joey Jones
133	John McCue
125	Dennis Herod

(Herbert and Jones played in World War One)

Consecutive Appearances

Only five players (all defenders) have made over 100 consecutive League appearances for the club:

Tony Allen	121	17 March 1960 – 27 March 1963
Arthur Turner	118	27 April 1935 – 12 March 1938
Tom Holford	105	14 March 1903 – 17 February 1906
Alan Dodd	102	10 January 1976 – 29 April 1978
Bob McGrory	101	27 March 1926 – 29 September 1928

● Allen, in fact, played in 148 consecutive games for the Potters (March 1960-March 1963) with his total including 27 Cup-ties.

Appearance Fact File

Wing-half Eric Skeels holds the record for most senior appearances by a player for Stoke City. Over a period of 17 seasons from 1959-60 to 1975-76, he lined up in 606 competitive games for the Potters.

To make up the top 10 appearance-makers behind Skeels (at competitive level) we have full-back John McCue 542, another full-back (and later manager) Bob McGrory 511, centre-half Denis Smith 493, co-defender Alan Bloor 484, goalkeeper Peter Fox 477, full-back Tony Allen 473, long-serving defender Jackie Marsh 444, inside-forward Frank Bowyer 436 and versatile defender Frank Mountford 425.

Including the wartime periods, John McCue is the club's record holder for most appearances in all games with 675 while Frank Mountford amassed 608. And then we have Skeels 606, Bowyer 598, McGrory 511, Smith 493, Bloor 484, Tommy Sale 483, Fox 477 and Allen 473. The totals for Skeels, Smith, Bloor, Allen and Marsh include substitute appearances in the various competitions they played in.

NB: In December 1996 Peter Shilton, then of Leyton Orient, became the first footballer in history to appear in 1,000 Football League games. Earlier he had made 286 League appearances for Leicester, 110 for Stoke, 202 for Nottingham Forest, 188 for Southampton, 175 for Derby County, 34 for Plymouth Argyle and one for Bolton.

ARCHIBALD, Robert F.

A diminutive outside-left, born in Strathaven, Lanarkshire, in November 1894, Bobby Archibald joined Stoke in the summer of 1925 from Third Lanark. After scoring on his debut for the Potters in a 3-0 home win over Stockport County, he quickly became an established member of the side and went on to appear in 276 games for the club, claiming 40 goals. He gained a Third Division North championship medal at the end of his second season at The Vic and after giving the club superb service for seven full seasons, he left the Potteries for Barnsley in the summer of 1932, being replaced by future England international Joe Johnston. During a fine career, Archibald also served with Albion Rovers, Aberdeen, Glasgow Rangers and Raith Rovers (all before Stoke) and, in fact, he had two separate spells with Third Lanark. During World War One he played (and served) in France, Belgium, Denmark, Italy and South America. He retired in May 1937 through injury and went back home to Scotland (Glasgow) where he became an Insurance Agent, scouting from time to time for Bradford City. Archibald's brother, John, kept goal for Albion Rovers, Chelsea, Reading, Newcastle United, Grimsby Town and Darlington, and his daughter became an airline stewardess with Icelandic Airways. Bobby Archibald was 71 when he died after a short illness in 1966.

ARMITAGE, Leonard

At schoolboy level, Yorkshireman Len Armitage was regarded as a terrific talent and after gaining a winners' medal with Sheffield in the Final of the English School's Shield in 1914, several top-class managers sought his signature. In the end he joined his home-town club, Sheffield Wednesday, and then, after World War One, became one of the first players to sign for the restructured Leeds United side, scoring the Elland Road club's first-ever League goal. He then had a spell with Wigan Borough before moving to Stoke in March 1924. Originally an out-and-out centre-forward, Armitage was as 'strong as a bull' and was utterly fearless. He had a tremendous engine being able to cover acres of ground during every game he played in. He helped Stoke win the Third Division North title in 1926-27 and represented the FA XI against South Africa two years later. At the end of the 1931-32 season – with 19 goals in 200 appearances under his belt for the Potters – he left The Victoria Ground for non-League Rhyl and within four months had moved back to Stoke-on-Trent to sign for City's arch rivals, Port Vale. The grandson of a Yorkshire cricketer, Len Armitage died at Wortley in 1972, aged 73.

ARROWSMITH, Arthur

A native of Wolverhampton, Arrowsmith was a Junior international inside-forward who represented the Birmingham Association against Scotland's Juniors in 1906. He joined Stoke from Coventry City and in season 1906-07 scored eight goals in 37 League and Cup appearances for the Potters, following up with one goal in 11 outings the following year. He left The Victoria Ground in May 1908 to sign for his hometown club Wolverhampton Wanderers. He died c.1954, aged 74.

ARSENAL

Stoke's playing record against Arsenal:
Football League

Venue	P	W	D	L	F	A
Home	37	15	13	9	47	38
Away	37	5	5	27	21	74
Totals	74	20	18	36	68	112

FA Cup

Venue	P	W	D	L	F	A
Home	1	0	0	1	0	1
Away	7	0	2	5	8	17
Totals	8	0	2	6	8	18

League Cup

Venue	P	W	D	L	F	A
Home	1	0	1	0	1	1
Away	2	0	0	2	2	8

Stoke's best League victory over the Gunners is 5-0, achieved at The Victoria Ground in September 1970. That day a crowd of 18,163 saw in-from City destroy the Londoners with some fine, attacking football. John Ritchie led the goal-rush with two excellent strikes. The Potters also won 4-1 at home in December 1964 when Ritchie again scored twice.

FA Cup winners Arsenal, thanks mainly to a hat-trick by Doug Lishman, beat Stoke City 5-2 at The Victoria Ground in May 1950, having thrashed the Potters 6-0 at Highbury a month earlier. The Londoners also won 4-0 at home in March 1938 and again in September 1984, as well as registering a 4-1 triumph in front of their own supporters in December 1938 and by the same score, also at Highbury, in April 1952.

The last Stoke-Arsenal League game played at The Victoria Ground was in the First Division in March 1985 when a meagre crowd of 7,371 saw the Potters win 2-0 with goals from Ian Painter (penalty) and defender Paul Dyson.

The first League meeting between the clubs took place in November 1904 (Division One) when Arsenal ran out winners 2-1 in London.

The return fixture that season saw Stoke gain sweet revenge with a 2-0 victory. Freddie Rouse and Jack Hall were the scorers before 6,000 fans.

A record crowd for a game at The Victoria Ground – 51,373 – saw Stoke and Arsenal play out a 0-0 draw in the First Division on 29 March 1937.

Crowds of 62,000 saw the Arsenal-Stoke successive League matches a Highbury in October 1946 and September 1947.

In FA Cup action, almost 42,000 fans saw Arsenal beat Stoke 4-1 at Highbury in a sixth-round tie in March 1928, and the following year the Gunners again put the Potters out of the competition, winning a third-round contest by 2-1 at home before a 30,762 crowd.

In season 1970-71 and again in 1971-72, Stoke were eliminated by Arsenal at the semi-final stage – each time after a replay. In the former competition, a crowd of 54,770 witnessed the 2-2 draw at Hillsborough before the Gunners took the replay 2-0 at Villa Park in front of an audience of 62,356. Then 12 months later, almost 47,000 spectators watched the goalless draw at Sheffield Wednesday's stadium before Arsenal went through to Wembley by winning the Villa Park replay 3-2 in front of 49,247 supporters. Arsenal went on to win the trophy in 1971, but as holders they lost 1-0 to Leeds United in the 1972 Final.

The two League Cup clashes took place in 1996-97, and after an exciting 1-1 draw at Stoke, Arsenal progressed into the fourth-round by winning the replay 5-2 at Highbury in front of the live BSkyB TV cameras and a crowd of 33,962. Mike Sheron scored both the Potters' goals, the first a real beauty.

Players with both clubs: Ian Allinson, Steve Bould, George Brown, Lee Chapman, Eddie Clamp, John Devine, Lee Dixon, George Eastham, Billy Herbert, David Herd, Alan Hudson, Joe Murphy, Jimmy Robertson, Jack Robinson, Dr Leigh Richmond Roose and Brian Talbot.

Alan Ball played for Arsenal and later managed Stoke, as did another international, Jock Rutherford, before and after World War One.

Paul Barron played one game for Stoke and later became goalkeeping coach at Villa Park. Fred Streete was physiotherapist with Stoke (1968-71) and Arsenal (1971-83).

ARTHERN, Thomas

An inside-forward, Arthern (some references state Atherton) made only one League appearance for the Potters in 1891. Born in Stoke in 1868, he played for Hanley Town and Congleton either side his service at The Victoria Ground.

ASHINGTON

Stoke's playing record against Ashington is:
Football League

Venue	P	W	D	L	F	A
Home	1	1	0	0	7	0
Away	1	1	0	0	2	0
Totals	2	2	0	0	9	0

These two games were in the League Division Three North in season 1926-27. Charlie Wilson hit five goals in Stoke's 7-0 win in September, while in the return fixture in the North-East, Josh Williams and Johnny Eyres earned Potters the double with an efficient 2-0 victory.

ASHWORTH, Samuel Bolton

Sam Ashworth was a fine defender, who remained an amateur for most of his career. Born in Fenton in 1881, he certainly travelled round the country and during his playing days served with the following clubs: Stoke Alliance, Fenton Town, Stafford Wednesday, Stafford Rangers, Stoke Nomads, Stoke (1901-03), Manchester City, Everton, Burslem Port Vale, Reading, Oxford City (whilst on holiday), Richmond Association FC, North Staffs Nomads and Northern Nomads. He appeared in 39 games for Stoke, and was secretary and founder-member of the North Staffs Nomads. In 1903-04, he represented the Football League as an Everton player and also collected an FA Cup winners' medal and a League runners-up medal with Manchester City in that same year (being one of only three amateurs to win an FA Cup medal this century). In 1906 he was involved in a soccer scandal at Manchester City, being accused of earning money over and above his normal expenses. Ashworth was found guilty and, along with 17 others, was ordered never to play for City again. He was also fined £25. An architect and surveyor by profession, Ashworth later became a Stoke director (1920) and was chief architect to the Stoke-on-Trent Education Committee when he died in December 1925.

ASPREY, William

Born in Wolverhampton on 11 September 1936, Asprey was signed by Stoke City boss Frank Taylor in 1953 from under the nose of his counterpart at Molineux, Stan Cullis. Asprey, who had been a Wolves

Bill Asprey

fan as a lad, developed quickly at The Victoria Ground and after establishing himself in the first team during the 1957-58 season, he went from strength to strength, performing superbly well either as a full-back (his preferred position), occasionally as a central defender and from time to time as a makeshift striker. Indeed, in January 1961 he netted a hat-trick while wearing the number-eight shirt against Charlton Athletic. When he left the club in 1966, Asprey had amassed a fine record of 341 appearances and 26 goals. He had helped Stoke win the Second Division title in 1963 and reach the League Cup final the following year. He joined Oldham Athletic from Stoke for £19,000 and after a brief spell with Port Vale, he took up coaching, first with Sheffield Wednesday, then Coventry City as well as spells with Wolves and West Bromwich Albion and in Zimbabwe (where he was director of Football) and the Middle East. In 1979 he took over as manager of Oxford United and then returned to The Victoria Ground as assistant to Richie Barker in 1981. Two years later he replaced Barker in the hot seat and held the position for two seasons before poor results coupled with his own ill-health saw him replaced by Mick Mills. He later became a hotelier on the South Coast.

NB: Stoke won only 14 of the 67 League games when Asprey was in charge.

ASTON VILLA

Stoke's playing record against Aston Villa is:

Football League

Venue	P	W	D	L	F	A
Home	44	18	13	13	66	54
Away	44	6	7	31	36	108
Totals	88	24	20	44	102	162

FA Cup

Venue	P	W	D	L	F	A
Home	5	1	3	1	8	6
Away	5	2	1	2	7	12
Totals	10	3	4	3	15	18

League Cup

Venue	P	W	D	L	F	A
Away	1	0	0	1	1	3

Stoke City's best win of the 24 recorded against Villa in the League is 6-1 at The Victoria Ground in December 1966 (Division One). Ex-Villa winger Harry Burrows scored a hat-trick for the Potters that day before of a 20,232 crowd.

Villa's best win over Stoke is 6-0 at Aston in December 1894.

The first-ever League games in 1888-89 ended Villa 5 Stoke 1 in Aston and Stoke 1 Villa 1 at The Victoria Ground. Villa also defeated the Potters 6-1 at home in December 1889 and 5-1 in Birmingham in September 1893. Another heavy Stoke League defeat was 6-2 at Villa Park in May 1950.

When Villa won the Second Division championship in 1959-60, Stoke held them to a 3-3 draw at The Victoria Ground.

Dennis Herod, the Stoke goalkeeper, was injured in the away League game at Villa Park in February 1952 and as a makeshift winger he scored in his side's 3-2 win.

Stoke first met Villa in the FA competition in January 1890 and they beat one of the finest club sides in the country by 3-0 at The Victoria Ground to enter the third qualifying round.

In January 1914, Villa, the FA Cup holders, beat Stoke 4-0 in a first-round tie before 26,094 fans at Villa Park.

Stoke and Villa met each other three times in the FA Cup third round in January 1958. After 1-1 and 3-3 draws, Stoke eventually went through by winning a second replay 2-0 at Molineux before a 37,702 crowd. Tim Coleman and Bobby Cairns scored the goals.

Players with both clubs: Jimmy Adam, Noel Blake, Harry Burrows, Martin Carruthers, Arthur Cartlage, Billy Dickson, Arthur Dixon (Stoke reserve 1889), Peter Dowds, Archie Dyke, John Gidman, Adrian Heath, Ian King (Villa junior, Stoke reserve), Jimmy Lee, Harry Leigh, Aaron Lockett, Alex McClure, Jack Palethorpe, Leigh Palin, Mike Pejic, Jack Robinson, Dr Leigh Richmond Roose, John Roxburgh, Geoff Scott (youth), Simon Stainrod, Edwin Stevenson, Tommy Thompson, Mark Walters, Mart Watkins, Tommy Weston, Jack Whitley, Tom Wilkes, Josh Williams, Alf Wood and John Woodward.

Paul Barron, who had one game for Stoke, became goalkeeping coach at Villa Park in 1995.

ASTON VILLA RESERVES

When Stoke played in the Birmingham & District League during the early 100s, they met Villa's second XI on six occasions.

Venue	P	W	D	L	F	A
Home	3	3	0	0	10	6
Away	3	0	0	3	2	10
Totals	6	3	0	3	12	16

A crowd of around 12,000 saw Stoke beat Villa 5-3 at home in September 1908.

Stoke were also knocked out of the Birmingham League Cup in 1909-10 by Villa Reserves who won 2-1 at Aston in a third-round tie.

ATTENDANCES

Large crowds

The biggest crowd ever to assemble at The Victoria Ground did so on 29 March 1937, when Arsenal were the visitors for a First Division game. That day 51,373 fans packed inside to witness the 0-0 draw.

The second biggest League crowd at The Vic was 47,609 v Blackpool (Division One) in December 1947, while 46,990 saw the local derby with Port Vale (Division Two) in September 1954.

Stoke's highest FA Cup crowd at The Vic was 50,735 v Bolton Wanderers on 2 March 1946 for a sixth-round 1st leg tie. The attendance for the fourth-round FA Cup-tie with Blackburn Rovers in January 1962 was 49,486, while 49,091 saw the sixth-round replay with Manchester United in March 1972.

The biggest League Cup audience at The Victoria Ground was that of 42,233 v Manchester United, fourth-round 2nd replay, in November 1971.

The biggest crowd ever to watch Stoke City in action is 97,852 at Wembley Stadium on 4 March 1972 for the League Cup Final against Chelsea.

A crowd of 84,569 saw Manchester City beat Stoke City 1-0 in a sixth-round FA Cup-tie at Maine Road on 3 March 1934.

Later that year, on 15 September 1934, some 60,000 fans witnessed the First Division League game between Manchester City and the Potters on the same ground.

A crowd of 65,419 saw the Bolton Wanderers-Stoke City 2nd leg of the sixth-round FA Cup-tie at Burnden Park on 9 March 1946.

Earlier that season, the Sheffield Wednesday-Stoke City FA Cup game at Hillsborough was seen by an audience of 62,728.

There were 65,681 fans at the Tottenham Hotspur-Stoke City third-round FA Cup-tie at White Hart Lane on 11 January 1947.

Some 68,189 fans were present at the Chelsea v Stoke City First Division game at Stamford Bridge on 12 October 1946 and there were 62,013 spectators in attendance at Highbury when Arsenal played Stoke a week later, also in the League.

Twelve months after that, on 20 September 1947, another bumper crowd of 62,067 saw the Arsenal-Stoke First Division match in North London, and there were 62,125 supporters assembled at St James' Park for the Newcastle United-Stoke City fifth-round FA Cup-tie on 10 February 1951.

A massive gate of 66,199 saw the vital Second Division promotion encounter between Chelsea and Stoke City at Stamford Bridge on 11 May 1963 and there were 63,497 inside Old Trafford when Manchester United beat Stoke 2-0 in a third round FA Cup-tie on 28 January 1967.

Four months later – on 13 May 1967 – a crowd of 63,071 packed into Old Trafford to see League Champions United held 0-0 by Stoke City.

The 1971 FA Cup semi-final replay between Arsenal and Stoke at Villa Park on 31 March attracted a crowd of 62,356.

When Stoke were on tour in 1964, an estimated crowd of around 80,000 saw them play Universidad in Chile.

And there were 65,000 fans present in the Nou Camp Stadium when Stoke defeated the Spanish giants Barcelona 3-2 in a friendly there in the summer of 1969. David Herd scored twice for the Potters who led 3-0 at half-time.

Low crowds

The lowest gate for a senior Stoke home game (League or Cup) is 1,000 v Manchester, FA Cup, 10 November 1883; v Crewe Alexandra at The County Cricket Ground, Football Alliance, 8 November 1890; v Newton Heath, Division One, 7 January 1893; v Birmingham, Division One, 27 October 1894; and v Burnley, Division One, 7 December 1895.

The lowest crowd at The Victoria Ground since 1946 has been that of 4,070 v Ipswich Town, Division Two, on 30 March 1960.

The lowest attendance for a Stoke away game at competitive level is 200 – against Halesowen, Birmingham League, 14 November 1908.

Other attendances under the 1,000 mark have been: 600 away at West Bromwich Albion, Division One, 26 November 1892; 300 at Burnley, Division One, 14 March 1896; 500 at Lincoln City, Division Two, 14 December 1907; 500 at Stafford Rangers, Birmingham League, 4 April 1910; 600 at Dudley, Birmingham League, 11 February 1911; 600 at Aberdare, Southern League Division Two, 22 November 1913 and 500 at Mardy, Southern League Division Two, 1 September 1914.

A crowd of just 7,800 saw the Manchester United v Stoke City First Division game at Maine Road on 5 February 1947.

Boothen End fans pictured in the 1970s.

Seasonal Averages

Stoke's best average home Football League attendance for a season has been 31,099 (in 1947-48). They averaged 30,863 in 1946-47 and 30,315 in 1963-64.

Stoke's lowest average home gate for a season was 3,275 in 1889-90; they averaged 3,684 in 1891-92 and 3,775 in 1888-89.

Playing in the Football Alliance in 1890-91, Stoke's average turnout at home was 2,136.

During their first two seasons of Southern League football, Stoke's home attendances averaged 3,500 in 1909-10 and 3,636 in 1910-11.

Ups and downs

Stoke's biggest seasonal increase in their average home League gate was achieved in 1962-63 when it went up by 9,675, from 15,751 to 25,426.

Stoke's worst decline in the average home League gate was suffered in season 1953-54 – down by 9,874 from 27,883 to 18,009.

In 1974-75, Stoke's average home gate in the First Division was 27,011. Ten years later it was down to 10,697 – and in 1985-86 the average turnout was 8,288 – the lowest at The Victoria Ground for 78 years.

In the first season after World War One, the average League attendance at The Victoria Ground was 12,334. It rose to over 19,000 in 1922-23, dropped to 10,420 in 1929-30 and shot up again to 24,595 in 1937-38.

Attendance records

A record League crowd at Vale Park – 40,066 – witnessed the local derby against Stoke City on 25 April 1955 (Division Two).

Tranmere Rovers' record attendance at Prenton Park – 24,426 – was set when Stoke City were the visitors for a fourth-round FA Cup-tie on 5 February 1972.

Oakwell attracted its biggest crowd when Stoke City played Barnsley there in a fifth-round FA Cup-tie on 15 February 1936.

Wartime attendances

Stoke's average home gate during the transitional season of 1945-46 was 14,260.

During World War One, Stoke averaged 6,604 in 1915-16, exactly 5,600 in 1916-17, almost 9,000 in 1917-18 and 11,847 in 1918-19.

Their home attendances fluctuated during World War Two – the lowest being 1,547 in 1940-41.

Stoke's best single home gate in Regional League/Cup games during the period 1939-46 was 28,387 v Chesterfield (League North) on 3 November 1945.

Stoke had ten home attendances of less than 900 during season 1940-41. Their lowest turnout was 300.

AUSTERBERRY, Horace Denham

Stoke's seventh manager, 'Denny' Austerberry was born in Hanley in February 1868 and was assistant schoolmaster to Tom Slaney at St John's School in Hanley. He also reported on Stoke's matches. A strict disciplinarian he once suspended three players for drinking champagne in breach of club rules. He had a good eye for talent and brought many fine players to the club. Stoke won only 134 games out of the 382 they played at League level when he was in charge of team affairs. He was 78 when he died in 1946 (See MANAGERS).

AUTOGLASS TROPHY

Stoke have played 13 matches in the Autoglass Trophy competition. Their full record reads:

Venue	P	W	D	L	F	A
Home	8	5	2	1	20	10
Away	5	5	0	0	7	0
Totals	13	10	2	1	27	10

Stoke entered this competition for the first time in season 1991-92 and they went on to win the trophy, beating Stockport County 1-0 at Wembley with a fine goal from striker Mark Stein. There were 48,339 fans inside the Empire Stadium for that final, more than 30,000 of them Stokies.

En route to Wembley, Stoke City defeated Walsall twice (2-0 away and 3-1 at home), Cardiff City (h) 3-0, Leyton Orient (a) 1-0 and Peterborough United (a) in the semi-final second leg also by 1-0 with a great strike from Paul Ware, this after having drawn 3-3 at home with Posh in the first game.

As holders of the trophy, Stoke reached the area semi-final the

Stoke celebrate victory over Stockport County at Wembley in 1992, when they won the Autoglass Trophy at the first attempt.

following season before going out 1-0 to arch rivals Port Vale at The Victoria Ground. In the earlier rounds, the Potters defeated Wrexham (a) 2-0, Barnet (h) 4-1 (when Steve Foley scored a hat-trick) and West Bromwich Albion (h) 2-1, as well as drawing with near neighbours Crewe Alexandra 2-2 at The Victoria Ground.

AWAY WINS

Stoke's best ever away win at senior level is 6-0 – achieved at Gigg Lane, Bury in a Second Division game on 13 March 1954.

They also beat Wrexham 6-2 in February 1927 (Division Three North) and Bristol City by the same score in February 1930 (Division Two).

Stoke's biggest away win in the FA Cup is 5-2 at Wigan Borough in January 1926, while in the League Cup (in terms of goals scored) it is 4-2 at Bristol Rovers in November 1971.

Stoke's heaviest away defeat at League level is 10-0 at Preston in September 1889. They lost 9-3 at Darwen in October 1891; 8-0 at Everton in November 1889 and Blackburn in January 1890.

Their heaviest away reverse in the FA Cup is 8-0 in a qualifying round v Wolverhampton Wanderers in February 1890.

The most away wins recorded by Stoke in a Football League season is 12 in 1932-33 (Division Two).

The Potters failed to win a single away League game in seasons 1891-92, 1893-94, 1897-98, 1968-69 and 1984-85.

AXCELL, A. Charles

Outside-left Axcell was born in Leigh-on-Sea in 1882 and joined Stoke from Burton United in 1906. He was given just three League outings by the club before returning to Burton United in 1907, later assisting Southend United. Axcell played initially for Leigh Ramblers before spending two seasons (from August 1904) with Fulham.

BACOS, Desmond P.

Born in Wynberg, Johannesburg on 13 November 1950, Bacos, an inside-forward, made just two appearances for Stoke City in 1977-78. Before moving to The Victoria Ground he served with Highlands Park (South Africa), Chelsea (on trial), Grinaker Rangers, Hellenic and Los Angeles Aztecs. And after leaving the Potters he once more had spells with Highlands Park, Grinaker Rangers (as player-manager in the late 1980s) and Hellenic, as well as Dion Cosmos and Mondeor.

BADDELEY, Amos

Inside-left Amos Baddeley from Fegg Hayes, was 19 years of age when he followed his brother George to The Victoria Ground in November 1906. But when the club folded in the summer of 1908, he went off to play for Blackpool, returning to the Potteries for a second spell at The Victoria Ground in July 1909. After re-establishing himself in the first team, Baddeley, who was only 5ft 6ins tall, went on to score a total of 56 goals in 101 games for the club before transferring to Walsall in April 1912. One of Baddeley's goals is the fastest ever scored by a Stoke player (from kick-off at the start of a game). He achieved this feat playing against West Bromwich Albion Reserves in a Birmingham & District League game at The Victoria Ground on 30 October 1909 when he found the net after just eight seconds – but Stoke still lost the game 3-1. After retiring from League soccer, he became player-manager of first Abertillery and then Ebbw Vale. Baddeley died in North Staffordshire c.1955.

BADDELEY, George

Brother of Amos, George Baddeley, a splendid wing-half, was born in Fegg Hayes in May 1874 and died in West Bromwich in July 1952. His career started at Pitshill FC and after a spell with Biddulph, he joined Stoke in 1900. He captained the side for several years and in eight seasons at The Victoria Ground (up to 1908) he scored 19 goals in 225

George Baddeley

League and Cup appearances for the Potters. When Stoke lost their League status Baddeley moved to West Bromwich Albion for £250. He spent six seasons at The Hawthorns and during that time helped the Baggies win the Second Division championship (1911) and reach the FA Cup Final 12 months later. He retired in 1914 after more than 150 outings for the Black Country club. He later became a publican in West Bromwich, taking over the Crown & Cushion.

NB: George Baddeley holds the record of being the oldest player ever to appear in a Football League game for West Bromwich Albion – he was almost 40 years of age when he lined up against Sheffield Wednesday on 18 April 1914.

NB: Baddeley twisted his knee in his 99th consecutive game for Stoke v Liverpool on Boxing Day 1905.

BADDELEY, Samuel

Another member of the Baddeley family, Sam, a strong tackling, highly competitive right-half, was born at Norton in the Moors in 1884. He joined Stoke in 1907 when Burslem Port Vale went bust, having earlier served with the Ball Green and Endon clubs. A very consistent player, he scored nine goals in 203 first-team appearances for Stoke up to 1915 when he announced his retirement. He died c.1960.

BADDELEY, Thomas

The fourth member of the Baddeley clan, goalkeeper Tom was born in

Bycars on 2 November 1874 and commenced his career with Burslem Swifts in 1890. Two years later he signed for Burslem Port Vale, and moved to Wolverhampton Wanderers for £40 in the summer of 1896. He spent 11 seasons at Molineux (up to 1907) making 315 appearances. He then switched his allegiance to Yorkshire to sign for Bradford Park Avenue (as a founder member of that club). During March and April 1910 he played eight games for Stoke (owing too Jack Robinson being indisposed) and finally called it a day in 1911. Winner of five full England caps (1903-04), Baddeley could throw a ball out to up to 50 yards (an unusual feature for a 'keeper of his era); he was a good shot-shopper, and accumulated well over 400 appearances at club level during a fine career. He died in Burslem on 24 September 1948.

BAILEY, Horace Peter

Goalkeeper Bailey – known as 'H.P.' – was capped five times by England senior level and on four occasions by the amateur team, and he also won an Olympic Gold medal for Great Britain at soccer in 1908. A small man, standing only 5ft 8ins tall, he had a massive pair of hands and could kick long and true. An amateur throughout his career, Bailey was born in Derby on 3 July 1881 and while working full-time as a rating officer with the Midland Railway Company based in Derby, he played for Derby County (from 1899), Ripley Athletic, Leicester Imperial, Leicester Fosse, Derby County (again) and Birmingham prior to joining Stoke in November 1910 (he was recruited after the ageing Jack Robertson had been taken ill). One of the most famous goalkeepers in the land, he unfortunately made only one Birmingham League appearance for the Potters (a 6-2 win over Wrexham) before returning for a second spell at St Andrew's. Bailey retired in May 1913. He died at Biggleswade on 1 August 1960, aged 79.

NB: *Bailey conceded 12 goals while playing for Leicester Fosse against Nottingham Forest in a First Division game in 1908.*

BAILEY, Thomas

Originally a centre-forward, Bailey arrived at The Victoria Ground in 1912 as a half-back from Stoke Priory. He scored once in 35 games for the Potters, up to 1915, when he joined Hanley Swifts. He was born in Stoke in 1888.

BAINES, Paul

Inside-forward who made two League appearances for Stoke in 1991. Born in Tamworth on 15 January 1972, he joined the club in 1990 and left after two years. He later had trials with Tamworth and Walsall and then played for both Tamworth and Atherstone United (on loan).

BAIRD, William

A centre-forward, born in Glasgow in 1876, Baird had three League outings for Stoke in 1896 after joining the club from Greenock Morton. He left the Potteries for St Bernard's after only a few months at The Vic.

BAKER, Charles

Baker, described as a 'neat dribbler' had two spells with Stoke as an inside-forward: April 1889 to August 1892 and from January 1893 to June 1894. Born in Stafford in February 1870, he played for Stafford Rangers initially, and in between his two terms at The Victoria Ground he assisted Wolverhampton Wanderers (1891-93). When he left the Potteries, second time round, Baker went to Southampton St Mary's and later came back to play again for Stafford Rangers before retiring in 1900 to pursue a shoemaking trade. He scored 13 goals in 38 senior games for Stoke and was presented with a gold medal on his departure from The Dell. He died c.1940.

BAKER, Frank

Stoke manager Bob McGrory pipped Wolves' boss Major Frank Buckley for Baker's signature in 1936. The Potteries-born outside-right, who had driven a laundry van whilst playing as an amateur with Port Vale in their Cheshire League team, went on to give the club excellent service over the next 13 years or so, appearing in 174 League and Cup games and scoring 33 goals either side of World War Two. He also turned out occasionally during the hostilities, occupying both wing positions. Baker was 33 when he retired in 1951 through injury (he broke his leg at least three times). On leaving football he became a fish and chip shop proprietor in Fenton. He died in Stoke-on-Trent in 1989.

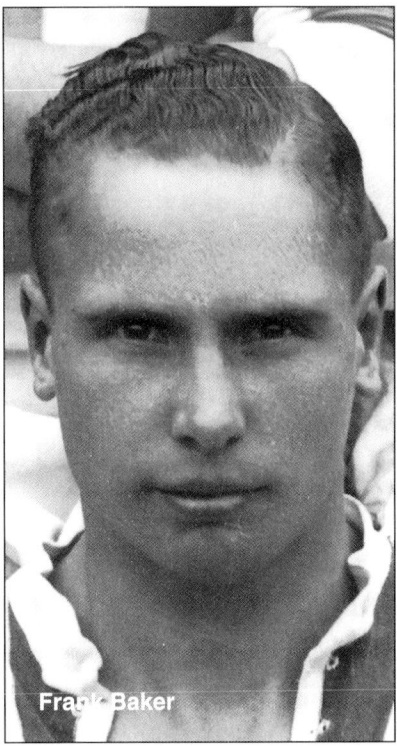
Frank Baker

BALL, Alan junior

Alan Ball

Stoke City manager from November 1989 to February 1991. Ball started his footballing life in 1961 as an apprentice with Blackpool. He was in charge at The Victoria Ground for 58 League games of which Stoke won only 15 (losing 23). He was still associated with the game in 1997 (See MANAGERS).

BALL, James Alan senior

Born at Farnworth on 23 September 1924. Alan Ball's father was an inside-forward with Bolton Boys' Federation, Southport (1945-47), Birmingham City (1947-48), Southport (again), Oldham Athletic (1950-52), Rochdale, Oswestry Town (as player-manager 1952-53), Borough United, Ashton United (manager 1959-60), Nantwich Town (manager), Stoke City (coach 1972), Halifax Town (two spells as manager), Preston North End (manager 1973-74), Southport (manager 1974-75) and Blackpool (scout 1980-81). He also managed five clubs in Sweden. He died tragically in a motoring accident in West Cyprus on 2 January 1982 where he had accepted a short-term coaching position prior to resuming as boss of Vester Haringe (Sweden).

BALLHAM, Joseph Lewis

Another player who had two separate spells with Stoke – from August to October 1886 and from September 1890 to April 1892. An orthodox outside-right, Ballham was born in the Potteries in 1867 and played his early football with Stoke Locomotive, had a brief spell with Stoke in 1886 and from 1886 to 1890 starred for Burslem Port Vale. He returned to The Victoria Ground and spent two more seasons with the Potters, retiring in the summer of 1892, having scored 14 goals in a total of 45 senior games for Stoke. His brother, Edgar, also played for the Vale (1890).

BAMBER, John David

A 6ft 3in striker, good in the air, Bamber was born deep in Rugby League territory, in St Helens on 1 February 1959. He started off with his home town's soccer team, moving to Winsford United before attending and playing for Manchester University. He signed for Blackpool in 1979 to start his League career which saw him play, in turn, for Coventry City, Walsall, Portsmouth, Swindon Town, Watford, Stoke City (from December 1988 to February 1990), Hull City and Blackpool (again). Bamber scored 12 goals in 49 appearances for the Potters who paid £190,000 for his signature and then sold him for £130,000. In his career Bamber netted almost 190 goals in well over 500 League and Cup appearances.

NB: Alan Ball sold Bamber three times during his managerial career.

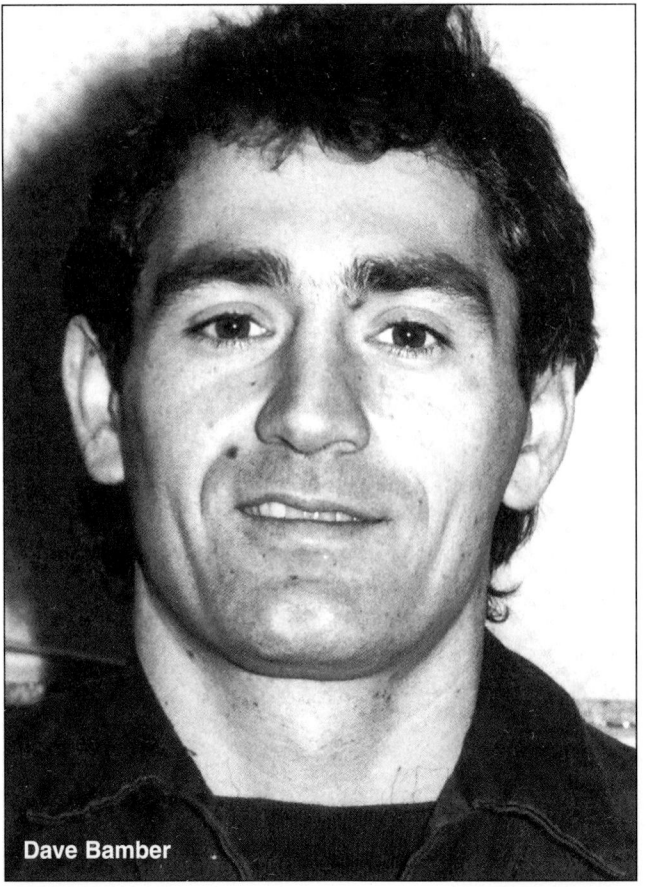
Dave Bamber

BAMBER, John Belfield

Centre-half Bamber was a member of Stoke's playing staff from 1932 to 1939 during which time he was given 24 first-team outings, scoring one goal. Born in Preston in June 1912, he played for the 'A' team at

John Bamber

Deepdale before assisting Fleetwood Town from where he moved to The Victoria Ground as reserve to Arthur Turner. In fact, Bamber skippered Stoke's second XI on several occasions. When war broke out he went to Swynnerton to work as a joiner in a reserved occupation. He moved back to his native Preston in the mid-1940s when he was also called up by the Hertfordshire Yeomanry, going over to Normandy with the Second Army. He did not resume his footballing career after the hostilities

BANKS, Gordon, OBE

Banks was, by far the finest goalkeeper in the world during the period 1968-71; some people in football even classed him as being the greatest goalkeeper ever. That tremendous save from Pele's downward

BALL - BANKS

Gordon Banks

Ritchie Barker

header in the 1970 World Cup Finals in Mexico is still, to this day, being shown on TV in countries all over the world – and is rated to have been the greatest save ever made in top-class football. At the time Banks was a Stoke City player, having joined the club in as a 29-year-old in the summer of 1967 from Leicester City for a mere £52,000. A Yorkshireman, born in Tinsley, Sheffield in December 1937, Banks played his early football with Millspaugh Steelworks FC (two spells) and Rawmarsh Welfare. In 1954 he signed for Chesterfield and turned professional at Saltergate in September 1955. He went on to appear in 23 League games for the Spireites also gaining an FA Youth Cup runners-up medal before transferring to Filbert Street in May 1959. For Leicester he added a further 293 League outings to his tally and played for them against Stoke City in the 1964 League Cup Final, and in two losing FA Cup Finals (v Spurs in 1961 and Manchester United two years later). He won the first of his 73 full England caps in April 1963 (against Scotland) having already played twice for the Under-23 side. He later represented the Football League on six occasions. A year before moving to The Victoria Ground he gained a World Cup winners' medal when England defeated West Germany at Wembley and his haul of caps when he switched from Filbert Street to the Potteries stood at 37 – making him Leicester's most-capped player at that time. He therefore added 36 more to his collection with the Potters and is now Stoke's most-capped player at full international level. Awarded the OBE in the Queen's Honours List in 1970 (after his World Cup heroics), Banks appeared in a total of 246 senior games for Stoke, gaining a League Cup winners' tankard in 1972, when he was also named both Footballer of the Year and Sportsman of the Year In 1977 he was voted the NASL 'Goalkeeper of the Year' when serving with Fort Lauderdale Strikers. This came five years after he had been involved in a horrific car smash which cost him the sight in his right eye and forced him into an early retirement from League football in this country. This accident took place five miles from Ashley Heath on 22 October 1972 when his Ford Granada crashed head-on with an Austin van. An immensely likeable man, Banks coached at The Victoria Ground after retiring and he also assisted on the coaching staff at Vale Park before becoming general manager of Telford United. He later ran his own sports promotion agency.

NB: When Fort Lauderdale lured him over to America, Banks' first thoughts were that he was joining a circus act, and admitted to seeing bill-boards revealing: "Roll-up, roll-up – come and see the greatest one-eyed goalkeeper in the world."

BANNISTER, Gary

Bannister had a fine career as a goalscorer in League Football. Born in Warrington in July 1960, he played, in turn, for Coventry City (apprentice June 1976, professional May 1978), Sheffield Wednesday (1981-84), Queen's Park Rangers (1984-88), Coventry City, for a second spell (1988-90), West Bromwich Albion (1990-92), Oxford United (on loan in 1992), Nottingham Forest (1992-93), Stoke City (signed on a 'free' in May 1993 and released in May 1994), Hong Kong Royals (briefly in the summer of 1994), Lincoln City (1994-95) and Darlington (1995-96). Bannister's transfer fees totalled £850,000 and when he was forced to retire in the summer of 1996 (with a back injury) his statistics read: 206 goals in 621 League and Cup appearances at club level. For Stoke his record was two goals scored in 18 outings. He was capped once by England at Under-21 level. and helped Darlington reach the 1996 Play-off final at Wembley.

BARKER, Alfred J.

Stoke's manager from May 1908 (when the new club was formed as a limited company) to April 1914. Born in the Potteries in 1873, Barker, a former League referee, did so much to save the club from going to the wall and when he left The Victoria Ground his departure left a sour taste in the mouth (See MANAGERS).

BARKER, Richard

Richie Barker entered League football at the age of 28 when he joined Derby County whom he helped win the Second Division title in 1969. He later served with Notts County (gaining a Fourth Division championship medal with the Magpies). But after breaking his leg playing for Peterborough, he moved into management, first as assistant to Alan Durban at Shrewsbury. When Durban left for Stoke, Barker moved up to the manager's hot seat. Ten months later he went to Wolves as their assistant manager before joining Stoke in 1981. Under his leadership, the Potters won only 30 of their 101 League games (losing 48). He returned briefly to Meadow Lane and later worked in Greece and Egypt prior to becoming Ron Atkinson's assistant at Sheffield Wednesday (See MANAGERS).

BARKER, William

Sadly centre-forward Barker's career ended with a broken leg, suffered in season 1949-50 after he had played in just one League game for Stoke City v Manchester City at Maine Road in October 1949. Born in Stoke on 31 May 1924, he joined the club in October 1948, but was always a reserve-team player at The Victoria Ground.

BARNES, Paul Lance

Paul Barnes

Striker Paul Barnes started his playing days with Notts County, moving to Stoke at the age of 22 for £30,000 in March 1990. He scored four goals in 29 appearances for the Potters and after a loan spell with Chesterfield he switched to York City in July 1992 for £50,000. He did extremely well at Bootham Crescent, netting 85 goals in 179 outings for the Minstermen, before he was signed by Birmingham City boss Barry Fry for £350,000 in March 1996. Barnes was born in Leicester on 16 November 1967.

BARNET

Stoke have met Barnet just once in senior competition, beating them 4-1 at home in a second round Autoglass Trophy game in January 1993. Steve Foley scored a hat-trick in this game which was attended by 8,892 fans.

Players with both clubs: Keith Berstchin, Billy Herbert, Kenny Lowe, Gerry McMahon and Dave Regis.

BARNSLEY

Stoke's playing record against Barnsley is:

Football League

Venue	P	W	D	L	F	A
Home	25	15	7	3	42	17
Away	25	4	5	16	25	48
Totals	50	19	12	19	67	65

FA Cup

	P	W	D	L	F	A
Home	1	0	1	0	3	3
Away	2	0	0	2	2	4
Totals	3	0	1	2	5	7

Stoke's best victory over the Tykes (in terms of goals scored) is 5-4 at The Victoria Ground in October 1993 (Division One). That day a crowd of 14,674 saw defenders Fleming and Bishop concede own-goals for the visitors.

Barnsley beat Stoke 5-2 at Oakwell in October 1987 (Division Two) to register their best win over the Potters.

The 50th League meeting between the clubs ended in a 1-0 win for Stoke at The Victoria Ground on Boxing Day 1996 when a crowd of over 19,000 saw Mike Sheron score the only goal.

The 3-3 FA Cup draw took place at The Victoria Ground in January 1989 before 18,540 fans (paying £65,065 at the gate), and Stoke's goals were scored by players whose surnames began with the letter B – Beagrie (Peter), Berry (George) and Bamber (Dave). Stoke were 3-1 down with 15 minutes remaining but battled back to earn a replay with Beagrie's late equaliser.

More than 50 years earlier, in an FA Cup fifth-round tie at Oakwell in February 1936, a record attendance of 40,255 saw Barnsley win 2-1 with goals from Gallacher and Hine.

Players with both clubs: Bobby Archibald, Wayne Biggins, Steve Davis (Stoke reserve), Peter Fox, Jimmy Hay, Harry Leigh, Ian Moores, Alf Owen, Brian Sherratt, John Short and Fred Tomlinson. Charlie Bishop was a Stoke junior (1986-87) who later played over 140 games for Barnsley and Frank Taylor, who managed Stoke City between 1952 and 1960, was born in Barnsley.

BARR, Robert

Scottish centre-forward, born in Kilmarnock in 1865, Barr had three League games for Stoke in season 1888-89, having signed from Hurlford. He left The Victoria Ground for Abercorn and during his career also assisted Preston North End and Bury,

BARRETT, Scott

An efficient goalkeeper who was introduced to League Football by Wolverhampton Wanderers in the mid-1980s. Born in Ilkeston in April 1963, he played initially for his home-town club, Ilkeston Town and was a youngster with Notts County and a reserve with Derby County before making 35 appearances for Wolves. He moved from Molineux to Stoke City for £10,000 in July 1987 and played in 60 first-team games for the Potters, up to August 1991, when he signed for Colchester United – this after loan spells at both Layer Road and

Stockport County in 1990. He left Colchester for Gillingham in August 1992 and switched to Cambridge United three years later. On his day Barrett was an excellent goalkeeper but he did have his moments of inconsistency.

BARRON, Paul G.

Tall, well-built goalkeeper who had one League outing for Stoke City, in January 1985, playing against Leicester City (away) whilst on loan from West Bromwich Albion. Born in Woolwich in September 1953, his career started with Slough Town, and from July 1976 to May 1990 he also served with Plymouth Argyle, Arsenal, Queen's Park Rangers, Reading (on loan), Cheltenham Town and Welling United, amassing 240 League appearances in total. He was goalkeeping coach at Aston Villa 1995-97.

BARROW

Stoke's playing record against Barrow reads:
Football League

Venue	P	W	D	L	F	A
Home	1	1	0	0	4	0
Away	1	0	1	0	0	0
Totals	2	1	1	0	4	0

FA Cup

Venue	P	W	D	L	F	A
Home	1	1	0	0	3	1

Stoke met Barrow in two Third Division North League games in season 1926-27. At The Victoria Ground, a crowd of 9,638 saw Charlie Wilson score a hat-trick in a 4-0 win.

The FA Cup-tie was in the fifth qualifying round in season 1913-14 and a crowd of 10,000 saw Billy Herbert score twice in Stoke's win.

Players with both clubs: David Brown, Tony Ford, Verdi Godwin, Jim Harbot, Kenny Lowe, Edgar Powell, Alan Suddick and Tommy Thompson.

Former Stoke and England centre-forward Fred Pentland later managed Barrow, while Mark Harrison, the ex-Stoke goalkeeper, became assistant manager-coach at Holker Street.

BARRY TOWN

Stoke's playing record against Barry is:
Southern League

Venue	P	W	D	L	F	A
Home	2	2	0	0	6	0
Away	2	0	2	0	1	1
Totals	4	2	2	0	7	1

These four games were in the old Southern League Division Two in the two campaigns leading up to World War One. In 1913-14 Stoke recorded their best win over Barry, beating them 7-1 at The Victoria Ground when Alf Smith and Joey Jones both netted twice. The following season Barry were beaten 2-0 in the Potteries.

Inside-forward Edgar Powell played for both Barry and Stoke.

BASNETT, A. Frederick

Useful inside-forward, born in Stoke in 1924, Fred Basnett played in just two FA Cup games for the club in 1946, having arrived at The Victoria Ground as a professional in late 1941. When time allowed from his RAF duty, he appeared in several wartime matches (as well as guesting for Northampton Town) and left the Potters for Northwich Victoria. Basnett's brother, Albert, also played for Stoke during World War Two, turning professional in February 1942.

BATEMAN, George

Solid, strong-kicking full-back who made six League appearances for Stoke during two spells with the club – between September 1890 and April 1893 – deputising for the England international Alf Underwood on four occasions. Born in the Potteries c.1866, he joined The Victoria Ground playing staff from Burslem Port Vale, returned to Vale briefly and left Stoke, second time round, for Northwich Victoria in 1893.

BAXTER, John

With Tom Baddeley due to retire, Stoke chose Baxter as their reserve goalkeeper to Jack Robertson for the 1910-11 campaign. Born in Wigan on 24 December 1889, he remained an amateur throughout his career and, in fact, a month before signing for the Potters, he had been on trial at Derby County. Baxter made six League appearances for Stoke, following his transfer from Tunstall Park, after a trial with Derby County, having earlier assisted Burslem Liverpool Road FC, and Congleton White Star. He left the Potters for Macclesfield in the summer of 1911.

BEACHILL, Arthur

A rugged full-back and contemporary of Bob McGrory, Billy Spencer and Charlie Scrimshaw, Beachill, made 136 senior appearances for the Potters spread over a period of eight years – from September 1926 to May 1934. Born at Monk Bretton on 21 May 1905, Beachill played initially for Monk Bretton FC and then for Rotherham County and Frickley Colliery before teaming up with Stoke. He left The Victoria Ground for Millwall and later assisted Wellington Town. He sadly died on 12 April 1943 after suffering a heart attack in Fletcher Road, Stoke, whilst returning home from Hyde & Sons Foundry, where he was on essential munitions work.

BEAGRIE, Peter

A very talented footballer with an exceptionally good left-foot, Beagrie starred on the wing in 61 games for Stoke City between August 1988 and October 1989 when he was transferred to Everton for £750,000. Beagrie, born in Middlesbrough on 28 November 1965, had earlier served with Guisborough and with his

Peter Beagrie

home-town club at Ayresome Park (1983-86), as well as Sheffield United (1986-88) and after leaving Goodison Park, and after a loan spell with Sunderland (1991) he went to Manchester City for £1.1 million in March 1994, playing for them in the Premiership. Capped twice by England 'B' and twice for the Under-21s, Beagrie has now amassed over 400 senior appearances as a professional.

BECKETT, Roy W.

Born in Stoke-on-Trent on 20 March 1928, half-back Beckett played for the Milton Youth Club and Burslem Albion before signing professional forms for Stoke City in April 1945. He scored once in 15 outings for the Potters before leaving the club for Northwich Victoria in 1953.

BECKFORD, Jason Neil

Between 1985 and 1996, Beckford was a right-sided attacking midfield player with Manchester City, Blackburn Rovers, Port Vale, Birmingham City, Bury, Stoke City (for six months duration: August-December 1994), Millwall and Northampton Town. He appeared in five senior games for the Potters and was never really a regular first-teamer with any of his clubs. He was born in Manchester in February 1970 and his brother, Darren, a striker, played for Manchester City, Bury, Port Vale, Oldham Athletic, Norwich City and Hearts.

BEBBINGTON, Richard Keith

A speedy outside-left who scored 22 goals in 124 games for the Potters whom he served as a professional from August 1960 to August 1966, having joined the club as an amateur in 1958 after unsuccessful trials with Northwich Victoria. Born in the village of Cuddington near Nantwich on 4 August 1943, he had trials early on with Northwich Victoria and appeared for Stoke in the 1964 League Cup Final v Leicester City. After leaving The Victoria Ground, he served with Oldham Athletic (sold for £26,000 plus George Kinnell in 1966) and then Rochdale, pulling out of League soccer in 1974 to join Winsford United. In his later years he played in midfield.

BEESTON, Carl Frederick

An enterprising but injury-prone midfield player who, in 1997, celebrated 14 years with Stoke City during which time he appeared in 271 first-team matches (17 goals scored). Born in Stoke on 30 June 1967, he gained an England Under-21 cap v USSR in 1987-88 and also helped the Potters win the Second Division championship in 1992-93. After failing to regain his first-team place at The Victoria Ground, in January 1997 he was loaned out to Third Division Hereford United.

BENBOW, Leonard

Centre-forward with a determined approach who was born in Oswestry c.1877. Benbow spent just the one season at The Victoria Ground (1900-01) during which time he scored four goals in 23 League appearances. He started his career with Oswestry United and then assisted Shrewsbury Town before teaming up with Nottingham Forest (1897-1900). He made over 50 senior appearances for Forest prior to joining Stoke whom he left for Northampton Town (1901-06). Benbow also assisted Port Vale, albeit briefly.

BENEFIT & TESTIMONIAL MATCHES

One of the first players to be granted a benefit by Stoke was Fred Johnson against the Corinthians in 1901.

Potters' wing-half Len Armitage was awarded a benefit match v Tottenham Hotspur in the Football League Division Two on 3 May 1930 when only 6,570 fans turned up instead of the anticipated 13,000.

Bobby Archibald's benefit game saw Stoke play FA Cup winners West Bromwich Albion (h) in the Second Division on 30 April 1931. The Victoria Ground's second biggest crowd of the season attended – over 26,000.

Full-back George Bourne and winger John Malkin had a joint Testimonial game at The Victoria Ground in 1956-57. Bourne received £855 as his share of the funds.

A TV audience of around 112 million watched Stan Matthews' farewell match at The Victoria Ground in April 1965 when Eurovision chose to beam the action across the North Sea and English Channel.

For Gordon Banks' Testimonial match on 12 December 1973, a crowd of 20,664 watched a Stoke side which included great stars like Eusebio and Bobby Charlton, lose 2-1 to Manchester United.

Among the other Stoke players to have had testimonials or benefit matches at The Victoria Ground are defenders Tony Allen and Eric Skeels (joint game v Derby County in February 1969); George Berry (v Port Vale in August 1990), Alan Bloor, Ian Cranson, Alan Dodd (v Port Vale, 1982), Peter Fox (v Everton in 1989), John McCue (October 1961), Denis Smith (April 1980), Dennis Viollet (May 1967), while ex-Potters' manager Tony Waddington was granted a testimonial in April 1987 when current and former Stokies starred in a Saint v Greavsie match.

In April 1913 a benefit match was arranged by Stoke on behalf of their former goalkeeper Tom Wilkes, who had fallen on hard times.

In November 1970 Stoke played East Fife (away) in a benefit match for Jock Dewar.

Former Stoke defender Arthur Turner was granted a testimonial match in October 1972 when the Potters met Wolves at Oxford United's Manor Ground.

Ex-Potter Tony Bentley's testimonial saw Stoke City play his club Southend United at Roots Hall in May 1972.

Tony Waddington took his Stoke City side to Maine Road to play Manchester City in Johnny Hart's testimonial match in May 1974.

Goalkeeper Alan Kelly of Preston celebrated his testimonial with a game against Stoke at Deepdale in November 1974.

Another 'keeper, Colin Boulton of Derby County, had his testimonial v Stoke City at The Baseball Ground in April 1975.

The following month (May 1975) Stoke visited Aston Villa to play in Mick Wright's testimonial match.

Stoke visited Port Vale for Phil Sproson's testimonial in March 1988 and played Dundee United in a testimonial for defender John Clark in 1994.

BENNETT, Edward

One of Stoke's earliest utility forwards, Bennett scored four goals in his three FA Cup appearances for the club in the early 1880s. Born in Stoke in 1862, he was with Stoke St Peter's initially and after leaving Stoke he played for Leek Welfare.

BENSON, Harold Lewis

Born in Hartshill on 22 January 1883, full-back Benson appeared in 91 League and FA Cup games for Stoke in six seasons up to April 1907. Strong in the tackle, he joined the Potters in May 1901 from Porthill, having previously assisted Shelton Albion, and he left The Victoria Ground for Northampton Town, later serving Port Vale from December 1908. It is believed that Benson, who worked as an office clerk, died locally (Stone) c.1953.

BENT, Junior

A 5ft 5ins Yorkshireman, born in Huddersfield on 1 March 1970, Bent, an out-and-out winger, used mainly down the right, had one League game for Stoke in March 1992 while on loan from Bristol City. He had been with Huddersfield Town and Burnley (on loan) prior to that, and joined Shrewsbury Town in season 1996-97 after more than 190 appearances for the Ashton Gate club.

BENTLEY, Anthony

Utility-forward Bentley was born in Stoke-on-Trent on 20 December 1939, and did well at schoolboy level before making his senior debut for Stoke City as an outside-right in 1958 at the age of 18. He went on to score 15 times in 51 League and Cup outings for the Potters, up to May 1961 when he joined Southend United for £1,500. After being successfully converted into a full-back, he proceeded to give the Roots Hall club excellent service, amassing more than 400 senior appearances, while skippering the Shrimpers many times and receiving two testimonials. On retirement in 1971, Bentley turned down an offer from Port Vale and quit football to go into catering and teaching in the Folkestone area.

BENTLEY, Arthur

Stockily built inside-forward, born in Longton in 1871, Bentley joined Stoke from Sandbach Ramblers in the summer of 1896 and played one season for the Potters as a reserve, making five League appearances before moving back to his former club.

BENTLEY, Frank William

Strapping centre-half with a solid frame, Bentley scored once in five League and Cup appearances for Stoke during March 1908. Born at Butt Lane (Staffs) on 9 October 1884, he played for his local club, Butt Lane FC prior to serving Stoke from June 1907 and after leaving The Victoria Ground he moved to London to play in 52 games for Tottenham Hotspur (July 1908-August 1912) and a handful for Brentford (1912-13). He died in Stoke-on-Trent in October 1958.

BENTLEY, William J.

During his career hard-tackling left-back Bill Bentley appeared in 296 League games for Stoke City, Blackpool and Port Vale. Born at Longton on 21 October 1947, he joined Stoke as a junior from St Gregory's School and turned professional in October 1964. After gaining England youth honours, he made his League debut at the age of 18 and went on to score twice in 53 first-team outings for the Potters before transferring to Bloomfield Road for £30,000 in January 1969. He was at Vale Park from July 1977 to May 1979 and rounded off his career with Stafford Rangers.

BENTON, John D.

Goalkeeper Jack Benton had two spells with Stoke – from March 1904 to March 1906 and from September 1908 to April 1910. Born in Newcastle (Staffs) in 1878, Benton started out with his local team Newcastle Swifts and then played for the North Staffordshire Regiment before switching to Northern Ireland where he assisted Glentoran. Whilst there he represented the Irish League on three occasions. Benton then travelled to South Africa where he assisted the Transvaal Police team. On his return to England, in March 1904, Stoke moved in and brought him to The Victoria Ground just in time for him to make his League debut against Sheffield Wednesday at Hillsborough (replacing Tom Wilkes). Jack Whitley then became first choice between the posts in 1904-05 and the following season, with Benton in the Reserves, Welsh international Richmond Roose was re-signed. At this juncture Benton, now a permanent fixture in the second XI, chose to revisit Ireland to play again for Glentoran. He rejoined Stoke in 1908 and took his appearance tally up to nine before retiring in 1910 through injury. He remained with the club as trainer until 1918, having taken the job on a temporary basis initially in 1908.

BERNARD, Michael

A hard-tackling, resourceful wing-half who could also play at full-back, Bernard accumulated a fine record during his six years in Stoke City's first team, appearing in 177 League and Cup games and scoring 11 goals. Born in Shrewsbury in 1948, he joined the playing staff at The Victoria Ground as a teenager in 1964 and turned professional two years later. From Stoke he went to Everton, joining the Merseysiders for £140,000 in 1972, and later played for Oldham Athletic before retiring (through injury) to become a publican in Chester. He later returned to soccer by becoming Football in the Community Officer at Crewe Alexandra, later working on the Commercial side at Gresty Road. Capped three times by England at Under-23 level, Bernard helped Stoke win the 1972 League Cup Final.

Micky Bernard

George Berry

BERRY, George F.

A strong-tackling, determined and wholehearted central defender who became a firm favourite with the Stoke fans following his transfer from Wolverhampton Wanderers in the summer of 1982. Born to Welsh parents in the town of Rostrop in (West) Germany in 1957, Berry joined the Molineux club as a youngster in 1973 (after trials with Ipswich Town) and went on to appear in 160 League and Cup games for the Wolves, helping them win the Football League Cup in 1980. For Stoke, he starred in 260 competitive matches, scoring 30 goals, a third of them from the penalty spot. He had a loan spell with Doncaster Rovers in 1984 and rounded off his senior career by having brief spells with Peterborough United, Preston North End and Aldershot. In 1992 he teamed up with Stafford Rangers, becoming their commercial manager when they were in the GM Vauxhall Conference. Four years later Berry left Stafford to take a full-time job with the PFA, working alongside Chief Executive Gordon Taylor, Pat Nevin and Brendon Batson. Berry won five full caps for Wales – his first ironically against West Germany.

BERTSCHIN, Keith Edwin

Bertschin scored with his first kick in League Football – for Ipswich Town against Arsenal at Highbury in April 1976. After that he continued to do well as a marksman and netted well over 150 goals in 450 games during

Keith Bertschin

the next 16 years or so while playing for the Portman Road club, Birmingham City, Norwich City, Jacksonville Teamen (NASL), Stoke City (signed for £80,000 in November 1984 and transferred for £32,500 in March 1987), Sunderland (with whom he gained a Third Division championship medal in 1988), Walsall, Chester City and Aldershot. His record at The Victoria Ground was 33 goals in 103 outings. Born in Enfield on 25 August 1956, Bertschin started out with Barnet as a youngster and while at Ipswich he was capped by England at both youth and Under-21 levels. On leaving top-class football, he played for Worcester City (1994-95) and then Atherstone Town, Oldbury Town and Solihull Borough, teaming up with another ex-Stokie, Paul Dyson, with the latter club.

BESWICK, David

Reserve-team goalkeeper at The Victoria Ground during the early

1930s, initially to Dick Williams and then to Norman Lewis, Beswick was given nine senior outings between the posts, and he did well. Born in Stoke in February 1910, he played his early football with Mount Pleasant FC (1927-29) and signed for the Potters initially as an amateur in April 1928, turning professional the following March. He stayed at The Victoria Ground for five years before leaving to join Walsall in November 1933.

NB: Beswick was not associated with the famous pottery family.

BESWICK, John Ewart

No relation to Dave (above) Jack Beswick was an intelligent but determined 6ft 1in centre-half, being a first-class header of the ball who thought hard and long about his game, giving nothing away. Born in Macclesfield, on 5 April 1897, he had two spells at The Victoria Ground – from April 1921 to April 1924 and from August 1925 to December 1927, when he retired through injury. One of the most distinguished amateurs to serve the club, being a member of the famous Longton pottery family (Samuel Macadam Beswick was his elder brother), he attended Longton High School and played for Congleton Town before joining Stoke and again prior to his return to the club. He scored twice in his 63 appearances in a Stoke shirt and was a member of the Third Division North championship winning side in 1926-27. He died in Stoke in February 1978.

BETTANY, Frederick

An inside or centre-forward, born in Stoke in 1862, Bettany was given two FA Cup outings by the Potters in 1885. Besides Stoke, he also assisted Tunstall Park and Newcastle (Staffs).

BEVANS, Stanley

Stoke City was Bevans' only Football League club. He was at The Victoria Ground for five and a half years (from April 1951 to November 1955) during which time he scored once in 15 senior appearances for the Potters as a forward. Born in Kingsley on 16 April 1934, he left Stoke for Macclesfield Town and later served with Heanor Town, Freehay Rovers and Bolton SC. He was one of the youngest players ever to appear in a Stoke shirt – aged 17 years, five months when he made his debut against Tottenham Hotspur (home) in September 1951.

BIGGINS, Wayne

Striker Biggins was born in Sheffield on 20 November 1961 and his first League club was Lincoln City (1977-81). After that he did well in the goalscoring stakes, first with King's Lynn and Matlock Town in non-League circles and thereafter with Burnley, Norwich City, Manchester City, Stoke City (who signed him for £250,000 in August 1988 and then sold him for £200,000 in October 1992 under the freedom of contract agreement), Burnley (again), Glasgow Celtic, Stoke City (for a second spell: signed in March 1994 for £125,000 and given a free to join Oxford United in July 1995 after a loan spell with Luton) and Wigan Athletic (November 1995 onwards). An Autoglass Trophy winner with Stoke in 1992, Biggins had netted 150 goals in more than 500 senior appearances at club level (to 1997). His two spells at The Victoria Ground realised 61 goals in 181 League and Cup outings.

BILEY, Alan Paul

Wayne Biggins

Biley had an excellent goalscoring record during his first-class career which saw him play for the following clubs: Luton Town (1973), Cambridge United (1975), Derby County (1980), Everton (1981), Stoke City (on loan in 1982, netting once in eight outings), Portsmouth (also in 1982), Brighton & Hove Albion (1985), New York Express (NASL), Cambridge United (again, 1986), Brest, Panionios (Greece) and finally Swindon Town (1988). He scored well over 150 League goals in less than 350 appearances. Biley, who was born in Leighton Buzzard on 26 February 1957, ended his nomadic career with non-League Welton Rangers before taking over as manager of Ely Town.

BIRCH, Percy

Goalkeeper Birch played in three League games for Stoke in 1885. Born in the Potteries in 1860, he assisted Stoke Priory in 1883-84 and after leaving Stoke served with Cobridge.

BIRMINGHAM CITY

(Formerly Small Heath Alliance and Small Heath)
Stoke's playing record against the Blues:

Football League

Venue	P	W	D	L	F	A
Home	39	26	8	5	71	34
Away	39	11	9	19	42	52
Totals	78	37	17	24	113	86

Football Alliance

Venue	P	W	D	L	F	A
Home	1	1	0	0	4	2
Away	1	0	0	1	1	5
Totals	2	1	0	1	5	7

FA Cup

Venue	P	W	D	L	F	A
Home	3	1	2	0	7	4
Away	3	1	1*	1	3	3
Totals	6	2	3	1	10	7

*This was a third place Play-off game in 1971 which ended 0-0 before Blues won 4-3 on penalties.

Autoglass Trophy

Venue	P	W	D	L	F	A
Home	1	1	0	0	3	1

Anglo-Italian Cup

Venue	P	W	D	L	F	A
Home	1	1	0	0	2	0

Texaco Cup

	P	W	D	L	F	A
Home	1	0	1	0	0	0
Away	1	0	1*	0	0	0

*After a 0-0 aggregate over two legs of a Group 1 tie, Blues beat Stoke 3-1 on penalties at the end of the second game at St Andrew's in October 1973.

Stoke's best League win over Blues is 6-1 at home in October 1895. Joe Schofield hit a hat-trick and the crowd was 8,000.

Stoke won 6-3 at The Victoria Ground in January 1939 when England star Freddie Steele scored four of the Potters' goals.

Stoke also won 5-0 at St Andrew's in September 1935 with a rare hat-trick from Stanley Matthews and two strikes from Joe Johnson; 5-2 at home in November 1973 (John Ritchie scored twice) and 4-1 away in September 1982 (a brace here for Mark Chamberlain).

Steele hit another hat-trick in a 4-2 home win over Blues in September 1936. The last minute of the Blues v Stoke City Second Division match at St Andrew's on 29 February 1992 was played out behind closed doors. The referee Roger Wiseman took both teams off the field following a pitch invasion by Blues' supporters after Paul Barnes had equalised for the Potters with barely 60 seconds remaining. The ground was emptied and the remainder of the game played at walking pace in a deserted stadium. The final result was 1-1.

Playing under their former name of Small Heath, Birmingham's best victory over Stoke is 5-1 in the Football Alliance in November 1890. Their best Football League win is 4-2 in November 1894. Birmingham also won a League game by 4-2 at home in November 1894 (Division One).

Stoke went 13 home League games without defeat against Blues between 1922 and 1965.

Under 11,000 – one of the lowest crowds for a League game between the clubs – assembled at The Victoria Ground on a bitterly cold Friday evening in January 1997 to watch Stoke beat Blues 1-0 in a BSkyB televised game. Ray Wallace scored the vital goal in the first-half.

Freddie Steele scored a hat-trick in Stoke's 4-1 win over Blues in the third round of the FA Cup in January 1937.

Blues fielded a weakened team when they visited The Victoria Ground for an Autoglass Trophy game in December 1991 which Stoke won 3-1.

Cyril Trigg scored five goals in Birmingham's 6-2 wartime Southern regional League win over Stoke in November 1940.

Players with both clubs: Horace Bailey, Jason Beckford, Keith Bertschin, Arthur Box, Noel Blake, Peter Bullock, Wayne Clarke, Ian Clarkson, Sammy Cole (Stoke junior 1892), Gerry Daly, Louie Donowa, Keith Downing, Bill Finney, George Gallimore, Howard Gayle, John Gayle, Nigel Gleghorn, Jimmy Greenhoff, Billy Haines, Jack Hall, Roger Jones, Howard Kendall, Terry Lees, Arthur Leonard, Kenny Lowe, Alex McClure, Vince Overson, Jack Peart, Fred Pentland, Paul Peschisolido, Graham Potter, Mark Prudhoe, Dave Regis, goalkeeper Bill Robertson, Mark Sale, Geoff Scott, Barry Siddall (non-contract with Blues), Andy Smith, Simon Sturridge and Arthur Turner.

Turner also managed Blues while Lou Macari managed at both clubs, having two spells with Stoke. Mick Mills was player-manager of Stoke City and later became assistant manager of Blues (1996) and Chic Bates was assistant manager-coach at both clubs (under Macari). Brian Caswell was a coach with both Stoke and Birmingham City. Peter Henderson was physiotherapist at both Birmingham City and Stoke City (under Lou Macari's management). Alan Ball senior was a player with Blues (1947) and later coach with Stoke City (1972). *NB: Four players who later joined Stoke, top-scored for Birmingham between 1980 and 1991: Keith Bertschin, Howard Gayle, Wayne Clarke (twice) and Nigel Gleghorn.*

BIRMINGHAM RESERVES

Stoke played Blues' second string six times during their Birmingham & District League days before World War One, the details being:

Venue	P	W	D	L	F	A
Home	3	2	0	1	10	3
Away	3	2	0	1	7	6
Total	6	4	0	2	17	9

Stoke won 4-0 in November 1909 and 6-2 in January 1911, both matches at St Andrew's.

BIRMINGHAM LEAGUE CUP

Stoke competed in this competition in season 1909-10.
They played four matches, the results of which were:
Rd 1   v Brierley Hill Alliance (h) draw 2-2
Rd 1R v Brierley Hill Alliance (a) won 5-0
Rd 2   v Stourbridge (h) won 3-1
Rd 3   v Aston Villa Reserves (a) lost 1-2

Amos Baddeley scored four goals in that 5-0 win at Brierley Hill.

BIRMINGHAM & DISTRICT LEAGUE

Stoke's first team played in the Birmingham & District League for three seasons: 1908 to 1911 inclusive.
Their record for each season was as follows:

Season	P	W	D	L	F	A	Pts	Pos
1908-09	34	13	5	16	71	64	31	8th
1909-10	34	17	7	10	83	48	37	7th
1910-11	34	24	2	8	95	48	50	1st
Totals	102	54	14	34	249	160	118	-

● When winning the championship in 1910-11, Stoke lost only one home match while winning the other 16.

● Their biggest Birmingham League victory out of the 54 recorded was 10-0 v Halesowen (home) in April 1911 when Alf Smith scored five goals.

● An 8-1 reverse away to West Bromwich Albion Reserves in October 1908 was Stoke's heaviest Birmingham League defeat.

BIRMINGHAM ST GEORGE'S

Stoke's playing record against St George's:
Football Alliance

Venue	P	W	D	L	F	A
Home	1	1	0	0	6	3
Away	1	0	0	1	2	5
Totals	2	1	0	1	8	8

These games were played in season 1891-92 – on 13 September at The

Victoria Ground when Charlie Baker scored four times in Stoke's 6-3 win, while the return match took place on 18 October in Birmingham when St George's gained sweet revenge.

BIRMINGHAM TRANSPORT

Stoke met the Transport team in the first qualifying round of the FA Cup in October 1914 and came through narrow victors by 3-2.

BITHELL, Brian

Bithell graduated via the Stoke youth scheme (set up when George Eastham was manager in the early 1970s). He went on to make 18 appearances for the club in two seasons, but after a loan spell with Port Vale and a sending-off at West Brom, he was then transferred to Wimbledon for £5,000 in December 1977. A wing-half with good balance, he was born in Winsford in October 1956 and joined Stoke as a teenager in 1973, turning professional on his 18th birthday.

BLACKBURN ROVERS

Stoke's playing record against Blackburn Rovers, who were also founder members of the Football League in 1888:

Football League

Venue	P	W	D	L	F	A
Home	39	22	8	9	76	42
Away	39	6	5	28	37	101
Totals	78	28	13	37	113	143

FA Cup

Venue	P	W	D	L	F	A
Home	2	1	0	1	1	1
Away	1	0	0	1	0	1
Totals	3	1	0	2	1	2

League Cup

Venue	P	W	D	L	F	A
Home	1	0	0	1	0	1
Away	1	0	1	0	1	1
Totals	2	0	1	1	1	2

Stoke beat Rovers 6-2 at The Victoria Ground on 31 October 1903 when six different names figured on the Potters' scoresheet.

Stoke also won 5-1 at home in April 1895, while in reverse, Rovers walloped the Potters 8-0 at Ewood Park on 4 January 1890, this being only the fourth meeting between the clubs.

The very first League clash saw Rovers beat Stoke 5-2 at home in October 1888. Stoke gained revenge later that season by winning 2-1.

Rovers also beat Stoke 5-3 in March 1892, 5-0 in April 1894, 6-0 in in September 1894 and 6-1 in February 1902 – all at home.

A hat-trick from Joey Schofield earned Stoke a point from a 3-3 away draw with Rovers in February 1893.

In the Lancashire Section Primary Competition in November 1917, Stoke rattled in a total 24 goals in successive games against Rovers. They beat them 16-0 at home with Bob Whittingham (4), Ted Turner (4) and Billy Herbert (3) leading the route, and a week later Rovers were hammered 8-1 at Ewood Park when Whittingham netted twice as did Henry Howell and Jack Bridgett.

The following season, in the same competition, Stoke beat Blackburn 7-0 at home and 6-0 away. Arthur Lockett scored a hat-trick in the first game and Herbert in the second.

In the transitional League season of 1945-46, Stoke beat Rovers 5-0 a home a week after losing 5-1 at Ewood Park

Stoke played with only ten men for the duration of their home Football League game against Blackburn Rovers on 14 December 1889. The missing player was Harry Simpson. Rovers won 3-0.

A controversial penalty decision (subsequently scored by England winger Bryan Douglas) saw Rovers through 1-0 against Stoke in a fourth-round FA Cup-tie at The Victoria Ground in January 1962 when the crowd was 49,486

Players with both clubs: Jason Beckford, Percy Brooke, Viv Busby, Joe Clennell, Peter Dobing, Howard Gayle, Verdi Godwin, David Gregory, Geoff Hickson (amateur with Rovers), Roger Jones, Howard Kendall, Bert Mitchell, Fred Pentland, Bert Ralphs, Tommy Sale, Bill Sawyers, Jimmy Swarbrick, Dennis Thorley, Roy Vernon and Tom Williamson.

Asa Hartford was assistant manager-coach at both Rovers (under Kenny Dalglish) and Stoke City (under Joe Jordan). Sammy Chung was assistant manager at Stoke and scout for Blackburn Rovers.

BLACKIE, Sidney

Reserve centre-forward from Gateshead who played in two League games for Stoke in January 1925, deputising for Len Armitage against Leicester City and Port Vale. He joined the club from Hebden Bridge FC and left for Southend United.

BLACKPOOL

Stoke's playing record against Blackpool is:

Football League

Venue	P	W	D	L	F	A
Home	26	11	8	7	47	32
Away	26	7	8	11	30	39
Totals	52	18	16	18	77	71

FA Cup

Venue	P	W	D	L	F	A
Home	3	2	1	0	8	2
Away	1	1	0	0	1	0
Totals	4	3	1	0	9	2

Stoke's best win over the Seasiders at League level is 4-0 at The Victoria Ground in December 1952 when a crowd of 19,382 saw Harry Oscroft lead the goal-rush with a fine double.

The Potters also won 4-1 at home in December 1946 when 30,000 saw Stan Matthews net against his future club. Blackpool beat Stoke 4-2 at Bloomfield Road in December 1950 and again at home in November 1951 when Willie McIntosh scored twice for the Potters in front of a near 20,000 crowd.

Frank Mountford split the casing on the ball when he converted a penalty to give Stoke a 1-0 home win over Blackpool in the First Division in November 1951.

Over 30,000 fans saw Matthews, Frank Soo and Tommy Sale score for Stoke in their 3-0 home FA Cup win over Blackpool in January 1934.

Thirty one years later in January 1965, John Ritchie (2) and Dennis Viollet (2) were on target in Stoke's 4-1 third round FA Cup triumph over the Seasiders at The Victoria Ground when the turnout was 38,651.

Players with both clubs: Amos Baddeley, Dave Bamber, Walter Bussey, Joe Clennell, Archie Dyke, Tony Ellis, Harold Hardman, Dave

Hockaday, Jim Martin, Stanley Matthews, Willie McIntosh, Hugh McMahon, Jackie Mudie, Carl Muggleton, Fred Pentland, Paul Richardson, Barry Siddall, Alan Suddick, Bob Whittingham and Jim Williams.

Alan Ball played for and managed Blackpool and was also manager of Stoke. Ball's father, Alan senior, was a scout with Blackpool and coach at Stoke. Terry Lees had trials with Blackpool and also played for Stoke. And Verdi Godwin was a Stoke player who later scouted for the Seasiders.

BLAKE, Noel Lloyd George

A fiercely competitive defender, Blake was built like a heavyweight boxer. Commanding in the air, strong and fearless on the ground, he was a match for any bustling centre-forward and never shirked a tackle. Born in Jamaica in January 1962, he was educated at Alderlea School and as a youngster played for Wilhemena Boys before joining Sutton Coldfield Town in April 1978. After a spell with Walsall as a non-contract player, he signed professional forms for Aston Villa in August 1979. Then, following a month on loan with Shrewsbury Town (March 1982) he was transferred to Birmingham City for £55,000 in the September of that same year, and went on to make almost 100 senior appearances for the Blues. In August 1984, he was sold to Portsmouth for £150,000 and four years later switched to Leeds United for a fee of £175,000. Stoke paid £160,000 for his services in February 1990 and during his stay at The Victoria Ground (to May 1992) he scored three goals in 92 League and Cup games. After leaving Stoke, Blake had a spells with Bradford City and also in Scotland with Dun-

Noel Blake

dee before moving due south to team up with his former Potters colleague Peter Fox at Exeter City.

BLYTH SPARTANS

Stoke's playing record against the Spartans is:

FA Cup

Venue	P	W	D	L	F	A
Home	1	0	0	1	2	3
Away	1	1	0	0	3	0
Totals	2	1	0	1	5	3

In January 1922 Stoke travelled north for a first-round tie and won comfortably by 3-0, Jimmy Broad scoring twice.

Then in February 1978, non-League Blyth caused a major shock when they knocked Second Division Stoke out of the competition in the fourth round, winning 3-2 at The Victoria Ground before an 18,765 crowd. Alan A'Court was caretaker manager of the Potters at the time of this debacle.

BLOOR, Alan

Nicknamed 'Bluto', Alan Bloor was a local lad who certainly reached the top. At junior level he was one of the star defenders for Uttoxeter Road CP and then Queensbury Road senior schools and he also represented Stoke-on-Trent Schoolboys, going on to win England youth caps, skippering his country at this level. Born in Stoke-on-Trent in March 1943, he signed professional forms for the Potters on his 17th birthday, but had to bide his time, for manager Tony

Alan Bloor

Waddington would not be rushed into introducing Bloor to first-team action. Indeed, it was not until 1961-62 that Bloor finally entered League Football and then it was not until 1965 that he finally established himself in the first XI. But from then on, he never looked back. He went from strength to strength and in the next 12 seasons, mainly as partner to Denis Smith, he was an inspiring figure in Stoke's defence. He eventually amassed a total of 484 first-team appearances for the club, scoring 19 goals. He was a member of Stoke's 1972 League Cup and 1973 Watney Cup winning teams and during his time at The Victoria Ground he received praise from many of the country's top managers, including Sir Matt Busby, Ron Greenwood and Bill Shankly. After serving Stoke City for 18 years, Bloor moved across town to join Port Vale, initially as player and youth-team coach, and then later as manager, albeit not a happy reign. After leaving Vale Park he became successful in a carpet business in his native Longton.

BOARDMAN, Albert

Boardman was a capable goalkeeper, who actually played the last of his four League games for Stoke in the left-back position against Nottingham Forest in September 1896, replacing 'flu victim Jack Eccles at the 11th hour after after his replacement Peter Durber failed to receive a postcard requiring him to play. Indeed, Stoke turned up at Nottingham with only ten men; Boardman arrived 37 minutes after the kick-off with manager-secretary Billy Rowley. Stoke lost the game 4-0. Born in Stoke-on-Trent in February 1870, Boardman was recruited from neighbours Burslem Port Vale in June 1894 and left the Potters to play for Dresden United in the summer of 1897.

BOGOTA AFFAIR

On the 8 May 1950, two Stoke City players, centre-half Neil Franklin and forward George Mountford, along with Charlie Mitten of Manchester United and Everton's Billy Higgins, with their respective families, packed their bags and left Britain en route to South America via New York, to play their football in Colombia, a country outside the jurisdiction of FIFA.

Franklin, Mountford and Mitten joined Independiente Sante Fe of Bogota, while Higgins signed for the Millionaires Club, along with the great Spaniard, Alfredo di Stefano.

Their departure from these shores created a major talking point in English soccer circles and indeed throughout the footballing world.

In truth, prior to his departure, Franklin's relationship with Stoke City had been somewhat uneasy for quite a while – and rumours of renewed problems had been rumbling since the previous spring. Franklin had declined to go with England to the World Cup finals that year and when they heard the news that he was set to travel overseas, the FA made this announcement:

'The reports and rumours that Franklin is to take up a coaching position in America during the close season or play football for the Sante Fe club, must be disregarded in view of the letter which he has sent to the FA in which he stated that the reason he wished to be exempted (from the World Cup) was that he just could not possibly leave home during the summer months because of his wife's health. We have been in touch with him since the receipt of his letter and he has confirmed what he has written."

Walter Winterbottom, the England team manager, had made three attempts to persuade Franklin to change his mind and join his squad for the World Cup finals, but he drew a blank each time. The FA also sent telegrams on the Tuesday giving all four players involved a last chance to pull out of the Bogota experience – but the die was cast.

The national and local papers gave extensive coverage of the infamous affair for, after all, Franklin had just played his 37th consecutive game in an England shirt (27 at senior level and 10 in wartime internationals) which was a record at the time, and gives a good and clear indication of his stature in the game.

From his hotel in New York, Franklin was reported as saying that he had not left England secretly. He had received a much better offer and the chance of a super holiday with his family. He did not sign a contract for Indepediente Sante Fe – just an agreement 'to look over the place'. The position of head coach was available (if required) with George Mountford as his assistant.

Reports of the inducements made to tempt the players abounded with large signing-on fees of around 20,000 dollars (£3,400 each) plus 1,000 pesos per match (another £170).

There was free house thrown in along with servants, and additionally Mrs Franklin, who was expecting a baby in the August, was promised the best medical attention possible.

A large crowd assembled at the airport to welcome the four English players to Bogota, and by this time, Jimmy Guthrie, leader of the Players' Union was heavily involved in the situation and threatened to issue a High Court injunction if the two Stoke players were banned. This was clearly a body blow for players' freedom.

For the record, the maximum wage in the Football League in 1950 was £12 a week in the winter and £10 in the summer.

The Colombians appreciated the skills of the Stoke duo, particularly the footwork and pace of Mountford who set the fans talking by netting a hat-trick in a practice match.

Franklin and Mountford made their debuts for Sante Fe in the Colombian Premier League on the 14 May and they started off with a 3-2 victory over Medallin, Mountford having a hand in two of the goals and then scoring their winner himself, much to the delight of the 22,000 crowd.

Expectador, the local paper in Sante Fe, stated: 'The players left the field to the chants of "Long Live Britain".'

The players and their wives were treated like royalty, but there was political unrest in the country, and the social life out there left a lot to be desired, no one could travel around the towns after 6.30pm.

Inside two months Franklin was back in England, fed up with Colombian football and both his Stoke City and England careers in tatters.

He never donned a Potters' shirt again and in February 1951 was transferred to Hull City for £22,500.

As for Mountford, he completed the season with Sante Fe and returned to England. He rejoined Stoke and after serving a suspension, turned out for the first team again.

It was thought that a third Stoke player – possibly Johnny Malkin – had also set his sights on going to Colombia, but nothing was proven in this field.

BOLTON WANDERERS

Stoke's playing record against Bolton is:
Football League

Venue	P	W	D	L	F	A
Home	36	19	6	11	73	35
Away	36	8	11	17	43	67
Totals	72	27	17	28	116	102

FA Cup

Home	2	1	0	1	4	4
Away	3	0	1	2	3	6
Totals	5	1	1	3	7	10

League Cup
Home   1   1   0   0   3   0

Stoke registered their best League win over the Wanderers at The Victoria Ground in January 1893, beating them 6-0 with Teddy Evans scoring a hat-trick in front of 4,500 fans.

In contrast Bolton's best League win over the Potters is 5-0 – at Burnden Park in February 1890. The Trotters also won 4-0 at home in September 1994.

In October 1892 eight goals were shared in a thrilling 4-4 League game at Bolton.

When the Trotters drew 1-1 at The Victoria Ground in the last League game of the 1994-95 season, they were on the brink of the Premiership which they gained entry to via the Wembley Play-off Ffinal against Reading.

Bolton scored in each of their first 17 home Football League games against Stoke (1888-1936).

The Potters ran in 15 goals against the Trotters in three successive home League games in the 1890s, winning 6-0, 5-0 and 5-0 again in that order.

Stoke from the Second Division beat Bolton from the First 4-2 in a fourth-round FA Cup-tie at The Victoria Ground in January 1928. Charlie Wilson scored twice for the Potters in front of 24,868 fans.

A third-round FA Cup-tie between Bolton and Stoke at Burnden Park was the first-ever Sunday game for both clubs – and it was the Trotters who celebrated by winning a closely fought contest 3-2.

After knocking Stoke out of the FA Cup in the fifth round in season 1957-58 Bolton went on to win the trophy, beating Manchester United 2-0 in the Final.

The Trotters beat Stoke 9-3 in a Lancashire Section Primary Competition in 1916-17, while the Potters gained revenge with a 7-1 victory in the same competition in December 1918.

The score of the First Division clash between Stoke and Bolton at the start of the ill-fated 1939-40 season was 2-1 in favour of the Potters. When the teams met again at the start of the 1946-47 campaign, Stoke again defeated the Trotters by the same scoreline of 2-1.

Players with both clubs: Harry Brigham, Paul Crooks, Dickie Cunliffe, Billy Dickson, Mick Doyle, John Dreyer, Tony Ellis, Arthur Fielding, Tony Henry, Billy Herbert, Tom Kay, Tony 'Zico' Kelly, Jim McGeachan, Wally McReddie, Ian Moores, Robbie Savage, Peter Shilton, Barry Siddall, Jack Tennant and Jim Turner.

Future Stoke boss Tom Mather was Bolton Wanderers' assistant secretary (pre-war) who later became manager at Burnden Park (1915-19). Asa Hartford played for Bolton and later became assistant manager at Stoke City. Verdi Godwin was a Stoke player who later acted as scout for the Wanderers.

BOLTON DISASTER OF 1946

In season 1945-46 Stoke City made progress to the sixth round of the FA Cup and were paired with Bolton Wanderers, the tie to be played over two legs. The first game at The Victoria Ground on 2 March resulted in a 2-0 win for Bolton and consequently the Trotters were red-hot favourites to enter the semi-finals.

Thousands of fans flocked to Burnden Park for the return leg a week later and it was reported that the ground attendance record could be broken. In fact, the official figure given was 65,419 – which was around 4,500 below the record which had been set in 1933. A combined total of 116,154 spectators witnessed the two legs in 1946.

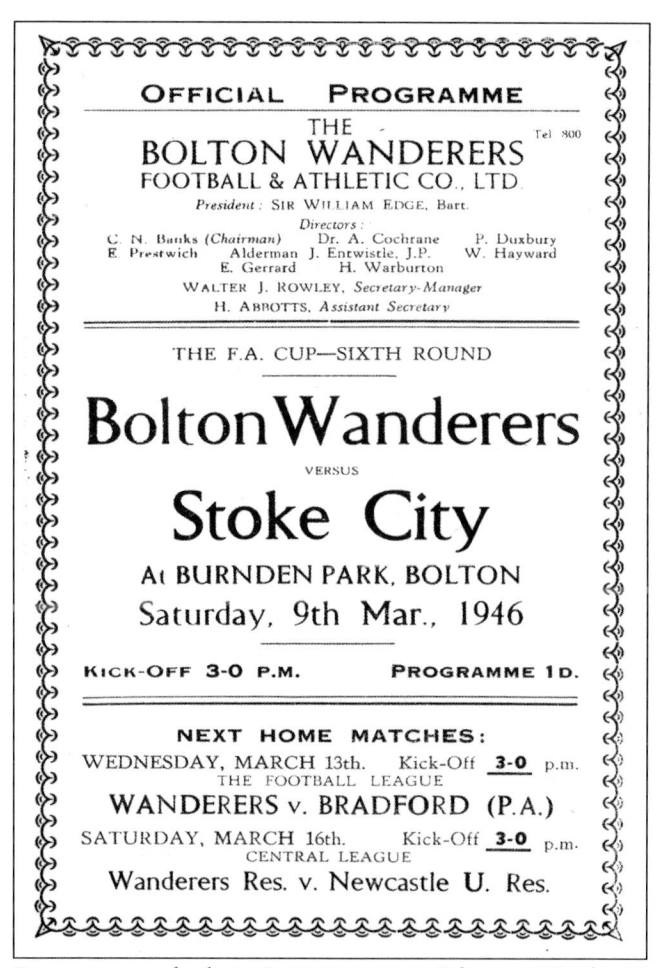

Programme cover for the tragic FA Cup game at Bolton in 1946, when 33 spectators were killed in the crush as over 65,000 squeezed into Burnden Park to see the game between the Trotters and the Potters.

Unfortunately, during the first half of the match at Burnden the crush barriers gave way on the terraces and in the mayhem that followed, 33 spectators were killed and another 520 injured, some of them seriously. The game itself was delayed for a short time while stewards, police and the emergency services sorted things out. The players did not know what had happened at first, but when they were told some of them broke down and shed tears.

BONNYMAN, Philip

A Glaswegian midfielder, born in February 1954, Bonnyman started off in his native Scotland, playing for Anniesland Wanderers. He then played for Glasgow Rangers and Hamilton Academical before joining Carlisle United in 1976. Four years later he went to Chesterfield and in 1982 was transferred to Grimsby Town. He was aged 32 when he played seven games on loan for Stoke City during the 1985-86 season. Bonnyman later played for Darlington and Dunfermline Athletic and retired in 1990 with more than 500 club appearances under his belt.

BOOTE, George

Boote was one of four different goalkeepers utilised by Stoke in four matches. He played in the 1-1 home League draw with Nottingham Forest in the First Division on 5 October 1901 – his only outing for the club. Always a reserve at The Victoria Ground, he was allowed to leave the club to join Lonsdale Rovers in 1902 when Dr Leigh Richmond

Roose arrived. Born in Stoke in 1878, Boote was signed from St Peter's Bards as cover for Tom Wilkes. He died c.1940.

BOOTH, Alderman H.

Booth was chairman of Stoke City FC for 15 years (1936-51). He took over the mantle from Mr A.J.C.Sherwin and in turn handed over the duties to Mr T.A.Preece.

BOOTLE

Stoke's playing record against Bootle:
Football Alliance

Venue	P	W	D	L	F	A
Home	1	1	0	0	2	1
Away	1	0	1	0	2	2
Totals	2	1	1	0	4	3

These games were played in 1890-91. On 15 November a brace of goals by outside-left Billy Dunn gave the Potters a 2-1 home victory, while in the return fixture on Merseyside on 6 December, Dunn and Charlie Baker netted to earn Stoke a point from a 2-2 draw.

BOUGHEY, Darren

'Dodger' Boughey, a outside-right, born in Newcastle (Staffs) in November 1970, graduated through the junior ranks at Stoke and went on to make 10 first-team appearances for the club before moving to Macclesfield Town on a free transfer in 1992. Whilst at The Victoria Ground he also played on loan with Wigan Athletic and Exeter City and after Macclesfield Town (April 1992) had a spell with Stafford Rangers.

BOULD, Stephen Andrew

After scoring seven goals in 211 League and Cup games for Stoke City and appearing in 11 matches on loan with Torquay United in 1982, Steve Bould became Tony Adams' long-standing partner at the heart of the Arsenal defence, and when the 1996-97 season ended Bould had amassed close on 400 appearances for the Gunners. Born in Stoke-on-Trent on 16 November 1962, he joined the apprentice ranks at The Victoria Ground as a 16-year-old and turned professional in November 1980. He made the number-five shirt his own at The Victoria Ground in 1983 and was a regular in the senior side until his tribunal-set £390,000 transfer to Arsenal in the June 1988. A strong,

Steve Bould

determined player, powerful in the air, keen and assured on the ground, he suffered back problems as a Stoke player and has gone through the same pain barrier (as well as being plagued by a number of thigh and leg injuries) whilst at Highbury, yet has still managed to collect medals for two First Division championship triumphs (1989 and 1991) and a European Cup-winners' Cup Final victory in 1994 with the London club. He has also been capped twice by England at senior level and once for the 'B' team. A great competitor at any level.

BOULLIMIER, Lucien Emile

Despite his name, Boullimier was, in fact, born in Penkhull, Stoke-on-Trent in 1874. The son of the famous Parisian ceramic artist Anton Boullimier, who was employed by Mintons, right-half Lucien Boullimier was a decent wing-half who, besides playing seven League games for Stoke during the 1896-97 season, was also employed by Royal Worcester, and he was also a very good opera singer, a respected actor and a pretty successful artist. In 1897, he left Stoke for Burslem Port Vale. In the summer of 1903 he went over to America to pursue his artistic career, and on his return after a year he continued playing football, this time for Northampton. In season 1905-06 he was back with Port Vale (one game). He died in Stoke-on-Trent c.1948.
NB: Lucien's brother, Leon Antony, kept goal for Stoke's reserve team, Burslem Port Vale, Lincoln City, Brighton & Hove Albion and Northampton Town.

BOULTON, Ernest

Centre-forward Boulton scored six goals in 11 Southern League and Birmingham League games for Stoke during the second half of the 1910-11 season, deputising initially for Billy Smith and then taking over as leader of the attack when key players were injured. Born in Hanley in 1889, he served in the Grenadier Guards before signing for Stoke and unfortunately his career was cut short through injury, Boulton being forced to retire in 1912.

BOURNE, Albert

Burslem-born full-back who played in one senior game for Stoke against Warwick County in the first qualifying round of the FA Cup in October 1888 when he stood in for Tommy Clare. Born at Chesterton in 1862, Bourne, who joined Stoke from church football, was never a candidate for regular first-team duty and he stayed at the club for just a year, leaving in April 1889 for Tunstall Rovers.

BOURNE, George

A product of Middleport County Modern School, Bourne assisted a number of local teams including Park Road Youth Club, Thomas Hughes (Pottery) and Burslem Albion before signing as an amateur for Stoke City in June 1950, turning professional after completing his National Service in 1951. Born in Burslem on 5 March 1932, he was originally a forward, but was successfully converted into a fine right-back at The Victoria Ground and went on to score one goal in 109 outings for the Potters. Sadly a serious leg injury ended Bourne's career at the age of 24. he was awarded a testimonial and given a club grant which the press reported as being £855 – nothing near the princely sum received by players these days.

BOURNEMOUTH AFC

Stoke's playing record against Bournemouth is:
Football League

Venue	P	W	D	L	F	A
Home	6	3	2	1	7	6
Away	6	2	3	1	6	5
Totals	12	5	5	2	13	11

League Cup

Venue	P	W	D	L	F	A
Home	1	1	0	0	2	1

The first League encounter between the Potters and the Cherries took place at The Victoria Ground in October 1987 (Division Two). That day a crowd of 8,104 saw Tony Ford give Stoke all three points with the game's only goal.

The return fixture at Bournemouth later in the season resulted in a 0-0 draw.

Stoke doubled up over the Cherries in 1988-89, winning 2-1 at home and 1-0 away.

Former England left-back Derek Statham scored his first goal for Stoke to earn a point from a 1-1 draw at Bournemouth in 1990-91.

The last two meetings between the clubs at League level took place in 1992-93. Mark Stein scored both goals in Stoke's 2-0 home win and he was again on target in the 1-1 draw at Dean Court.

When Bournemouth won their first League game at Stoke (3-1 in 1990-91) they did so against ten men following the dismissal of Mick Kennedy.

The League Cup clash was in the fourth round in November 1963 when John Ritchie scored both Stoke's goals in front of 9,766 freezing spectators.

Players with both clubs: David Kevan, Roger Jones, Nicky Morgan, David Puckett, Dave Regis, Colin Russell, Kevin Russell, Robbie Savage, Keith Scott, Brian Siddall and Andrew Smith.

BOWERS, Ian

A competent full-back in his own right, 'Danny' Bowers was born in Audley on 16 January 1955 and graduated through the junior ranks at Stoke, turning professional in 1972. He made his League debut two years later along with Peter Shilton against Wolves, and went on to appear in 46 senior games for the Potters, scoring two goals. After a loan spell with Shrewsbury Town (1977) he left The Victoria Ground for Crewe Alexandra for £8,000 in July 1979 and quit top-class football in 1983 after making 175 League appearances for the Alex. He later played for Audley & District FC and Bignall End Swan FC.

BOWMAN, John William

A native of Middlesbrough (born on 23 April 1879) wing-half Bowman was discovered by Burslem Port Vale in junior football (1898) and after a short spell there he switched to Stoke in August 1899. A teetotaller and non-smoker, Bowman was also an exceptional swimmer and a pretty smart athlete who ran any distance from 11 yards to 10 miles. He had four League outings for Stoke before transferring to Queen's Park Rangers in 1901. After that he went to

Norwich City, first as a player, and later held the position of player-manager of the East Anglian club for two seasons (1905-07). He died in Salisbury in January 1943.

BOWYER, Frank

Inside-forward Bowyer joined Stoke City in June 1937 soon after leaving Birches Head School. He developed quickly and turned professional in the summer of 1939. Unfortunately World War Two disrupted his career at the outset and it was not until February 1948, at the age of 26, that he finally played in the Football League and FA Cup competitions. However, during the hostilities Bowyer did extremely well for the Potters, scoring 62 goals in 162 Regional League and Cup matches. Thereafter, up until 1960, he went on to add 436 more senior appearances to his tally, netting another 149 goals – to become one of the finest marksmen in Stoke's history, finishing only three goals short of Freddie Steele's record of 140 League goals for the club. A quality player with excellent shot (in both feet) Bowyer, who was born in Chesterton on 10 April 1922, went on tour with the FA to Canada in the summer of 1950. After 23 years service with Stoke, Bowyer finally left the club in the summer of 1960 and played briefly for Macclesfield Town before retiring two years later.

BOX, Arthur

Box was a squarely built goalkeeper who played in 39 League games for Stoke between August 1907 and September 1909. Born in Hanley in September 1884, he was a pupil at Wellington Road School and assisted Hanley Villa and Northwood Mission as a junior before having trials at The Victoria Ground (1904). He then had three excellent years with Burslem Port Vale, where he became their chief penalty-taker. He returned as a permanent player with Stoke in 1907-08, leaving the Potters second time round for Birmingham for £100, later assisting Leek Victoria and Croydon Common (1910-11) and Crewe Alexandra from 1911, through World War One to 1921. Box died in Stoke-on-Trent c.1950

BOXLEY, David

Black Country centre-forward, born in Cradley Heath in 1890, Boxley scored four goals in eight League outings for Stoke in the first season after World War One. He was signed by the Potters from Cradley St Luke's in the summer of 1919 and left The Victoria Ground for Dudley Town the following summer. He later assisted Old Hill Wanderers and Smethwick Town.

BRACEWELL, Paul William

Bracewell joined Stoke City as a junior straight from school in 1976. He battled on through the intermediate sides into the Reserves and finally became an established first-team player in 1980, having made his League debut before his 18th birthday. A skilful midfielder, with excellent passing ability, Bracewell went on to score six goals in 141 senior games for the Potters before transferring to Sunderland for £250,000 in June 1983, signed by former Stoke boss Alan Durban. He left Roker Park after a season to join another former Stokie, Howard Kendall, at Everton – the fee: £425,000. Whilst at Goodison Park, Bracewell gained three full England caps (to add to his 13 he had already won at Under-21 level, two of them when at Stoke). He returned to Roker Park for £250,000 in 1989 and three years later he went the short journey to Newcastle United, the fee another £250,000. Always a valuable member of the team, Bracewell suffered his fair share of injury problems during the late 1980s/early '90s, but he bounced back every time and in 1995 he joined Sunderland for the third time. £100,000 exchanged hands on this occasion and he duly helped guide the Wearsiders into the Premiership. During his stay with Everton, Bracewell, who was born on the Wirral in July 1962, won European Cup-winners' Cup and First Division championship medals in 1984-85, and over a period of seven years, between 1985 and 1992, he played in four successive losing FA Cup Finals. At the end of the 1996-97 season, Bracewell (who by now had been promoted to assistant manager-coach at Roker Park) had taken his appearance tally at club level to close to the 650 mark.

BRADBURY, William

Left-half Bradbury made 31 League and Cup appearances for Stoke – all in season 1910-11. Born in Sudbury, Derbyshire in 1884, he served with May Bank FC, Newcastle Swifts, Burslem Port Vale and Fegg Hayes before moving to The Victoria Ground, and after leaving the Potters he played briefly for Aberdare, then Oldham Athletic (two spells: 1911-13 and 1919-22, making 73 appearances in total), Scunthorpe and Lindsay United (1913-19) and Rochdale (1922-23). Bradbury was awarded the Military Medal during World War One and after leaving football he became a publican in Burton upon Trent. His son, Tom Bradbury, played for Derby County.

BRADFORD CITY

Stoke's playing record against the Bantams is:
Football League

Venue	P	W	D	L	F	A
Home	17	11	4	2	29	12
Away	17	3	4	10	19	31
Totals	34	14	8	12	48	43

Data Systems Cup

Home	1	1	0	0	2	1

Stoke's best League win over the Bantams is 4-1 – achieved on two occasions: at home in May 1933 and at Valley Parade in January 1988.

Stoke were presented with the Second Division championship trophy before that victory in 1933 and a crowd of 17,380 saw Bobby Liddle score twice in a comfortable celebratory victory.

In contrast Stoke had four different marksmen in that win at Bradford in 1988 – Nicky Morgan, Tony Ford, Lee Dixon and Tony Henry.

Bradford's best League triumph over Stoke is 6-0 at home in March 1908 (Division Two) when Frank O'Rourke scored a hat-trick in front of 14,996 fans.

The Full Members' Cup-tie took place in November 1989. George Berry (penalty) and Dave Bamber scored for the Potters before a crowd of 4,616.

Players with both clubs: Jeff Cook, John Dreyer, Jack Forrest, Peter Griffiths, Harold Hardman, Sam Higginson, Peter Jackson, Robbie James, Mick Kennedy, Jock Kirton, Harry Leese, Tommy Little, Eric McManus, George Mulholland, Leigh Palin, Ben Prosser, Robbie Savage, Ronnie Sinclair, Billy Smith, Tim Steele, Jack Stirling, Albert 'Tinker' Whitehurst, Bob Whittingham, Louis Williams and Alf Wood.

Jack Peart played for Stoke (pre-World War One) and later became manager of Bradford City (1930-35), likewise Chris Kamara, ex-Stokie, who was appointed into the hot seat at Valley Parade (The Pulse Stadium) in November 1995. Ex-Stoke player Jack Peart later managed Bradford City as did Peter Jackson.

BRADFORD PARK AVENUE

Stoke's playing record against Park Avenue is:
Football League

Venue	P	W	D	L	F	A
Home	7	4	2	1	10	3
Away	7	1	2	4	12	16
Totals	14	5	4	5	22	19

FA Cup

Home	2	1	0	1	4	2
Away	1	0	1	0	1	1
Totals	3	1	1	1	5	3

The last time the teams met at League level was in 1932-33 when the Potters became Second Division champions. That season Stoke won 4-0 at home to register their best win over the Yorkshire side and drew 2-2 away.

Harry Sellars, Joey Mawson, Bobby Liddle and Harry Ware scored in that home victory which was witnessed by just 7,962 fans – the lowest of the season at The Victoria Ground.

Players with both clubs: Tom Baddeley, Norman Lewis, Tom Little, Jock Stirling and Alf Wood.

BRADLEY, James Edwin

Wing-half Bradley, a model of consistency who tackled with great judgement, had two separate spells at The Victoria Ground and all told scored six goals in 256 League and Cup games for the club. Born at Goldenhill in May 1881, he signed for Stoke as a 16-year-old in February 1898, and was a regular in the side right up until 1905 when he transferred to Liverpool after refusing to go to Plymouth Argyle. Bradley did very well on Merseyside, gaining a League championship medal with the Reds in 1906. A great practical joker, he played for Reading for a short time before returning to Stoke in 1913 after having his contract terminated at Elm Park after he had tossed the full Reading kit into the bath. Back at Stoke, he helped the Potters win their Southern League Division Two title in 1915 and when war arrived he quit playing top-class soccer and started work for the Stoke-on-Trent Highways Department, coaching the Reserves at The Victoria Ground in his spare time. Bradley died in Blackpool on 12 March 1954.

NB: His brother Martin played for Sheffield United, Grimsby Town and Bristol Rovers.

BRADSHAW, Joseph

Bradshaw replaced Harry Lockett as Stoke's secretary-manager in August 1890. But he only last a short while, handing over his duties to Arthur Reeves halfway through the 1891-92 season (See MANAGERS).

BRENTFORD

Stoke's playing record against Brentford is:

Football League

Venue	P	W	D	L	F	A
Home	8	5	3	0	21	10
Away	8	2	3	3	9	6
Totals	16	7	6	3	30	16

Southern League

Venue	P	W	D	L	F	A
Home	4	3	1	0	7	2
Away	4	1	1	2	5	8
Totals	8	4	2	2	12	10

Stoke are unbeaten at home at competitive level against the Bees and their best victory to date over the Londoners is 5-1 at The Victoria Ground in April 1937 (League Division One). Freddie Steele notched a smart hat-trick that day in front of 18,349 spectators. Stoke also won 4-1 at Griffin Park in December 1946 (Division One) with three-goal Syd Peppitt the star man, and 4-0 in London in March 1991 (Division Three).

Stanley Matthews netted twice in Stoke's excellent 3-0 victory over Brentford in December 1937.

Brentford ran up their best win over Stoke in February 1913, winning a Southern League Division One game 4-2 at Griffin Park.

Stoke won five successive home Football League games v Brentford between 1935 and 1946, scoring 15 goals against six.

Players with both clubs: Frank Bentley, Gary Brooke, Verdi Godwin, Chris Kamara, Tony Parks, Fred Pentland, Fred Rouse and Jimmy Swarbrick. Pentland later returned to Griffin Park as coach.

BRIDGETT, George Arthur

A fleet and markedly unselfish outside-left, outstandingly quick and dangerous, with terrific shot (he once sent the ball straight through the net when scoring for Sunderland against Stoke), Arthur Bridgett won 11 caps for England between 1905 and 1909 (never finishing on the losing side). Unfortunately from the club's point of view, he spent only a few months with Stoke during the early part of the 1902-03 season when he appeared in just seven League games. He was a player who Stoke certainly let slip through their fingers – for he became an exceptionally fine footballer, playing in well over 320 senior matches for Sunderland scoring 112 goals. A religious man who wouldn't play on holy days, Bridgett was born in Forsbrook (Staffs) 11 October 1882, and started playing football at Stoke St Peter's School. He then did well for Burslem Park and Trentham before joining Stoke. He left The Victoria Ground for Roker Park in January 1907 where he stayed until July 1912 when he was appointed manager of South Shields, later taking over as boss of neighbouring North Shields. He returned to play League Football with Port Vale in August 1923 and scored seven goals in 14 games before ending his career with Sandbach Ramblers, retiring in May 1926. He died in Newcastle (Staffs) in the summer of 1954.

BRIDGWOOD, Gerald

Scorer of eight goals in 111 League and Cup games for Stoke between 1961 and 1969, Bridgwood was a product of the youth scheme at The Victoria Ground and was given his senior debut at the age of 16 versus Brighton at home in April 1961 – the second youngest player in Stoke's history behind Peter Bullock. A winger, with good pace and neat footwork, he was born in Stoke-on-Trent in October 1944 and joined The Victoria Ground playing staff in 1960, turning professional on his 17th birthday. He left Stoke for Shrewsbury Town in a £12,000 deal in February 1969 and spent five seasons at Gay Meadow. On retiring from League football he became a publican and turned out for both Telford United and Burton Albion until hanging up his boots in the late 1970s.

BRIERLEY HILL ALLIANCE

Stoke met the Black Country club six times in Birmingham League action during the early 1900s. Their full playing record is:

Birmingham League

Venue	P	W	D	L	F	A
Home	3	3	0	0	10	2
Away	3	2	1	0	9	7
Totals	6	5	1	0	19	9

FA Cup

Venue	P	W	D	L	F	A
Home	1	1	0	0	1	0

Birmingham League Cup

Venue	P	W	D	L	F	A
Home	1	0	1	0	2	2
Away	1	1	0	0	5	0
Totals	2	1	1	0	7	2

Stoke's best League win of the five recorded was 4-1 at home in December 1909 when Arthur Griffiths scored twice. The Potters also won 4-3 away in October 1908 when Fred Groves netted two goals.

The FA Cup-tie was played in October 1914 in the third qualifying round, and a crowd of 2,000 saw the Potters win 1-0 with a goal from the former Chester player, Fred McCarthy.

Amos Baddeley struck home four of the goals for Stoke in their 5-0 win at Brierley Hill in a Birmingham League Cup first-round replay in 1909-10.

BRIGHAM, Harold

Stoke City boss Bob McGrory beat off a number of big-named clubs to land the signature of full-back Brigham from Frickley Colliery FC in May 1936. At the time the press described the Yorkshire defender, who had been on Bolton Wanderers books as an amateur, as 'the most coveted player in the Midland League'. Brigham, who was born in Selby on 19 November 1914, quickly bedded himself into the Stoke side and went on to appear in 119 senior games for the club, plus another 101 during the hostilities, when he also guested for Chester and Wrexham. In November 1946, at the age of 32, he left The Victoria Ground to join Nottingham Forest for £4,000 and ended his career with non-League Gainsborough Trinity after a spell with York City.

BRIGHT, David John

Bright, a striker, made just one substitute League appearance in Stoke's colours, at home to Reading in November 1990. Born in Bathavon on 5 September 1972. He joined the club straight from school and after loan spells with Stromsnasbruck IF, Newcastle Town and Tamworth, he joined Clevedon Town in the summer of 1991.

BRIGHTON & HOVE ALBION

Stoke's playing record against Brighton is:

Football League

Venue	P	W	D	L	F	A
Home	15	5	7	3	19	15
Away	15	3	7	5	16	17
Totals	30	8	14	8	35	32

Southern League

Venue	P	W	D	L	F	A
Home	2	2	0	0	6	2
Away	2	0	0	2	1	7
Totals	4	2	0	2	7	9

Of their 10 wins over Albion, Stoke's best has been 4-1 (away) in April 1990 (League Division Two) when Tony Ellis scored twice in front of a 9,600 crowd.

Brighton's highest victory has also been by 4-0 – at home in a Southern League game played in December 1911.

Players with both clubs: Alan Biley, Mark Chamberlain, Eph Colclough, Joe Corrigan, Johnny Eyres, Jack Hall, Harry Mellor, David Parkes, Tom Robertson, John Ruggiero, Kevin Russell, Mickey Thomas and Harry Watson.

Walter Gould played for Albion and was later coach and assistant manager at Stoke, while Stoke reserve Mike Trusson played 15 League games for Brighton (1987-88).

BRIGHTWELL, David John

Defender Brightwell played twice for Stoke City on loan from Manchester City in September 1995. Younger brother of Ian, who also served with Manchester City, Brightwell junior started his career at Maine Road in 1986, turned professional in 1988 and went on to appear in 53 first-team games for the Maine Road club before transferring to Bradford City for £30,000 in December 1995. In between times he also went on loan to Chester City (1991) and Lincoln City. Son of the Olympic athletes Robbie Brightwell and Ann Packer, he was born in Lutterworth on 7 January 1971.

BRINDLEY, Horace

Outside-left, born in Newcastle (Staffs) in 1897, Brindley was 25 years of age when he joined Stoke from Knutton Villa in 1904. He played only four League games for the Potters before leaving the club the following year for Crewe Alexandra, quickly switching to Norwich City. During a useful career he also served with Chester, Blackpool, Queen's Park Rangers and Lincoln City (at various levels).

BRISTOL CITY

Stoke's playing record against City is:

League

Venue	P	W	D	L	F	A
Home	19	13	3	3	39	18
Away	19	5	7	7	20	31
Totals	38	18	10	10	59	49

FA Cup

Venue	P	W	D	L	F	A
Home	1	0	0	1	1	3
Away	1	0	1	0	0	0
Totals	2	0	1	1	1	3

League Cup

Venue	P	W	D	L	F	A
Away	1	0	0	1	0	1

Watney Cup

Venue	P	W	D	L	F	A
Home	1	1	0	0	4	1

Charlie Wilson scored four times when Stoke recorded their best win over Bristol City, beating them 6-2 at home in a Second Division match in February 1930.

Nine years earlier at Ashton Gate Stoke had crashed to their heaviest defeat against City, losing 4-1 in April 1921.

The FA Cup games were played in season 1994-95 when Stoke did the hard work by drawing away only to lose the replay 3-1 after extra-time.

Stoke's 1-0 League Cup defeat was suffered at Bristol in August 1977 when the crowd was over 17,800.

The Watney Cup victory came in the semi-final of the 1973-74 competition when a crowd of 13,812 saw Geoff Hurst, Mike Pejic, Jimmy Greenhoff and Terry Conroy score for Stoke to take them into the Final against Hull City.

Players with both clubs: Paul Allen, Julian Bent, Tommy Broad, Joe Brough, Arthur Capes, Joe Johnson, Tony Kelly, Fred Molyneux, Jim Martin, Willie Maxwell, Nicky Morgan, Mark Prudhoe, Alex Raisbeck, Ken Scattergood, Ronnie Sinclair and Cyril Watkin. Kelly, at the age of 16 years, 244 days, is the youngest player ever to appear for the Bristol club in a League game when making his debut in October 1982.

Joe Jordan managed both Stoke City and Bristol City. Denis Smith played for Stoke and later managed Bristol City.

Former Stoke goalkeeper Mark Harrison became Bristol City's youth-team coach.

BRISTOL ROVERS

Stoke's playing record against Rovers is:

Football League

Venue	P	W	D	L	F	A
Home	11	7	1	3	22	16
Away	11	1	2	8	9	23
Totals	22	8	3	11	31	39

Southern League

Venue	P	W	D	L	F	A
Home	2	2	0	0	5	2
Away	2	0	1	1	2	6
Totals	4	2	1	1	7	8

FA Cup

Venue	P	W	D	L	F	A
Away	1	1	0	0	1	0

League Cup

Venue	P	W	D	L	F	A
Away	1	1	0	0	4	2

Most games between the two clubs have been fairly close. Stoke's best win is 3-1 while Rovers' has been 4-0. Stoke achieved their triumph on the last day of the 1911-12 Southern League season (27 April) at The Victoria Ground when the crowd was 5,000. They also won 3-2 at home in December 1977 (League Division Two) when Howard Kendall with a penalty figured on the scoresheet. Rovers' 4-0 victory came at home in a Southern League match in March 1913. They also won 4-1 at Eastville in April 1978 (League Division Two).

Players with both clubs: Arthur Cartlidge, John Chalmers, Joe Clennell, Brian Doyle, Billy Draycott, Jack Howshall, George Lennon, Wilf Phillips, Paul Randall, Arthur Rowley, Carl Saunders, Sam Spencer, Louis Williams and Ian Wright.

'Chic' Bates played for Rovers and later became assistant manager at Stoke City. Dennis Rofe was coach and then manager of Bristol Rovers (1991-92) before becoming coach at Stoke (1993). Alan Ball junior was a player with Rovers and later Stoke City manager.

BRITANNIA STADIUM

In the summer of 1997, after more than 119 years at The Victoria Ground (from March 1878) Stoke City Football Club moved to a new 28,000 all-seater ground known as The Britannia Stadium. Situated at Trentham Lakes, less than a mile from their old site, it cost £14.7 million to build and has every facility available.

On Monday 20 January 1997, it was announced at a press conference, that the Britannia Building Society, one of the country's leading mutuals, had agreed to sponsor the new Stoke City community stadium at a cost £1.3 million over 10 years, thus allowing part of the company's name (Britannia) to form part of the title of the ground (The Britannia Stadium).

Stadium Fact File

● The two-tier main West Stand can accommodate 8,900 spectators, including sponsors and press/media personnel.

● The North Stand (behind one goal) which is linked to the East Stand, accommodates 14,300 supporters.

● The South Stand has room for 5,000 visiting supporters. This stand can also be sub-divided into three equal parts, enabling up to 3,500 seats to be made available to home fans if required.

● There are spaces for 160 disabled spectators, elevated and covered with ample toilet facilities.

● The playing pitch is of international size (approx. 115 yards long by 75 yards wide). There is under-soil heating and a synthetic running surface round the perimeter.

● The ground has 50 Executive Boxes situated on two levels in the main Stand with private lounges and full catering facilities.

● There is a function room/banqueting suite for 350 diners overlooking the pitch.

● A vice-presidents' Suite can cater for 250 supporters with seats in the directors' Box.

● There is a bar for the 1,000 Legend Club members whose seats in the main stand are based on two floors.

● Two upper tier executive concourses in the main Stand provide top of the range facilities for 2,250 Premier Club members.

● There are three lifts – two for supporters, one for goods.

● The match sponsorship room caters for 40 people.

● There are separate rooms for the players, first aid personnel, the club's physiotherapist, the press and media, and matchday photographers plus a separate weight/exercise room.

Work under way on one of the stands at Stoke City's new home.

- The matchday control room is equipped with full up-to-date CCTV and PA facilities.

- There is in-house TV, satellite and video facilities to most suites and some concourses.

- A dedicated and independent club accommodation and administration block is located in the south-west corner of the stadium and there are also two ticket offices set in opposite corners of the stadium.

- The official club shop, lottery office and Community Programme Office are all based in the main stand, along with two classrooms.

- The ground is fully-equipped with a dedicated security system plus security rooms.

- There are spaces for 650 cars on the stadium site with 1,600 additional parking spaces located to the south of the stadium.

BRITTLETON, James Thomas

Surprisingly Brittleton was over 41 years of age when he moved from Sheffield Wednesday to Stoke City in the summer of 1920. He had made 353 League appearances for the Hillsborough club and had starred in their 1907 FA Cup Final win over Everton as well as gaining five full England caps. Born in Winsford, Cheshire on 23 April 1879, Brittleton, a well built, sturdy full-back or right-half, who had exceptional kicking ability, played his early football as a centre-half with Winsford Celtic and Winsford United. He then broke into League action with Stockport County (45 League outings). From Edgeley Park he moved to Sheffield Wednesday during the early part of the twentieth century and he went on to appear in 343 League matches for the Owls. He left The Victoria Ground in the summer of 1925 after scoring five times in 123 League and Cup games for Stoke, and returned home to play for Winsford United (1924), finally retiring in 1926. In his long career Brittleton made 512 appearances in the Football League. He had his last outing for Stoke shortly after his 46th birthday and therefore held the title of the club's oldest player for 40 years, until Stan Matthews came along and played his last match at the age of 50 in 1965. Brittleton, who was keen fisherman, died in Winsford on 22 February 1955.

NB: Tom's son, John, played for Aston Villa and Chester.

BROAD, James

Jimmy Broad was a fine goalscorer and a footballing nomad, who played all over the country during a career which spanned 24 years. Born in Stalybridge on 10 November 1891, the son of a Manchester City trainer, he began his exploits as a goalkeeper (and not as a goalscorer) in non-League circles in 1907 with St Mark's (West Gorton) and continued them (as a goalie) with Stalybridge Celtic (1908), Manchester City (November 1909), Oldham Athletic (August 1913), Blackburn Rovers and Greenock Morton, both as a wartime guest, Millwall Athletic (April 1919), Stoke City (£2,000 – June 1921 to November 1924), Sittingbourne (guest), Everton (signed from Stoke for £1,400), New Brighton (December 1925), Watford (September 1926), Caernarvon Town (June 1927), Taunton United (September 1928) and Fleetwood (August 1931) before becoming groundsman at Chelmsford City (late 1931). Broad was a clever player and a great finisher who had the knack of being in the right place at the right time. He scored for every club he served including five in 10 starts for Oldham, 32 in 39 appearances for Millwall in season 1919-20 and 67 in 116 first-team matches for Stoke. One of England's early 'exports', Broad coached overseas in Coruna, Las Palmas, Barcelona, Geneva, Italy, Turkey, South Africa, Norway and Holland, mainly in the 1920s. In fact, shortly after leaving The Victoria Ground for Goodison Park, he went to Spain to coach Barcelona. His brothers Wilf (with Manchester City and Millwall) and Tommy (see below) were both useful footballers. Jimmy Broad died at Chelmsford on 22 August 1963, aged 71.

NB: Broad, wearing a kilt, turned up at Millwall immediately after the war and asked for a trial (he had been in the Royal Scots Guards during the hostilities). His request was granted and in an early game for Millwall Reserves, he scored all his side's goals in an 8-1 win over Spurs' second XI. He was signed up immediately.

BROAD, Thomas Higginson

Unlike his brother Jimmy (above) Tommy Broad was an orthodox outside-right, whom the press described as being 'of the tearaway class, who runs like a greyhound.' He was certainly quick, but very erratic in his overall play. Born in Stalybridge on 31 July 1887, Broad started out with Redgate Albion and after a brief spell with Denton Wanderers, he had trials with Manchester City (1903). He failed to impress at City and joined the Openshaw Lads' Club from where he moved to West Bromwich Albion in September 1905. From The Hawthorns he went to Chesterfield (February 1908) and joined Oldham Athletic for £250 in May 1909. He played in almost 100 games for the Latics before transferring to Bristol City in May 1912. His next move took him to Maine Road (March 1919) and two years later he was signed by Stoke manager Arthur Shallcross, who paid £500 for his signature on 26 May, 1921. Broad did well at The Victoria Ground, scoring four goals in 89 appearances for the Potters who then allowed him to leave for Southampton for £250 in July 1924. After appearing in 399 League games, he gallantly ended his career with spells at Weymouth and Rhyl Athletic, retiring *c.*1928. Star of Oldham's promotion-winning side in 1910, Broad won an England Junior international cap v Scotland in April 1906 and he also played once for the Football League representative side. He died soon after England had won the World Cup in 1966.

BROADHURST, Joseph

A right-half, born in Stoke in 1862, Broadhurst played once for the Potters – in an FA Cup-tie against West Bromwich Albion (away) in January 1888. He played for Leek before and after serving Stoke and later assisted Arcadians.

BRODIE. David

Recruited from Scottish football, wing-half David Brodie (who was born in Paisley in 1863) joined Stoke in December 1889 after good spells with his native Paisley and Abercorn. He helped the Potters win the Football Alliance and in 1897 moved across town to sign for neighbouring Burslem Port Vale. He scored three goals in 218 first-team appearances for Stoke. A strong, forceful player, he enjoyed a battle and was always totally committed to playing football at whatever level.

BROOKE, Garry James

Midfielder Brooke had a loan spell at The Victoria Ground in season 1989-90 when he played in eight League games. A Londoner from Bethnal Green (born in November 1960) he scored twice when making his debut for Tottenham Hotspur in 1978 (his first club) and during his career which spanned 15 years he also assisted GAIS (Gothenburg), Norwich City, Groningen (Holland), Wimbledon, Brentford, Reading, Wivenhoe Town (1991-92) and Romford. He was named as substitute three times by Spurs in FA Cup Finals.

BROOKE, Percy

Full-back Brooke represented the Welsh League shortly after joining Aberdare from Stoke in July 1921. Born in Kidsgrove in May 1893, he was playing in defence for Kidsgrove Wellington when Stoke moved in and brought him to The Victoria Ground soon after the war (December 1919). He was given 12 first-team outings before his release and after skippering Aberdare he served with Swindon Town and Accrington Stanley and Blackburn Rovers.

BROOKES, Gilbert Henry

Giant goalkeeper Brookes (6ft 1in tall) made 14 appearances between the posts for Stoke during the 1922-23 season, stepping in as a replacement for the injured Les Scott. Born in Churchill near Kidderminster in June 1895, he did well with Kidderminster Harriers and Shrewsbury Town before moving to The Victoria Ground for £300 in May 1922. After leaving Stoke on a free transfer in the summer of 1923, Brookes had spells with Swansea Town, Luton Town and Merthyr Town.

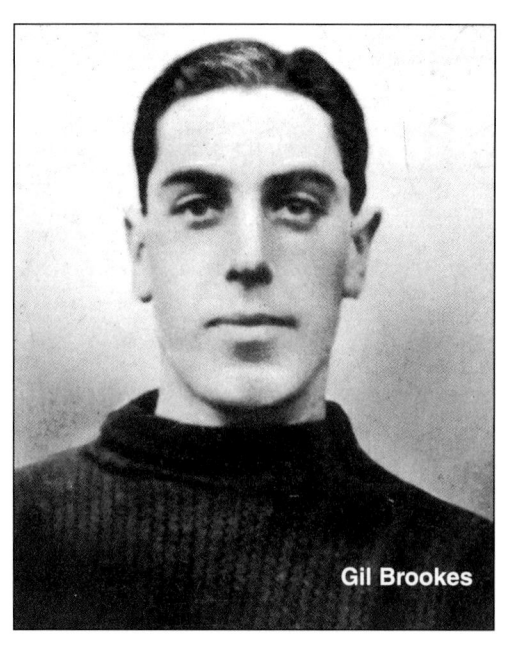

BROOKES, Isaac

Brookes was a well-respected cricketer during the 1890s, being the wicketkeeper for Staffordshire County. He was persuaded to play in goal for Stoke in an emergency during the period from November 1890 to March 1902 – and he did well in a total of 17 Football Alliance and FA Cup games, helping the Potters with the Alliance championship in his first season. Born in Bilston in May 1861, he later turned out for Northwich Victoria.

BROOKES, John

Left-half Brookes, from Stoke-on-Trent (born 8 February 1927) made just two League appearances for the club during his four-and-a-half years at The Victoria Ground (December 1946 to May 1951). He joined Stoke as a teenager and left for Eccleshall Town.

BROOKFIELD, Arthur

Scorer of two goals in 10 games for Stoke between January and September 1895, outside-right Brookfield was first reserve during his brief stay at the club. Born in Stoke in 1870, he joined the club from Longton Atlas and left to play for Crewe Alexandra.

BROOMHALL, Arthur

Goalkeeper Broomhall played in one FA Cup-tie for Stoke – against Crewe Alexandra in November 1886, replacing Billy Rowley. He let in half-a-dozen goals that day as Stoke went out of the competition 6-4 after extra-time. Broomhall, who was born in Stoke in 1860, played for Burslem Port Vale before joining the Potters and for Hanley Town afterwards.

BROUGH, Henry Burton

Right-half Harry Burton spent three and a half seasons at The

Victoria Ground – 1923 to 1926 – and during that time he appeared in 85 League games for Stoke, scoring one goal – against Coventry City in September 1924. Born in Gainsborough in December 1896, he moved to Sheffield with his parents and skippered the Sheffield Schoolboys' side, attracting the attention of several leading clubs. After playing briefly for Kilnhurst, he joined Huddersfield Town. From there he went to York City only to return to Leeds Road soon after. He signed for Stoke in February 1923 – and his career was ended by injury during the 1925-26 campaign when he played in only five matches. He continued to live in the Potteries for the rest of his life, passing away at Longton, in March 1975.

BROUGH, Joseph

One League outing was all wing-half Brough managed during his brief association with Stoke in season 1907-08. Born locally in Burslem on 9 November 1886, he started off as a centre-forward with Burslem Park Boys, Smallthorne FC and Burslem Port Vale before signing for the Potters in September 1907. He then went on to assist Tottenham Hotspur (three games), Liverpool (August 1910-January 1912), Bristol City (January 1912-April 1913) and the Vale again (May 1913-June 1915). Ill-health hampered his stay with Spurs.

BROWN, David (Carre)

Inside or centre-forward David Brown was born in Broughty Ferry, near Dundee on 26 November c.1887 and was well into his 30s when he joined Stoke from Dundee in October 1919 for a fee of £1,200. The Stoke management team thought he would be the answer to their scoring problems, but sadly he never really hit it off in the Potteries and after netting 17 goals in 52 League and Cup appearances for the club, he was transferred to Notts County in July 1921. During his playing career, Brown, who was a good ball player, with 'capital shot' also served with Dundee St Joseph's (his first club), Dundee (March 1911), Morton, Peebles Rovers (from July 1913) and Dundee (again, from March 1914). After leaving Meadow Lane, he returned to Scotland to play for Kilmarnock (August 1922), Darlington (August 1923 – signed for £80), Crewe Alexandra (June 1926) and Barrow (June 1927 to March 1928). He struck 74 goals in only 97 games for Darlington, helping the Quakers win the Third Division North title in 1924-25. In the summer of 1933 he returned to The Feethams as reserve-team manager. During World War One, Brown guested for Glasgow Rangers (1917), Port Vale (1918), Nottingham Forest, Birmingham and represented the North of Scotland. He died c.1970, aged 78.

BROWN, George Gerald

Brown was an amateur, who played on the left-wing for Millwall, Sheffield United, Woolwich Arsenal Reserves, Stoke (September-December 1904) and Norwich City. He had eight League games for the Potters but never really settled in the area. A Welshman, born in Aberdare in June 1870, he was a coalminer before taking up football.

BROWN, Horace R.

One of the many versatile players in Stoke's early years, Brown lined up in four FA Cup-ties for the club between November 1883 and October 1886, as well as in many friendly matches. In fact, he played outside-right in the first-ever Stoke Cup game against Manchester in November 1883 and later on he starred at centre-half and left-back. He was born in Potteries in 1860 and from 1886-88 served with Stoke St Peter's.

BROWN, James Frederick

Born and bred in Brierley Hill in the Black Country, quick moving inside or centre-forward Fred Brown began his career with Great Bridge Celtic, and after a brief association with Kidderminster Harriers he joined Stoke in April 1907 at the age of 21. He went on to score 11 goals in 29 League and Cup games for the Potters before transferring to West Bromwich Albion for £210 in May 1908. In 1910 he returned to Kidderminster and later assisted Walsall Swifts before retiring in 1915. Brown died in May 1939.

BROWN, John F.P.

Outside-left Jackie Brown, who was born in Liverpool c.1888, scored seven goals in 15 League games for Stoke in season 1910-11. Formerly with Orrell, he was signed from Manchester City and stayed just the one term at The Victoria Ground before transferring to nearby Port Vale.

BROWN, Roy H.

A useful utility player, Brown scored 14 goals in 74 peacetime games for Stoke City (1946-53). Born in the Potteries on 20 December 1923, he played his early football for the club during the latter stages of the war and after spending 11 years at The Victoria Ground, moved to Watford for a fee of £3,500, a month after the Coronation of Queen Elizabeth II. Later Brown served with Chelmsford City and died in Watford on 8 November 1989, aged 65. Brown's brother, Doug was appointed trainer at Stoke in 1963-64.

BULLER, Joseph

As a miner in County Durham, Buller played his early football for Chilton Colliery and Spennymoor United before joining Hartlepool United in 1930. In April 1932 a fee of £250 took him to The Victoria Ground and although he stayed with Stoke for four seasons, he only managed seven senior outings as a wing-half, being just short of First Division quality. He left Stoke for Aldershot for £100 in August 1936 and called it a day from top-class football in season 1939-40. Buller was born in Chilton, County Durham in 1909.

BULLOCK, Albert

As a reserve inside-forward, Bullock scored one goal in his five League games for Stoke between April and October 1909. Born in the Potteries c.1884, he was a useful marksman for Bucknall before joining Stoke and after leaving The Victoria Ground he had a brief spell with Stafford Rangers.

BULLOCK, Peter L.

The youngest footballer ever to appear for Stoke City in a League game, Bullock was just 16 years, 153 days old when he made his debut against Swansea Town on 19 April 1958. This was the first of 46 senior appearances for Bullock who also scored 15 goals from the inside or centre-forward positions. Born in Stoke on 17 November 1941, he won international honours for England as a schoolboy and later played for his country at youth-team level. Bullock's career suffered a set-back when he broke a leg whilst on tour with Stoke in Morocco. He took time to recover and after regaining full fitness he went on to have a useful career although from time to time injuries halted his progress. After leaving the Potters he did well with Birmingham City (signed from Stoke for £10,000 in March 1962), Southend United, Colchester United (for whom he netted 33 goals in 95 League games), Exeter City and Walsall. He pulled out of top-class football in 1969.

NB: Bullock's brother, Michael, also played for Birmingham City as well as Oxford United, Leyton Orient and Halifax Town, and when he was manager at The Shay he had Peter's son Simon with him as a player at the club.

BURGESS, Charles

Burgess was a cool and solid defender who tackled tigerishly but was never flustered, always playing a cool, calculated game of football. Born in Church Lawton on Christmas Day 1883, he was a farmer at Field Farm and played his early soccer with Butt Lane Swifts from where he moved to Stoke in March 1901, actually signing the appropriate forms on top of a haystack on his father's farm. When Stoke went bust Burgess went to play for Manchester City (from July 1908), but a knee injury hampered his performances and he was forced to retire. He made 195 appearances in Stoke's defence. Burgess died at Hartshill, Stoke-on-Trent a fortnight before his 73rd birthday in 1956.

BURNLEY

Stoke's playing record against Burnley is:

Football League

Venue	P	W	D	L	F	A
Home	36	24	7	5	85	41
Away	36	10	8	18	42	63
Totals	72	34	15	23	127	104

Test Matches

Venue	P	W	D	L	F	A
Home	1	0	1	0	0	0
Away	1	1	0	0	2	0

FA Cup

Venue	P	W	D	L	F	A
Home	2	2	0	0	10	2
Away	5	1	1	3	5	7
Totals	7	3	1	3	15	9

League Cup

Venue	P	W	D	L	F	A
Home	2	0	1	1	0	2
Away	1	0	0	1	1	2
Totals	3	0	1	2	1	4

As founder members of the Football League, the first two games in season 1888-89 ended in two home victories – Stoke winning 4-3 and Burnley 2-1.

Stoke's best League victory over the Clarets is 5-1 at The Victoria Ground in March 1895 (Division One). A crowd of 3,000 saw Joey Schofield have a splendid game, scoring two goals and laying on two more for his colleagues. Stoke also won 4-0 at The Victoria Ground in April 1974 (Division One) when Ritche struck home two penalties. Three 4-1 home victories came in November 1891, when Billy Dickson scored a superb individual goal, in September 1898 and March 1976, when defender Denis Smith got two goals.

Burnley's biggest win over Stoke at League level is 4-0 – achieved in September 1893 (Division One), in March 1948, in February 1952 and April 1968 – all at home. They also won 4-1 at Turf Moor in September 1891 and 4-1 in December 1965 (having lost 3-1 at Stoke 24 hours earlier).

A crowd of 32,279 witnessed a pulsating 4-4 draw at The Victoria Ground in November 1963 when John Ritchie netted twice for Stoke, and there were seven-goal thrillers at The Victoria Ground in March 1890 which ended in an excellent 4-3 victory for Burnley and again in December 1966 when on this occasion the Potters claimed victory by 4-3.

When Stoke won the Second Division title in 1932-33 they beat Burnley 3-0 at home (with a Joe Johnson hat-trick) and 2-1 away. Syd Peppitt also hit a treble in Stoke's 3-0 home League win in March 1948 and Frank Bowyer did likewise nine months later in a 3-1 win at Turf Moor on Christmas Day 1948.

The First Division League game between Stoke and Burnley, played at The Victoria Ground on 23 December 1889, ended in a 2-1 win for the home side. But Bob McCormick of Stoke suffered a chest injury during the match which resulted in the crowd invading the pitch. Burnley lodged a protest which was upheld and the game was replayed on 10 March 1890. This time Burnley won 4-3.

The two Test matches were played at the end of the 1897-98 season and by taking three points off Burnley (and two off Newcastle United) Stoke held on to the First Division status.

Stoke's best FA Cup win over Burnley is 7-1 at home in a second-round replay in February 1896. Tommy Hyslop scored four of the Potters' goals that day in a rather one-sided contest.

Stoke actually lost an FA Cup game in 1946 to Burnley yet remained in the tournament. They met the Lancashire side over two legs in the third round in 1945-46. After winning their home game 3-1 (with a hat-trick from Freddie Steele) Stoke lost the return leg at Turf Moor by 2-1 but still went through 4-3 on aggregate.

In 1917-18, playing in the Lancashire Primary Section, Stoke defeated Burnley 9-0 at The Victoria Ground.

Players with both clubs: Wayne Biggins, Charlie Bishop (Stoke junior), Steve Davis (Stoke reserve), Lee Dixon, Alex Elder, John Gayle, Nigel Gleghorn, Peter Hampton, Adrian Heath, Mark Higgins, Jimmy Hill, Zeke Johnson, James Lindsay (Stoke reserve 1899), Doug Newlands, Bob McGrory, Jimmy McIlroy, Len Mudie, Vince Overson, Louis Page, Leigh Palin, Billy Robson, Kevin Russell, Barry Siddall, Dennis Tueart and Tom Walker. Heath later went back to Turf Moor as team manager (1996).

BURNS, William S.

Durham-born centre-forward, who scored twice in his three League games for Stoke in February 1931 when deputising for Wilf Kirkham. He joined the Potters from the amateur club Crook Town at the age of 23 in October 1930, and after leaving The Victoria Ground, played for Stockport County and then Rotherham United. An amateur throughout his career, Burns was only 5ft 5ins tall and weighed under 9st.

BURROWS, Harold

Good, old-fashioned outside-left with a terrific shot, Burrows had a fine career, playing for Aston Villa, Stoke City and Plymouth Argyle in the First and Second Divisions. Born near the racecourse at Haydock Park on 17 March 1941, Burrows was a pupil at St Joseph's School in Wigan and he left there to sign for Aston Villa, stepping up to professional status in March 1958. He spent seven seasons with the Birmingham-based club, during which time he won an England Under-23 cap and appeared in two League Cup Finals, in 1961 and 1963, gaining a winners' medal in the former. He also helped Villa win promotion as Second Division champions in 1959-60 and netted 73 goals in his 181 senior outings in the 'claret and blue' strip. He was transferred to Stoke City for £27,000 on deadline day, in March 1965 and became an instant hit with the Potters' fans. He was twice joint top scorer at The Victoria Ground and when he left the club for Plymouth in June 1973, he had amassed a fine record of 79 goals in 281 League and Cup appearances. He spent just a year at Home Park, helping Argyle win promotion from Division Three while taking his overall appearance tally in League Football to past the 400 mark. In the mid-1970s Burrows played in several Charity Matches for Villa All Stars. He finally hung up his boots in 1978 when he returned to the area to run a pub near to Mow Cop.

NB: Burrows scored a hat-trick for Stoke against Villa in a First Division League game in 1966-67.

BURTON, Matthew

A player who could occupy both the inside-left and left-wing positions, Burton joined Stoke in January 1920 from Chesterfield, having guested during World War One for Everton. Born in Grassmoor in 1897, he scored twice in his nine outings for the Potters and he left the club for Wrexham in June 1921, top-scoring for the Welsh club in in his only season at The Racecourse Ground. Later on in his career he served with New Brighton, Rhos and Connah's Quay and Shotton.

BURTON, Richard A.

Reserve centre-half with Stoke in season 1913-14, Burton played in just two Southern League games, the first against Aberdare (away) in November and the second at Pontypridd in April. Born in Stoke in 1889, he played for North Staffs Nomads prior to and after leaving The Victoria Ground.

BURTON UNITED

Stoke's playing record against Burton is:
Birmingham League

Venue	P	W	D	L	F	A
Home	2	1	0	1	5	1
Away	2	1	0	1	8	3
Totals	4	2	0	2	13	4

Southern League

Venue	P	W	D	L	F	A
Home	1	1	0	0	5	0
Away	1	0	0	1	0	2
Totals	2	1	0	1	5	2

Stoke beat United 8-0 at home in a Birmingham League game in January 1910, Amos Baddeley scoring a hat-trick. And in the same season of Southern League football, Stoke doubled up over United, winning 5-0 at home and 7-1 away. Baddeley was again in top form, scoring five times in the latter game and once in the former.

Players with both clubs: Charlie Axcell and Alf Smith.

BURY

Stoke's playing record against Bury is:
Football League

Venue	P	W	D	L	F	A
Home	28	16	4	8	52	32
Away	28	9	4	15	38	47
Totals	56	25	8	23	90	79

FA Cup

Venue	P	W	D	L	F	A
Home	1	0	1	0	1	1
Away	8	2	3	3	12	17
Totals	9	2	4	3	13	18

The last time he teams met at League level was in season 1991-92 (Division Three). Bury won 2-1 at Stoke in front of a 12,385 crowd while the Potters were 3-1 victors at Gigg Lane, Ton Ellis scoring twice in front of a disappointing crowd of 3,245.

Stoke's best win of the 25 recorded over the Shakers in the League, is 6-0 at home in March 1954 (Division Two). Harry Oscroft and Frank Bowyer both scored twice apiece that day and the crowd was 13,763. This is also Stoke's best away win in the Football League.

Johnny King netted a hat-trick in Stoke's 3-0 home win over Bury the following season when, in fact, the teams actually met each other on seven occasions (twice in the League and five times in the FA Cup).

Bury claimed a 5-2 scoreline at home on Christmas Eve 1898 to record their best League win over the Potters. They also registered two 4-2 home victories (1896 and 1901).

Stanley Matthews made his Football League debut for Stoke City against Bury at Gigg Lane on 19 March 1932.

That long drawn out FA Cup battle took place in January 1955 in the third round. After a 1-1 draw at Gigg Lane, the replay also ended all square after extra-time with the same result. The second replay and third game at neutral Goodison Park finished level at 3-3 (aet) and the third replay at Gigg Lane also ended in stalemate at 2-2 (aet). Finally, after 9 hours 22 minutes of football Stoke finally came through winners by 3-2 at Old Trafford. The five games had been watched by 72,478 spectators. This is the fourth longest FA Cup-tie on record (See FA CUP).

In a wartime Regional League game at Gigg Lane in December 1939, Bury beat Stoke 7-6.

Players with both clubs: Tony Allen, Jason Beckford, Wilf Chadwick, Don Clegg, Lee Dixon, Ted Evans, David Goodwin, David Gregory, Willie Hendry, Mark Higgins, Tony 'Zico' Kelly, Alec Lindsay, James Lindsay (Stoke reserve 1899), Fred McCarthy, Sammy McIlroy, Ernie Mullinex, Ian Scott, Mike Sheron, Barry Siddall (loan at Gigg Lane), Alan Suddick and Ted Wordley.

Charlie Bishop was Stoke reserve who went on to play 136 games for Bury (1987-91); Harry Pearson played for Bury and was later Stoke's trainer for 15 years (1936-51).

BUSBY, Vivian Dennis

Yet another nationwide club-hopper, Busby, who was born in Slough on 19 June 1949, served with 12 different clubs (as player, coach or manager etc.) between 1968 and 1983. He started off with Wycombe Wanderers (1968) and thereafter played, in turn, for Luton Town (1970), Newcastle United (1971), Fulham (1973 – FA Cup Finalist in 1975), Norwich City (1976), Stoke City (from November 1977), Sheffield United (on loan, 1980), Tulsa Roughnecks (NASL – March 1980 for £30,000), Blackburn Rovers (1981), Tulsa (again) and York City as player-coach from August 1982 and then assistant manager from 1984 to May 1987. Busby's next appointment was that of assistant manager (to ex-Stokie Denis Smith) at Sunderland (May 1987 to December 1991) and then he took over as team boss of Hartlepool United (February to May 1993) later joining Howard Kendall at Sheffield United as coach. He scored 73 goals in more than 300 League appearances in his playing career and his record for Stoke was 12 strikes in 60 senior outings (22 as substitute).

BUSSEY, Walter

Bussey spent nine seasons at The Victoria Ground. He joined the club as an amateur in March 1924, turned professional the following year (November) and stayed until the summer of 1933 when he transferred to Blackpool. A workmanlike striker who could play in all three central forward positions, Bussey was born in Eckington on 6 December 1904. He served with several local junior sides including Denaby United, Aughton Celtic, Dinnington Main and Anston Athletic before making the move to The Victoria Ground. Stoke manager Tom Mather thought very highly of Bussey who gained a regular place in the side in 1926-27 when he helped Stoke win the Third Division North title. Bussey went on to appear in 197 senior games for the Potters, scoring 49 goals before switching to Bloomfield Road. He later played for Swansea Town and Exeter City, retiring from football in 1939. He remained in the West Country and died in Exeter in January 1982.

BUTLER, John Edward

A consistent and dependable defender, Butler was Stoke's regular right-back for most of his six and a half years at The Victoria Ground, although occasionally he was asked to play in other positions. Born in Liverpool on 7 February 1962, he played for Prescot Cables before becoming a full-time professional with Wigan Athletic in January 1982. After 302 appearances for the Springfield Park club he was transferred to Stoke for £75,000 in December 1988 and went straight into the side against Manchester City on the Boxing Day. Butler held his position, producing some excellent performances and he went on to amass a personal record for the club of 319 League and Cup appearances and nine goals. He helped Stoke win the Autoglass Trophy at Wembley in 1992 and a year later was a key member of their Second Division championship-winning side. At the age of 33 Butler left The Victoria Ground and returned to Wigan on a free transfer in June 1995 and when the 1996-97 season ended he had taken his overall record of senior appearances at club level to well past the 700 mark.

CAERNARVON WANDERERS

Stoke recorded one of their best-ever victories in the FA Cup when they hammered luckless Caernarvon Wanderers 10-1 in a first qualifying round tie at The Victoria Ground on 30 October 1886. Three players shared the goals for Stoke that day – Alf Edge (5), Teddy Bennett (3) and full-back Tommy Clare (2). The attendance was 5,000.

CAERPHILLY

Stoke's record against the Welsh club is:
Southern League

Venue	P	W	D	L	F	A
Home	1	1	0	0	4	0
Away	1	1	0	0	5	1
Totals	2	2	0	0	9	1

These two games were played over the Christmas period in season 1913-14. On Christmas Day, a crowd of 3,000 saw Alf Smith hit a hat-trick in Stoke's 5-1 win at Caerphilly and on Boxing Day, Stoke doubled up with another emphatic victory in front of 10,000 fans at The Victoria Ground.

CAIN, Thomas

Goalkeeper Cain (standing almost 6 feet tall and weighing over 12st) had under a season with Stoke, appearing in 14 first-team games. Born in Sunderland on 12 October 1872, he played for Hebburn Argyle before moving down to the Potteries (November 1893) and after his exploits with Stoke, he signed for Everton (April 1894). In October of the following year he was transferred to Southampton St Mary's and then had a brief spell with Grimsby Town (April-October 1896) before rejoining Hebburn Argyle. In January 1897 he signed for West Stanley and stayed with that club until retiring (through injury) in 1900. His move from Saints to Grimsby was for a club record fee of £20. Cain died in the summer of 1952.

CAIRNS, Robert

Stoke secured the services of the former Royal Albert and Third Lanark wing-half Bobby Cairns at Christmas 1953, bringing him down from Ayr United along with Joe Hutton. Neat and constructive, Cairns, who was born in Annathill in May 1929, scored 11 goals in 196 League and Cup games for the Potters up to July 1961 when he moved to Macclesfield Town.

CALLAGHAN, Aaron Joseph

Irish centre-half who, facing stiff opposition, appeared in 17 League and Cup games for Stoke during the mid-1980s. Born in Dublin on 8 October 1966, he signed as an apprentice for the Potters in February 1983 and turned professional in November of the following year. Capped by the Republic of Ireland at youth, Under-17 and Under-21 levels, he starred for his country in the four-nations European Under-21 tournament in Dourgess, France, in May 1986 and was immediately chased by Oldham Athletic. He finally joined the Latics for £10,000 five months later. While at Stoke Callaghan was loaned out to Crewe Alexandra (November 1985) and he signed for the Alex permanently for £15,000 in May 1988. He later assisted Preston North End and St Patrick's (Dublin).

CAMBRIDGE UNITED

Stoke's playing record against United:

Football League

Venue	P	W	D	L	F	A
Home	2	0	1	1	2	4
Away	2	1	0	1	1	3
Totals	4	1	1	2	3	7

League Cup

Venue	P	W	D	L	F	A
Home	1	0	0	1	1	2
Away	1	0	1	0	2	2
Totals	2	0	1	1	3	4

Stoke's only League win over United was achieved at The Abbey Stadium on 19 August 1978, this being the first ever meeting between the clubs. A crowd of 7,489 saw Paul Richardson net the only goal of a tightly fought contest.

The two League Cup games took place in season 1992-93, United going through 4-3 on aggregate after winning the return leg of a second-round tie in front of 10,732 fans at Stoke.

Players with both clubs: Neville Chamberlain, Wayne Ebanks, Kofi Nyamah, Geoff Scott and Mark Sale.

CAMERON, John

Glaswegian centre-forward who was one of many Scots who came south to play in English football during the 1890s. Born in 1868, he starred for Renton for three years from 1888, scoring over 30 goals. He managed four in nine League games for Stoke between September and November 1891 before returning to Scotland to play for Hibernian.

CAMPBELL, Kenneth

Campbell was a very popular and unassuming Scottish international goalkeeper who gained eight full caps for his country: 1920-22. He was born in Cambuslang on 6 September 1892 and was signed by Stoke from New Brighton in March 1923 to replace the former Sunderland goalkeeper Les Scott between the posts. He did well in his 35 League games for the Potters, but never really settled in the area and in November 1926 was transferred to Leicester City. Prior to New Brighton, he had served with Rutherglen Glencairn (Glasgow), Cambuslang Rangers (May 1911), Liverpool (April 1920) and Partick Thistle (June 1922) and after having over 80 games in goal for Leicester, he went back to New Brighton (May 1931) and retired two seasons later. He stayed in the area and, indeed, ran a successful sports shop in Wallasey which flourished for more than 60 years. Campbell amassed over 400 League and Cup appearances during his career, and was a Scottish Cup Final winner with Partick and an FA Cup Final loser with Liverpool. He died in Macclesfield on 28 April 1977.

CAPES, Adrian

Born in Burton upon Trent in 1873, Capes was a useful inside-forward who played for Burslem Port Vale before moving to The Victoria Ground in November 1905 (along with Harry Croxton). Brother of Arthur (below) he scored twice in 19 first-team outings for Stoke before returning to Vale in January 1907. He had played for Burton Wanderers (gaining a winners' medal in the Kettering District Charity Cup) and Nottingham Forest before joining Vale first time round. After his playing days were over, Capes became a publican in Smallthorne and was also a trainer with Port Vale. He died in Smallthorne in September 1955.

CAPES, Arthur John

Nicknamed 'Sailor' Capes was a quality centre-forward, born in Burton upon Trent in 1875, who netted 20 goals in 65 League and Cup games for Stoke during his two seasons at The Victoria Ground (June 1902 to May 1904). He started his career with Burton Wanderers and then played significantly well for Nottingham Forest, gaining an FA Cup winners' medal in 1898 when he scored twice in the 4-1 Final victory over Derby County. Described occasionally as 'an artisan or unpolished and workmanlike' player, Capes won one England cap (v Scotland) in April 1903 and he also represented the Football League. After leaving Stoke, he played for Bristol City and then Swindon Town. He scored over 80 goals in more than 380 League appearances during his career. He died in Burton on 26 February 1945.

CAPEWELL, William

Billy Capewell had two spells at The Victoria Ground. A tenacious half-back, born in Stoke-on-Trent in February 1878, he first played for the Potters in 1895-96, and then after assisting Reading, he returned to the club in 1899, staying until 1902. In all he appeared in 61 first-team games before retiring through injury.

CAPTAINS

Over the years Stoke have had many inspiring captains who have served the club greatly both on and off the field.

Secretary-manager-player Tom Slaney was captain of Stoke from 1875 to 1882, long before the team joined the Football League and, indeed, before the Potters began to play regularly in the FA Cup.

Full-back Tommy Clare was the first recognised team skipper of Stoke, at competitive level, leading the team into the Football League in 1888.

Wing-half George Baddeley was next in line, taking the club into the twentieth century. He captained the side right up until the club went bankrupt in 1908.

George Turner took over from Baddeley and he led the side until the outbreak of World War One, when Joey Jones took over the mantle.

Alec Milne and Charlie Parker both skippered the side after the hostilities, before the honour was taken up by Bob McGrory, who held office for a number of years.

Arthur Turner then had an excellent spell in charge, and he was followed by Frank Soo, Frank Mountford and Jock Kirton, John McCue and Bill Asprey, Tony Allen, Eddie Stuart and Eric Skeels. They, in turn, were succeeded by Peter Dobing, who led the Potters to League Cup glory at Wembley in 1972, Denis Smith, George Berry, Paul Dyson, Chris Kamara, Vince Overson, Ian Cranson and Larus Sigurdsson, among others.

● Goalkeeper Peter Shilton skippered England on 15 occasions (7 wins, 4 draws, 4 defeats) and Mick Mills captained his country on eight occasions (six wins).

CARDIFF CITY

Football League

Venue	P	W	D	L	F	A
Home	11	6	3	2	13	4
Away	11	3	2	6	16	22
Totals	22	9	5	8	29	26

Southern League

Venue	P	W	D	L	F	A
Home	1	1	0	0	5	0
Away	1	1	0	0	2	1
Totals	2	2	0	0	7	1

FA Cup

Venue	P	W	D	L	F	A
Home	2	2	0	0	6	2

Autoglass Trophy

Venue	P	W	D	L	F	A
Home	1	1	0	0	3	0

Playing in the Southern League in December 1910 Stoke recorded their best win over Cardiff, beating them 5-0 at The Victoria Ground.

Stoke's biggest Football League victory is 3-0 at home in November 1957 when Tim Coleman netted twice.

Cardiff's best win over the Potters is 5-2 at Ninian Park in a Second Division game in December 1957 when the crowd topped 30,000.

When the Welsh side gained promotion from the Second Division in 1959-60 they played out a cracking 4-4 draw with Stoke at Ninian Park on 21 November before a crowd of 21,448.

Stoke's two victories in the FA Cup were 4-1 in January 1968 when Harry Burrows (2) Willie Stevenson and Roy Vernon were the scorers, and 2-1 in January 1987 when Carl Saunders and Adrian Heath found the net.

The Autoglass Trophy game took place in January 1992, when 4,851 fans saw Wayne Biggins score two of Stoke's three goals.

Players with both clubs: Joe Clennell, Alan Curtis, Keith Downing, Sid Fursland, Philip Heath, Robbie James, George Kelly, Tony Kelly, David Kevan, Johnny King, George Latham and Kevin Russell.

Latham later became trainer at Cardiff. Alan Durban was manager of both Cardiff City (1984-86) and Stoke City.

CARLISLE UNITED

Stoke's playing record against the Cumbrians is:
Football League

Venue	P	W	D	L	F	A
Home	2	1	1	0	5	2
Away	2	1	0	1	2	3
Totals	4	2	1	1	7	5

Two League games were played in season 1974-75 (Division One) and two in 1985-86 (Division Two). Stoke completed the double over the Cumbrian side in the former campaign, winning 2-0 at Brunton Park (Alan Hudson and John Ritchie the scorers) and then 5-2 at The Victoria Ground (a hat-trick here for Terry Conroy and a goal each for Jimmy Greenhoff and Geoff Salmons). The games in 1985-86 ended in a 3-0 home victory for Carlisle and a 0-0 scoreline in the Potteries.

Players with both clubs: Phil Bonnyman, Bill Caton, Paul Crooks, George Daniels, Tony Gallimore, Jack Howshall, Doug Jones, Peter McArdle, David McAughtrie, Charlie Parker, Mark Prudhoe, Barry Siddall and Bob White.

Parker was player-coach with Carlisle and ex-Stoke full-back Peter Hampton became assistant manager of Carlisle United.

CARR, Clifford Paul

A diminutive right-back, Carr joined Fulham on leaving school in 1980. He quickly made the grade at Craven Cottage and rose to captain the first team, also representing England at Under-21 level. After more than 150 appearances for the London club, he was signed by Stoke City boss Mick Mills for £45,000 in July 1987. It took Carr time to settle in at The Victoria Ground following Stoke's poor start to the 1989-90 season and there was speculation within the camp that he would leave quickly. But Carr battled on and eventually established himself in the side and became very popular with the supporters. Unfortunately he never quite matched up to the manager's requirements, yet still made 144 appearances for the club, scoring one goal. In the summer of 1991, he was given a free transfer and after trials with Shrewsbury Town and Telford United, signed a one-year contract with Mansfield Town. He later linked up with former Stokie Mick Kennedy at Chesterfield. Carr, who was born in Hackney, London on 19 June 1964, worked for the Severn Trent Water Board in the mid-1990s, and was president of the Junior Potters during his final year at The Vic.

CARRUTHERS, Martin George

A determined striker who had three frustrating seasons at The Victoria Ground when he simply could not hold down a regular place in the first team. Quick off the mark with a workrate second to none, Carruthers started his professional career with Aston Villa in 1990. He had a loan spell with Hull City in October 1992 and was transferred to Stoke City for £300,000 in July 1993. During his time at Stoke he has been linked with Burnley and Fortuna Sittard, but chose to continue to play in the Reserves hoping for a first-team call-up. Born in Nottingham on 7 August 1972, Carruthers had a spell on loan with Peterborough United (November 1996) before joining Posh permanently the following month. He scored 20 goals in 119 games for the Potters.

CARTLIDGE, Arthur E.

Goalkeeper Cartlidge had two spells with Stoke. Standing over six feet tall, and weighing 14st, he was certainly well built with a safe pair of hands and strong kick. He was born in Stoke-on-Trent on 12 June 1880, and played initially for Penkhull Victoria before serving with Market Drayton. He joined Stoke, first time round, in May 1899, and made three League appearances as understudy to Tom Wilkes in his first half season at The Victoria Ground. In April 1901, he went to Bristol Rovers for whom he played in more than 250 games, helping them win the Southern League championship in 1905. Four years later he was transferred to Aston Villa and after 55 outings for the

Birmingham side, he returned to Stoke in April 1911 for £315 to start his second spell with the club. Cartlidge took his appearance tally with Stoke up to 45 before moving to South Shields in May 1912. He retired at the end of the 1914-15 season. He later returned to Stoke-on-Trent and died in the city in August 1940.

CASUALS (Corinthian)

Stoke met the famous London amateur side in the 1st qualifying round of the FA Cup in January 1892. A meagre crowd of just 1,200 attended The Victoria Ground to see Stoke win 3-0 with goals by Billy Dunn (2) and Ted Evans.
Billy Fearns played for both the Casuals and Stoke in the 1890s.

CATON, Clifford William

Bill Caton was the only Stoke player to be signed by the great Bill Shankly. This was in April 1950 when 'Shanks' was the manager of Carlisle United. The future Liverpool boss recruited Caton to Brunton Park for £3,.000 after the Stoke-born inside-forward had scored twice in 22 League games during his eight years at The Victoria Ground. Caton was 18 when he signed for Stoke during the war, and during the hostilities he guested for Wrexham and the Italian club, Benevento. After leaving Carlisle in 1952, he played for Chesterfield, Worcester City, Crewe Alexandra, Stafford Rangers, Mossley, Gresley Rovers, Congleton Town and Burslem Albion, also being a committee member, chairman and then president of the latter club. It's on record that Caton was an expert with penalties and from the 31 he took in the professional game, 29 were converted. He could also throw a ball a vast distance. In later life he took over a pub in Newcastle (Staffs).

CENTENARY

The club officially celebrated its centenary during the 1962-63 season (See FORMATION OF CLUB and REAL MADRID) But in later years it transpired that Stoke (City) FC was seemingly founded in 1868 – and therefore the celebrations were five years premature.

On 26 April 1976, Stoke visited neighbours Port Vale to celebrate their centenary.

CHADWICK, Richard

Half-back from Stoke-on-Trent who had one season at the club during which time he played in one FA Cup-tie against Caernarvon Wanderers in October 1886, Born in 1860, he played church football before joining the club and left to assist Longton Albion.

CHADWICK, Wilfred

Inside-forward Chadwick was a soccer 'wanderer' and during a lengthy career he served with eight different clubs at various levels – Bury Juniors, Nelson (1920-21), Rossendale United (for whom he hit 35 goals in 23 games), Everton (February 1922-November 1925), Leeds United (November 1925), Wolverhampton Wanderers (from August 1926), Stoke City (signed in May 1929 for £250) and Halifax Town (from October 1930 to May 1931). He was top-scorer at Goodison Park in 1923-24 with 30 goals and in all, netted 55 in his 109 appearances for the Merseysiders. Afterwards he struck 44 goals in 101 appearances for Wolves and netted twice in eight games for the Potters. In League action, Chadwick claimed 104 goals in 251 outings. A clever and sometimes very creative player, he was born in Bury on 7 September 1900 and died in the same Lancashire town in February 1975.

CHAIRMEN

Stoke have had a chairman, presiding over the board of directors, ever since the club became a professional body in 1885. Here are details of the men who have held the position at The Victoria Ground:

1885-87	Mr A.Fleming
1887-97	Mr S.Barker
1897-99	Mr J.T.Fenton
1899-1908	Mr W.A.Cowlishaw
1908-14	Rev A.E.Hurst
1914-24	Mr E.B.Reynish
1924-36	Mr A.J.C.Sherwin
1936-51	Ald H.Booth
1951-52	Mr T.A.Preece
1952-53	Mr E.Henshall
1953-55	Mr T.L.Duddell
1955-57	Mr G.W.Taylor
1957-59	Mr C.T.Salmon
1959-62	Mr A.A.Henshall
1962-66	Mr G.W.Taylor
1966-76	Mr A.A.Henshall
1976-80	Mr T.Degg
1980-83	Mr P.Axon
1983-85	Mr F.Edwards
1985-86	Mr S.Chubb
1986-97	Mr P.Coates

Alderman Booth held office a the longest period of time – 15 years including a difficult spell during World War Two.

Mr A.A.Hernshall is the only man (so far) to have held the position of Stoke City chairman on two separate occasions, covering a combined period of 13 years.

Mr Peter Coates has been in office for 11 years and is, of course, the first chairman to lead the club into new head-quarters (i.e. Trentham Ilkes).

CHALLINOR, John

Stoke captured the services of resilient former Witton Albion full-back Jack Challinor from under the noses of West Bromwich Albion, who had given him a trial only months before he agreed to sign for the Potters in November 1936. Challinor, who was born in Middlewich c.1917, was brought in as cover for Charlie Scrimshaw and Bill Winstanley, and he and another full-back, Harry Brigham, battled it out between them for a first-team place. Challinor waited 10 months before making his debut, replacing broken-leg victim Scrimshaw against Chelsea at Stamford Bridge, this being the first of 46 senior games for the club. He remained at Highfield Road until the outbreak of the war and after the hostilities Challinor went over to Northern Ireland to play for Linfield (Belfast) in season 1946-47.

CHALMERS, John

Centre-forward Chalmers was born locally in October 1884 and signed for Stoke in January 1906. He did well with the Potters and after scoring 19 goals in 43 League and Cup games, he, along with several other players, exited The Victoria Ground when the club folded in 1908. He quickly joined Bristol Rovers, but in November 1908, pulled out of competitive football to go and work in a factory. He retired in April 1915.

CHAMBERLAIN, Mark Valentine

Chamberlain, younger brother of Neville (below) started his career as a junior with Port Vale in 1977 and he was still in the game 20 years later, having also served in turn with Stoke City (August 1982 to September 1985), Sheffield Wednesday, Portsmouth (1988-94), Brighton & Hove Albion and Exeter City (August 1995 to date). Born in Stoke-on-Trent on 19 November 1961, Chamberlain, an out-and-out winger during the first 15 years in the game, made 110 appearances whilst at Vale Park and followed up by scoring 18 goals in 125 outings for Stoke who paid £135,000 for him from their arch neighbours. Whilst at The Victoria Ground Chamberlain won the first of his eight full England caps, having already represented his country at schoolboy, youth and Under-21 levels. Fast, with excellent ball control, he loved to run at defenders and could cross a ball with great precision. He left Stoke for Hillsborough in a £300,000 deal and when he joined Pompey the fee involved was £200,000. He teamed up with his former colleague at Stoke, Peter Fox, when he signed for struggling Exeter City. At the end of the 1996-97 season Chamberlain had taken his appearance tally in competitive football to past the 600 mark.

CHAMBERLAIN, Neville P.

After playing League football for 10 years (1978-88) with first Port Vale, then Stoke City (September 1982 to May 1984), Newport County (two spells, one on loan), Plymouth Argyle, Mansfield Town, Cambridge United and Doncaster Rovers, Chamberlain drifted into the lower reaches of non-League soccer and went on another mini tour, serving with Stafford Rangers, Worksop Town, Stafford Rangers

Lee Chapman

(again), Shepshed Charterhouse, Matlock Town, Leek Town, Shamblers FC, Rocester and Kynpersley Victoria (up to 1993). Unlike his brother, he never really hit the high spots and played only seven games for Stoke as a forward. Born in the Potteries on 22 January 1960, he nevertheless still amassed a total in excess of 350 appearances at senior club level, including 141 in the League for Port Vale.

CHAPMAN, Lee Roy

Lee Chapman's father, Roy, was a utility forward with Aston Villa, Lincoln City, Mansfield Town, Port Vale and Chester and he also managed several clubs including Stockport County, Stafford Rangers and Stourbridge. Lee's mother, Margaret, was also associated with football, being the secretary of the Stoke City manager Frank Taylor during the 1950s. Chapman junior, who was born in Lincoln on 5 December 1959, turned into a fine goalscorer, first hitting the headlines with Stoke City (as a junior in 1975 and a professional from June 1978) and thereafter with Arsenal (1982-83), Sunderland (1983-84), Sheffield Wednesday (1984-88), Nottingham Forest (1988-90), Leeds United (1990-93), Portsmouth (1993), West Ham United (1993), Southend United (on loan, 1995), Ipswich Town (1995-96), Leeds (again, on loan 1995) and Swansea City (1996). He also assisted Stafford Rangers at the start of his career and played also for Plymouth Argyle (on loan from Stoke in 1978) and in France with Niort (before Nottingham Forest). Capped once by England's 'B' team and once at Under-21 level, he gained a Second Division and First Division championship medals with Leeds in 1990 and 1992 respectively and earlier collected League Cup and Simod Cup prizes with Forest in 1989. His record as a Stoke City player was 38 goals in 107 appearances and all told, in his playing career in England at club level, Chapman revealed a fine set of statistics – 253 goals in 679 appearances. He retired at the end of the 1995-96 season to open a his own restaurant/wine bar in London.

CHARLTON ATHLETIC

Stoke's playing record against the Addicks is:
Football League

Venue	P	W	D	L	F	A
Home	27	16	7	4	52	28
Away	27	7	4	16	31	55
Total	54	23	11	20	83	83

League Cup

Away	2	1	0	1	4	6

Stoke's best League victory over Athletic is 6-3 – at The Victoria

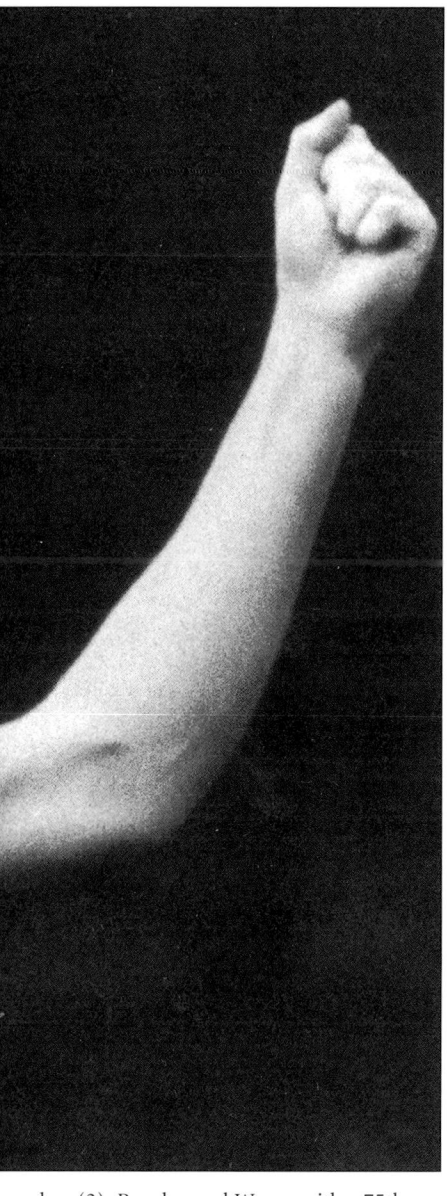

Ground in September 1962 (Division Two). Dennis Viollet scored four goals that day and 11,596 attended. Another good Potters victory was 5-3 in January 1961 when defender-cum-attacker Bill Aspey netted a smart hat-trick.

The first Football League game between the Potters and the Addicks took place in September 1929 (Division Two). A crowd of 16,648 at The Victoria Ground saw Stoke come back from a goal down to win 2-1 with strikes from Charlie Wilson and Wilf Chadwck.

The return game a week later ended all square at 4-4 after a titanic battle before 13,536 fans at The Valley. Stoke led 1-0 and 4-1 before the Londoners stormed back to grab a point. Walter Bussey (2) Wilson and Cull scored for the Potters, Whitlow (2), Pugsley and Wyper with a 75th equaliser replied for Athletic. Stoke overwhelmed Charlton 4-0 at home in October 1931 (Bobby Liddle netting twice) and in the first League game after World War Two (played on 31 August 1946) a crowd of 32,565 witnessed a 2-2 draw.

Almost six years later, in April 1952, almost 13,900 spectators saw Charlton crush the Potters 4-0 at The Valley with Gordon Hurst and Charlie Vaughan both scoring twice.

The following year (November 1952) Stoke lost 5-1 at Charlton with the South African Eddie Firmani scoring a hat-trick in front of 11,852 supporters at The Valley.

Stoke were the last team to play Charlton at The Valley before the ground was closed down and redeveloped. This was on 21 September 1985 when a crowd of 8,858 saw Athletic win 2-0 with late goals from Stuart and Lee.

In January 1997, two goals by Mike Sheron – his 20th and 21st strikes of the season – gave Stoke only their seventh League win at Charlton (2-1).

Stoke's one League Cup victory came at Charlton in round 4 of the 1978-79 competition when they won 3-2, Garth Crooks (a future Addicks player) netting an 87th-minute match-winning penalty before a crowd of almost 19,000. Sammy Irvine had put the Potters ahead after just 36 seconds, one of the fastest goals in the competition.

Players with both clubs: Garth Crooks, Jim Harbot, Vince Hilaire, Maurice Setters and Geoff Scott.

CHARNLEY, William

An outside-right, Will Charnley came down to the Potteries from Aberdeen for the 1919-20 season. He was given just two League outings by the club before returning to Scotland to play for Musselburgh. Born at Kirkham in 1895, he drifted out of football in the mid-1920s after suffering a spate of injuries.

CHELSEA

Stoke's playing record against the Blues is:
Football League

Venue	P	W	D	L	F	A
Home	34	15	6	13	51	37
Away	34	7	10	17	45	68
Total	68	22	16	30	96	105

FA Cup

Home	1	1	0	0	3	1
Away	1	0	0	1	2	3
Totals	2	1	0	1	5	4

League Cup

Home	4	2	2	0	8	3
Away	3	2	1	0	5	3
Totals	7	4	3	0	13	6

Stoke have registered two exciting 6-1 home League wins over Chelsea. The first in February 1939 saw Freddie Steele score a hat-trick, and in the second encounter, played in February 1947, both Alec Ormston and Syd Peppitt netted twice.

The Potters also won 5-2 at Chelsea in October 1946 (Ormston claiming a hat-trick this time) and earlier, they completed a fine double over the Pensioners in 1935-36 – winning 5-3 in London and 3-0 at The Victoria Ground, Tommy Sale finding the net in both matches.

Stoke's heaviest reverse against the Londoners is 4-0 at Stamford Bridge in October 1964.

A crowd of 66,199 saw champions Stoke beat Chelsea 1-0 at Stamford Bridge in a vital Second Division promotion game in May 1963, and nine years later, in March 1972, the Potters lifted their first major trophy when they beat Chelsea 2-1 in League Cup Final at Wembley (See FOOTBALL LEAGUE CUP).

In the same tournament in October 1974, Stoke beat Chelsea 6-2 at home in a third-round second replay after 2-2 and 1-1 draws at Stamford Bridge and The Victoria Ground respectively. Chelsea defenders Ron Harris and Mickey Droy both conceded own-goals in that eight-goal bonanza.

After holding Premiership side Chelsea to a draw at The Victoria Ground in a second-round 1st leg League Cup-tie in October 1995, Canadian international Paul Peschisolido netted the only goal in the return leg at Stamford Bridge to send Stoke into the next round.

Players with both clubs: Bill Dickie, Alan Hudson, Bill Robertson, Fred Rouse, Mark Stein, Mickey Thomas, Bob Whittingham and Jack Whitley. The latter became trainer at Stamford Bridge. Geoff Hurst played for Stoke and later managed Chelsea.

Dennis Rofe played for Chelsea and later became reserve-team coach at Stoke (1993). Verdi Godwin was a Stoke player who later did some scouting for Chelsea.

CHESHAM TOWN

Stoke's playing record against Chesham is:
Southern League

Venue	P	W	D	L	F	A
Home	1	1	0	0	3	0
Away	1	1	0	0	8	0
Totals	2	2	0	0	11	0

These games took place in season 1910-11. The Potters won 3-0 at home with a hat-trick from centre-forward Vic Horrocks, and then raced to an emphatic 8-0 victory away when Billy Smith and Ernie Boulton both registered trebles.

CHESTER (CITY)

Stoke's playing record against Chester is:
Football League

Venue	P	W	D	L	F	A
Home	3	1	0	2	6	4
Away	3	0	3	0	2	2
Total	6	1	3	2	8	6

FA Cup

Venue	P	W	D	L	F	A
Home	1	1	0	0	3	2
Away	1	0	1	0	0	0
Totals	2	1	1	0	3	2

Stoke's only League win over Chester was a 4-0 triumph at home in March 1993 when Mark Stein (2), Graham Shaw and Steve Foley found the net in front of 14,534 fans.

Stoke first played Chester at Moss Rose, Macclesfield in September 1990. Mickey Thomas put the Potters ahead but Chester's Neil Ellis earned his side a point with a smart header.

The two FA Cup games were played in 1946-47, Stoke winning 3-2 in a fourth-round mid-week replay when Freddie Steele scored twice.

Players with both clubs: Keith Bertschin, Horace Brindley, Lee Dixon, Paul A.Johnson, Tony Kelly, George Latham, Fred McCarthy, Alec Raisbeck, Paul Richardson, John Ruggiero, Barry Siddall, Clem Smith, Wilmot Turner and Dick Williams.

Mike Pejic played for Stoke and later managed Chester before returning as coach at The Victoria Ground. Alan A'Court was assistant manager at Chester and caretaker manager of Stoke City.

CHESTERFIELD

Stoke's playing record against the Spireites is:
Football League

Venue	P	W	D	L	F	A
Home	4	3	1	0	8	5
Away	4	3	1	0	10	5
Total	8	6	2	0	18	10

FA Cup

Venue	P	W	D	L	F	A
Home	1	1	0	0	2	1

League Cup

Venue	P	W	D	L	F	A
Home	2	2	0	0	3	1
Away	2	1	1	0	4	3
Totals	4	3	1	0	7	4

Stoke last played Chesterfield in season 1932-33 when they won the Second Division championship. The Potters were 2-1 victors in both matches, with the away victory setting them up for the star prize.

Stoke's best League win of the six recorded was a 4-2 scoreline at Chesterfield in 1907-08.

Stoke's FA Cup victory was achieved in a third-round tie in January 1972. when Terry Conroy and Peter Dobing found the net in front of 26,559 fans at The Victoria Ground.

Stoke knocked Chesterfield out of the League Cup after a replay in 1965-66, winning 2-1 at home following a 2-2 draw at Saltergate, and the Potters accounted for the Spireites 3-1 over two legs in a first-round League Cup-tie in season 1991-92.

Players with both clubs: Gordon Banks, Paul Barnes, Phil Bonnyman, Tommy Broad, Cliff Carr, Billy Caton, Herby Hales, Jimmy Hay, Charlie Hinks, Jack Howshall, Mick Kennedy, Fred McCarthy, Carl Muggleton, John Paxton, Bert Ralphs, Tom Revill, Geoff Salmons and Steve Waddington.

CHRISTIE, David

Stoke had several Scottish-born players at the club during the late 1890s/early 1900s and Christie was undoubtedly one of the best. A powerful half-back, able to occupy all three middle line positions, he was comfortable on the ball, had good technique and was never hurried. He played at The Victoria Ground from 1889 to 1895, scoring three goals in 135 League and FA Cup appearances. He moved to the Potteries from Forfar Athletic (where he had been since 1885) and rounded off his career with a brief spell at Dresden United. Christie was born in Forfar in 1867 and it is believed he returned to Scotland after retiring around the turn of the century.

CHURCH

During the early years there is no doubt whatsoever that the church played an important part in the history of Stoke Football Club. The vast strip of land which spread from Stoke church, to Church Street, to Lonsdale Street and upwards towards Campbell Road, was all glebe land and the Rector, Sir Lovelace Starmer, certainly encouraged many sporting games to be played on the land, including football, cricket, rugby and athletics. Stoke were among the many teams to play their football on church land and it is said that several of the club's early players belonged to the church in some small way.

The importance of the church was clearly indicated in documents around the turn of the century when the Reverend Charles H.Simpkinson, an avid supporter of football, agreed to rent the church land on a 21 year lease to the club – and this gave Stoke FC a valuable asset which undoubtedly helped the Potters enhance their ground improvements as the years rolled by.

CLAMP, Harold Edwin

Eddie Clamp was a tough, determined wing-half, who was dubbed 'Chopper' by the fans at Molineux. A great character during the 1950s and early '60s, he was one of the most aggressive players in League Football, never shirking a tackle, always totally committed and above all, a terrific competitor with a never-say-die attitude. Born in Coalville (Leicestershire) on 14 September 1934, he was a pupil at the village state school and actually joined Wolverhampton Wanderers halfway through his paper round. This was in 1949. Wolves' boss Stan Cullis immediately placed him in the club's nursery team, Wath

Wanderers, where his game developed rapidly. Clamp turned professional in April 1952 and made his senior debut in the 'old gold and black strip in March 1954 against Manchester United at Old Trafford in front of almost 39,000 fans. This was the start of a superb career for 'Chopper'. He went on to play in 241 League and Cup games for Wolves, winning two First Division championship medals (1958 and 1959) and an FA Cup winners' medal in 1960. He also received four England caps (1958) when he starred alongside his teammates Billy Wright and Bill Slater to form an all-Wolves half-back line. Clamp left Molineux in November 1961 to sign for Arsenal for £12,000, but he never settled in London and left Highbury after just 10 months, switching to Stoke City in September 1952 to be re-united with his former Wolves colleague Eddie Stuart. He helped the Potters regain their First Division status in 1963 and played in 62 games (two goals scored) during his time at The Victoria Ground before leaving for Peterborough United in October 1964. After a season at London Road (when he took his career tally up to 335 games) Clamp then had brief spells with Worcester City and Lower Gornal, and finally called it a day in 1970, although he still figured in the occasional charity match for Wolves Old Stars. Thereafter he ran his own business and was a regular visitor to both The Victoria Ground and Molineux right up until his death on 14 December 1995. Clamp's mother was the laundry lady at Molineux during the 1950s.

CLARE, Thomas

Full-back Clare was Stoke's first professional player as well as the club's first appointed team captain in the Football League. Born at Congleton in March 1865, he joined the club in 1884 after spells with Talke Rangers, Goldenhill Wanderers and Burslem Port Vale. A splendid header of the ball, he was quick off the mark, strong and purposeful in the tackle and ever-reliable, always working for his team. He made his senior debut in a Stoke jersey in 1885 and went on to amass a total of 251 League and Cup appearances for the club, scoring six goals, up to 1897. He represented Staffordshire on several occasions and gained four full England caps as a Stoke player and on leaving the club he had one League game for Manchester City (on trial) before rejoining Burslem Port Vale as player-coach (1898), retiring as a player three years later. He continued to coach the Valiants and was their manager in 1905-06, but soon afterwards he emigrated to Canada. He died in the town of Ladysmith, Vancouver on 27 December 1929, aged 64.

CLARK, Andrew

A forceful, strong-running left-back, who played in 59 games for Stoke during his two seasons with the club: 1901-03. Born in Leith, Midlothian, in August 1881, Clark assisted Hamilton Academical, Buckheaven United and Heart of Midlothian before moving down to the Potteries. He left The Victoria Ground to sign for Plymouth Argyle and later played for Leeds City (1906-07).

CLARK, John Brown

Rugged, well built utility defender, born in Edinburgh on 22 September 1964, who was signed from Dundee United for £150,000 in January 1994. Clark's family never settled in the Potteries and he spent less than eight months at The Victoria Ground, during which time he appeared in 18 games (one goal scored). He returned home to sign for Falkirk for £100,000 in September 1994, moving to Dunfermline Athletic in February 1996. A Scottish youth international, Clark netted 36 goals in 324 outings for the Dundee club whom he joined as a junior in 1979, turning professional in July 1981. Stoke played Dundee United in a Testimonial Match for Clark at Tannadice Park in 1994.

CLARKE, George

Clarke remained a part-time footballer throughout his career, occupying a half-back position, where, as a 'spoiler' he was both powerful and resolute. He scored four goals in 165 senior appearances for Stoke, spread over a period of 11 years, 1914-25, although he didn't actually enter first-team action until after the war, having suffered a broken leg while playing army football as a member of the the Liverpool Scottish Regiment serving in France during the hostilities. Born in Nantwich on 3 December 1894, he cost Stoke £125 plus the proceeds of a game between the two sides. In 1921-22 he helped Stoke win promotion to the First Division but after breaking his leg again (in a Cup-tie against Leeds United) he was never the same player again and eventually left The Victoria Ground for Crewe Alexandra. After retiring Clarke acted as a scout for the Alex. He died at Willaston near Nantwich on 30 July 1960.

CLARKE, Wayne

Wayne Clarke, from the famous Black Country footballing family which included the Leeds United and England star Allan, had scored for Wolverhampton Wanderers, Birmingham City, Everton (League Championship winner in 1987), Leicester City and Shrewsbury Town before joining Stoke, on loan, in March 1991. He stayed at the club for two months during which time he hit three goals in nine League outings. Clarke, born in Willenhall on 28 February 1961, had a second spell with Wolves and after giving Walsall good service, he went into non-League football with Telford United as player-manager in August 1995, resigning his position in November 1996. All told, Clarke netted over 130 goals in more than 500 League appearances during his senior career. He also played for England at schoolboy and youth team levels.

CLARKSON, Ian Stewart

After 96 first-team appearances for Stoke City, right-back Clarkson was given a free transfer by manager Lou Macari in the summer of 1996 and was quickly snapped up by Northampton Town. Born in Solihull on 4 December 1970, and a pupil at Tudor Grange school, he had 172 games for Birmingham City before moving to The Victoria Ground for £40,000 in September 1993, joining a band of former Blues players already with the Potters. Clarkson, a steady performer, returned to Stoke with the Cobblers for a Coca-Cola Cup game in season 1996-97.

CLAWLEY, George W.

Goalkeeper Clawley, who was 6ft 2ins tall and 12st 7lbs in weight, always wore a cap. He was one of the finest goalkeepers of his era, possessing all the physical requirements for a player in his position. He had two separate spells at The Victoria Ground and all told appeared in 96 League and Cup games for Stoke. Born in Scholar Green on 10 April 1875, he played for Crewe Alexandra (from August 1893) before joining the Potters for £10 in September 1894. He left The Victoria Ground for Southampton in May 1896 season, only to return to Stoke for a second time in May 1898, staying until the end of that campaign when he was transferred to Tottenham Hotspur. Unfortunately he broke a leg in his first season at White Hart Lane, but recovered in time to win an FA Cup winners' medal in 1901 and also figure in an England international trial (March 1903). Clawley, who was a big favourite with the supporters, later switched back to Southampton (July 1903 to May 1907). He won three Southern League championship medals with Southampton (1897, 1898 and 1904, the second as skipper of the team and represented both Hampshire County and the Southern League during the 1890s when a Saints player. Clawley appeared in 163 games for Southampton and 187 for Spurs and on announcing his retirement in 1907 he became landlord of the Wareham Arms Hotel in Southampton. He died in the Hampshire town on 16 July 1920, but was buried in Kidsgrove.

CLEAN SHEETS

Goalkeeper Roger Jones holds the record for keeping most clean sheets in a League season for the Potters. He was goalless in 20 of his 41 games in 1978-79 when the Potters won promotion to the First Division. Bob Dixon kept 18 clean sheets when Stoke won the Third Division North title in 1926-27.

CLEGG, Donald

Stoke's goalkeeping strength at the start of the 1950-51 season was exceptionally good, with Dennis Herod, Norman Wilkinson and Don Clegg all ready to claim the number-one position. It was Clegg who started off the campaign, being given just two League outings by manager Bob McGrory before he was dropped following two defeats. A Yorkshireman, born in Huddersfield on 2 June 1921, Clegg served his home-town club at Leeds Road before signing for Bury in July 1948. After 15 League games for the Shakers he moved to Stoke (June 1950) and in the summer of 1951 he left the Potteries to sign for Rossendale, retiring in 1956.

CLENNELL, Joseph

Born New Silksworth, County Durham on 19 February 1889, Inside-forward Joe Clennell first played junior football in with his hometown club, Silksworth United and then Seaham Harbour before turning professional with Blackpool (1910). His next move took him to Blackburn Rovers (1911) from where he switched to Everton, who paid a healthy sum for his services in January 1914. After scoring 33 goals in 74 senior games for the Merseysiders, and representing the Football League in 1920, he had a very successful spell in South Wales with Cardiff City (from October 1921 – netting 37 goals in 118 League appearances) before finding his way to Stoke in February 1925 at the age of 36. Yet despite being a soccer veteran, he still strived to give the Potters good value for their money, scoring nine goals in 35 appearances before moving on to Bristol Rovers (1926) and then Rochdale (1927). Thereafter, he became player-manager of Ebbw Vale, then Barry Town (1928-29) and Bangor Town, before going to the Lancashire non-League side, Great Harwood. Clennell later took charge of the Irish club, Distillery and he also coached Accrington Stanley (1934-35). Clennell was sadly killed in a car crash, nine days after his 76th birthday (28 February 1965).

CLEVELAND STOKERS

In the summer of 1966 when England were preparing to win the World Cup, Stoke City FC played in the US Soccer Tournament bearing the name of Cleveland Stokers. They failed to win any prizes as they completed 11 matches, ending with these statistics:

P	W	D	L	F	A
11	5	3	3	17	11

Stoke's best wins were those of 4-1 against both ADO, The Hague (Holland) and Dundee United.

During the trip Maurice Setters and Calvin Palmer were involved in a heated argument which result in the latter player being ordered home by manager Tony Waddington.

CLIFFORD, Hugh

After playing for Stoke, half-back Clifford illegally signed for Celtic in 1893 and was banned from English football for two years. Born in Glasgow in May 1866, he served with Renton and Carfin Shamrock (with Willie Naughton) before joining the Potters in September 1890. He scored twice in 34 senior appearances during his three-year stay at The Victoria Ground, and, in fact, walked out of The Victoria Ground in a temper and threatened to quit football altogether. After his ban had been served, Clifford played for Manchester City (July 1895-March 1896) and scored once in four games.

CLOWES, John A.

Clowes had two spells at The Victoria Ground (June 1950 to June 1952 and August 1955 to March 1956). A useful reserve inside-forward, he scored twice on his debut for Stoke in a 3-2 win over Wolverhampton Wanderers at Molineux in April 1951. He had four outings for the Potters altogether. Prior to Stoke Clowes, who was born at Alton on Guy Fawkes Day, 1929, had been with Crewe Alexandra, and in between his spells at The Victoria Ground he served with Shrewsbury Town and Wellington Town. He rounded off his career with Macclesfield Town (March 1956 to May 1957).

COACHES

Since Stoke (City) Football Club was formed in 1868, there have been several men who have held the position of coach, some while still active players at either first or second-team levels.

Here are details of some of the coaches who have served at The Victoria Ground over the years: Alan A'Court (also caretaker manager); Gordon Banks; Chic Bates (also assistant manager); Dougie Brown (trainer-coach 1960s); Sammy Chung (also assistant manager); Walker Gould (under George Eastham's managership); Len Graham (also assistant manager); George Jackson (youth team, late 1970s); Howard Kendall (as player-coach under manager Alan Durban); David Kevan; Cyril Lea (also under Durban); Jimmy McIlroy (under Tony Waddington); Frank Mountford (trainer-coach, under Waddington); Graham Paddon (also caretaker manager); Mike Pejic; ex-Motherwell, Leicester City and Mansfield Town player Bobby Roberts (under manager Bill Asprey) and former player Harry Sellars (1950s) who was also assistant manager to Bob McGrory.

COATES, Richard J.

Coates was a short, stocky centre-forward who had one Southern League game for Stoke, against Coventry City (at home) in January 1913. Born in Hanley in April 1889, he joined the Potters from Mardy FC in the summer of 1912 and left the club for Annfield Plain in May 1913.

COLCHESTER UNITED

Stoke City have yet to play United at competitive level.

Players with both clubs: Ian Allinson, Peter Bullock, Tony Kelly, John McClelland, Jack Palethorpe, Mark Sale and Brian Sherratt.

Neil Franklin player for Stoke and later managed Colchester. Alan Ball was manager of both Colchester United and Stoke City. Bobby Roberts was player-coach with Colchester (1973), then manager (1975-82) and later coach at Stoke City and Cyril Lea was coach at Stoke (1979) and later coach and then manager of Colchester (1983-86).

COLCLOUGH, Ephraim

Described as a 'versatile forward' Colclough played in three League games for Stoke between April 1899 and January 1900. Born in Blurton in June 1875, he was signed as a reserve striker early in 1899 from local junior football and was transferred to Watford in the summer of 1900, later playing for Brighton & Hove Albion (August 1901 to May 1902). It is believed that Colclough died in 1914.

COLEMAN, Neville J.

'Tim' Coleman holds the record for scoring most goals in a game for Stoke City – he netted seven times in an 8-0 victory over Lincoln in a Second Division fixture at The Victoria Ground on 23 February 1957. After this flourish outside-right Coleman failed to hit the target again for the Potters that season – but during his six years with the club he amassed a pretty useful set of statistics: 52 goals in 126 senior appearances. Born in Prescot on 29 January 1930, he moved to The Victoria Ground from Gorleston in Norfolk in 1953. He did his National Service in the RAF and actually assisted in providing the cost of buying himself out of the forces in the summer of 1955, when he immediately signed professional forms for the Potters. In the next season he established himself in the first XI. Coleman was transferred to Crewe Alexandra for £1,000 in February 1959 and went on to score 16 goals in 73 League outings for the Gresty Road club before pulling out of competitive football in 1961.

COLOURS

In the club's early days, black, blue, white and even claret shirts were donned by players with black shorts taking preference over white.

But when Stoke played their first match at The Victoria Ground in September 1883 (against Talke) the players donned red and white striped flannel shirts and white knickerbockers. And when they were forced to change (away from home) they usually wore white shirts and black shorts.

As time went by, so the strip changed and during the 1870s Stoke donned red and white hooped shirts with either white or black shorts. Into the 1880s they changed to wearing black and amber striped shirts and black shorts and then played in red and white stripes and black shorts, reverting back to red and amber stripes in 1891-92. Thereafter, players wore all red shirts and white shorts (early 1900s), they played in white shirts and black shorts for a time after that and then went back to plain red shirts until 1908. From then until the present day, the true colours of the club have been basically red and white striped shirts and white shorts, although occasionally, certainly in the 1980s, the design of the shirt changed somewhat from the traditional vertical stripes. In the mid-1980s the club's chosen kit was white shirts, red sleeves and red shorts as well as being red and white striped shirts with red sleeves and white shorts.

● For a time just after World War Two (when ration coupons were being used) the Stoke City players were forced to wear white shirts and black shorts instead lf their now traditional red and white striped shirts and white shorts.

COMMERCIAL DEPARTMENT

Stoke's first professional efforts to try and sell the club to the general public came about in October 1967 when a leading Northern-based journalist, Derek Hudson, was appointed as assistant manager at The Victoria Ground, not on the playing side it must be said. He was brought in to boost the 'commercial side' of the club and immediately changed the style, design and name of the matchday programmne, retitling it *The Ceramic City Clipper*. He also introduced a bevy of glamorous skimpy-dressed girls, known as the *jet set* who went round the ground selling programmes etc. Hudson also started the *Potters Bar* (a shop in fact) which contained Stoke City merchandise, and he also developed an agents' network with Golden Goal tickets being sold to supporters.

Cornishman Dudley Kernick (see under KERNICK) followed Hudson into the club's commercial department and he did an excellent job for a number of years before handing over the duties to the former Port Vale player, Mick Cullerton, in 1982. Having learned the 'business' with nearby Stafford Rangers, Scotsman Cullerton, who was born in Edinburgh in November 1948, remained at the club as commercial manager until 1994 when Jez Moxey, formerly with Partick Thistle, was brought in as chief executive – a position he still holds today.

Assistant commercial manager (under Cullerton) was Tony Tams, who combined his duties with those of programme editor, a job previously undertaken by David Capper.

'T.T.' as he is referred to, worked overtime on the matchday programme/magazine and was rewarded in 1991-92 when the *Wirrall Programme Club* voted the *Potters News* the best in the Third Division. When Moxey came to the club 'T.T.' was given the title of marketing services manager (as well as programme editor).

In 1995 the club introduced a Marketing Department which included Rob Bailey and later Wayne Archer with public relations officer Lorraine Hampson, who succeeded Maria Latham.

The Stoke City Lottery, the club's Prize Draw, the Golden Potters Club, scratchcards and Matchday Moneyspinner were all fund-raising elements introduced by the marketing department during the 1980s and 1990s – which brought thousands of pounds into the club.

The club shop was also developed considerably, more so from 1991 onwards, and in 1995 besides the one adjacent to the ground, a second store was opened in Stafford Street, Hanley. Paul Gerkin assumed the role of head manager with Paul Bradbury named as under manager.

NB Former player Alec Ormston worked in the club's promotion office after retiring.

COMMUNITY PROGRAMME

Stoke City have had a Football in the Community department within the club since the mid-1980s. Former players at The Victoria Ground, Brendon O'Callaghan and Paul Johnson, were two of the early community officers. and in 1995 Andy Morgan took over the reins with Adrian Hurst as his assistant. Their main responsibility is to go round the local schools coaching the youngsters and talking football in general, hoping that in years to come those children will be either players themselves or failing that ardent supporters of Stoke City FC.

CONNOR, Harold

A Liverpudlian, born on 26 December 1929, O'Connor played initially as a centre-forward for non-League side, Peterborough United, and after serving with and playing for the RAF (Halton) and assisting Marine Crosby, he joined Stoke City in March 1953 as reserve to Bill Finney. He appeared in only four matches for the club, scoring two goals (his first after only ten minutes of his debut against Sunderland) and then returned to Marine, later assisting New Brighton and Skelmersdale United. Connor, the last amateur to play senior football for Stoke City, was also a very fine athlete, especially on the track over middle distances (400-800 yards). In later years he chose to live in retirement in Maidstone, Kent.

CONROY, Gerald Anthony

Terry Conroy was a very popular player at The Victoria Ground. He was certainly the fans' favourite son from the day he joined the Potters from the Irish club, Glentoran for £10,000 in March 1967. Starting off in the Reserves and not being introduced to first-team action by manager Tony Waddington until six months after joining, the red-headed Dubliner, who was born in that fair city on 2 October 1946, wore the number-seven shirt in practically all of his 333 League and Cup games for Stoke (31 as sub), scoring 66 goals and laying on another 100 at least. A brilliant dribbler, he had pace, a superb bodyswerve and fierce shot in either foot – and above all, he had great stamina. He ran his socks off for Stoke City week after week and was rewarded with a League Cup winners' medal in 1972 when he starred in that 2-1 victory at Wembley over Chelsea. Capped by The Republic of Ireland 26 times, he left The Victoria Ground for the Hong Kong club Bulova on a free transfer in the summer of 1979 having spent 12 happy years in the Potteries. He returned to England and served with Crewe Alexandra from January 1980 to June 1981, scoring five goals in 37 League outings before hanging up his boots to concentrate on his business in the area. He turned out in a few charity matches from time to time and attends Stoke home games when ever possible.

Terry Conroy

CONSECUTIVE HOME MATCHES

Stoke played a total of eight League and FA Cup home games back to back between 7 November and 12 December 1910 – a club record. They won them all, including a 7-0 victory over Worcester City in the Cup and a 6-1 triumph over Wolverhampton Wanderers Reserves in the Birmingham League.

COOK, Albert

Cook was a well-respected amateur full-back, who could also play on the wing. He had two spells with the club – the first in February 1906, the second from September to December 1908 – and all told scored one goal in 12 first-team games. Cook was a smart footballer who started out with North Staffs Nomads and joined Stoke from Burslem Port Vale. He left to play for Stockport County and after returning to The Victoria Ground from Edgeley Park, he went back to the Vale, this time as a guest. Born in Burslem in February 1880, he also skippered the Burslem cricket club for many years. He died in Stoke-on-Trent c.1950.

COOK, Jeffrey W.

Born in Hartlepool on 14 March 1953, defender Cook played with Hellenic FC before joining Stoke in November 1977. He played 33 times for the Potters (5 goals scored) before transferring to Plymouth Argyle for £25,000 in 1981. He also assisted Bradford City (on loan from Stoke) and after leaving Home Park he served with Halifax Town, Worksop Town, North Ferriby United, Ferryhill Athletic and Hartlepool Town (as player-manager).

COPE, William Arthur

Cook was another fine full-back whose game was characterised by some beefy clearances despite the fact that he wore only a size 4 boot. Born in Burslem on 25 November 1884. Cook played for Mount Pleasant and Burslem Port Vale (from August 1904) before teaming up with Stoke in July 1907. At first he seemed to lack speed, but as time went by he developed into sound player with a fine tackle. He appeared in 31 League games for the Potters before transferring to Oldham Athletic for £300 in June 1908. He later played for, and skippered, West Ham United (1914-22) and also assisted Wrexham before returning to the area in 1923. He died in Stoke on 18 February 1937 at the early age of 52.

COPESTAKE, Joseph

Utility defender, born in Fenton in June 1859, Copestake played in two FA Cup-ties for Stoke in November 1883 – his only senior outings for the club. He served with Newcastle under Lyme and Stoke Town before and after his brief association with the Potters.

CORRIGAN, Thomas Joseph

Born in Manchester on 18 November 1948, Joe Corrigan at 6ft 5ins was one of the tallest goalkeepers in the game between 1967 and 1985 – and he is certainly one of the tallest footballers ever to don a Stoke shirt. An England international (capped nine times at senior level 1976-82, and once by the Under-23's) he played for Sale FC before becoming a professional with Manchester City in January 1967. He went on to appear in well over 500 games for the Maine Road club (476 in the League) up to June 1982, when he left to play in the States with Seattle Sounders. He returned to England to assist Brighton & Hove Albion for a season (1983-84) and the following term had loan spells with both Norwich City and Stoke City before retiring from first-class football. He had nine League outings for the Potters and while with Manchester City won two League Cup winners' medals (1970 & 1976) and was an FA Cup finalist in 1981.

COTTON, Harold Henry

Six foot goalkeeper Cotton was reserve to Bert Miller and Fred Rathbone during the 1908-09 season when he was given just two League outings (when Bert Miller was absent). A tall man, born in Crewe in January 1883, he had two spells with Burslem Port Vale and a brief association with Crewe Alexandra, before Stoke who signed him in October 1908 for £50. He played for Eccleshall after leaving The Victoria Ground. An ironsmith by trade, Cotton was certainly a sporting fellow who enjoyed fishing, cricket, swimming and athletics as well as soccer. He died in his native Crewe.

COTTON, John

Reserve-team full-back, born in Stoke-on-Trent on 2 March 1930, Cotton appeared in two League games for the Potters in April 1954. He joined the club, initially as a junior, and turned professional in May 1952. After leaving Stoke in October 1955, he played 14 times for Crewe Alexandra in the Third Division North.

COUPAR, Peter A.

Workmanlike centre-forward from Scotland, who came to Stoke in the summer of 1889 hoping to make a name for himself in English League football. Unfortunately he never quite fitted the bill and after scoring six times in his 17 first-team outings he had a brief spell with Newton Heath (Manchester United) before returning home to Scotland in the summer of 1891. Born in Dundee c.1863, who he played for, he moved to the Potteries and then Dundee again. In later years he emigrated to America.

COVENTRY CITY

Stoke's playing record against Coventry is:

Football League

Venue	P	W	D	L	F	A
Home	21	13	3	5	46	26
Away	21	6	3	12	19	33
Totals	42	19	6	17	65	59

Southern League

Home	3	2	0	1	7	3
Away	3	1	0	2	7	9
Totals	6	3	0	3	14	12

FA Cup

Away	1	0	0	1	0	1

League Cup

Away	1	0	0	1	1	2

Full Members' Cup

Home	1	1	0	0	3	0

The last time Coventry met Stoke in a Football League game was in season 1984-85 (Division One). A crowd of just under 9,900 saw the Sky Blues race to a convincing 4-0 win at Highfield Road while a meagre audience of 6,930 saw Stoke lose 1-0 at The Victoria Ground.

Stoke's best League win is 6-1 at home in December 1919 (Division Two) when Wilf Phillips (2), David Brown (2) and Bob Whittingham (2, one a penalty) found the net in front of a 20,000 crowd. Stoke also won a Southern League game by 5-1 at home in January 1915 when Arty Watkin netted a hat-trick.

Coventry's best victory is 5-2 – achieved twice: in September 1912 (Southern League) and in April 1977 (League Division One).

Stoke's 1-0 defeat in the FA Cup was in the fifth round in February 1987 when over 31,000 fans packed into Highfield Road.

Stoke's exit from the League Cup came in the fourth round of the 1973-74 competition.

The Full Members' Cup-tie was played in September 1985 when goals from Keith Bertschin (penalty), Carl Saunders and Carl Beeston gave the Potters a 3-0 victory in front of just 3,516 spectators.

Players with both clubs: Mickey Adams, Arthur Arrowsmith, Dave Bamber, Gary Bannister, Ernie Cull, Archie Dyke, Paul Dyson, Gareth Evans, Sean Flynn, Ashley Grimes, Mickey Gynn, Joey Jones, Alex McClure, Eric McManus, Ian Painter, Billy Poole, Maurice Setters, Peter Shilton, Jack Stirling, John Tudor and John Williams.

Dudley Kernick was a coach at Coventry City before becoming commercial manager of Stoke. Former Potters' cricketer-goalkeeper Arthur Jepson later acted scout Graham Paddon played for Coventry City and later became caretaker manager of Stoke (1991). Bobby Roberts was coach at Coventry City (1972-73) and later coach at Stoke. Arthur Jepson was a Stoke goalkeeper who later scouted for Coventry City.

COWAN, Thomas

Despite his lack of height, for a left-back Cowan can match anyone in the air and is no mean tackler on the ground. Born in Belshill, Scotland, on 28 August 1969, he played for Netherdale Boys Club before signing for Clyde in 1988. From there he went to Ibrox Park and made 15 appearances for Rangers prior to his transfer to Sheffield United for £350,000 in August 1991. Two years later he was taken on loan by Stoke City (October/November 1993) and played in 18 first-team games before returning to Bramall Lane from where he switched to Huddersfield Town for £150,000 in March 1994.

COWDEN, Stuart

Wing-half 'Ted' Cowden played in just one competitive game for Stoke City against Burnley in the third round of the FA Cup in January 1946. He had joined the club as an amateur in 1943, turned professional two years later and having failed to make an impact after the war he was transferred to Witton Albion in the summer of 1946. Cowden was born in Alsager c.1926.

COX, Walter

A local man from the Potteries (born in September 1860) Cox played right-half in Stoke's first-ever FA Cup game against Manchester in October 1883. During his career he also served with Talke Rangers, Burslem Swifts and Stoke St Peter's. He was secretary-manager of the club (1883-84) before handing over to Harry Lockett (See MANAGERS).

COXON, Thomas

Coxon was a clever, stocky outside-left who caused defenders plenty of problems. He had two spells at The Victoria Ground – from October 1903 to September 1905 and from May 1907 to May 1908. Born in Hanley on 10 June 1883, he played his early football with Burslem Port Vale (from 1902) and joined Stoke for £200. In between his time at The Vic he served with Middlesbrough (to June 1906) and the Vale (again) and after leaving the Potters, he joined Grimsby Town, later serving with Leyton, whom he joined for a tribunal-set fee of £50 in 1910, and Grimsby Rovers. All told Coxon, who in 1903 was rated one of he fastest wingers in Division Two, scored six goals in 38 appearances for Stoke and six in 61 outings for the Mariners. He died in Cleethorpes on 30 January 1942.

CRANSON, Ian

Cranson was a very experienced defender when he joined Stoke from Sheffield Wednesday for a club record fee of £450,000 in July 1989, having previously made 165 appearances for Ipswich Town and 35 for

Ian Cranson

the Owls. Born in Easington on 2 July 1964, he was an apprentice at Portman Road before turning professional in July 1982. Capped five times by England at Under-21 level whilst with Ipswich, he went to Hillsborough in March 1988, also for £450,000, but never really settled in Yorkshire. He has suffered his fair share of injuries during his career but when fit Cranson is a terrific defender who puts his heart and soul into the game. He helped Stoke win the Autoglass Trophy in 1992 and the Second Division title the following year. In November 1996, after a long-term injury, he decided to quit first-class soccer (on medical advice) having scored 12 goals in 281 senior appearances for the Potters and 15 in 481 club games in his career.

CREWE ALEXANDRA

Stoke's playing record against the Alex is:

Football League

Venue	P	W	D	L	F	A
Home	2	2	0	0	3	1
Away	2	2	0	0	4	1
Totals	4	4	0	0	7	2

Football Alliance

Home	1	0	1	0	2	2
Away	1	1	0	0	4	2
Totals	2	1	1	0	6	4

Birmingham & District League

Home	3	1	1	1	4	4
Away	3	0	0	3	4	8
Totals	6	1	1	4	8	12

FA Cup

Home	1	0	1	0	2	2
Away	2	0	0	2	4	7
Totals	3	0	1	2	6	9

Autoglass Trophy

Home	1	0	1	0	2	2

Stoke played their home Football Alliance game against the Alex on 8 November 1890 at The County Cricket Ground as The Victoria Ground was unfit. The game ended all square at 2-2.

Both teams have a best score against each other of 4-2 – Stoke claiming theirs away from home in January 1891 (Football Alliance) while the Alex registered their triumph in January 1910 (Birmingham League). Crewe also won 4-3 at The Victoria Ground in another Birmingham League game in January 1909.

The Potters and Crewe first opposed each other in the Football League Division Three North in 1926-27, winning both games, 2-1 at home and 2-0 away. The League Division Two matches in season 1990-91 also resulted in two victories for the Potters, 1-0 at home (when Mark Devlin found the net) and 2-1 at Gresty Road, where Wayne Biggins and Paul Ware were on target for the Potters.

After drawing 2-2 at Stoke in a 1st qualifying round of the FA Cup in October 1885, Crewe won the replay 1-0 a week later.

Twelve months on – in November 1886 – Crewe again beat Stoke 6-4 after extra-time in a marvellously entertaining second-round FA Cup-tie at Gresty Road. A crowd of 3,500 saw the game twist and turn throughout the normal 90 minutes before the Alex finally took a stranglehold on proceedings to win in extra-time.

Players with both clubs: Arthur Brookfield, David Brown, Aaron Callaghan, Billy Caton, George Clarke, George Clawley, John Clowes, Tim Coleman, Terry Conroy, Harry Cotton, John Cotton, Ernie Cull, Steve Davis (Stoke reserve), Paul Dyson, Bill Finney, Neil Franklin, David Goodwin, Jimmy Greenhoff, Len Hales, Sean Haselgrave, Frank Hesham, Geoff Hickson, Colin Hutchinson, Jimmy Jones, Joey Jones, John Love Jones, Jason Kearton, Johnny King, Fred Latham, John Lawton, Terry Lees, Harry Leese, Kevin Lewis, Aaron Lockett, Peter McArdle, Jack Maddock, John Mahoney, Graham Matthews, Joey Mawson, Ernie Millward, Billy Mould, Albert Mullard, Danny Noble, Calvin Palmer, Bert Ralphs, Don Ratcliffe, Paul Rennie, Paul Richardson, Jimmy Robertson, Valentine Rouse, Ian Scott, Harry Simpson, Alf Smith, Billy Spencer, Tom Thornton, Arthur Turner, Dennis Viollet, Mart Watkins, Billy Whitehurst, Don Whiston, Bob Whittingham, Bill Williamson, Harry Wootton. Bruce Grobbelaar was a non-contract player with Crewe who later kept goal for Stoke.

Tony Waddington was with Crewe before taking over as manager of Stoke City (he died in Crewe in 1994). Louis Page played for Stoke and later managed Alex likewise Harry Ware. Former Stoke player Jackie Mudie became assistant coach at Gresty Road. Alan A'Court was manager-coach of Crewe and caretaker manager of Stoke City. Mike Allen was physiotherapist at both Gresty Road and The Victoria Ground.

Former Stoke player Mike Bernard, became Football in the Community Officer with Crewe Alexandra and later worked on the commercial side at Gresty Road.

CRICKETING-FOOTBALLERS

In their long history, Stoke have had several footballers on their books who also did well on the cricket field, among them: Ike Brookes and Henry Hutsby (both of whom represented Staffordshire), Albert Cook (skipper of Burslem CC), Fred Houldsworth (Berkshire area), Alf Smith (vice-captain of Longton), Peter Dobing (12th man for Lancashire in a Roses match), Geoff Hurst (Essex), Tom Revill (Derbyshire), Arthur Jepson (Nottinghamshire) and Terry Lees (club cricketer in various villages), Alan Philpott (Stoke M.O. CC in North Staffs League), Arthur Turner (Silverdale CC) and Gary Hackett (Belbroughton CC).

Revill played for Derbyshire between 1913 and 1920, and scored 231 runs in 20 innings for an average of 14.43. Jepson hit over 6,300 runs (avg. 14.31) and took more than 1,000 wickets (avg. 29.06). He later became a Test Match umpire. Brookes was the Staffordshire County wicketkeeper, who played in goal for Stoke in 12 Football Alliance games during the 1890-91 season – and he was never once on the losing side.

CROOKS, Garth Anthony

They say that Stoke manager Tony Waddington signed Crooks after watching him kicking a ball up against a wall outside The Victoria Ground. Whether that story is true of not, Crooks went on to become an exceptionally fine goalscorer in a career which spanned 15 years. Born in the Potteries on 10 March 1958, he joined Stoke as an apprentice in 1974 and turned professional on his 18th birthday. He made his League debut against Coventry City the following month, the first of 164 appearances for the club, and he scored 53 goals. He was capped four times by England at Under-21 level, netting a hat-trick on his first outing against Bulgaria at a foggy Filbert Street. On leaving Stoke in the summer of 1980 (after rather heated relations with manager Alan Durban) Crooks signed for Tottenham Hotspur for £650,000, and the following year he gained the first of two

CREWE - CROOKS

Garth Crooks

successive FA Cup Final winners' medals and also collected a runners-up medal in the League Cup Final. After five years and more than 50 goals for Spurs, plus a loan spell with Manchester United (in November 1983) he moved from White Hart Lane to West Bromwich Albion for £100,000. In March 1987 he switched to Charlton Athletic for £75,000 and it was here when he started to have a spate of back injuries which eventually led to his retirement in November 1990. Thereafter he concentrated on being a radio and television journalist having previously been chairman of the PFA (1988-89).

CROOKS, Paul

A teenage forward with Bolton Wanderers, Crooks was born in Durham on 12 October 1966 and signed for Stoke as a teenager in July 1986. He never really made an impact at The Victoria Ground and appeared in only three senior games for the Potters (all as sub) before switching to Carlisle United. He later played for Rhyl, Bangor City and Blaenau Festiniog Amateurs.

CROSSTHWAITE, Harold

Outside-right Crossthwaite made 31 League appearances for Stoke. He joined the club halfway through the 1919-20 season from Stockport County where he had been since June 1912, and he returned to Edgeley Park in the summer of 1921, remaining there until May 1923 by which time he had taken his County record to 19 goals in 142 appearances. Born in Manchester in July 1899, he remained in Stockport until his death c.1968.

CROWD DISTURBANCES

On 23 December 1889 when Stoke played Burnley at The Victoria Ground in a League game, the visitors complained that they had been intimidated by the home players and their supporters, yet Potters' inside-right Bob McCormick suffered a badly injured breast-bone after a challenge from an opposing defender. With Stoke 2-1 up, the crowd invaded the pitch. Burnley protested to the League, demanding – and winning – a replay (4-3).

On 23 April 1910, Stoke's reserve side played hosts to their counterparts from across the city, Port Vale in a game to decide the North Staffordshire League Championship. The former Stoke goalkeeper Dick Roose was in the Vale line-up and he played a blinder in his side's 2-0 win. The home fans gave vent to their anger and man-handled the Welsh international off the pitch at the end, threatening to throw him into the River Trent. The police moved in and with the help of the Stoke directors and other club officials, calm was restored and Roose was taken to the safety of the boardroom, claiming afterwards that he thought the game was a friendly and not a vital League game.

At the commencement of the 1977-78 campaign, Second Division Mansfield Town provided Stoke with their first League game which the Potters lost 2-1 at Field Mill. The Stoke followers let themselves and the club down badly before, during and after the game, causing disturbances of a very severe nature.

Following a late, controversial match-deciding penalty scored by England's Bryan Douglas for Blackburn Rovers against Stoke City in a fourth-round FA Cup-tie, a whole band of Stoke fans took it to heart and one irate supporter even started legal proceedings against the referee.

On 29 February 1992, incensed home fans invaded the pitch after Paul Barnes of Stoke City had scored a late equaliser against Birmingham City at St Andrew's. Referee Roger Wiseman ordered the 22 players to the dressing room, told the police to clear the stadium and then played the remaining sixty seconds at walking pace is an empty ground.

There were ugly scenes at the end of the First Division Pplay-off semi-final, second leg clash between Stoke City and Leicester at The Victoria Ground in May 1996. Hundreds of Stoke fans poured on to the pitch after the final whistle, as the Leicester players celebrated with their fans. It took nine police horses, scores of stewards and a number of male and female beat constables some ten minutes to get the situation under control. It was a frightening time for some Leicester players who were pinned in one corner of the ground.

CROXTON, Harry

Former Burslem Park inside-right Croxton, who was born in North Staffordshire in February 1890, joined Stoke from Port Vale along with Adrian Capes in 1905. He remained at the club for three years before returning to the Vale in 1908. Basically a reserve, he scored once in 24 League and Cup appearances for Stoke.

CROYDON COMMON

Stoke's playing record against Croydon is:
Southern League

Venue	P	W	D	L	F	A
Home	2	1	1	0	7	3
Away	2	0	0	2	1	4
Totals	4	1	1	2	8	7

A crowd of just over 1,500 saw Stoke register their best win over Croydon – 6-2 at home in November 1910 – when both Jack Peart and Amos Baddeley netted twice.

CRYSTAL PALACE

Stoke's playing record against Palace is:
Football League

Venue	P	W	D	L	F	A
Home	18	7	7	4	25	18
Away	18	5	3	10	16	29
Total	36	12	10	14	41	47

Southern League

Venue	P	W	D	L	F	A
Home	2	1	1	0	2	1
Away	2	1	0	1	2	2
Totals	4	2	1	1	4	3

FA Cup

Venue	P	W	D	L	F	A
Home	1	1	0	0	1	0

The first time the teams met was in the Southern League in season 1911-12. Stoke won both games 2-1. Jack Peart figuring on the scoresheet in each time.

The initial Football League clash – on 3 December 1921 – Stoke swamped Palace 5-1 with four goals coming from Jimmy Broad. A week later Broad scored both goals as Stoke completed the double with a 2-0 victory.

Palace's best win over the Potters is also 5-1, achieved at Selhurst Park in November 1923 (Division Two).

A goal by Graham Shaw gave Stoke their 1-0 third-round FA Cup win over Palace at The Victoria Ground in January 1989.

Players with both clubs: Paul Barron, Billy Davies, Fred Groves, Charlie Hallam, Vince Hilaire, Sam Johnson, Joey Jones, Stewart Jump, Jack Palethorpe, Tom Ward and Mart Watkins.

CULL, John Ernest

During his career outside-right Cull played for Shrewsbury Town, Stoke City (signed for £1,000 in September 1925), Coventry City (April 1931), Shrewsbury Town again (August 1932), Crewe Alexandra (August 1933), Accrington Stanley (June 1934), Gateshead (July 1935) and Aldershot (January-May 1936). He retired to go into a steel factory. Born in Wolverhampton on 18 November 1900, Cull played local junior football before entering a more established and competitive game at the age of 17. He scored ten goals in 80 first-team appearances for Stoke, helping them win the Third Division North title in 1927. Standing 5ft 7ins tall, he could occupy either wing and in all netted 32 goals in a total of 182 League appearances. Cull died in Birmingham c.1979.

CUNLIFFE, Jack

Born in Wigan on 4 February 1930, 'Dickie' Cunliffe played amateur football for Bolton Wanderers and after a trial on the left-wing for Leeds United, he joined Port Vale in December 1950. At Vale Park, he became a firm favourite with the fans and went on to score 51 goals in 283 League appearances for the club, helping Vale win the Third Division North title in 1953-54 and reach the semi-finals of the FA Cup in the same season. He moved across to Stoke City in September 1959 for £2,000 (plus two players) and after netting three goals in 28 outings for the Potters, he finally dropped out of big-time football to sign for Macclesfield Town in September 1960.

CURTIS, Alan Thomas

Curtis was almost 32 when he joined Stoke on a month's loan from Southampton in March 1986. Born in Rhondda on 16 May 1954, he had previously played (and scored) for Swansea City (two spells) and Leeds United as well as gaining 35 full caps for Wales, plus others at Under-21 and Under-23 levels. After his Stoke days, he returned to The Dell and later assisted Cardiff City, Swansea (for a third time), Barry Town and Haverfordwest County. In his Football League career Curtis netted a total of 116 goals in 570 appearances. His had three outings for the Potters and he also won three Welsh Cup winners' medals.

DA COSTA, Hugo

The Portuguese utility player joined Stoke from Benfica before the start of the 1996-97 season after impressing manager Lou Macari during summer trials at The Victoria Ground. Well built, strong with dark hair. the 25-year-old had just four senior outings for the club before being released in October 1996 when he returned home.

DALE, James

Scotsman Jim Dale was a solid wing-half who played in four League games for Stoke in June 1894 after coming down to the Potteries from

Sunderland. Born in Motherwell in July 1869, he later assisted Southampton St Mary's (from October 1895) before returning to Scotland.

DALY, Gerald Anthony

Republic of Ireland international midfielder Gerry Daly struggled with injury during his time with Stoke City. He arrived at The Victoria Ground in March 1987, costing £15,000 from Shrewsbury Town and was hurt making his debut. But he battled on and scored twice 30 appearances for the club before leaving to team up with Dave Mackay at Doncaster Rovers, later taking over as player-manager of Telford United where he was succeeded by another ex-Stoke player, Wayne Clarke. Born in Cobra, Dublin, on 30 April 1954, Daly, who scored 13 times in his 46 full outings for his country, also earned one cap at Under-21 level. Brought over to England by Manchester United boss Tommy Docherty from Bohemians at the age of 19, he quickly helped United win the Second Division title in 1975 and also played in the FA Cup Final defeat by Southampton the following year. After a dispute with the 'Doc' Daly left Old Trafford for Derby County and then he netted 16 goals in the NASL for the New England Teamen over two seasons. Back in England he played, in turn, for Coventry City (1980-83), Leicester City (on loan) and Birmingham (1984-85) prior to joining Shrewsbury Town. In his Football League career, Daly amassed a fine record of 80 goals in 433 appearances.

DANIELS, George

Daniels was a half-back who played in two League games for Stoke during a relatively short stay with the club in season 1933-34. Born in Winsford in June 1913, he played initially for Altrincham and was registered with Leeds United as an amateur prior to joining the Potters, and after leaving Stoke he appeared in senior games for Torquay United, Crystal Palace (May 1937 to June 1939), Hartlepool United and finally Carlisle United, retiring during World War Two.

DARLINGTON

Stoke's playing record against the Quakers is:
Football League

Venue	P	W	D	L	F	A
Home	2	2	0	0	9	1
Away	2	2	0	0	3	1
Total	4	4	0	0	12	2

Two of the four encounters took place in season 1925-26 when the Potters were relegated from the Second Division. The Quakers lost 6-1 at Stoke and 2-1 at The Feethams. In the game at The Victoria Ground, Joe Clennell and outside-right Josh Williams both scored twice in front of an 13,811 crowd. The last time the teams met was in season 1991-92.

Players with both clubs: Gary Bannister, David Carre Brown, Paul Dyson, Tommy Flannigan, John Gidman, Graham Kavanagh, David McAughtrie, Tim Maloney, George Mulholland, Jimmy O'Neill, Don Ratcliffe, Phil Bonnyman, David McAughtrie and Barry Siddall.

DARWEN

Stoke's playing record against Darwen is:
Football League

Venue	P	W	D	L	F	A
Home	2	2	0	0	8	2
Away	2	0	0	2	4	12
Total	4	2	0	2	12	14

Football Alliance

Venue	P	W	D	L	F	A
Home	1	1	0	0	6	2
Away	1	0	1	0	3	3
Totals	2	1	1	0	9	5

The Lancashire cotton town side, Darwen, inflicted upon Stoke their second biggest League defeat when hammering them 9-3 at home in October 1893. Stoke, though, won all their three home games against Darwen in some style: 6-2 in the Football Alliance on Boxing Day 1890 when Edge and Turner both netted twice; 5-1 in the Football League December 1891, when Joey Schofield scored two goals, and 3-1, also in the Football League, in December 1893, when Schofield again hit a brace.

Players with both clubs: Charlie Hinks, Tom Lonie, Allan Maxwell, Billy Smith and Jack Whitley.

DAVIES, Lloyd E.

Davies was youngest of six brothers, five of whom played senior football with four representing Wales. He started out as an orthodox outside-left with Rhosymedre St John's (1898-99) and when he joined Druids FC he was switched to the defence where he occupied both full-back and the centre-half positions. Born in Cefn Mawr near Ruabon on 23 February 1877, had two spells at The Victoria Ground, the first commencing in July 1903 and ending the following May, and the second starting in December 1905 and going on until May 1908. In between times he played for Wellington Town and Swindon Town, and after leaving the Potters, second time round, Davies became the great Herbert Chapman's first ever signing. At the time Chapman was manager of Northampton Town and he paid £200 for Davies' signature. Davies was also the first Northampton own player to win a full cap. He moved from Elm Park to Reading in August 1920 and later returned to Northampton to coach them in the Football League. A totally committed player, Davies won 18 full caps for Wales (four while at Stoke) and he also gained a Southern League championship medal. He made over 300 Southern league appearances for Northampton. After quitting football, Davies, despite the threat of bankruptcy, ran a successful tobacconists shop in Cefn for many years, and he died in that village in October 1957.

NB: Davies' son, Ronald, played reserve-team football for Manchester United in the 1940s.

DAVIES, Harold Augustus

Harry Davies averaged a goal every four games for Stoke whom he served from 1922 to 1929 and again from early 1932 until 1938, when he left for Port Vale. An inside-forward, he possessed a lot of ability and always looked the part out on the field, often taking the ball in precarious positions and then opening up the play with either a splendidly struck pass, a swift turn of foot or a delicate manoeuvre. He was a class act and gave the fans plenty to cheer about. Born in Gainsborough on 29 January 1904, Davies came to Stoke's attention while playing for Bamfords Athletic (Uttoxeter). Son of the former Hull City and Wolves player of the same name, he joined the Potters as an 18-year-old in the summer of 1922 and was given his debut almost immediately, holding his place in the side until April 1929 when he was transferred to Huddersfield Town, who required him to replace Clem Stephenson who had become manager at Leeds Road. Davies had helped Stoke climb back into the Second Division in 1926-27 when he hit 15 vital League goals, and was twice selected to represent Staffordshire FA. In 1929 he came very close to winning a full England cap, being chosen as reserve in a trial match at Sheffield, but in the summer (after leaving Stoke) he went on tour to South Africa with the FA party, playing in two matches. With the Terriers Davies had two successful seasons, playing in the 1930 FA Cup Final when Town lost to Arsenal. He returned to Stoke early in 1932 after finding himself languishing in Huddersfield's Reserves and he was instrumental in seeing the Potters win the Second Division championship in 1932-33. He remained a permanent fixture in the first team and pushed his appearance total with the Potters up to 410 and his goal-haul to 101, reaching the century mark with a fine strike in a 3-1 win over Birmingham in February 1936. After a season in the second team at The Victoria Ground (Jimmy Westland had taken over at inside-left) Davies moved across town to Port Vale in a deal which brought Tom Ward to Stoke. He retired during the war and stayed in the Potteries until his death in April 1975. Besides being a fine footballer, Davies was also an extremely good billiards player and recorded seven three-figure breaks in his time, with a high of 135.

DAVIES, Harold Donald

Davies could play on either wing. An amateur footballer, he was quick over short distances but perhaps lacked ability which was required at a higher level. Born in the Potteries in June 1890, he spent the 1913-14 season at The Victoria Ground in between separate spells with Northern Nomads. He appeared in one Southern League game for Stoke (v Treharris).

DAVIES, William Charles

Like Lloyd Davies (above) Billy Davies was also a Welsh international who gained four full caps during a career which saw him play for Rhayader and Llandrindod Wells Schools, Knighton FC, Shrewsbury Town (1903-05), Stoke (December 1905-October 1907), Crystal Palace (two spells: October 1907-August 1908 and from September 1910-April 1915). Born in Forden, near Welshpool in June 1883, Davies was a fleet-footed winger with good ball control who scored once in 17 first-team outings for the Potters. When with Palace he linked up with J.J.Williams to form the only Welsh left-wing in top-class football. He netted 23 goals in 208 games for Palace and died in Wales c.1950.

DAVIES, William

Nicknamed 'Longton Billy' by his friends and colleagues, Davies was a useful inside-forward, serving Stoke for two seasons: 1907-09. He acquired a splendid scoring record – 16 goals in 31 appearances – before a serious knee injury (received in an FA Cup-tie v Sheffield Wednesday) forced him into an early retirement at the age of 23. Born in Longton in April 1886, he was a very popular fellow who played for Newcastle Rangers prior to Stoke. He died c.1942.

DAVIES, Samuel Storey

A reserve full-back, shaky at times, Davies was born at Marsden near Whitburn Colliery, Tyne and Wear, on 25 May 1900, and played for Marsden School and Whitburn FC before joining Stoke as an amateur in November 1923, turning professional two months later. His stayed at The Victoria Ground until the end of the season, moving to Tranmere Rovers in May 1925. He then served with Accrington Stanley (August-September 1926) and Spennymoor United (1926-28). Davies (now deceased) made only two first-team appearances for the Potters, replacing Tom Brittleton in both games against South Shields in March 1924.

DAWSON, Thomas

One-time miner in the North-East, Dawson first played football with Washington Colliery and then Chopwell Institute in the Northern League, and came south to Stoke in June 1924. A versatile defender, born in the town of Springwell, County Durham, on 15 December 1901, he had good heading ability and a strong right foot and remained at The Victoria Ground until the summer of 1932. In that time Dawson was given only 24 first-team outings due to the strength in depth at the club. He did, though, skipper the Reserves for six of those eight seasons and could well have been a regular with any other club if he had chosen to move on. In May 1932, Dawson was given a free transfer and switched to Clapton Orient, later playing for Gateshead, where he remained to become assistant and then head trainer. He died on 30 November 1977 in Washington, County Durham.

DEAKIN, Jack

A local man, born in Stoke-on-Trent in August 1873, Deakin played twice in Stoke's defence in season 1898-99, deputising for Alf Wood. He joined the club from Dresden United and left for Hanley Swifts.

DEATHS

● Jack Proctor was a registered player with Stoke when he was taken ill and died suddenly in 1893 of pneumonia.

● In the summer of 1927. Stoke centre-half Reg Hodgkins was admitted to Coventry Hospital for an appendix operation. Sadly, he never left his bed and three weeks later passed away, aged 24.

● Full-back Arthur Beachill was 37 when he died of a heart attack in

April 1943 while returning home from work at Hyde & Sons Foundry.

● Former Stoke City full-back Jack Kirby collapsed and died while playing in a reserve-team game for Wrexham in 1953. He was only 23 years of age.

● On 14th October 1968 promising Stoke goalkeeper Paul Shardlow collapsed and died during a training session after suffering a heart attack. He was 25.

● John Nibloe, ex-Stoke and then of Stockport County, was killed in a car crash in November 1964, aged 25.

● Stoke full-back Terry Ward died suddenly in 1963 at the age of 24.

● Former Stoke centre-half Ken Thomson was killed while out playing golf in 1969. He was 39.

● A handful of players who had been registered as either amateurs or professionals with Stoke lost their lives while serving their country in World Wars One and Two. These included: Billy Dixon (killed in France in 1916); Stan Ripley (killed in France in 1916, aged 23); Henry Salmon (killed in France in 1944).

● Centre-forward Bob Whittingham died just a month after leaving Stoke in April 1920.

● Stoke's 1920s Scottish-born defender Tom Williamson died in a Norwich house fire in 1988, aged 87.

● During an FA Cup game between Bolton Wanderers and Stoke City at Burnden Park on 9 March 1946, two crash barriers collapsed and as a result 33 fans were killed and more than 500 injured (See BOLTON WANDERERS).

DEBUTS

Scoring Debutants
Over the years several Stoke players have scored on their senior debuts for the club (League and Cup) and on the list over the last 20 years we have: John Tudor (1976-77), Alec Lindsay and Brendon O'Callaghan (1977-78), Paul Maguire and Iain Munro (1980-81), Sammy McIlroy and Alan Biley (1981-82), George Berry (1982-83), Graham Shaw and Louie Donowa (1985-86), Nicky Morgan (1986-87), Chris Kamara and Dave Bamber (1988-89), Wayne Biggins and Leigh Palin (1989-90), Mick Kennedy and Wayne Clarke (1990-91).

Tudor's early goal on his first appearance for the Potters v Ipswich Town in September 1976 was screened on BBC TV.

Stan Matthews (in 1934), Dennis Wilshaw (1955, as a Wolves player) and Mark Chamberlain (1982) all scored on their international debuts for England.

DEFEATS

Stoke's worst home defeat in League football is 6-1, suffered at the hands of Tottenham Hotspur on 15 September 1951 (Division One).

Their heaviest away defeat at League level is 10-0 at Preston in September 1889.

In FA Cup football, Wolves beat Stoke 8-0 at Molineux back in February 1890, while at The Victoria Ground, the Potters lost 4-0 at home to Everton in February 1905.

Newcastle United inflicted upon Stoke a 4-0 home beating in the League Cup in 1996.

In European competition, the German side FC Kaiserslauten beat Stoke 4-0 at home in September 1972. And Luton defeated Stoke 4-1 at Kenilworth Road in a Full Members' Cup-tie in March 1988.

Stoke lost 31 of their 42 First Division League games in season 1984-85.

In 1926-27, when winning the Third Division North title, the Potters suffered only six defeats (from of 42 starts). They lost the same number of League games when the won promotion from Division Two in 1978-79.

Stoke went 25 League games without defeat during season 1992-93 (from 5 September to 27 February inclusive).

DEFENSIVE RECORDS

Stoke's best defensive record in one full League season came in 1978-79 when they conceded only 31 goals in 42 games.

In contrast, the club's worst defensive record came in 1984-85 when they gave away 91 goals in 42 First Division matches.

DEMPSEY, Archibald

Centre-forward Dempsey played once for Stoke on loan from Preston North End against his own club in October 1888. Stoke arrived at Deepdale with only nine players (two having missed the early morning train). North End duly allowed Dempsey and Bill Smalley to make up the Stoke team, but the visitors still crashed to a 7-0 defeat. Born in Lancaster in 1864, Dempsey spent two seasons with without ever making their first team.

DEPLEDGE, Joseph

A Yorkshireman, born in Sheffield in February 1897, Depledge joined Stoke as a reserve defender in March 1923 from Rotherham United for £130. He made just five first-team appearances in his only season with the Potters before being freed to join Mansfield Town.

DERBY COUNTY

Stoke's playing record against the Rams is:
Football League

Venue	P	W	D	L	F	A
Home	57	26	21	10	94	66
Away	57	8	16	33	55	129
Total	114	34	37	43	149	195

FA Cup

Venue	P	W	D	L	F	A
Away	3	1	0	2	3	7

Anglo-Scottish Cup

Venue	P	W	D	L	F	A
Home	1	0	1	0	1	1
Away	1	0	0	1	2	3
Totals	2	1	1	0	3	4

Stoke and Derby County were both founder members of the Football

League and, in fact, the Potters have only met Wolverhampton Wanderers more times in the competition than the Rams.

Stoke's best win of the 34 registered so far at League level s 8-1 – at The Victoria Ground in September 1937. A crowd of almost 33,000 saw a rampant Potters side over-power the Rams with Freddie Steele scoring five goals and Jim Westland the other three.

Tom Hyslop netted a hat-trick in Stoke's 4-1 home League win in March 1895.

Les Johnston netted twice in a 4-1 home victory in September 1950 and John Ritchie got two in another 4-0 home win in December 1972.

Derby, too, have run up some impressive victories over Stoke, including a 7-3 scoreline at home during Stoke's 1925-26 Second Division relegation campaign on 24 October (the Rams' Harry Bedford netted a fine hat-trick). Among their other big wins have been those of: 5-2 (h) in December 1893; 5 1 (h) in November 1896; 5-0 (h) on Boxing Day 1903; 4-0 at The Victoria Ground and 5-1 (h) in season 1933-34; 5-0 (h) in September 1938 and 4-0 (h) September 1971. The Rams have also recorded a cluster of 4-1 victories.

The 114 League games involving the two clubs (1888 to 1996) have produced, on average, three goals per 90 minutes of football.

Stoke were undefeated in 17 successive home League games v Derby between 1953-54 to 1979-80 inclusive.

County dumped Stoke out of the FA Cup in the semi-final of 1898-99, winning 3-1 at Molineux before a 20,000 crowd. The Rams also won a third-round tie 3-0 at home in season 1902-03 while the Potters knocked out Derby 2-1 at The Baseball Ground in 1937-38.

Players with both clubs: George Antonio, Horace Bailey, Scott Barrett (Rams reserve), John Baxter (Derby trialist), Gerry Daly, Sean Flynn, Graham Harbey, Roger Jones, Eric Lowell, Bob Milarvie, Carl Muggleton, Jack Peart, Jack Robertson, Ken Scattergood, Peter Shilton, Ronnie Sinclair, Herby Smith, Mickey Thomas, Jim Turner, Dave Watson and Alf Wood.

Richie Barker was a player with Derby and manager of Stoke and Alan Durban played for and was later assistant manager of the Rams and he also managed the Potters.

DEVINE, John A.

Manager Mick Mills brought midfielder Devine to The Victoria Ground on a free transfer from Norwich City as a straight replacement for Alan Hudson in the summer of 1985, but the Dubliner's career with Stoke was ruined when he sadly broke his leg in five places during a game at Brighton (his 16th outing for the Potters). Born on 11 November 1958, he joined Arsenal as an apprentice in 1974, turned professional two years later and went to Carrow Road in August 1983 after making 89 League appearances for the Gunners. He added a further 53 League games to his tally with the Canaries (one goal scored) before linking up at Stoke. After regaining full fitness Devine, who was a tireless performer in the middle of the park, went on to play for IK Start in Norway (August 1986 to March 1988) and then visited India to play and coach out there for seven months. He returned home to Dublin to assist Shamrock Rovers and retired in 1995. Whilst at Highbury he played in two losing FA Cup Finals and gained a League Cup winners' medal with Norwich in 1985. He was also capped 12 times by the Republic of Ireland and played twice at Under-21 level. A keen singer, he married the runner-up in the Miss Universe contest in 1981.

DEVLIN, Mark Andrew

Scottish utility player Devlin was introduced to first-team football by Stoke City boss Alan Ball while still on YTS forms. This was in February 1991 when he came on as a substitute against Chester City. He was still at The Victoria Ground six years later, having taken his overall record to 65 appearances and two goals. Born in Irvine on 18 January 1973, Devlin played initially for Kilmarnock FC Boys Club and he had a trial with Raith Rovers in 1991-92 after failing to gain a regular place in the Potters senior side.

DICKIE, George

Outside-right who played in one League game for Stoke in September 1925 against Oldham Athletic at Boundary Park when the Potters lost 7-2. Born in Montrose in March 1905, Dickie played for Forres Mechanics prior to his brief association with Stoke. He stayed at The Victoria Ground for only two months before joining St Johnstone.

DICKIE, William Cunningham

A block cutter by trade, and a Sergeant Instructor during World War One, Cunningham was a tall, fair-haired, wholehearted Scottish defender, who cost Stoke £2,000 when signed from Chelsea in April 1921. Born in Kilmarnock on 2 May 1893, he had earlier been with Riccarton FC (1909), Kilbirnie, Ladeside (1910) and Kilmarnock (May 1912), moving to Stamford Bridge in April 1919. He appeared in 14 League games for the Potters before transferring to Sittingbourne in June 1922, later assisting Sheppey United (1932-33) before returning to Sittingbourne as a coach. Dickie also guested for Chelsea, Everton, Southport and Wrexham during World War One and won a London Cup winners' medal with Chelsea in April 1919. Dickie died at Sittingbourne on 15 January 1960.

DICKSON, William Alexander

Dickson was a talented inside-forward who scored four goals in a 10-2 win over Ireland in his only outing for Scotland in 1888 when he was a Dumbarton player. Born in Crail, Fife, on 27 August 1866, Dickson attended school in Dumfries and played for Dundee Strathmore early in his career. He served with Dundee for a while and then had a spell with Sunderland, up to August 1889 when he switched to Aston Villa, for whom he scored 34 goals in 64 outings, skippering them on several occasions as well as appearing in the 1892 FA Cup Final. Three months after that game against West Bromwich Albion which Villa lost 3-0, Dickson joined Stoke and he stayed at The Victoria Ground for five years, until injury forced him to quit in the summer of 1897. He scored 48 goals in 134 outings for the Potters. Upon his retirement he became coach at the club and was also a licensee in the town. He

died in Stoke on 1 June 1910.
NB: Dickson's brother played for Preston North End.

DIXON, Lee Michael

Right-back Lee Dixon followed Steve Bould to Highbury (from Stoke). Bould went for £390,000, Dixon for £400,000, the latter joining the Gunners in January 1988 after scoring five goals in 88 games for the Potters following his £40,000 transfer from Bury in July 1986. Born in Manchester on 17 March 1964, Dixon played initially as an apprentice for Burnley, turning professional at Turf Moor in July 1982. He then assisted Chester City before moving to Gigg Lane in July 1985. A fine attacking player, Dixon has strength, ability and courage and besides winning 21 full and 4 'B' caps for England, he also helped Arsenal twice win the First Division title (1989 and 1991), the FA Cup in 1993 and the European Cup-winners' Cup in 1994. At the end of the 1996-97 his League record at club level stood at more than 500 appearances.

DIXON, Robert Hewitson

Bob Dixon was a courageous goalkeeper, who was spotted by an eagle-eyed scout plying his trade in Durham with West Stanley (the club where another goalkeeper Dick Herron came from in 1911). He was quickly recruited to The Victoria Ground, signing for the Potters in January 1923, initially as deputy to Les Scott. Dixon bided his time in the Reserves, becoming first choice between the posts at Stoke within a year, and despite the competition from Scottish international Kenny Campbell (signed in March 1923), he went on to accumulate a total of 200 League and Cup appearances for the club, helping the team carry off the Third Division North title in 1926-27 when he missed only one game. Born in sight of the coalface at Easington near Whitehaven on 30 August 1904, Dixon remained at The Victoria Ground for six years, leaving the Potters for West Ham United in March 1929. He was understudy to England's Ted Hufton at Upton Park, but later had a good spell in the senior side. He was forced to quit the game with a knee injury in the early 1930s and at this juncture Dixon returned to Stoke to become mine host of The Prince of Wales pub in Sandford Hill as well as doing good business renting out holiday caravans at Lytham St Anne's. Just before the war, Dixon was offered a coaching job in Turkey which he turned down. His wife, Daisy, played football and cricket for England Ladies.

DOBING, Peter A.

Dobing was signed by manager Tony Waddington from Manchester City for what was to prove a bargain fee of £37,500 in the summer of 1963, a week or so after Stoke had gained promotion to the First Division. A quality player, Dobing could occupy a number of positions in the forward-line and became a firm favourite with the fans. Born in Manchester on 1 December 1938, his father was a Rugby League professional, but it was at soccer that Dobing junior excelled. He began his career by playing a few games for Crewe Rangers prior to linking up with Blackburn Rovers in 1954, turning professional at the age of 17. He went on to score 89 goals in 179 League games for the Ewood Park side, collecting an FA Cup runners-up medal in 1960. From Rovers he moved to Manchester City in July 1961 and scored 31 times in 82 League games before joining Stoke. Dobing, who was capped seven times at Under-23 level by England and represented the Football League three times (scoring a hat-trick against the League of Ireland in Dublin) went on to net 94 goals in 372 League and Cup

Peter Dobing

appearances for the Potters, captaining them to glory in the 1972 league Cup Final at Wembley, having earlier collected a runners-up medal in the same competition in his first season at The Victoria Ground. Dobing certainly gave Stoke ten years' excellent service, up to May 1973 when he was forced to retire through injury. Unfortunately Dobing's disciplinary record left a lot to be desired and in 1970 he served a nine-week suspension which was an English record at the time, although than ban didn't affect Dobing (or Stoke) as the player was suffering from a broken leg at the time. He then became a pottery worker in Longton, and still lives in the area today.

NB: Dobing was a very useful cricketer and once came on as 12th man for Lancashire against Yorkshire in a Roses Match in the County Championship.

DODD, Alan

When he was declared ready for first-team action, Dodd had to fight for a place in Stoke's League side with the likes of Denis Smith and Alan Bloor – but he battled on and eventually gained a regular spot in the side (1973) and went on to amass a fine set of statistics for the club – four goals scored in a total of 416 appearances (in two spells). Born in Stoke-on-Trent on 20 September 1953, 'Doddy' joined the junior ranks at The Victoria Ground on leaving school in 1969 and turned professional in October 1970. He made his first-team debut in November 1972 and after establishing in the side, became a class player, with a lot of skill, being strong in both aerial and ground confrontations. Despite his form he never gained full England honours, collecting just six Under-23 caps for his efforts. Nevertheless, as a club man, Dodd was quite superb and he was eventually sold to Wolverhampton Wanderers for £40,000 in November 1982 after more than 12 years at Stoke. He helped Wolves won promotion back to the First Division but after 99 outings for the Black Country team he returned to Stoke under manager Bill Asprey in January 1985, initially on a monthly contract. He stayed with the club until the end of the season when he went over to Sweden to assist Elfsborg. He then played for GAIS Gothenburg and Elfsborg (again) before having two League games for Port Vale in 1986. Dodd later

Alan Dodd

turned out for Cork City, Landskrona Bols and non-Leaguers Rocester and Goldenhill Wanderers before returning to Rocester as player-coach (1992-93).

DONCASTER ROVERS

Stoke's playing record against Rovers is:
Football League

Venue	P	W	D	L	F	A
Home	6	2	4	0	11	5
Away	6	2	1	3	7	11
Total	12	4	5	3	18	16

FA Cup

	P	W	D	L	F	A
Away	1	0	0	1	0	1

League Cup

	P	W	D	L	F	A
Away	1	0	0	1	1	3

The last time Stoke and Rovers met at League level was in season 1957-58 (Division Two). The Potters won 1-0 at Belle Vue and were held to a 0-0 draw at The Victoria Ground.

The previous season (in the same Division) Rovers recorded their best win over Stoke, beating them 4-0 at home. Stoke's biggest triumph was a 5-2 scoreline at The Victoria Ground in December 1955 when over 15,000 fans saw Johnny King (2), Andy Graver, Frank Bowyer and Tom Coleman find the Rovers' net.

Players with both clubs: Neville Chamberlain, Gerry Daly, John Flowers, Lee Fowler, Harry Gregg, Andy Holmes, John Lumsden, Hugh McMahon, Alec Milne, John Nibloe, Brendon O'Callaghan, Mark Prudhoe, Paul Reece, Colin Russell, Jimmy Wallace and Billy Whitehurst.

Maurice Setters, ex-Stoke City defender, later became manager of Doncaster Rovers.

Irish international Len Graham was a player with Doncaster before taking over as assistant manager-coach at Stoke in June 1960. Brian Caswell played for Doncaster Rovers and later was a coach with Stoke.

DONOWA, Brian Louie

A fast-raiding outside-right, born in Ipswich on 24 September 1964, Donowa came to Stoke on a month's loan from Norwich City (his first club) in January 1986 and scored once in five outings for the Potters. Capped three times by England at Under-21 level, he gained a Milk Cup winners' medal with the Canaries (1985) and left the Norfolk club for Deportivo La Coruna in a £400,000 deal soon after leaving Stoke. He then had a spell in Holland with Willem II and in 1989 transferred to Ipswich Town. From there he went to Bristol City (1990) and a year later he switched to Birmingham City for £60,000. While at St Andrew's he served with Burnley, Shrewsbury Town, Walsall and Peterborough United, all on loan before signing permanently for Posh early in 1997.

DOWD, Henry William

Goalkeeper Harry Dowd had a fine career which spanned 14 years: 1960-74. Born in Salford, Manchester on 4 July 1938, he played for Blackley Imperial Chemical Industries FC before turning professional with Manchester City in July 1960. He appeared in more than 200 games during a ten-year period at Maine Road which incorporated a loan spell with Stoke City in October 1969 when he was given three League outings and one with Charlton Athletic in August 1970. After leaving Maine Road he made 121 League appearances for Oldham Athletic and retired in June 1974. Dowd scored a goal for Manchester City in the 1-1 draw against Bury in February 1964 after moving out to the wing following an injury.

DOWDS, Peter

Dowds was a dogged defender, rather stone-faced, unhurried in his ways, who took over the centre-half duties from John Proctor in 1893-94 – his only season with Stoke. Born in Johnstone, Renfrew, on 11 December 1867, he gained a full Scottish cap as a Celtic player (v Ireland in 1891) and also won a Scottish Cup winners' medal while at Parkhead. A heavy drinker, he had a short spell with Aston Villa (21 games) before arriving at The Victoria Ground, and in his only season with the Potters (1893-94) he made 24 first-team appearances. Dowds then returned to Celtic, but sadly, on 2 September 1895, after a serious chest complaint, he died suddenly, aged 27.

DOWNING, Keith Gordon

Nicknamed 'psycho' Downing is a hard-working impetuous midfielder, who is often in trouble with referees for his over-robust style of play. But that's his nature – he is totally committed to playing football and gives his all each and every time he takes the field. Born in Oldbury, West Midlands, on 23 July 1965, he had an unsuccessful spell with Chelsea as a teenager and after a spell with Mile Oak Rovers (near Tamworth) he joined Notts County in May 1985. From Meadow Lane he switched to Wolverhampton Wanderers on a free transfer in August 1987 and went on to appear in 228 games for the Molineux club, helping them win both the Third and Fourth Division championships (in successive seasons) and the Sherpa Van Trophy prior to signing for Birmingham City in July 1993. Twelve months later he came to Stoke City and made 24 appearances for the Potters before joining Cardiff City in August 1995, switching to Hereford United after just a month at Ninian Park. Under his former manager Graham Turner, he helped the Bulls reach the Third Division Play-offs in 1996.

DOYLE, Joseph Brian

Full-back Brian Doyle played in 19 first-team games for Stoke during the early 1950s. Born in Manchester on 15 July 1930, he worked at Salford Docks and served with Lostock Green before moving to The Victoria Ground in March 1951. He left the Potters for Exeter City in April 1954 and went on to play in exactly 100 League games for the Grecians before ending his senior career with Bristol Rovers (August 1957 to June 1959). He later managed Stockport County (1972-74). Doyle died of ill health on 22 December 1990, aged 62.

DOYLE, Michael

Defender Mick Doyle had a fine playing career which spanned 20 years: 1964-84. Born in Manchester on 25 November 1946, he joined the staff at Maine Road as a 16-year-old and turned professional with City in May 1964. He developed quickly and went on to appear in 448 League games for the Light Blues, up to June 1978, when he was recruited by Stoke City. As a Manchester City player, he gained five England caps, eight more at Under-23 level and twice represented the

Mick Doyle

Football League. He also earned winners' medals with City for victories in the Football League Championship in 1968, the FA Cup the following year, in two League Cup Finals of 1970 and 1976, in the European Cup-winners' Cup, also in 1970, for the Second Division championship in 1966 and the Charity Shield in 1968 and he received a collection of runners-up medals as well. Manager Alan Durban, who had played against Doyle on a number of occasions, paid £50,000 to bring the respected defender to The Victoria Ground and it was money well spent. Doyle had a little over three excellent seasons with the Potters, scoring six goals in 128 appearances before falling out with boss Richie Barker after a game against Manchester United. He never wore a Stoke jersey again, and in January 1982 was transferred to Bolton Wanderers for a fee of £10,000. In his first two games for the Trotters he conceded an own-goal and was then sent-off. Doyle finished his career with Rochdale (1983-84) and hung up his boots with more than 700 senior appearances under his belt (627 in the Football League).

DRAWS

Stoke played out a record number of 19 drawn League games during the 1989-90 season. In contrast they never registered a single draw in their 30 Football League games in 1895-96.

The club's highest scoring draw is 4-4 – achieved six times at League level: away at Bolton Wanderers in 1892-93, Charlton Athletic in 1929-30 and Cardiff City 1959-60, and at home to Burnley and Sheffield Wednesday in 1963-64 and Luton Town in 1982-83.

Stoke played out four successive draws against Bury in the third round of the FA Cup in January 1955.

DRAYCOTT, William Levi

Born at Newhall, near Derby, on 15 February 1869, wing-half Draycott was signed by Stoke from Burslem Port Vale in June 1891 – to boost the squad at The Victoria Ground – and his debut was one to forget as Stoke crashed 9-3 to Darwen. Over the next three years Draycott had only one more outing before leaving the club for Burton Wanderers. He later served with Newton Heath, Bedminster, Bristol Rovers, Wellingborough (1901-02) and Luton Town.

DREYER, John Paul

A versatile defender, Dreyer occupied every position across the back line during the period 1985 to 1997, and he also appeared in midfield as well. A real dogged footballer, totally committed, he was born at Alnwick on 11 June 1963. He played at first for Wallington FC and entered League Football with Oxford United, who secured his services in January 1985. Loan spells with Torquay United and Fulham preceded his move from The Manor Ground to Luton Town for £140,000 in June 1988. From Kenilworth Road he switched to Stoke City on a free transfer in July 1994 and made 60 senior appearances for the Potters, scoring four goals. He left The Victoria Ground for Bradford City in November 1996 for a fee of £25,000. Dreyer also played four games on loan to Bolton Wanderers in March/April 1995 when he was unable to get into Stoke's first team.

DUDLEY TOWN

Stoke's playing record against Dudley Town in the Birmingham & District League (1908-11) was:

Venue	P	W	D	L	F	A
Home	3	3	0	0	15	3
Away	3	0	1	2	6	8
Totals	6	3	1	2	21	11

The first meeting, on 24 October 1908, resulted in a 4-0 win for Stoke. The following season, Stoke won 6-1 at home but lost 5-4 away, and in 1910-11, the Potters were 5-2 victors at The Victoria Ground when Jack Peart scored a hat-trick.

Among the players who served with both clubs is Ike Turner.

DUNN, William

Outside-left Billy Dunn was another Scottish import. He moved to the Potteries from East Stirlingshire in November 1889 and stayed until January 1893 when he signed briefly for Hednesford Town, returning to Scotland in 1894. Born in Stirling in April 1875, Dunn (now deceased) scored 21 goals in 71 first-team outings for Stoke, helping the team win the Football Alliance title in 1891.

DURBAN, William Alan

Manager of Stoke City for almost three and a half years (1978-81) the former Welsh international midfielder (27 full caps) surprisingly quit The Victoria Ground saying: "I wish to manage a big club." He went to Sunderland where he stayed until 1984 and later managed Cardiff City, returning later as assistant manager at his former club Derby County and Sunderland as chief scout (1995). In all, Durban appeared in 554 Football League games between 1959 and 1978, scoring 135 goals. He had a fairly even League record as a manager with the Potters with 53 wins and 47 draws from a total of 142 matches in charge (See MANAGERS).

DURBER, Peter

Spotted playing locally for Wood Lane FC and Audley, left-back Durber finally arrived at Stoke in May 1896. He stayed for a couple of seasons, making 30 first-team appearances before leaving The Victoria Ground, with a group of other players, to sign for Southampton. He became a big favourite with the fans at The Dell, enjoying a lot of success including an appearance in the 1900 FA Cup Final and an England trial in that same year (South v North). In fact, a lot of people were surprised he didn't win a full cap for he was a polished performer, a strong tackler, and a player who was never afraid to get 'stuck'. After 52 games for the Saints, Durber rejoined Stoke in the summer of 1900 and made 35 more appearances for the Potteries club before moving north to Glossop, from where he joined Northampton Town, retiring in 1906 to go into the licensing trade in Stoke. He was born at Wood Lane (Staffs) in April 1873 and died in the Potteries.

DURHAM CITY

Stoke's record against Durham is:
Football League

Venue	P	W	D	L	F	A
Home	1	1	0	0	4	0
Away	1	1	0	0	2	1
Totals	2	2	0	0	6	1

Stoke met Durham twice in the Division Three North in 1926-27. A crowd of 7,382 saw Stoke win 4-0 at The Victoria Ground in early January and for the return fixture in mid-April, the turnout was under 3,000.

Played with both clubs: Peter McArdle and Joey Mawson.

DYKE, Archibald Samuel

Archie Dyke was a clever outside-left who had two spells at The Victoria ground – from August 1909 to December 1912 and from August 1913 to April 1914. Born in Newcastle (Staffs) in September 1891, he played, first of all, for Newcastle PSA and then Chesterton (before Stoke). He served with Port Vale (during the second half of the 1912-13 season) and after leaving the Potters second time round he joined Aston Villa for £500 (February 1914). Understudy to Charlie Wallace at Villa Park he made only nine appearances for the Birmingham-based club. He didn't play at top-class level after the war.

DYSON, Paul Anthony

Dyson was a tall central defender who relied on his positional sense rather than his pace. He was good in the air and possessed a timely tackle. Born in Kings Heath, Birmingham, on 27 December 1959, he joined Stoke from Coventry City in July 1983 for £150,000, being brought in by manager Richie Barker to replace Dave Watson. 'Dec' served the Potters for three seasons, making 123 appearances and scoring five goals before moving to West Bromwich Albion for £60,000 in March 1986 – sold by Mick Mills who replaced him with Steve Bould. After a good spell at The Hawthorns Dyson moved to Darlington (1989) and later assisted Crewe Alexandra, Telford United and Solihull Borough, taking over as player-manager of the latter club in 1996. Capped four times by England at Under-21 level (all gained whilst at Highfield Road) Dyson amassed over 400 senior appearances for his four Football League clubs.

EARDLEY, Frank

Inside-forward Eardley scored two goals in three League games for Stoke during the months of March and April, 1909. Born at Hanley in June 1885, he played for Tunstall Park and Goldenhill Wanderers before moving to The Victoria Ground in the summer of 1908, and left the Potters for Port Vale, later assisting Hanley Town (from 1911) and Meir Social (1912). He made his debut for the Vale against Stoke Reserves in a North Staffs League game.

EARDLEY, William George

Outside-right Billy Eardley (no relation to Frank, above) was born in Tunstall in December 1871 and played for Burslem Port Vale (two

George Eastham

spells: May 1894 and September 1895) and Newcastle Swifts (early 1895) before joining Stoke in August 1896. He spent just one season at The Victoria Ground, scoring once in his ten League games for the Potters, when he deputised for Freddie Johnson. He later played for a number of minor teams in the North Staffs area.

EASTHAM, George Edward, OBE

Eastham was an exceptionally talented inside-forward who netted his fair share of goals as well as making scores more for his colleagues. Born in Blackpool on 23 September 1936, he started off playing with the

Bipsham church team and Highfield Youth Club and then joined the Irish League club, Ards, where his father was player-manager. A gifted schemer, able to pass the ball inch-perfect, he moved to Newcastle United in May 1956 and hit 29 goals in 124 League outings for the Geordies. While at St James' Park Eastham was involved in the famous court case which finally broke the 'retain and transfer' system, and after winning that long-winded case he moved south to join Arsenal in October 1960 for £47,500. He did exceedingly well at Highbury and scored over 40 goals for the Gunners in 207 First Division appearances before Tony Waddington stepped in and brought him to Stoke for £35,000. This was on 18 August 1966, shortly after England had won the World Cup when Eastham was in Alf Ramsey's squad. He went on to claim five goals in 239 appearances for the Potters, his most valuable strike being the winner in the 1972 League Cup Final against Chelsea when, at their age of 35 years 161 days, he became the oldest player to receive a winners' medal. Just prior to that Wembley triumph, Eastham had started to develop his coaching qualities and, in fact, between February and October 1971, he had gone over to South Africa, playing on loan with Cape Town Spurs and later as player-manager of Hellenic. Back with Stoke, after retiring as a player (1975) he took the position of assistant to manager Waddington and when 'Waddo' was dismissed in March 1977, Eastham took over the hot seat at The Victoria Ground. Awarded the OBE in 1973, he held the position for barely a year, Alan Durban taking over the reins in February 1978. Eastham emigrated to his beloved South Africa where he set up his own business called Hat Trick and in his spare time coached football to the black youngsters in the townships around Cape Town (See MANAGERS).

EASTWOOD, Cecil Milner

A Yorkshireman, born at Tadcaster in June 1894, left-half Eastwood was a vital cog in the Stoke side during their 1926-27 Third Division North championship winning season. He played initially for Castleford Town (in Rugby League territory), Plymouth Argyle (103 League appearances) and then Preston North End before teaming up with Stoke in June 1926. Unfortunately during his second season at The Vic Eastwood found himself playing more in the Reserves than in the first team, and this led to him leaving the club in August 1928 for Stockport County. He had 48 outings for the Potters.

EBANKS, Michael Wayne Anthony

Full-back Ebanks who was born near the Longbridge car factory in Birmingham in October 1964, was taken on loan by Stoke boss Bill Asprey from West Bromwich Albion during the 1984-85 season when the club were short of defenders. He played in 12 League matches for the Potters before returning to The Hawthorns. In March 1985 he joined Port Vale and in 1987 was a non-contract player with Cambridge United.

EBBW VALE

Stoke's record against Ebbw Vale is:
Southern League

Venue	P	W	D	L	F	A
Home	1	1	0	0	10	0
Away	1	1	0	0	1	0
Totals	2	2	0	0	11	0

These two matches took place in 1914-15 and 'Arty' Watkin (5) and Alf Smith (4) led the goal-rush at The Victoria Ground.

Former Stoke inside-forward Amos Baddeley was player-manager of Ebbw Vale for a short period just prior to the outbreak of World War One. And 1920s Stokie Joe Clennell also managed the Welsh club.

ECCLES, John

Despite his light frame, full-back Jack Eccles was a resolute defender who had to battle for a first-team place early on along with the formidable duo of Tommy Clare and Alf Underwood. But Eccles hung in there and he went on to score one goal in 193 senior games for Stoke, whom he joined from London Road FC in March 1890. He spent just 11 years at The Victoria Ground, during which time he twice represented the Football League and must have been mighty close to winning a full England cap. After Stoke, he had a short spell in Burslem Port Vale's reserve side and then returned to The Victoria Ground as Stoke's trainer in 1902, taking over a similar position with Birmingham before World War One. Born in Stoke-on-Trent on 31 March 1869, Eccles was said to have been a dour man although he did produce 14 children, one of whom – Joe – went on to play for Aston Villa, Coventry City and West Ham United. Jack died in Small Heath, Birmingham on 2 February 1932.

EDGE, Alfred

Alf Edge was an exceptionally fine footballer, a versatile forward, who had loads of skill, was quick over short distances and never gave up the ghost. Born in Hanley c.1866, he played for Goldenhill for three seasons (from 1882) and then Stoke (September 1885 to May 1891). He then had an awkward spell with Newton Heath (now Manchester United) and whilst there was suspended for signing for Notts Jardines without knowledge of the Lancashire club. After a subsequent FA inquiry, the ban was lifted and he quickly rejoined the Potters for a second spell. This lasted for just a few months (early in 1893) and thereafter he assisted Northwich Victoria. Edge was awarded a gold medal by the Stoke directors for his services to the club – he scored 28 goals in 69 League and Cup appearances and helped the Potters win the Football Alliance title in 1891. He was also a member of the club's first-ever League team against West Brom on 8 September 1888 – and he also holds the record for scoring most goals in an FA Cup-tie for Stoke – five in a 10-1 home win over Caernarvon Wanderers in October 1886. He died in April 1941.

ELDER, Alex R.

Left-back Elder made his Football League debut for Burnley during their championship-winning season of 1959-60. This was the first of 330 senior games for the Clarets whom he served for eight years. A wartime baby, born in Lisburn, Northern Ireland, on 25 April 1941, Elder played for Glentoran on the Emerald Isle before moving to Turf Moor in January 1959. He impressed so much that he was quickly introduced to first-team action and despite breaking a leg in 1963 he remained a regular in the side until his departure to Stoke City for £50,000 in August 1967. He spent five seasons at The Victoria Ground, adding another 100 appearances (one goal scored) to his tally at senior level. He won six caps for Ireland whilst at Stoke, having earlier collected 34 with Burnley. He left the Potteries in the summer of 1973 on a free transfer and signed for Leek Town, near his north Staffordshire home.

ELLIOTT, Frank Frederick George

Goalkeeper Elliott played in 23 competitive games for Stoke, taking took over the duties in 1953 when Bill Robertson was unavailable. A Welshman, born in Merthyr Tydfil on 23 July 1929, he played for his home-town club during the middle and late '40s and then won a Welsh Cup winners' medal in 1951 with Swansea Town, whom he joined in September 1949. He moved to The Victoria Ground initially on trial in November 1952, signing full-time the following month, but left the Potteries for Fulham in March 1954 after failing to hold down a regular place in the side. Elliott, strong and well developed, made 25 League appearances for the Cottagers before winding down his professional career by having 63 League outings for Mansfield Town (July 1956 to May 1958).

ELLIS, Anthony Robert

Ellis scored 20 goals in 93 League and Cup games for Stoke City between December 1989 and August 1992. Born in Salford on 20 October 1964, he played initially for Poets Corner FC, Horwich RMI, Bolton Wanderers (on trial) and Northwich Victoria before signing as a full-time professional for Bolton in August 1986. From Burnden Park he moved to Preston North End for £23,000 in 1987 and after serving Stoke, he went on to have a second spell at Deepdale (returning there in a player-exchange deal involving Graham Shaw) before moving to Blackpool for £165,000 in July 1994. A proven goalscorer, Ellis has now netted over 150 goals in more than 450 senior games.

Tony Ellis

ELLIS, John Albert

Prior to joining Stoke, at the age of 24, in January 1914, Manchester-born half-back or inside-forward Jack Ellis played for Salford United and Witton Albion. Unfortunately he never really made an impact at The Victoria Ground and appeared in just three League games (all in 1913-14). Described as 'craft and tricky' he left the club when the war in Europe forced the termination of competitive football, at the end of the following season. He later signed for Stalybridge Celtic (July 1919) before returning to Witton Albion in October 1923. He also assisted Eccles United and guested for Manchester United in several matches during the hostilities.

EUROPEAN COMPETITIONS

Stoke played in the UEFA Cup competition in 1972-73 and again in 1974-75, participating in a total of four matches. They also competed in the Anglo-Italian tournament during the early 1970s and again in the 1990s (See ANGLO-ITALIAN TOURNAMENT and UEFA CUP).

EVANS, Arthur W.

Goalkeeper Evans had nine outings for the Potters during the early part of the 1893-94 season when he took over from Billy Rowley. Born in Stoke in April 1868 he played local Church football prior to his spell at The Victoria Ground which began in August 1893 and ended in the summer of 1894 after Tom Cain had taken over between the posts. He assisted Barlaston Swifts until the turn of the century.

EVANS, Gareth Ivan

Rejected by Coventry City as a teenager, inside-forward Evans broke through with Rotherham United and after a loan spell with Northampton Town, he signed for the Scottish club, Hibernian for whom he went on to appear in more than 150 games. He had a month with Stoke City (September/October 1990) when he scored twice in seven games before returning to Easter Road. Born in Coventry on 14 January 1967, Evans won a Skol Cup winners' medal with Hibs in 1982.

EVANS, John

Outside-left Jack Evans was born and bred in the Black Country. A West Bromwich man (born 12 July 1900) he played for West Bromwich Standard and Ewells FC before making the breakthrough with Sheffield United in 1923. A year later he moved to Stoke and made 12 League appearances for the Potters before switching his allegiance to Nantwich Victoria in May 1925. He later served with Stalybridge Connaughts.

EVANS. John Edward

Ted 'Jammer' Evans was the first Stoke player ever to be sent off – being dismissed in a League game against Everton on Merseyside on 12 November 1892. The result was a 2-2 draw. Evans, born in Fenton in April 1868 was a real tough guy, a forward who loved to dribble his way through a defence. He played initially for Newcastle Swifts and was a regular in the Stokie for more than three seasons between September 1891 and April 1895, during which time he scored 19 goals in 62 first-team appearances. After Stoke he played for Bury and returned to the Potteries in August 1896 to assist Port Vale, retiring three years later to work in a factory.

EVANS, Raymond Leslie

Evans was a powerfully-built full-back, a fine overlapper who got in some good crosses. His career centred on London before joining Stoke City in August 1979 for £120,000. Born in Edmonton on 20 September

1949, he developed via Edmonton Boys and Middlesex Schools and joined Tottenham Hotspur as an apprentice in 1965, turning professional two years later. He went on to make over 200 appearances for Spurs before serving with Millwall and then Fulham. During his time with the three London-based clubs, he had two separate spells in the NASL with St Louis Stars and California Surf. At The Victoria Ground he quickly fitted in to the manager's style of play, and netted two goals in 105 outings for the Potters, skippering the side at times before an unfortunate training ground incident blighted his stay at the club. In March 1982 he returned to America to join Seattle Sounders with whom he ended his playing career soon after they had lost to New York Cosmos in the Super Bowl. Evans remained in Seattle and still coaches there today.

EVER-PRESENTS

Just 63 players have been ever-present in a Football League season for the Potters, with four of them – Bill Asprey, Tommy Clare, Bob McGrory and Arthur Turner (all defenders) – appearing in every game in a campaign three times apiece.

Clare also played in all games in the Football Alliance in 1890-91.

Tony Allen, George Baddeley, Frank Bowyer, David Brodie, Harry Burrows, Bill Dickson, Alan Dodd, Peter Fox, Nigel Gleghorn, Tom Holford, John McCue, Eric Skeels, Frank Soo and Alf Underwood all had League ever-present records on two occasions. Brodie also appeared in every game in the Alliance in 1890-91.

EVERTON

Stoke's playing record against Everton is:
Football League
Venue	P	W	D	L	F	A
Home	52	20	16	16	71	63
Away	52	7	11	34	41	120
Totals	104	27	27	50	111	183

FA Cup
Home	5	2	1	2	5	8
Away	3	1	0	2	4	9
Totals	8	3	1	4	9	17

As founder members of the Football League, Stoke and Everton have been playing against each other at competitive level for well over 100 years and it is the Merseysiders who have, by far, the better set of statistics as far as results are concerned. Stoke's best League win of the 27 so far registered is 4-1 at home in January 1923 (Division One) when the crowd was 15,000.

Everton's best is an emphatic 8-0, achieved at Goodison Park in January 1890. They also won successive home games by 6-2 in April 1894 and 7-2 in December 1895. Another big Everton win was 6-2 at Goodison Park in October 1969 when Stoke lost goalkeeper John Farmer who was replaced by Denis Smith. The last League encounter between he teams was in April 1985 when Everton went on to win the First Division title after beating Stoke 2-0 a The Victoria Ground before a crowd of 18,258.

The first Stoke player ever to be sent-off in a League game was Teddy Evans, dismissed for foul play against Everton in November 1892.

Alf Edge scored a hat-trick when Stoke beat Everton 4-2 in an FA Cup-tie in February 1890, but eight years later the Merseysiders gained sweet revenge by knocking Stoke out the competition in 1897-98, beating them 5-1 at home after a 0-0 draw in the Potteries. Everton also won 4-0 at Stoke in season 1904-05. In May 1971, at Crystal Palace's Selhurst Park ground, Stoke and Everton played for third and fourth place in the FA Cup – and Everton came out on top, winning 3-2.

There were 11 goals scored in a Stoke-Everton wartime game in season 1941-42. The Potters won 8-3 at The Victoria Ground with a hat-trick from Tommy Sale.

Players with both clubs: Neil Adams, Sam Ashworth, Peter Beagrie, Mike Bernard, Alan Biley, Paul Bracewell, Jimmy Broad, Matt Burton, Tom Cain, Wilf Chadwick, Wayne Clarke, Joe Clennell, Bill Dickie, Albert Farmer, John Gidman, Harold Hardman, Adrian Heath, Mark Higgins, Howard Kendall, George Latham (Everton trialist), Allan Maxwell, John Moore, Jimmy O'Neill, Mike Pejic, Dr Leigh Richmond Roose, Fred Rouse, Tommy Sale, Paddy Sheridan, Mickey Thomas, Joe Turner, Roy Vernon and Jack Whitely.

Alan Ball was a player at Everton and later manager at The Victoria Ground. Asa Hartford was an Everton midfielder who later became assistant manager-coach at Stoke City.

Former Stokie Mark Harrison later became goalkeeping coach at Goodison Park.

EXETER CITY

Stoke's playing record against the Grecians is:
Football League
Venue	P	W	D	L	F	A
Home	3	2	1	0	8	4
Away	3	0	2	1	2	4
Totals	6	2	3	1	10	8

Southern League
Home	2	0	0	2	1	5
Away	2	0	1	1	1	2
Totals	4	0	1	3	2	7

FA Cup
Home	2	1	1	0	3	0
Away	3	1	2	0	3	2
Totals	5	2	3	0	6	2

Stoke and Exeter met four times in the Southern League before World War One (1911-13). The other six League meetings came in the Third Division (1990-93). Stoke beat the Grecians 5-2 at The Victoria Ground in March 1992 when Ashley Grimes scored his only goal for the Potters. In season 1909-10 Stoke met Exeter three times in the FA Cup, the Potters eventually going through 2-1 after a second replay at neutral Craven Cottage. The teams met again in the same competition in 1955-56 and again the Potters came out best, winning 3-0 at home after a 0-0 draw.

Players with both clubs: Noel Blake, Darren Boughey, Peter Bullock, Walter Bussey, Mark Chamberlain, Brian Doyle, Peter Fox, Graham Harbey (Exeter trialist), Vince Hilaire, Robert Lister, Peter McArdle, Jason Percival (Stoke junior), Jack Robinson, Maurice Setters, Tim Steele and Enos Whittaker. Goalkeeper Robinson had already won 11 England caps when he joined the Potters from Exeter in May 1909. Fox became player-manager at St James' Park, while former England star Alan Ball also managed Exeter City as well as Stoke City.

EYRES, John

Inside-forward Eyres was associated with Stoke for a period of seven years without really establishing himself in the first team. Born in Northwich on 20 March 1899, he had spells with his home-town club and Witton Albion before Stoke paid £250 for his services in June 1922. After scoring 23 goals in 65 League games for the Potters, he was transferred to Walsall in May 1929 for a modest fee which Eyres received himself as part of a benefit. After that he became something of a nomad, and played, in turn, for Brighton & Hove Albion, Bristol Rovers, York City and Gainsborough Trinity. He retired in 1936 and died c.1975.

FAMILY CONNECTIONS

Brotherly love

Edgar and Harry Montford (from Newtown) were the first brothers to be associated with Stoke. They played together at the club in the late 1880s.

Hanley-born brothers John and Billy Tunnicliffe were at Stoke in season 1888-89, the latter being a member of the club's first League side v West Bromwich Albion.

The Owen brothers – Alf and Wally – were associated with Stoke during the period from 1886 to 1908, with Alf following his older brother to the club.

England international Arthur 'Sailor' Capes and his brother Adrian were at The Victoria Ground during the early 1900s. Arthur was at the club 18 months before his brother. The brothers Capes also played for Nottingham Forest.

George and Amos Baddeley from Fegg Hayes were Stokies together in 1907. Between them they made over 320 senior appearances for the club, their respective careers at The Victoria Ground overlapped each other.

Forwards Tommy and Jimmy Broad from Stalybridge, came to the club soon after World War One to 'beef up' the front-line. They were at The Vic from 1921 top 1924. Jimmy also coached Las Palmas and Barcelona. They were paired together in the Stoke forward-line a record 79 times.

The Stoke careers of the Watkin brothers, 'Arty' and Frank, ran back to back: 1913-26. 'Arty' had two spells with the club and made 177 appearances to Frank's five.

Aberdonians Doug and Jim Westland, recruited by manager Bob McGrory, gave Stoke good service during the inter war years. They played together in the same Stoke team just twice, with West Brom getting thumped 10-3 the first time they were teammates (in February, 1937).

In wartime football, brothers Albert and Fred Basnett were together at The Victoria Ground.

Since World War Two, brothers Derek and Terry Ward made over 100 appearances between them for the Potters (1952-62), Derek on the right-wing, Terry at full-back.

The Pejics – centre-half Mel and full-back Mike – played for Stoke City in the 1970s. Mel made only one senior appearance for the club, but after leaving The Victoria Ground, he amassed had over 400 games for Hereford United (1980-91). Mike had 336 outings for Stoke City and gained England honours during his lengthy career which also saw him serve with Aston Villa and Everton. He later returned to the club as coach, under Lou Macari.

Mark and Neville Chamberlain both played League Football for Port Vale and Stoke City. Mark was the more pronounced player at Stoke and earned England recognition before moving to Sheffield Wednesday. He had over 120 games for the club whereas Neville played just seven times in Stoke's colours.

Brothers Lee and Jonathan Chapman were on Stoke's books together as YTS lads before Lee finally made it as a professional.

Late 1980s goalkeeper Kevin Lewis was the nephew of 1970s full-back Kevin William Lewis.

Brothers, Peter and John Birks were YTS apprentices at The Victoria Ground at the same time in the late 1990s. Neither made the first XI.

Paul and Marc Barnes signed for Stoke City, on YTS forms in the 1990s. Paul went on to make the grade at a higher level.

Roy Brown was a post-war Stoke player while his brother later joined the club as trainer (1963-64).

The last set of brothers to join Stoke were Steve and Mark Taaffe in 1996.

Family Links

● Alan Ball senior and his son, Alan Ball junior, were chief scout and manager respectively at Stoke City after they had retired as players.

● As Stoke City's manager, Tony Waddington had his son, Steve, in the first team at The Victoria Ground.

● The uncle and nephew combination of the same name – Kevin Lewis and Kevin Lewis – were both members of the playing staff at Stoke.

● Between them, Harry and Johnny Sellars (father and son respectively) made over 800 senior appearances for Stoke. Both were wing-halves – Harry from 1924-35 and Johnny from 1947-58.

● David Ritchie was a reserve at Stoke in the 1970s, having watched his more illustrious father, John, score regularly at The Victoria Ground when he was a lad.

● Manager Lou Macari had his two sons with him at The Victoria Ground during the 1990s – Mike, who made the first team, and Paul, both of whom were forwards.

● The Icelandic duo of Toddy Orlygsson and his cousin, Larus Sigurdsson, both played for Stoke City in the 1990s.

● Tom Holford was the cousin of Wilf Kirkham, and both players were associated with Stoke and Port Vale.

FARMER, Albert

Farmer was a gritty half-back who played in three League games and three FA Cup-ties for Stoke during his two seasons with the club: 1888-90. Born in the Potteries in July 1864, he had a few games for Everton before moving to The Victoria Ground but was never a serious contender for a regular place in the side and left the club for Newton Heath (Manchester).

FARMER, George D.

Left/half-back Farmer (no relation to Albert) played in one FA Cup-tie for Stoke v Crewe Alexandra in November 1886. Born in the Potteries in April 1862, he played for Tunstall before joining Stoke and for Burslem Swifts afterwards (1887-89).

FARMER, John

Farmer was keeping goal for Chatterley Boys' Club when Stoke spotted his enormous talent and brought him to The Victoria Ground in 1964. Born in Biddulph on 31 August 1947, Farmer attended a rugby-playing school as a lad, but never wanted to handle the oval ball, and chose the round ball game instead. He never regretted it. He made his debut for the Potters in a League match against Arsenal in January 1966 at the age of 18 (still one of the youngest men ever to don the goalkeeper's jersey for the club) and from that day on his confidence soared, although occasionally his performances did suffer through lack of concentration and he had a certain Gordon Banks as his superior. Farmer won an England Under-23 cap in November 1967 (v Wales) and he steadily built on his appearance record, eventually amassing a grand total of 185, a total cut short owing to Banks's presence and Peter Shilton's arrival. Nevertheless Farmer, who guested for West Bromwich Albion on a pre-season tour in 1972 and had two games on loan with Leicester City in 1974, remained a loyal and dedicated player for Stoke City right up until he left The Victoria Ground for Northwich Victoria in 1975. He later became factory manager for Smiths Crisps, based in Cheadle, near Stockport.

FARRELL, John

Centre-forward Jack Farrell spent two seasons at The Victoria Ground – three years apart. He first played for Stoke from October 1894 to April 1895 and returned for a second time for the 1898-99 campaign. In all he scored 12 goals in 42 League and FA Cup appearances for the Potters. Born in Tunstall in August 1873, he started out with Dresden United at the age of 17 and in between his spells with the Potters he served with Southampton St Mary's. He went back to The Dell after his second stint with Stoke and later he played for New Brighton Tower (June 1900-April 1901), Northampton Town (May 1901-May 1902) and West Ham United (June 1902 to May 1904). When he joined Southampton (in 1895) his arrival was described as a 'great catch at £40.' A fast and tricky player, very reliable with a level-headed approach, Farrell won two Southern League championship medals with Saints (1897 and 1898) and he also played in the 1900 FA Cup Final defeat v Bury. All told he scored 54 goals in 97 outings during his two spells at The Dell, including a haul of 13 in 20 games in their first championship-winning season. On retiring he returned to Tunstall where he became a publican. Farrell died in Stoke on 22 February 1947.

FARRELL, Stephen

A native of Scotland (born in Kilmarnock in March 1973), midfielder Farrell made two substitute League appearances for Stoke in season 1989-90. Having skippered the club's youth team, it was thought that he would make the grade in the senior side, but sadly that didn't materialise and left The Victoria Ground in May 1990 for St Mirren.

FARROW, Desmond A.

Rugged defender Des Farrow, a former amateur with Leicester City, was one of manager Frank Taylor's early signings for Stoke City. He was brought to The Victoria Ground from Queen's Park Rangers in 1952 in a £4,000 cash/player deal, involving George Mountford. He failed to impress at Stoke and made only eight League appearances before joining Peterborough United in May 1955 on a free transfer. Farrow was born in Peterborough in February 1926.

FERNS, William

There are references to this footballer's name being spelt Fearns. A typically stern Scottish half-back, he played in four League games for Stoke midway through the 1896-97 season, having signed for the club in April 1894. Born in Glasgow in September 1871, he remained an amateur throughout his career and either side his service with the Potters, he played for the famous Corinthians club.

FESTIVAL OF BRITAIN

To celebrate the Festival of Britain, Stoke played three friendly matches, all in May 1951, two at home against the Dutch side Schiedam VC (won 2-1) and the Portuguese team FC Oporto (won 2-0) and one away at Mansfield Town (drew 1-1).

FIELDING, Abraham Ross

Fielding was a talented outside-right, who came from a well respected North Staffordshire family. He had two useful spells with Stoke: the first in 1901-1902 and the second from 1904 to 1908. He scored 12 goals in a combined total of 109 senior appearances. Born in Trentham in January 1880, Fielding, who weighed barely 10st, joined the Potters initially from Florence Colliery FC. And before returning to The Victoria Ground for his second term of office, he played for both Nottingham Forest and West Bromwich Albion. In fact, the Baggies' secretary-manager Fred Everiss and one of the club's directors joined Fielding while he was out enjoying himself on a fox hunt. He signed the appropriate forms out in the countryside. He died c.1952.

FIELDING, Arthur John

Inside-forward Archie Fielding, a local lad, born in Hanley in April

1883, played briefly for Bolton Wanderers Reserves in 1906 before going to work down the pit. He then assisted Florence Colliery FC and joined Stoke in August 1908. He made only three Birmingham & District League appearances for the Potters during the season (as deputy for Owen and Gorman) and left the club in June 1910 to sign for Burslem Port Vale where he stayed for one season before going back to Florence Colliery.

FINANCIAL DIFFICULTIES

As the nineteenth century gave way to the twentieth, it was common knowledge that Stoke FC was in financial trouble. There had been several public appeals for funds and a certain amount of money had been raised – but not enough. The club's directors continued to scan Scotland in an attempt to sign players for practically peanuts, but in truth those they did recruit weren't all that good. The team itself had flirted with relegation for a number of seasons and they had hardly put together a decent Cup run.

Secretary-manager Horace Austerberry attempted to guide the club along, aided and abetted by chairman Mr W.A.Cowlishaw, but it was hard going. Thankfully things picked up and a major crisis was averted.

However, Stoke's financial situation started to get somewhat uneasy again as the 1904-05 season was drawing to its close, and the next three years were very difficult ones for the club. Lack of money was now a major concern for the directors and even the supporters. Apathy reigned and a loss of £1,100 (a lot of cash in those days) was incurred. Wholesale disposal of players was inevitable as the board, still chaired at this by Mr Cowlishaw, tottered on the brink. Before the 1905-06 campaign kicked off several players left the club, including half-back Tom Holford (sold to Manchester City to the annoyance of the fans) as the directors tried to gain extra cash. It was tough going for all concerned.

The club was in dire straits – no money, only a few good players, low attendances and above all the team was slipping down the ladder, heading fast for obscurity. Stoke, in fact, went out of the League at the end of the 1907-08 season and at the time there was little or no money in the bank – and the pile of bills was mounting all the time.

In June 1908, a new club was born – Stoke Football Club (1908) Ltd. A new seven-man board of directors came to office under chairman, the Reverend A.E.Hurst, and things started to improve, slowly at first, but more rapidly thereafter until the club got on to a more substantial footing. It was no easy matter.money was still tight, but gradually the situation eased as the attendances increased, albeit very slowly.

On the resumption of competitive soccer in 1919, after Stoke, had regained their Football League status, the financial situation within the club was described as 'sound'.

There have been a few close calls regarding cash flow since the early 1920s, but Stoke City FC survived and it is now looking forward to a new life at a new ground.

FINNEY, Charles William Thomas

A teenage centre-forward with Edensor Youth Club and an amateur under the managership of the former Stoke centre-half Arthur Turner with Crewe Alexandra, Bill Finney moved to The Victoria Ground in May 1949 as a part-time professional – and it was not until October 1951 that he signed as a full-time 'pro' for the Potters. Born in Stoke on 5 September 1931, Finney was given his debut in an away League game at Old Trafford in October 1952, and he scored (with a stunning left-footer) to celebrate the occasion as Stoke beat Manchester United 2-0 in front of almost 29,000 fans. Come 1955 Stoke manager Frank Taylor began to look elsewhere for a central striker and Finney knew his time was up as a Potter. In November of that year – after netting 15 goals in 62 senior appearances – he was transferred to Birmingham City for £7,000, who were managed by the same Arthur Turner. Finney later played for Queen's Park Rangers, Crewe (again), Rochdale and Cheltenham Town, retiring in 1960.

FIRSTS

● First recorded game: (as Stoke Ramblers) v E.W.May's XV (friendly) on 7 October 1868 at The Victoria Ground (1-1 draw).

● First goalscorer: Henry John Almond (v May's XV) in above match.

● First game at The Victoria Ground: Stoke v Talke Rangers (friendly) 28 March 1878 (won 1-0).

● First FA Cup-tie: v Manchester (h) 10 October 1883 (lost 1-2).

● First FA Cup win: 10-1 v Caernarvon Wanderers (h) 30 October 1886.

● First FA Cup hat-trick: Alf Edge (5 goals) v Caernarvon (in the above match).

● First Football League match: v West Bromwich Albion (h) 8 September 1888 (lost 0-2).

● First Football League victory: 3-0 v Notts County (h) 22 September 1888.

● First Football League hat-trick: by David Ramsey v Accrington (h) 1 March 1890.

● First double figure League defeat: 0-10 v Preston North End (a) 14 September 1889.

● First double-figure League victory: 10-3 v West Bromwich Albion (h) 4 February 1937 (Division One).

● First Divisional League triumph: Division Three North championship in season 1926-27.

● First Football League Cup-tie: v Doncaster Rovers (a) 18 October 1960 (lost 1-3).

● First League Cup win: 1-0 v Southend United (a) 13 September 1961.

● First League Cup scorer: Tommy Hymers (Doncaster Rovers) own-goal in the above game in 1960.

● First Stoke City scorer in League Cup: Peter Bullock v Southend United (in the above away game in September 1961).

- First European competitive match: v FC Kaiserslautern (h) UEFA Cup 13 September 1972 (won 3-1).

- First European goalscorer: Terry Conroy in above match in 1972.

- First player to make 100 League appearances for club: Alf Underwood in season 1892-93.

- First player to reach 200 League appearances for club: Tommy Clare in 1896-97.

- First player to reach the 300 League appearances: Bob McGrory in 1931-32.

- First player to reach 400 League appearances: John McCue in 1959-60.

- First player to make 500 League appearances: Eric Skeels in 1974-75.

- First player to score 100 League goals for club: Charlie Wilson, reaching milestone in 1929-30.

- First Stoke player to be capped at full international level: Teddy Johnson for England v Wales at Wrexham on 15 March 1880.

- First Scotsman capped for club: Tommy Hyslop v England in 1896.

- First Welshmen capped: Mart Watkins, Dr Leigh Richmond Roose and Sammy Meredith v England in 1902.

- First Irishman capped as Stoke player: Jack Sheridan v England in 1905.

- First Stokie to win a Republic of Ireland cap: Terry Conroy v Czechoslovakia in 1960.

- First Stoke player to be sent-off in League game: Ted Evans v Everton (a) 12 November 1892.

FLANNIGAN, Thomas

Scottish inside-forward with a good left foot who sadly never fitted into Stoke's plans during his two years at the club, during which time he appeared in just four League games. Born in Edinburgh on 27 April 1908, he often showed a great deal of determination and courage, but lacked that extra bit of finesse required to be a quality footballer. Flannigan began his career as a junior with Edinburgh Emmett and after a brief spell with Dundee, he joined the Potters in July 1927. In the summer of 1929 he went to Hull City for £500, but again failed to establish himself in the Tigers' line-up, and after being placed on the list with a £750 tag on his head, he drifted somewhat, and went on to assist Loughborough Corinthians, Darlington, Rochdale, Buxton, Stafford Rangers, St Etienne (in France – for three months in 1933) and Shrewsbury Town. He finally quit soccer in May 1934 to concentrate on his hairdressing business. Flannigan died in Darlington on 23 May 1981.

FLOODLIGHTS

Floodlights were first installed at The Victoria Ground in 1956, and the first game under the lights took place on 10 October that year when Stoke City played near neighbours Port Vale in the Second Division. A crowd of almost 39,000 saw the Potters win 3-1 with goals from Tim Coleman (2) and George Kelly.

The first FA Cup-tie under The Victoria Ground floodlights saw Stoke beat West Ham United 1-0 in a third-round replay in January 1961.

On 27 February 1890, Stoke defeated Crewe Alexandra 3-1 in a home friendly match which was played under Wells Lights.

Stoke were the visitors when the floodlights were first switched on in Holland's Olympic Stadium in Amsterdam in 1936-37. Stoke beat an Amsterdam XI 1-0 to celebrate the occasion.

The first foreign club side to visit The Victoria Ground for a floodlit friendly was FC Radnicki (Yugoslavia) who were beaten 3-0 in 1956.

Stoke played friendly matches to officially open the floodlights at the following grounds: Worcester City in February 1953, Shrewsbury Town in November 1959 and Bangor City in March 1970.

From October 1979 to its closure in May 1997, The Victoria Ground was the only football stadium in the country which had two different pairs of floodlights.

FLOWERS, John E.

Flowers, a tall, constructive wing-half, spent six years at The Victoria Ground (June 1960 to August 1966) during which time he appeared in only nine senior games for the Potters. He then joined Doncaster Rovers for £10,000 and amassed 164 League appearances up to August 1971 when he switched back to the Potteries to sign for Port Vale. Brother of the Wolves and England wing-half, Ron Flowers and married for a time to the women's World Darts champion, Maureen, Flowers, who was born in Doncaster on 26 August 1944, has also worked as a postman.

FLYNN, Sean

Midfielder Flynn was born in Birmingham on 13 March 1968, and played initially for the West Midlands non-League club Halesowen Town before moving to Coventry City for £20,000 in December 1991. After more than 100 appearances for the Sky Blues he was transferred to Derby County for £250,000 in August 1995, being part of a £1m transfer deal – and in his first season at the Baseball Ground helped the Rams into the Premiership. A strong, determined player, with heaps of energy, Flynn made five appearancers for the Potters during the latter stages of the 1996-97 campaign after signing on loan from Derby a fortnight after his 29th birthday.

FOLEY, Stephen

Tough-tackling midfielder Steve Foley began his career as an apprentice at Anfield in 1978. He spent four years there but never made Liverpool's first XI. Following a loan spell with Fulham (December 1983) he was transferred to Grimsby Town in August 1984 and scored five goals in 40 appearances for the Mariners before moving to Sheffield United in August 1985. After 79 outings and 18 goals for the Blades he went to Swindon Town for £40,000 (June 1987) and added 190 appearances and 29 goals to his playing record with the Robins prior to joining Stoke City for £50,000 in January 1992. Foley, who was born in Liverpool on 4 October 1962, stayed at The Victoria Ground for two-and-a-half years, helping the Potters win the Autoglass Trophy at Wembley in 1992 and the Second Division title the following season. He scored 13 goals in 135 games for the Potters, including a hat-trick against Barnet (h) in an Autoglass Trophy match in January 1993. He left The Victoria Ground for Lincoln City in July 1994 and then had a month's trial with Bradford City in October 1995 before slipping into non-League football.

FOOTBALL ALLIANCE

After losing their Football League status, Stoke participated in the Football Alliance for just the one season – 1890-91 – and they ended up as champions with this record:

Venue	P	W	D	L	F	A	Pts
Home	11	9	2	0	33	15	20
Away	11	4	5	2	24	24	13
Totals	22	13	7	2	57	39	33

Stoke had three points to spare over second-placed Sunderland Albion after an excellent season. Their best victory (of the 13 registered) was 6-2 over Darwen (at home) on Boxing Day. They also beat Sheffield Wednesday 5-1 and Birmingham St George's 6-3, both at The Victoria Ground. Their heaviest defeat was suffered at Small Heath (Birmingham) where they went down 5-1 on 1 November. Alf Edge finished up as top-scorer with 12 goals, while three other players each netted 11.

The home game with Crewe Alexandra on 8 November (2-2) was staged at the local cricket ground as The Vic was unfit for use.

FA CUP

Stoke first entered the FA Cup competition for season 1883-84, their initial game being against Manchester (at home) in the first qualifying round on 10 November which they lost 2-1 before a crowd of 1,000. Teddy Johnson scored the Potters goal.

Since then Stoke have played a further 281 games in the FA Cup, their full record (up to 1997) being:

Venue	P	W	D	L	F	A
Home	130	68	36	26	263	126
Away	152	32	42	78	172	273
Totals	282	100	78	104	435	399

*Includes two Play-off games in 1971 and 1972.

Stoke's biggest wins in the FA Cup (all at home):

11-0	v Stourbridge	1914-15
10-1	v Caernarvon Wanderers	1886-87
7-0	v Worcester City	1910-11
7-1	v Burnley	1895-96
6-0	v Grimsby Town	1896-97
6-1	v Gillingham	1927-28
5-0	v Tottenham Hotspur	1895-96
5-0	v Glossop North End	1896-97
5-0	v Lincoln City	1907-08
6-2	v Hartlepools United	1953-54

Their biggest away win is 5-2 at Wigan Borough in 1925-26

Stoke's heaviest FA Cup defeats:
(All suffered away from home except Everton in 1904-05)

0-8	v Wolverhampton W	1886-87
3-6	v Swansea Town	1925-26
4-6	v Crewe Alexandra	1886-87
0-5	v Sheffield Wednesday	1908-09
1-5	v Everton	1897-98
1-5	v Preston North End	1936-37
0-4	v Wolverhampton W	1889-90*
0-4	v Sunderland	1891-92
0-4	v Everton	1904-05
0-4	v Aston Villa	1913-14
0-4	v Aston Villa	1921-22

* Following this 4-0 defeat, Stoke protested over the state of the Wolves' ground. Their appeal was upheld and a replay arranged. Wolves were unduly worried and they went out and doubled their score (from the first meeting) and thrashed Stoke 8-0 in the rearranged fixture which was staged on the same ground in Dudley Road.

Ousted by the Minnows

Since entering the Football League as founder members in 1888, Stoke have been knocked out of the FA Cup on four occasions by non-League opposition: In October 1888, they fell to Warwick County in a qualifying round after choosing to field their reserve team; in December 1926 they were ousted by Rhyl (after three games); in February 1978 they fell at home to Blyth Spartans and in January 1994 were knocked out (after a replay) by Telford United.

FA Cup Best

Stoke's best efforts in the FA Cup have been in seasons 1898-99, 1970-71 and 1971-72, when they reached the semi-final stage each time. After ousting Sheffield Wednesday, Birmingham and Tottenham Hotspur in 1898-99, Derby County dented Stoke's hopes of a Final appearance by winning the semi-final 3-1 at Molineux in front of a 20,000 crowd.

In 1970-71, Stoke's Cup exploits ended against Arsenal (the eventual double winners that season). After knocking out Millwall, Huddersfield Town (at the third attempt), Ipswich Town and Hull City, Stoke fell to the Gunners in a semi-final replay at Villa Park by 2-0 in front of a 62,356 crowd, after a nail-biting 2-2 draw at Hillsborough which saw Arsenal equalise late on.

The following season it was Arsenal again who prevented Stoke from making it to Wembley. In the earlier rounds the Potters accounted for Chesterfield, Tranmere Rovers, Hull City and Manchester United, but sadly they failed to get the better of the team from Highbury, who won the Goodison Park replay 2-1 (after a 1-1 draw at Villa Park).

Longest FA Cup-tie

The longest FA Cup-tie Stoke City have been involved in, was their third-round clash with Bury in January 1955 which went to a fourth replay and lasted 9 hours 22 minutes. This is the fourth longest tie in the competition – behind Alvechurch v Oxford City in 1971 (11 hours); Leyton v Ilford in 1924 (9 hrs, 40 mins) and Barrow v Gillingham, also in 1924 (9 hrs, 30 mins).

FOOTBALL LEAGUE

League clubs never met

Of the present-day clubs in the English Premiership and Nationwide Leagues, Stoke have yet to play the following in League competition: Barnet, Colchester United, Gillingham, Hereford United, Scarborough, Wycombe Wanderers and York City.

First League season

1888-89 was the first season of League Football in England and Stoke, one of the 12 founder members, played 22 matches, the results being:

Opponents	Home	Away
Accrington	2-4	0-2
Aston Villa	1-1	1-5
Blackburn Rovers	2-1	2-5
Bolton Wanderers	2-2	1-2
Burnley	4-3	1-2
Derby County	1-1	1-2
Everton	0-0	1-2
Notts County	3-0	3-0
Preston North End	0-3	0-7
West Bromwich A	0-2	0-2
Wolverhampton W	0-1	1-4

Stoke finished the season bottom of the pile with this disappointing record:

Venue	P	W	D	L	F	A	Pts
Home	11	3	4	4	15	18	10
Away	11	1	0	10	11	33	2
Totals	22	4	4	14	26	51	12

Bob McSkimming top-scored for Stoke, claiming six of their 26 goals. McSkimming, along with full-back Alf Underwood, were the only ever-presents in the team. And a total of 26 players were utilised by the club during this first season – all of them making the Football League debuts.

First League game

Stoke's first League game was at home to the FA Cup holders West Bromwich Albion on 8 September 1888. A crowd of 4,524 saw them beaten 2-0 fielding this team – Rowley; Clare, Underwood; Ramsey, Shutt, Smith; Sayer, McSkimming, Staton, Edge, Tunnicliffe.

Wilson and Woodhall scored for Albion who in winning became the first team to top of the Football League (on goal average).

Worst starts to a League season

Stoke's worst ever start to a Football League season came at the beginning of the 1906-07 campaign when they lost their opening four matches. Indeed, Stoke did not record a single League victory in any of their first eight games.

In 1922-23 they collected only two points from their initial eight fixtures and in 1951-52 Stoke drew only two matches in their first 11 Division One games.

League Wins

Stoke's best League win is 10-3 v West Bromwich Albion (home) in February 1937, while their best away victory is 6-0 at Bury in March 1954.

Clean Sheets

Stoke's defence have kept clean sheets in 26% of all the Football League games they have played since 1888.

Fewest Goals

By netting just 24 goals in their 42 First Division games in season 1984-85, Stoke City attained the worst scoring record in Football League history based on a programme of 40 or more games.

Longest & Shortest League seasons

Here are the three longest League seasons Stoke have been involved in:

The Stoke team which won the old Second Division championship in 1962-63, the second time this had been achieved by the club.

The Stoke team of 1906-07, which made the worst-ever start to a League season in the club's history, losing their opening four matches.

287 days   31 August 1946 to 14 June 1947
280 days   10 August 1968 to 17 May 1969
279 days   18 August 1962 to 24 May 1963
The shortest League season was that of 205 days in 1889-90.

Long Service
Four men, all associated with Stoke City Football Club, had lengthy career at top-class level. Stanley Matthews played League football for almost 33 years (1932-65); Peter Shilton's League career spanned close on 31 years (1966-97); Tom Holford was a League player for well over 25 years (1898-1924) and Jock Rutherford starred as a winger for a shade over 25 years (1902-27).

Sunday League games
Stoke's first Sunday League game was against Chelsea at The Victoria Ground on 27 January 1974 (Division One). A crowd of almost 32,000 turned out to see Stoke win 1-0. Former England World Cup hero Geoff Hurst scored the deciding goal from a disputed penalty awarded nine minutes from time for a foul on Alan Hudson, a former Chelsea man.

Since then Stoke have played several matches, both at home and away, on a Sunday, especially since 1992-93.

Unchanged team
Stoke City manager Tom Mather fielded an unchanged team in 15 consecutive League Division Two games between 19 September and 25 December 1931. The team was: Lewis; McGrory, Beachill, Robertson, Turner, H. Sellars; Liddle, Bussey, Mawson, Sale, Archibald.

Christmas Holiday League games
Stoke played 28 Football League games on a Christmas Day morning from 1891 to 1954. This is Stoke's Christmas Day record:

Venue	P	W	D	L	F	A	Pts
Home	8	7	0	1	16	7	14
Away	20	5	4	11	28	43	14
Totals	28	12	4	12	44	50	28

● Their best victory was a 5-1 triumph at Grimsby Town in 1937, while their heaviest defeat came at Sheffield Wednesday in 1897 (lost 4-0).

● The team Stoke have met most times on 25 December is Preston North End Between 1891 and 1900 there were five First Division encounters and Stoke won just once, 1-0 at home in 1895.

Void League games
At the start of the ill-fated 1939-40 season, prior to the outbreak of World War Two, Stoke (along with all the other clubs in the country) played three League matches which were subsequently declared null and void owing to the hostilities in Europe.
Here are details of Stoke's three matches played in Division One:
26 August 1939 v Charlton Athletic (h) 4-0 (Soo, Smith 2, Sale)
28 August 1939 v Bolton Wanderers (h) 1-2 (Gallacher)
2 September 1939 v Middlesbrough (a) 2-2 (Sale 2)

League Sequences
Undefeated games: 25 (September 1992 to February 1993).
Undefeated home games: 23 (December 1973 to December 1974).
Undefeated away games: 12 (September 1992 to January 1993).
Games without a win: 17 (September 1984 to 22 December 1984 & 22 April 1989 to 14 October 1989).
Games without a home win: 9 (April to November 1963).
Games without an away win: 30 (January 1897 to December 1899).
Successive defeats: 11 (April to August 1985).
Successive home wins: 11 (March to December 1895).

● Stoke's record breaking sequence of 25 unbeaten League games commenced with a 0-0 home draw with Bolton Wanderers at The Victoria Ground and ended with a 1-0 defeat at Leyton Orient. During this run, the Potters won 17 and drew eight of their 25 fixtures.

Home Form
Stoke have never completed a Football League programme with an unbeaten home record: they lost one game in each of the following seasons: 1893-94 (Division One), 1921-22 (Division Two), 1923-24 (Division Two), 1926-27 (Division Three North) and 1931-32 (Division Two).

The highest number of wins registered in a League season has been 17 – in 1926-27 and 1992-93.

Re-Election
After finishing bottom of the first Football League table in 1888-89, Stoke, along with the three clubs who had finished immediately above them, had to apply for re-election. Thankfully, Stoke with ten votes, finished top of the poll and duly held on to their status in the newly-formed Football League.

The following season, to their obvious disappointment, Stoke again finished in last place in the League and once again they had to seek re-election – but this time they missed out, Sunderland replacing them for the 1890-91 campaign.

First Division
As founder members of the Football League in 1888, over the past 109 years Stoke (City) have played in the First Division for a total of 56 seasons, including an unbroken run of 16 years from 1891-92 to 1906-07 inclusive. They have yet to win the First Division title, their highest placing to date being fourth, achieved three times in 1935-36, 1946-47 and 1995-96.

This is Stoke's record in the First Division:

P	W	D	L	F	A	Pts
2,038	680	484	874	2,498	3,194	1,906

Second Division
Stoke played Second Division football for the first time in season 1907-08. Since then they have spent a further 30 seasons in this section, winning the championship in 1932-33, thirty years later in 1962-63 and again in 1992-93 after the lower Divisions had been restructured. They went to the top of the table in the latter campaign after after beating Blackpool at Bloomfield Road in November and held pole position until the last ball was kicked, finishing with 93 points, three ahead of second-placed Bolton Wanderers.

This is Stoke's full record of Second Division soccer:

P	W	D	L	F	A	Pts
1,404	551	361	492	2,009	1,843	1,585

Third Division
Stoke were relegated to the Third Division North for the first time in 1926. But thankfully, for all concerned, they made an immediate return, winning back their Second Division place at the first attempt after remaining on top of the table from the word go. They completed ten doubles over their opponents and took the championship by beating Accrington Stanley 1-0 on 23 April 1927. They eventually finished five points clear of runners-up Rochdale (63-58). Charlie Wilson top-scored, thus equalling Jimmy Broad's then record of 25 goals in a League season.

The club's next visit to the Third Division was in 1990-91 when they finished in their lowest-ever League position of 14th. The following season, under the guidance of manager Lou Macari, the Potters made the Play-offs only to lose out to Stockport County over two legs. Following the restructuring of the lower Divisions by the Football League's governing bodies, Stoke found themselves in Division Two in 1992-93, but straightaway they won that section to re-enter the 'new' First Division.

Stoke's full record of Third Division (including North) football is:

P	W	D	L	F	A	Pts
180	91	47	42	289	182	293

This is Stoke's Football League record: 1888 to 1997

P	W	D	L	F	A	Pts
3,622	1,322	892	1,408	4,796	5,219	3,784

FOOTBALL LEAGUE CUP

At the AGM of the Football League in May 1960, a proposal to introduce the Football League Cup was carried by 31 votes to 16. Entry to the competition was optional at the time, but Stoke decided to enter at the outset and have participated in the said competition ever since, winning the trophy once (in 1972).

Stoke's full record in the League Cup 1960-97 inclusive:

Venue	P	W	D	L	F	A
Home	58	27	21	10	82	51
Away	67	25	11	31	86	102
Totals	125	52	32	41	168	153

Wins and Losses
Stoke's biggest home League Cup win is 6-2 v Chelsea in 1974-75 while away their best victory has been 4-2 at Bristol Rovers in 1971-72.

Stoke's heaviest League Cup defeats have been 4-0 at home to Newcastle United in 1995 and 5-2 away at Arsenal in 1996. They lost 4-1 at Charlton in 1961.

Wembley Glory
Stoke City won the Football League Cup at Wembley on 4 March 1972, beating the favourites Chelsea 2-1 in the Final. The teams that day (in front of an attendance of 97,852) were as follows:

Chelsea: Bonetti; Mulligan (sub Baldwin), Harris; Hollins, Dempsey, Webb; Cooke, Garland, Osgood, Hudson, Houseman.
Stoke City: Banks; Marsh, Pejic; Bernard, Smith, Bloor; Conroy, Greenhoff (sub Mahoney), Ritchie, Dobing, Eastham.

Stoke scored after only five minutes when George Eastham found Terry Conroy free inside the penalty area, and the Republican of Ireland star planted a firm header past the stranded Peter Bonetti.

Then game developed into a very entertaining affair with chances being created and missed at both ends, Gordon Banks pulling off one superb save from Alan Hudson (later to play for Stoke).

The skills of Eastham and Hudson, Charlie Cooke and Peter Dobing stood out, and so did the defensive qualities of Denis Smith and Alan Bloor for Stoke and David Webb and John Dempsey for Chelsea. It was intriguing to watch.

A minute from half-time Chelsea drew level when Webb's cross found Peter Osgood, who managed to hook his shot wide of Banks as he fell to the ground.

Chelsea continued to force the pace after the interval and although

Stoke players Jimmy Greenhoff, Denis Smith, Gordon Banks and Alan Bloor celebrate with the League Cup after the victory over Chelsea in 1972.

John Ritchie had a goal ruled out for offside, Stoke had to battle to stay in the game. They did just that – and with the game racing towards a climax, they swooped to take the trophy.

The winning goal came in the 73rd minute – and it was scored by the veteran himself, Eastham. Conroy's deep cross was headed down by John Ritchie for Jimmy Greenhoff, whose shot was saved by Bonetti. The ball, though, broke free to the unmarked Eastham who drove it back into the net from five yards. Stoke had won – and how the fans celebrated.

Longest League Cup-tie

Stoke's longest League Cup-tie to date has been their semi-final clash with West Ham United in season 1971-72. The tie itself went to four matches, and it lasted a shade over seven hours. Stoke finally went through 3-2 at Old Trafford in the second replay.

Unbeaten run

Stoke were unbeaten in their first 15 home League Cup-ties (from 16 October 1963 to 15 November 1967 inclusive).

Most appearances & goals

Peter Dobing made a record 40 League Cup appearances for Stoke City and John Ritchie netted a record 18 League Cup goals.

FOOTBALL LEAGUE JUBILEE FUND

At the start of the 1938-39 and 1939-40 seasons, Stoke City played their Staffordshire rivals Wolverhampton Wanderers in two friendlies under the auspices of Football League Jubilee Fund matches. The details were:

20 August 1938   Wolves 4 Stoke City 3   Att: 18,186
19 August 1939   Stoke City 2 Wolves 4   Att: 5,289

● Dickie Dorsett hit a hat-trick for Wolves in the 1939 fixture.

FOOTBALLER OF THE YEAR

Stoke City players Stanley Matthews and Gordon Banks were voted Footballer of the Year in 1963 and 1972 respectively by the Football Writers' Association.

● Matthews, in fact, was the first player ever to receive the Footballer of the Year award, doing so in 1948 when with Blackpool.

● In 1956, Matthews (still at Bloomfield Road) had the honour of being voted the first European Footballer of the Year.

● Former Stoke City goalkeeper Peter Shilton received the PFA Player of the Year award in 1978 and the PFA Merit Award for services to football in 1990.

● Ex-Stoke City midfielder Howard Kendall was twice voted Manager of the Year when in charge at Everton: 1985 and 1987.

FORD, Anthony

When he made his Football League debut for Grimsby Town on 4 October 1975 as substitute against Walsall, Tony Ford became the youngest player ever to appear for the Mariners in a first-class game, being just 16 years, 143 days old. And he still holds that record today. Born in Grimsby on 14 May 1959, Ford joined his home-town club on leaving school in 1974 and he stayed at Blundell Park for 12 seasons, scoring 60 goals in 410 League and Cup appearances as well as having a loan spell with Sunderland (in March 1986). He moved from Grimsby to Stoke City for £35,000 on the transfer deadline of 1986 and did very well at The Victoria Ground, mainly as an orthodox outside-right, although during his career he has filled in at right-back, right-half and inside-forward. He netted 14 times in 135 outings for the Potters before switching to West Bromwich Albion for £50,000 in March 1989. He made 128 appearances in less than three years at The Hawthorns and in November 1991 returned to Blundell Park for a second spell where he added another 72 outings (3 goals) to his Mariners' collection. A loan spell with Bradford City (September/October 1993) preceded his move to Scunthorpe United in August 1994. Early in the 1996-97 season Ford joined Barrow and from there he became player-manager Steve Parkin's assistant at Mansfield Town (December 1996). Ford made well over 800 appearances at senior club level (104 goals scored). While with West Brom he gained two England 'B' caps, and during his first stint with Grimsby, gained a Third Division championship medal (1980) and a League Cup Group winners' medal (1982).

FORD, Peter Leslie

For six seasons during the 1950s Ford acted as understudy to centre-half Ken Thomson and played in 14 League games for the Potters. Born in Etruria, Stoke-on-Trent, on 10 August 1933, Ford played for Cannon Street Youth Club and was an amateur with West Bromwich Albion prior to signing professional forms for the Potters in May 1953, and even then he had to wait almost four years before making his senior debut. But being a loyal and dedicated club man, he battled on regardless and eventually left The Victoria Ground in September 1959 to sign for rivals Port Vale in a deal which also saw City's Harry Oscroft move across town in exchange for Dickie Cunliffe plus a £2,000 cash adjustment. Ford went on to make over 125 appearances for the Valiants before drifting into non-League football, having two spells with Macclesfield Town (August 1963) and also assisting Stafford Rangers, Hanley Town (as manager) and Milton United (as coach).

FORD, Stephen D.

After starting his career with Lewes, inside-forward Ford, who was born in Shoreham-on-Sea on 17 February 1959, joined Stoke City's professional staff in June 1981 for £2,000. He failed to settle down in the Potteries and after just two senior games for the club, moved on to Stafford Rangers (April 1983). Later on he served with the A.E.L. Sports club of Limasol (in Cyprus) represented Finn Harps in Ireland and also assisted two intermediate club sides in Hong Kong.

FOREIGN-BORN PLAYERS

Over the years Stoke (City) have had 15 foreign-born players registered with the club: Des Bakos (born in South Africa); George Berry (Rostrop, West Germany, but later to play for Wales); Noel Blake (Kingston, Jamaica); Hugo Da Costa (Portugal); Bruce Grobbelaar (Durban, South Africa); Jason Kearton (Ipswich, Australia); Jack Kirby (America); Toddy Orlygsson (Odense, Iceland); Paul Peschisolido (Scarborough, Canada); Hans Segers (Eindhoven, Holland); Larus Sigurdsson (Akureyri, Iceland); Mark Stein (Capetown, South Africa); Eddie Stuart (Johannesburg, South Africa); Ernie Tapai (Yugoslavia – but a naturalised Australia) and Loek Ursem (Holland).

● Stoke's very first professional foreign import was the Dutchman Loek Ursem who was recruited from AZ '67 Alkmaar for £85,000 in July 1979.

- In 1965-66 Stoke boss Tony Waddington was fined 100 guineas for fielding unsigned Swedish international Sven Larrson in the friendly match against Moscow Dynamo.

- In the summer of 1993, Stoke City manager Lou Macari signed the Icelandic midfielder Toddy Orlygsson from Nottingham Forest and then in October 1994 Macari recruited Orlygsson's cousin, Larus Sigurdsson.

- Three goalkeepers, Dutchman Hans Segers from Nottingham Forest (in February 1987), the Australian Jason Kearton from Everton (in August 1991) and the Durban-born Zimbabwean international Bruce Grobbelaar from Liverpool (March 1993) all played on loan with Stoke during the months indicated.

- Canadian international striker Paul Peschisolido was with Stoke City from August 1994 to March 1996.

- Norwegian striker Trond Egal Soltvedt had trials at The Victoria Ground in November 1994, and in this same year Stoke gave a trial to Prince Polley (South Africa), but he was not retained, leaving to join Twente Enschede in Holland, while at the start of the 1996-97 season Lou Macari gave a senior debut to the Portuguese utility player Hugo Da Costa.

- During the 1996-97 campaign Stoke had a number of players with foreign extractions turn out in their reserve, intermediate and Lancashire League teams, including Conics, Heinola, Jensen, Jermanis, Nonkavarka, Schanomaan, Solsberg, Ziukus, Gianfranco Circatti (from Cosenza), Hubert Busby and Olafur Gottskalksson.

- In 1965-66 Stoke boss Tony Waddington wanted to sign the Swede Sven Larrson and actually played him in a friendly against Moscow Dynamo. In the end permission was denied and Stoke were fined £105 for the efforts.

FORESTER, Reginald

Wing-half Forester was one of the few players to serve the Potters before, during and after World War One. Born in Penkhull in May 1892, he played for Kidsgrove Wellington before having a dozen or so games in Manchester City's reserve team (from October 1912). He signed for Stoke in September 1913 for £300 and had just one outing in the Southern League before war broke out. During the hostilities he served as a sergeant in the machine Gun Corps, being involved in the action in Mesopatamia and Russia. He was not demobbed until 1919 when he returned to The Victoria Ground, adding another seven League outings to his tally. He finally left The Victoria Ground in July 1922 to sign for Macclesfield Town, later assisting Congleton Town. Prior to taking up football Forrester trained as artist with Mintons and on retiring became decorating manager of Johnsons Brothers (Imperial Pottery) in Hanley. He died at Newcastle under Lyme on 9 December 1959.

FORMATION OF CLUB

The story goes that during the summer of 1863 a number of former pupils (believed to have attended Charterhouse School) formed a football team (it could have been to play either soccer or rugby, or both) when they were taken on as apprentices at the North Staffordshire Railway Works (Stoke),

Among them, so past reference books reveal, were the following: Armand, Bell, Matthews and Philpott. But on checking through the official Charterhouse School register: 1769 to 1872, compiled by R.L.Arrowsmith and published by Phillimore & County Ltd. in 1874, no such people are listed for that era.

However, around that time there was another school in existence called Stoke St Peter's and it is understood that the headmaster, Mr J.W. Thomas, who was also the secretary of The Victoria Athletic Club, was a very keen and active sportsman, and consequently it is quite feasible that football (soccer) was being played in the Stoke area. But little evidence exists as to whether or not any organised matches ever took place.

Then, surprisingly, five years later, in the issue of *The Field* magazine of 26 September 1868, it stated: 'At Stoke-upon-Trent a new club has been formed for the practice of the Association Rules, under the charge of H.J.Almand, one of the most prominent performers in the Charterhouse School Eleven of last year.'

The references made to both Mr Almand and to Charterhouse School are true. Yet, although the spelling of the founder himself is different, the pronunciation of 'Armand' and 'Almand' is almost identical and there is, of course, quite a huge gap between the historic formation date which was previously believed to be that of 1863 and the one given in *The Field*. (1868).

FORREST, John

Centre-forward Jack Forrest, born in Lanarkshire in September 1878, was one of the many Scots who crossed the border to try to establish themselves in English League football in the late 1890s/early 1900s. He left Motherwell for Stoke in August 1902, but played in only six matches (three goals scored) before leaving for Bradford City in May 1903. Forrest later served with Hamilton Academical (January 1906 to June 1907). He scored 24 goals in 58 games for Bradford.

FORRESTER, Thomas

No relation to Reg above, Tom Forrester was a utility forward who could play in any position. He spent just two seasons at the club, making one FA Cup appearance in October 1888 against Warwick County. Born in Stoke in June 1864, he assisted Trentham FC before joining the Potters, and Stoke St Peter's after leaving The Victoria Ground. He later had two seasons with Manchester City (October 1892 to May 1894).

FORRESTER, William

Outside-left Billy Forrester was born in Stoke in August 1869 and played in one Football League game for the club – in a 3-0 defeat at Accrington in January 1892 when he replaced Billy Dunn. He played for Hanley Town either side of his season at The Victoria Ground.

FORSYTH, Richard Michael

In 1994 Forsyth was playing in the GM Vauxhall Conference with

Richard Forsyth

Kidderminster Harriers. The following year he was battling it out in midfield for Birmingham City in the Football League, having joined Blues from Aggborough for £50,000 on 13 July 1995. A well-built, strong tackling player with a powerful right-foot shot, he went on to 41 appearances during his season at St Andrew's but when Trevor Francis replaced Barry Fry as manager, Forsyth left and joined Stoke City in July 1996 for £200,000. Prior to teaming up with Blues, he helped Harriers win the GM Vauxhall Conference and also represented the FA XI. Forsyth, who can also occupy a full-back role, was born in Dudley on 3 October 1970 and he hit 8 goals in 44 appearances in his first season at The Victoria Ground.

FOSTER, Arthur

Reserve full-back Archie Foster made seven League appearances for Stoke during his two seasons with the club (1893-95), his debut coming at Everton. Born at Fenton in September 1869, he played initially for Hanley Town and after leaving The Victoria Ground he linked up with Oswestry Town, later assisting Chirk.

FOSTER, Emmanuel

Goalkeeper Manny Foster's only game at senior level for Stoke was against Bolton Wanderers (away) in a First Division game on 11 September 1946. That day over 25,000 fans saw the Potters lose 3-2. Foster was understudy at the time to Dennis Herod, but was passed over when cricketer-footballer Arthur Jepson took over the green jersey until Herod returned. Born in Wolstanton on 4 December 1921, Foster joined the Potters from Mow Cop FC in March 1943 and made 27 appearances for the club during the wartime period. He left The Victoria Ground for Stafford Rangers in May 1947.

FOWLER, Lee

Able to play as a full-back or central defender, Fowler started off as a trainee at The Victoria Ground in 1985 and stayed at Stoke until May 1992 when he moved to Preston North End. He made 65 appearances for the Potters. Born at Eastwood, Nottingham on 26 January 1969, Fowler served with Doncaster Rovers after leaving Deepdale and later assisted Telford United.

FOX, Peter David

Fox holds the record for most appearances as a goalkeeper for Stoke City. He spent more than 15 years at The Victoria Ground – from March 1978 to July 1993 – and in that time turned out in 477 first-

Peter Fox

team matches, helping the Potters win the Autoglass Trophy at Wembley in 1992 and the Second Division championship 12 months later. A very consistent performer throughout his career, Fox was not a flashy type of player, always doing the simple things easy while dealing with the harder ones efficiently and competently. Born in Scunthorpe on 5 July 1957, he joined Sheffield Wednesday as a junior and after turning professional went on to play in 52 games for the Owls. After a loan spell with Barnsley, he left Hillsborough for The Victoria Ground for £15,000 and after a loan spell with Linfield (September/October 1992) he left the Potters for Exeter City on a free transfer in July 1993, taking over as player-manager at St James' Park in the summer of 1995. Holder of a full FA coaching badge, Fox passed the 650 appearance-mark (all levels) in 1996, the year he retired as a player to concentrate full-time as boss of the Grecians.

FRANKLIN, Cornelius

Neil Franklin was a superb centre-half, certainly one of the finest defenders ever to pull on the number-five shirt for Stoke City and, indeed, for England. Born in Shelton, Stoke-on-Trent on 24 January 1922, he starred for one of the club's nursery sides – Stoke Old Boys – before turning professional at The Victoria Ground in January 1939. Despite the war in Europe, he made tremendous progress and played in 186 games for the Potters during the hostilities as well as appearing representing England. When peacetime football returned, in 1946, he was regarded as the country's best centre-half, being positive in everything he did (tackling, passing, heading) and he went on to make 142 League and 20 FA Cup appearances for Stoke as well as adding 27 full caps to the ten he gained in wartime and Victory internationals. Franklin also represented England's 'B' team and played three times for the Football League side. In 1950, after turning down an invitation to go to the World Cup Finals with England, Franklin decided to try his luck in South America by signing for the Colombian-based club, Sante Fe of Bogota with his club-mate George Mountford. Colombia was outside the jurisdiction of FIFA and there was a lot of discussion about Franklin's move (See BOGOTA AFFAIR). The trip was short-lived, but Franklin, sadly, never played for Stoke again, and soon after his return to England was transferred to Hull City in February 1951, where he teamed up with his England colleague, Raich Carter, who was manager of the Tigers. After leaving Hull, Franklin assisted Crewe Alexandra, Stockport County and Mansfield Town, the latter briefly as player-coach. He moved into football management in August 1958, first as player-boss of Wellington Town. and then at Sankeys FC of Wellington (1961-62), retiring as a player in December 1962 having relinquished his position as manager six months earlier. After a brief spell in Cyprus, with Appoel Nicosia (February 1963) he returned to England to manage Colchester United, from November 1963 to May 1968, when he was dismissed. After leaving football, he kept a pub in the village of Oswaldtwistle and later in Sandon (near Stafford). He attended The Victoria Ground whenever possible, right up until his death, in Stoke-on-Trent on 9 February 1996.

FRASER, William

Scottish outside-right Bill Fraser played in three League games for Stoke in September 1891 at a time when the position was causing some concern. He failed to impress and moved back to his native homeland before the turn of the year, re-signing for Renton. He was born in Glasgow in June 1868.

FRIENDLY MATCHES

Down the years Stoke have played almost 1,000 friendly matches at first team level. The first (as Stoke Ramblers) was against E.W. May's XV (1-1 draw) on 17 October 1868 (at the local cricket ground in Lonsdale Street).

Stoke's first friendly win came in that same season – 2-0 against Newcastle VL.

On 28 March 1878, Stoke played – and beat – Talke Rangers 1-0 in a friendly match to officially open The Victoria Ground.

Stoke's first friendly abroad took them to Holland in April 1934 when they defeated the Swallows Club of Amsterdam by 2-1.

Teams whom Stoke have met in friendlies (but not in major competitions) include: Middlesbrough Ironopolis (twice in 1891-92),

New Brighton (Tower) (1897-98 and 1923-24), Wycombe Wanderers (1906-07) and Hereford United.

FULHAM

Stoke's playing record against the Cottagers:
Football League

Venue	P	W	D	L	F	A
Home	29	13	7	9	50	31
Away	29	9	7	13	40	55
Totals	58	22	14	22	90	86

League Cup

Venue	P	W	D	L	F	A
Home	1	1	0	0	1	0
Away	1	0	0	1	2	3
Totals	2	1	0	1	3	3

The first two League games between the clubs took place in season 1907-08 (Division Two) when Stoke won 6-1 at home yet lost 5-1 in London. That six-goal romp took place at The Victoria Ground on 21 December and is the Potters' best victory over the Cottagers to date. Freddie Brown scored a hat-trick that afternoon in front of 6,000 spectators. Stoke had earlier run up a 5-0 scoreline in January 1926 when Dick Johnson netted four times. The Potters also won 5-1 at The Vic and 5-1 at Craven Cottage in season 1927-28, Charlie Wilson scoring in both games, including a hat-trick in the home fixture in March.

'Tim' Coleman scored a hat-trick in Stoke's 4-3 League win at Fulham in November 1957.

Fulham's best League win over Stoke is 6-1 at Craven Cottage on the opening day of the 1958-59 campaign (Division Two). They also won 5-0 at Craven Cottage in September 1951 (Division One).

Stoke played Exeter City at Fulham in an FA Cup fifth qualifying round 2nd replay in December 1910 and won 2-1 before 3,000 fans.

Stanley Matthews played his last and 461st Football League game of his career against Fulham at The Victoria Ground on 6 February 1965 – five days after his 50th birthday. He helped Stoke win 3-1 in front of almost 28,600 fans.

Players with both clubs: Mickey Adams (player-manager of Fulham), Charlie Axcell, Viv Busby, Cliff Carr, John Dreyer, Frank Elliott, Ray Evans, Steve Foley, Howard Gayle, Stewart Jump, Tony Parks and Brian Talbot. ex-Stokie Jack Peart later became manager of Fulham.

FULL MEMBERS' CUP

This competition ran during the second half of the 1980s and Stoke entered on two separate occasions, their results being:
Season 1985-86
v Coventry City (home) – Won 3-0
v Millwall (away) – Draw 2-2
v Oxford United (home) – Lost 0-1
Season 1986-87
v Sheffield United (home) – Lost 1-2
Stoke's full record in the Full Members' Cup is:

Venue	P	W	D	L	F	A
Home	3	1	0	2	4	3
Away	1	0	1	0	2	2
Totals	4	1	1	2	6	5

FURSLAND, Sydney

Welsh miner Fursland was a gritty left-half who played his early football with his home-town club, Llwynpia, the village where he was born in April 1916. He graduated to become a full-time professional with Cardiff City, but stayed at Ninian Park for just a season (1934-35) before moving to Bangor City. Nine days later he was signed by Stoke City who beat off the challenge of several other League clubs for his signature. Fursland's stay at The Victoria Ground lasted for three-and-a-half years, which he spent mostly in the Reserves, making just four senior appearances and scoring one goal. He quit top-class football shortly before the outbreak of World War Two and retired in 1944.

GADSDEN, Herbert

Goalkeeper Gadsden's 76 first-team appearances for the Potters during the three seasons prior to World War One (1912-15) were made consecutively. Born at Bulwell in September 1893, he was recruited from Standen Hall Victoria (Notts & Derbyshire League) following the departure of Arthur Cartlidge and quickly established himself in the side, producing many fine displays. He was in goal for the Potters when they achieved their record FA Cup win of 11-0 v Stourbridge in 1914. Gadsden (now deceased) did not rejoin Stoke after the war, signing for Mansfield Invicta instead. He later assisted Notts Rangers.

GAINSBOROUGH TRINITY

Stoke's playing record against Trinity is:
Football League

Venue	P	W	D	L	F	A
Home	1	1	0	0	5	0
Away	1	0	0	1	0	2
Totals	2	1	0	1	5	2

FA Cup

Venue	P	W	D	L	F	A
Home	1	0	1	0	1	1
Away	2	1	1	0	5	4
Totals	3	1	2	0	6	5

The two League games between the clubs took place in season 1907-08 (Division Two) and 5,000 fans saw Tom Holford (2), Ross Fielding, Jimmy Gemmill and Mart Watkins score for the Potters in that five-goal romp at The Victoria Ground in early October.

After two evenly matched contests in a second round FA Cup-tie in February 1908, Stoke finally came through winners by 3-2.

Former Stoke City midfielder Geoff Salmons had a spell with Gainsborough Trinity (1981-82) and 1960s/70s player John Worsdale also served with both clubs.

GALLACHER, Patrick

Scottish international inside-forward 'Patsy' Gallacher cost Stoke £5,000 when manager Bob McGrory recruited him from Sunderland on 29 November 1938. Already the holder of a League Championship medal (1936) and an FA Cup winners' medal (1937), Gallacher was a fine footballer, an all-rounder, quick-thinking and fine dribbler, who could also head the ball with power. Born in Bridge of Weir,

Patsy Gallacher

Renfrewshire on 21 August 1909, he played for Linwood Schools, Linwood St Connels and Bridge of Weir FC before joining Sunderland in September 1928. Capped against Ireland in 1935 Gallacher made 307 senior appearances for the Roker Park club, scoring 108 goals. He had four League outings for the Potters before the war and in September 1939 joined the RAF He was player-manager of Weymouth for a short spell in the mid-1940s, but then retired to run a business in London, returning to Scotland as an engineer. Gallacher died at Greenock on 4 January 1992, aged 82.

GALLIMORE, Anthony Mark

After 11 games for Stoke City, whom he served from June 1988 to March 1993, and two separate loan spells with Carlisle United (October 1991 & February 1992), left-back Tony Gallimore officially joined the Cumbrian side for £15,000 in March 1993. He went on to appear in 164 games for the Brunton Park outfit, helping them win the Third Division championship in 1995. In March 1996 he was transferred to Grimsby Town for £125,000 to replace Gary Croft. Born in Crewe on 21 February 1972, Gallimore is a strong tackler who plays with coolness and competency.

GALLIMORE, George

Dribbling utility forward who was very unpredictable at times, often over-running the ball, but on his day was a fine footballer. Born in East Vale, Longton in April 1884, Gallimore played for East Vale FC before joining Stoke in May 1903, although he may well have escaped the clutches of the Potters after signing for Hanley Swifts on the wrong registration form. But Stoke quickly stepped in to bring him to The Victoria Ground. Over the next five years he scored 17 goals in 85 outings for the Potters, before leaving The Victoria Ground for Sheffield United in the summer of 1908, when Stoke went bust. He transferred to Birmingham in April 1910 and later returned to the Potteries area to assist Leek Town (1911-12) and East Vale (1912-14). Gallimore died in Stoke in 1949, aged 65.

GATE RECEIPTS

Progressive list of how the gate receipts record was broken at The Victoria Ground (1965 onwards):

£190,350	v Arsenal, Coca-Cola Cup	23 Oct 1996
£188,005	v Newcastle United, League Cup	25 Oct 1995
£129,767	v Port Vale, FA Cup	16 Nov 1992
£119,865	v Port Vale, League Division Two	24 Oct 1992
£109,056	v Liverpool, League Cup	9 Oct 1991
£96,045	v Liverpool, FA Cup	9 Jan 1988
£58,023	v Manchester United, Division One	20 Dec 1981
£43,007	v Manchester City, Division One	1 Sep 1981
£33,739	v Liverpool, Division One	23 Apr 1980
£31,673	v Sunderland, FA Cup	14 Feb 1976
£22,064	v Manchester United, FA Cup	3 Jan 1965

● In October 1891, from the home First Division League game with Aston Villa, the takings at the gate amounted to £420.

● The highest gate receipts taken from a League game at The Victoria Ground have been £176,764 v Manchester City, Division One, on 24 August 1996.

GAYLE, Howard A.

A Liverpudlian (born on 18 May 1958) Gayle was a purposeful forward with pace and good skills who scored twice in six outings for Stoke in April/May 1987 when he was on trial at The Victoria Ground. Prior to his association with the Potters, he had served, in turn, with Bedford FC (a Merseyside Sunday League side), Liverpool, Fulham, Birmingham City and Newcastle United (the last three on loan), Birmingham (again), Sunderland and Dallas Sidekicks (NASL). And after Stoke he played for Blackburn Rovers, Carlisle United (on loan), Wrexham (as a trialist) and Halifax Town. Capped three times by England at Under-21 level, he received a Milk Cup runners-up with Sunderland in 1985.

GAYLE, John

At 6ft 4ins tall and 13st 4lbs in weight, Gayle was one of the tallest and heaviest strikers in League football in the 1990s. A real beefy player, he was born in Bromsgrove on 30 July 1964 and starred for Burton Albion before making his Football League debut with Wimbledon in 1989. From Plough Lane he switched to Birmingham City for £175,000 in November 1990, and after a loan spell with Walsall and a

John Gayle

superb Wembley scoring display in for Blues in their Freight Rover Trophy triumph in 1991, he switched to Coventry City for £100,000 in September 1993. Unfortunately Gayle never fitted in at Highfield Road, or at his next club, Burnley, whom he joined in August 1994, and it was no surprise when his former boss at St Andrew's, Lou Macari, bought him to Stoke for £70,000 in January 1995, basically as a squad member. He failed to hold down a regular place in the first team at The Victoria Ground and in March 1996 was loaned out to Gillingham. After netting four goals in 33 games, Gayle left the Potters in February 1997, joining Northampton Town for £15,000. By the end of the season he had helped Northampton win promotion from Division Three.

GEE, Frederick

Centre-forward Gee scored five goals in 21 games for the Potters in two seasons with the club: 1888-1890. Born in Handsworth, Birmingham in June 1872, he played for the city's Edgbaston club before moving to Stoke and after leaving The Victoria Ground Gee served with Pershore Swifts and Kings Heath.

GEMMILL, James

Born in Glasgow in January 1880, inside-forward joined Stoke in July 1907 from Sunderland. He netted twice in 11 outings for the Potters before moving to Leeds City in December of that same year. He returned to Roker Park for a second spell in May 1910 and two years later signed for Third Lanark. In all he scored 46 goals in 227 League and FA Cup games for Sunderland

GIBBONS, Ian K.

One of the few men to make one substitute appearance for Stoke – Gibbons, a outside-right, had his only outing against Crystal Palace in April 1988. Born in Stoke-on-Trent on 8 February 1970, after leaving The Victoria Ground in June 1988 he played non-League football for Hilberry FC, Florence Colliery, Newcastle Town (two spells), Coalville Wanderers, Eastwood and Rocester.

GIBLIN, Edmund John

An amateur wartime signing by Stoke from Tunstall BC in February 1943, Giblin turned professional in April 1944 and played only one senior game for the club, as a left-half against Manchester United at Old Trafford in October 1947. He left The Victoria Ground in 1948, signing for neighbours Stafford Rangers. Giblin was born a mile from Stoke's ground on 29 June 1923.

GIDMAN, John

Gidman was a quality right-back, exceptionally quick in recovery and a player, who loved to overlap at every opportunity. Born in Garston, Liverpool on 10 January 1954, he played schoolboy football on Merseyside and joined Anfield's apprentice staff in June 1969. Not retained by Liverpool, he signed for Aston Villa as a professional in August 1971. He went on to score nine goals in 243 appearances for the Villians, gaining Youth Cup and League Cup winners' medals in 1972 and 1977 respectively as well as collecting one full England cap, four at Under-23 level, two 'B' and one with the youth team. From Villa he switched to Everton for £650,000 in October 1979 (Pat Heard was also involved in the deal) and two years later he signed for Manchester United for £450,000 (August 1981), returned to Wembley in 1985 to help the Reds win the FA Cup. A spell with Manchester City (October 1986 to August 1988) preceded his move to Stoke and during his short stay in the Potteries he made just 13 League appearances, leaving for Darlington on a free transfer in January 1989. In a long professional career Gidman, who suffered a nasty eye injury on Bonfire Night 1974 which caused him to miss the League Cup Final v Norwich City four months later, accumulated more than 500 senior appearances at club level.

John Gidman

GILLINGHAM (New Brompton)

Stoke's playing record against the Gills is:
Southern League

Venue	P	W	D	L	F	A
Home	2	1	0	1	2	2
Away	2	0	2	0	1	1
Totals	4	1	2	1	3	3

FA Cup
Home 1 1 0 0 6 1
League Cup
Home 1 1 0 0 2 0
Away 1 1 0 0 1 0
Totals 2 2 0 0 3 0

The four League encounters between the Potters and the Gills (New Brompton) took place in seasons 1911-12 & 1912-13 in the Southern League Division One. The first two resulted in a 2-0 home win for Stoke and a 1-1 away draw. The following season the 'Gills' won 2-0 at The Vic and were held 0-0 at home.

On target for Stoke in their emphatic 6-1 FA Cup victory over Gillingham in a third-round tie in January 1928 were Charlie Wilson (2), Tom Williamson, Bobby Archibald, Walter Bussey and Harry Davies. The attendance was 5,234.

The two League Cup clashes were second round affairs in 1987-88 when the Potters went through 3-0 on aggregate, Graham Shaw scoring both goals in the home leg.

Players with both clubs: Mickey Adams, Bill Godley, Jimmy Harbot, Joe Hutton, Tony Parks and Paddy Sheridan.

GLEGHORN, Nigel William

'Gleggy' as he is called, has a fine left foot and gave Stoke excellent service on the left-side of midfield for almost four years. Born in Seaham on 12 August 1962, he played for the local team, Seaham Red Star before becoming a professional with Ipswich Town (August 1985). He made 84 appearances for the Suffolk-based club up to August 1988 when he was transferred to Manchester City for £47,500. He remained at Maine Road for a season, playing in 39 first-team matches. His next move, in September 1989, took him to Birmingham City and 'Gleggy' did well at St Andrew's, amassing 176 appearances and scoring 43 goals. In October 1992, a year after helping Blues win the Freight Rover Trophy at Wembley, he joined Stoke City for £100,000, and at the end of his first season at The Victoria Ground collected a winners' medal as the Potters took the Second Division title. In the summer of 1996 'Gleggy' (after 31 goals in 208 outings) left Stoke to join Burnley on a free transfer, with Vince Overson.

NB: Gleghorn was also a capable stand-in goalkeeper.

GLOSSOP NORTH END

Stoke's playing record against Glossop is:
Football League

Venue	P	W	D	L	F	A
Home	2	2	0	0	5	0
Away	2	1	0	1	3	2
Totals	4	3	0	1	8	2

FA Cup
Home 2 2 0 0 6 0
Away 1 1 0 0 3 2
Totals 3 3 0 0 9 2

A crowd of 7,000 saw Stoke beat Glossop 4-0 at The Victoria Ground on 19 October 1907 (Division One) this being their best win of the three in that competition. Four different players scored the goals including a real crackerjack from Ross Fielding.

Stoke beat Glossop 5-0 at home in a first round FA Cup-tie in January 1897 (Willie Maxwell scored twice) and then scraped home 1-0 in a qualifying round in the 1900-01 competition.

In their away FA Cup against North End in February 1903, Stoke had to fight all the way before scraping a narrow 3-2 victory.

Players with both clubs: Peter Duber, Billy Herbert, Jack Kennedy, James Lindsay (Stoke reserve 1899), Ernie Millward and Frank Whitehouse.

GOALSCORING

Here are details of Stoke's leading goalscorers in Football League, FA Cup, Football League and wartime competitions:

Stoke's George Berry scores a spectacular goal against Arsenal on the first day of the 1982-83 season.

Football League
140 Freddie Steele
137 Frank Bowyer
135 John Ritchie
110 Charlie Wilson
106 Johnny King
103 Harry Oscroft
98 Tommy Sale
92 Harry Davies
84 Joey Schofield
82 Peter Dobing
76 Jimmy Greenhoff
75 Willie Maxwell

FA Cup
19 Freddie Steele
15 John Ritchie
13 Arty Watkin
12 Frank Bowyer
11 Jimmy Greenhoff
10 Willie Maxwell
9 Harry Davies
8 Terry Conroy
8 Stan Matthews
8 Joey Schofield
8 Charlie Wilson

League Cup
18 John Ritchie
9 Peter Dobing
9 Jimmy Greenhoff
8 Mark Stein

Wartime
179 Tommy Sale
86 Bob Whittingham
81 Freddie Steele
64 Billy Herbert
58 Alf Basnett
56 Frank Bowyer
54 Frank Mountford
42 Henry Howell
37 George Mountford
32 Bobby Liddle
(Whittingham, Herbert and Howell played in World War One)

Top 10 Stoke scorers (all competitions)
282 Tommy Sale
240 Freddie Steele
205 Frank Bowyer
176 John Ritchie
118 Charlie Wilson
113 Johnny King

107   Harry Oscroft
101   Harry Davies
101   Jimmy Greenhoff
96   Bobby Liddle

Most League & Cup Goals Scored in Season
(By team)
179   in 1910-11 (167 League, 12 FA Cup)
149   in 1909-10 (131 League, 7 FA Cup, 11 Birmingham League Cup)
104   in 1963-64 (77 League, 19 League Cup and 8 FA Cup)
96   in 1946-47 (90 League, 6 FA Cup)
95   in 1926-27 (92 in League, 3 FA Cup)
92   in 1992-93 (73 in League, 8 League Cup, 1 FA Cup, 10 AGT)

● The most goals scored by Stoke in a Football League season is 92 (1926-27).

(By player)
38   Arthur Griffiths in 1909-10 (36 League, 1 FA Cup, 1 Birmingham League Cup)
38   Charlie Wilson in 1927-28 (32 League, 6 FA Cup)
36   Freddie Steele in 1936-37 (33 League, 3 FA Cup)
35   Alf Smith in 1910-11 (31 League, 4 FA Cup)
34   Jack Peart in 1910-11 (31 League, 3 FA Cup)
33   Mark Stein in 1992-93 (26 League, 4 League Cup, 3 Autoglass Trophy)
31   Freddie Steele in 1946-47 (29 League, 2 FA Cup)

● Steele (with a total of 33) holds the record for most League goals scored in a season.

Most Goals Scored in a Game
(By team)
Football League: 10 v West Bromwich Albion (h) February 1937
FA Cup: 11 v Stourbridge (h) September 1914
League Cup: 6 v Chelsea (h) October 1975
UEFA Cup: 3 v Kaiserslautern (h) September 1972
Birmingham League: 10 v Halesowen Town (h) April 1911 Southern League: 11 v Merthyr Town (h) September 1909
Football Alliance: 6 v Birmingham. St George (h) September 1890 and Darwen (h) December 1890
Birmingham League Cup: 5 v Brierley Hill Alliance (a) October 1909
United Counties League: 5 v West Bromwich Albion (h) March 1894
Anglo-Scottish Cup: 4 v Motherwell (h) September 1971
Anglo-Italian Cup: 3 v Wolverhampton Wanderers (a) August 1993
Watney Cup: 4 v Bristol City (h) August 1973
Full Members' Cup: 3 v Coventry (h) September 1985 and Portsmouth (a) November 1987
Freight Rover Trophy: 1 v Northampton Town (h) November 1990
Autoglass Trophy: 4 v Barnet (h) January 1993
Staffordshire Cup: 26 v Mow Cop (h) September 1877
FA Youth Cup: 14 v Kidderminster Harriers (h) September 1954
Other matches: 10 v Stromsgodset (away) friendly, June 1984
World War One: 16 v Blackburn Rovers (h) November 1917
World War Two: 9 v Wolverhampton Wanderers (h) January 1944

Most Goals Scored in a Game involving Stoke:
26 – Stoke 26 Mow Cop 0 – Staffordshire Cup, 1st round, 1877-78.

No goals 'for'
Stoke failed to score in 25 of their 42 League matches in 1984-85 and were relegated from the First Division. They went eight consecutive games without a goal from 29 December to 16 March inclusive, playing three at home and five away.

When the Potters were demoted to the Second Division in 1976-77 they did so after failing to score in 24 of their 42 League games. They managed only one goal in their first 11 away games and netted only three times in the first 17. And when they went down from the Second to the Third Division in 1989-90, Stoke failed to hit the net in 22 of their 46 matches.

From 9 March to 13 April 1957, Stoke went six consecutive League games without scoring.

In their last nine League games of 1971-72 (after winning the League Cup) Stoke netted only twice (one of them an own-goal).

In 1972, Stoke failed to score in seven consecutive away games – from 24 April to 30 August.

The club's longest consecutive sequence of home games without a goal is four, achieved twice: in 1922-23 and 1924-25.

No goals 'against'
Stoke's defence did not concede a goal in five consecutive League games in 1970-71 and they repeated that feat in 1978-79.

On two occasions (1924 and again in 1932-33) Stoke went seven consecutive home League matches without conceding a goal.

In season 1969-70 Stoke kept a clean sheet in five successive away games.

Goal Talk

● The fastest goal scored by a Stoke player (from kick-off at the start of a game) was claimed by Amos Baddeley against West Bromwich Albion Reserves in a Birmingham & District League game at The Victoria Ground on 30 October 1909. The goal was timed at eight seconds. Stoke still lost the game 3-1.

● One of the quickest goals ever conceded by Stoke came after just 10 seconds, scored by Norwich City's Keith O'Neill in a Nationwide League game at Carrow Road on 12 April 1997.

● Mike Sheron set a new club record by scoring in seven successive League games for the Potters between 23 March and 17 April 1996. When he netted against Charlton Athletic at The Victoria Ground in mid-April, he broke the previous record of scoring in six games which was then shared by John Ritchie (1960s) and Harry Wilson (1920s).

● Willie Maxwell top-scored for the Potters in each of five successive First Division seasons: 1896-97 to 1900-01 inclusive.

● Freddie Steele was Stoke's leading marksmen in five seasons either side of World War Two: 1936-39 and 1946-48.

● Joey Schofield topped the Stoke scoring charts in four out of five seasons during the 1890s and Charlie Wilson was leading goal-getter four seasons on the trot (1926-30).

● Jimmy Broad (1921-24), Tommy Sale (1933-36), Frank Bowyer (1948-51), John Ritchie (1963-66 and 1969-72) all headed the Stoke City goalscoring list three years running.

- Bowyer topped the charts six times between 1948 and 1960.

- Ritchie was Stoke's leading marksman a record seven times during his two spells at The Victoria Ground.

- Two players – Dennis Viollet (22) and Jackie Mudie (20) – scored 20 or more goals for Stoke City in season 1962-63.

- Neville 'Tim' Coleman top-scored for the Potters in season 1956-57 with a total of 27 goals – all netted before 1 March – and included his haul was that seven-goal feat against Lincoln City in February 1957.

- On 9 December 1957, Stoke beat Swansea Town 6-2 in a home Second Division match, and five of the Potters' goals were scored between the 10th and 40th minutes. The Swans also scored before the interval, making it six goals in the first-half.

- During Stoke City's Third Division North championship-winning season of 1926-27, Charlie Wilson netted 19 goals in 12 games including five in a 7-0 romp against Ashington.

- In the transitional League campaign of 1945-46, Stoke's star centre-forward Freddie Steele netted 15 goals in the first 10 matches including hat-tricks against Middlesbrough (won 5-4) and Sheffield United (won 3-0).

- John Ritchie hit 13 goals in nine First Division games in the middle of the 1963-64 season, including a treble against Sheffield Wednesday whom he also served during his career.

- Wayne Biggins had a superb run of scoring 12 goals in 12 games from the start of the 1991-92 season.

GODFREY, Thomas

Scotsman Godfrey was a sturdy half-back who played for Stoke for a couple of seasons: August 1927 to April 1929. Born in Stenhousemuir in October 1904, he played for his home-town club before having 10 first-team outings for the Potters, leaving The Victoria Ground to join Walsall. After 42 outings for the saddlers in 1930-31 he went on to assist Swindon Town. Godfrey died in Redditch in December 1983.

GODLEY, William

Inside-forward Godley scored once in three senior games for Stoke after joining the club in April 1904. Reserve to Hall, Holcroft and Sheridan, he joined the Potters from Middlesbrough (whom he served since December 1902). Godley was born in Durham in September 1879 and during a lengthy career he also served with New Brompton (Gillingham) and Reading.

GODWIN, Verdi

Born in Blackburn on 11 February 1926, Godwin, a useful inside or centre-forward, played for Blackburn Rovers and Manchester City before joining Stoke City for £3,000 in June 1949. His outings were limited at The Victoria Ground and he managed only 23 first-team appearances (two goals scored) before moving on to Mansfield Town in a player/cash exchange deal in January 1950. He later assisted Middlesbrough and Grimsby Town (each time as a Trialist), Brentford, Southport, Barrow, Tranmere Rovers, Kings Lynn, Macclesfield Town, Netherfield and New Brighton. He retired from playing football in 1964, aged 38, but continued in the game itself, acting as scout for Blackpool, Chelsea, Plymouth Argyle, Liverpool (two spells), Vancouver Whitecaps, Bolton Wanderers and Wimbledon. He was perhaps responsible more than anyone else for spotting the talent of Steve Heighway, Paul Mariner and Tony Waiters (all became full internationals) and he also arranged for the Whitecaps to release Peter Beardsley to Carlisle United in 1979.

GOODWIN, David

A centre-forward and scorer of three goals in his 29 appearances for Stoke City, Goodwin was a useful performer on his day, always giving a good account of himself. Born in Nantwich on 15 October 1954, he joined Stoke City as an apprentice in 1970 and turned professional two years later. After a loan spell with Workington in October 1976, he left The Victoria Ground for Mansfield Town 13 months later and further spells followed with Bury, Rochdale and Crewe Alexandra before dropping out of League football in 1983. He later assisted Macclesfield Town, Alsager United, Kidsgrove Athletic and Hanley Town.

GORMAN, John

A proper down-to-earth Black Country inside-forward with a splendid physique and enormous willpower, Gorman scored seven goals in 17 outings for Stoke in season 1908-09 when acting as reserve striker. Born in Dudley in April 1892, he served with Old Hill, Wolverhampton Wanderers (1905-07) and Halesowen Town before joining the Potters, and after leaving The Victoria Ground he assisted Dudley Town and Cradley Heath.

GRAVER, Andrew Martin

Willington FC, Annfield Plain, Newcastle United, Lincoln City (twice) and Leicester City were Graver's clubs before he signed for Stoke City in November 1955 for £11,000. He was already an established marksmen when he moved to The Victoria Ground, having scored 111 goals in 187 League games for Lincoln, but unfortunately he never really settled with Stoke and after hitting 14 goals in 42 appearances, he was sold to Boston United for a £1,000 in September 1957. He had a third spell with Lincoln City before winding down his career at Skegness Town (from July 1961) and Ilkeston Town (July-November 1963). Between June 1964 and October 1965 he was youth-team coach at Sincil Bank and after that acted as scout for Lincoln City. Born in Craghead on 12 September 1927, centre-forward Graver, who played alongside that prolific goalscorer Arthur Rowley at Filbert Street, netted 159 goals in 325 League games (1947 to 1961).

GREAVES, Thomas

Stoke picked up robust centre-forward Greaves from the local side Goldenhill Villa in July 1908 to add cover to the front-line. He stayed at The Victoria Ground for two seasons during which time he scored five goals in 13 appearances before moving on to Hanley Swifts. In 1913 Greaves, who was born in Hanley in April 1888, also assisted Stoke as a guest during World War One and he eventually quit playing football to became a referee.

GREENHOFF, James

Jimmy Greenhoff was a quality footballer who gave Stoke supreme service over a number of years. A big favourite with the fans, he had the power to turn a match round with one fleeting movement either with his own scoring ability or with his distinctive knack of laying on a chance for a colleague. He was certainly unlucky not to have won a full England cap, for there were few better inside-forwards around when Greenhoff was at his peak. Born in Barnsley on 19 June 1946, the elder brother of Brian (ex-Leeds and Manchester United) Greenhoff senior, did well with Barnsley Schools and Yorkshire Boys before scoring 21 goals in 94 League games for Leeds United, whom served from 1961 (as an apprentice) until August 1968. In this same year he won a League Cup winners' medal (v Arsenal) as well as playing in the first leg of that year's Fairs Cup Final v Ferencvaros which United eventually won. Greenhoff was then transferred to Birmingham City for £70,000 and spent a season at St Andrew's, hitting 15 goals in 36 senior outings for the Blues. In August 1969, Tony Waddington lured him to Stoke for £100,000 and immediately he made an impact in the Potteries. In 1972 he was a key member of City's League Cup winning side and his seven-year stay at The Victoria Ground yielded 101 goals in 338 first-team appearances. After leaving the Potters for Old Trafford in a £120,000 deal in November 1976 (reluctantly it must be said, although the club had a financial problem at the time) Greenhoff went on to score 36 goals in 122 outings for the Reds, gaining an FA Cup winners' medal in 1977 (when he scored against Liverpool) and a loser's medal two years later. He switched to Crewe Alexandra in December 1980, and later had a brief spell at manager at Gresty Road. Thereafter he went to Canada to play for Toronto Blizzard, and rounded off his career with two seasons at Port Vale (1981-83) and a term as player-manager of Rochdale, returning as coach at Vale Park. Greenhoff finished with a League record of 146 goals in 571 appearances and besides winning five England Under-21 caps, he also represented the Football League XI. After retiring in May 1984, he spent a few months coaching youngsters at various Butlins Holiday Camps while also working as an insurance broker. He now lives in Alsager.

NB: Greenhoff's terrific volleyed goal for Stoke in a 3-0 win over his former club Birmingham City at St Andrew's in December 1974, was duly voted Goal of the Season on ATV.

GREGG, Henry

Four months after surviving the Munich air crash, Harry Gregg was proving himself one of the finest goalkeepers in the game when he excelled between the posts for Northern Ireland in the 1958 World Cup Finals in Sweden. In that competition he was superb as the Irish reached the quarter-finals. Gregg had performed heroically on that snow-covered air strip in Germany, helping dazed and injured survivors from the wreckage, going back several times to have a last look to see if anyone was in trouble. He was praised highly for his noble efforts. Born in Magherafelt, County

Derry on 25 October 1932, and a former schoolboy international, he won amateur caps for Ireland and represented the Irish League as a Coleraine player prior to signing professional forms for Doncaster Rovers in October 1952. He won nine full caps whilst with Second Division Rovers and was noted for his habit of standing well outside the penalty area urging his team on as they attacked. After 93 League games for the Belle Vue club Gregg was transferred to Manchester United for a then British record fee for a goalkeeper of £23,500 in December 1957. Five months later he was controversially bundled over the goal-line by Bolton's Nat Lofthouse in the FA Cup Final. After 24 games for his country Gregg was eventually replaced by Pat Jennings. In all Gregg played in 247 competitive games for the Reds up to December 1966 when he joined Stoke City. But a severe shoulder injury restricted him to just two outings for the Potters whom he left in May 1967 to become manager of Shrewsbury Town. He subsequently took charge of Swansea City and Crewe Alexandra, coached the Kiton Sports Club (Kuwait) and for a short time was assistant to Lou Macari at Swindon Town before losing his job in a clash of personalities.

GREGORY, David H.

Gregory, a utility forward, spent 14 years in League football (1973-87) during which time he scored for the following teams: Peterborough United (his home-town club – born on 6 October 1951), Stoke City (June 1977 to September 1978), Blackburn Rovers (on loan from Stoke), Bury, Portsmouth, Wrexham and Peterborough (again). His first club was Chatteris Town and after leaving Posh in 1987, he assisted Kings Lynn. Gregory hit four goals in 25 outings for Stoke, who paid £50,000 for his signature from London Road and then sold him to Bury for £30,000.

GREWER, James

Jimmy Grewer played 84 times in Stoke's first XI between June 1894 and December 1897, being the first Potters' player to pass the 75 appearance mark in the centre-half position. A powerful defender, born in Dundee in February 1865, he joined the Potters from Sunderland Albion having previously been associated with Middlesbrough Ironopolis. He left The Victoria Ground for Gravesend & Northfleet, retiring in 1902. He died c.1950.

GRIEVE, James

Defender Jock Grieve was born in Edinburgh in April 1887 and after moving south from Scotland he was suspended sine die by the FA after being sent-off as a Watford player. earlier in his career he served with Hibernian and Distillery (Belfast) and joined Stoke from Watford for £200 in August 1911. He scored once in 24 League and Cup games for the Potters before transferring north to South Shields in the summer of 1912. He later returned to Scotland where he died c.1955.

GRIFFIN, Andrew

Left-back Griffin made his senior debut following injuries to Nigel Worthington and the sale of John Dreyer during the first part of the 1996-97 season. Born on 7 March 1979, in Rugby League territory at Wigan, he joined Stoke's YTS ranks on leaving school and made rapid progress into the first XI, much to the delight of his manager and coaches. In February 1997 Griffin was called up to the England Under-18 squad and was later named in the Under-20 party for the mini World Cup in Malaysia. When the season ended he had taken his total of appearances record with Stoke up to 36 (1 goal).

GRIFFITHS, Arthur

Griffiths had two spells at The Victoria Ground as a goalscoring outside-right or inside-forward. Born at Hartshill in February 1885, he played junior football in the Potteries before initially signing for Stoke on 24 September 1905. His first spell lasted three years, Griffiths joining the exodus of players who left the The Victoria Ground when the Potters went out of the League at the end of the 1907-08 campaign. He quickly returned to big-time football, however, by signing for Oldham Athletic (5 August 1908) and scored four goals in 25 games for the Latics prior to his return to Stoke in June 1909. Three years later he went to Wrexham (15 August 1912) and retired in 1915. All told for Stoke Griffiths netted 51 times in 121 games, top-scoring in 1909-10 with 38 goals. On his second debut for the club, he hit a hat-trick in an 11-1 Southern League win over Merthyr Town (September 1909). Army officer Griffiths spent 20 months serving in the trenches in France during World War One as well as guesting for Oldham in 1917. He died c.1944.

GRIFFITHS, Arthur

No relation to any of the Griffithses, Archie played four League games for the Potters in November/December 1938, taking over from Frank Baker on the left-wing. Born in Tonypandy in September 1915, his career saw him serve with Torquay United, Barry Town, Cheltenham, Newry Town, Glenavon and Alexander Rochdale before he found his way to The Victoria Ground in the summer of 1938. He left Stoke when World War Two broke out and played non-League football prior to his retirement after the hostilities.

GRIFFITHS, Edwin

Griffiths (an amateur throughout his career) was an orthodox outside-right who scored once in 11 games for Stoke between August 1908 and May 1910. Born in Hanley in February 1883, and an Old

Carthusian, educated at Charterhouse School, he played for North Staffs Nomads prior to joining the Potters and after leaving The Victoria Ground returned to the Nomads.

GRIFFITHS, Peter J.

Scorer of five goals in 64 senior appearances for Stoke City between November 1980 and July 1984, Griffiths was born in Barnstaple, Devon on 14 August 1957 and was being chased by a number of clubs while playing for Bideford Town during the late 1970s. But he chose the Potters and did well during his three and a half years at The Victoria Ground. A loan spell with Bradford City preceded his departure from Stoke to Port Vale in July 1984, and from there he went to Australia to play for Salisbury United, returning later to that country to assist Newcastle K.B. (May 1986). Griffiths also played for Stafford Rangers, Northwich Victoria, Matlock Town, Milton United and Nantwich Town.

GRIMES, Ashley A.

During his playing career red-haired Grimes was capped 17 times by the Republic of Ireland at senior level and twice by the Under-21s. A midfielder, winger or full-back, he played for the Bohemians, made over 100 appearances for Manchester United (1977-83), had more than 30 outings for Coventry City and turned out in 75 League matches for Luton Town before assisting Osasuna in Spain (1988). He returned to England to join Stoke City in December 1991 and had 15 outings (one goal scored) prior to his retirement in June 1992, following a serious knee injury. Grimes, who was born Dublin on 2 August 1957, and a close friend of Lou Macari's (they played together at Old Trafford) then concentrated on the coaching side at The Victoria Ground and went briefly to Celtic with Macari, before returning with his manager in October 1994.

GRIMSBY TOWN

Stoke's playing record against the Mariners:

Football League

Venue	P	W	D	L	F	A
Home	25	16	6	3	51	14
Away	25	6	10	9	32	35
Totals	50	22	16	12	83	49

Football Alliance

Home	1	1	0	0	2	1
Away	1	0	1	0	1	1
Totals	2	1	1	0	3	2

FA Cup

Home	3	2	1	0	9	1
Away	1	0	1	0	1	1
Totals	4	2	2	0	10	2

Stoke's best Football League win over the Mariners is 5-0 (h) in March 1908 (Division Two), while Grimsby's best was their 4-1 success at Blundell Park in August 1956, also in Division Two.

On Christmas Day 1937, Stoke beat Grimsby 5-1 at The Victoria Ground and then ran up a 5-2 victory at Blundell Park in April 1947 when Freddie Steele struck a hat-trick. The first two meetings between the clubs at League club took place in 1901-02 (Division Two) when Stoke won 2-1 away and 2-0 at home, Mart Watkins scoring in both games.

Stoke met Grimsby three times in a third-round FA Cup-tie in January 1987 and after two 0-0 draws the Potters finally went through 6-0 at The Victoria Ground when both Nicky Morgan and Carl Saunders scored twice. The crowd was 12,087.

In season 1895-96 Stoke visited Grimsby and were beaten 7-6 in a highly entertaining friendly.

Players with both clubs: Phil Bonnyman, Tommy Cain, Tom Coxon, Steve Foley, Tony Ford, Verdi Godwin, Joe Johnson, Sam McAllister, Harry Mellor, Mark Prudhoe, Paul Reece, Brian Rice, Fred Rouse, Jimmy Swarbrick and Tom Ward.

Ford holds the record for being the youngest League debutant for Grimsby. He was 16 years, 143 days old when he came on as a substitute against Walsall on 4 October 1975 (See AGE).

Bobby Roberts was manager of Grimsby Town (1987-88) and later coach at Stoke City.

GROBBELAAR, Bruce David

Born in Durban, South Africa, on 6 October 1957, goalkeeper Bruce Grobbelaar played his early football with Vancouver Whitecaps and after a trial with West Bromwich Albion, he joined Crewe Alexandra (on loan). He continued to impress in the NASL (with the Whitecaps) and in 1981, Liverpool paid £250,000 for his services to bring him to Anfield. With the Reds he did exceedingly well and went on to win medals galore as well as massing 628 senior appearances for the Merseysiders up to August 1994 when he was transferred to Southampton. In March 1993, he came to Stoke on a month's loan and

Ashley Grimes

made four League appearances. Three years later he left The Dell to join Second Division newcomers Plymouth Argyle, carrying on his shoulders the burden that he was under suspicion for match-fixing. In January/February/March 1997, Grobbelaar, along with fellow goalkeeper Hans Segers, striker John Fashanu and a Malaysian businessman, Heng Suan Lim, appeared at Winchester Crown Court accused of match-rigging. The jury could not reach a decision and a re-trial was ordered for later in the year.

GROVES, Frederick

Groves developed his skills in local junior football in his native Lincoln playing for South Bar FC before joining the professional ranks at Sincil Bank in August 1909. In July 1910 he switched to Worksop Town and in June 1911 was signed by Sheffield United for £100. A hard-working inside-right, he left Bramall Lane for Huddersfield Town in August 1912 for £50 and a year later returned for a second spell with Worksop. In the last season before World War One Groves assisted Portsmouth and in 1919 he teamed up with Tranmere Rovers, eventually signing for Stoke for £750 in November 1921. He made his debut four hours after signing for the Potters, lining up against Notts County. Sadly he failed to settle in at The Victoria Ground and after scoring 13 goals in 46 appearances, he was sold to Crystal Palace for £250 in August 1924. Before retiring in 1928, Groves served with Rhyl Athletic and Sutton Town (Notts). He was born in Lincoln on 6 May 1892 and died in that city on 8 December 1980.

GUEST PLAYERS

Stoke, like every major club in the country, utilised guest players during the First and Second World Wars, while at the same time, several Stokies guested for other clubs. During World War One period of 1915-18, Stoke were blessed with the services of England internationals Sid Bowser (WBA) and Harry Hampton (Aston Villa) while in World War Two, they recruited Edwin Blunt (Northampton Town), John Boothway (Manchester City), Arthur Cunliffe (Hull City), Harry Griffiths (Port Vale), Jack Griffiths (Manchester United), Lol Hamlett (Bolton Wanderers), Eric Hayward (Blackpool), Eric Longland (local), George Marks (Arsenal), Les Micklewright (Stafford Rangers), John Oakes (Charlton), Tom Pearson (Newcastle United), Billy Pointon (Port Vale), Jim Simpson (Chesterfield), Billy Tunnicliffe (Bournemouth), Emlyn Williams (Preston), Sid Williams (Bristol City) and Horace Wright (Wolverhampton Wanderers) along with ex-Stokies Doug Jones (Carlisle), Charlie Scrimshaw (Middlesbrough), Arthur Turner (Birmingham) and Harry Ware (Norwich), plus a few others.

Stoke players who guested for other clubs included: George Antonio (Aldershot, Leeds, Nottingham Forest, Notts County and Wrexham), Frank Baker (Linfield and Wrexham), Alf Basnett (Crewe), Fred Basnett (Derry City and Northampton), Frank Bowyer (Derby County), Harry Brigham (Derby County and Wrexham), Jack Challinor (Derby County, Doncaster, Leeds, Nottingham Forest and Notts County), Neil Franklin (Wolves and Wrexham), Sid Fursland (Cardiff and Swansea), Patsy Gallacher (Charlton, Crystal Palace, Dundee, Fulham, Luton and Notts County), Eric Hampson (Fulham), Dennis Herod (Wrexham), Jock Kirton (Leeds, Nottingham Forest and Notts County), Stan Matthews (Blackpool and Wrexham), Billy Mould (Linfield), Frank Mountford (Derby County), George Mountford (Crewe and Kidderminster Harriers), George Oldham (Derry City), Alec Ormston (Linfield and Middlesbrough), Syd Peppitt (Linfield, Middlesbrough and Newcastle), Tommy Sale (Wrexham), Clem Smith (Arsenal, Charlton, Clapton Orient, Crewe, Fulham, Halifax, Leicester, Rotherham, Southampton, Watford, West Ham and Wrexham), Frank Soo (Blackburn, Brentford, Chelsea, Everton, Millwall, Reading and Wrexham), Freddie Steele (Bradford Park Avenue, Doncaster, Leeds, Leicester, Northampton, Nottingham Forest, Notts County and Sheffield United), Jack Tennant (Southport and Wrexham), Arthur Tutin (Crewe and Wrexham), Doug Westland (Nottingham Forest and Raith), Jim Westland (Doncaster), Norman Wilkinson (Doncaster, Sheffield Wednesday and Nottingham Forest) and George A.Wright (Port Vale).

GYNN, Michael

An industrious midfielder, born in Peterborough on 19 August 1961, Gynn played in 156 League games for his home-town club before joining Coventry in August 1983. He stayed at Highfield Road for ten years, making more than 240 senior appearances for the Sky Blues and gaining an FA Cup winners' medal in 1987. In August 1993 he joined the Potters, but stayed only a season at The Victoria Ground, adding 28 more outings to his tally prior to assisting Kings Lynn, Stamford and Corby Town (February 1997).

HACKETT, Gary Stuart

Right or outside-left Gary Hackett started out with local sides Lye Town and Bromsgrove Rovers before signing full-time professional forms for Shrewsbury Town in 1983 at a fee of £5,000. From Gay Meadow he went to Aberdeen for £80,000 in 1987 and a year later was secured by Stoke City for £110,000 (March 1988). He spent two years at The Victoria Ground, scoring seven goals in 84 games for the Potters before transferring to West Bromwich Albion for £70,000. Hackett, a useful club cricketer with Belbroughton CC, next played for Peterborough United and after a spell with Chester City, he went back into non-League football with Stourbridge (one game) and Halesowen Town (mid-1990s). He was born in Stourbridge on 11 October 1962.

HAINES, Wilfred Henry

A short, stocky outside-right, born at Stone in June 1882, Haines played for Mount Pleasant Alliance and Newcastle Swifts before having a season with Stoke (1905-06) during which time he played in three League games. He then assisted Hanley Swifts and Stafford Rangers, up to July 1908, when he signed for Birmingham for £250. Like at The Victoria Ground, he failed to impress at St Andrew's and left Blues for Leek United in August 1909, later having a second spell at Stafford Rangers. He retired in 1915.

HALES, Herbert

Herby Hales was a busy outside-left with a sound understanding of the game who loved to hug the touchline. Born in Kettering in July 1908, he played his early football with Peterborough & Fletton United, joining Stoke in August 1930 as reserve to Bob Archibald. He made only one League appearance for the Potters (v Bradford City at home on Boxing Day 1930) and at the end of that season was transferred to Preston North End. He played over 60 times for the Deepdale club and later assisted Nottingham Forest, Chesterfield and Stockport County (22 appearances in 1934-35) before retiring during the war.

HALES, Leonard

An amateur inside-forward from Crewe, Len Hales had two spells with the Potters, the first on loan, and totalled 20 senior appearances (scoring four goals). Born in February 1872, he was registered with Crewe Alexandra from 1889 and played on loan with the Potters in December 1898. He returned to Crewe before having a much longer stay at The Victoria Ground (from August 1901-to April 1902). He was injured during his latter weeks with Stoke and decided to retire at the age of 30. He later went into business in Northwich.

HALESOWEN (Town)

Stoke's playing record against Halesowen:
Southern League

Venue	P	W	D	L	F	A
Home	3	2	0	1	14	1
Away	3	1	0	2	2	4
Totals	6	3	0	3	16	5

These six matches were all played in the Birmingham & District League over a three-year period: 1908-11. Stoke's best win of the three they registered was a 10-1 scoreline at The Victoria Ground on 8 April 1911 when Alf Smith (5) and Albert Savage (3) led the goal rush in front of 10,500 fans.

Players with both clubs: Gary Hackett and Sean Flynn.

HALIFAX TOWN

Stoke's playing record against Halifax is:
Football League

Venue	P	W	D	L	F	A
Home	1	1	0	0	5	1
Away	1	0	1	0	2	2
Totals	2	1	1	0	7	3

FA Cup

Venue	P	W	D	L	F	A
Home	1	0	1	0	1	1
Away	2	1	0	1	3	1
Totals	3	1	1	1	4	2

League Cup

Venue	P	W	D	L	F	A
Home	1	1	0	0	3	0

Stoke's home win was an emphatic 5-1 victory in their last Third Division North match in the championship-winning season of 1926-27. A crowd of 10,280 at The Victoria Ground saw Harry Davies (2), Johnny Eyres (2) and Bob Archibald score for the Potters. Archibald also scored at Halifax earlier in the season. Terry Conroy hit a hat-trick in Stoke's 3-0 home League Cup second-round victory over Halifax in September 1974 when the crowd was 17.805.

Players with both clubs: Wilf Chadwick, Jeff Cook, Howard Gayle, Ellis Hall, Tony Kelly, Mick Kennedy, Jim Martin, Fred Pentland, Alex Raisbeck, Ronnie Sinclair, Clem Smith and Roy Vernon.

Alan Ball senior had two spells as manager of Halifax Town and was also coach at Stoke (1972).

HALL, Ellis

Hall was a rock solid centre-half, powerful in the air, strong on the ground who was described in some circles as being a 'rare spoiler'. He was born in Ecclesfield near Sheffield on 22 June 1889 and was 38 years of age when he finally hung up his boots after a long and reasonably successful career. He started out with local church side Ecclesfield Bible Class FC in 1906 before joining Hull City. Unfortunately he failed to make an impression with the Humberside club, and left for Hastings, later playing one game for Millwall (v Crystal Palace in December 1907) prior to signing for St Leonard's. He joined Stoke from the latter club in the summer of 1909 and his debut came in an 11-0 win over Merthyr Town. Hall stayed only a season at The Victoria Ground during which time he scored four goals in 49 competitive matches, helping the Potters win the Southern League Division Two (Western) title. In June 1910 he moved to Huddersfield Town and followed up with spells at South Shields, Goole Town (guest), Hamilton Academical, Halifax Town, Rochdale and Consett. Hall played in more than 100 senior games for Hamilton and in 115 League matches for Halifax. He officially retired in 1927 and died in 1949 after a short illness.

NB: His brothers Harry (Hull City) and Ben (Derby County) both played professional football.

HALL, John Henry

Despite standing only 5ft 9ins tall, Jack Hall was terrific marksman whose career took him all over the country, starting with Hucknall Boys Club in 1898 and ending with Hucknall Town in 1917. In between times he served with Newark Town, Nottingham Forest (as a trialist), Mansfield Town (also on trial), Stoke (from October 1904 to June 1906), Brighton & Hove Albion, Middlesbrough, Leicester Fosse and Birmingham (for £750, December 1910-May 1915). All told he registered more than 150 goals at club level including 48 in 103 appearances for Birmingham and 18 in 55 games for the Potters. After World War One he went over to Holland to coach Feyenoord. Hall was born at Hucknall (Notts) on 3 July 1883 and died in Nottingham in 1938.

HALL, Victor

Amateur half-back Vic Hall spent a fortnight on loan at The Victoria

Ground and played once in Stoke's first team – against Aberdare at home in November 1910 (Southern League). Now deceased, he was born in Ashton c.1886 and was registered with Macclesfield at the time he served with the Potters.

HALL, Wilfred

Goalkeeper Hall was born near Haydock Park racecourse on 14 October 1934. Despite his height (only 5ft 8ins) he was well built, with good reflexes and a safe pair of hands. He played initially for Earlstown FC before joining Stoke City in October 1953, vying with Bill Robertson for a first-team place and having 45 games on loan for Worcester City in season 1954-55. In fact, he took 18 months to break into the Potters' first XI and then went on to appear in 57 League and Cup games for the Potters, up to June 1960, when he was transferred to Ipswich Town for £2,000 after six-and-a-half years with the club. He stayed at Portman Road for two seasons, making 16 League appearances (as deputy to Roy Bailey) before rounding off his career in non-League football with Stafford Rangers Two spells), Altrincham and Macclesfield Town.

HALLAM, Clifford Charles

Inside-forward Charlie Hallam was born in Longton on 17 January 1902. He played for Sandford Hill Primitives, once for Port Vale (in November 1922) and had two separate spells with Sandbach Ramblers prior to joining Stoke in August 1924. He stayed three years at The Victoria Ground, mainly as a reserve, and was given 33 senior outings (two goals scored). He played in 10 League games when the Potters won the Third Division North title in 1926-27. Hallam left Stoke for Crystal Palace in June 1927 and after scoring twice in two games for the Londoners was transferred a year later to Stafford Rangers, later assisting Hednesford Town. He died at Fenton on 20 March 1970.

HAMNETT, Abraham Samuel

Enterprising outside-right from Runcorn (born in February 1882) Abe Hamnett played nine games for Stoke in the Birmingham & District League during the second half of the 1909-10 season after transferring from Birkenhead FC. He left The Victoria Ground after just six months and signed for Annfield Plain, later serving with Crewe All Saints.

HAMNETT, Robert

No relation to Abe (above) Bob Hamnett, also an outside-right, was born in Manchester in April 1889 and appeared in five Southern League games for Stoke between January and April 1914, scoring two goals, both against Mardy (away – won 2-1). He joined the club on a short-term basis from Fenton FC and left The Victoria Ground for Burslem United, later assisting Ashton Rangers.

HAMPSON, Eric

Defender Hampson joined Stoke as a professional in May 1939 after serving with Summerbank. During the war he guested for Fulham and stayed at The Victoria Ground until 1952. Born at Norton on 11 November 1921, he played most of his football in the Reserves, and was given just eight League appearances by manager Bob McGrory, his debut coming against Manchester City on New Year's Day 1949 when he took over at right-back from Billy Mould. His other outings were all at right-half. He left the Potters for Stafford Rangers whom he later managed.

HAMPTON, Peter John

Former England youth international left-back with pace, good ball control and excellent temperament, Hampton appeared in 156 League and Cup games for the Potters during a four-year stay at The Victoria Ground (August 1980 to August 1984). Born in Oldham on 12 September 1954, he joined Leeds United as a teenager and moved to The Victoria Ground for £165,000 after 68 First Division outings for the Yorkshire club. He left the Potters for Burnley and later assisted Rochdale and Carlisle United, becoming trainer/physiotherapist at Brunton Park in 1993. Hampson played in 355 League games during his career.

HARBEY, Graham Keith

Stoke boss Lou Macari paid £80,000 for Graham Harbey from West Bromwich Albion in August 1992. The left-back was out of contract at The Hawthorns, and his manager at the time of his move, Ossie

Ardiles, was ironically giving evidence against Macari at court and the two bosses were not allowed to speak to each other. The fee was fixed by tribunal. Born in Chesterfield on 29 August 1964. Harbey signed apprentice forms for Derby County as a 16-year-old and turned professional at The Baseball Ground in August 1982. He played in 40 League games for the Rams before moving to Ipswich Town in July 1987. After a bout of injuries and 28 outings for the Potters, Harbey left The Victoria Ground in the summer of 1994. He had trails with Exeter City and Gresley Rovers before joining Burton Albion for the 1994-95 season.

HARBOT, James Willie

Lancastrian Jimmy Harbot played amateur football for the Royal Naval Depot (Chatham) and Gillingham before signing professional forms for Charlton Athletic in August 1932. Then a forward, he was quickly converted into a hard-tackling full-back, but starred in only one League game for the Addicks, scoring in a 1-1 draw at Manchester United in September 1932. In August 1933 he moved from The Valley to Barrow and spent a season at Holker Street before switching to Stoke City in May 1934. He was freed at the end of the 1936-37 campaign after making just two senior outings for the Potters, his only League game coming in that epic 10-3 win over West Bromwich Albion in February 1937. Harbot, who was born in Bolton on 16 August 1907, signed for Torquay United on leaving Stoke (May 1937) and later assisted Chorley Town (1938-39). In his long career he made only 42 League appearances, spending most of his time playing reserve-team football.

HARDING, William

Right-half Harding made five Birmingham & District League appearances for Stoke at the start of the 1908-09 season. Born in Hanley in July 1883, he played Wolstanton RS prior to his brief association with the Potters and after leaving the The Victoria Ground he served with Ribbendale.

HARDMAN, Harold Payne

Amateur outside-left Hardman was one of the Edwardian game's finest footballers. Small and elusive, he was a confident, ball-player with pace, strong shot and an appetite for hard work. Born at Kirkmanshulme, Manchester on 4 April 1882, he served with Blackpool and Everton early in his career, and won an Olympic Games soccer Gold Medal for Great Britain in 1908, the year he left Goodison Park to join Manchester United. He had also appeared for England in 10 amateur and four senior internationals, helping his country beat France 16-0 in Paris in an amateur encounter in 1906-07. Hardman appeared in successive FA Cup Finals for the Merseysiders (1906 and 1907) earning a winners' medal in the latter, thus joining Manchester City's Sam Ashworth (another ex-Stokie) and the Reverend Kenneth Hunt of Wolverhampton Wanderers, as the only amateurs to win such medals this century. Hardman made only four appearances during his brief spell at Old Trafford and after assisting Bradford City, he signed for Stoke in February 1911. He did well at The Victoria Ground and scored ten goals in 55 appearances for the Potters before announcing his retirement in 1913. After World War One he went on to become one of the game's greatest administrators. A solicitor with offices in the centre of Manchester, he was chairman at Old Trafford from 1951 until his death in June 1965 when he was succeeded by Louis Edwards, father of the current United chairman, Martin. Hardman was also an FA councillor, president of the Lancashire FA and was associated with the Central League. Thankfully he chose not to travel with the Manchester United party to Yugoslavia for the game against Red Star Belgrade in February 1958 when, of course, on the homeward journey, the plane crashed at Munich air port.

HARGREAVES, Frederick J.

Hargreaves was a fine amateur centre-forward who scored twice on his Birmingham & District League debut for Stoke against Wrexham in December 1908. Born in North Yorkshire in June 1884, he played for Leeds City before agreeing to assist Stoke, and after receiving a serious leg injury, he decided to quit competitive football in the summer of 1909, although he did play at a lower level until the outbreak of World War One.

HARGREAVES, Henry

No relation to Fred (above) Harry Hargreaves was a local man, born in Wolstanton in August 1893 who played outside-right for Newcastle Town before joining Stoke in August 1912. He was one of the quickest players of his time, especially over 20-30 yards but after scoring four goals in 38 first-team games for the Potters he was sadly killed in action during World War One (1916).

HARRIS, George

Inside-left Harris made his Stoke debut in a 6-1 League defeat at Sunderland in November of 1900, and at the halfway stage of the following campaign he had established himself in the first team. He went on to score three times in 15 matches, but then managed just seven League outings (2 goals) in 1902-03 before transferring to Reading (May 1904). He blossomed at Elm Park (11 goals in 28 games) and this form led to him taking part in an England international trial. From May 1905 to May 1907 he made 48 appearances for Southampton (nine goals) but then surprisingly announced his retirement from first-class football to take over a hostelry in Tutbury near Burton upon Trent. In 1908-09 he had occasional game for the local side Tutbury Town. Harris was born in Rocester c.1878 and played his early football with Uttoxeter Town.

HARRISON, Mark Simon

Harrison's chances of keeping goal for Stoke on a regular basis were severely restricted owing to the presence of Peter Fox. Born in Derby on 11 December 1960, he was a junior at the Baseball Ground and with Nottingham Forest, and an apprentice with Southampton, turning professional at The Dell in 1978. He failed to break into Saints' first team and moved to Port Vale in February 1980. From there he switched to The Victoria Ground (in August 1982) in a £150,000 joint deal involving Mark Chamberlain (Harrison's fee being levelled out at £15,000). But owing to a troublesome knee injury (and Fox) he managed only eight senior appearances for the Potters before transferring to Cape Town City (South Africa) in November 1983. He later played for Hellenic (SA). Kettering Town, Stafford Rangers and Telford United. He then became manager of the South African club, Clyde before returning to England as youth-team coach at Bristol City, later taking over as goalkeeping coach at Everton, before becoming assistant manager-coach of Barrow, serving as player-manager of Stafford Rangers and then as reserve-team coach at Oxford United. Harrison received an insurance pay-out for the injury received whilst at Stoke.

HARTLEPOOL (United)

Stoke's playing record against the Pool is:

Football League

Venue	P	W	D	L	F	A
Home	3	2	0	1	6	4
Away	3	2	1	0	6	3
Totals	6	4	1	1	12	7

FA Cup

Home	1	1	0	0	6	2

The first two meetings took place during Stoke's Third Division North championship-winning campaign of 1926-27 and the Potters won them both by the same scoreline of 3-1. Charlie Wilson netted twice in each game.

A crowd of almost 24,000 witnessed the third round FA Cup-tie at Stoke in January 1954 when Frank Bowyer scored four times for in-form City.

Players with both clubs: Joe Butler, George Daniels, Kenny Lowe, Carl Muggleton, Charlie Parker, Mark Prudhoe, Barry Siddall and Ken Thomson.

Ex-Stoke striker Viv Busby managed Hartlepool United during the early 1990s.

HARTSHORNE, Arthur

Stoke swooped to sign bulky full-back Hartshorne and his colleague Teddy Holdcroft from neighbours Burslem Port Vale in April 1903. A fine defender, strong and resourceful, Hartshorne was born at Moxley near Darlaston in December 1880, and played for Moxley White Star and then Wolverhampton Wanderers (December 1900 to June 1902) before having over 30 outings for the Vale. A well-built player, who occasionally looked overweight, he could be quite brilliant at times and his performances belied his bulky frame. He went on to appear in 56 League and Cup games for the Potters and after leaving The Victoria Ground, in April 1905 had two weeks with Aston Villa before signing for Southampton. He made 30 appearances for Saints, but never really settled in the south of England and moved to Northampton Town in May 1906. He died c.1945.

HASLEGRAVE, Sean M.

Haslegrave scored eight goals in 139 senior appearances for Stoke City between 1968 and 1976. A local midfielder (born 7 June 1951) he left The Victoria Ground for Nottingham Forest for £35,000 and after serving with Preston North End, York City (two spells), Crewe Alexandra and Torquay United, he pulled out of League football in 1988 with almost 600 senior outings under his belt (491 in the Football League).

HASSALL, Charles

Solidly-built goalkeeper who played in one FA Cup-tie for Stoke, deputising for Billy Rowley against Warwick County in October 1888 (lost 1-2). Born in Hanley in June 1863 Hassall spent only one season with the club having previously assisted Jude's FC He left for Leek Town.

HAT-TRICKS

Over the years Stoke players between them have scored 192 hat-tricks in competitive matches (including wartime Regional games). Here is a breakdown:

Competition	Total
Football League	88
FA Cup	16
Football Alliance	1

Autoglass Trophy	1
Southern League	22
Birmingham League	7
Birmingham League Cup	1
World War One	15
World War Two	41
Total	192

Hat-trick Talk

● Tommy Sale has scored most hat-tricks for Stoke City – 28 in all competitions during his two spells with the club: 1930-36 and 1938-45. Twenty-three of his trebles were claimed in wartime football with 12 coming in 1941-42, which included a six-timer (a double hat-trick) v Walsall a League Cup qualifying game.

● England international Freddie Steele hit 24 hat-tricks for the Potters, ten during wartime football including an FA Cup treble v Bolton in 1945-46. He, too, scored a 'six-timer' against Wolves in 1942-43 as well as two 'fives' in Football League action, versus West Bromwich Albion (in a 10-3 victory in February 1937) and against Derby County the following season.

● George Paterson scored a hat-trick on his League debut for Stoke against Middlesbrough in September 1925.

● Three players, Billy Herbert (1913-19), Arty Watkin (1914-22) and Charlie Wilson (1926-30) each scored eight hat-tricks for the Potters; Archie Smith claimed six (1910-15); Johnny King five (1953-61) and both Jack Peart (1910-11) and John Ritchie (1963-74) four apiece.

● Watkin scored five trebles in season 1914-15 while Peart claimed four in 1910-11.

● Between them Stoke players scored 12 hat-tricks in 1910-11 and 13 in the wartime campaign of 1941-42.

● Three players scored hat-tricks in Stoke's 16-0 victory over Blackburn Rovers in a wartime game in season 1917-18: Bob Whittingham (4), Ed Turner (3) and Billy Herbert (3).

● Amos Baddeley scored a five-timer and a hat-trick in separate games against Burton United in 1909-10.

● Charlie Wilson scored seven goals in the two League games v Bristol City in season 1929-30 – a hat-trick and a four-timer.

● Tommy Sale hit a 'five' and a hat-trick in Stoke's two wartime games against Tranmere Rovers in 1941-42 and in the same season he notched nine goals in the two matches against Walsall (a 'six' and a 'three').

● George Mountford netted a 'five' and a 'four' in the two wartime fixtures versus Port Vale in 1944-45.

● Stoke's first Football League hat-trick was registered by David Ramsey v Accrington in March 1890 and the club's first FA Cup treble was secured by Alf Edge (with five goals) against Caernarvon Wanderers in October 1886.

● Neville 'Tim' Coleman scored seven goals in an 8-0 League win over Lincoln City in February 1957.

● Bill Asprey, normally a defender, scored a hat-trick from the centre-forward position for Stoke against Charlton Athletic in a Second Division League game in 1960-61.

● Harry Burrows netted a hat-trick against his former club Aston Villa in Stoke's 6-1 League win at The Victoria Ground in 1966-67.

● John Ritchie scored a First Division hat-trick against Sheffield Wednesday in 1963-64 and weighed in with a four-timer against the Owls the following season. He moved to Hillsborough in 1966.

● Garth Crooks netted a hat-trick against his future club, West Bromwich Albion in a 3-2 home win in 1979-80 and Lee Chapman did likewise for Stoke against Leeds United in 1980-81.

● And Crooks is also one of the youngest players (at 20 years, one week, one day) to score a League hat-trick for the Potters, doing so against Blackburn Rovers in March 1978. Chapman was 20 years, 345 days old when he registered a treble v Norwich City in November 1980.

● Steve Foley is the last Stoke City player to score a hat-trick – against Barnet in the Autoglass Trophy in 1992-93.

● West Bromwich Albion full-back Bobby Cram hit a hat-trick in his side's 5-3 First Division win over Stoke City at The Hawthorns in September 1964.

HAWE, Richard

Raven-haired Dick Haw was one of several half-backs recruited by Stoke for the 1908-09 season and was given just three outings – all in the Birmingham & District League – before being released to rejoin Goldenhill United in 1911. Born in the Goldenhill district of Stoke-on-Trent in June 1883, Hawe spent all his career in the Potteries, and besides Stoke played for a number of other local teams including Goldenhill Juniors, Goldenhill St Joseph's, Tunstall Park, Goldenhill Wanderers (two spells) and Goldenhill Villa. He died c.1940.

HAWKINS, A. Crop

Right-half was Hawkins' best position, although during his career he also lined up at full-back and centre-half. An amateur, born in Stoke in August 1893, he played for Stoke St Peter's before making four appearances for the Potters between September 1912 and April 1914. He signed for Stoke United in the season before World War One.

HAWORTH, Jack

Centre-forward Haworth made six League appearances for Stoke – four in 1903-04 and two the following season – and he scored two goals, the first on his debut against Sunderland in March 1904. A strong burly footballer, born in Nelson in March 1883, he was brought to The Victoria Ground from Colne and left the Potters to play for Netherfield, later serving Darwen Institute.

HAY, James

Teak-tough Scottish full-back, cool under pressure and a player who feared no one, Hay served with Renfrew Victoria, Barnsley and Chesterfield before teaming up with Stoke in the summer of 1909 at the age of 33. Born in Lanark, Renfrewshire in June 1876, he stayed at The Victoria Ground for two and a half years, making 80 first-team appearances for the Potters, scoring one goal. His debut came in the Southern League against Merthyr Town when the Potters won 11-0. Hay retired in December 1911 and went to Barnsley to take over a pub. He died c.1940.

HEAMES, William Thomas H.

Scorer of three goals in 19 games for Stoke during the latter part of the nineteenth century, Heames was an out-and-out outside-left with good pace and temperament. Born in Middleport in July 1869, he played for Middleport Athletic and Middleport Alma before joining the Potters in August 1893 and after spending four seasons at The Victoria Ground he moved to Burslem Port Vale in August 1897. He remained with the Vale until May 1904 during which time he amassed 254 appearances, scoring 28 goals.

HEATH, Adrian Paul

A nippy, darting forward, sharp and incisive in the box, but not such a prolific goalscorer as might be expected. Heath had two spells with the Potters: 1977-82 and again in 1992, and all told scored 17 goals in 118 appearances. Born in Knutton on 11 January 1961, he joined the apprentice staff at The Victoria Ground on leaving school and turned professional on his eighteenth birthday, having made his debut as a 17-year-old. In January 1982 Heath was transferred to Everton for £700,000 and in the next six years netted 93 goals in 307 outings for the Merseysiders, helping them twice win the First Division title (in 1985 and 1987) and the FA Cup in 1984, as well as appearing in four Charity Shield winning sides at Wembley. From Goodison Park he switched to Espanol (in Spain) for £600,000, only to return to England to sign for Aston Villa for £360,000 in August 1989. Six months later he went north to Manchester City (for £300,000) and returned for his second spell with the Potters in March 1992, joining for a fee of £50,000. Heath's next move, in August 1992, took him to Burnley on a free transfer and at Turf Moor he did supremely well, netting 35 goals in 143 outings. But then in December 1995 he moved to Sheffield United where he became player-assistant manager to his former teammate at Stoke, Howard Kendall. In March 1996, Heath left Bramall Lane and returned to Burnley where he was appointed manager in succession to Jimmy Mullen. In his playing career (which ended in 1996) Heath knocked in more than 150 goals in 604 senior appearances at club level. He also won one England 'B' cap and eight at Under-21 level.

HEATH, Philip Adrian

A fast-raiding winger, born in Stoke on 24 November 1964, Phil Heath (no relation to Adrian above) scored

19 goals in 179 appearances during his eight years at The Victoria Ground. Naturally right-footed, he had plenty of skill, showed a lot of endeavour and was pretty quick over short distances, and at times caught the eye of scouts from both Derby County and Everton. He played for the Potters from June 1980 to June 1988, when he moved to Oxford United for £80,000. Thereafter he had spells with Cardiff City, Port Vale (trial), Aldershot and Aylesbury United before quitting football to concentrate on his pottery business in Stoke-on-Trent.

HEIGHT

Over the years Stoke (like all other clubs) have had their fair share of tall players on their books with the following perhaps among the tallest to have donned the famous Potters' strip (pre 1939): goalkeepers George Clawley, Jack Whitley, and Tom Wilkes; defenders Harry Benson, Tom Stanford and Tommy Clare (from the 1880s); half-backs Jimmy Bradley, Jimmy Grewer and Sammy Meston (who weighed 14st 10lbs); forwards Teddy Holdcroft and Tommy Hyslop (1890/1900s – the latter was 6ft 4ins); full-back Charlie Burgess (1900s);, defenders Bob McGrory, Bill Winstanley and Jack Bamber (1930s), and since World War Two: goalkeepers Frank Elliott, Bill Robertson, John Farmer and Joe Corrigan (who was 6ft 5ins); full-backs Bill Asprey, John McCue and Eddie Stuart; central defenders Noel Blake, Alan Bloor, Steve Bould, Alan Dodd, Mark Higgins, Denis Smith and Ken Thomson; forwards Dave Bamber, Lee Chapman, John Gayle (6ft 3ins and 15st 4lbs), George Kelly, Ian Moores, Brendon O'Callaghan, Dave Regis, John Ritchie and Keith Scott.

Giant 6ft 7ins striker Kevin Francis (Derby County, Stockport County and Birmingham City) is the tallest player ever to line up in a first-class game against the Potters.

Among the smaller brigade (those of 5ft 5ins and below) who have served Stoke are defenders Steve Parkin and Tom Holford and forwards Bobby Archibald, Amos Baddeley, Fred Brown, Keith Bebbington, Adrian Heath, Joe Hutton, Johnny Malkin, Billy Tempest and Josh Williams, the latter weighing only 8st 11lbs.

HEGGARTY, Archibald

Irishman Archie Heggarty, from Belfast, had one season at The Victoria Ground – 1912-13 – when he scored once in 22 first-team games. A outside-right with good pace and fair amount of skill, he was born in August 1884 and joined the Potters from Belfast Distillery. He left Stoke for Tottenham Hotspur, but made only one first-team appearance at White Hart Lane before returning to Ireland to play briefly for Belfast Crusaders.

HELME, Jack Albert

An amateur inside-left who played for Stoke during the latter stages of the 1920-21 season, making four League appearances. On leaving The Victoria Ground, Helme returned to his former club Altrincham. He was born in Altrincham c.1887.

HEMMING, Christopher A.J.

The ginger-haired utility defender from Newcastle-under-Lyme hit the national sporting headlines when he had a pace-maker fitted at the peak of his career – and he then stunned everyone by bouncing back to continue his career as a professional footballer. Having graduated through the junior ranks, Hemming made his League debut for the Potters on his 18th birthday against Tottenham Hotspur at White Hart Lane on 13 April 1984 – this being the first of 105 games for the club at senior level (two goals scored). He stayed at The Victoria Ground until August 1989 when he transferred to Hereford United for £25,000, following a loan spell with Wigan Athletic. After spending two years at Edgar Street he switched to Merthyr Tydfil and later assisted Macclesfield Town and Stafford Rangers.

HENDRY, William Henry

Hendry was centre-forward in the West Bromwich Albion team which beat Stoke 2-0 in the club's first-ever Football League game on 8 September 1888. A craggy Scotsman, born in Dundee in June 1864, he was a prolific goalscorer north of the border and was among a posse of Scottish footballers who migrated south to try their luck in England. Hendry succeeded, to a certain degree and amassed a useful record of more than 200 senior appearances. He had scored for Dundee Invergowrie Schools, Dundee (as an amateur trialist), Dunblane Thistle and Dundee Wanderers (1886) prior to signing for West Brom in August 1888. He came to Stoke towards the end of that initial League season (March 1889) and after being converted into a centre-half, he netted once for the Potters in 16 outings before transferring briefly to Kidderminster Harriers (in 1990). He later did well with Preston North End (1890-91), Sheffield United (1891-95), skippering the Blades to promotion, Dundee (again in 1896), Bury (1896-97) and Brighton United, from 1898 to 1900 when he retired through ill-health. Unfortunately he was twice in trouble as a West Brom player – first he was suspended for a month by the Football League for fighting with Sneddon of Bolton Wanderers (November 1888 and then banished from the club for being drunk in training. Hendry apparently died of consumption in November 1900, aged 26.

HENRY, Anthony

Stoke manager Mick Mills paid Oldham Athletic £40,000 to bring midfielder Tony Henry to The Victoria Ground in December 1987 – and he did a useful job as the playmaker in the centre of the park although never really winning over the support of the fans. He skippered the team occasionally and, going on to score 11 goals in 70 appearances for the Potters. Born in Houghton-le-Spring on 26 November 1957, Henry had earlier gained an FA Cup runners-up medal with Manchester City in 1981 before moving to Bolton

Wanderers from where he joined the Latics in March 1983. He initially signed a two-and-a-half year contract with Stoke, but left the club prematurely, joining the Japanese side Mazda FC in June 1989. He later played for Shrewsbury Town (1990-92) and then Witton Albion (1994-95). In his League career Henry made over 480 appearances and netted 80 goals.

HERBERT, William Edward

Billy Herbert, a true Cockney, played inside or outside-left during a useful career which spanned almost 12 years. Born in Canning Town, London c.November 1888, he played initially for Walthamstow Grange, Barnet, Woolwich Arsenal, Glossop North End and Gravesend United before joining Stoke in December 1912 when the Potters were in the Southern League. He made his debut for the club on Christmas Day 1912 against the club he supported as a lad – West Ham United – and served at The Victoria Ground right up until November 1919 when he moved north to Bolton Wanderers, later assisting Wigan Borough (September 1921). One of the few players to don a Stoke jersey at senior level before, during and after the 1914-18 hostilities, Herbert (now deceased) was a fine attacker, who enjoyed running with the ball. He won a Southern League championship medal with the Potters in 1915 and in wartime football he scored 64 goals in 135 outings. His peacetime record with Stoke was 28 goals in 67 first-team appearances.

HERD, David George

Centre-forward David Herd played alongside his father, George, for Stockport County before moving to Arsenal for £8,000 in August 1954. At Highbury, he began to score regularly and in the next seven seasons netted 97 goals in 166 First Division matches for the Gunners. In July 1961, he was transferred to Manchester United for £35,000 and two years later scored at Wembley when Leicester City were defeated 3-1 in the FA Cup. Twice a League championship winner with the Reds in 1964-65 and again in 1966-67, Herd was capped five times by Scotland and during his time at Old Trafford, he scored 144 times in 263 League and Cup matches (114 goals coming in the top flight). Stoke City boss Tony Waddington enticed Herd (then aged 34) to The Victoria Ground on a free transfer in July 1968, and in the next two-and-a-half years he scored 11 goals in 48 first-team outings for the Potters. Herd, who was born in Hamilton on 15 April 1934, wound down his career in Ireland playing for Waterford (1970-72).

NB: In November 1966, Herd scored an unusual hat-trick for United against Sunderland – netting past three different goalkeepers: Jim Montgomery, his replacement Charlie Hurley and then John Parke. Herd went on to hit a fourth goal in United's 5-0 win. Herd also kept goal for United, replacing the injured Harry Gregg during a League game against Liverpool in November 1963.

David and his father Alex Herd, who died in August 1982, were players together at Stockport.

HEREFORD UNITED

Stoke have yet to oppose the Bulls in a major competition, although they have met each other in a friendly game in 1976-77 when the Potters won 1-0 at Edgar Street.

Players with both clubs: Carl Beeston, Keith Downing, Chris Hemming, Joe Johnson, George Mountford, Alec Ormston, Mel Pejic, Kevin Russell, Brett Williams and John Williams.

HEROD, Dennis J.

Goalkeeper Dennis Herod had the distinction of scoring a vital League goal for Stoke – in a 3-2 win against Aston Villa in an away First Division match on 16 February 1952, after being put out to grass (on the wing) following an injury. One of a bevy of young talent to emerge during and immediately after World War Two, Herod, who was born in Basford on 27 October 1923, signed as a junior at The Victoria Ground in the summer of 1940, having assisted Trent Vale United from 1937. Although relatively small for a goalkeeper, he stood 5ft 9ins tall, he was exceptionally sound in his ground work and quite fearless and acrobatic when he was called into action. He had 120 wartime outings for the Potters, and also served in the armed forces in Europe where he he was wounded in battle. On being demobbed, Herod became first-choice goalkeeper at Stoke, beating off the challenge of Norman Wilkinson and Arthur Jepson. Besides his wartime activities, he made well over 300 appearances (215 in League and FA Cup) during his 13 years' association with the club, which came to an end in July 1953 when he moved to Stockport County for a fee of just £750. After leaving competitive football two years later he ventured into the greengrocery business and occasionally turned out for his adopted club, Newcastle Town. He makes an occasional visit to The Victoria Ground, his last in 1996.

HERRON, Richard

Dick Herron was a useful goalkeeper with Stoke during the four seasons leading up to World War One and during the hostilities. One of the shortest goalkeepers to play for the club at 5ft 7ins, Herron was born near the coalface in the town of West Stanley, County Durham in January 1890. Known as 'Invincible Dick' he played for his hometown club before moving down to the Midlands to join Stoke in March 1911. He was quickly embedded into the first XI (replacing Jack Robinson) and went on to appear in 46 peacetime games for the Potters plus another 74 during the first part of the war, before he was tragically killed whilst on active service in France in April 1917.

HESHAM, John Frank

Outside-right Frank Hesham had a useful career which ended after 18 years when he was sadly killed while serving with the Royal Garrison Artillery in France on 17 November 1915. Born near Hyde Road, the ground of Manchester City, in December 1880, he played, in turn, for Gorton St Francis FC (from 1897), Manchester City (23 January 1901), Accrington Stanley (1903), Stoke (4 May 1904 to 30 June 1906), Leyton (briefly in season 1906-07), Oldham Athletic (30 August 1907), Preston North End (16 September 1909 for £25), Croydon Common (6 November 1909), Crewe Alexandra (1910) and Newton Heath Alliance (September 1913-May 1914). When deputising for that great Welsh wing wizard Billy Meredith at Manchester City, Hesham was described as 'an earnest and conscientious player, full of dash and judgement'. He came to Stoke with a good reputation after scoring well for his first two major clubs, but he never really fitted into the plan of attack at The Victoria Ground and after scoring once in 17 starts for the Potters he moved to Leyton and then to Boundary Park.

HICKSON, Geoffrey G.

Goalkeeper Hickson played in 11 League games for the Potters over a 16 month period: December 1959 to May 1961. Born in Crewe on 26 September 1939, he was an amateur with Blackburn Rovers before turning professional at The Victoria Ground in August 1957. Reserve to Wilf Hall and Bill Robertson, he had to wait almost two years before making his debut (v Sunderland at Roker Park). He did well, never letting the side down, but after conceding five goals at Liverpool he was replaced by new signing Tommy Younger (ironically ex-Liverpool) and went into the Reserves. Hickson wasn't happy and desperate for first-team football, he left Stoke in July 1962, moving to neighbours Crewe Alexandra. After more than 100 games for the Alex he assisted Port Vale (17 outings on loan over a four month period in 1968) before ending his senior career with spells at both Southport and Shrewsbury Town and also in South Africa with Cape Town City. Some people said that Hickson was given away by the club far too quickly.

HIGGINS, Mark

Higgins, born in Buxton on 29 September 1958, and a former England youth international, was a valuable member of Everton's defence for a number of years until sidelined by a niggling groin injury in 1983. He was ready to quit the professional game on medical advice after some 200 appearances for the Merseysiders, but persevered and following a hernia operation, and a two-year break, he bounced back and joined Manchester United in December 1985. He regained full fitness at Old Trafford and after a handful of League outings for the Reds he went to Bury (January 1987), moving to Stoke

City at the age of 30 year for £150,000 in the summer 1988. Potters' boss Mick Mills gambled on Higgins and to a certain extent it was a good move, with the defender chalking up 44 appearances (one goal scored) in his first two seasons at The Victoria Ground. Unfortunately he didn't figure in the first team at the start of the 1990-91 campaign and in December his three-year contract was cancelled, allowing him to witch to Burnley. Sadly, after just two months at Turf Moor, injury again forced Higgins out of the game and within a short time he had decided to hang up his boots.
NB: Mark's father, John, played over 200 games at centre-half for Bolton Wanderers (1952-61).

HIGGINSON, Samuel

Higginson could play in a number of attacking positions with centre-forward his best. He served with Tunstall Casuals and Goldenhill Wanderers prior to joining Stoke in August 1899 after a series of impressive displays in prearranged practice matches. Born in Tunstall in 1880, he spent five excellent seasons at The Victoria Ground during which time he scored 23 goals in 124 senior appearances before transferring to Reading in June 1904. After leaving Elm Park he had a short association with Bradford City and moved back to the Potteries on quitting the game in 1908. On his day Higginson was a clever footballer, a good mover and tidy passer of the ball whose finishing sadly let him down far too many times. He died c.1945.

HILAIRE, Vincent Mark

Born in Forrest Hill, London, on 10 October 1959, outside-left Hilaire played for Crystal Palace, San Jose Earthquakes (on loan), Luton Town, Portsmouth and Leeds United before having a loan spell at Stoke. There followed another loan spell with Oldham Athletic before he joined the Potters permanently in November 1990. He scored three goals in 17 games for Stoke all told before leaving the club for Exeter City, later assisting Waterlooville. Capped by England at youth-team level, Hilaire went on to win nine Under-21 caps and one for the 'B' team and also helped Crystal Palace win the Second Division title in 1979. He made over 500 club appearances as a professional.

HILL, James

Hill was an experienced footballer when he joined Stoke from Burnley in January 1897. He had previously given good service to St Mirren (summer of 1886 to December 1889) and was approached by New Brighton Tower before moving to the Potteries. Born in Paisley c.1865, Hill was a versatile forward with perhaps the left-wing his best position, who scored 13 goals in 35 League and Cup appearances for Stoke. Ironically he left The Victoria Ground in May 1898 for New Brighton Tower and later returned to Scotland where he ended his career.

HILL, Thomas

A well-built centre-forward who scored twice in five League games for Stoke during the first half of the 1897-98 season. Born in Market Drayton in June 1871, Hill played for his home-town club before joining the Potters and after leaving The Victoria Ground he served with Leicester Nomads.

HINGERTY, James

Another useful centre-forward who found it difficult to adapt to competitive League football and in a brief career with Stoke scored eight goals in 24 first-team appearances between January 1897 and February 1898. Born in Walsall in December 1875, he came out of the North Staffs Regiment to play for the Potters and after leaving the club he assisted non-League side Rushden.

HINKS, Charles Henry

Born in Manchester in September 1880, outside-left Hinks played for Darwen and Manchester City before teaming up with Stockport County in 1901 (one appearance). From Edgeley Park he switched to Stoke (September 1903) but managed only one League outing for the Potters, helping them beat Liverpool 5-2 at home in a First Division match a month after signing. He left the Potters for Altrincham in May 1904.

HOBSON, J.W.Francis

Local-born half-back, born in Smallthorne in June 1889, Hobson played once in Stoke's first team – against Stafford Rangers in a Birmingham & District League game in April 1911. He had assisted Smallthorne Amateurs as a youngster and after leaving The Victoria Ground a month after his only outing, he signed for Audley, later assisting Rocester.

Dave Hockaday

HOCKADAY, David

A well- built defender who also mans midfield, Hockaday, a native of Billingham (born on 9 November 1957) played for Billingham Synthonia prior to making 178 appearances for Blackpool (1975-83). He followed up with 308 outings for Swindon Town (winning a Fourth Division championship medal in 1988) and 83 for Hull City before having seven League games on loan at Stoke (March/April 1993). After leaving Boothferry Park he assisted Shrewsbury Town.

HODGE, Peter

A native of Dunfermline, Hodge combined refereeing in the Scottish Second Division with soccer administration. He was involved with several clubs north of the border and was, in fact, Raith Rovers' first ever team manager (1907-12). He became Stoke's manager in June 1914, and did a fine job, steering the side to the Southern League championship at the end of his first season in charge. He returned home to his native Scotland during the war when he rejoined Raith Rovers, taking over Leicester Fosse in September 1919. He led the Foxes to the Second Division title in 1925 but 12 months later was appointed manager of Manchester City, leading them out at Wembley for the FA Cup Final of 1926 (v Bolton Wanderers). In March 1932 Hodge signed Matt Busby for City, yet soon afterwards returned to Filbert Street as boss. He died in August 1934 while still in office at Leicester (See MANAGERS).

HODGKIN, Ernest

Hodgkin at 5ft 7ins and less than 12 stone, was one of the smallest and lightest central defenders of his era. Yet he never shirked a tackle, always battled hard and long against some of the toughest forwards around and never gave less than 100 per cent effort out on the park. Born in Grassmore near Chesterfield in 1891, he played his early football for Mansfield Mechanics before signing professional forms for Sunderland. He left Roker Park for The Victoria Ground in April 1912 and lined up at both left-half and centre-half for the Potters, deputising in the latter position for Joey Jones. In February 1913, after scoring once in 29 games, he was suspended by the Stoke directors for one month for a breach of club discipline. He left the Vic at the end of the season and signed for Billingham in the North-East.

HODGKINS, Thomas Reginald

Born in Nuneaton, Warwickshire in January 1903, Reg Hodgkins joined the Potters from Hinckley United in September 1925 with a reputation of being a fearless defender, well proportioned with a strong tackle. He certainly looked the part and did well in reserve-team matches before making his senior debut. Unfortunately injuries upset his rhythm and he managed only five League outings in two seasons at The Victoria Ground. Early in July 1927 Hodgkins was admitted to Coventry Hospital for an appendix operation. Sadly, he never left his bed and three weeks later passed away, aged 24.

HOLDCROFT, Hugh Edward

Long-striding inside-forward who scored 11 goals in 43 League and Cup games for Stoke during the early part of the twentieth century. Born in Tunstall in July 1882, he played 18 times in defence for Burslem Port Vale (from October 1901) before transferring to The

Victoria Ground for £500 in March 1903, in a deal which also involved Arthur Hartshorne. In 1905 he was taken ill with heart trouble and was out of the game for three years until a specialist consultant advised him to continue light training in 1908. However, he failed to regain his first-team place and retired from first-class football at the age of 26. He died at Norton on 4 February 1952.

HOLDITCH COLLIERY

Following the tragic loss of many coalminers' lives at the Holditch Colliery in 1937, Stoke City played the great Scottish side Glasgow Rangers in a friendly at The Victoria Ground on Tuesday 19 October 1937 in a game in aid of the Holditch Colliery Disaster Relief Fund. The game ended 0-0 before a 25,000 crowd.

HOLFORD, Thomas

For seven seasons – 1901-08 – 'Dirty Tommy' Holford, who stood 5ft 5ins tall and weighed barely 9st, was an inspirational character in Stoke's defence. A rugged, non-nonsense performer, sometimes referred to as 'pugnacious' he occupied a number of positions, and it is said that his name went on the team-sheet first for every game. Born in Hanley on 28 January 1878, and the cousin of Wilf Kirkham, Holford came out with Granville's Night School and played next for Cobridge before joining Stoke as a professional in May 1898. He took time to 'bed in' at The Victoria Ground and, indeed, it was not until the 1901-02 campaign that he finally established himself in the first team. He won an England cap in 1903 and remained with Stoke until the club went bust in 1908, scoring 33 goals in 269 appearances. He then switched to Manchester City, who went on to win the Second Division championship with Holford in their team. In May 1914 he joined Port Vale as player-manager and went on to serve Stoke's arch rivals for 38 years, in his original capacity and later as scout (1935-39) and then as trainer throughout World War Two (from July 1939 to July 1946). He had earlier guested for Nottingham Forest during the World War One. So desperate were the Vale for players in 1924 that Holford came out of retirement to play for them at the age of 46, thus taking his overall appearance record for the club to 141 (nine goals scored). He is still the oldest footballer ever to don a Vale jersey at senior level. Holford, who was appointed full-time team manager of Vale in June 1932, holding office until September 1935 when he was relieved of his duties, actually played competitive League football for 25 years, 201 days – from 17 September 1898 to 5 April 1924 – died at Blurton, Stoke-on-Trent on 6 April 1964.
NB: Holford played his 100th consecutive game for the Potters at Liverpool on New Year's Day 1906.

HOLFORD, Wilfred

Holford, no relation to Tom (above) was a useful half-back who played in four FA Cup games for Stoke between November 1886 and September 1888. Born in Cobridge in March 1862, he assisted several local sides, including Boothen Victoria and Stoke Priory, before joining the Potters, but during his last season at The Victoria Ground he suffered a serious knee injury which forced him into an early retirement. He died in Stoke c.1930.

HOLMES, Andrew J.

Holmes' career with Stoke City was plagued by injury and he appeared in only 11 senior games for the club before leaving to join Doncaster Rovers in 1990. A defender, born in the Potteries on 7 January 1969, after leaving Parkway Clayton FC he came through the ranks at The Victoria Ground under the guidance of Tony Lacey, but leg and a serious back injury kept him out of action for 18 months. With such a wealth of defensive cover at the club, Holmes was allowed to leave for Belle Vue. A broken leg interrupted his progress with Rovers and although he regained full fitness (again) he finally quit top-class football on medical advice at the age of 22. He went to work in the family's picture framing business combining this with outings for Leek Town.

HOLMES, William H.

A well-built centre-forward who scored four goals in nine senior appearances for the Potters during his short stay at The Victoria Ground (1912-14). Born in Stone c.1889, he played for Leek Alexandra and Darlaston prior to signing for Stoke and after leaving the club served with Mid-Rhondda.

HOLT, Harold

Welsh amateur centre-half who played in one game for Stoke – against West Bromwich Albion Reserves in an away Birmingham & District League game in January 1911. Born in Aberystwyth in July 1889, he played for his home-town club as well as for Wrexham and Mold.

HOPE, Richard

Scottish inside-forward who came to Stoke in attempt to establish himself in English football. He played in only two Southern League games, in September 1914, before returning home to sign for Port Glasgow. He was born in the Gorbals district of Glasgow in January 1890 and before assisting the Potters, had scored over 20 goals for Glasgow St Peter's.

HORNE, Brian

England Under-21 international (capped five times) Horne kept goal in almost 200 games for Millwall (1985-92). He also had loan spells at Watford, Middlesbrough, Woking and Stoke City (two outings) early in the 1992-93 season and Sunderland, before leaving The Den for Portsmouth, from where he moved to Hartlepool United (August 1994). Horne was born in Billericay on 5 October 1967.

HORROCKS, Victor

Another local player who could occupy either wing-half position or any of the three central striking berths with centre-forward perhaps his best role. Born in Goldenhill in October 1884, he served with the Burslem Boys Club and Goldenhill Wanderers before joining the Potters briefly in 1903. He left the club to sign for Talke United, later assisting Sandyford and Goldenhill United prior to registering with Port Vale in April 1905. All told, he had 38 games for the Valiants up to May 1907, when he returned to Goldenhill United. He then had a second spell with Stoke (from September 1908 to September 1911) and ended his playing career with Congleton Town (1912-13). Horrocks netted eight goals in 21 appearances up for the Potters, including a hat-trick v Wellington in a Birmingham League game. He died at Hartshill on 7 January 1922.

HOULDSWORTH, Frederick S.Charlton

Goalkeeper Houldsworth, 5ft 9ins tall and 11st 3lbs in weight, was born in Henley-on-Thames on 29 May 1911, and while serving in the Surrey Corps, played for the British Army team against Belgium (1932). He began his soccer career in earnest as an amateur with Swindon Town before transferring to Stoke City for £750 in April 1935. Reserve to Ken Scattergood and Norman Lewis, he played in only two League games for the Potters before switching to Ipswich Town in May 1935, later playing for Reading (1938-39). A keen club cricketer, he later became an umpire at Framlington College where he was employed. Houldsworth died in 1994.

HOWE, Thomas

Reserve full-back (to Bob McGrory) Howe was born in Wolverhampton on 25 May 1890 and played works football for Sunbeam Motors before joining Stoke in May 1921. He stayed at The Victoria Ground for five years, having a couple of decent runs in the first team, the best in 1923-24. In all, he scored twice in 56 outings before being placed on the transfer list in May 1926. He finally signed for Featherstone Rovers (a local team) after eight months out of the game.

HOWITT, Robert G.

Howitt, a hardworking, purposeful half-back, was never the most popular player around The Victoria Ground, yet always gave 100 per-cent effort out on the field. His professional career began with Partick Thistle before he broke into League Football with Sheffield United in July 1955. He went on to score 30 goals in 88 League games for the Blades up to April 1958, when he joined Stoke City for £8,000. In five seasons at The Victoria Ground, Howitt, who was born in Glasgow on 15 July 1929, hit 16 goals in exactly 150 first-team appearances for the Potters, helping them win the Second Division championship in 1962-63. He retired in the summer of 1963 and after coaching Morton, he was appointed manager of Motherwell and actually brought the Well down to Stoke for an Anglo-Scottish Cup-tie. He later scouted for the Potters north of the border.

HOWSHALL, John Henry

Stoke signed Howshall as an amateur from Dresden Juniors in May 1931. He stayed at The Victoria Ground for three seasons during which time he made just one League appearance, lining up against Wolverhampton Wanderers in September 1933 when he replaced Harry Sellars at left-half. In June 1934 he moved to Chesterfield and later assisted Southport (51 League games), Bristol Rovers, Accrington Stanley, Carlisle United, Northwich Victoria and Wigan Athletic. During the war he served in the RAF and played football on a regular basis for the various units. Howshall was born at Normacot on 12 July 1912 and died at Shelton on Christmas Eve, 1962.

NB: Howshall's brother, Tom, played for Southport and also assisted Stoke as a guest during World War Two, while his other brother's son, Gerry, was a wing-half with West Bromwich Albion during the 1960s.

HOWSHALL, Samuel

Reserve outside-left Howshall scored twice in his only senior outing for Stoke against Stourbridge in a Birmingham & District League game in September 1908. Born in Cobridge in July 1883, he had spells with Newcastle Swifts, Burslem Port Vale (from May 1903 to May 1905) and Salisbury Town and Clapton Orient before spending a season with the Potters. He left The Victoria Ground for Merthyr Town.

HUDDERSFIELD TOWN

Stoke's playing record against the Terriers is:

Football League

Venue	P	W	D	L	F	A
Home	31	15	11	5	54	26
Away	31	9	8	14	38	48
Totals	62	24	19	19	92	74

FA Cup

	P	W	D	L	F	A
Home	1	0	1	0	3	3
Away	2	1	1	0	1	0
Totals	3	1	2	0	4	3

League Cup

	P	W	D	L	F	A
Home	1	0	1	0	0	0
Away	1	1	0	0	2	0
Totals	2	1	1	0	2	0

Stoke have registered two 5-1 League wins over the Terriers – the first in February 1957 when over 27,000 attended The Victoria Ground and the second in December 1958 when a crowd of 13,000 saw former England star Dennis Wilshaw scored twice for the Potters – both games were in Division Two. Stoke also won 4-1 at Leeds Road in a First Division game in December 1934 when Tommy Sale netted twice; by the same score on the same ground in December 1938 when Sale this time netted a hat-trick, and they came storming back from 2-0 down to beat the Yorkshire club 3-2 at The Victoria Ground in a League game in September 1996 when Mike Sheron netted a dramatic late winner. Huddersfield Town's biggest League victory over Stoke is 4-0, achieved at home in March 1950. The first two League games between the two clubs took place in season 1919-20 when Huddersfield doubled-up by winning 1-0 at Stoke and 3-0 at Leeds Road.

Stanley Matthews made his second debut for Stoke against Huddersfield in a Second Division game at The Victoria Ground in October 1961. Almost 36,000 fans turned out (around 27,500 up on the previous home gate) to see Matthews lead his side to a thrilling 3-0 victory.

All three FA Cup encounters took place in season 1970-71 when, after a 3-3 draw at Stoke and a 0-0 scoreline at Huddersfield, the Potters finally won the second replay by 1-0 at Old Trafford thanks to a Jimmy Greenhoff goal. The two League Cup matches were played in 1983-84, when goals by Steve Bould and Paul Maguire sent the Potters through to the fourth round.

Players with both clubs: Julian Bent, Harry Brough, Don Clegg, Tom Cowan, Harry Davies, Fred Groves, Ellis Hall, Mick Kennedy, Sam McAllister, Ernie Millward, Derek Parkin, Edgar Powell, Billy Robson, Dr Leigh Richmond Roose, Colin Russell, Billy Smith, George Stentiford, Harry Taylor, Billy Tempest, Bob White, Norman Wilkinson, Josh Williams and Charlie Wilson.

HUDSON, Alan Anthony

Hudson was one of the most gifted footballers of his generation – an inside-forward who at times could make the ball talk. He had two spells at The Victoria Ground – the first from January 1974 to December 1976 and the second from January 1984 to September 1985. He appeared in a combined total of 170 League and Cup games for the Potters, scoring nine goals. Born in London in Chelsea on 21 June 1951, Hudson started his career as an apprentice at Stamford Bridge, turning professional there in June 1968. He struck 14 goals in 189 League and Cup games for the Blues, helping them win the European Cup-winners' Cup in 1971. And 10 months after lining up for Chelsea against Stoke in the 1972 League Cup Final, he left the bright lights of London and moved to The Victoria Ground for £240,000. He left the Potteries for Arsenal in a £200,000 deal after picking up an FA Cup losers' medal with the Gunners in 1978 and having a brief spell with Seattle Sounders in the NASL and assisting Hercules Alicante in Spain, he returned to Stamford Bridge for a second spell in August 1983. Six months later he was back at Stoke who paid £22,500 for his services, a fee which was partly offset by the sale of Mickey Thomas to the Londoners. Hudson remained in the Potteries for the rest of his career, retiring from competitive football with a knee injury soon after the 1985-86 season had got under way. Capped twice by England at senior level and ten times by the Under-21s, he scored 19 goals in a total of 324 League appearances for his three English clubs. In the 1990s Hudson went into the nightclub business in London.

NB: *In 1974-75 Hudson was voted the Most Exciting Young Player in England.*

HUGHES, Dennis

Hughes made only one League appearance for Stoke City – playing at outside-right against Huddersfield Town (home) in August 1950. He was born in the Potteries on 9 April 1931 and was recruited by the club as a 17-year-old (in September 1948). He stayed at The Victoria Ground for two seasons before moving to Congleton in May 1950.

HULL CITY

Stoke's playing record against the Tigers is:

Football League

Venue	P	W	D	L	F	A
Home	22	11	7	4	38	19
Away	22	7	6	9	23	31
Totals	44	18	13	13	61	50

FA Cup

	P	W	D	L	F	A
Home	3	2	1	0	7	3
Away	1	1	0	0	3	2
Totals	4	3	1	0	10	5

Watney Cup Final

	P	W	D	L	F	A
Home	1	1	0	0	2	0

Stoke's best League win over the Tigers is 4-0 (away) in November 1986, when Tony Ford had a superb game, scoring one of the goals in front of 5,252 fans. In contrast, Hull's best win over Stoke is 7-1 at Anlaby Road in November 1921. They also won 4-0 at Boothferry Park in March 1960.

Potters' goalkeeper Scott Barrett saved a penalty in a 4-1 home in over Hull in March 1989 (Division Two).

A bumper crowd of 41,452 packed into Boothferry Park to see Stoke beat Hull 3-2 in a memorable sixth-round FA Cup-tie in March 1971 when John Ritchie (2) and Terry Conroy scored for the Potters in front of the TV cameras.

The following season Stoke repeated their Cup success over the Tigers, this time beating them 4-1 at home in a fifth-round clash when Jimmy Greenhoff found the net twice before 34,558 fans.

The Final of the Watney Cup was played at The Victoria Ground in August 1973 when Jimmy Greenhoff's two goals gave the Potters victory.

Players with both clubs: Dave Bamber, Harry Davies, Stuart Eccleston (Stoke reserve), Tommy Flannigan, Neil Franklin, Ellis Hall, Dave Hockaday, Alf Jordan, Tony Kelly, Leigh Palin and Billy Whitehurst.

Frank Taylor was assistant manager at Hull before taking over as manager of Stoke City (1952) and Cyril Lea was coach-assistant manager at Boothferry Park (1980) after his brief spell as coach at Stoke. Stuart Ecckleston, ex-Stoke reserve, played 23 League games for Hull (1981-82).

HULSE, Robert

Hulse had a short career in League football, playing twice for Stoke City in the First Division in the late 1960s. Born in Crewe on 5 November 1948, he came to The Victoria Ground from Nantwich Town in April 1967 and stayed until May 1968. Hulse emigrated to Australia in the summer of 1969.

HURST, Geoffrey Charles

In 1966 Geoff Hurst became the first footballer ever to score a hat-trick in a World Cup Final, doing so in England's 4-2 win over West Germany at Wembley. Born in Ashton-under-Lyne on 8 December 1941, Hurst junior played for Halstead Chelmsford City as a teenager before joining West Ham United's apprentice staff in 1958. He turned professional at Upton Park in April 1959 and from then until August 1972 when he moved to The Victoria Ground, he proved himself to be one of greatest marksmen in Hammers' history by netting 252 goals in a total of 502 senior appearances. Whilst with the London club Hurst netted 24 goals in 49 internationals for England, also winning four Under-23 caps and playing six times for the Football League side. He was an FA Cup and European Cup-winners' Cup winner with the

Hammers in 1964 and 1965 respectively, and played in the 1966 League Cup Final defeat against West Brom. When he left the Hammers for Stoke the fee involved was £75,000 – money well spent by manager Tony Waddington – for Hurst went on to scored 37 goals in 128 games for the Potters, up to August 1975 when he was transferred to West Bromwich Albion for £20,000 after having guested for Cape Town City during his association with the Potters. He was 34 at that time he left Stoke and spent barely a season at The Hawthorns, leaving the Baggies to serve briefly with Cork Celtic, and Seattle Sounders (NASL). He came back to England as player-manager of Telford United and thereafter had a spell as coach in charge of England's Under-21 side, later acting as assistant manager of the full England squad (under his former boss at West Ham, Ron Greenwood). In the late 1970s he was made coach at Stamford Bridge and managed Chelsea from 1979 to 1981 prior to going over to coach in Kuwait. A useful cricketer in his time, Hurst represented Essex at County level, and whilst with Stoke he also ran a pub in Whitmore. He later became a director of Motorplan, a top Insurance company.
NB: *Hurst's father, Charles, was a professional footballer with Oldham Athletic, Bristol Rovers and Rochdale.*

HUTCHINSON, Colin

Utility forward Hutchinson was a reserve at The Victoria Ground for six years: 1952-58, during which time he was given nine League outings, lining up at outside-right, inside-right and inside-left, and he actually make his debut as a 17-year-old against Middlesbrough. Born in Lanchester. near Consett, County Durham on 20 October 1936, he played for Crook Hall FC before moving to Stoke, initially as an amateur, and during his National Service in the RAF he unfortunately broke his leg which set him back as a player and he never recaptured his true form. He had a loan spell with Crewe Alexandra before leaving the Potters in the summer of 1958 to sign for Stafford Rangers. He became a very successful manager of Rangers and later did a good job in charge of first Nantwich Town and then Droylesden. Quite often he was seen in the directors' box at The Victoria Ground in his fee hours outside the running of a successful stationery business in Newcastle (Staffs).

HUTCHINSON, William

Hutchinson was Stoke's reserve outside-right during the club's first League season of 1888-89, and played once in the first team against Derby County (away). A well-built footballer, born in Stoke in July 1870, he served with Fenton RS and Long Eaton either side his season at The Victoria Ground.

HUTSBY, Henry

A good, competent full-back from a footballing family Hutsby was born in Norton Bridge on 4 January 1886. He was educated at Alleyne's Grammar School and then served as an amateur with Stafford FC, Stafford Wednesday, Stafford Excelsior and Stafford Wesleyans, as well as Northern Nomads and Stone Town before joining Stoke as an amateur with his close friend Albert Pitt in the summer of 1908. After a short time at The Victoria Ground he turned professional and went on to make 37 senior appearances (32 in his first season) before leaving to play briefly for Wrexham. A very useful club cricketer, he later returned to Stafford where he died on 30 December 1971 after a good innings.

HUTTON, Joseph

A Scotsman from Dundee (born on 18 November 1927) inside-forward Hutton played for Albion Rovers, Leytonstone, Reading and Ayr United before moving to Stoke in December 1953 at the same time as Bobby Cairns. A diminutive inside-forward (5ft 4ins tall and 10st in weight) Hutton made a fine start to his career at The Victoria Ground when scoring in a 5-0 drubbing of Swansea Town. But his outings were restricted to just 37 (eight goals scored) during his four-year stay in the Potteries, this due to the form of Messrs. Bowyer, King and Kelly. In August 1957 he left Stoke for Gillingham in a £3,000 deal and later served with Millwall and Poole Town before retiring in 1962. He scored 22 goals in 103 League games all told.

HYSLOP, Thomas

An ex-Scots Guardsman, Hyslop was a tall, rangy centre or inside-forward, fast over the ground with a powerful right-foot shot. Born in Mauchline, Ayrshire in June 1874, he played his early soccer with Elderslie FC before assisting Millwall Athletic and then Sunderland, who actually bought him out of the Army on 25 January 1894. He went on to score ten goals in 19 games before leaving Roker Park for Stoke on 20 March 1895 with the League Championship already destined for Sunderland (Hyslop had played in 12 games that season). He became an instant success at The Victoria Ground, being the first Stokie ever to score a hat-trick on his debut – in a 4-1 home win over Derby County three days after signing. Hyslop stayed with the Potters for just over a season, and in July 1896, he switched to Glasgow to join Rangers where, in two years, he added two Scottish Cup winners' medals to his collection. In August 1898 he returned to Stoke for a further season and took his record with the Potters to 30 goals in only 49 appearances before going back to Scotland for a second stint at Ibrox Park. Hyslop, who won two Scottish caps – one with Stoke, the other with Rangers, both against England in the mid-1890s – rounded off an impressive career by assisting Partick Thistle. He died in Glasgow c.1950.

ILKESTON

Stoke beat Ilkeston 2-0 at home in the fourth qualifying round of the FA Cup in November 1909. A crowd of 2,000 saw former Aston Villa man Harry Leigh and Billy Smith score the goals.

Goalkeeper Paul Reece had two League outings for Stoke in 1987 and later joined Ilkeston (1996). Striker Andy Graver also served with both clubs.

INJURIES

During their long history Stoke have, like several other clubs, lost the services of many key players through injury. The full list is far too long to print here, but among those you have lost out through various injuries are defender Ian Cranson, who was forced to quit the game in November 1996 after a prolonged leg injury.

● Hard case defender Denis Smith was one of the most unluckiest of Stoke footballers. During his time with the club (1968-82) he suffered five fractured legs, four broken noses, a cracked ankle, a broken collar-bone, a chipped spine, several dislocations, half-a-dozen finger and toe breaks, concussion and hundreds of cuts which subsequently required stitches.

● Both Peter Dobing and Willie Stevenson suffered double leg fractures while playing for Stoke in successive matches, against Ipswich Town and Tottenham Hotspur respectively in October 1970. Stevenson received his injury after coming on as a sub.

● Dai Nicholas fractured his skull in a motor cycling accident in 1923.

● Gordon Banks was involved in a serious car crash in 1972 which resulted in him losing an eye and quitting professional football.

● On 7 October 1899, the Stoke players were involved in a railway accident on their way back from Wolverhampton. The train they were in ran into the rear carriage of another one standing at Stafford railway station and wrecked it. Jack Eccles was tossed through the door and the injuries he suffered kept him out of the game for a month.

● Former Stoke defender Joey Jones lost the sight of an eye in 1925 after heading the lace in the ball while playing for Crewe Alexandra.

INTERNATIONAL POTTERS

Here are details of players who have won full international caps for their country whilst registered with Stoke (City) Football Club:

Australia
E.Tapei (1).
Canada
Paul Peschisolido (1).
England
Tony Allen (3), Gordon Banks (36), Arthur Capes (1), Mark Chamberlain (8). Tommy Clare (4), Neil Franklin (27), Alan Hudson (2), Tom Holford (1), Teddy Johnson (1), Joe Johnson (5), Arthur Lockett (1), Stanley Matthews (18), Billy Rowley (2), Mike Pejic (4), Jimmy Sayer (1), Joey Schofield (3), Peter Shilton (3), George Shutt (1), Freddie Steele (6), Jim Turner (1), Dave Watson (2), Alf Underwood (2).
Iceland
Toddy Orlygsson (4), Larus Sigurdsson (3).
Northern Ireland
Alex Elder (6), Bobby Irvine (1), Jimmy McIlroy (4), Sammy McIlroy (26), Paddy Sheridan (1), Sammy Smyth (1), Nigel Worthington (2).
Republic of Ireland
Terry Conroy (27), Gerry McMahon (3), Brendon O'Callaghan (7).
Scotland
Tom Hyslop (1), Willie Maxwell (1).
Wales
George Berry (1), Lloyd Davies (4), Robbie James (12), Roy John (6), John Love Jones (1), Joey Jones (10), John Mahoney (31), Sammy Meredith (3), Dai Nicholas (1), Dr Leigh Richmond Roose (9), Mickey Thomas (10), Roy Vernon (10), Mart Watkins (4).

WARTIME/VICTORY INTERNATIONALS
Details of Stoke players who represented their country during wartime internationals between 1939 and 1945 and in Victory internationals in seasons 1919-20 and 1945-46:
England
Neil Franklin (10), Stanley Matthews (29), Charlie Parker (1), Frank Soo (8).
Scotland
Jock Kirton (1).
Wales
Joey Jones (2).

REPRESENTATIVE HONOURS
Details of other international/representative honours gained by Stoke players:
Great Britain XI
Stanley Matthews (1).
All Ireland XI
Terry Conroy (1).
England FA XI
L.Armitage (2), Harry Davies (2), Johnny King (3), Josh Williams (2).
The Rest
Stanley Matthews (1).
England XI
Gordon Banks (1), Stanley Matthews (1).
Scotland XI
Stanley Matthews (1).
England Under-21
Carl Beeston (1), Paul Bracewell (4), Mark Chamberlain (4), Lee Chapman (1), Garth Crooks (4), Adrian Heath (5), Ian Painter (1), Steve Parkin (5).
Republic of Ireland Under-21
Aaron Callaghan (2).
Iceland Under-21
Larus Suigurdsson (2).
England Under-23
Tony Allen (7), Mike Bernard (3), Alan Dodd (6), John Farmer (1), Jimmy Greenhoff (1), Alan Hudson (1), Ian Moores (2), Mike Pejic (8).
Wales Under-23
John Mahoney (2).
England 'B'
Neil Franklin (1).
Young England
Tony Allen (2).
Football League
Tony Allen (2), Gordon Banks (2), Arthur Capes (1), Tommy Clare (1), Alan Dodd (1), George Eastham (1), Jack Eccles (2), Jack Farrell (1), Neil Franklin (5), Jimmy Greenhoff (1), Fred Johnson (1), Stanley Matthews (9), Alec Ormston (3), John Ritchie (1), Fred Rouse (2), Billy Rowley (1), Joey Schofield (2), Peter Shilton (1), Denis Smith (1), Freddie Steele (2), Jim Turner (3).
Southern League XI
Jack Peart (3).
Irish League XI
Frank Baker (1), Alec Ormston (1).
Football League Select XI
Joey Schofield (1).
Football League XI
Harry Brigham (1), Stanley Matthews (5), Tommy Sale (1).

A-Z OF STOKE CITY

Professionals XI
Len Armitage (1).

England Amateur XI
Len Hales (1).

England Junior International
Archie Smith (1).

FA XI
Frank Bowyer (1), Harry Brigham (1), Neil Franklin (6), John McCue (4), Stanley Matthews (4), Billy Mould (1), Alec Ormston (1), Frank Soo (3), Freddie Steele (1), Norman Wilkinson (1).

Staffordshire County FA
George Bateman (1), Tommy Clare (4), Harry Davies (3), Teddy Johnson (2), Billy Rowley (4), Joey Schofield (5), George Shutt (2), Elijah Smith (2), Alf Underwood (3).

Birmingham FA
Arthur Arrowsmith (1), Teddy Johnson (4), George Shutt (3).

Army XI
George Clarke (2), Jock Kirton (1), Stanley Matthews (1), Freddie Steele (2).

RAF XI
Neil Franklin (4), Stanley Matthews (18), Frank Soo (23).

RAF North West
Stanley Matthews (1), Frank Soo (1).

Northern Command
Jock Kirton (1), Freddie Steele (1).

AA Command
George Antonio (1), Jack Challinor (2), Jock Kirton (4), Stanley Matthews (2), Freddie Steele (2), Jim Westland (4), Norman Wilkinson (2).

Western Command
Roy Brown (1), Arthur Cumberbridge (1), Frank Mountford (1).

Combined Services
Stanley Matthews (4).

Army in Scotland
Jock Kirton (3).

FA Services XI
Neil Franklin (1), Stanley Matthews (2), Frank Soo (1).

London District XI
Stanley Matthews (1).

INTERNATIONAL TRIALS

England
Tommy Clare (2), Fred Johnson (1), Joe Johnson (1), Stanley Matthews (2), Billy Rowley (4), Jimmy Sayer (1), Joey Schofield (2), George Shutt (2), Jim Turner (1), Alf Underwood (2).

Scotland
Jack Kennedy (1), Tom Hyslop (1), Willie Maxwell (4), Tom Robertson (1).

Wales
Joey Jones (1).

Welsh Amateur Trial
Joey Jones (1).

Players (v Gentlemen).
George Shutt (1).

YOUTH INTERNATIONALS

England
Tony Allen, Bill Bentley, Mike Bernard, Alan Bloor, Darren Boughey, Derek Buckley, Peter Bullock, Steve Davis, Brian Hulse, Ian Painter, Steve Parkin.

Republic of Ireland
Aaron Callaghan.

Scotland
David McAughtrie.

Wales
Stuart Roberts.

England Under-18 & Under-20
A.Griffin.

INTERNATIONAL CHIT CHAT

Three players
Stoke have provided three players for a full international side on four separate occasions:
1892 – Clare, Rowley and Underwood (England).
1902 – Meredith, Roose and Watkins (Wales).
1904 – Davies, Meredith and Roose (Wales).
1937 – Johnson, Matthews and Steele (England).

Players for both sides
Stoke have supplied players for both sides in full internationals as follows:
1965 – Irvine (Northern Ireland) and Vernon (Wales).
1967 – Banks (England) and Elder (Northern Ireland).
1967 – Banks (England) and Vernon & Mahoney (Wales).
1969 – Banks (England) and Elder (Northern Ireland).
1974 – Pejic (England) and Mahoney (Wales).
1977 – Mahoney (Wales) and Shilton (England).

International Facts & Figures

● Peter Shilton went on to win a record 125 caps for England.

● Gordon Banks won a total of 73 England caps in his career.

● Dave Watson was capped 65 times by England.

● Stanley Matthews played in 54 full internationals for England.

● Between them the two McIlroys, Jimmy and Sammy, won a total of 143 Northern Ireland caps (55 and 88 respectively).

● John Mahoney and Mickey Thomas both won 51 caps in their careers for Wales.

● Nigel Worthington won 50 caps for Northern Ireland before joining Stoke City in 1996.

● Freddie Steele scored eight goals in his six appearances for England including a hat-trick in a 4-0 win v Sweden in 1947.

● Stanley Matthews also scored a hat-trick for England in a 5-4 win over Czechoslovakia in 1937.

● Before he moved to Stoke, Dennis Wilshaw (Wolves) scored four goals in England's 7-2 win over Scotland in 1955.

● Geoff Hurst scored 24 goals in 49 internationals for England before joining Stoke – and this included a hat-trick in the 1966 World Cup Final.

● Both Tommy Sale and Stanley Matthews were on target for the Football League v an All British XI in 1940.

● During the First and Second World Wars, Stoke had guest players assist them who had previously won full international caps and they were: (World War One) Sid Bowser (WBA), Sammy Brooks (Wolves) and Harry Hampton (Aston Villa) and (World War two) Tom Pearson (Scotland).

IPSWICH TOWN

This is Stoke's playing record against Ipswich:

Football League

Venue	P	W	D	L	F	A
Home	27	11	8	8	45	30
Away	27	6	5	16	26	59
Totals	54	17	13	24	71	89

FA Cup

Venue	P	W	D	L	F	A
Home	3	2	1	0	2	0
Away	2	1	1	0	2	1
Totals	5	3	2	0	4	1

League Cup

Venue	P	W	D	L	F	A
Home	1	1	0	0	2	1
Away	2	1	0	1	3	3
Totals	3	2	0	1	5	4

Stoke inflicted upon Ipswich a 9-1 League defeat at The Victoria Ground on 21 March 1964. That day a crowd of 16,168 saw a rampant Potters outfit completely destroy the Suffolk side who, two years earlier, had won the First Division championship. On target for Waddington's Wonders were Dennis Viollet (3), Jimmy McIlroy (2), John Ritchie (2), Peter Dobing and Keith Bebbington. The Potters also beat Ipswich 5-1 at home in October 1957 when both George Kelly and Harry Oscroft netted twice. Ipswich's best win over the Potters is 5-0 at Portman Road in September 1983. Town also won 4-0 at home in January 1981, by 4-1 (also at home) in 1995 and 4-2 in the Potteries in October 1990. The teams played out two exciting 3-3 draws at Stoke – in November 1969 and then in February 1972 (both in Division One).

Stuart Roberts, at the age 17 years, 258 days became the youngest goalkeeper ever to appear for Stoke in a League game when he lined up in the home game against Ipswich in December 1984 when the visitors won 2-0.

On their way to the semi-final stage of the 1970-71 FA Cup competition, Stoke overcame Ipswich Town in a fifth-round replay at The Victoria Ground when Denis Smith netted the only goal of the game in front of 30,232 fans.

Stoke's two League Cup wins over Ipswich were by the same scoreline of 2-1 – at home in October 1967 and away in October 1972.

Players with both clubs: George Berry (trialist at Ipswich), Keith Bertschin, Lee Chapman, Ian Cranson, Louie Donowa, Nigel Gleghorn, Wilf Hall, Graham Harbey, Fred Houldsworth, Mick Mills (also Stoke manager), Phil Morgan (reserve for both), Jimmy Robertson, Brian Siddall, Brian Talbot and Josh Williams.

Cyril Lea was a player with Ipswich (107 League games) and later coached at Portman Road, who later became assistant manager-coach at Stoke (under Alan Durban) August 1979-80.

IRVINE, Robert J.

Northern Ireland international goalkeeper who won eight full caps, one at Under-23 level and two as a schoolboy. Born in Carrickfergus on 17 January 1942, Irvine played for Linfield before joining Stoke City for £6,000 in June 1963, signed to replace fellow countryman Jimmy O'Neill. He played in the first seven League games of that season, but then lost his place to another new signing, Lawrie Leslie. Irvine was out of the side until April when he came back for three more League games and also played in the second leg of the League Cup Final against Leicester City. He was given just 19 more outings with the Potters before leaving the club in May 1966. In fact, his career at The Victoria Ground ended five months earlier after a penalty incident in a third round FA Cup-tie against Walsall a game the Saddlers won 2-0. Manager Waddington was livid with Irvine's antics and never picked him again. The Irishman left to join Altrincham on a free transfer. Irvine's brother, Willie, played centre-forward for Burnley.

IRVINE, Samuel

Scottish-born midfield player who scored 12 goals in 77 first-team outings for Stoke City between August 1978 and February 1980. A native of Glasgow (born 1956) Sammy Irvine played for Shrewsbury Town from 1972 under manager Alan Durban who then bought him to The Victoria Ground for £60,000 after he had taken over as boss of the Potters. Unfortunately for Stoke, Irvine was involved in a horrific car crash in February 1980 and although he recovered from his injuries, he was forced to quit football and became a licensee.

ISLE OF MAN SOCCER FESTIVAL

Stoke first entered this pre-season competition in July 1985 when they defeated Manchester City 2-1, an Island XI 5-0 and Carlisle United 1-0 before losing to Blackburn Rovers 1-0.

The following year the Potters returned to the island and this time defeated Hearts 1-0, drew 0-0 with the Bohemians and lost 1-0 to Wigan.

In July 1987, after victories over the IOM XI 3-1, Wigan Athletic 2-0 and Dundee 1-0 and a 1-1 draw against Hibernian, Stoke finally won the trophy at the third attempt.

After a year elsewhere, Stoke City went back again in 1989 and again remained unbeaten, accounting for Blackpool 3-1 and drawing with Motherwell 1-1 and Wrexham, 2-2 which failed to get them into the Final.

However, in 1991, the Potters won the tournament for a second time after easing through with wins over the IOM XI 7-0, the Dutch side SC Cambuur 2-0 and Sunderland 2-0.

Confidently the Potters went on to retain the Cup the following year with victories over the IOM XI 4-1, their old adversaries Wigan Athletic 2-0 and Wrexham 5-1.

They haven't been back to the island for a tournament since.

This is Stoke's full record in this competition:

P	W	D	L	F	A
20	14	2	4	44	11

JACKSON, George

Jackson had a relatively short career as a midfielder, playing in just 10 games for Stoke City during the second half of the 1971-72 season before injury forced an early retirement. Born in Stretford (Manchester) on 10 February 1952 he joined the groundstaff at The Victoria Ground in 1967 and turned professional in July 1969. He made his debut on New Year's day 1972 (at Huddersfield) and at the end of that season went over to play for Cape Town City in South Africa. Over there he suffered a serious leg injury from which resulted in him calling it a day (at senior level) at the age of 20. He later returned to the club as coach to Stoke's 'B' team.

JACKSON, John

Centre-forward Jackson, from North Staffs had a superb record with Stoke – scoring three goals in four League games in 1947. Born in Newcastle on 7 January 1923, he joined the club from Alsager FC in May 1941, but had to wait six years before making his senior debut (owing to the war). He had a loan spell with Congleton Town during the hostilities and left The Victoria Ground for Northwich Victoria in 1952. A second spell with Congleton preceded a stint with his last club Leek Town (1955-56). Jackson died at Endon in June 1992, aged 69.

JACKSON, Wilbert (Peter)

Born in the quaintly-named Yorkshire town of Luddendonfoot on 4 August 1904, Jackson (also known as Peter and nicknamed 'Jammy Legs') came south to play for Stoke in April 1924 from Hebden Bridge. He stayed in the Potteries for 10 years, making 73 first-team appearances and scoring one goal against Southampton in a vital Second Division championship victory in March 1933 when the Potters were going for the title. A sturdy half-back with fearsome tackle, Jackson was never really a regular in the side, his best season coming in 1930-31 when he had 22 outings. Nevertheless, he was a dedicated clubman and always gave a good account of himself at whatever level he played. After leaving The Victoria Ground in 1934, he assisted Southend United and Congleton Town only to return to the club as assistant manager to Bob McGrory 12 months later. From that point on, Jackson's managerial career blossomed. He became boss of Wrexham (1950-54) and then Bradford City (1955-61) and after leaving Valley Parade he became a Stoke City scout. His twin sons, Peter and David, both played for Bradford City. Jackson died in Shipley on 9 May 1986.

JAMES, Charles

Reserve defender from Longton (born September 1882), James spent six seasons at The Victoria Ground during which time he appeared in 13 first-team games, lining in up both full-back positions as well as right-half and centre-half. A hard-working player, he served with Halmerend FC before joining Stoke in the summer of 1908 and after leaving the club in May 1914, assisted Florence Colliery. James was unfortunate to concede four penalties in season 1913-14, all for handball.

JAMES, Robert Mark

Welsh international midfielder with power and stamina, a real workhorse who scored seven goals in 56 appearances for Stoke during his short spell with the club: July 1983 to October 1984. Born at Gorseinon near Swansea in 1967, Robbie James cost £160,000 from Swansea City (signed by Richie Barker) and was sold to QPR for £100,000, the money received being invested in striker Keith Bertschin. Capped 47 times by Wales at senior level and thrice by the Under-21s, he played for Leicester City after leaving Loftus Road in 1987 and returned to Swansea in 1988, finally ending his League career with Bradford City. He gained a League Cup runners-up medal with QPR (1986) and collected four Welsh Cup winners medals with Swansea. As a teenager (before joining the 'Swans') he was on Cardiff City's books and also had a brief spell with Arsenal.

JARVIS, George H.

Strong-limbed utility player who came down from Scotland to try his luck in English football immediately after World War One. He made a big impact and scored ten goals in 30 Second Division games for the Potters in 1919-20 when he occupied six different positions, four in the forward-line. Unfortunately Jarvis became homesick and left The Victoria Ground halfway through the following season after taking his appearance tally up to 33. Born in Glasgow in June 1893, he played for Cambuslang Rangers as a teenager and joined Stoke from Celtic for £300. On his return to Scotland he signed for Clydebank. During World War One he had guested for at least six other Scottish League sides.

JEPSON, Arthur E.

Jepson was perhaps better known in sporting circles as an all-round cricketer rather than a goalkeeper. In 390 matches for Nottinghamshire County Cricket Club, between 1938 and 1959, as a hard-hitting lower order batsman he scored 6,369 runs (avg. 14.31); and as right-arm fast medium bowler, took 1,051 wickets (avg. 29.08) with a best of 8-45. A close fielder, he claimed 201 catches and achieved his best seasonal haul of wickets (115) in 1947. As a footballer (over the period 1934-50) he appeared between the posts in more than 300 League and Cup games at various levels for Grantham Town, Mansfield Town, Burslem Port Vale, Stoke City, Lincoln City, Northwich Victoria, Gloucester City and Hinckley United (player-manager). He then became manager of Hinckley Athletic and later acted as scout for both Coventry City and Middlesbrough. Born in Selston, Notts on 12 July 1915, Jepson joined the Potters from arch rivals Vale for £3.750 in September 1946 and in that same year he suffered a spinal injury which put him into temporary retirement, but he bounced back and stayed another two years, finally leaving The Victoria Ground for Sincil Bank in December 1948 after 32 senior outings for the Potters. On retiring as an active 'sportsman' in 1960, Jepson became a first-class cricket umpire, standing in both County and Test matches until 1985. He also scouted for both Coventry City and Middlesbrough and had a brief spell as manager of Hinckley Athletic from July 1963. Jepson died in Kirby-in-Ashfield c.1994.

JOHN, William Ronald 'Roy'

A player who started off as a centre-forward, then performed as a full-back before finally settling down in goal, a position in which he excelled, appearing for Wales in 13 full internationals and one in wartime. Born at Briton Ferry near Neath in 1911, Roy John was a useful goalscorer for both his school team and Briton Ferry Athletic before joining Swansea Town in 1927. Here he was converted him into a left-back but after trials with Manchester United (1928) he left the Vetch Field for Walsall. He went on to amass 93 appearances for the Saddlers, eventually leaving Fellows Park for Stoke City in April 1932 – and he had the pleasure of saving a penalty on his debut for the Potters (v Bradford PA). He helped the Potters win the Second Division title in 1932-33 and appeared in 76 games for the club, up to May 1934, when he moved to Preston North End, later serving with Sheffield United, Manchester United, Newport County and Swansea Town (again) until the outbreak of World War Two. During the hostilities John guested for Blackburn Rovers, Bolton Wanderers, Burnley, Southport and Swansea and in 1942 he starred for a Welsh XI v the RAF (this being his last game at any level). On quitting football he became a hotel manager and after taking over a pub in Swansea he went to work for British Steel. John was also a very fine club cricketer, acting as batsman/wicketkeeper for Briton Ferry CC. He died in July 1973 at Port Talbot.

JOHNSON, Edward

Utility forward Teddy Johnson was Stoke's first full international, being capped by England v Ireland in February 1884, and he scored two goals in an 8-1 victory. Born in Birmingham in June 1862, he represented the Birmingham FA and England v Wales in March 1880 while with Saltley College and after joining Stoke (September 1883) he played for Staffordshire. A robust player, with good technique, he lined up at centre-forward in Stoke's first-ever FA Cup-tie against Manchester two months after joining the club, this being his only senior appearance for the Potters before announcing his retirement, through injury during the 1884-85 season.

JOHNSON, Frederick James

An excellent outside-right, six feet tall, Fred Johnson first made the grade with a local side, Stoke St Peter's, whom he joined at the age of 12. Born in Stoke-on-Trent c.1877, he was secured by Stoke in 1895 and made his debut that same year – the first of 196 senior appearances for the club (20 goals scored). A player with good pace and crossing ability, Johnson represented the Football League against the Irish League during his Stoke career which ended in 1903 when he retired. Two years earlier he was granted a benefit game v the famous Corinthians amateur side which finished 3-3 at The Victoria Ground.

JOHNSON, Joseph Alfred

One-time fishmonger who became an England international outside-left, Joe Johnson was a fine player who loved to start his runs deep in

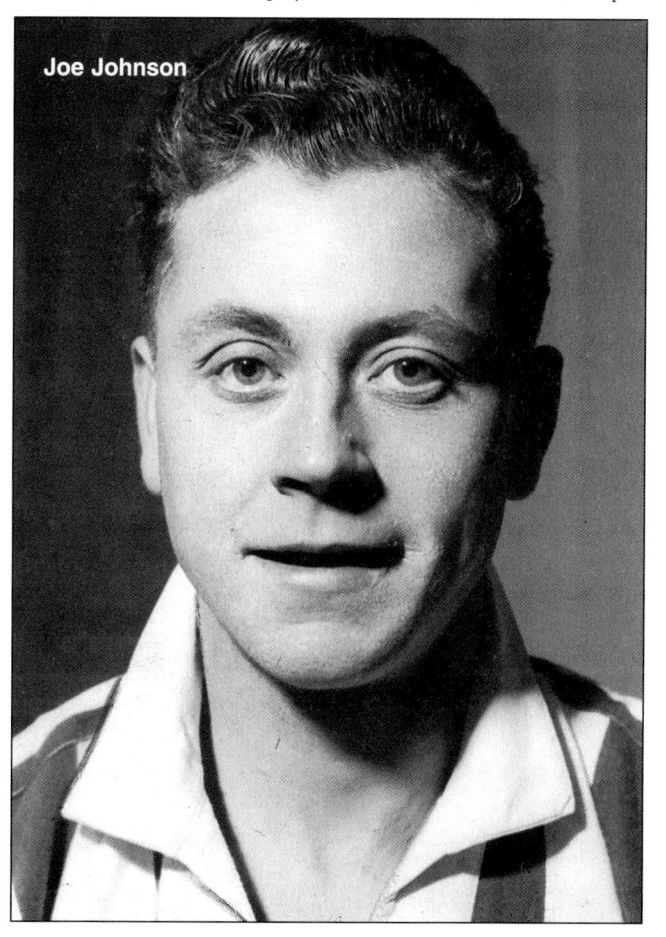

Joe Johnson

his own half of the field. He often cut in fast to shoot at goal. Indeed, he had an excellent scoring record during his soccer career which saw him serve with Cleethorpes Royal Saints, Scunthorpe United, Bristol City, Stoke City (from May 1932 to August 1937 – signed for £250), West Bromwich Albion (sold for £6,000), Northwich Victoria and Hereford United. He also guested for Crewe Alexandra, Leicester City and Notts County during the war. Born in Grimsby on 4 April 1911, Johnson won five England caps, lining up on the opposite flank to his Stoke colleague, Stan Matthews. He scored 57 goals in 193 games for Stoke and helped them win the Second Division championship in 1933. After leaving football Johnson ran the cafe-restaurant in Dartmouth Park, West Bromwich for many years and died in that town on 8 August 1983, aged 72.

JOHNSON, Paul

Introduced to League football by manager Alan Durban, left-back Johnson looked set for a bright future in the game, but when Peter Hampton arrived from Leeds, his days were numbered at The Victoria Ground and in May 1981 he was transferred to Shrewsbury Town for £20,000. Born in Stoke-on-Trent on 25 May 1959, Johnson served his apprenticeship with the Potters and signed professional forms at the age of 17. He made 34 first-team appearances for City and went on to top the 200 mark during a fine spell at Gay Meadow. In July 1987 he switched to York City, but was given a free transfer by the Minstermen after a year at Bootham Crescent. He then returned to Stoke as Community Development Officer, a position he held until 1995. He turned out for Macclesfield Town in the GMVC during the early 1990s.

JOHNSON, Paul A.

A local lad (born in Blurton in 1965) Johnson was a firm favourite with the Stoke crowd, but often took some stick on away grounds because of his build (12st 2lbs for a man of 5ft 6ins tall). He was a determined midfielder, nevertheless, who appeared in a total of 60 senior games and 270 at reserve team level for the Potters whom he served from 1974 to 1982. He left The Victoria Ground on a free transfer for Chester and later played for Altrincham, Buxton, Stafford Rangers and Leek Town, as well as a loan spell with the American club, California Lasers.

JOHNSON, Richard Kemp

An out-and-out goalscoring centre-forward with speed and superb ball control, who netted 25 times in 83 League and Cup games for Stoke during his four-and-a-half years with the club (February 1925 to September 1929). Born in Gateshead in 1897, Dick Johnson started his career with Felling Colliery. He then had a good spell with Liverpool where he won a Second Division championship medal (1923) before transferring to Stoke for £1,200. He left The Victoria Ground for New Brighton (receiving a fee as his accrued share of a small benefit) and rounded off his playing days with Connah's Quay. Johnson died c.1960.

JOHNSON, Samuel

Born in Kidsgrove on 19 October 1901, Sammy Johnson arrived at The Victoria Ground from Goldenhill Wanderers in October 1924 and spent two seasons with the Potters during which time he appeared in 40 League and Cup games as a tough-tackling left-half. After leaving Stoke he played for Swindon Town, York City, Southport and Crystal Palace, retiring from competitive football in 1939.

JOHNSTON, Leslie Hamilton

A Glaswegian inside-forward (born in 1920) who scored 22 goals in 92 League and Cup games for the Potters between 1949 and 1953 after Stoke manager Bob McGrory had paid a club record fee of £9,000 to Celtic for his services. Already a Scottish international (2 caps) Johnston started off well at The Victoria Ground, but was then struck down by injury and loss of form which eventually resulted in him leaving the Potteries for Shrewsbury Town in the summer of 1953 for £2,000. He then had a spell with Hinckley Town, Leek Town, Clover Dairies FC and Wolstanton United – and, in fact, he continued to play regularly in 5-a-side games until he was 50. Johnson also refereed certain matches as well. Prior to joining Celtic, he had served with Clydebank, Hibernian and Clyde (two spells), and in one wartime international v England in April 1945, he came on as sub for Scotland and scored in a 6-1 defeat before 133,000 fans at Hampden Park. In 1949 it was reported that Johnston, who was described as a 'strolling player', had had more money spent on him in transfer fees than any other footballer in the game.

JOHNSTON, Ezekiel

Goalkeeper Johnston was signed from Glentoran on 30 November 1896 and went straight into the Stoke team against Derby County a week after joining the Potters. He did well, playing in 18 League and Cup games during the second-half of that season (helping the team avoid relegation) and in 25 the following campaign. Then Stoke secured the services of Tom Wilkes from Aston Villa and Johnston quickly departed, joining Belfast Celtic. Born in Northern Ireland c.1870, he first played for Glentoran before moving to Burnley in February 1894. He left Turf Moor in April 1895 and returned for a second spell in his homeland with Glentoran.

JONES, Alfred

Amateur outside-left who scored once in five League outings for the Potters in the 1924-25 season when the position he occupied was causing some concern in the camp. Born in Hanley in March 1902, he played for Congleton Town either side of his spell at The Victoria Ground and during his career he also assisted Port Vale and Crewe Alexandra.

JONES. David Douglas

During the final week of the 1938-39 season Stoke manager Bob McGrory was in a predicament with two of his senior goalkeepers – Wilkinson and Westland – both unavailable and he decided to gamble by recruiting the Welsh amateur international Doug Jones to The Victoria Ground to bridge the gap. Born in Blaenau Festiniog on 8 September 1914, Jones made his debut against Leeds United at Elland Road on the last day of the League programme (6 May) and he performed tremendously well in a 0-0 draw before 18,000 fans. This was his only appearance for the Potters and during the summer Leeds even asked about his availability, but instead of joining the Yorkshire club, Jones chose Carlisle United instead. the war, however, disrupted his career and although he returned to Stoke as a guest during the hostilities, he resumed his career at Brunton Park in 1946, going on to appear in 66 League games in two seasons. He ended his playing career with Northwich Victoria (1948-50).

JONES, Gerry

Outside-left Jones played in just seven League games for Stoke in the mid-1960s. Born in Middleport on 30 December 1945, he joined the club as a youngster in 1962 and left The Victoria Ground for Stafford Rangers in June 1967. He later played for Macclesfield Town.

JONES, James Love

Stoke signed 19-year-old inside-forward Love three days after seeing him play decidedly well for Rhyl against Birkenhead in December 1905, and he made a splendid start to his League career by scoring on his Potters' debut against one of the strongest teams in the land, Newcastle United. He held his place in the side (injuries apart) for the rest of the season when he also gained the first of two full caps for Wales when he replaced Archie Green against Scotland in March 1906. Born in Rhyl in April 1885, Jones then lost his place in the side and struggled somewhat over the next season and a half. After scoring three goals in 13 League games for Stoke, he was transferred to Crewe Alexandra in November 1907. Again he failed to hold down a regular first-team place there and in March 1909 switched to Middlesbrough, before signing for Portsmouth in June 1911. Two years later, when still at Fratton Park, he fell ill with tuberculosis and returned home to Rhyl where he sadly died a few months later (21 December 1913) aged 28.

JONES, Joseph Thomas

One of the select band of players who appeared for Stoke before, during and after World War One, Joey Jones was a Welshman, born in the village of Rhosymedre near Ruabon on 9 January 1888. Known as 'The Old Warhorse' Jones joined the club from Treharris (with George Smart) in 1911 having previously played for Cefn Albion and Wrexham. He went on to wear Stoke's colours until 1920, making 129 appearances as a defender and scoring 12 goals. He also gained 10 full caps for his country (and in his career he actually totalled 15). Jones, who skippered the team to the runners-up spot in successive wartime seasons of Lancashire Section football in 1917-18 and 1918-19, left The Victoria Ground for Crystal Palace for £150. He next played for Crewe Alexandra and in 1925, sadly lost the sight of an eye after heading the lace in one of those old fashioned leather footballs. He died in Stoke-on-Trent on 23 July 1941.

JONES, Roger

A very consistent goalkeeper with good reflexes who served a number of clubs during a lengthy career which spanned 23 years. Born in Upton-on-Severn on 8 November 1946, Jones started out as an apprentice with Portsmouth in 1962 and thereafter played, in turn, for Bournemouth, Blackburn Rovers, Newcastle United, Stoke City (1977-80), Derby County (£25,000 in 1980), Birmingham City (on loan) and York City, up to 1985 when he retired to go into coaching (first at York and then with Sunderland). He made over 750 appearances all told, 112 for the Potters whom he helped win promotion from the Second Division in 1978-79, keeping a club record 20 clean sheets in the process. Jones also gained a Third Division championship with Blackburn (1974-75), a Fourth Division prize with York City (1983-84, when former Stoke defender Denis Smith was in charge at Bootham Crescent) and was capped by England at Under-23 level during his time at Ewood Park. Jones was still playing football for Loggerheads FC at the age of 41.

JONES, Roy

Centre-half who changed his name by deed poll from Roy Shufflebottom in 1948, Jones made his debut for the Potters in November 1943 against West Bromwich Albion in League North game at The Hawthorns. After the hostilities he became a full-time professional with the club but his senior outings were limited simply because he was understudy to the England pivot Neil Franklin. Jones went on to appear in just seven Football League matches before leaving The Victoria Ground at the end of the 1949-50 season to join Congleton Town. He was born in Stoke-on-Trent on 29 August 1924.

JONES, Thomas James

Inside or outside-left who played local junior football for Newcastle Boys, Congleton Hornets and Newcastle Swifts before signing for Stoke in May 1899. Born in Newcastle in November 1876, he spent 18 months at The Victoria Ground, scoring nine goals in 29 first-team appearances before moving to Crewe Alexandra. His debut for Stoke was the reigning League champions Aston Villa (away) just before Christmas 1899.

JORDAN Alfred R.

Right-half who played twice for the Potters in 1923-24 after signing for the club from Willowfield FC He left The Victoria Ground for Hull City. Born in Belfast c.1900, he later played for Bristol Rovers (1926-27) but did not appear in their first team. His elder brother, David Jordan, also played for Hull City as well as Ards, Wolves, and Crystal Palace.

JORDAN, Frank

Versatile forward who scored twice in 10 Southern League games for Stoke in season 1911-12 when he occupied four different positions in the front-line. Born c.1888, he joined the club from Reading, and left The Victoria Ground for Merthyr Town.

JORDAN, Joseph

Jordan managed Stoke City for just 10 months – from November 1993 to September 1994. He took over the reins from Lou Macari and duly handed them back to his fellow Scot when he left The Victoria Ground. Born in Carluke on 15 December 1951, Jordan was a robust striker, scoring goals, in turn, for Blantyre Celtic, Greenock Morton, Leeds United (1970), Manchester United (1978), AC Milan and Verona (in Italy), Southampton (1983) and Bristol City. He netted over 140 goals in some 600 appearances at club level and also gained 52 caps for Scotland. He was player-manager at Ashton Gate towards the end of his spell with Bristol City and in 1990 he took charge of Hearts, moving to Stoke from Tynecastle. He is now back in charge of Bristol City (re-appointed in November 1994) (See MANAGERS).

JUMP, Stewart P.

Jump graduated through the junior ranks at The Victoria Ground and made his senior debut in 1970. Basically a reserve defender, he was always hovering on the edge of the first team, yet had a good 1971-72 campaign when he played in 30 matches. In December 1973, Stoke boss Tony Waddington sold Jump to Crystal Palace for £70,000. Born in Crumpshall, near Manchester on 27 January 1962, Jump made over 80 League appearances for the London club and after a loan spell with Fulham (January 1977) he decided to go over to play in the NASL where he spent seven years assisting Tampa Bay Rowdies, Houston Hurricane and Minnesota Kicks. When the USA celebrated its bicentennial, he lined up for Team America against England, this being the highlight of his career.

KAMARA, Christopher

Currently manager of Bradford City (he moved into the hot-seat in November 1995), Middlesbrough-born Kamara led the Valley Paraders to a Wembley Play-off Final victory at the end of that 1995-96 season. He had a fine playing career himself which spanned 20 years (from 1973-93) when he starred for Portsmouth (two spells), Swindon Town (two spells) Brentford, Stoke City (1988-90), Leeds United, Sheffield United and Luton

Joe Jordan

Chris Kamara

Town, joining Bradford City in the summer of 1993 as assistant manager to Lennie Lawrence. Kamara amassed well over 700 appearances at club level (71 for Stoke) being a strong tackling defender or midfielder, who is now passing all his experience on to the young players at Bradford. Kamara was born on Christmas Day 1957 and cost the Potters' manager Mick Mills £27,500 in July 1988 after being involved in an unsavoury incident while playing for Swindon at Shrewsbury which ultimately led to a court appearance (Macari was the Swindon boss at the time). He left Stoke for Elland Road in a £150,000 deal in January 1900 and at the end of that season gained a Second Division championship medal with the Yorkshire club. This followed his Fourth Division medal won with Swindon four years earlier. Kamara also collected a runners-up medal in the Associate Members Cup Final with Brentford (1985).

KASHER, Joseph W.R.

Between 1910 and 1915, sturdy defender Joe Kasher (6ft 2ins tall) played in the north-east of England for Hunwick Juniors, Willington and Crook Town. During World War One he served as a Petty Officer in the Royal Naval Division and was drafted to France where he was held prisoner for two years. In mid-May 1919, he joined Sunderland as a professional and after 90 games for the Wearsiders, moved to Stoke for £1,200 on 18 October 1922. A well-built centre-half, strong in heading, he certainly had that military look about him on the field where he marshalled his fellow defenders accordingly. Born in Willington, County Durham on 14 January 1894, Kasher scored once in 55 games for the Potters and then left the club in May 1924, after failing to agree terms for a new contract. Rather disgusted 'big Joe' returned home to Willington where he played part-time for Carlisle United in the North-Eastern League. In June 1925 he was snapped by Accringtoin Stanley for £1,000 and made 47 appearances during his two years at Peel Park before retiring to take over The Park Hotel next to Stanley's ground. Kasher was the oldest former Stoke player when, at the age of almost 98, he died in Middlesbrough on 8 January 1992.

KAVANAGH, Graham

A strong-running left-sided midfielder with good vision and positional sense, Kavanagh was recruited by Stoke City manager Lou Macari from Premiership club Middlesbrough on a month's loan in mid-September 1996 – around the same time his fellow countryman, Gerry McMahon, was bought from Spurs. Born in Dublin on 2 December 1973, Kavanagh began his career with Home Farm in 1989, joining Middlesbrough in August 1991 as a full-time professional. He did well at Ayresome Park and although having several other players to contend with for a first-team place, he still managed well over 40 senior outings for the Teessiders, although in February 1994 he did have a loan spell with Darlington. Following the arrival of manager Bryan Robson and the move to The Riverside Stadium in the summer of 1994, Middlesbrough suddenly became overloaded with midfielders and eventually Kavanagh was allowed to depart to Stoke. He signed permanently for the Potters for £250,000 in October 1996 and at the end of his first season with the club he had scored four goals in 42 appearances. Prior to moving to The Victoria Ground Kavanagh had represented his country at schoolboy and youth team levels and had also collected nine Under-21 caps for the Republic of Ireland. Kavanagh scored Stoke's last League goal at The Victoria Ground against West Bromwich Albion on 4 May 1997.

KAY, Thomas

Stoke recruited goalkeeper Tom Kay in April 1919 – as they prepared to renew their acquaintance with the Football League after a break of 11 years. Born in Mossley Common near Manchester c.1892, he previously served with Walkden FC (in the Lancashire Combination), Bolton Wanderers (as a reserve) and Rochdale. He cost the Potters £300, and gave the club excellent service until the summer of 1922 when retired from football after suffering a bout of poor health. He played in 77 League and Cup games for Stoke (71 in succession) and in all kept 25 clean sheets. He died c.1940.

KEARTON, Jason Brett

Born in Ipswich, Australia, on 9 September 1969, goalkeeper Kearton made 17 appearances for Stoke City on loan to the club from Everton during the early part of the 1991-92 season. The following year he also had loan spells with Blackpool and Notts County and assisted Preston North End in March 1996. First reserve to Neville Southall at Goodison Park since 1988 when he left Brisbane Lions to try his luck in England, Kearton played less than a dozen games for the Merseysiders prior to leaving for Crewe Alexandra in 1996. He was a member of the Crewe team which beat Brentford in the 1997 Division Two Play-off Final.

KEEN, Kevin Ian

Hardworking right-sided midfield player with good pace and excellent vision. He was bought for £300,000 from Wolverhampton Wanderers in October 1994 at a time when the Potters' engine-room needed stoking up. And he did a useful job before losing his place in the side in 1996. Born in Amersham, on 25 February 1967, Keen played for West Ham United from 1982 (first as an apprentice and then as a professional, March 1984) until moving to Molineux in July 1993 for £600,000. A former England schoolboy and youth international, he made over 270 appearances for the Hammers and followed up with 54 for Wolves. At the end of the 1996-97 season his record with Stoke was six goals in 79 senior appearances.

Kevin Keen

NB. Keen's father, Mike, led Queen's Park Rangers to victory League Cup Final at Wembley and to the Third Division title in the 1966-67 season.

KELLY, Anthony Gerald 'Zico'

After being released by Liverpool and spending a year with Prescot Cables, Kelly helped Wigan Athletic win the Freight Rover Trophy at Wembley in 1985 and since then he's amassed well over 500 appearances as a hard-working midfield player who occasionally has looked rather overweight. After Wigan he served with Stoke City (1986-87, scoring four goals in 44 appearances for the Potters), West Bromwich Albion, Chester City, Colchester United, Shrewsbury Town, Bolton Wanderers, Port Vale, Millwall, Peterborough United, two more spells with Wigan, Altrincham, Halifax Town and Sligo Rovers. Kelly was born in Prescot in October 1964.

KELLY, Charles

Inside-forward Kelly scored five goals in 28 first-team outings for the Potters in the mid-1920s. Born at Sandbach in Cheshire in 1894, he played for his local team, Sandbach Ramblers, before moving to The Victoria Ground in 1923. After three years with Stoke he left the club to join Tranmere Rovers.

KELLY, Christopher

Well-built centre-half or full-back, Kelly had 20 senior games for the Potters (one goal scored) during the 1908-09 season. Born in Tunstall in 1887, he played for Goldenhill Wanderers immediately before signing for Stoke and left the club for Denaby United. He later spent two years with Leeds City 1910-12).

KELLY, George L.

Well-proportioned Scottish inside-forward, tall and rangy who scored 37 goals in 73 first-team outings for Stoke City between March 1956 and March 1958. Born in Aberdeen on 29 June 1933, Kelly was not yet 23 when joined the Potters from home-town club at Pittodrie for £4,000, and he left The Victoria Ground for Cardiff City for a fee of £20,000 (good business on the part of Stoke's boss Frank Taylor). Nicknamed 'Spider' and 'Grace', Kelly also played for Stockport County (July 1959 to May 1960).

KELLY, Nyrere Anthony

No relation to Tony (above) this 'Tony' Kelly was born in the heart of England, at Meriden in February 1966. A fast raiding utility forward, he was an apprentice with Bristol City and played briefly for Dulwich Hamlet, Cheshunt, Enfield, St Albans City and on loan with Gimonas Cycle (Sweden) before joining Stoke City as a full-time professional in January 1990 for £20,000. He went on to score eight goals in 68 appearances for the Potters and after loan spells with Hull City and Cardiff City, he left The Victoria Ground for Bury in September 1993, later transferring to Leyton Orient (July 1995).

KENDALL, Howard

Kendall became the second youngest player ever to appear in an FA Cup Final when he lined up for Preston North End against West Ham United in May 1964 at the age of 17 years 345 days*. A fine wing-half, it was sad that he never won a full England cap, for he was one of the finest players in his position during the late 1960s/early '70s and six appearances at Under-23 level and a game for the Football League representative side were all the honours he received. Born at Ryton-on-Tyne in May 1946, Kendall moved from Preston to Everton in March 1967. A year later he again played in an FA Cup Final and in 1970 he helped the Goodison Park side win the League championship. From Everton he moved to Birmingham City and in 1977 he joined Stoke for £40,000 (being George Eastham's best signing for the club). Kendall made 91 appearances (10 goals scored) in two seasons at The Victoria Ground before switching to Blackburn Rovers. He returned to Goodison Park as a non-contract player in 1981 and after taking over as manager of the Merseysiders, he called it a day (as a player) in 1982 with over 700 League and Cup appearances under his belt at club level. He had a terrific run in charge at Everton, winning two League championships, the FA Cup, the European Cup-winners' Cup and three Charity Shields. He left Goodison Park in 1987 to take over Atletico Madrid, two years later he was appointed manager of Manchester City and went back to Everton as their manager in 1990. It is very rare for someone to make a go of it second time round at a previous club, and this was the case as Kendall was not a success. After a short spell out of the game, he coached the Greek club Xanthi whom he brought over for a pre-season friendly to Stoke in 1994. He then became manager of Notts County (1995) and later that year (December) moved into the hot-seat at Sheffield United to replace Dave Bassett. In 1997 he saw his Blades side beaten by a last-minute Crystal Palace goal in the First Division Play-off Final at Wembley. Kendall then returned to Everton as manager for the third time.

* Jimmy Prinsep was 17 years, 245 days old when he played for Clapham Rovers v Old Etonians in the 1879 FA Cup Final and later,

Howard Kendall

Paul Allen (later a Stoke City player) starred for West Ham v Arsenal in the 1980 Final at the age of 17 years 256 days.
NB: Kendall is one of a handful of men to have featured in an FA Cup as a player (with Preston) and manager (of Everton).

KENNEDY, John

Edinburgh-born inside-forward, who was one of a plethora of Scots who ventured south to try their luck in English football during the 1890s. Jack Kennedy was a strong, muscular player who joined Stoke from Hibernian in the spring of 1898. He went on to score 12 goals in 70 appearances for the club before joining Glossop North End after two years in the Potteries. He later returned to his native Scotland and died *c*.1940, aged 67.

KENNEDY, Michael Francis Martin

Capped twice by the Republic of Ireland at senior level and once by the Under-21s, tough-tackling midfielder Mick Kennedy started his career in 1977 as a junior with Halifax Town and he was still playing non-League soccer in 1997 at the age of 36. Born in Salford on 9 April 1961, he remained at The Shay until August 1980 when he joined Huddersfield Town. From Leeds Road he moved to Middlesbrough (August 1982) and two years later switched to Portsmouth, transferring to Bradford City in January 1988, playing next for Leicester City and then Luton Town. His association with Stoke began in the summer of 1990 when he was signed from Kenilworth Road by his ex-Pompey boss Alan Ball for £250,000. It ended in May 1992 when he joined Chesterfield, having had, said the press 'a torrid time under manager Lou Macari.' Kennedy scored three goals in 65 outings for the Potters.

KERNICK, Dudley Henry John

Stoke City's commercial manager from 1970 to 1982 (when he was succeeded by Mick Cullerton), Kernick was born in Cornwall in August 1921 and as a player he served with Tintagel FC, Torquay United, Northampton Town, Birmingham City, Shrewsbury Town, Kettering Town and Nuneaton Borough, becoming player-coach and then manager-secretary of the latter club. A qualified FA coach he left Nuneaton to move on to the coaching side at Coventry City and from there he transferred to Stoke City as CM in 1970. Although born in England Kernick actually represented a Welsh XI during the war, playing a Birmingham XI at St Andrew's in 1941, this because Wales were a player short. After leaving Stoke he dropped out of football, writing is autobiography called: *Who The Hell Is Dudley Kernick*. His son, Max, went over to America some years ago to work in football.

KETTERING TOWN

Stoke's record against Kettering is:
Southern League

Venue	P	W	D	L	F	A
Home	1	1	0	0	8	1
Away	1	1	0	0	5	1
Totals	2	2	0	0	13	2

Stoke played Kettering in Southern League Division Two in season 1910-11. A crowd of 3,000 saw Jack Peart hit a hat-trick in the 8-1 home win while Amos Baddeley scored twice to lead the goal-spree at Kettering where the attendance was 5,000.

Players with both clubs: Kofi Nyamah and former England centre-half Dave Watson both for Stoke and Kettering Town.

Dudley Kernick was a player with Kettering who later became Stoke City's commercial manager.

KEVAN, David John

Hard-working midfield player with Notts County, Stoke City (1990-93), AFC Bournemouth, Cardiff City and Maidstone United, who was forced to quit the game through injury in January 1995, at the age of 27. Kevan, from Wigtown, scored twice in 102 first-team appearances for the Potters and had 89 League outings whilst at Meadow Lane from where he moved to The Victoria Ground for £75,000. Kevan later returned to coach the Stoke City youth team (March 1997).

KIDDERMINSTER HARRIERS

Stoke's playing record against the Harriers is:
Birmingham & District League

Venue	P	W	D	L	F	A
Home	3	3	0	0	12	3
Away	3	0	1	2	4	6
Totals	6	3	1	2	16	9

These six games were played between 1908-11.

Stoke's three home wins were by 3-1, 4-2 and 5-0 in that order, with Harry Leese scoring twice in each of the last two encounters.

Wilf Kirkham and Ike Turner are two of the players who served with both Stoke and Kidderminster.

KIERNAN, Thomas

A Scotsman from Coatbridge near Dumfries (Queen of the South territory) inside-forward Tom Kiernan was recruited to The Victoria Ground camp by manager Bob McGrory from Celtic in September

1947 for a club record fee of £8,000. He was brought to bolster up the side. He had been a regular first teamer at Parkhead and represented the Scottish League, but sadly he never quite fitted the bill at Stoke and after 15 months' service during which time he hit seven goals in 30 appearances, he left the Potteries and joined Luton Town for £7,000, a shrewd bit of business on the part of McGrory. Kiernan, who was born on 22 October 1918, later returned to Scotland.

KING, John W.

Scorer of 113 goals in 371 games for the Potters during the 1950s, Johnny King was a naturally left-footed player, who had a pair of excellent shooting boots and was a very consistent performer around The Victoria Road. Born in Wrenbury on 9 August 1932, King played initially for Crewe Alexandra where he teamed up on the left with Frank Blunstone who later became an England international. While Blunstone went to Chelsea, King made his way to Stoke, signing for the Potters in September 1953 for £8,000. Standing at just 5ft 7ins tall, King quickly settled into the City attack and became a big favourite with the supporters, being a regular marksman season after season with his best term coming in 1954-55 (20 goals). He is one of only a handful of players who have scored over 100 League goals for the Potters. From The Vic King moved to Cardiff City for £12,000 in May 1961 and a year later he returned to Gresty Road, retiring in 1967 after chalking up a record of 128 goals in 365 League games. King played for the FA XI while with the Alex.

NB: King, in partnership with Stoke reserve of the mid-1950s George Kell, formed a fine double partnership at tennis and were on the brink of making the Wimbledon championships.

KINNELL, George

Kinnell, cousin of the legendary former Scottish international wing-half Jim Baxter, scored eight goals in 111 games for Stoke City over a period of three years. A utility defender, strong and fearless, and able to occupy any position across the back line, and occasionally in attack, Kinnell was born in Cowdenbeath on 22 December 1937 and played for Crossgates Primitives and Aberdeen (from March 1959) before joining Stoke City on 15 November 1963 for £27,000. He left The Victoria Ground (along with Keith Bebbington) for Oldham Athletic in August 1966 in a combined deal worth £26,000, thus teaming up again with his former Stoke colleague Jimmy McIlroy, who had taken over as manager of the Latics. Surprisingly he stayed just three months at Boundary Park before transferring to Sunderland (19 October 1966). Kinnell later played for Middlesbrough (from October 1968).

KIRK, Stephen D.

Full-back Steve Kirk appeared in 12 League games for the Potters during the second half of the 1981-82 season. A Scotsman, born in Kirkcaldy on 3 January 1963, he played for East Fife before transferring south to The Victoria Ground in May 1980 for £10,000. He left the club in June 1982, after failing to command a regular place in the side, and signed for Partick Thistle. He later assisted East Fife (again) and Motherwell, for whom he appeared in almost 250 League games. He had 135 outings for Fife.

KIRKBY, John

Jack Kirby – the first overseas footballer to play for Stoke City – was only 23 when he collapsed and died during a reserve-team game with Wrexham in 1953. A stocky full-back, born in North America on 29 November 1929, he appeared in just one First Division game for Stoke against Middlesbrough (away) in April 1949 (1-1 draw). He had earlier assisted Banks o'Dee FC and joined the Potters in December 1946. He left for Wrexham in a £500 deal a fortnight after his only senior outing for the Potters.

KIRKHAM, Wilfred Thomas

An outstanding goalscorer with Port Vale, Kirkham always seemed to do well against Stoke and it was perhaps no surprise when the City manager and directors decided that they wanted him at The Victoria Ground. Kirkham, who was at Cobridge on 26 November 1901, signed for Stoke for £2,800 in May 1929 – and immediately the fans thought that the 27-year-old would continue his marksmanship at The Vic. He did score well enough – but in truth, never really settled down in his new surroundings and although he rattled in 30 goals in just 51 League games for the Potters, Kirkham returned to the Vale in January 1932. He went on to register a club record 164 League and Cup goals for the Valiants from where he switched to Kidderminster Harriers in the summer of 1933, taking the position as headmaster at Cobridge School at the same time. Cousin of Tom Holford, Kirkham played his early football with the Cobridge Church side and after unsuccessful trails with Stoke, he went off to assist Congleton Town, becoming an amateur with Burslem Port Vale in April 1920. He had several games with Shelton United (from November 1923 onwards) before registering at Sheffield Teacher Training College, going back to the Vale as a trialist in August 1923 before signing professional forms soon afterwards. After retiring as player, he moved to the south of England and died in Bournemouth on 20 October 1974, aged 73.

KIRTON, John

Jock Kirton's career was interrupted by seven years of World War Two but he still managed to attain a terrific record for the Potters by appearing in 249 peacetime matches and 65 in wartime. An Aberdonian, born in March 1916, Kirton was a splendid wing-half who was brought to Stoke by fellow Scot Bob McGrory in November 1935 having earlier won schoolboy caps for his country when playing for St Marchers in Aberdeen and the Banks o'Dee FC Messrs. Tutin and Soo were in the wing-half berths when Kirton arrived at the club, but he bided his time and eventually gained a regular first-team place,

John Kirton

lining up behind Joe Johnson down Stoke's right-hand flank. After 18 years at The Victoria Ground, Kirton moved on to Bradford City in July 1953 after quitting League football he played out his time with Hinckley Athletic and Downings FC before returning to his adopted home town of Stoke to retire. He died in the City General Hospital in March 1996, aged 80.

KNOTT, Percy

Knott was reserve goalkeeper at The Victoria Ground to Tom Kay during the second and third seasons after World War One. Knott, who was born in Hartshill in July 1899, signed from Hartshill White Star, he initially joined the Potters as an amateur in August 1920, signing as a full-time professional two months later. He made his debut in February 1921 – the first of 30 senior games for Stoke during his seven years with the club, the last five as a permanent reserve to the likes of Bob Dixon, Kenny Campbell, Jim Lee and Les Scott. He left The Victoria Ground in September 1927 to join Queen's Park Rangers. In 1961 he emigrated to South Africa where he died in 1972.

LACEY, Anthony John

Lacey was initially a player with Stoke City, making his League debut at the age of 24 in 1968. He was later employed by the club as youth-team coach and also had two spells as caretaker manager in the mid-1980s (during Bill Asprey's reign). Born in Leek on 18 March 1944, Lacey was a pupil (and player) at Leek CSOB and St Luke's College, Exeter, where he studied before turning to soccer. He left The Victoria Ground in 1970 for neighbouring Port Vale for £3,000 and after 215 appearances for the Valiants he ended his playing career with Rochdale and Stafford Rangers before returning to Stoke as coach, being responsible for bringing forward some excellent stars. His second spell at The Vic ended in 1996.

LATHAM, Frederick

Following the success they had with ex-Crewe Alexandra goalkeeper George Clawley, Stoke returned to their Gresty Road neighbours to sign Fred Latham in May 1896. He started off well and played in five League games, but then Billy Rowley was recalled and Latham found himself out in the cold. In May 1897 he duly returned to Crewe, the town where he was born in July 1876.

LATHAM, Capt George MC

Welsh international half-back who played eight Southern League games for Stoke in the 1910-11 season. Born in Newtown on 1 January 1881, he was educated at New Road School, Newton, and played for the local team (Newtown FC) in 1897-98 before going off to fight in the Boer War (to 1901). When in South Africa he played occasionally for Caledonian FC, briefly coming home to have a trial with Everton. On leaving the armed forces he rejoined Newtown, and in the summer of 1902 was transferred to Liverpool, for whom he served for seven years, only having 18 senior outings. In June 1909 he moved to Southport Central and then on to Stoke (September 1910 to March 1911). In April 1911 he was recruited by Cardiff City as head trainer – and when the Welsh side an injury crisis in 1922 he came out of retirement to play in a League game at Blackburn, aged 41, being the oldest debutant in the Welsh club's history. Having collected his first cap for Wales against Scotland in 1905, Latham won his tenth and last v Ireland in 1913 as a last minute replacement when the national team found they were a man short. Latham remained as trainer at Cardiff until May 1932 when he switched north to Chester, also as trainer. But two years later he was back at Cardiff. During World War One he had served as a captain in the 7th battalion, Royal Welsh Fusiliers on the Turkish front, and earned the Military Cross. In the first battle of Gaza in March 1917, Latham's party of 40 men were successful in overpowering the Turkish line, only to learn that HQ had, the previous night, ordered the withdrawal on the basis of reports that around 7,000 Turkish reinforcements were on their way. The line was abandoned and then reoccupied by the Turks only for the RWF to be ordered to retake the position once again. Throughout the 1920s Latham enjoyed a reputation as a trainer of rare skill – and indeed he acted as manager to the Great Britain Olympic team in 1924 and also played an important role in Cardiff's sensational FA Cup Final victory over mighty Arsenal in 1927. In 1936 Latham was seriously injured in a cycling accident and ill-health later forced him to quit soccer and retire to his beloved Newtown where he sadly died a few months before the outbreak of World War Two (9 July 1939). Latham did a terrific amount of charity work, raising hundreds of pounds for the Newtown Hospital where his mother was matron. It is said that during his time at Cardiff he never failed to send his mum a telegram after each match giving her the score.
NB: In his memory Newtown's football ground is called Latham Park.

LAWTON, George

Signed from Porthill FC in July 1901, Lawton played once in goal for Stoke in a 4-2 defeat at Bury in three months after joining. He was born in Tunstall in December 1880, and on leaving The Victoria Ground early in 1902, he signed for Tunstall, playing out the rest of his career at a lower level of football.

LAWTON, George

Standard outside-right born in Stoke in August 1862, Latham played 17 games for the Potters (3 goals scored) during the late 1880s. He joined the club in the summer of 1885 from Stoke St Peter's and left The Victoria Ground in January 1886 for Burslem Port Vale, whom he left after scoring three times in 13 outings. He later assisted Belvedere FC.

LAWTON, John K.

Lawton hit three goals in nine League appearances for Stoke City in 1955. A useful reserve-team centre-forward, born in Woore on 6 July 1936, he played initially for Crewe Alexandra and joined the Potters in June 1954. Three years later, after failing to establish himself in the first XI, he moved to Winsford United (August 1957).

LEE, James Thomas

Stoke paid £750 to Aston Villa for goalkeeper Jimmy Lee in the summer of 1921 He had made just 18 appearances for Villa during the first two seasons after World War One (mainly in place of Sam Hardy) and was keen to make a name for himself at The Victoria Ground. He did well for the Potters, appearing in 24 matches in 1921-22 before he fell away and moved to Macclesfield. Born in Brierley Hill on 12 April 1892, Lee, a good shot-stopper who used his legs exceptionally well, played for Cradley Heath St Luke's and Wulfrians before joining Villa. He died in Dudley in 1955.

LEECH, William

Billy Leech, born in Newcastle-under-Lyme in 1875, played locally for Newcastle White Star and Newcastle Swifts before joining Tottenham Hotspur as an out-and-out winger, very tricky, who could occupy the wing-half or inside-forward positions. He failed to make the grade with the London club and in June 1899 returned to the Potteries to sign for Burslem Port Vale. After a season there when he made 36 appearances, he moved to Stoke (May 1900) and remained at The Victoria Ground until 1903, spending the latter campaign in the Reserves. In all, Leech scored twice in 50 League and Cup games for the club and after leaving The Vic he served with Plymouth Argyle and Leicester Fosse, helping the latter win promotion in 1908 when he was an ever-present in their ranks. He remained at Filbert Street as reserve-team coach and trainer and he died in Leicester on 24 November 1934.

LEEDS CITY

Stoke's playing record against City is:
Football League

Venue	P	W	D	L	F	A
Home	1	1	0	0	2	1
Away	1	1	0	0	1	0
Totals	2	2	0	0	3	1

These two games were in the Second Division in season 1907-08. George Baddeley scored Stoke's winner at Leeds with what was described as a 'capital shot'.

Players with both clubs: Andy Clark, Jimmy Gemmill, Fred Hargreaves, Chris Kelly, Ben Prosser and Jack Whitely.

LEEDS UNITED

Stoke's playing record against United is:
Football League

Venue	P	W	D	L	F	A
Home	39	20	7	12	90	55
Away	39	5	9	25	27	74
Totals	78	25	16	37	117	129

FA Cup

Venue	P	W	D	L	F	A
Away	2	0	0	2	1	4

League Cup

Venue	P	W	D	L	F	A
Home	1	1	0	0	2	1
Away	1	0	0	1	0	2
Totals	2	1	0	1	2	3

Zenith Data Systems Cup

Venue	P	W	D	L	F	A
Home	1	0	1*	0	2	2

* Leeds won 5-4 on penalties

Stoke's best win of their 25 registered so far is 8-1 at The Victoria Ground on 27 August 1934 (Division One). Stanley Matthews was in terrific form that day and scored four of the goals with Joe Johnson and Tommy Sale each netting twice. The crowd was 24,555 – and the game marked the home debut of goalkeeper Ken Scattergood who was hardly troubled throughout the 90 minutes. This is still Leeds' all-time record defeat.

Two more impressive Stoke victories were those of 6-2 and 7-2, both in home Second Division matches in August 1985 and December 1986 respectively. Surprisingly only 7,047 fans saw the first encounter when Keith Bertschin (2), Mark Chamberlain (2), George Berry and Chris Maskery netted for the in-form Potters. For the second clash 12,358 spectators turned up to see Nicky Morgan (3), Carl Saunders, Lee Dixon, Tony Kelly and Tony Ford score for City.

Arty Watkin scored a hat-trick in Stoke's 4-0 home win over United in November 1920.

Leeds' best League win over Stoke is 5-1 – achieved twice – at Elland Road in December 1927 and on the same ground in March 1969 when they went on to win the First Division title. Leeds also won a seven-goal thriller at Stoke in March 1932 by 4-3.

When Stoke beat United 3-2 at The Victoria Ground on 23 February 1974, it brought to an end the Yorkshire club's unbeaten run of 30 consecutive League games (29 from the start of the season).

Stoke and Leeds have met twice in the FA Cup competition – and it was United who came on tops on both occasions – winning 1-0 in January 1912 and 3-1 in January 1963, each time at Elland Road, the second after 12 postponements due to the atrocious weather.

Stanley Matthews played his last League game for Stoke in a 3-1 win over Leeds at Elland Road before transferring to Blackpool in 1947.

Players with both clubs: Len Armitage, Noel Blake, Wilf Chadwick, Lee Chapman, Alan Curtis, George Daniels (amateur with Leeds), Jimmy Greenhoff, Peter Hampton, Vince Hilaire, Chris Kamara, Ronnie Sinclair, Mickey Thomas, Ray Wallace and Tommy Younger.

Frank Taylor was assistant manager of Leeds and later boss of

Stoke's five goalscorers celebrate after the 7-2 win over Leeds United in December 1987. From left to right are Lee Dixon, Carl Saunders, Nicky Morgan (who scored a hat-trick), Tony Kelly and Tony Ford.

Stoke City. Brian Caswell played for Leeds United and later became reserve-team coach at Stoke.

LEES, Terence

Versatile full-back who was understudy to more established players at each of the clubs he served in a longish career. Born in Stoke-on-Trent on 30 June 1952, he began his career at The Victoria Ground, turning pro in July 1969. He went on to appear 29 League and Cup games for the Potters and after a loan spell with Crewe Alexandra in March 1975, he left for Port Vale five months later for £2,000. From Vale Park (where he made 47 appearances) he went over to Holland where, in three years, he assisted Sparta Rotterdam, Rhoda JC and Kerkerade, returning to England to sign for Birmingham City (August 1979). After two seasons at St Andrew's he joined Newport County (August 1981) and followed on with spells in Hong Kong with Morning Star FC, Blackpool (on trial), Altrincham and Stafford Rangers before spending another season in League football with Scunthorpe United on a non-contract basis in 1984-85. He managed Hanley Town in 1985-86 and then did likewise with Kidsgrove Athletic, later acting as assistant manager of Meir KA and then as boss of Ball Haye Green. On retirement (c.1993) Lees, who was also a useful club cricketer, became a sports shop manager in his native Potteries.

LEESE, Harold

Half-back Harry Leese was born in from Goldenhill in 1886 and scored 29 goals in 124 League and Cup games during two spells with the Potters between September 1909 and May 1913. Strong and competitive, and able to play in a number of positions including full-back and half-back, he served initially with Smallthorne and Goldenhill Villa before joining Stoke in the summer of 1909 and after a brief association with Bradford City, he returned to The Victoria Ground and then left again for neighbours Port Vale in 1913. After serving in World War One, Leese went back to the Vale and took his appearance tally up to 57, before rounding off his career with spells at Crewe Alexandra and Goldenhill Wanderers. He died in the 1950s.

LEICESTER CITY (FOSSE)

Stoke's playing record against Leicester is as follows:

Football League

Venue	P	W	D	L	F	A
Home	34	19	9	6	51	30
Away	34	5	12	17	34	59
Totals	68	24	21	23	85	89

League Play-offs (1995-96)

Venue	P	W	D	L	F	A
Home	1	0	0	1	0	1
Away	1	0	1	0	0	0
Totals	2	0	1	1	0	1

FA Cup

Venue	P	W	D	L	F	A
Home	4	2	1	1	8	5
Away	5	0	3	2	6	11
Totals	9	2	4	3	14	16

League Cup
Home   2   0   1   1   2   2
Away   1   0   0   1   2   3
Totals   3   0   1   2   4   5
Simod Cup
Away*   1   0*   1   0   0   0
* Stoke won 5-3 on penalties.

Stoke's best win at League level over Leicester is 4-3 (away) in a Second Division match on a bone-hard pitch in February 1922 when some 21,000 fans saw Fred Groves net twice for the Potters.

In contrast, Leicester's best win over Stoke in League competition has been 5-0 at Filbert Street on 27 August 1923 when the turnout was 14,500.

The Play-off matches took place at the end of the 1995-96 season and after Stoke had held out for a 0-0 draw at Leicester, midfielder Gary Parker sent the Foxes through to Wembley (and eventually into the Premiership) with the only goal in the second leg at The Victoria Ground.

The Simod Cup-tie was played at Filbert Street in December 1987 when Stoke's scorers from the penalty shoot-out were George Berry, Lee Dixon, Carl Saunders, Cliff Carr and Graham Shaw.

Three players who made their League debuts for Stoke against Leicester are Terry Conroy, Ian Moores and Paul Barron.

Players with both clubs: Horace Bailey, Gordon Banks, Junior Bent, Kenny Campbell, Wayne Clarke, Gerry Daly, John Farmer, Des Farrow, Andy Graver, Jack Hall, Robbie James, Mick Kennedy, Arthur Leonard, Billy Leech (also trainer-coach at Leicester), Tom Lonie, Carl Muggleton, Alf S.Owen, Billy Rowley, John Roxburgh, Kevin Russell, Geoff Salmons, Geoff Scott, Peter Shilton, Frank Soo, Tony Spearing and Bill Williamson.

Peter Hodge managed both Leicester City (1919-26) and Stoke City as did Tom Mather, who was in charge at Leicester in season 1945-46 having had a lengthy spell at The Victoria Ground (1923-35).

Louis Page was a player with Stoke who later became a 1950s scout for Leicester City. Bobby Roberts was a player with Leicester and coach with Stoke before returning to Filbert Street as coach in 1988. Dennis Rofe played for Leicester and was appointed reserve-team coach at Stoke in 1993. Cyril Lea was coach at Stoke in 1979 and later coach (1986) and then youth development officer at Leicester (May 1987 to May 1989).

LEIGH, Walter Harold

Outside-right Harry Leigh played for Aston Villa (along with his brother Herbert) before joining Barnsley from where he moved to The Victoria Ground in 1909. He went on to star for the Potters in 70 first-team games, scoring 14 goals. He left Stoke for Winsford United in 1911 and failed to appear in competitive football after World War One, He was born in Lymm, Cheshire in 1888.

LENAGHAN, John

Centre-forward Jack Lenaghan scored ten goals in 37 League appearances for Stoke between December 1911 and March 1913. Born in Southbank c.1888, he played for Mardy FC before moving to The Victoria Ground and on leaving the Potters signed for Chirk. A strong, robust player, he had the pleasure of netting a hat-trick on his debut for Stoke in a 4-3 home win over West Ham United in a Southern League game.

LENNON, George

Lennon played as a full-back for St Mirren, Ayr United and Luton Town before transferring to Stoke for £500 in March 1923. Reserve to Bob McGrory his chances were limited at The Victoria Ground and after just three League games he left the Potteries for Bristol Rovers in May 1925. Born in Kilwinning, Scotland in May 1900, he made over 107 League appearances for Luton

LENNOX, Steven J.M.

Scottish midfielder, born in Aberdeen on 16 November 1964, Lennox played in two League games for the Potters (one as sub) during the second half of the 1982-83 season. He joined the club as a junior, turned professional in December 1981 and before leaving The Victoria Ground in the summer of 1984, he had 11 outings on loan with Torquay United. He later played for Montrose, Forfar Athletic, Peterhead (in the Highland League) and East Fife.

LEONARD, Arthur Ralph (also Arthur Leonard Bamford)

Scorer of three goals in 14 games for the Potters, inside-forward Leonard was born in Leicester in 1874 and joined his first major club, Birmingham, in bizarre circumstances. The Blues had watched Leonard play for Glentoran in November 1921, and a few hours after the game they signed him for £120. Also present at that same match were representatives of Leicester Fosse who recognised Leonard as their 'missing player" Bamford. When approached, Leonard bolted and went missing for several days, sending a telegram to his wife saying that he had gone to America. He later resurfaced in Bristol and was persuaded to return to Birmingham to see out the 1901-02 season, with the club paying Leicester a further £20 for the trouble caused. A real bag of tricks, able to use both feet, Leonard became a big hit with the fans and stayed with Blues until January 1904, scoring 26 goals in 75 appearances before transferring to Stoke. He left The Victoria Ground without really making much of an impact and signed for Reading, later serving with Clapton Orient, St Bernard's and Plymouth Argyle. Before registering as a player with Leicester in 1895, Leonard had served with the 17th Leicestershire Regiment and after 'deserting' Filbert Street he had spells with both Rushden Town and Sheppey United prior to going over to Ireland. He died c.1950.

LESLIE, Steven

A diminutive Scottish central midfielder who made two substitute appearances for Stoke during a brief association with the club, his first in the Anglo-Italian Cup competition v Ancona in September 1994. Born in Dumfries on 6 February 1976, he attended and played for West Park School and was a junior with Motherwell before joining Clydebank in 1991. He was brought down to the Potteries by manager Lou Macari, who signed him in March 1993, and at the end of his first season gained a Midland Youth Cup winners' medal. Unfortunately he was not retained and was given a free transfer in May 1995 when he returned to his native homeland.

LESLIE, Lawrence

A very capable goalkeeper, good on his line, Lawrie Leslie played in 97 senior games for Stoke over a period of two years – 1963 to 1965. A Scot, born in Edinburgh in 1935, and capped five times by his country, he also played for Hibernian, Airdrieonians and Southend United and joined Stoke for £14,000 from West Ham United, leaving the club for Millwall on a free transfer at the end of the 1964-65 campaign. In all Leslie made over 200 League appearances in his career.

LEWIS, Arthur Norman

A very capable goalkeeper who played for the Potters for over six years – to 1935 – making 170 senior appearances (159 in the Football League). Born in Wolverhampton on 13 June 1908, he played for his school team and after a useful spell with the Sunbeam Works team (he was an assembler on the shop floor) joined his home-town club, Wolves, as a professional in July 1928. He left Molineux for The Victoria Ground for a fee of £250, being signed by Stoke boss Tom Mather as cover for Dick Williams in May 1929. Lewis, 5ft 10ins tall and over 12st in weight, eventually gained a regular first-team place at The Victoria Ground in 1930 and was replaced in the team by the former Huddersfield Town goalkeeper Norman Wilkinson. Lewis himself moved on to Bradford Park Avenue (May 1936 for £300) and later served with Tranmere Rovers (from November 1936, signed for £250, to 1939), playing in 58 senior games for the Prenton Park club and helping them win the Third Division North title in 1938. Lewis retired from active football in 1942

LEWIS, Frederick

Right-half Lewis spent two seasons as a reserve at West Bromwich Albion before joining Stoke in April 1910. He made two appearances for the Potters and left the club in May 1911 for Cradley St Luke's, later serving Dudley Town and Brierley Hill. Lewis was born in Birmingham in 1886 and was educated in Handsworth.

LEWIS, John E.

A well-built half-back who came to Stoke from the Welsh club Merthyr Town in January 1934 to bolster up the reserve side. He made only three first-team appearances before injury forced him into an early retirement in 1936. Born in Porthcawl, Glamorgan in 1912, Lewis had done very well in Welsh football and was seen to be just the right type of player Stoke needed to develop. Sadly Lewis' career was short-lived.

LEWIS, Kevin

Injuries interrupted Lewis's career as a full-back with Stoke. He managed only one substitute appearance for the Potters in 1988-89 before leaving for Stafford Rangers (August 1989). Born in Hull on 17 October 1970, Lewis had trials with Mansfield Town during his stay at Stoke. He is nephew to Kevin Lewis (below).

LEWIS, Kevin William

Lewis was also born in Hull on 25 September 1952. He was signed by Stoke boss Tony Waddington from Manchester United in July 1972 after having served a lengthy suspension. A utility defender, he remained at The Victoria Ground for seven seasons, making just 16 first-team appearances. In 1977 he went on loan to Cape Town City and won a League championship medal while out in South Africa, also breaking a leg which kept him out of action for almost two years. He eventually joined Crewe Alexandra in June 1979 before moving into non-League football as player-manager of Telford United and then Leek Town. He later became licensee of the Dyer Arms.

LEYTON

Stoke's playing record against Leyton:
Southern League

Venue	P	W	D	L	F	A
Home	1	0	1	0	0	0
Away	1	0	0	1	0	2
Totals	2	0	1	1	0	2

These two games were in the Southern League in season 1911-12.

Also Stoke beat Leyton 3-1 (away) in another Southern League game in September 1914. But the London club withdrew from the competition in mid-season and consequently the fixture was declared null and void.

LEYTON ORIENT (also Clapton Orient & Orient)

This is Stoke's full playing record against Orient:
Football League

Venue	P	W	D	L	F	A
Home	19	9	4	6	32	17
Away	19	7	1	11	29	29
Totals	38	16	5	17	61	46

League Cup

Venue	P	W	D	L	F	A
Home	1	0	0	1	1	2
Away	1	1	0	0	2	1
Totals	2	1	0	1	3	3*

* Orient won 3-2 on penalties (see below)

Autoglass Trophy

Venue	P	W	D	L	F	A
Away	1	1	0	0	1	0

Stoke's best League win over Orient is 7-1, achieved at The Victoria

Ground on 22 September 1956 (Division Two). That day a crowd of almost 20,000 saw six different players find the net for the Potters with Harry Oscroft netting twice and Bobby Cairns almost bursting the ball with his penalty kick. Stoke also won 5-1 at home in March 1978 when Steve Waddington netted twice.

Orient's best victory over Stoke at League level is 4-0 at home in March 1926 (Division Two) when 8,000 attended Brisbane Road on a bitterly cold day.

Orient's centre-forward Tommy Johnston scored on four of his five visits to Stoke's Victoria Ground during the 1950s.

When the teams met in the second round of the League Cup in 1988-89, Orient won 3-2 on penalties after the scores had finished level at 3-3 over two legs. The Autoglass Trophy clash took place in 1991-92.

Players with both clubs: Tom Coxon, Tommy Dawson, Frank Hesham, Sam Howshall, Tony Kelly, Arthur Leonard, Sam Meredith, Ian Moores, Wilf Phillips, Peter Shilton, Herby Smith, Enos Whittaker and Chris Zoricich (Stoke trialist from New Zealand).

Gilbert Swinburne Glidden was Orient's first-team trainer in the early 1950s (making two appearances for the O's in an emergency). He later became Stoke City's physiotherapist-trainer (1952-54). Dennis Rofe played as a full-back for Orient and in 1993 was made reserve-team coach a Stoke.

Jock Rutherford played briefly for Orient after leaving is managerial post with Stoke in 1923. Cyril Lea played 205 League games for Orient and was later Stoke's coach-assistant manager (1979-80).

● On 22 December 1996, goalkeeper Peter Shilton made his record-breaking 1,000th Football League appearance when he lined up for Orient against Brighton – and just like he had done in his first-ever League game back in 1966, he kept a clean sheet as his side won 2-0.

LIDDLE, Robert

Discovered playing on the right wing for Washington Colliery in the North-East by Stoke City scouts, Bobby Liddle became one of the star performers at The Victoria Ground for more than a decade. Born in Gateshead on 11 April 1908, he joined Stoke in January 1928 at the age of 19 and the following season broke into the first team, establishing himself in the senior side in 1929-30. He went on to score 64 goals in 314 League and Cup games for the Potters as a utility forward up to World War Two, collecting a Second Division championship medal in 1932-33. During the first half of the war, Liddle made a further 152 appearances (28 goals scored) before becoming a trainer at the club, a position he held until 1953. In all he gave Stoke City FC 25 years service. Standing 5ft 6ins tall and weighing 10st 7lbs, for quite some time Stoke had Stan Matthews and Joe Johnson as their regular wingers, so Liddle was used as an inside-right and he did extremely well, often performing with great zest both at home and away. He died in Nottingham in 1972, aged 64.

LIMITED COMPANY

In August 1895, Stoke Football Club became a Limited Liability Company and at the same time former goalkeeper Billy Rowley was appointed secretary-manager at The Victoria Ground. When the 'new' Stoke Football Club was formed in 1908 it retained his Limited Liability status.

LINCOLN CITY

Stoke's playing record against Lincoln City reads:

Football League

Venue	P	W	D	L	F	A
Home	12	9	2	1	38	10
Away	12	6	2	4	21	18
Totals	24	15	4	5	59	28

FA Cup

Venue	P	W	D	L	F	A
Home	2	2	0	0	9	0

League Cup

Venue	P	W	D	L	F	A
Away	1	0	0	1	1	2

Stoke's best victory of their 17 recorded at League level over the Imps is 8-0, achieved in February 1957 (see match report below), while Lincoln's best win over the Potters is 3-0, accomplished at Sincil Bank in September 1959 (Division Two).

Stoke whipped Lincoln 6-1 at home in another Second Division match in September 1959 when Dennis Wilshaw (3) and Tony Bentley (2) led the goal-rush. The Potters also beat Lincoln 4-1 at The Victoria Ground in 1953-54 (Division Two) when Johnny King scored twice, and they repeated that scoreline away from home the following season when winger Harry Oscroft hit a hat-trick. In the return fixture in 1954-55, inside-forward Frank Bowyer claimed three goals of Stoke's goals in their excellent 4-2 home win over the 'Imps.'.

Players with both clubs: Gary Bannister, Steve Foley, Andy Graver, Fred Groves, Arthur Jepson, Eric McManus, Harry Pugh, Jack Robertson, Keith Scott, Barry Siddall, Jack Whitley, Bobby Windsor (Stoke reserve) and Jack Worsdale.

Graver scored a record 143 League goals for Lincoln.

Stoke City 8 Lincoln City 0

On bitterly cold afternoon on 23 February 1957, a Victoria Ground crowd of 10,790 (almost a third of the average gate) saw one man – outside-right Neville 'Tim' Coleman – set a new scoring record for Stoke City. That day, the 27-year-old outside-right netted seven goals (from eight efforts) in a Second Division League game against Lincoln City.

In the first half, Stoke, defending the Boothen End, played some excellent football and went in at the break leading 4-0. The pattern of play continued during the second half as the Potters doubled their goal-tally to run out convincing winners by 8-0. As stated, the majority of the scoring was done by one man, the dynamic 'Tim' Coleman and this is how those eight goals went in:

7 mins   Hutton hooked a cross from the left into Coleman's path and the winger did the rest.
18 mins Kelly's right-wing cross fell straight to Coleman who took the ball in his stride to score with ease.
20 mins Kelly's floated cross hung in the air and before goalkeeper or defenders could react, the alert Coleman swooped to complete his hat-trick.
32 mins Emery slipped in trying to intercept a pass, allowing Coleman in to score from 10 yards.
48 mins Johnny King hit the net this time, scoring from an acute angle.
50 mins King's corner was deflected into Coleman's path and the winger did the business from close range.
73 mins King led a raid down the right and from his cross Coleman banged home his sixth goal.
82 mins The best goal of the game. Kelly crossed from the right, Coleman, timing his run to perfection, dived forward to plant a firm header wide of the Lincoln 'keeper Downie.

The ball, suitably autographed, was presented to Coleman after the game by the Stoke City players, manager and directors. The media made such a fuss over Coleman, but amazingly that was his lot, for he failed to score again for the Potters that season.

LINDSAY, Alec

Blond left-back Lindsay played in 126 League games for Bury and 170 for Liverpool before joining Stoke City for £25,000 in August 1977. A very competent defender, who was capped four times by England at full international level as well as a youth-team player, Lindsay scored three goals in 22 games for the Potters before quitting the club to go to join Oakland Stompers in America in March 1978 for £7,000. Later on he served with Toronto Blizzard and Newton FC Lindsay was born in Bury on 27 February 1948.

LISTER, Robert

Nimble outside-left whose only senior appearance for the Potters was against Fulham in a Second Division game at Craven Cottage in November 1927 when he laid on two goals in a 5-1 victory. Born in Fife in June 1901, Lister played for Hearts and Dunfermline Athletic before moving to The Victoria Ground. He left Stoke for West Ham United early in 1929 and in 1930-31 served with Exeter City. Later on he had spells with Rhyl and Shrewsbury Town.

LITTLE, Thomas Stewart Colquhoun

Scorer of one goal in 21 Second Division games for Stoke during the early 1920s, Tommy Little was a useful centre-forward who, prior to joining the Potters in December 1920, had netted 106 times in 232 League outings for Bradford Park Avenue. Born in Ilford, Essex, on 27 February 1890, he played for Ilford FC (1907) and Southend United (from August-November 1908) before moving to Bradford. Little was forced to retire through injury in 1922.

LIVERPOOL

Stoke's playing record against Liverpool is:
Football League

Venue	P	W	D	L	F	A
Home	53	23	18	12	77	55
Away	53	3	9	41	36	121
Totals	106	26	27	53	113	176

FA Cup

Home	2	0	2	0	0	0
Away	4	0	0	4	0	6
Totals	6	0	2	4	0	6

League Cup

Home	1	0	0	1	2	3
Away	2	0	1	1	3	4
Totals	3	0	1	2	5	7

Stoke's best League win over the Merseysiders is 6-1 at The Victoria Ground on 6 February 1897 (Division One). That day, a crowd of 7,000 saw Joey Schofield and Jimmy Hill both score twice for the Potters.

Liverpool's best over Stoke is 7-0, which they achieved on 4 January 1902 (Division One) when the gate topped 10,000. An outbreak of food poisoning left Stoke with just seven fit players for this game at Anfield and deploying a revolutionary 1-8-2 formation (with four members of the side basically unfit) the Potters simply couldn't contain the Reds for whom Andy McGuigan scored five times.

Stoke beat Liverpool 5-2 at home in October 1903 and 4-2 in the Potteries in March 1955 (Division Two), while Liverpool have run up some fine home wins over the Potters including those of 4-0 in October 1897, 5-0 in April 1935, 4-0 in March 1949, 5-1 in March 1960, 6-1 in December 1963, 5-3 in April 1976, 4-0 in December 1976 (in front of 50,371 fans) and 5-1 in March 1983. The Reds also won 5-1 at The Victoria Ground in March 1982 when the turnout was a disappointing 16,758.

Over 35,500 fans witnessed a seven-goal thriller between the teams at The Victoria Ground in March 1959 when Dennis Wilshaw was in fine form with two goals for City.

A crowd of 49,000 saw Liverpool, the holders, beat Stoke 2-0 at Anfield in an FA Cup-tie in 1975 and eight years later, on the same ground in the same competition, there were 36,666 fans present to see Liverpool repeat that scoreline.

Liverpool knocked the Potters out of the FA Cup again in season 1987-88, winning the Anfield replay 1-0 after a goalless draw at The Victoria Ground.

Stoke had a great battle against Liverpool in the League Cup in season 1991-92 before going out 5-4 on aggregate. After a 2-2 draw at The Victoria Ground, Liverpool won 3-2 at Anfield despite two strikes from Wayne Biggins (one a penalty).

Players with both clubs: Jimmy Bradley, Joe Brough, Kenny Campbell, Steve Foley, Howard Gayle, John Gidman, Bruce Grobbelaar, Dick Johnson, Tony Kelly, George Latham, Alec Lindsay, Carl Muggleton, Louis Page, Mark Prudhoe (on loan at Anfield), Alec Raisbeck, Tom Robertson, Jack Robinson, Dr Leigh Richmond Roose, Colin Russell, Robbie Savage, Sammy Smyth, Willie Stevenson, Harry Taylor, Jack Tennant, Mark Walters, Albert Whitehurst and Tommy Younger. Raisbeck later scouted for Liverpool.

Alan A'Court was a outside-left with Liverpool who later became caretaker manager-coach of Stoke City. And Verdi Godwin was a player with Stoke who later had two spells on the Anfield scouting staff.

LLANELLY

Stoke's record against the Welsh club:
Southern League

Venue	P	W	D	L	F	A
Home	2	2	0	0	5	2
Away	2	1	0	1	2	3
Totals	4	3	0	1	7	5

These four games were played during seasons 1913-14 and 1914-15. 'Arty' Watkin scored a hat-trick in Stoke's 3-1 home win in November 1914 – their best victory of the three recorded over Llanelly. The Welsh club's only success was a 2-0 triumph at home seven months earlier, in March 1914.

LOCKER, William

Inside-forward Bill Locker was a 'one game wonder' for Stoke –

having his only outing for the club in November 1889, a 2-1 home defeat at the hands of reigning League and Cup double-winners Preston North End. Born in Nottingham in 1864 he played initially for Long Eaton Rangers and after his brief association with the Potters he returned home to play for Notts County.

LOCKETT, Arthur H.

Regarded as a 'swift outside-left' with energy and pace, Lockett gained England international honours when capped against Ireland in February 1903 (won 4-0) and represented the Football League the following year. Born at Alsagers Bank in August 1877, he played for Crewe Alexandra before joining Stoke in May 1900, and went on to score seven goals in 73 senior appearances for the Potters before leaving The Victoria Ground for Aston Villa in a £40 transaction in May 1903. A player who loved to dribble with the ball, he later played for Preston North End (September 1905-July 1908), Watford (1908-May 1912) and finally Port Vale, although he never made Vale's first XI. He died in c.1950.

LOCKETT, Harry

Lockett was Stoke's manager from April 1884 to August 1890 and it was he who took the club into the Football League in 1888 and he was also in charge when professionalism was introduced, agreeing to pay the better, more established players at the club the princely sum of two shillings and sixpence a week (13p).

It was Lockett who represented Stoke at a meeting called at Anderton's Hall Hotel on the 23 March 1888 to discuss the formation of the Football League proposed by Aston Villa's chief, William McGregor. Lockett later became the Football League's first secretary, having his headquarters at No.8 Parker's Terrace, Etruria (later renamed 177 Brick Kiln Lane). Initially the post of League secretary was an elected position, but eventually Lockett became a full-time paid employee of the League, merging the job with that of treasurer. Lockett held the secretarial positions simultaneously with both Stoke and the Football League, but in the end he relinquished the appointment at The Victoria Ground to concentrate solely on his League duties.

LONGEST SEASONS

Stoke's League season in 1962-63 lasted nine months and four days – from 18 August to 22 May inclusive.

The 1995-96 campaign spanned nine months and three days finishing with the second leg of the Play-off semi-final against Leicester City. And the 1981-82 season lasted 8 months and 21 days, from 29 August to 20 May.

LONG SERVICE

In 1997 Stoke City secretary Mike Potts completed 38 years' service with the club. He joined The Victoria Ground office staff initially on a part-time basis in 1959, was then upgraded to assistant secretary and then to secretary in succession to Bill Williams in July 1977.

Bob McGrory spent over 31 years at The Victoria Ground – joining as a player in April 1921 and then rounding off his stay at The Victoria Ground as a manager (from June 1935 to May 1952).

Stoke City's current secretary Mike Potts has now completed 38 years service with the club (since 1959). He acted as assistant secretary to Bill Williams before taking over his present position in July 1973.

Tony Waddington's association with the club spanned 25 years. It began in 1952 when he joined as a coach. Five years later he was appointed assistant manager (to Frank Taylor) and then became team manager himself in June 1960, holding office until March 1977.

Stanley Matthews had two separate spells with Stoke – 1932-47 and 1961-65 – for a total of 20 years (inclusive); Alan Bloor was with the club for 17 years (1961-78) and Eric Skeels was a player at The Vic for 16 years (1960-76).

For 43 years (from August 1924 to May 1967) part-time commissionaire Fred Bradley never missed a first-team match at The Victoria Ground – he never saw one either. For he was confined to the main entrance to the ground where he sat or stood for seven hours each game – being in position three hours before kick-off, right up until the final guest left.

LONIE, Thomas

Centre-forward Lonie scored four goals in nine League games for Stoke in 1895. Born in Dundee in 1872, he played for his local clubs, Dundee Harp and Dundee prior to coming down to the Potteries. Unfortunately he only stayed with Stoke for three months, later assisting Leicester Fosse, Notts County, Darwen and Dundee Wanderers.

LOWE, Kenneth

Long-striding 6ft 1in midfield player who made 13 appearances for Stoke City between August and December 1993. Born near the racecourse at Sedgefield on 6 November 1961, Lowe started out as an apprentice with Hartlepool United in 1977, turning professional in November 1978. He had a spell with Billingham in 1984 and then served with Spearwood FC (in Australia), Gateshead, Morecambe and Barrow before establishing himself with Scarborough in January 1988. He returned to Barrow in April 1989 and two years later was signed by Barnet for £40,000. He joined Stoke on a free transfer from Underhill and left The Victoria Ground for Birmingham City for £75,000. He had loan spells with Carlisle United and Hartlepool United during

Kenny Lowe

his stay at St Andrew's, which ended in the summer of 1996 when he returned to non-League soccer.

LOWELL, Eric James

After a fairly lean time with Derby County, inside-forward Lowell joined Stoke City in May 1955, and he did well in his seven first-team appearances for the Potters, scoring three goals. However, he failed to maintain that excellent form and left the club for Stafford Rangers in 1957. He was born in Cheadle on 8 March 1935.

LUMSDEN, John W.

Born in Edinburgh on 15 December 1960, inside-forward Lumsden was 19 years of age when he moved from East Fife to Stoke City in January 1980 for £40,000. Sadly, he never settled in the Potteries and made only six appearances (four as sub) for the club before returning to Scotland after an unsuccessful trial with Doncaster Rovers.

LUMSDON, John David

Born at Newcastle-upon-Tyne on 30 July 1956, right-back John Lumsdon graduated through the junior ranks at The Vic and played 28 games for Stoke (November 1975 and October 1977). He had a loan spell with Port Vale in March 1978 (five League games) and after leaving the Potters, served with Telford United.

LUTON TOWN

Stoke's playing record against the Hatters is:
Football League

Venue	P	W	D	L	F	A
Home	14	5	6	3	26	20
Away	14	5	5	4	13	19
Totals	28	10	11	7	39	39

Southern League

Venue	P	W	D	L	F	A
Home	2	1	0	1	5	5
Away	2	0	1	1	2	3
Totals	4	1	1	2	7	8

FA Cup

Venue	P	W	D	L	F	A
Home	1	0	0	1	2	3
Away	1	0	1	0	1	1
Totals	2	0	1	1	3	4

Simod Cup

Venue	P	W	D	L	F	A
Away	1	0	0	1	1	4

Stoke's best win over the Hatters at League level is 5-0 – achieved at The Victoria Ground as recently as 4 November 1995 (Division One) when a crowd of 9,382 saw a late goal rush following an early first-half strike from the Canadian international Paul Peschisolido. The other four Potters' goals came from Simon Sturridge (2), John Gayle and Nigel Gleghorn (all of them scored in the last 17 minutes). Luton's best League victory over Stoke came at their Kenilworth Road stadium in November 1993 when debutant goalkeeper Gordon Marshall had a nightmare against the Hatters attackers. Stoke, in fact, were 2-0 up in this game through Dave Regis and Linton (own-goal) but caved in afterwards with the unlucky Marshall at fault with at least three of the goals.

The two third-round FA Cup games were played in season 1984-85 when the Potters did the hard work by drawing at Luton, but then lost out in the replay before a 9,917 crowd at The Victoria Ground. Goalkeeper Stuart Roberts, at the age of 17, played for Stoke in both these matches against the Hatters.

In the Simod Cup-tie, played in March 1988, Graham Shaw scored for Stoke who were well and truly beaten by the Finalists of that year, the Hatters before a 4,480 crowd at Kenilworth Road. Brian Stein (Mark's brother) scored twice for Luton that evening.

Players with both clubs: Jimmy Adam, Ian Allinson, Viv Busby, Billy Draycott, John Dreyer, Ashley Grimes, Vince Hilaire, Mick Kennedy, Tommy Kiernan, George Lennon, Alex McClure, Bert Mitchell, Fred Molyneux, Frank Soo and Mark Stein.

McALINDEN, James

Stoke manager Bob McGrory signed Irishman McAlinden from Portsmouth in September 1947 for a club record fee of £7,000. He was said to be the 'right man' to fill the problematic inside-left position. A tall, well-balanced player, McAlinden was inconsistent at Stoke and after scoring twice in 36 League and FA Cup appearances for the Potters, he left the club in October 1947 to join Southend United for £6,000. Born in Belfast on 31 December 1917, McAlinden (a teetotaller and non-smoker) had a fine career on the whole. After winning schoolboy and junior international honours and representing the Irish League, he was capped six times at senior level by his country – twice by Eire and on four occasions by Northern Ireland. Educated at Milford School (Belfast), he started his career with Glentoran and after a good spell with Belfast Celtic, he joined Pompey with whom he won an FA Cup winners' medal (v Wolves) in 1939. After leaving Southend in 1954 McAlinden became player-manager of Glentoran, later taking the same position with Distillery and Droghedra United. As boss of Distillery, he nurtured Martin O'Neill (the current boss of Leicester City). In the 1960s and '70s he scouted periodically for Liverpool before retiring to live in Belfast where he died in 1994.

McALLISTER, Samuel

Utility forward McAllister scored four goals in 16 senior games for

Stoke in 1908-09 – his only season with the club. Born in Scotland c.1882, it is believed he played as a teenager for Motherwell and was a reserve with West Ham United, Grimsby Town, Huddersfield Town and Wrexham before joining the Potters. After leaving The Victoria Ground he returned home to assist Port Glasgow.

McARDLE, Peter

Orthodox outside-left with Stoke during 1933-34 and 1934-35, he scored once in seven First Division matches when replacing Joe Johnson. Born in Durham in 1914, he played for Durham City before joining Stoke and after leaving the Potters McArdle served with Exeter City (nine outings in 1935-36), Carlisle United, Stockport County (four games in 1937-38), Gateshead and Crewe Alexandra.

Lou Macari

MACARI, Lou (Luigi)

Born in Edinburgh on 7 June 1949, Macari played junior football with St Michael's Academy (Kilwinning) Kilmarnock Amateurs and Kilwinning Rangers, and senior football for Celtic (June 1966 to January 1963), Manchester United (January 1973 to July 1984) and Swindon Town (May 1984 to May 1985) winning three League championships and two Scottish Cups while with the Glasgow club and an FA Cup medal with United (1977). He was also capped 24 times by his country to go with those he gained at schoolboy, youth and Under-23 levels. He started his managerial exploits as player-boss of Swindon Town in 1984-85, taking over as team manager after two seasons and holding office at The County Ground until 1989. He then served with West Ham (1989-90) and Birmingham (1990-91) before being appointed manager of Stoke (first time round) in May 1991. He then left The Vic for a brief sojourn with Celtic (from November 1993), returning to the Potteries in October 1994, holding office until May 1997 when he quit the club for the second time. As a manager he guided Swindon to the Fourth Division title in 1986 and promotion to Division Two the following year. In 1991 he took Birmingham to victory in the Leyland DAF Cup Final at Wembley and followed up with success in the Autoglass Trophy with Stoke in 1992 and promotion from Division Two in 1993. As a player Macari scored almost 150 goals in over 600 competitive games (88 in 391 for Manchester United). He managed Stoke (in his two spells) in 250 League games, winning 108.

NB: At 5ft 6ins, Macari is one of the smallest footballers ever to play for Scotland.

MACARI, Michael

Mike Macari is the son of manager Lou. A useful striker, born at Kilwinning, Scotland on 4 February

Mike Macari

1973, he made his debut for the Potters as sub against Barnsley in September 1996 after graduating through the junior ranks at West Ham and then at The Victoria Ground to where he moved from the London club in May 1991 when his father took over at Stoke following his spell in charge at Upton Park. At the end of the 1996-97 season, Macari had scored three goals in 32 senior appearances for Stoke City.

McAUGHTRIE, David

Stoke City scout Neville Briggs sent McAughtrie down to the Potteries from Ayr Boys Club in the summer of 1979. A 6ft 1in defender, he certainly had the build to become a professional footballer and after making steady progress (and winning five youth caps for his country) he was taken on as a full-time professional at The Victoria Ground by manager Alan Durban in January 1981, having made his League debut at the age of 17 against high-flying Nottingham Forest, who won 5-0 against a depleted Stoke side. McAughtrie was born in Newcummock, Ayrshire on 30 January 1963 and went on to appear in 89 senior games for the club (33 as sub). But when Bill Asprey took over as manager unfortunately he became surplus to requirements and eventually left the club for Carlisle United in July 1984, switching across country to York City in June 1985 and then on to Darlington in July 1987. He came out of League football and signed for Northwich Victoria in 1988, winning a Staffordshire Senior Cup and mid-Cheshire Senior Cup winners medals before extending his career with spells at Bishop Auckland and Harrogate Town.

McCARTHY, Frederick

A former Tranmere Rovers inside-forward, McCarthy joined Stoke from Chester in the summer of 1914, choosing the Potters instead of Middlesbrough, who had also been interested in signing him. He was a useful goalscorer and netted eight times in 11 games for the Potters in that last season prior to World War One. Born in Birkenhead in June 1890, he worked in Liverpool as a teenager and opted for Stoke because he wanted to continue in his line of work. During his spell at The Victoria Ground he became something of a hero when, on returning home, he dived from the quayside at Liverpool docks to save a potential suicide attempt. Guesting for Port Vale and Bury during the hostilities, McCarthy later played for Chesterfield, Willenhall and Stafford Rangers before retiring in 1929.

McCLELLAND, John W.

An inside-forward who played in four League games for the Potters in 1952. Born in Colchester on 11 August 1930, he joined Stoke from his home-town club at Layer Road and had two years at The Victoria Ground before transferring to Swindon in June 1954. He later assisted Rochdale (1955-56).

McCLURE, Alexander

A player with a fine physique and excellent positional sense, McClure was the fulcrum of the Birmingham defence in almost 200 games in 11 years (1912-23) during which time he gained a Second Division championship medal (1921) and twice represented the Football League. He moved to rivals Aston Villa, but only spent a season there before switching his allegiance to Stoke in October 1924. Born in Workington in April 1894, and a former Grangemouth junior, McClure gave the Potters good service in 31 senior outings prior to his departure to Coventry in March 1926. He later served with Walsall, Bromsgrove Rovers, Luton (1927) and Market Harborough, and during his time at Kenilworth Road he coached the colts team. On retiring in 1928 he went back to St Andrew's, first as youth manager (to 1932) and then as assistant manager (to 1934), earning the reputation as a hard task-master. After leaving football McClure worked for Rudge Motor Cycles and thereafter ran a successful haulage company in Small Heath. He died in Birmingham on 8 August 1973.

McCORMICK, Robert

Scottish international outside-right who won one full cap with Abercorn in 1886. Born in Paisley in 1872, McCormick scored twice in 12 League games for Stoke during his brief stay at The Victoria Ground which lasted four months from September to December 1889. He joined the club from Abercorn and returned there after feeling homesick.

McCOLL, James

Another Scottish import, McColl was a thick-set, robust centre-forward who had a useful career north of the border where he served with Hibernian, Leith Athletic, Glasgow Celtic and Partick Thistle. Born in Glasgow in 1896, he came to Stoke in July 1920 from Parkhead and had a reasonable season at The Victoria Ground, scoring five goals in 27 League appearances before returning to Thistle.

McCUE, John William

Full-back John McCue had a fine career at The Victoria Ground. Born at Longton on 22 August 1922, he was a pupil at Longton school and joined Stoke as a 15-year-old in 1937, turning professional in April 1940. Proportionally right for a defender, he was strong in every department of full-back play, kicking long and true, a fine tackler and determined in every sense of the word. Not a dirty player, he never shirked a challenge and always gave 100 per-cent effort on the field. A great club man, McCue played in 502 League games and 40 FA Cup-ties for the Potters (two goals scored) as well as in 133 wartime matches. He broke Bob McGrory's appearance record for the club and only Eric Skeels has played in more first-class games for the Potters than McCue. He made his debut against Mansfield in September 1940 and after establishing himself at the club, he remained a permanent fixture in the side for 14 years, eventually making way for Tony Allen. McCue left The Victoria Ground in September 1960, joining Oldham Athletic at the age of 38. He made 56 appearances for the Latics in two years at Boundary Park, and later played for Macclesfield (1962-63). A qualified PE instructor in Stoke, McCue skippered the Potters several times and was indeed one of the finest players ever to don a Stoke City jersey.

McDAID, John

McDaid, an inside-forward, played in four League games for Stoke after arriving at the club in September 1930, initially as an amateur, signing as a professional three weeks later. Born in Londonderry in 1909, he assisted Heptonstall (before Stoke) and after leaving The Victoria Ground in May 1932 he joined Belfast Crusaders on a free transfer.

McDONALD, Edward

Signed from Burslem Port Vale in August 1896, right or left-half Ted McDonald made two League appearances for the Potters before returning to his former club in May 1897. Two-and-a-half years later (November 1899) after taking his appearance tally for the Valiants past the century mark and gaining a Staffordshire Cup winners' medal, he signed for Notts County for a substantial fee. He later played for Portsmouth. Born in Newcastle (Staffs) in June 1876, McDonald played his early football with Newcastle FC and during his first spell with the Vale (1894-96) he was described as a 'resourceful player.' He died in October 1938.

McDONALD, Michael F.

In October 1972, following Gordon Banks' terrible car accident, Stoke manager Tony Waddington reinforced his goalkeeping availability by signing Mike McDonald from Clydebank for £20,000 instead of Bobby Clark, the Scottish national. Himself a Scotsman, born in Glasgow on 8 November 1950, McDonald, who had five youth caps to his name when he arrived at The Vic, went on to play in nine first-team games for Stoke in two seasons (1972-74) before leaving for Hibernian in June 1974 for £22,000. After his spell at Easter Road he assisted Dundee, Berwick Rangers and St Johnstone, helping the latter win the Scottish First Division title. He later became manager of Gala Fairydean.

McDONALD, William James

A dashing Scottish inside-forward, born in Inverness c.1877, McDonald played for Stoke in the 1901-02 season, scoring three goals in nine League games. He joined the Potters from Derby County for whom he had starred alongside Steve Bloomer in the 1899 FA Cup Final. He was previously with Dundee (from June 1898) and returned to Dens Park on his departure from The Victoria Ground.

McGEACHAN, James

A very talented but tempestuous centre-half who had a good career both in Scotland and in England. Born in Edinburgh in February 1871, he was playing exceedingly well for Hibernian when Celtic moved in for him at the start of the 1894-95 season. McGeachan certainly thought above a move to Glasgow but instead of joining the Scottish giants he chose Bolton Wanderers, moving to Burnden Park in November 1894. Three years later he was suspended by the Wanderers' committee for failing to travel for an away game at Sheffield. This ban was lifted, but in the interim period he had lost his place in the team to Bobby Brown and was subsequently transferred to Stoke for £150 (December 1897). He spent only three months at The Victoria Ground, making six League appearances for the Potters before being suspended sine die for misconduct. He left Stoke in February 1898 to return to Hibs and then, surprisingly McGeachan went back to Bolton for a second spell in 1899, finally retiring in 1901 (through injury). He scored five goals in 81 appearances during his time at Bolton. He died c.1935.

McGILLIVRAY, John

Centre-half McGillivray joined Stoke from Southport Central in August 1911. He had previously been with Berry's Association and Manchester United, signing initially for the Old Trafford club as an amateur in January 1907, turning professional the following month. He spent just a season with the Potters, making 25 League appearances before leaving the club to join Dartford (August 1912). He was born in Broughton, Lancashire in 1889.

McGROARTY, James

An Irishman, born in Londonderry on 30 August 1957, outside-right McGroarty was secured by Stoke in September 1977 for £7,000 from Finn Harps, having earlier leant his football with the Tammaherin Youth Club. He spent almost three years at The Victoria Ground, scoring twice in nine first-team appearances before returning to Finn Harps (May 1980). He later served with Glenavon and Crusaders prior to taking over as manager of Dungiven Celtic (1993).

McGRORY, Robert

Bob McGrory joined Stoke in April 1921 after service with Dumbarton and Burnley for whom he made three League appearances. He stayed at The Victoria Ground for the next 31 years, as a player and then manager. Born in Bishoptown on 17 October 1891, and a Scot through and through, he was an apprentice joiner on Clydeside before taking up football. He never regretted that decision and had a fine career in the game, performing supremely well at right full-back for the Potters. A strong-tackling defender, whose positional sense was second to none, he was hardly ever flustered, playing the game wholeheartedly and was very rarely spoken to by the referee. McGrory went on to appear in 511 League and Cup games for the player in 1934-35. When Mather left The Vic for Newcastle United in June 1935, McGrory was asked to take over the managerial hot-seat. He took to it like a duck to water and made hardly changes in the personnel at the club. He gradually replaced the ageing players with younger ones and steadily built up a useful side. One of his best buys was Tommy Sale. In the summer of 1952, McGrory stepped down as boss, handing over the reins to Frank Taylor, having managed the team in 192 League games of which 90 ended in victories. He remained in close contact with the club until his death in Glasgow on 24 May 1954.

McILROY, James

One of the greatest inside-forwards of his time, McIlroy at times could make the ball talk. He was a superb footballer who loved to play the passing game, being the vital 'cog' in the Burnley midfield from 1950 to 1963, when he made a total of 497 first-team appearances for the Turf Moor club and scored 131 goals, besides making at least double that number for his colleagues. He was born in Lambeg, a small village south of Lisburn, Belfast on 25 October 1931, and from the age of three kicked a ball around the back garden, encouraged by his father, Harry, a part-timer with Distillery and his uncle, Willie, a professional with Portadown. McIlroy practised constantly and on leaving school at the age of 15, he joined Craigavil FC near Bangor. In August 1949 he became a professional with Glentoran, one of his teammates being Billy Bingham. He developed rapidly and Burnley

Jimmy McIlroy

Potters, skippering the team for quite some time. He made his debut in May 1921 and played his last first-team game 14 years later in May 1935 when well past his 43rd birthday. In 1932 he had actually stepped down from regular first-team football to take over the running of Stoke's reserve team but injuries meant that he was recalled to senior action much to the delight of manager Tom Mather. McGrory appeared in all 42 League games in his final season as a

signed him for £8,000 in March 1950, giving him his debut against Sunderland in a First Division game seven months later. McIlroy became an established member of the side and during his time at Turf Moor helped Burnley win the League title in 1960 and reach the FA Cup Final two years later when he also finished runner-up behind his teammate Jimmy Adamson in the Footballer of the Year poll. After being placed on the transfer list, McIlroy was snapped up by Stoke boss Tony Waddington for £25,000 in March 1963. He did a terrific job at The Victoria Ground, helping the Potters win the Second Division title by scoring six vital goals in 18 matches at the end of that season. He went on to net 19 times in 116 outings for the Potters before joining Oldham Athletic as manager on 28 January 1966, coming out of retirement to sign up again as a player within two months while also retaining the position as team boss. He resigned from Boundary Park on 28 August 1968 to return to Stoke as first-team coach. He later did a similar job at Bolton before becoming assistant manager at Burnden Park in 1970, only to resign after just 28 days in charge. Capped 55 times by Northern Ireland (1951-65), McIlroy also represented Great Britain against the Rest of Europe in 1955 and played twice for a Football League XI in 1960.

McILROY, Samuel B. MBE

Sammy McIlroy was Stoke's record signing when he joined the club from Manchester United for £350,000 in February 1982. Potters' boss Richie Barker had raised the cash from the sale of Adrian Heath to Everton for £700,000. Born in Belfast on 2 August 1954, McIlroy (no relation to Jimmy) scored 71 goals in 418 appearances during his 11 years at Old Trafford, helping United win the FA Cup in 1977 and reach the Final in 1976 and 1979, as well as gaining a Second Division championship medal in 1975. Capped 88 times by Northern Ireland at senior level and once by the Under-23s, he signed for Manchester United as a 15-year-old and turned professional under Matt Busby in September 1969. He made his League debut in the Manchester derby in 1971 before 63,024 fans at Maine Road. At Stoke he did well for the first two years, but then found himself playing in a struggling side and after scoring 14 goals in 144 games for the Potters, was transferred free of charge to Manchester City (August 1985). He later played for FC Orgryte (Sweden) before having a second spell at Maine Road. In March 1987, McIlroy signed for Bury and after serving with FC Moedling (Austria), Bury (again) and Preston North End (player-coach) he was appointed player-manager of Northwich Victoria, later taking the position as manager of Macclesfield Town whom he led into the Football League in 1997. In his Football League career McIlroy amassed 510 appearances and scored 90 goals.

McINTOSH, William D.

Scorer of six goals in 27 games for Stoke City between September 1951 and November 1952, McIntosh, a Glaswegian utility forward, born on 7 December 1919, cost the Potters £10,000 from Blackpool. Earlier in his career he had scored for St Johnstone (1945-46) and Preston North End (46 goals in 91 League games including two hat-tricks in a week in September 1946). After leaving The Victoria Ground he assisted Walsall. It is believed he died c.1985.

MacKENZIE, Neil

Blond midfielder who broke into Stoke's first team during the 1996-97 campaign after playing intermediate and reserve-team football with West Bromwich Albion (1993-95). He moved to The Victoria Ground in August 1995 and at May 1997 had scored once goals in 22 games for the Potters. MacKenzie was born in Birmingham on 15 April 1976.

McLAREN, Douglas David

Played one game for Stoke as a late replacement of Turner v Burnley in September 1892. A reserve inside-left, born in Hanley c.1870, he stayed at the club for just a season.

McMAHON, Gerard Joseph

Right-sided midfielder, with good skills and an appetite for hard work, Gerry McMahon joined Stoke City from Tottenham Hotspur for £300,000 in September 1996 after trials with the German side Eintracht Frankfurt and the Italian club Udinese. He made his debut for the Potters against Northampton Town in a Coca-Cola Cup game 24 hours after putting pen to paper. Born in Belfast on 29 December 1973, he played for Glenavon before entering the English soccer scene with Tottenham Hotspur in July 1992 for £100,000. Capped by his country (Northern Ireland) at schoolboy, youth, Under-21, 'B' and senior levels, he was loaned out to Barnet (October 1994) during his four years with Spurs for whom he made 20 appearances. By May 1997 he had scored three goals in 39 games for Stoke.

McMAHON, Hugh

Tall, well-built centre-half who scored once in eight League games for Stoke in the early 1930s, McMahon was born in Saltcoats in 1907 and came to the Potteries from Blackpool during the summer of 1931. Brought in as cover for the injured Arthur Turner, he played in the first XI during the opening month of the season and then appeared twice in the inside-left position after Christmas. He never really settled at the club and left in March 1932 for Wrexham, the club he went on to serve for three years making over 150 senior appearances. He also played for Doncaster Rovers.

McMANUS, Charles Eric

Goalkeeper McManus won amateur caps for Northern Ireland while representing Coleraine (1966-67). He moved into English football with Coventry in August 1968, and thereafter served with Notts County, Stoke (from October 1979 to August 1982), Lincoln (on loan), Bradford City, Middlesbrough and Peterborough (the latter two also on loan), Tranmere (1986-87) and Boston United (September 1987 to May 1988). In all he appeared in well over 450 senior games (396 in the Football League – 229 with Notts County and 113 for Bradford). In June 1990 he was appointed youth development officer-coach at Walsall. Born in Limavady on 14 November 1950, McManus, tall and courageous, had just four outings with the Potters, all in 1981-82 when he deputised for Peter Fox.

McNALLY, Mark

McNally was born in Motherwell on 10 March 1971 and was a junior with Celtic before turning professional at Parkhead in May 1987. A stern defender, totally committed, he went on to play over 150 games for the Glasgow club, winning two Scottish Under-21 caps as well as gaining a Scottish Cup winners' medal in 1995. In December of that year he moved to Southend United for £100,000 and made over 50 appearances for the Shrimpers prior to moving to The Victoria Ground for £120,000 on 27 March 1997. He played in three first-team games for Stoke at the end of that season.

McREDDIE, Walter William

Scottish inside-forward Wally McReddie had two spells with the Potters during the last decade or so before the turn of the century. Born in Lochee in 1871, he played his early football with Lochee &

Harp FC, joining Stoke, first time round, in August 1889. He stayed with the club just five months, moving to Middlesbrough Ironopolis, only to return to The Victoria Ground in September 1893 for another year when he left to play for Manchester City. In total, McReddie scored 14 goals in 52 appearances for the Potters. He also assisted Bolton Wanderers and Glasgow Celtic in a career which ended in 1902 through injury.

McSKIMMING, Robert

One of Stoke's first real goalscorers, McSkimming played in the club's opening League game against West Bromwich Albion in September 1888 and finished up as leading marksman at the end of that campaign. He scored a lot of goals for the Potters in friendly matches, but at senior level he managed only six in 22 appearances. Born in Kilmarnock in 1870, and a fine sprinter at various Scottish athletics meetings, he came to Stoke from Hurlford in July 1888 having previously assisted his home-town club, Kilmarnock. He left the Vic for Burslem Port Vale in May 1889 and after 17 games for the Valiants joined Stone Town (1891) after being released owing to business commitments. It is thought he returned to Scotland before World War One.

McVAY, James

Born in the North-East at Wallsend in 1889, centre-half McVay suffered with his health during his brief stay at The Victoria Ground which lasted eight months (February-October 1913). In that time he played in 12 League games for the Potters, whom he joined from Wallsend Swifts. He left The Vic for Barnard Castle and retired in 1915.

MADDISON, John Arden Brown

Born at Chester-le-Street on 12 February 1900, defender Jack Maddison played for Usworth Colliery before joining Stoke in November 1923. He only appeared in one first-team game for the Potters, lining up in the left-half position against Stockport (h) on 2 February 1924. Almost nine months later, on 31 October, he was transferred to Port Vale. He had over 50 outings for the Valiants up to May 1927 when he moved to Oldham Athletic, later assisting Mansfield, Nimes (France), Gresley Rovers and Sutton United. He died in Rugeley on 19 August 1987.

MADDOCK, John

After monitoring the progress of hard-kicking right-back Maddock since he was a teenager with Bignall End, Stoke finally brought him to The Victoria Ground from Audley FC in September 1916. He made over 40 appearances in wartime football and then continued to impress during the 1919-20 League campaign. But then his form began to wane and after a lean spell, found himself in the Reserves where he stayed until leaving for Macclesfield, having scored four goals in 23 senior outings for the Potters. He signed for Port Vale in August 1923 and was a regular in the Valiants side by 1925. He went on to score 12 goals in 184 games for Stoke's arch rivals, up to July 1931, when he transferred to Crewe. A fine penalty-taker, he later assisted Nantwich and Audley, the town where he was born on 24 November 1896. Maddock died in Normacot on 27 October 1972.

MAGUIRE, Paul Bernard

A fast-raiding outside-left or wide midfield player from Glasgow (born 21 August 1956) Paul Maguire played for Kilbirnie Ladeside and spent four seasons with Shrewsbury Town before signing for Stoke for £262,000 in September 1980. Terrific with corner-kicks and also a penalty expert, he was a big favourite with the fans at The Victoria Ground and went on to give the Potters wonderful service, scoring 25 goals in 125 appearances, including all four (two penalties) in an emphatic victory over Wolves at The Victoria Ground in May 1984, this being his last game for the Potters before leaving for Tacoma Stars (USA). Maguire returned to England to join Port Vale in June 1985 and immediately became a regular with the Valiants, helping them win promotion from the Fourth Division in his first season. In May 1988, after scoring 27 goals in 147 outings for Vale he became player-assistant manager of Northwich Victoria, later acting as caretaker-boss. He left football in 1992.

MAHONEY, John Francis

Crewe Alexandra sold 'Josh' Mahoney to Stoke for what was to prove a bargain fee of £19,500 in March 1967. In the next ten years the Welsh midfielder scored 28 goals in 329 appearances for the Potters, gained a League Cup winners' medal in 1972 and became an established international, eventually winning 51 full caps (1968-83) plus three at Under-23 level. Born in Cardiff on 20 September 1946, Mahoney played for Ashton United before making 18 League appearances for Crewe, whom he served as a professional from March 1966. He left The Victoria Ground for Middlesbrough in a £90,000 deal in August 1977, and two years later, after 77 League games for the Ayresome Park club, he joined Swansea City for £100,000. He added a further 110 League outings to his tally while at The Vetch Field before becoming player-manager of Bangor City (September 1984) leading the non-League club into Europe via the Cup-winners' Cup after guiding them to a Welsh Cup Final victory in 1981. Mahoney also had three seasons in charge of Newport County (August 1988-May 1991) prior to returning to Bangor for a second spell. He also managed the Welsh semi-professional side v England and in fact played with his cousin, John Toshack at Swansea. Mahoney amassed a total of 489 League appearances for his four major clubs.

MAIDSTONE UNITED

Stoke have never played Maidstone at senior level and only one player, David Kevan, has been associated with both clubs.

MALE, Christopher

Midfielder Chris Male made one substitute appearance for Stoke, coming on against Northampton Town in the Freight Rover Trophy in November 1990. Born in Portsmouth on 16 June 1972, he joined the Potters from Fratton Park in July 1990, returning to Hampshire to sign for Waterlooville in 1993 after failing to settle in the North Midlands. Whilst at Stoke he also had a loan spell with Newcastle Town.

MALKIN, John

Diminutive outside-right Malkin hit 27 goals in 190 League and FA Cup games for the Potters. A positive player, born at Longton on 9 November 1925, he was unlucky to have a certain Stanley Matthews vying for the number-seven shirt with him during his time at The Victoria Ground, but when Matthews left for Blackpool in 1947, Malkin took over on the right wing and did exceedingly well. A pupil at Queensbury Road School, he didn't play football in earnest until he was in the Army, being spotted in the BAOR team. Word got back to Stoke boss Bob McGrory and almost immediately the impressive Malkin was signed as a professional at the age of 18. Unfortunately he damaged knee ligaments in a game at Filbert Street in 1956 which forced him to give up competitive football. He later had a joint testimonial with full-back George Bourne and received £855, plus a club grant. Malkin died in Stoke-on-Trent on 19 May 1994.

MALONEY, Timothy George

Useful outside-left from the North-East of England who scored once in eight League games for the Potters during the 1931-32 season when he replaced first Bobby Archibald and then Harry Taylor. Born in Middlesbrough in 1908, he was signed from Darlington (initially as Archilbald's understudy) but never settled in the Potteries and returned north to sign for Southbank FC in June 1932.

MANAGERS

Prior to 1874 Stoke Football Club was run by a committee which comprised a chairman, vice-chairman, four other members and at least two players, one being the captain.

The first manager to take office was Tom Slaney in 1874.
Here is a full list of Stoke City managers from 1874 to 1997

Manager	Term of Office
Thomas Charles Slaney	August 1874 – May 1883
Walter Cox	June 1883 – April 1884
Harry Lockett	April 1884 – August 1890
Joseph A. Bradshaw	August 1890 – January 1892
Arthur Reeves	January 1892 – May 1895
William Spencer Rowley	May 1895 – August 1897
Horace Denham Austerberry	September 1897 – May 1908
Alfred J. Barker	May 1908 – April 1914
Peter Hodge	June 1914 – April 1915
Joseph Alfred Schofield	May 1915 – January 1919
Arthur John Shallcross	February 1919 – March 1923
John Rutherford	March – April 1923
Thomas Mather	October 1923 – June 1935
Robert McGrory	June 1935 – May 1952
Frank Taylor	June 1952 – June 1960
Anthony Waddington	June 1960 – March 1977
George Edward Eastham, OBE	March 1977 – January 1978
Alan A'Court*	January 1978
William Alan Durban	February 1978 – June 1981
Richard J. Barker	June 1981 – December 1983
William Asprey	January 1983 – May 1985
Michael Dennis Mills, MBE	May 1985 – November 1989
Alan Ball	November 1989 – February 1991
Graham Charles Paddon*	February – May 1991
Lou Macari	May 1991 – November 1993
Joseph Jordan	November 1993 – October 1994
Lou Macari	October 1994 – May 1997
Chic Bates	July 1997 –

* caretaker manager.

Managerial Matter

● Slaney was a teacher by profession who was also a player with Stoke. He was later a referee and helped form the Staffordshire F A.

● Cox was another ex-Stoke player.

● Lockett took the club into the Football League in 1888 and later became the League's secretary.

● Bradshaw led Stoke to the Football Alliance title in 1891.

● Reeves was the man who blended local-born players Rowley, Clare and Underwood as well as recruiting several stars from Scotland.

● Rowley was the first former League player to take over as Stoke's manager (See ROWLEY, William Spencer).

MAIDSTONE - MANAGERS

● Austerberry was assistant schoolmaster to Slaney at St John's School, Hanley. Known as 'Denny' he spent 11 years in charge, taking Stoke into the FA Cup semi-finals. He quit the club to become a journalist and later ran his own news agency. He also rose to a high level in the Masonic movement and later became an Estate Agent in Longton. He died in Stoke-on-Trent in April 1946, aged 78.

● Barker got the club back on its feet after it had gone into liquidation in 1908. He resigned in 1914 after doing an exceptionally fine job at The Victoria Ground.

● Hodge was a qualified referee in Scotland and was honorary secretary of Dunfermline Athletic. He was Raith Rovers' first manager (1907) and after leaving Stoke went back to Raith, later taking charge at Leicester Fosse (1919-26), Manchester City (1926-32) and Leicester (again). He died soon after seeing Leicester beaten by Portsmouth in the 1934 FA Cup semi-final.

● Schofield was a Stoke player and England international who managed Port Vale (See SCHOFIELD, Joseph Alfred).

● Shallcross played for Leek prior to becoming a Football League referee. He led Stoke to promotion from Division Two in season 1921-22.

● Rutherford spent barely a month in charge at Stoke. The former Newcastle United, Arsenal and England winger, who guested for Fulham and Chelsea during World War One, won three League championship medals in the early 1900s (with Newcastle) as well as an FA Cup medal (1910). After Stoke he made a brief comeback as a player with Clapton Orient and later coached non-League side Tufnell Park.

● Mather had been associated with Manchester City, Bolton and Southend before taking over at Stoke, whom he guided to the Third Division North and then Second Division championships in 1927 and 1933 respectively. He was the man who introduced Stanley Matthews to League Football. Mather managed Newcastle after Stoke and later on was in charge of Leicester (1945-46) and Kilmarnock (1947-48) (See MATHER, Thomas).

● McGrory was a fine defender with Stoke before taking over from Mather as manager (See McGRORY, Robert).

● Taylor was a defender with Wolverhampton Wanderers and played in the 1939 FA Cup Final. In 1948 he was appointed manager of Scarborough, became Major Frank Buckley's assistant at Hull after that and following a spell with Leeds in the same capacity, he took over as manager of Stoke. He played for England in a wartime international at Hampden Park in front of 133,000 fans. His brother Jack managed both Leeds and QPR and they lined up as full-back partners with Wolves.

● Waddington, without doubt, has been Stoke's greatest-ever manager, serving the club in that capacity for 17 years. In his time at The Victoria Ground, Stoke won the Second Division title (1963) and the League Cup at Wembley (1972). He signed many fine players including Stan Matthews (second time round) (See WADDINGTON, Anthony).

● A'Court was a outside-left with Liverpool, who also played for England at senior and Under-23 levels. He was also manager-coach at Crewe Alexandra and assistant manager at Chester.

● Eastham, an England international midfielder, played League football for both Newcastle and Arsenal before joining Stoke (See EASTHAM, George Edward, OBE).

● Durban had a fine playing career as an inside-forward or wing-half with Shrewsbury, Derby County and Wales (gaining 27 full caps). He managed Sunderland and Cardiff after Stoke, and later returned to the Baseball Ground as assistant manager (See DURBAN, William Alan).

● Barker played League Football for Derby County, Notts County and Peterborough United before becoming coach at Shrewsbury Town in 1974. He then took over as manager at Gay Meadow and after a brief spell on the staff at Molineux, he joined Stoke. He lost his job through player-power despite making over £600,000 profit for the club during his reign in office (See BARKER, Richie).

● Asprey was a fine player with Stoke, making over 340 appearances for the club (See ASPREY, William).

● Mills was a full-back with Ipswich and Southampton before joining Stoke as player-manager. He gained a winners' medal in both the FA Cup and UEFA Cup Finals with Ipswich and also won 42 England caps. He played in more than 700 games as a professional. After leaving Stoke, Mills managed Colchester, was assistant manager at Coventry (under his former teammate Terry Butcher) and acted as chief scout at Sheffield Wednesday before becoming Trevor Francis's assistant at Birmingham in 1996-97 (See MILLS, Michael, MBE).

● Ball, like Mills (above) had a fine playing career. A World Cup winner with England for whom he won 72 caps, he also starred in midfield for Blackpool, Everton, Arsenal, Southampton and Bristol Rovers as well as Vancouver Whitecaps and Philadelphia Fury in the NASL and Bulova in Hong Kong. He appeared in more than 900 competitive matches and as a manager, he first took charge of Blackpool (1978-79) and then guided Portsmouth into the top flight for the first time in 28 years in 1987. After serving as assistant to Mills at The Victoria Ground, Ball was given the manager's job at Stoke. On leaving the club, he had spells in charge of Exeter, Southampton and Manchester City (1995-96) and for a time was on the England coaching staff under Graham Taylor. When Ball was transferred from Everton to Arsenal for £220,000 in December 1971, he was the costliest footballer in Britain at that time (See BALL, Alan junior).

● Manchester-born Paddon played League football as an inside-forward (1968-82) for Coventry, Norwich (two spells), West Ham and Millwall, making 415 appearances and scoring 38 goals. He also won one England Under-23 cap.

● Macari was a fine goalscorer with Celtic and Manchester United, as well as playing international football for Scotland. He has also managed Swindon Town, West Ham, Birmingham and Celtic, and became the first man to return to Stoke for a second spell as manager (See MACARI, Lou).

A-Z OF STOKE CITY

Assistant managers
Included in the list of men who have held the position of assistant manager at Stoke City are (in A-Z order): former Shrewsbury striker Philip D. 'Chic' Bates (under Lou Macari); the Oxford, Watford and Reading post war player and former Wolves boss Cyril 'Sammy' Chung (under Mick Mills); Walter Gould (assistant to both Alan Durban and Richie Barker); the Northern Ireland international and Doncaster and Torquay defender W.G.Leonard Graham (right-hand man to Tony Waddington); the ex-West Bromwich Albion, Manchester City, Everton, Nottingham Forest, Norwich, Oldham, Stockport and Scotland midfielder Richard Asa Hartford (under Joe Jordan); Cyril Lea (under Alan Durban); Harry Sellars, and former player (under Bob McGrory) and Arthur Owen Turner, another ex-Stoke player (under Frank Taylor).

● Bates was born in West Bromwich in 1949 and was a regular marksman for Stourbridge, Shrewsbury (64 League goals scored: 1974-78 & 1980-86), Swindon (15 goals) and Bristol Rovers. He appeared over 400 matches and halfway through his second spell at Gay Meadow, he was appointed player-manager. In 1987 he went back to Swindon as assistant to Lou Macari, later following him to Birmingham, Stoke, Celtic and then back to Stoke for a second spell as coach-assistant manager of the Potters. When Macari left Celtic to rejoin Stoke, Bates stayed for a while as caretaker manager. In July 1997 he became manager at Stoke following the departure of Macari.

Stoke Players Who Became Football Club Managers:
Mickey Adams (Fulham); Bill Asprey (Oxford United, Stoke City); Gordon Banks (Telford United); Alan Bloor (Port Vale); Jack Bowman (Norwich City); Viv Busby (Hartlepool United); Tommy Clare (Port Vale); Wayne Clarke (Telford United); Joe Clennell (Distillery); Doug Clifford (Manchester City); Tim Coleman (Notts County); Walter Cox (Stoke City); Brian Doyle (Stockport County, Workington); George Eastham (Stoke City); Peter Fox (Exeter City); Neil Franklin (Colchester United, Apoel Cyprus); Jimmy Greenhoff (Rochdale); Harry Gregg (Carlisle United, Crewe Alexandra, Shrewsbury Town, Swansea City); Eric Hampson (Stafford Rangers); Adrian Heath (Burnley); David Herd (Lincoln City); George Oldham (Hitchin Town); Tom Holford (Port Vale); Bobby Howitt (Motherwell); Geoff Hurst (Chelsea); Wilbur (Peter) Jackson (Bradford City, Wrexham); Robbie James (Merthyr Tydfil); Roy John (Torquay United); Chris Kamara (Bradford City); Howard Kendall (Atletico Bilbao, Everton; Blackburn Rovers, Manchester City, Notts County, Sheffield United); Bob McGrory (Stoke City); Jimmy McIlroy (Bolton Wanderers, Oldham Athletic); Sammy McIlroy (Northwich Victoria); Stanley Matthews (Port Vale); Mick Mills (Stoke City); Jackie Mudie (Port Vale); Iain Munro (Hamilton Academical, St Mirren, Raith Rovers); Louis Page (Chester, Newport County, Swindon Town, Yeovil Town); Steve Parkin (Mansfield Town); Jack Peart (Bradford City, Fulham, Rochdale); Mike Pejic (Chester City); Alex Raisbeck (Bath City, Bristol City, Chester, Hamilton Academical, Halifax Town); Billy Rowley (Stoke City); Joey Schofield (Port Vale, Stoke City); Maurice Setters (Doncaster Rovers); Peter Shilton (Plymouth Argyle); Tom Slaney (Stoke City); Denis Smith (Bristol City, Oxford United, Sunderland, York City); Frank Soo (Scunthorpe United); Simon Stainrod (Falkirk, Dundee and Ayr United); Freddie Steele (Mansfield Town, Port Vale); Brian Talbot (West Bromwich Albion, Fulham, Hibernians of Malta); Arthur Turner (Birmingham City, Crewe Alexandra, Oxford United); Dennis Viollet (Crewe Alexandra, Linfield); Harry Ware (Crewe Alexandra); Billy Wooton (Halifax Town, Oldham Athletic, Northwich Victoria) and Tommy Younger (Falkirk).

Managerial Comment
● Three of Port Vale's first seven full-time secretary-managers were all ex-Stoke players – Tommy Clare, Tom Holford and Joey Schofield. Over the years seven former Potters have become Vale managers: three named above plus Freddie Steele, Stanley Matthews, Jackie Mudie and Alan Bloor.

● Former England winger Joe Rutherford was signed as player-manager by Stoke in March 1923, but never turned out for the club.

● Cyril Lea (Stoke's coach-assistant manager in 1979-80) was the Welsh National team coach-manager in 1981.

MANCHESTER

Stoke's first-ever opponents in the FA (English) Cup competition were Manchester whom they met in a qualifying round tie at The Victoria Ground on 10 November 1883. Despite a goal from Teddy Johnson, the visitors won the game 2-1 in front of 1,000 spectators. The Stoke team was: Birch; Stanford, Mellor; Cox, Shutt, E.Smith; H.R.Brown, Yates, Johnson, E.Wilson and Bennett.

MANCHESTER CITY

Stoke's playing record against City is:
Football League

Venue	P	W	D	L	F	A
Home	37	23	6	8	63	31
Away	37	5	11	21	30	63
Totals	74	28	17	29	93	94

FA Cup

Venue	P	W	D	L	F	A
Home	2	1	0	1	2	2
Away	3	1	0	2	3	4
Totals	5	2	0	3	5	6

League Cup

Venue	P	W	D	L	F	A
Home	3	2	1*	0	5	1
Away	3	0	0	3	0	6
Totals	6	2	1	3	5	7

* Stoke lost 9-8 on penalties after a second-round tie in October 1981 had finished level at 2-2 over two legs.

Stoke's best League win over City is 5-1, achieved at The Victoria Ground on 23 September 1972 (Division One). Jimmy Greenhoff netted a hat-trick that afternoon in front of a near 26,500 crowd. Stoke also won 4-0 at home in February 1975 (Division One) when Ian Moores was in fine form, scoring twice in front of 32,007 fans.

The Potters' heaviest defeat is 4-1, suffered at Maine Road in September 1970 when Manchester City were on a high following their successes in both the League Cup and European Cup Winners' Cup the previous season.

In-form Stan Matthews was on target in Stoke's 3-2 League win over City at The Victoria Ground in February 1938. He also helped lay on both his side's other goals for Tom Ward.

Defender Mike Doyle conceded an own-goal to give Stoke a 2-1 League win at Maine Road on April Fool's Day 1972. Doyle was later to play for Stoke.

Sammy McIlroy scored Stoke's winner in their 1-0 League victory over his former club Manchester City in April 1983.

In season 1921-22 Stoke drew 1-1 at home and were beaten 2-1

MANCHESTER

away by Manchester City. Both Stoke's goals came from Jimmy Broad, who had played for the Maine Road club earlier in his career.

A crowd of over 21,000 saw the Potters beat demoted City 2-1 at home in a Nationwide League Division One game in August 1996.

Stoke City replaced Manchester City in the First Division for season 1963-64.

A record crowd of 84,569 packed into Maine Road to witness the sixth-round FA Cup-tie between City and Stoke in March 1934 which the home side won 1-0. The Potters lost both their League games to City in this same season.

Stoke progressed through to the 1964 League Cup Final by defeating Manchester City over two legs in the semi-final, winning 2-1 on aggregate (2-0 at home, 0-1 away).

That 17 goal League Cup penalty shoot-out bonanza took place at The Victoria Ground on the evening of 28 October 1981. Messrs. Evans, O'Callaghan, Heath, Bracewell, Johnson, Smith, Hampton and Dodd scored from the spot for the Potters but Lee Chapman's miss meant that Manchester City went through to the third round.

Players with both clubs: Sam Ashworth, Jason Beckford, David Brightwell, Jimmy Broad, Tommy Broad, Jack Brown, Charlie Burgess, Wayne Clarke, Nigel Gleghorn, Hugh Clifford, Joe Corrigan, Peter Dobing, Harry Dowd, Mike Doyle, Reg Forrester, John Gidman, Verdi Godwin, Adrian Heath, Tony Henry, Frank Hesham, Charlie Hinks, Tom Holford, Sammy McIlroy, Wally McReddie, Bob Milarvie, Billy Owen, Ian Scott, Barry Siddall, Harry Taylor, Dennis Tueart and Dave Watson.

Alan Ball managed both clubs, as did Peter Hodge, who was at Maine Road for six years (1926-232). Howard Kendall played for Stoke and later managed at Maine Road. Asa Hartford played for Manchester City and was assistant manager at both clubs thereafter, also acting as caretaker-boss at Maine Road in 1996. Tom Mather was assistant secretary at Manchester City and Stoke manager for 12 years from 1923.

Stoke's £100,000 signing from Birmingham Jimmy Greenhoff celebrates a goal, with Manchester City's Mick Doyle, who later was to join Stoke, also in picture.

The other half of a great partnership, John Ritchie, in action from the same game, with Manchester City's goalkeeper Joe Corrigan.

MANCHESTER UNITED

Stoke's playing record against United is:

Football League

Venue	P	W	D	L	F	A
Home	36	16	11	9	62	41
Away	36	6	13	17	30	63
Totals	72	22	24	26	92	104

Test Matches

Venue	P	W	D	L	F	A
Away	1	1	0	0	3	0

Football Alliance

Venue	P	W	D	L	F	A
Home	1	1	0	0	2	1
Away	1	1	0	0	1	0
Totals	2	2	0	0	3	1

FA Cup

Venue	P	W	D	L	F	A
Home	4	1	3	0	5	4
Away	5	0	3	2	6	11
Totals	9	1	6	2	11	15

League Cup

Venue	P	W	D	L	F	A
Home	3	2	1	0	4	2
Away	2	0	1	1	1	3
Totals	5	2	2	1	5	5

Stoke's best League win over United (then Newton Heath) is 7-1 – at The Victoria Ground (Division One) on 7 January 1893. Just on 1,000 fans saw this game in which Billy Dickson netted a fine hat-trick for the Potters. United won the return fixture two months later by 1-0.

Stoke were relegated from the First Division at the end of 1984-85, and during that campaign they crashed to their heaviest League defeat at the hands of United, losing 5-0 at old Trafford on 6 April before a near 43,000 crowd. Mark Hughes and Jesper Olsen both scored twice for United.

Denis Law scored four times in United's second biggest League win over Stoke – 5-2 at Old Trafford in December 1963. This was the first time the teams had met each other since Stoke's relegation campaign 10 years earlier.

United also beat Stoke 4-1 at home in February 1907 (Division One); 4-0 at home in September 1951 (when Jack Rowley hit a hat-trick); 4-2 at The Victoria Ground in March 1968 (as they headed towards European Cup glory) and 4-0 at Old Trafford in September 1979 when defender Gordon McQueen netted twice.

When Stoke were relegated from the First Division in 1953, they completed the double over United, winning 3-1 at home and 2-0 away.

Over 61,000 fans saw Stoke hold League champions United to a 0-0 draw at Old Trafford in May 1967.

The final nail was driven into Manchester United's relegation coffin when they were beaten 1-0 by Stoke in the last League game of 1973-74. John Ritchie scored the all-important goal in front of 27,392 Victoria Ground fans.

Alan Bloor's goal gave Stoke a fine 1-0 League win at Old Trafford in April 1976 before 53,879 supporters.

A six-goal thriller ended all square at 3-3 between Stoke and United at The Victoria Ground in May 1977. Garth Crooks (later to play for United) netted twice for the Potters. who were on their way into the Second Division at the time.

The Test Match at the end of the 1894-95 season was staged at neutral Burslem Port Vale's ground and victory enabled the Potters to retain the First Division status.

Almost 100,000 spectators witnessed the two fourth-round FA Cup games between Stoke and United in 1964-65. There were 49,032 present at The Victoria Ground when the teams drew 0-0 and 50,874 saw United win the replay 1-0.

A crowd of 63,497 assembled at Old Trafford to see United beat Stoke 2-0 in a third-round FA Cup-tie in January 1967.

Stoke and United met each other seven times in 1971-72 – twice in the First Division, three times in the League Cup and in two FA Cup games. The League clashes ended 1-1 at Stoke and 3-0 to United at Old Trafford. The three fourth-round League Cup encounters were witnessed by a combined total of 130,124 fans and in the end it was Stoke who went through, winning a second replay 2-1 at The Victoria Ground after 1-1 and 0-0 draws.

A crowd of just 7,800 saw the United-Stoke First Division game at Maine Road in February 1947 (Old Trafford was closed owing to wartime bomb damage).

The two FA Cup matches both attracted big crowds. There were 53,820 fans at Old Trafford to see former United star Jimmy Greenhoff score to earn Stoke a 1-1 draw, and then 49,091 attended the replay as the Potters went through to the semi-finals with a 2-1 victory after extra-time.

Stoke were beaten by United in a second-round League Cup-tie in 1993-94. It was 2-1 to the Potters at The Victoria Ground (Mark Stein scoring twice), but in front of 41,387 fans at Old Trafford, United won 2-0 to squeeze through 3-2 on aggregate.

Players with both clubs: Peter Coupar (United reserve), Garth Crooks, Gerry Daly, Billy Draycott, Alf Edge, Albert Farmer, Reg Forrester (United trialist), John Gidman, Jimmy Greenhoff, Harry Gregg, Ashley Grimes, Harold Hardman, David Herd, Frank Hesham, Mark Higgins, Roy John, Kevin Lewis, John McGillivray, Sammy McIlroy, Bob Milarvie, Louis Page, Bob Ramsey, Billy Robertson, Maurice Setters, Mickey Thomas and Dennis Viollet.

Joe Jordan and Lou Macari were both goalscoring forwards with Manchester United who later became managers of Stoke City. Norman Tapkin was a goalkeeper with United who later became Stoke's trainer (1952-60). Former Stoke City manager Tony Waddington was an amateur with United in the 1940s.

MANSFIELD TOWN

Stoke's playing record against the Stags is:
Football League

Venue	P	W	D	L	F	A
Home	3	2	1	0	8	2
Away	3	1	1	1	5	2
Totals	6	3	2	1	13	4

FA Cup

Venue	P	W	D	L	F	A
Away	1	1	0	0	4	2

League Cup

Venue	P	W	D	L	F	A
Home	1	0	1	0	2	2
Away	1	1	0	0	3	1
Totals	2	1	1	0	5	3

Freight Rover Trophy

Venue	P	W	D	L	F	A
Away	1	0	0	1	0	3

The first two Football League encounters were played in 1977-78 (Division Two). Mansfield gained a point from a 1-1 draw at Stoke after winning their home match 2-1.

In the FA Cup-tie at Field Mill in January 1948, Stoke player-to-be Harry Oscroft and Len Butt (penalty) scored for the 'Stags' while future Town player-manager Freddie Steele with a brace, Tommy Kiernan and Johnny Sellars, netted for the Potters.

The Freight Rover Cup game was played on a waterlogged Field Mill pitch in season 1990-91.

Players with both clubs: George Antonio, Cliff Carr, Neville Chamberlain, Joe Depledge, Frank Elliott, Verdi Godwin, David Goodwin, Arthur Jepson, Kevin Lewis, Bill Moore, Harry Oscroft, Steve Parkin (later manager of the Stags), Mark Smith, Freddie Steele (who became player-manager at Mansfield) and Jim Westland. Tony Ford joined Parkin as player and assistant manager at Field Mill during 1996-97. Bobby Roberts played for Mansfield and later became coach at The Victoria Ground.

MARDY

Stoke's playing record against Mardy:
Southern League

Venue	P	W	D	L	F	A
Home	1	1	0	0	4	0
Away	1	1	0	0	2	1
Totals	2	2	0	0	6	1

Stoke's emphatic 4-0 home win was achieved in April 1914 when a crowd of 3,000 saw Dick Smith (2), Henry Hargreaves and Arty Watkin score the goals to complete the double over Mardy following their 2-1 away success earlier in the month.

Stoke also played away at Mardy in a Southern League game on 1 September 1914. The Potters were beaten 2-1 in front of just 500 spectators, but before the return fixture could be staged, Mardy resigned from the competition and that initial result was expunged from the record books.

Players with both clubs: Richard Coates and Jack Lenaghan.

MARSH, John H.

Jackie Marsh followed a number of local born players of his generation to The Victoria Ground – and like Messrs. Bloor, Pejic and Smith, he went on to the ultimate accolade of gaining a League Cup winners' medal in 1972. An exceptionally fine full-back, his deep crosses were a feature of his play in the 1960s and '70s, and indeed, he played an important role in the club's success. Born in Stoke-on-Trent on 31 May 1948, Marsh joined the Potters on leaving school, turned professional in in June 1965 and made his Football League debut against Arsenal at Highbury in August 1967 – the first of 444 senior appearances for the club (two goals scored). His last game in a Stoke City shirt was in March 1979 and he now lies in eighth place in the club's all-time appearance list. After spells in America with Los Angeles Aztecs and in Hong Kong with Bulova, he wound down his career with Northwich Victoria, retiring in 1984.

MARSHALL, Gordon George Banks

Goalkeeper Marshall had a nightmare debut for Stoke, conceding six goals at Luton in a First Division League game in November 1993 after joining the Potters on loan from Celtic. He went on to appear in 13 senior games for Stoke – his last in January 1994 – after which he returned to Parkhead. Born in Edinburgh on 19 April 1964, Marshall played for Tynecastle FC (1979), Glasgow Rangers (January 1980), East Stirlingshire (on loan), Broxburn Juniors (November 1982), East Fife (December 1982), Falkirk (March 1987), before joining Celtic in August 1991. A Scottish international, he passed the milestone of 500 appearances at club level in season 1996-97 when he was still with Celtic.

NB. Marshall's cousin, Scott, is a defender with Arsenal.

MARTIN, James Colin

Scorer of one goal in 16 League appearances for Stoke in the first two seasons after World War One (1919-21) Jimmy Martin was a useful centre-forward with good pace. Born at Basford on 2 December 1898, he played for Stoke St Peter's before joining the Potters for £750 in July 1916, and on leaving The Victoria Ground in June 1921, he signed for Aberdare Athletic. During his 24-year career (1914-38) he also assisted Wolverhampton Wanderers (from September 1923), Reading (July 1924), Aberdare (again, June 1925), Bristol City (May 1926), Blackpool (February 1928), Southend United (February 1929), Halifax Town (July 1929) and Congleton Town (August 1930-May 1931). Martin died in Stoke on 27 June 1969.

MARTIN, John Alan

A versatile half-back or inside-forward, born at Smallthorne on 23 November 1923, Alan Martin played for Nettlebank Villa before signing for Port Vale as an amateur in February 1941. He turned professional in December 1942 and went on to become an established member of the Valiants League side, being an ever-present in 1947-48 and 1948-49. He left the Vale for Stoke City in an exchange deal involving Albert Mullard plus £10,000 in September 1951 and went on to give the Potters excellent service, scoring six goals in 115 first-class games. In March 1955 he moved from The Victoria Ground to Bangor City, but then returned to Vale Park as a part-time professional in July 1957, but was rarely selected during his second spell at the the club. He was given a free transfer in May 1959 after having taken his record to 30 goals in 201 appearances covering eight different positions. He later became player-manager of Nantwich Town and also coached the juniors at Vale Park.

MASKERY, Christopher P.

Born in Stoke-on-Trent on 25 September 1964, midfielder Chris Maskery actually retired from football twice. He joined the Potters as a youngster, turned professional on his 18th birthday and went on to score five goals in 108 appearances for Stoke before moving to Stafford Rangers on a free transfer in the summer of 1987. Injuries interrupted his career during his later years at The Victoria Ground hence him deciding to call it a day at senior level.

MASSEY, Alfred W.

Right-half Alf Massey appeared in two League games for the Potters during January-February 1939 when he came into a re-adjusted middle-line owing to the absence of Jock Kirton. A strong tackler, his career was unfortunately cut short through injury in 1944. He was born in Stoke in 1916 and joined the Potters as a teenager.

MATCHES

The most competitive matches played by Stoke in a full season is 71 in 1971-72 (42 League, 12 League Cup, 9 FA Cup, 4 Anglo-Scottish Cup and four Anglo-Italian Cup). Five friendly games were also played in this campaign for an overall total of 76.

The team completed 62 first-class matches in 1991-92 (plus 12 other games) for a tally of 74 while a total of 60 competitive games were fulfilled in 1993-94 (plus a further 10 friendlies).

MATHER, Thomas

Tom Mather was Stoke's manager from October 1923 to May 1935. In those 12 years the Potters played almost 500 Football League games of which 212 resulted in victories and only 167 in defeats. Born in Chorley in the summer of 1888, Mather worked as assistant secretary at both Manchester City and Bolton Wanderers, and later became club secretary and then secretary-manager at Burnden Park, taking the

Tom Mather

latter post in June 1915. Four of the next the five years of football were, of course, marred by World War One and then, in August 1920 he joined Southend United as their manager, holding office until his transfer to The Victoria Ground. He took his time in revamping the playing side at Stoke and in 1926-27 the Third Division North championship was won. After narrowly missing promotion again shortly afterwards, Mather finally guided the Potters into the top flight in 1933, having signed Bob McGrory (his successor in the manager's seat) as well as introducing the Stanley Matthews to League action. Mather was a fine manager, working with little or now cash and when he left The Victoria Ground for Newcastle United in May 1935, a lot of people were bitterly upset and disappointed at his departure. After World War Two, Mather was appointed manager of Leicester City, and he stayed at Filbert Street for nine months before ending his soccer career in charge of the Scottish club Kilmarnock. He retired to the Potteries where he died on 29 March 1957, aged 68.

Stanley Matthews

MATTHEWS, Graham

No relation to Sir Stan, this Matthews was a utility forward, born in Stoke-on-Trent on 2 November 1942. He joined the club as a teenager in 1958, turned professional a year later, on his 17th birthday, and went on to score five goals in 20 appearances for the Potters before moving to Walsall. He later played for Crewe Alexandra (1965-67). In his League career as a whole, Matthews netted 43 goals in 139 outings.

MATTHEWS, Stanley, Sir, CBE

The son of Hanley's famous boxing-barber, Jack Matthews, Stan was one of the greatest footballers in the world for at least 20 years from 1937. A marvelously gifted outside-right, with scintillating pace over 20-30 yards, he was a brilliant dribbler, great crosser of the ball and such a big asset to the team. Born in Hanley on 1 February 1915, on leaving Wellington Road School, he did general office work with a local firm while also on the groundstaff at The Victoria Ground. He turned professional without hesitation on his 17th birthday, having represented England at Schoolboy level in 1929. He made his League debut for Stoke on 19 March 1932 in the away game at Bury, but it was a further two years before Matthews established himself in the Potters' first team. Occupying the right-wing berth, which he retained throughout his career both as a club player and England international, he won the first of his 54 full England caps in September 1934 (v Wales), scoring in a 4-0 win in Cardiff. During the 1939-46 period, Matthews appeared in a 24 wartime and five Victory internationals, and he also represented the Football League, the Football League XI and the FA XI. In 1947 he played for Great Britain, confirming that he was the finest outside-right in the game. His first stay at Stoke ended in May 1947 when, aged 32, and after a lot of uncertainty, he moved to Blackpool for £11,500. Matthews did well at Bloomfield Road, teaming up with future Stokie Jackie Mudie. He helped the Seasiders win the FA Cup in 1953, after previously collecting two runners-up medals in 1948 and 1951, and scored 17 goals in 379 appearances for the Lancashire side before returning to The Victoria Ground in a blaze of publicity in October 1961, signing in front of the TV cameras for £2,500. Matthews was 46 at the time, yet it transpired that he had four years left in him as a footballer with the Potters. When he made his second debut for Stoke v Huddersfield, the gate at The Vic increased from 8,409 to almost 36,000. His presence sent a buzz of excitement right through the club. Promotion back to the First Division was gained in 1963 and two years later, following a League game v Fulham on 6 February 1965, just five days after his 50th birthday, Matthews retired from competitive football with well over 800 games under his belt, 701 in the Football League (332 with Stoke and 369 for Blackpool). His Stoke record (in two spells) was 355 senior appearances and 62 goals. He was knighted in 1965 (having received the CBE nine years earlier); in 1948 and 1963 he was voted Footballer of the Year and was European Footballer of the Year in 1956. Always keeping himself fit, after leaving Stoke, Matthews went round the world, coaching in many countries including Africa and both the Far and Middle East. He returned as team manager of Port Vale in 1967-68 before choosing to live in Malta, where he took charge of Hibernians, the club later managed by ex-Stoke player Brian Talbot. He later resided in Canada, but always felt for the Potteries and in the late 1980s he returned home while also retaining holiday accommodation in Tenerife. In 1989, 'Sir Stan' was officially appointed president of Stoke City Football Club, and he was presented with the Midlands Sports Personality of the Year in 1994.

NB: Prior to an FA Cup-tie between Stoke and Sheffield United in 1946, Matthews went down with the influenza. A doctor prescribed medicine similar to that used by Luftwaffe crews on bombing missions during the war. These worked perfectly, for Matthews recovered to help Stoke win 1-0.

NB: Matthews played League football for 32 years, 324 days from his debut for Stoke on 19 March 1932 to his last Potters' outing on 6 February 1965. His international career spanned almost 23 years and is the oldest player ever to win a full England cap, aged 42 years, 103 days v Denmark in May 1957.

MAWSON, Joseph Spence

'No frills' centre-forward Joey Mawson was a miner brought up in the Durham coalfield. He played his early football with the amateur side Crook Town and then served with Durham City and Washington Colliery before moving south to sign professional forms for Stoke City in January 1929. He made his debut a month after joining the Potters and went on to score 50 goals in 93 appearances during his four years at The Victoria Ground, finishing up as top-scorer in 1931-32 and 1932-33, gaining a Second Division championship medal in the latter campaign. In the summer of 1933 he was transferred to Nottingham Forest and later played for Stockport County, Linfield and Crewe Alexandra, retiring during the war. Mawson was born in Brandon Colliery on 26 October 1905 and died in Stoke-on-Trent on 10 September 1959.

MAXWELL, Allan

Centre-forward Maxwell joined Stoke from Darwen in exchange for a set of wrought iron gates. The Scottish striker – born in Glasgow in 1870 – scored six goals in 37 League and FA Cup games for the Potters between February 1896 and April 1897. He left The Victoria Ground and returned home to play for St Bernard's. Earlier in his career he had assisted Cambuslang Rangers and Everton, netting 16 goals in 53 games during his two-year stay with the Merseysiders (October 1891 to November 1893).

MAXWELL, James F.

Wing-half Jimmy Maxwell was born in Glasgow in 1900. He played for Arbroath before signing for Stoke in the summer of 1925. He remained at The Victoria Ground for just one season, transferring to Watford in May 1927.

MAXWELL, William Sturrock

Inside-forward Willie Maxwell was a solicitor's clerk, working in Dundee and playing for Heart of Midlothian when he decided that he wanted to move to the Potteries to take up a similar position and also sign for Stoke. This was in 1894. Twelve months later he finally arrived at The Victoria Ground and went on to give the Potters excellent service, scoring 85 goals in 173 senior appearances and gaining one full Scottish cap in the next six seasons, up to 1901, when he was transferred to Third Lanark for £250. After that he assisted Sunderland, Millwall Athletic and Bristol City, for whom he netted 62 goals in 128 outings and won a Second Division championship medal, before retiring in 1909. Later that same year Maxwell took to coaching with the Belgium club, Leopold FC of Brussels and during the 1920s coached the Belgium national side. He was born in Arbroath on 21 September 1876 and died in 1940.

MAYER, Wilfred

Reserve outside-right Mayer played in one League game for the Potters against Chelsea (home) in March 1935 (lost 1-0). Born in Etruria, Stoke-on-Trent on 18 February 1912, he started out with Newcastle PSA and was recruited from Downings Collieries in August 1932, He left The Victoria Ground for Southampton in March 1937 for £650 and played in 14 League games for Saints (in a number of forward position) before moving to Wellington Town in 1938. Two years later he won a Welsh Cup winners' medal and retired in 1943. Mayer died in Stoke on 5 April 1979.

MEAKIN, Harry

Full-back Meakin was given 41 League and Cup outings by Stoke City between August 1946 and January 1950. A competent player, with a fair degree of doggedness, Meakin was born in Stoke-on-Trent on 8 September 1919 and joined the Potters from Summerbank FC in November 1945. It was a pity he had Messrs. Mould and McCue to contest with for a first-team place. Meakin left The Victoria Ground for Northwich Victoria in May 1950.

MEAKIN, Samuel Stanley

Left-half Sammy Meakin spent a season with Stoke, playing in one FA Cup-tie against Burslem Port Vale in October 1887, when he helped the Potters win 1-0. Born locally in Fenton in 1860, he played for Tunstall and Burslem Swifts either side his brief spell at The Victoria Ground.

MELLOR, Harold Halden

Inside-forward Harry Mellor, who was born in Stoke in 1878, started his career with Burslem Port Vale and after a brief spell with Dresden United he joined Stoke in the summer of 1897. He netted four goals in 35 appearances for the Potters and then spent 16 months with Grimsby Town (from June 1900 to October 1901), having 33 games for the Mariners and helping them win the Second Division title. After suffering a bad injury early in that 1901-02 season Mellor announced his retirement and duly returned to the Potteries. An attempted comeback with Brighton & Hove Albion in October 1903 proved abortive.

MELLOR, James

Mellor made one FA Cup appearance for Stoke, replacing Joey Schofield at outside-left against Nottingham Forest in February 1895. Born in Stoke in 1870 he joined the Potters from Dresden United and left for nearby Stone after spending just a season at The Victoria Ground.

MELLOR, Sydney

Scorer of one goal in 11 League games for Stoke, inside-forward Mellor was born in Leek c.1898, and joined the Potters from Leek Town shortly after World War One. He left the club for Congleton Town in the summer of 1921 after two complete seasons at The Victoria Ground.

MEREDITH, Samuel

Older brother of the great wing wizard, Billy Meredith, Sammy was, in contrast, a tough-tackling, ever-reliable full-back, who joined Stoke from Chirk in May 1901. He stayed at The Victoria Ground for four seasons, making exactly 50 League and Cup appearances. A Welsh international, born in Trefonch near Chirk on 5 September 1872, Meredith won eight full caps (1900-07). He left Stoke in June 1905 for Leyton, staying there until announcing his retirement in 1910 after amassing 94 Southern League appearances for the London club. In fact, he was forced to give up football after developing a wasting disease. He became a publican and kept the Jolly Forgeman at Newbridge near Ruabon before moving to Gorton (Manchester) to become a landlord for Hardy's brewery. Meredith died in Gorton on Christmas Day 1921.

MERRITT, Wilfred

Understudy to Billy Rowley for three seasons (1888-91) goalkeeper Merritt played in just five senior games for Stoke, one in the FA Cup when Wolves won a replayed tie 8-0 in February 1890. Born in Leek in November 1864, Merritt played for his home-town club before and after serving the Potters.

MERTHYR TOWN (Tydfil)

Stoke's playing record against Merthyr:
Southern League

Venue	P	W	D	L	F	A
Home	4	4	0	0	21	1
Away	4	1	1	2	5	6
Totals	8	5	1	2	26	7

Stoke beat Merthyr 11-0 at The Victoria Ground on the opening day of the 1909-10 Southern League season. Billy Smith (4) and Arthur Griffiths (3) led the goal-chase in front of 4,000 fans. England international goalkeeper Jack Robinson (aged 39) made his debut for Stoke in this same game.

Later in the month Stoke completed the double over the Welsh side by winning 4-2 in the valleys.

Stoke also registered a 4-0 home win over Merthyr in October 1914, having beaten them 4-1 at The Vic in January 1911.

Players with both clubs: Gary Brooke, Chris Hemming, Sam Howshall, Robbie James (player-manager of Merthyr), Frank Jordan, Jack Lewis, Dai Nicholas (Merthyr trialist), Edgar Powell and Billy Poole. Bob McGrory was a player with Stoke who also managed both clubs.

MESTON, Samuel

A gargantuan figure, right-half or inside-forward Meston (6ft 2ins tall and 14st 10lbs in weight) scored four goals in 19 first-team games for Stoke between March 1894 and February 1895. Known as 'Long Tom' (for his long-range shooting) he was born in Arbroath on 16 January 1872 and joined the Potters from his home-town club Arbroath Victoria in January 1894. He left The Victoria Ground for Southampton St Mary's in April 1895 and while at The Dell won six Southern League championship medals and two FA Cup runners-up medals. He made 288 Southern League appearances for Saints (20 goals scored) the second highest tally for the club behind Bert Lee, while only Terry Paine and Nick Holmes had more FA Cup outings for Saints than Meston who later assisted Salisbury City (1906), Croydon Common (as player-trainer 1907), Salisbury City again (1909), Chandlers Ford, Eastleigh Athletic (1913) and then Bishopstoke WMSC as trainer (1923). In the 1920s while working as a brake-fitter's mate at Eastleigh Railway Works, Meston starred in several charity games for an ex-Saints XI. His son, Samuel William, joined the playing staff at The Dell in 1922. Meston senior died at Ashurst, Hampshire on 14 August 1948.

MID RHONDDA

Stoke's playing record against the Welsh club is:
Southern League

Venue	P	W	D	L	F	A
Home	2	2	0	0	9	0
Away	2	1	0	1	4	4
Totals	4	3	0	1	13	4

Stoke beat Mid Rhondda 8-0 at The Victoria Ground in November 1914 helped by three goals from 'Arty' Watkin and a brace from Dick Smith. Smith scored both Stoke goals in the return fixture that season when 'Rhondda' revenged that heavy defeat by winning 4-2.

The previous season Stoke had completed the double over the Welsh side, winning 1-0 at home and 2-0 away. The latter result was achieved on a muddy, undersized, sloping and dangerous bumpy pitch.

Winger Sam Spencer played for both Stoke and Mid Rhondda in the 1920s.

MIDDLESBROUGH

Stoke's playing record against 'Boro is:
Football League

Venue	P	W	D	L	F	A
Home	42	24	9	9	75	45
Away	42	6	10	26	36	81
Totals	84	30	19	35	111	126

FA Cup

Venue	P	W	D	L	F	A
Home	1	1	0	0	3	1
Away	1	0	0	1	1	4
Totals	2	1	0	1	4	5

League Cup

Venue	P	W	D	L	F	A
Home	1	0	1	0	1	1
Away	1	1	0	0	2	1
Totals	2	1	1	0	3	2

The Potters' best League victory over 'Boro is 6-2 while their heaviest defeat has been 6-1.

That 6-2 win was achieved at The Victoria Ground in September 1936, when Freddie Steele (3), Joe Johnson (2) and Stan Matthews found the net for the Potters.

Stoke also defeated 'Boro 4-0 at home in September 1925 when George Paterson, making his debut, scored a hat-trick.

Another hat-trick hero for Stoke was Tim Coleman who netted all his side's goals in a 3-1 home win over 'Boro in December 1956 (Division Two).

'Boro ran up that 6-1 scoreline at Ayresome Park in a First Division game in November 1933. England's George Camsell scored twice for 'Boro and helped lay on three more goals for his colleagues before a disappointing crowd of under 7,000.

'Boro also beat Stoke 5-0 at home in successive First Division matches in April and December 1906; ran up a 5-1 victory at home on the last day of 1938; won a Second Division match by 5-2, also at home, in March 1956 and then repeated that score at The Victoria Ground in December 1959.

A nine-goal thriller at Middlesbrough in a First Division game on 7 September 1946 ended in victory for the home team by 5-4. Freddie Steele netted another hat-trick for Stoke, while Mick Fenton scored four times for 'Boro. The official crowd figure was 43,685.

Stoke's home First Division game with Middlesbrough on 17 January 1976 was played at Vale Park following storm damage to The Victoria Ground. A crowd of over 21,000 saw Stoke win 1-0, Ian Moores the scorer.

Mick Fenton scored for Middlesbrough against Stoke in the void Division One game on 2 September 1939 and did so again when the teams met in the first League season after the war (7 September 1946).

Middlesbrough won only twice in 17 League visits to Stoke between 1956 and 1994.

Players with both clubs: Tom Coxon, Bill Godley, Verdi Godwin, Jack Hall, John Love Jones, Graham Kavanagh, George Kinnell, Eric McManus, John Mahoney, Bert Mitchell, Mick Kennedy, Fred Pentland, Don Ratcliffe, Jimmy Robertson ('Boro junior), Geoff Scott, Charlie Scrimshaw, Jack Stirling, Ken Thomson and Josh Williams. Arthur Jepson was a goalkeeper with Stoke, who later became scout for Middlesbrough.

MIDDLESBROUGH IRONOPOLIS

Stoke have not met Ironopolis at competitive level, although the teams have played each other in friendly encounters, the last being in season 1892-93 when Stoke were beaten 3-0 on Teesside but won their home game 1-0.

Players with both clubs: Jimmy Grewer and Wally McReddie.

MILARVIE, Robert

Born in Pollockshields, Scotland, in 1864, Bob Milarvie was a useful outside-left who played for Pollockshields FC and Hibernian before joining Stoke in May 1888. He did reasonably well with the Potters, scoring five goals in 15 first-team games before signing for neighbours Port Vale in June 1899. He made only one friendly appearance for the Valiants before the club was censured by the Football Association for playing him illegally because Milarvie had, in fact, earlier signed for Derby County. The Rams won the battle to secure his services. Milarvie later assisted Newton Heath (from August 1890) and Ardwick (later Manchester City) from 1891 to 1896. He scored 26 goals in more than 120 League and Cup games during his career. Milarvie died in Gorton in November 1912.

MILLER, W. Albert Bertrand

Goalkeeper Bert Miller was born in Newcastle (Staffordshire) c.1880. He played for Tunstall Park (two spells), Port Vale (two spells, the first in 1902 as a trialist) and Norwich City before joining Stoke in the summer of 1908 from the former club. An amateur throughout his career, he made 11 first-team appearances for the Potters before leaving the club for Leek United in April 1909. Founder member of the May Bank Cup competition, as well as a plethora of other local League appointments, he qualified as a solicitor's clerk in 1907 and helped Tunstall win the North Staffs District Premier League championship. Among the other non-League clubs Miller assisted before teaming up with Stoke were: Newcastle St Giles, Newcastle Swifts, Cross Heath, Burslem Liverpool Road, Blackpool Etrurians, Stafford Rangers and Stone Town. He retired in the summer of 1912.

MILLER, John

Physically strong, moustachioed outside-left Jack Miller was a useful footballer who gave Stoke good service over a two year period, August 1905 to May 1907, during which time he scored five goals in 63 appearances. Born in Hednesford in 1875, he joined Wolverhampton Wanderers from Hednesford Town in September 1895, initially as cover for Scotsman David Black and Alf Griffin. He eventually amassed a record of 49 goals in 249 games for the Wanderers, being virtually an ever-present in the side from September 1896 to November 1904. He moved from Molineux to The Victoria Ground for £400 and after leaving Stoke Miller served briefly with Willenhall before retiring to become a publican in 1910.

MILLS, Michael Denis MBE

Mills was Stoke's manager from May 1985 to November 1989 – and during the four and a half years he was in charge, the Potters played over 200 competitive games (190 in the Football League of which Mills himself appeared in 44). As a player, Mills occupied, in the main, the left-back position, amassing almost 700 League appearances for Ipswich Town (1965-82) after having been rejected as a teenager by Portsmouth. He won FA Cup and UEFA Cup winners medals while at Portman Road and gained 42 full England caps plus five at Under-23 level, skippering his country eight times, including matches in the 1982 World Cup finals. He joined Southampton for £100,000 in November 1982 and added another 103 League appearances to his tally with the Saints before moving to Stoke as a player-manager, retiring as a player in 1988. With hardly any money to spend, Mills was unable to bring quality players to the club and this led to him quitting his position at The Victoria Ground after a run of poor results and performances saw the crowds drop alarmingly. He later managed Colchester United. and in 1996 was appointed assistant to Trevor Francis at Birmingham City. Mills was born in Godalming, Surrey on 4 January 1949.

MILLWALL (Athletic)

Stoke's playing record against the Lions is:

Football League

Venue	P	W	D	L	F	A
Home	13	6	3	4	17	13
Away	13	4	4	5	15	18
Totals	26	10	7	9	32	31

Southern League

Home	2	1	0	1	7	2
Away	2	1	0	1	3	6
Totals	4	2	0	2	10	8

FA Cup

Home	2	2	0	0	6	1
Away	1	0	1	0	0	0
Totals	3	2	1	0	6	1

League Cup

Home	2	1	1	0	1	0
Away	2	0	0	2	1	4
Totals	4	1	1	2	2	4

Full Members' Cup

Away	1	0	1	0	2	2

On 9 December 1911 Millwall beat Stoke 5-1 in a Southern League game in London, but the Potters quickly gained revenge by winning the return fixture in April by 7-0, Jack Lenaghan leading the goal glut with a hat-trick.

Stoke beat Millwall 4-3 at The Victoria Ground in an exciting First Division game in April 1995 when Nigel Gleghorn scored twice. The Potters winner came from Kevin keen in the final minute.

Simon Sturridge notched two goals when Stoke beat Millwall 3-2 at The New Den on 27 April 1996 – their last Football League encounter against the Lions, who were relegated at the end of that campaign.

After a goalless draw in London, Stoke beat Millwall 4-0 in a third round FA Cup replay in January 1936 with Freddie Steele scoring a cracking hat-trick.

On their way to the FA Cup semi-finals in 1970-71, Stoke ousted Millwall from the competition in the third round, beating them 2-1 at The Victoria Ground before 21,398 fans.

It was certainly cold at Cold Blow Lane when Stoke drew 2-2 with Millwall in the Full Members' Cup-tie there in October 1985 in front of only 1,741 fans.

Players with both clubs: Arthur Beachill, Jimmy Broad, Tommy Broad, George Brown, Ellis Hall, Brian Horne, Joe Hutton, Tom Hyslop, Lawrie Leslie, Willie Maxwell, Wilf Phillips and Henry Salmon.

Graham Paddon played for Millwall and later became assistant and then caretaker manager of Stoke.

MILLWARD, Douglas

A utility forward, Millward had one game in Stoke's colours, lining up at inside-left in a fifth-round FA Cup-tie against West Bromwich Albion in January 1888. Born in Stoke in 1866, he played for Stoke Priory before signing for the Potters and on leaving The Victoria Ground (after one season) he joined Leek Town.

MILLWARD, Ernest Foster

No relation to Doug (above) Ernie Millward was an amateur outside-left who had a useful career in the game, serving with Cobridge Church, Biddulph Mission, Glossop North End, Wrexham, Stoke (briefly), Port Vale (2 appearances in 1907), Stoke again (from August 1908 to May 1910), Hanley Swifts, Huddersfield Town and Crewe Alexandra. Born at Hartshill in 1887, he was regular in the first XI during his two seasons at The Victoria Ground and scored 25 goals in 78 first-team outings for the Potters. Millward died in Bournemouth on 23 June 1962.

MILNE, Alexander James

Left-back Milne made 276 League and Cup appearances for Stoke between October 1912 (after signing from Hebburn Argyle) and May 1936, when he moved to Doncaster Rovers. Born in Hebburn-on-Tyne on 29 September 1889, he initially started out as a defender with Hebburn Old Boys and always looked the part, a rugged, no-nonsense tackler with strong kick. He did not play much during the wartime period (1915-19) when he was called back to the north-east to work on munitions. He played on until he was almost 41, retiring in May 1930. Milne died in Doncaster in 1970.

Alex Milne

MITCHELL, Albert James

Bert Mitchell, born in Stoke-on-Trent on 22 January 1922, had a useful career as an inside-forward. He won an England 'B' cap and played for Burslem Albion, Stoke City (May 1941-February 1948), Blackburn Rovers, Kettering Town, Northampton Town (1949-51), Luton Town, Middlesbrough (195-56), Southport, Wellington Town, Kidderminster Harriers and finally Stafford Rangers, whom he also managed. Mitchell netted twice in his 10 League outings for the Potters.

MOLYNEUX, Frederick

Molyneux was a capable centre-forward who scored five goals in 16 League and Cup games for Stoke. A Lancastrian, born in Bolton in 1878, he came out of the third Batallion of the Grenadier Guards to play for Stoke whom he served from February 1898 to March 1899, when he moved to Bristol City (making five appearances up to 1900). During his career Molyneux also played for Berwick Rangers and Luton Town.

MONTFORD, Edgar William John

Born on the English/Welsh border at Knighton near Welshpool c.1859, Edgar Montford played for Newtown prior to a five-year spell with Stoke (1885-1890). A reliable defender able to play as a full-back or wing-half, he made just seven League and Cup appearances for the Potters in that time before leaving the club for join his brother at Leek Town. After leaving football he became a Collector of Taxes for Hanley, Stoke and Fenton, and was clerk to the Mucclestone Parochial Church Council, living in Knighton, when he died on 22 November 1940.

MONTFORD, Harold E.

Inside or centre-forward Harry Montford, younger brother of Edgar (above), was born in Newtown in 1865, and he, too, assisted his home-town club before joining Stoke for the club's first season in the Football League (1888-89). He played in two first-team games before he went off to play for Leek Town.
NB: *The Montfords were the first set of brothers to represent Stoke at football.*

MOORE, Albert Edward

Moore remained an amateur inside-forward throughout his playing career which he spent entirely in the North Staffordshire area, assisting Normacot, Stoke (1921-22) and Burslem Swifts. He played in just one Football League game for the Potters v Bradford Park Avenue in November 1921 (lost 1-0). Moore was born in Longton in 1898.

MOORE, John

Half-back Moore made 13 appearances for Stoke City during the 1967-68 season. Born in Liverpool on 9 September 1945, he was an amateur with Everton before signing professional forms for Stoke City in July 1963. He remained at The Victoria Ground – playing mainly as a reserve – until August 1968, when he moved to Shrewsbury Town, later assisting Swansea City (January-May 1973). Moore made over over 150 appearances during his five seasons at Gay Meadow.

MOORE, Thomas

A Scotsman, born in Arbroath *c*.1864, Moore made one League appearance for Stoke in the very first season of the competition, lining up at centre-forward in a 2-1 defeat at Bolton in October 1888. He came down to try his luck on the English soccer scene from Arbroath and returned to the same club after failing to settle (or impress) in the Potteries.

MOORE, William

Born in New Washington, County Durham in the spring of 1916, Billy Moore was a useful half-back who played for Walker Celtic before appearing in four League games for Stoke City during his two seasons at The Victoria Ground: 1936-38. He left the club to join Mansfield Town before retiring after the war to take up a coaching position with Notts County who at the time were managed by Eric Houghton. Moore looked after the likes of Jackie Sewell and Tommy Lawton at Meadow Lane and when Houghton left to take over at his former club, Aston Villa in 1953, Moore went with him as his assistant, seeing Villa win the FA Cup at Wembley in 1957. In December of that year he took over as team manager at Walsall and in 1960 guided them to the Fourth Division championship. And 12 months later took them into the Second Division. Moore left Fellows Park to become scout of Fulham in November 1963, but returned for a second spell in charge of the Saddlers from February 1969. He remained there for another three years, until financial problems began to hit the club. He resigned his post in March 1972 following a disagreement with the coach, John Smith who later took over the reins as team boss. Moore quit football at that point and took over a hotel in Stafford. He died in 1982.

MOORES, Ian Richard

Over a period of 12 years, Ian Moores, a gangling sometimes awkward-looking striker, standing 6ft 2ins tall and weighing well over 13st, served with five different clubs, amassing a total of 225 League appearances and scoring 49 goals. Born in Newcastle-under-Lyme on 5 October 1954, he joined Stoke City after playing for Staffordshire Schools and turned professional at The Victoria Ground in June 1972 – three months after the Potters had lifted their first ever trophy (the League Cup). After making his debut for the Potters in April 1974, he went on to net 15 goals for Stoke in 57 senior outings before leaving the club for Tottenham Hotspur in August 1976 for £90,000. A year or so after leaving Stoke, Moores scored a hat-trick for Spurs in a 9-0 Second Division win over Bristol Rovers and in the summer of 1977 he played in Australia with the Western Suburbs club, Sydney. A little over a year later (in October 1978) he moved across London to sign for Leyton Orient for £55,000, and in seasons 1982-83 he assisted both Bolton Wanderers (July-August) and Barnsley (February) on loan. Moores then did well in Cyprus with Apoel, gaining both League and Cup winners' medals before returning to England to play non-League football with Newcastle Town, later assisting Tamworth prior to having a brief spell in Sweden with Landskrona Bols followed by a trial period with Port Vale. Moores was capped twice by England at Under-23 level while at Stoke.

MOORWOOD, John E.

Jack Moorwood played nine League games at centre-half for Stoke during the second half of the 1920-21 season when he lined up across the middle with George Clarke and Dickie Smith. A strong tackler, he had good positional sense, but lacked that extra yard of pace. Born in Chesterfield in 1898, he joined the Potters from Alfreton for £300 and left The Victoria Ground for Wrexham.

MORGAN, Nicholas

Nicky Morgan had a fine career as an out-and-out striker. A Londoner, born in East Ham on 30 October 1959, he started out with West Ham United as an apprentice, turning professional at Upton Park in November 1977. He spent over five years with the Hammers, never really establishing himself in the first team. In March 1983 he went to Portsmouth and after doing much better with Pompey (32 goals in 95 League outings), he switched to Stoke in November 1986 for £50,000. He spent three and a half seasons at The Victoria Ground during which time he claimed 26 goals in his 104 senior appearances before transferring to Bristol City for £30,000 in March 1990, later playing for AFC Bournemouth. In his League career as a whole Morgan hit over 100 goals in more than 300 games.

MOULD, William

Born at Great Chell on 6 October 1919, defender Billy Mould played as a full-back and centre-half for Stoke City in a total of 194 League and Cup games plus another 83 in wartime competitions. He was a fine player, dedicated to the game who replaced Arthur Turner at the heart of the Stoke defence. He joined the Potters from Summerbank FC as a junior in 1936 (along with Alec Ormston) and went on to serve the club until July 1962 when he was given a free transfer to join Crewe Alexandra. During the hostilities he was wounded in the leg while serving with the Royal Artillery in Normandy and spent a short time in Ireland with a handful of other Stokies including Syd Peppitt and Ormston. Mould captained the side several times and was a fine club man. He retired from football, in May 1954 to concentrate on the his successful sports-outfitters business.

MOUNTFORD, Frank

The versatile Frank Mountford had a fine career with Stoke City. Born in Askern, near Doncaster on 30 March 1923 he came down to the Potteries with his family at an early age and joined the club as a youngster in 1937 while still at Bradley Junior School. After turning professional during the war, he held down a regular place in the side for 13 years (from 1942) and eventually accumulated a total of 425 senior appearances for the Potters (25 goals scored) as well as turning out in another 183 wartime fixtures (54 goals) when he also guested for Derby County. Only nine players have appeared in more competitive games for the Potters than Mountford and, indeed, only one man – John McCue with 675 – has amassed more than Mountford's tally of 608 first-team outings. Able to play in a variety of positions including those of full-back, centre-half and centre-forward, Mountford was a big favourite with The Victoria Ground fans and he was always totally committed to playing football, never shirking a tackle, always giving 110 per-cent out on the park. After hanging up his boots in 1958 he moved behind the scenes at Stoke, first as a trainer and then as coach, holding office until Alan Durban arrived as team manager. Mountford remained in close contact with the club and attended several of Stoke's home games right up until the mid-eighties.
NB: Mountford scored a record 14 penalties in peacetime League and Cup competitions for Stoke City as well as netting another six in wartime football.

MOUNTFORD, George Frederick

No relation to Frank (above) George Mountford was born in Kidderminster on 30 March 1931 and died in that town on 14 June 1973. Either an outside-right or inside-right, he was signed by Stoke City from Kidderminster Harriers in 1942 for a fee of just £40. He made 95 wartime appearances for the Potters (37 goals scored), playing mainly on the wing when Stanley Matthews was unavailable, and after the hostilities he became a regular member in the side, especially after Matthews had moved to Blackpool. Mountford added 29 goals in 158 peacetime League and FA Cup games to his Stoke record before going to South America with clubmate Neil Franklin in 1950 (See BOGOTA AFFAIR). Known as 'Bald Arrow" in Colombia. Mountford was a star performer with the Independiente Sante Fe club and during that 1950-51 season over there he scored and made plenty of goals. On his return to England he was immediately suspended and after serving his punishment returned to The Victoria Ground (October 1952) but was quickly exchanged with Des Farrow of Queen's Park Rangers by manager Frank Taylor. He played 34 League games for Rangers and then dropped out of the big-time by signing for Hereford United, later returning to his former club Kidderminster Harriers and ending his career with Lockheed Leamington. On retirement Mountford became a GPO engineer based near his home in Kidderminster.

MOW COP

Stoke well and truly crushed luckless Mow Cop 26-0 in a Staffordshire Cup first-round tie in season 1877-78. Thereafter, the Potters knocked out Hanley Rovers 2-0, Leek 1-0 and Ashbourne 1-0 in the semi-final before they collected their first trophy, accounting for Talke Rangers, also by a 1-0 scoreline, in the final.

Match reports contradict each other as to who were Stoke's scorers against Mow Cop, but one generally assumes that Tom Slaney scored at least nine goals and Teddy Johnson six.
Goalkeeper Manny Foster was signed by Stoke from Mow Cop during World War Two.

MUDIE, John Knight

Jackie Mudie was a diminutive inside-forward who had an exceptionally fine playing career which saw him amass a total of 463 League appearances (184 goals) and win 17 full caps for Scotland. Born in Dundee on 10 April 1930, one of seven brothers, all of them footballers, Mudie played initially for Dunkeld Amateurs and Dundee

Jackie Mudie

Stobswell before signing as a professional for Dundee. He left there for Blackpool in 1945, turned professional in May 1947 and six years later helped the Seasiders win the FA Cup (4-3 v Bolton) when he played in the same forward-line as a certain Stanley Matthews. With Stoke manager Tony Waddington recruiting experience footballers in an effort to win promotion from the Second Division, Mudie was lured to The Victoria Ground in March 1961 for £7,000, and he did a terrific job, scoring 33 goals in 93 senior outings, helping the Potters win back their place in the top flight in 1963. In November 1963, along with Ron Wilson and £12,000, he was sold to rivals Port Vale where he became caretaker manager in February 1965, taking over as player-manager the following month. With the team doing badly, Mudie resigned his position for personal reasons in May 1967 after scoring 11 goals in 64 outings for the Valiants. Thereafter he became player-manager of Oswestry Town, was assistant coach at Crewe Alexandra after that, and then acted as trainer-coach to Eastwood and managed Northwich Victoria prior to taking up a scouting position with Johannesburg Rangers in South Africa. Mudie died in Hatshill on 2 March 1992.

MUDIE, Leonard

Scottish inside-forward Len Mudie scored once in three League outings for the Potters during the first half of the 1889-90 season after moving down from Burnley for whom he played in one League game, ironically against Stoke on 8 December 1888. A temperamental player, he never settled in the Potteries and after an argument with the committee, left The Victoria Ground before the turn of the year and signed for Dundee Wanderers. Born in Forfar in 1872, he had started his career in Scotland.

MUGGLETON, Carl David

A fine shot-stopper, goal-keeper Carl Muggleton joined Stoke from Celtic for £150,000 on 21 July 1994. Managed by Lou Macari at Parkhead, he teamed up with his former boss at The Victoria Ground and in his first season with the Potters appeared in 31 senior games. Born in Leicester on 13 September 1968, Muggleton went to Filbert Street as a junior and turned professional there in September 1986. Over the next eight years, besides having 54 outings for the Foxes he played on loan with Chesterfield, Blackpool, Hartlepool United, Stockport County and Stoke City (August-September 1993, when he was given nine games) and in January 1994 moved to Celtic for £150,000. He played 13 times for the Scottish giants prior to his transfer to Stoke – and since then he's also played on loan for both Rotherham United and Sheffield United. Capped once by England at Under-21 level, Muggleton had first Ronnie Sinclair and then Mark Prudhoe fighting it out with him for first-team football at The Victoria Ground. His Stoke record at May 1997 was 74 appearances.

MULHOLLAND, George R.

Resilient Scottish full-back, born in Ayr on 4 April 1928, Mulholland developed through the junior ranks at The Victoria Ground and went on to make just three League appearances for the Potters, all of them during the second half of the 1950-51 season. Unable to command a regular place in the side, he eventually left Stoke for Bradford City in July 1953 and made well over 300 senior appearances for the Valley Paraders before moving on to Darlington in July 1960. He quit League soccer in 1963 after more than 400 games as a professional.

MULLARD, Albert Thomas

Born in Tamworth on 22 November 1920, Mullard was an adaptable player who could do a good job as an half-back or as an inside or centre-forward. As strong as an ox, he was courageous, determined and totally committed to playing football. He assisted Hinckley United, Walsall (July 1938) and Crewe Alexandra before joining Stoke City in August 1950. He scored five goals in 23 appearances for the Potters up to September 1951 when he moved to Port Vale for £10,000 plus Alan Martin. he did very well at Vale Park, scoring 23 goals in 179 first-team matches, helping the Valiants reach the FA Cup semi-final and win the Third Division title in 1953-54. He lost his place early in 1956 and was then transferred to Northwich Victoria in May of that year, later playing and working for Wednesbury Tube (Wolverhampton Works League). Mullard died in Bilston on 27 May 1984.

NB: Mullard was a prisoner-of-war for four years during World War Two.

MULLINEUX, Ernest

Right-back Mullineux was born in Norwood c.1879. He played his early football as a centre-half with Burslem Park before joining Port Vale in May 1900. He did very well with the Valiants and made 132 appearances for them before moving to Bury for £600 in December 1904. He spent two years at Gigg Lane and in the summer of 1906 switched his allegiance back to the Potteries with Stoke. A schoolteacher in Hanley, who combined his educational work with that of playing football, Mullineux had 19 outings in his first season, 13 in his second and from then until 1912, was a regular member of the team, amassing in total 186 League and Cup appearances for the Potters before winding down his career with Wellington Town (1914-15). Mullineux died in Bucknall on 3 August 1960.

MUNRO, Alexander Iain Fordyce

A fine full-back on his day, Munro was a £165,000 purchase by Stoke manager Alan Durban from St Mirren in October 1980. He played 34 competitive games for the Potters (one goal scored) before transferring to Sunderland for £150,000 in August 1981 – signed again by Durban who was now in the hot seat at Roker Park. Born in Uddingston on 24 August 1951, Munro won seven full caps for Scotland and before joining St Mirren he had served with Hibernian, Glasgow Rangers and Dundee United. He appeared in 80 League games for Sunderland and more than 400 in his professional career all told. After retiring as a player, in May 1986, Munro took over as manager of Hamilton Academical. He later managed St Mirren and was then boss of Raith Rovers, September 1996 to April 1997.

MURPHY, Joseph

A solid half-back or inside-forward, Joe Murphy wore a wig and was called 'Judge' by his teammates. Born in Stockton-on-Tees in 1873, he played for Hibernian before joining Stoke in the summer of 1897. He had 56 games for the Potters (two goals scored) and was transferred to Arsenal towards the end of April 1899. He later played for Raith Rovers (May 1900-02). He had over 50 first-team games for the Gunners in various competitions.

MYATT, Herbert T.

Born in Stoke c.1884, outside-right Myatt scored twice in four Birmingham & District League games for the Potters in season 1908-09 after joining the club from Stone Town. He left The Victoria Ground at the end of that season and signed for Stafford Rangers.

NAUGHTON, William A.

'Chippy' Naughton, an inveterate practical joker, was suspended from football for playing as an amateur while receiving payments. This happened in mid-1891, a year or so after he had joined Stoke from Carfin Shamrock where he had been after failing to establish himself in Celtic's first team. Born in Glasgow in 1866, Naughton was a useful outside-right who could cross a ball to perfection. He spent five seasons at The Victoria Ground during which time he scored 25 goals in 101 senior appearances. He left the Potters for Southampton St Mary's in April 1895 and netted 18 times in his 47 outings for Saints, helping them win the Southern League Shield. In May 1898 he returned to Scotland to sign for Hibernian.

NELSON

Stoke's playing record against Nelson is:
Football League

Venue	P	W	D	L	F	A
Home	2	2	0	0	8	1
Away	2	0	0	2	0	3
Totals	4	2	0	2	8	4

Stoke first met Nelson in season 1923-24 when the teams were in the Second Division. A crowd of 12,150 saw the Potters win 4-0 at The Victoria Ground on 22 September (Harry Davies scored twice), and there were 12,000 fans present for the return fixture a week later when Nelson took the points with a 2-0 victory.

The other two League meetings were in the Third Division North in 1926-27 when Stoke won 4-1 at home but lost 1-0 away.

Players with both clubs: Wilf Chadwick and Billy Smith.

NEUTRAL GROUNDS

Stoke have appeared in over 20 Cup replays on neutral grounds.

The first time they were asked to play on a neutral ground was in March 1899 when they lost to Derby County at Molineux in the FA Cup semi-final. Stoke then lost twice to Arsenal in FA Cup semi-finals replays – first in 1971 at Villa Park (after drawing at Hillsborough) and in 1972 at Goodison Park (after a stalemate at Villa Park).

In the 1972 League Cup, Stoke defeated West Ham United in the semi-final at neutral Old Trafford in a second replay after drawing at Hillsborough.

Wembley, of course, is another neutral ground on which Stoke have played – in the 1972 League Cup final v Chelsea and in the 1992 Autoglass Trophy Final v Stockport County – winning both games.

Other FA Cup replays played on a neutral ground involving Stoke:

1906-07	v West Bromwich Albion (Villa Park)	0-2
1907-08	v Gainsborough Trinity (Nottingham)	3-2
1909-10	v Exeter City (Exeter Rugby Ground)	1-1
1909-10	v Exeter City (Craven Cottage)	2-1
1926-27	v Rhyl (Old Trafford)	1-2
1930-31	v Manchester United (Anfield)	2-4
1931-32	v Sunderland (Maine Road)	2-1
1954-55	v Bury (Goodison Park)	3-3
1954-55	v Bury (Old Trafford)	3-2
1957-58	v Aston Villa (Molineux)	2-0
1960-61	v Aldershot (Molineux)	3-0
1970-71	v Huddersfield Town (Old Trafford)	1-0

● In May 1971 Stoke played Everton at Crystal Palace's Selhurst Park ground for the third/fourth place prize in the FA Cup.

● In season 1890-91 Stoke played their home Football Alliance game with Crewe Alexandra at the County Cricket Ground after The Victoria Ground had been declared unfit.

● Stoke won a vital Test Match against Newton Heath (Manchester United) at Burslem on 27 April 1895.

● Following storm damage at The Victoria Ground, Stoke played their home First Division game against Middlesbrough on 17 January 1976 at Vale Park.

NEW BRIGHTON

Stoke's playing record against New Brighton is:
Football League

Venue	P	W	D	L	F	A
Home	1	0	1	0	1	1
Away	1	0	0	1	0	5
Totals	2	0	1	1	1	6

These two Third Division North League games were played in season 1926-27. Just 4,000 fans saw Stoke hammered 5-0 away from home and 12,209 spectators witnessed the 1-1 draw at The Victoria Ground as the Potters edged towards to the championship.

Players with both clubs: Jimmy Broad, Kenny Campbell, Dick Johnson and John Spencer.

NEW BRIGHTON TOWER

Stoke have never played Tower at competitive level. although they did meet up in a friendly match in season 1897-98 when the Potters lost an away game 2-0.

Players with both clubs: Jimmy Hill and Harry Simpson.

NEWCASTLE UNITED

Stoke's playing record against United is:
Football League

Venue	P	W	D	L	F	A
Home	33	17	9	7	52	29
Away	33	3	6	24	26	82
Totals	66	20	15	31	78	111

Test Matches

Venue	P	W	D	L	F	A
Home	1	1	0	0	1	0
Away	1	0	0	1	1	2
Totals	2	1	0	1	2	2

FA Cup

Venue	P	W	D	L	F	A
Home	2	0	1	1	3	5
Away	3	0	0	3	3	7
Totals	5	0	1	4	6	12

League Cup

Venue	P	W	D	L	F	A
Home	1	0	0	1	0	4
Away	1	0	0	1	0	3
Totals	2	0	0	2	0	7

The first of the 66 League encounters between the two teams took place on 24 September 1898 when a crowd of 7,500 witnessed a goalless draw at The Victoria Ground. The return fixture on 21 January 1899 ended in a convincing 3-0 win for United before a crowd of 4,000.

On 14 September 1901, United beat Stoke 5-1 at St James' Park and the following season (on 6 September 1902) the Geordies won their home League game by 5-0, a victory they repeated to a goal on 24 April 1906 and again 63 years later in April 1969.

Stoke, however, quickly gained revenge for the drubbing they suffered at the start of the 1902-03 campaign when they also ran up a 5-0 scoreline at The Victoria Ground on 3 January 1903 before a crowd of 8,000 who saw Arthur Lockett score two fine goals. This is Stoke's best-ever win over Newcastle (League or Cup).

Newcastle ran up their best League win over United on the opening day of the 1951-52 First Division season, winning 6-0 at St James' Park on 18 August before a crowd of over 47,000. 'Wor' Jackie Milburn scored a hat-trick that afternoon.

For the return fixture that season (on 15 December) a crowd of over 25,000 assembled at The Victoria Ground to witness a nine-goal thriller which went Newcastle's way by 5-4. Sammy Smyth scored twice for Stoke, while Reg Davies and George Robledo each found the net twice for United.

Stoke were relegated from the First Division at the end of the 1952-53 season but not before they had doubled up over FA Cup holders Newcastle, winning 1-0 at home and 2-1 away.

When Stoke won the Second Division title in 1962-63, they lost 5-2 at Newcastle at a crucial stage in the season, but they recovered their composure to ease into the top flight.

Two goals by Roy Vernon (one a real cracker) helped Stoke beat United 4-0 in a one-sided First Division home game in September 1965.

Almost 60,000 fans witnessed a 2-2 draw between the Potters and United at Newcastle in September 1948.

Both League games in 1899-1900 finished level at 2-2.

Stoke played United in two Test Matches in a mini League at the end of the 1897-98 season to decide their First Division status. The Potters won the League and retained their place in the top flight.

Newcastle knocked Stoke out of the Coca-Cola Cup in October 1995, winning a third-round tie 4-0 at The Victoria Ground before a 23,000 crowd. Peter Beardsley scored twice for United.

Players with both clubs: Viv Busby, George Eastham, Howard Gayle, Andy Graver, Roger Jones, James Lindsay (Stoke reserve 1899), Jack Peart, Alan Suddick, Tommy Thompson, John Tudor, Harry Ware and Billy Whitehurst.

Graham Stokoe was a junior at St James' Park before joining Stoke.

Tom Mather managed both Newcastle United and Stoke City while Norman Tapkin was a goalkeeper with United who later served eight years as Stoke's trainer (1952-60).

Outside-right Jock Rutherford played for United and was manager of Stoke in 1923.

NEWLANDS, Douglas

Newlands was useful outside-right who scored 23 goals in 104 games for Burnley before joining Stoke for £15,000 in July 1959. He hit eight goals in his 34 appearances for the Potters who released him to St Johnstone in September 1960. Born in Edinburgh on 29 October 1931, Newlands had played initially for Forres Mechanics, Aberdeen, St Johnstone and Aberdeen (again) and later in his career, he served with Airdrieonians and Forfar Athletic, the latter as player-manager.

NEWPORT COUNTY

Stoke's playing record against County is:
Southern League

Venue	P	W	D	L	F	A
Home	2	2	0	0	5	1
Away	2	1	0	1	3	3
Totals	4	3	0	1	8	4

All four matches were played in the Southern League Division Two during the last two seasons before World War One. Stoke won 2-0 at home in 1913-14 and 3-1 the following year. Their one away victory came in December 1914 (1-0).

Players with both clubs: Neville Chamberlain, Roy John, Terry Lees, George Oldham and Tom Thornton. Louis Page played for Stoke and later managed Newport, as did Welsh international John Mahoney.

NIBLOE, John

Nibloe was a tough Yorkshireman, born in Sheffield on 1 June 1939, who played centre-forward for Sheffield United before transferring to Stoke City for £3,000 in October 1961, After a year at The Victoria Ground during which time he scored five goals in 23 outings for the Potters, he was sold to Doncaster Rovers for £5,000 (October 1962).

He rounded off his League career with Stockport County. Nibloe was tragically killed in a car crash in Stocksbridge on 12 November 1964.

NICHOLAS, David Sidney

After being capped by Wales at schoolboy level on 1912, Dai Nicholas was given trials by Merthyr Town, but unfortunately the war intervened and he was recruited to the Royal Navy. When the hostilities were over he played several games as an amateur for Swansea Town before turning professional with Merthyr Town in October 1918 – and in this same month he entered Camarthan Training College to train as a teacher. Born on 12 August 1897 in Aberdare, Glamorgan, Nicholas attended Aberdare Grammar School (to 1914). Described as a 'speedy outside-left' he played for Merthyr until March 1922 when he moved to Stoke for £1,000. He went on to score four goals in 58 games for the Potters up to November 1924 when he was transferred to Swansea Town having now secured a teaching appointment in his native Aberdare for whom he scored 13 goals in 150 games. He later played for Aberavon Athletic and retired in May 1930. During his time at The Victoria Ground, Nicholas was involved in a serious motor cycling accident in 1923 which resulted in a fractured skull. He went on to add three full caps to his collection, gaining one whilst with Stoke (v Scotland in 1923). In later years Nicholas became headmaster of Abernany School (Aberdare) and was involved in the administration of schoolboy football, serving on the Welsh Schools FA. He died in Aberdare on 7 April 1982.

NICKNAMES

Ever since football began in earnest over 125 years ago, hundreds of players up and down the country had been given nicknames, either by their family, friends, club and team colleagues or supporters.

Here are some nicknames given to Stoke players: Rev Ernest 'Churchy' Wilson (1870s); 'Jimmy the Greyhound' Sayer (1880s); Elijah 'Father' Smith (1880s); Ted 'Jammer' Evans (1890s); 'Long Tom' Meston (1895-95); Willie 'Chippy' Naughton (1890s); Joe 'Judge' Murphy (1890s – a half-back so-called because he wore a wig); Dave 'Lauchie' Thomson 91890s); 'Dirty Tommy' Holford (1898-1908); Albert 'Hairpin' Sturgess (early 1900s); Frank 'Tinker' Whitehouse (1900-05), Arthur 'Sailor' Capes (1902-04); 'Longton Billy' Davies (1907-09); Ernie 'White Nob' Mullineux (1907-14); Joey 'The Old Warhorse' Jones (1911-20); 'Invincible Dick' Herron (goalkeeper, 1911-15); Arthur 'Arty' Watkin (1913-25), Peter 'Jammy Legs' Jackson (1920s); Bobby 'Steve' Archibald (1925-31 – so called because he looked distinctly like the champion flat race jockey Steve Donoghue); Jack (S.O.S.) Palethorpe (1930s); Freddie 'Nobby' Steele (1933-49); George 'Grace' Kelly (1950s); Ron 'Chunky' Wilson, Eddie 'Chopper' Clamp (1960s); Peter 'Motor Mouse' Griffiths; Peter 'Shilts' Shilton; Paul 'Piggy' Johnson; Kevin 'Bomber' Sheldon; Derek 'Squeak' Parkin; 'Ally' Pickering; Tony 'Zico' Kelly; 'Toddy' Orlygsson, Steve 'Billy' Parkin; Kevin 'Rooster' Russell; 'Ziggy' Sigurdsson, Mark 'Steino' Stein and Wayne 'Bertie' Biggins

There was also manager Tony 'Waddo' Waddington with son Steve also having the same nickname.

And you have had 'Banksy', 'Doddy' 'Smithy', 'Foxy' (etc. etc.) with the letter 'y' having been added the the players' surname. And of course there was the 'Golden One' – Mark Stein (during his first spell at Stoke).

NIXON, William

Amateur outside-right, born in Stoke in 1886, Billy Nixon appeared in two League games for Stoke (both in April 1912). He served with Trentham FC before moving to The Victoria Ground and was sadly killed in action while serving France in 1916.

NOBLE, Daniel

After performing exceedingly well as a teenager for the Hull boys team which reached the English Schools FA Cup Final, goalkeeper Danny Noble was recruited as a junior by Stoke and made good progress through the ranks to sign for professional forms for the Potters in 1988. By this time he had also represented England at youth-team level, but was unable to break into Stoke's first team owing to the form of a certain Peter Fox. In fact, he made just two appearances for the club before being given a free transfer in May 1991 when he joined Crewe Alexandra. Noble was born in Hull on 21 September 1970.

NORTHAMPTON TOWN

Stoke's playing record against the Cobblers is:

Football League

Venue	P	W	D	L	F	A
Home	1	1	0	0	6	2
Away	1	0	0	1	0	1
Totals	2	1	0	1	6	3

Southern League

Venue	P	W	D	L	F	A
Home	2	2	0	0	2	0
Away	2	0	0	2	1	12
Totals	4	2	0	2	3	12

FA Cup

Venue	P	W	D	L	F	A
Home	1	1	0	0	3	0
Away	1	0	1	0	2	2
Totals	2	1	1	0	5	2

League Cup

Venue	P	W	D	L	F	A
Home	1	1	0	0	1	0
Away	2	2	0	0	5	2
Totals	3	3	0	0	6	2

Freight Rover Trophy

Venue	P	W	D	L	F	A
Home	1	0	1	0	1	1

Stoke were hammered 9-0 by Northampton Town in a Southern League First Division game on 4 January 1913 – their heaviest senior defeat against the Cobblers.

The Potters also lost 10-0 at Northampton in a Regional wartime game in season 1941-42.

Stoke's best win over Northampton is 6-2 at home in a First Division League game on 12 February 1966, when 16,525 fans saw big John Ritchie lead the goal-charge with a four-timer.

The Cobblers battled hard and long before losing a first-round Coca-Cola League Cup-tie 3-1 on aggregate to Stoke in September 1996, Mike Sheron scoring both Potters' goals in their 2-1 away win.

Players with both clubs: Ian Clarkson, Lloyd Davies, Peter Durber, Gareth Evans, Jack Farrell, John Gayle, Arthur Hartshorne, Bert Mitchell, Louis Page, Geoff Scott, Joe Turner, Mart Watkins and Brett Williams.

Dudley Kernick was a Northampton player who later became commercial manager at The Victoria Ground.

NORTHWICH VICTORIA

Players with both clubs: Keith Bebbington (Vics trialist) Ike Brookes, Alf Edge, Johnny Eyres, John Farmer, Peter Griffiths, Arthur Jepson, Stanley Jesse, Joe Johnson, Doug Jones, Jackie Marsh, Harry Meakin, Albert Mullard, James Mulligan (Stoke junior), Mike Pejic (coach-manager of the Vics), Bob Ramsey, Albert 'Eddie' Raynor, Tommy Sale, Paul Shardlow, Brian Siddall, Jesse Stanley and Jim Wallace.

Two ex-Stoke players, Harry Ware and Jack Mudie, both became manager of Northwich Victoria after their respective retirements, while former Potters' midfielder Sammy McIlroy was player-manager of the Vics during the 1990s.

NORWICH CITY

Stoke's playing record against the Canaries is:

Football League

Venue	P	W	D	L	F	A
Home	15	8	4	3	24	13
Away	15	2	5	8	11	31
Totals	30	10	9	11	35	44

Southern League

Venue	P	W	D	L	F	A
Home	2	0	1	1	1	2
Away	2	0	0	2	1	3
Totals	4	0	1	3	2	5

FA Cup

Venue	P	W	D	L	F	A
Home	1	0	0	1	0	1

League Cup

Venue	P	W	D	L	F	A
Home	2	2	0	0	4	2

The first meetings between the clubs were in season 1911-12 (Southern League Division One). Norwich won 2-1 at home and drew 1-1 at Stoke.

Stoke's best win over the Canaries is 3-0 at home on 20 October 1962 when Dennis Viollet (2) and Graham Matthews were on target in a Second Division match.

Norwich's best victory over Stoke is 6-0 at Carrow Road five months later (March 1963) when the Potters were chasing the title.

The FA Cup-tie was a third-round clash at Stoke in January 1982 when 12,805 fans saw Norwich's Jack Ross score the deciding goal.

Former Ipswich Town star, Nigel Gleghorn, returned to East Anglia to score Stoke's goal in their 1-0 win at Carrow Road in season 1995-96.

Players with both clubs: Neil Adams, Keith Bertschin, Gary Brooke, George Brown, Viv Busby, Joe Corrigan, John Devine, Louie Donowa, Bert Miller, Jack Peart, Keith Scott, Tony Spearing, Albert Sturgess, Harry Ware and Tom Williamson.

Asa Hartford played for the Canaries (winning a League Cup winners' medal in 1985) and later became assistant manager at Stoke.

Graham Paddon played for Norwich City and later became assistant and then caretaker manager at Stoke. Alan A'Court was player-coach at Norwich City and later caretaker manager-coach of Stoke, while Sammy Chung played for the Canaries and later became assistant manager at Stoke.

NOTTINGHAM FOREST

Stoke's playing record against Forest is:

Football League

Venue	P	W	D	L	F	A
Home	45	16	13	16	59	52
Away	45	12	10	23	55	82
Totals	90	28	23	39	114	134

Football Alliance

Venue	P	W	D	L	F	A
Home	1	1	0	0	2	1
Away	1	0	1	0	2	2
Totals	2	1	1	0	4	3

FA Cup

Venue	P	W	D	L	F	A
Home	2	0	2	0	1	1
Away	3	1	0	2	2	4
Totals	5	1	2	2	3	5

The teams first met at competitive level in the 1890-91 Football Alliance season when Stoke won 2-1 at home and drew 2-2 at Trent Bridge.

The first Football League meetings took place in 1892-93 (Division One) when the Potters completed the double over Forest, winning 4-3 away (being the first team to play a League game at Forest's Town Ground – 10 September) and 3-0 at The Victoria Ground.

Stoke's best League win over the East Midlands rivals is 6-0 while Forest's best over City is 5-4.

Stoke registered their six-goal romp at The Victoria Ground in March 1930 (Division Two). That day just 5,369 fans turned out to see the Potters turn on the style with Wilf Kirkham claiming a hat-trick.

They also won 4-0 at home in March 1906; by the same score in September 1920 (a hat-trick here for Arty Watkin) and 5-1 at The City Ground in August 1928.

All Stoke's goals in their 3-0 home League win over Forest in August 1954, were scored by Johnny King, two from the penalty spot.

That 5-4 Forest success was at The City Ground in a Second Division match on 19 September 1953. A crowd of 22,690 saw Frank Bowyer. Johnny Malkin (2) and Johnny Sellars score for Stoke in reply to goals from Alan Moore (3), Jack Burkitt and Ron Leverton for the home side.

Forest also won 4-0 in November 1895, by the same score in September 1896 and by 5-0 in August 1980 (all at home) followed by a 4-1 triumph at Stoke in March 1985.

When Stoke won the Second Division title in 1932-33, they lost both their League games to Forest by 1-0 in successive days in December.

Stoke and Forest played out five successive League draws between 1969 and 1972, four of which were goalless.

Arthur Capes scored against his former club Forest when Stoke won a second-round FA Cup replay by 2-0 in February 1903.

Players with both clubs: Adrian Capes, Arthur Capes, Lee Chapman, Gary Bannister, Herby Hales, Sean Haselgrave, Joey Mawson, Toddy Orlygsson, Leigh Palin, Calvin Palmer, David Puckett, Brian Rice, Paul Richardson, Hans Segers, Brian Sherratt, Peter Shilton, Ronnie Sinclair, Mark Smith and Brett Williams.

Asa Hartford played for Forest and later became assistant manager at Stoke.

NOTTS COUNTY

Stoke's playing record against County is:

Football League

Venue	P	W	D	L	F	A
Home	33	15	10	8	48	26
Away	33	10	8	15	38	56
Totals	66	25	18	23	86	82

FA Cup
Home	1	0	0	1	0	2
Away	1	0	0	1	0	1
Totals	2	0	0	2	0	3

League Cup
Away	1	0	0	1	1	3

Anglo-Italian Cup
Home	1	0	1*	0	0	0
Away	1	0	1	0	0	0
Totals	2	0	2	0	0	0

As founder members of the Football League, Stoke and County first met in this competition on 22 September 1888 before a crowd of 3,000 at The Victoria Ground. The Potters came out on top, winners by 3-0 – their first success at this level. Bill Tunnicliffe (2) and Bob McSkimming scored the goals. Later in the season Stoke completed the double by winning 3-0 at County.

Stoke recorded their best League win over County on 8 September 1956 (Division Two). That day County were crushed 6-0 with Tim Coleman netting twice before an 18,564 crowd. The Potters also won 5-0 at home in April 1929 when Charlie Wilson netted a hat-trick and

Ironically County registered their best League success over Stoke later on in that season, beating them 5-0 at Meadow Lane on 12 January.

County also beat Stoke 4-0 at home in a First Division match in December 1982.

Paul Richardson's goal not only gave Stoke a 1-0 win over County at Meadow Lane on 5 May 1979, it also earned the Potters promotion back to the First Division. Stoke had won 2-0 at The Vic earlier in the season.

The Anglo-Italian Cup games comprised the two-legged English Final in season 1994-95 and after a stalemate at Meadow Lane, County went through to Wembley by winning the penalty shoot-out at The Victoria Ground by 3-2.

Players with both clubs: Scott Barrett, David Brown, Tom Cowan, Keith Downing, David Kevan, Bill Locker, Tom Lonie, Ted McDonald, Eric McManus, Jack Peart, Paul Reece, Dave Regis, Dave Watson and John Williams.

Richie Barker was a player with and later manager of Notts County and boss of Stoke City. Howard Kendall was a player with Stoke City and manager of Notts County.

NUMBERING OF PLAYERS

Stoke players first had numbers sewn on to their jerseys for their Football League Jubilee Fund game with Wolverhampton Wanderers on 19 August 1939 – a game they lost 4-2.

The first League game played by Stoke with players wearing numbered shirts was against Charlton Athletic at The Victoria Ground (Division One) on 31 August 1946 (2-2 draw) and the first FA Cup-tie featuring numbered players was Stoke v Burnley (home) in the third round on 5 January 1946 (won 3-1).

NYAMAH, Kofi

Versatile left-footed player able to occupy a midfield or striking position, Nyamah joined the Potters from Kettering Town for £25,000 halfway through the 1996-97 season and made his senior debut as sub in the televised League game against Oxford United on 7 February 1997. Born in Islington, London, on 20 June 1975, he joined Cambridge United as a YTS lad in 1991, turned professional in May 1993 and before leaving the Abbey Stadium for Kettering the summer of 1996, he had a loan spell with Stevenage Borough. He scored three goals in 33 appearances for Cambridge. He had six substitute outings for Stoke.

O'CALLAGHAN, Brendon R.

A Yorkshireman, born in Bradford on 23 July 1955, O'Callaghan gave Stoke City Football Club excellent service for almost seven years, scoring 47 goals in 294 appearances while occupying a variety of positions, including those of central defender and centre-forward. He was recruited by Potters' manager Alan Durban from Doncaster Rovers for £40,000 in March 1978, and indeed he was Durban's first capture – and what a bargain buy he turned out to be. He had netted 77 goals in 212 games during his four-and-a-half years at Belle Vue and was just the man Stoke needed to boost their attack. He made a terrific start to his career at The Victoria Ground, coming on as substitute against Hull City and scoring with his first touch in 1-0 win – surely the fastest goal ever recorded by a Stoke player from the time he set foot on the pitch. O'Callaghan top-scored the following season with 15 goals as Stoke won promotion to the First Division, and in May 1979 he was called into the Republic of Ireland squad, making his international debut against West Germany in Dublin, the first of seven full caps he received. Standing almost 6ft 3ins tall, O'Callaghan was exceptionally good in the air and was no mean footballer on the ground either. He was a splendid target man, and was always dangerous at set pieces and at corner-kicks, especially those floated over by Paul Maguire. In February 1985 O'Callaghan moved to Oldham Athletic for £30,000 but in his first game for the Latics he suffered a groin injury which eventually ended his League career, although he did turn out for Newcastle Town in 1990. After football he worked in the pottery industry in Stoke-on-Trent and later became Community Development Officer at The Victoria Ground.

OLD WESTMINSTERS

The Potters defeated the London amateur side 3-0 at home in the 1st qualifying round of the FA Cup in January 1890. Gee, Sayer and Ramsey scored the goals and the crowd was given as 3,000.

OLDHAM, George

Oldham played two League games for Stoke in season 1938-39, replacing Jack Tennant at left-back for the away games against Liverpool and Middlesbrough in late December. Born in Tintwhistle on 20 April 1920, Oldham was signed from Mottram Central (a Manchester club) but he drifted away from The Victoria Ground during the war, when he guested for Aldershot and Stockport County. In September 1946 he signed for Newport County and made around 70 appearances for the Welsh club before becoming player-coach and then manager of Hitchin Town and later coach with Hebburn Town. On retiring from football, Oldham chose to live in Luton.

OLDHAM ATHLETIC

Stoke's playing record against the Latics is:

Football League

Venue	P	W	D	L	F	A
Home	22	8	6	8	32	21
Away	22	4	5	13	24	48
Totals	44	12	11	21	56	69

FA Cup

Venue	P	W	D	L	F	A
Home	3	1	0	2	5	3
Away	1	0	1	0	0	0
Totals	4	1	1	2	5	3

The first League meeting between the two clubs was in September 1907 (Division Two). A crowd of 12,000 at The Victoria Ground saw the Latics win 3-1 with Jim Swarbrick (later to play for Stoke) among their scorers. Oldham also won their home game later in the season by the same scoreline.

Stoke's best League victory over the Latics is 4-0 – achieved twice, each time at The Victoria Ground in Second Division matches. The first was on the evening of 8 September 1930 when ex-Port Vale star Wilf Kirkham netted a hat-trick in front of 15,055 fans and then on 17 September 1932 when Joe Johnson and Joey Mawson each netted twice before 13,528 spectators.

In September 1927, the Latics inflicted upon Stoke a 7-2 hammering at Boundary Park in front of 6,680 fans. Arthur Ormston netted five times for the home side.

When Oldham beat the Potters 5-0 at Boundary Park in March 1930 three of their goals were scored by Stewart Littlewood. The crowd for this game was over 17,700. The Latics also beat Stoke 4-1 at home in August 1922 and during Stoke's Second Division promotion-winning season of 1978-79, they met the Latics four times – twice in the League and twice in the FA Cup. The League games finished 1-1 at Boundary Park and 4-0 to Stoke in the return fixture when Garth Crooks scored twice. In the Cup, Oldham won a replayed third-round tie at Stoke by 1-0 (Ian Wood on target) after the initial contest had been postponed at half-time owing to the slippery snow-covered pitch at The Victoria Ground with the Potters 2-0 ahead. Almost 16,000 attended the first tie and there were 16,554 present at the second.

Players with both clubs: Neil Adams, Bill Asprey, Keith Bebbington, Micky Bernard, Bill Bradbury, Jimmy Broad, Tommy Broad, Aaron Callaghan, Billy Cope, Harry Dowd, Tony Ellis, Arthur Griffiths, Tony Henry, Frank Hesham, George Kinnell, John McCue, Jimmy McIlroy, Arden Maddison, Brendon O'Callaghan, Toddy Orlygsson, Alan Philpott, Simon Stainrod and Jimmy Swarbrick. Irish international McIlroy also managed the Latics while Asa Hartford was an Oldham player who later became assistant manager at Stoke. Alan Ball senior was a player with Oldham Athletic and later coach at Stoke.

ONE GAME WONDERS

Over the years several players have appeared in just one League or Cup game for Stoke City, and these include (since World War Two) defender Mel Pejic, goalkeepers Paul Barron and Hans Segers (both on loan), Ian Gibbons, Reg Pickup, Brian Sherratt (another goalkeeper), Shaun Wade and John Kirby.

Gibbons, in fact, holds the record for the shortest playing career as a Stokie. He came on as substitute against Crystal Palace three minutes from the end of a Second Division League game in April 1988 – his only outing for the club. Wade also had made just one substitute appearance for the Potters in 1994.

Mel Pejic, after his solitary outing for Stoke in 1979-80, went on to appear in well over 400 games for Hereford United whom he served until 1991.

O'NEILL, James Anthony

Born in Dublin's fair city on 13 October 1931, goalkeeper O'Neill was among a multitude of important signings made by Stoke manager Tony Waddington as he steadily assembled his team for a promotion push in the early 1960s. Just £2,000 was spent on the Republic of Ireland international who joined the Potters from Everton with 17 full caps under his belt, O'Neill had commenced his career with Buffin United before having 11 superb years at Goodison Park during which time he made 213 senior appearances. Ever-reliable, a safe-handler of the ball, he was particularly good with crosses and was rated one of the best goalkeepers in Europe in 1955. O'Neill kept 48 clean sheets in his total of 149 games for the Potters, helping them win the Second Division title in 1962-63. In March 1964 he was transferred to Darlington and then went on to serve in 48 games with Port Vale (under boss Stan Matthews). He had a loan spell with Cork Celtic (December 1966) and after being released by Vale in May 1967, he decided to announce his retirement from competitive football. O'Neill went into the taxi business on Merseyside and still makes the occasional visit to watch Stoke's home matches.

ORLYGSSON, Thorvaldur

Icelandic international who played as an orthodox outside-right with his first club, KA Akureyri (Iceland) and then with Nottingham Forest before being converted into an aggressive goalscoring midfielder with Stoke City. Born in Odense, Denmark on 2 August 1966, Toddy Orlygsson moved into the Football League in December 1989 when he joined Nottingham Forest for £175,000. He went on to score four goals 45 outings for the City Ground club before moving to Stoke on a free transfer in August 1993, after failing to hold down a regular place in Forest's first team. He became a firm favourite with the Potters' fans and in the 28 months he spent at the club he netted 19 times 102 appearances before leaving for Oldham Athletic in December 1995 in a deal worth £180,000.

ORMSTON, Alexander

A diminutive but enterprising outside-left who joined Stoke City as a 17-year-old from the club's nursery side, Summerbank FC. Born in Hanley on 10 February 1919, Ormston went to Wellington Road School and represented both Hanley Boys and Stoke Schools as well as having a trial for England schoolboys as a teenager. He signed professional forms at The Victoria Ground in 1937 and made his senior debut v Sunderland in November of that year – the first of 192 appearances for the Potters (30 goals scored). He played for the Football League XI three times in the late 1940s before transferring to Hereford United in 1951, finishing his career with spells at Stafford Rangers and then Runcorn. After retiring Ormston spent a short time in Loggerheads Sanatorium as he fought to regain full health. He became a publican in Hanley and also worked in the colliery offices and for a Madeley pottery firm as well as assisting at The Victoria Ground in the club's promotions office. Ormston died at Bentilee on 12 July 1975, aged 56.

OSCROFT, Harold

Born in Mansfield on 10 March 1926, Harry Oscroft was a terrific outside-left who took over the number-11 shirt from Alec Ormston. He started his playing career with Mansfield Colliery FC, and after a spell with Sheffield United he joined his home-town club, Mansfield Town, whom he served from April 1947 to January 1950 when he joined Stoke City in a deal set up by manager Bob McGrory and former Potters' star Freddie Steele who was then boss at Field Mill. Verdi Godwin was also involved in the transaction when a cheque for £8,000 was paid to the Stags. Oscroft settled in quickly at The Vic and he went from strength to strength, scoring some vital goals on the way. He held his place in the side until the end of the 1958-59 season and although still fit and well he switched his allegiance to Vale Park going there with reserve centre-half Peter Ford, plus £2,000, thus allowing Dickie Cunliffe to move to Stoke as his replacement. Oscroft scored 107 goals in 349 games for the Potters and added 12 more in 51 games for the Vale before moving into non-League football as player-manager of Brantham Athletic in June 1961, guiding them to victory in the Suffolk Senior Cup the following year. He later had a few games with Sutton United, and also starred in various Charity matches before taking up residence in Manningtree, where he worked for a local plastics company. He retired in 1988.

OSWESTRY TOWN

Stoke defeated Oswestry 3-0 at home in a third-round FA Cup-tie in November 1887. Edge, Ballham and Owen scored the goals in front of 3,000 spectators.

Forward Len Benbow, goalkeeper Stuart Roberts and full-back Billy Twemlow is among the handful of players who have been associated with both Stoke and Oswestry, while ex-Stoke City star Jackie Mudie became player-manager of Oswestry. Alan Ball senior was player-manager of Oswestry and later coach at Stoke City.

OVER WANDERERS

Three weeks before taking on Oswestry, Stoke had visited the Wanderers in a second-round FA Cup-tie on 5 November 1887. They won comfortably by 3-0, the goals coming from Edge, Lawton and Owen. The attendance was given as 1,000.

OVERSEAS PLAYERS

The great Brazilian footballer Pele played for his club side Santos in a friendly match against Stoke City at The Victoria Ground in September 1969 and he led his side to a 3-2 win before a 23,000 crowd.

OVERSEAS TOURS (GAMES)

The first time Stoke City Football Club travelled abroad to play a soccer match was in April 1934 when they met the Swallows Club (Amsterdam) in a friendly and won 2-1.

At the end of the following season the Potters made the trip by boat to Denmark where they played three matches, two against a Copenhagen Select XI, winning them both, while in 1936-37 they again went over to Holland and defeated an Amsterdam XI 1-0.

It was 20 years before Stoke went abroad again, this time to Europe, including France. They played six games in all, against Schweningen, Ulm, Forbach, Olympique Nice, Singen and FC Nice.

In 1958-59 the Potters played a handful of games in Morocco with fixtures against Casablanca Morocco, a Royal Army team, a Bavarian XI and a Gibraltar Select.

In 1961-62, the Potters went to Turkey; in 1962-63 they played in Israel and at the end of the 1963-64 campaign manager Waddington took his players on a demanding and what seemed like a round the world tour to Austria, Portugal, Colombia, Chile and Argentina where they played in front of some massive crowds including one of 80,000 in Santiago against Universidad of Chile (0-0). In Colombia they lost 3-2 to Santa Fe, the club for whom two former Stokies, Neil Franklin and George Mountford had played in 1950.

After the 1964-65 season had ended, Stoke travelled 20,000 miles to Sweden, Finland and USSR where they played six matches, and in 1965-66 the team visited Holland where they met Feyenoord and Ajax, Hong Kong and America when, under the name of Cleveland Stokers, they entered the US Soccer tournament, playing in 11 matches.

In 1967-68 Stoke played Asante Kotoko in Japan and in May 1969 they took the long trip over to the Belgian Congo where the faced a representative side in Kinshasha, returning via Spain where they played three friendlies, one against Barcelona (won 3-2).

Excellent away games against DOS Utrecht, PSV Eindhoven, Olympique Marseilles, Real Mallorca and Olympiakos (Greece) plus others, preceded a tremendous tour to Australia and New Zealand at the end of the 1972-73 season. Down Under the Potters played 11 games in front of mediocre attendances, winning seven of them, including an 8-1 triumph over Otago when John Ritchie scored all the Potters goals.

Further long (and a few short) tours followed during the mid to late 1970s when the Potters played in countries such as Cyprus, France (three separate clashes with AS Monaco), Belgium, Morocco, Norway, Israel, the Congo (v Kinshasha again), Spain, Indonesia, Holland (v Ajax), Portugal (v Oporto and Nijmegen), Italy (v Genoa) and Crete.

During the 1980s, the club visited Greece on two occasions, playing games against AEK Athens and Panathinaikos, Barbados, Tunisia, Saudi Arabia, and the USA (v Tampa Bay Rowdies). Twice the team went to the sun of Trinidad and Tobago and they also made four separate visits to Scandinavia where, in 1983, they ran up their only overseas double-figure score, beating Stromsund 10-1.

The last time Stoke City travelled overseas was in 1993 when they visited Africa to play six matches against local teams, winning five and drawing the other.

NB: When competing in the Anglo-Italian and UEFA Cup competitions Stoke ventured into Italy, Holland and Germany.

OVERSON, Vincent David

An essentially right-footed central defender, strong and uncompromising, whose battling qualities, particularly in the air, were always his strong points. Born in Kettering on 15 May 1962, Vince Overson joined Burnley as a youngster and turned professional at Turf Moor in November 1979 after having represented England at youth-team level. As a regular member of the Clarets' side, he helped them win the Third Division title in 1983 and then went on to amass a fine record for the Lancashire club, appearing in 249 League and Cup games (seven goals scored) before moving to Birmingham City on a free transfer in June 1986. At St Andrew's he continued to perform with resilience and in five seasons with Birmingham City he netted four times in 213 senior outings, helping Blues win the Freight Rover Trophy at Wembley in 1991. Managed at St Andrew's by Lou Macari, he followed his boss to Stoke City in August 1991 in a deal worth £55,000 – and within 12 months was playing at Wembley again, this time in the Final of the Autoglass Trophy (v Stockport County) which Stoke won 1-0. He then helped the Potters win the Second Division championship (1993) and thereafter proceeded to take his total of senior appearances for the club up to 216 (seven goals scored) prior to completing a full circle by returning to Burnley in August 1996. Overson was close to the personal milestone of of 700 club appearances in 1997.

NB: *Overson played alongside his younger brother Richard in five League games for Burnley in season 1979-80.*

OWEN, Alfred Sydney

Born in Newcaste-under-Lyme *c.*1885, the younger brother of Wally Owen (see below) Alf Owen was a versatile forward who had three spells with Stoke. He was an England amateur international while with North Staffs Nomads, the club he served before joining Stoke (first time round) in 1906. He stayed at The Victoria Ground for only a short time and after a brief spell with Stockport County, he rejoined the Potters in April 1908, remaining there until the end of the year by which time he had taken his overall record with the club to six goals in 10 games. He next joined Leicester Fosse and later played for Newcastle Town and Blackpool prior to signing for Stoke once more in 1909, although he never played another first-team game. In October 1907 and again in September 1908, Owen guested for Port Vale, and during his career he also assisted Northern Nomads and English Wanderers. He died in Blackpool on 22 August 1925.

NB: *Owen became the first secretary of the Players' Union.*

OWEN, James

Manchester-born centre-forward who was 25 years of age when he made his senior debut for Stoke in 1889-90. He scored twice in three League games at the end of that campaign, but was not retained for the following season, returning to his former club Newton Heath (Manchester United).

OWEN, Walter

Born in Stoke in 1864, Owen played as a utility forward for Stoke St Peter's before joining Stoke in October 1886. He stayed two years at The Victoria Ground, making six FA Cup appearances and scoring four goals before signing for Long Eaton Rangers.

OWEN, William A.

Born in Newcastle-under-Lyme *c.*1884, and elder brother of Alf (above), Wally (or Billy) Owen was an amateur defender whose career was spent with North Staffs Nomads, Stoke (August-October 1909), Manchester City (second XI) and Port Vale (July 1911-February 1912). He played in two League games for Stoke and in one reserve-team game for the Vale.

OXFORD UNITED

Stoke's playing record against United is:

Football League

Venue	P	W	D	L	F	A
Home	4	2	1	1	5	4
Away	4	0	0	4	3	11
Totals	8	2	1	5	8	15

FA Cup

Home	1	1	0	0	3	2
Away	1	0	1	0	0	0
Totals	2	1	1	0	3	2

League Cup

Home	1	1	0	0	2	0
Away	1	0	1	0	1	1

Full Members' Cup

Home	1	0	0	1	0	1

The first League meetings were staged in season 1988-89 (Division Two). Tony Henry gave the Potters a 1-0 home victory in late December, while United won their home match 3-2 in April when Stoke's Chris Hemming received his marching orders for a foul on John Durnin.

Stoke have registered just two home League wins over the U's – 1-0 on New Year's Eve, 1988, when George Berry found the net in front of 10,552 freezing supporters, and 2-1 in February 1997 when Neil MacKenzie scored his first senior goal for the Potters in front of the Sky Sports cameras and just 8,609 live fans. Denis Smith was the Oxford manager for this game.

Stoke have lost all their four away League games at Oxford, their heaviest reverse being that of 4-1 in October 1996.

Oxford replaced Stoke in the First Division for season 1985-86.

In the FA Cup in 1969-70, Stoke progressed into the fourth round after beating Oxford 3-2 in a replay with two goals from John Ritchie and another from Willie Stevenson.

A certain John Aldridge gave United victory in the Full Members' Cup-tie played at Stoke in November 1985.

Players with both clubs: John Dreyer, Philip Heath, Tony Parks, Paul Reece, Carl Saunders, Brian Sherratt, Tony Spearing, Mark Stein, Albert Whitehurst and Brett Williams.

Former Stoke defender Bill Asprey was Oxford boss in 1979-80 and another former Stokie, centre-half Denis Smith, was manager at Oxford in the 1990s, while Arthur Turner, a pre-war Stoke player, was in charge of Oxford for 10 years (1959-69). Asa Hartford played for Forest and later became Stoke's assistant manager. Ex-Stoke goalkeeper Mark Harrison became reserve-team coach at Oxford. Sammy Chung was a player with Oxford and later became assistant manager at Stoke.

PAGE, Louis Antonio

Born in Kirkdale, Liverpool on 27 March 1899, Louis Page was one of four brothers, all of whom went on to play professional football and represent their country (England) at baseball. He excelled in Liverpool schoolboy soccer matches and once scored ten goals in game from the inside-left (number-ten) position. Basically an inside-forward or outside-left, he served with Sudley Juniors and had trials with Everton before joining South Liverpool FC in 1918. A year later he went to Stoke as a professional and after scoring once in 21 League outings for the Potters he left The Victoria Ground for Northampton Town in November 1921. He did exceedingly well with the Cobblers, netting 22 goals in 122 League outings up to May 1925 when he moved to Burnley for what was described as a 'big fee'. As part of the deal, Jack Tresadern left Turf Moor to become player-manager of Northampton. Page became an instant hit with the Burnley supporters and in the next seven seasons he claimed 115 goals in 259 appearances for the Lancashire club. In April 1926 he scored in a double hat-trick when the Clarets beat Birmingham 7-1 at Turf Moor and during the next 12 months he was capped seven time by England, scoring his only international goal in a 9-1 destruction of Belgium in Brussels in May 1927. In March 1932, after Burnley had been relegated to the Second Division, Page was sold to Manchester United. From Old Trafford he went to Port Vale (October 1932), subsequently signing for Yeovil & Petters United as player-manager in July 1933. After a spell in charge of Newport County, he went on to become trainer/coach of the Irish League club Glentoran, manager of Carlton FC (Liverpool), Swindon Town after World War Two (1945-53) and, in fact, helped plan Burnley's downfall in the FA Cup in 1948. For three years up to 1956 Page managed Chester, after which he acted as senior scout for Leicester City. A painful illness then interrupted his life and sadly he died in Prenton, Birkenhead on 11 October 1959, aged 60.

PAINTER, Ian J.

Striker Ian Painter graduated through the junior ranks at The Victoria Ground, having joined the club as an apprentice in 1980 and becoming a professional in December 1982. He made his Football League debut 24 hours before his 18th birthday against Everton on 27 December 1982 – the first of 123 senior appearances for the Potters (24 goals scored). An England youth and Under-21 international, injury restricted his progress during he mid-eighties and when Mick Mills took over as manager at The Victoria Ground Painter became surplus to requirements. He left the club for Coventry City in a a £75,000 deal in July 1986 and four years later (after more injury problems) he was out of the first-class game, doing part-time coaching whilst running his own sports shop in his native Womborne near Wolverhampton. Painter returned to the game in 1995 when he became manager of West Midlands-based club Bilston United.

PALETHORPE, John T.

Centre-forward Jack (nicknamed S.O.S.) Palethorpe was a well-built, strong running footballer with an eye for goal. Born in Leicester in July 1911, he was a shoemaker before starting out on the soccer circuit, first as an amateur with Maidenhead United (in the Spartan League, 1927-28) and then with Crystal Palace (1929) before Reading gave him his first professional contract and a taste of League action.

Joe Palethorpe

From March 1933 to January 1934 he was with Stoke City, who paid £3,000 for his services from Elm Park. He did well for the Potters, netting 11 goals in 21 first-team appearances before transferring to Preston North End who he assisted until December 1934. He then had a half decent spell with Sheffield Wednesday, scoring 17 times in 34 games for the Owls and helping them win the FA Cup (v WBA) in 1935. Six months after that Wembley triumph Palethorpe was sold to Aston Villa who were signing players from all sources in a bold but unsuccessful bid to stave off relegation to the Second Division. He rounded off his playing career with a second spell at Crystal Palace (October 1936) and a brief association with Colchester United, retiring during the early part of the war. Palethorpe died in May 1984.

PALIN, Leigh G.

A reserve with Aston Villa, midfielder Palin, who won England youth honours as a teenager, never made a first-team appearance for the Birmingham club, and after a loan spell with Shrewsbury Town (in December 1984, when he made his Football League debut) he was transferred to Nottingham Forest in November 1985. He failed to get into the senior side at The City Ground and in October 1986 was sold to Bradford City. At Valley Parade he did well and made almost 100 League and Cup appearances for the Yorkshire club in three years. He joined Stoke City for £95,000 in September 1989 (after a loan spell), but never really established himself in the team and after 23 outings (three goals scored) he left The Victoria Ground for Hull City in a £100,000 deal in March 1990. He later assisted Rochdale (loan) before quitting League football in 1992.

PALMER, Calvin Ian

Palmer started his playing career with Skegness Town before becoming a full-time professional with Nottingham Forest in March 1958. A full-back or right-half, he spent over five years at The City Ground, making 90 League appearances. In September 1963 he became one of Tony Waddington's early signings for Stoke City, a fee of £35,000 being agreed. Palmer, who was born in Skegness on 21 October 1940, was brought in to boost the midfield as the Potters sought to establish themselves back in the First Division and at the end of his first season with the Potters he gained a League Cup runners-up medal. Palmer, who effectively replaced hard-man Eddie Clamp in the number-four shirt, did very well in his four-and-a-half years stay at The Victoria Ground, and accumulated a fine record of 27 goals in 196 senior appearances. A heated argument with Maurice Setters on the training field in 1966 was perhaps blown up out of all proportions, but it cost Palmer a place on Stoke's American tour. Fiercely competitive, and very popular with the Stoke fans, Palmer was eventually transferred to Sunderland for £70,000 in February 1968 – a move that really didn't pay off for him – and after brief spells in South Africa with Cape Town and with Crewe Alexandra, he quit top-class football in 1972. He now lives in Skegness.

PARKER, Charles W.

Born at Seaham harbour on 1 September 1892, and recruited from the North-East non-League club Hartlepool B.D. in January 1914, centre-half Charlie Palmer became one of the greatest defenders ever to don the red and white striped shirt of Stoke. He quickly established himself in the Potters' Southern League side and in the first season after World War One (1919-20), following Stoke's re-admission into the Football League and after he had been capped by England in a Victory international v Wales, he had an outstanding campaign, being the cornerstone of the back division. Many fans (and club officials) were disappointed that Palmer never received full international recognition, for he was a terrific player. After scoring five goals in 79 appearances for Stoke he was sold to Sunderland in September 1920 when, at the age of 28, he was certainly at the peak of his career. His move stunned the The Victoria Ground faithful and for sometime afterwards his leaving caused a lot of debate. He spent nine seasons at Roker Park and then had a spell with Carlisle United (as player-coach) before rounding off his playing days with Blyth Spartans.

PARKES, David

Parkes, who was born in Lye, in the heart of the Black Country, on 17 June 1892, was one of several centre-halves utilised by Stoke during the immediate post World War One period. He made only six League appearances for the club in 1920-21 following his £120 transfer from Sheffield Wednesday. He had earlier played for Brighton & Hove Albion and after leaving The Victoria Ground he signed for Rochdale (May 1921) for whom he went on to play in well over 300 games before retiring in 1930.

PARKIN, Derek

Stoke manager Richie Barker secured the services of full-back Derek 'Squeak' Parkin from his former club Wolverhampton Wanderers on a free transfer in March 1982. Parkin, who was born in Newcastle-upon-Tyne on 2 January 1948, appeared in a club record 609 senior appearances (501 in the Football League) during his 14 years at

Calvin Palmer

Molineux. He helped Wolves twice win the League Cup (1974 and 1980) and also the Second Division championship in 1977, as well as gaining five caps for England at Under-23 level and representing the Football League. Never a reckless tackler, he was a steady rather that enthusiastic defender, who had a wonderful left foot and always tried to use the ball rather than kick it long and aimlessly downfield. He started his League career with Huddersfield Town as a junior, turning professional at Leeds Road in May 1965. He moved to Molineux on St Valentine's Day 1968 for £80,000. Parkin spent a season at The Victoria Ground, making 45 appearances for the Potters. He then retired to concentrate on his landscape gardening exploits near Bridgnorth. A fine handicap golfer, Parkin now resides in the same locality as Bert Williams and Willie Carr, two former Wolves players.

PARKIN, Stephen John

Born in Mansfield on 7 November 1965, Parkin ('Billy' to his fans) became the youngest manager in the Premiership and Nationwide Leagues in 1996 when he took over the hot seat at Mansfield Town. As a full-back with Stoke (1982-89) he hit five goals in 137 appearances before transferring to West Bromwich Albion for £190,000. He left The Hawthorns for Field Mill in 1992. Honoured six times by the England Under-21 side, he also gained nine schoolboy and five youth caps and prior to taking over as manager, he was player-coach at Field Mill. Halfway through the 1996-97 campaign Parkin installed his former Stoke colleague, Tony Ford, as his assistant at Field Mill.

PARKS, Anthony

Goalkeeper Parks had three outings for Stoke on loan from West ham in September 1992. Born in Hackney on 26 January 1963, he joined Tottenham Hotspur in 1979 and whilst at White Hart Lane was loaned out to Oxford United, Gillingham, Brentford, QPR, Fulham and Southend before transferring to Upton Park. After Stoke he had a spell with Falkirk. He was a UEFA Cup winner with Spurs in 1984.

PARSONS, Edward

Hard-tackling right half-back Teddy Parsons, who was described in the local press as 'a player of vigorous stamp who used his weight', scored one goal in 65 League and FA Cup games for Stoke between October 1897 and September 1900. Born Stafford in 1878, he moved to Stoke from his home-town club Stafford Rangers in May 1896 and left The Victoria Ground for Featherstone Rangers in May 1901. His best season at The Vic was 1899-1900 when he had 33 outings.

PARTNERSHIPS

Since the club first started to play competitive football in 1880s, there have been many outstanding partnerships within the Stoke team either at full-back, in central defence, in midfield, as well as in attack.

Alan Bloor and Denis Smith hold the club record for most senior appearances as a defensive duo. Between 1968 and 1978 they played together in almost 250 first-class games for the Potters.

Bob McGrory and Billy Spencer lined up as full-back partners in 240 games (1926-35) while Bill Asprey and Tony Allen together donned the respective number-two and number-three shirts for the Potters in over 160 matches (1960-66).

Defenders Frank Mountford and Ken Thomson played alongside each other in more than 130 League and FA Cup fixtures for Stoke in the 1950s; Tommy Clare and Alf Underwood were Stoke's full-backs in 118 games during the late 1880s/early 1890s and McGrory and Alec Milne were City's regular full-backs in 112 matches in the 1920s.

Other outstanding partnerships include the Stoke midfield of Paul Bracewell, Mickey Thomas and Sammy McIlroy (1980s); John Butler and Lee Sandford at full-back (1990s); the half-back line of George Baddeley, Tom Holford and Jimmy Bradley in the early 1900s and the middle-line of Arthur Tutin, Arthur Turner and Frank Soo in the 1930s.

And you can readily add as superb goalscoring duos the following: Freddie Rouse and Jack Hall (1900s), Arthur Griffiths and Billy Smith and Jack Peart and Billy Smith (1910-13), Jimmy Broad and 'Arty' Watkin (early 1920s), Harry Davies and Charlie Wilson (late 1920s), Tommy Sale and Freddie Steele (1930s), Johnny King and Harry Oscroft (mid-1950s), Jackie Mudie and Dennis Viollet (1962-64), John Ritchie with Viollet, Peter Dobing and Roy Vernon (mid-late 1960s), Ritchie and Jimmy Greenhoff (early 1970s), Nicky Morgan and Carl Saunders (late 1980s) and Wayne Biggins and Mark Stein (early 1990s).

Goalkeeper Billy Rowley and full-backs Clare and Underwood played together as a trio in Stoke's first XI in more than 100 games between 1887 and 1893 – and indeed, all three represented England in the same full international match against Ireland in March 1892 (won 2-0).

There are many, many more famous double-acts, far too many to list here, who have given Stoke City excellent service over the years.

PATERSON, George F.

Scottish centre-forward Jock Paterson had the pleasure of scoring a hat-trick on his Football League debut for Stoke against Middlesbrough at The Victoria Ground on 26 September 1925 when he was introduced into the attack in place of the injured Dick Johnson. Born in Lochgelly in 1904, Paterson had joined the Potters from his home-town club, Lochgelly United in the summer of 1925, but unfortunately a leg injury ruined his chances of making further progress at Stoke and he left for East Fife in December 1925 after registering a total of four goals in seven appearances.

PAXTON, John

Inside-forward, born at West Stanley in 1890, Jack Paxton scored once in three Southern League games for Stoke in April 1911. Signed from West Stanley FC basically as a reserve, he left The Victoria Ground at the end of that season and joined Chesterfield.

PEACOCK, James

Jimmy Peacock was a local half-back (born in Stoke in 1871) who signed for the Potters from Dresden United in the summer of 1896. He played in one Football League game – against Wolverhampton Wanderers at home (won 2-1) – before leaving The Victoria Ground for Saltgates FC in May 1897.

PEART, John George

A prolific goalscoring centre-forward throughout his career, Jack Peart was born in South Shields on 3 October 1888. He played for South Shields Adelaide and Sheffield United before joining Stoke in July 1910. He netted 41 goals in just 47 appearances for the Potters – and indeed his record would have been even better had he not been sidelined with a broken **?????** from mid-December 1910 to September 1911. After leaving The Victoria Ground he went to Newcastle United (March 1912 for £600) and then served, in turn, with Notts County, Rochdale and Barnsley (as a a guest), Leeds City, Birmingham, Derby County and Ebbw Vale (as player-manager). In January 1922, he transferred himself to Port Vale, but he was now almost 34 years of age and coming to the end of a fine career. After suffering injury problems, he left the Vale in May 1922 and moved to Norwich City, later becoming player-manager of Rochdale and then boss of Bradford City and Fulham. He died in Paddington, London, on 3 September 1948.

PEJIC, Mel

Full-back Pejic played in one League game for Stoke, lining up in the home fixture against Ipswich Town in January 1980 in place of Ray Evans. Younger brother of Mike (below) Mel was born in Newcastle-under-Lyme of 27 April 1959, and joined the Potters straight from school, turning professional in July 1977. He spent three seasons in Stoke's Reserves before transferring to Hereford United in June 1980. At Edgar Street he did supremely well and in the next 12 years went on to appear 412 first-team matches for the Bulls. He then assisted Wrexham (1992-94).

PEJIC, Michael

Born nine years before his brother at Chesterton on 25 January 1950, Mike Pejic was also a full-back and he too amassed a sound number of appearances at club level. He emerged through the junior ranks at The Victoria Ground to sign professional forms on his 18th birthday. He developed rapidly and after establishing himself in the Potters' first team, he quickly gained England Under-23 honours, eventually securing eight caps at this level and later winning four with the seniors. Pejic collected a League Cup winners' medal at Wembley in 1972, and went on to amass a total of 336 competitive appearances for the Potters (8 goals scored) before transferring to Everton for £135,000 in February 1977. He later moved to Aston Villa (September 1979) but a niggling groin injury forced him into early retirement (1980) after he had made 360 League appearances all told. After trying his hand, unsuccessfully, at farming he returned to the football stage as coach-manager of Leek Town and then took a similar position with Northwich Victoria before teaming up with Port Vale as assistant to manager John Rudge. He came back to Stoke City as a coach under Lou Macari in 1996.

PENALTY KICK

The penalty kick first came into being in Irish League football in 1890-91 – following a successful proposal by Irish FA committee member and Milton Everton goalkeeper Billy McCrum. But it was not introduced into the rules of the Football League until season 1891-92 and perhaps Stoke had a hand in helping it into our way of life.

An FA Cup-tie between Notts County and Stoke in February 1891, had only nine minutes left to play. County were ahead 1-0 but as Stoke attacked, the ball was handled on the line by a desperate County defender to deny the visitors an equalising goal.

Match referee John Lewis of Blackburn duly awarded Stoke a free-kick, just inches from the goal-line. All the County players lined up between the two posts and quite simply there was no way through for the Stoke player about to take the kick. Thus the ball was blasted into the 'wall' and County escaped.

Mr Lewis recognised the the lack of equity and as a former player and at the time a distinguished football legislator, he persuaded the authorities to have second thoughts on McCrum's proposal at the League's next AGM in June 1891. The committee digested the penalty-kick proposal (again) and this time it was was approved – and it was added into the rules of the game for the start of the 1891-92 campaign.

● On 12 September 1892, Stoke were 1-0 down at home to Aston Villa in a First Division match when, with two minutes remaining, the referee awarded the Potters a penalty. Immediately the visitors' hefty goalkeeper Bill Dunning grabbed hold of the ball and booted it clean out of the ground. Before it was retrieved, the 90 minutes had elapsed and the ref blew for full-time. The laws were changed soon afterwards to allow time to be added on for a penalty-kick to be taken.

● The first Stoke player to score from a penalty kick was Tom Hyslop against Sunderland in a League Division One game at The Victoria Ground on 14 March 1896 when the Potters raced to a 5-0 win.

● Frank Mountford holds the record for most successful penalty conversations for the Potters. He netted a total of 14 in League and Cup games for the club, including five in season 1949-50. He also netted six times from the spot in wartime football.

● Defender Charlie James, who was basically a reserve-team player at The Victoria Ground, conceded four penalties in 1913-14 – all for hand-ball.

● Goalkeeper Dick Williams saved a penalty on his League debut for Stoke against Lincoln City in April 1927 as the Potters raced towards the Third Division North title.

● Towards the end of the 1970-71 FA Cup semi-final with Arsenal at Hillsborough, Stoke were leading 1-0 when their midfielder John Mahoney pulled off a fine goalkeeping save from Frank McLintock's header. But his, and Stoke's joy lasted barely 20 seconds as Peter Storey stepped up to slam home the resulting penalty to earn his side a replay which they won 2-1 at Villa Park.

Penalty shoot-outs

Stoke lost 4-3 to Motherwell on penalties after the Anglo-Scottish Cup-tie between the clubs in September 1970 had finished level at 2-2 after the two legs.

Stoke went down 4-3 on penalties away to Birmingham City in the game to decide third and fourth place in the FA Cup in August 1972. The score was 0-0 after normal and extra-time.

Birmingham City again defeated Stoke 3-1 on penalties in a Texaco Cup Group 2 match at St Andrew's in October 1973. The two-legged contest had earlier finished goalless.

After battling it out to finish 2-2 on aggregate, the Stoke-Manchester City second-round League Cup-tie in October 1981 went to a penalty shoot-out – and it was the Maine Road club who came out on top, winning 9-8 after a titanic, nail-biting contest. at The Victoria Ground.

The Simod Cup-tie between Stoke and Leicester City at Filbert Street in December 1987 went Stoke's way 5-3 after a penalty shoot-out. The scoreline was 0-0 after two hours of normal outfield play.

The following year, Stoke beat Leyton Orient 3-2 on penalties at The Victoria Ground to win a second-round League Cup-tie after the teams had fought out a 3-3 scoreline over the two legs.

In mid-December 1989 Stoke were squeezed out of the Full Members' Cup by Leeds United who won a penalty shoot-out 5-4 at The Victoria Ground after the teams had ended up level at 2-2.

Notts County prevented Stoke City from reaching Wembley in 1995. when they won a decisive penalty shoot-out 3-2 in the Area Final of the Autoglass Trophy following two 0-0 draws, the first at Meadow Lane.

PENTLAND, Frederick Beaconsfield

Centre-forward/inside-left Fred Pentland was born in Wolverhampton on 18 September 1883. A very fine footballer in his own right, he played initially for Willenhall Swifts then Avondale Juniors before signing for Small Heath (Birmingham) in August 1900. He made only one appearance for Blues in three seasons before joining Blackpool in June 1903. Six months later he was recruited by Blackburn Rovers and in May 1906 switched to Brentford. From Griffin Park he switched to Middlesbrough (June 1908 – after helping the Bees win the Southern League title) and from Ayresome Park he joined Halifax Town (of the Midland League) in August 1912. He left the Yorkshire club for Stoke on 4 February 1913 for a substantial fee and stayed at The Victoria Ground for 10 months, up to 18 December 1913, when, after netting six times in 12 outings for the Potters, he was transferred back to Halifax. Capped five times by England, Pentland played his last professional game of football for the Shaymen in April 1915 in the Bradford Charity Cup semi-final replay at Heckmondwike where he received a bad knee injury which eventually forced him to retire. In May 1914 Pentland secured, what was considered at the time, an important position with the German Olympic Council. Stationed initially at Karlsruhe, Baden, he was to assist with the coaching of the German athletes in readiness for the scheduled Olympic Games of 1916 which were to take place in Berlin. However, World War One prevented them from taking place, and presumably Pentland's work was wasted. After the hostilities were over he coached in France (1920), took a similar position with Atletico Bilbao (1921-36) and Brentford (1936-37) and then managed Barrow (January 1938-September 1939).

NB: Pentland was the son of a former Lord Mayor of Birmingham who was a fond admirer of Benjamin Disraeli, Earl of Beaconsfield after whom his son was named. He was in Spain when the Civil War started and in Cumbria when World War Two began.

PEPPITT, Sydney

Born in Hanley on 8 September 1919, and a pupil at Cannon Street

School, Syd Peppitt won three England Schoolboy caps as a utility forward in 1934 and after joining Stoke as an amateur, he turned professional at the age of 17. Although battling for a place with Stan Matthews and Freddie Steele, plus a few others, he worked perilously hard and went on to give the Potters excellent service over the next 13 years, during which time he scored 29 goals in 106 peacetime appearances. He also amassed a wartime record of 31 goals in 61 outings despite spending quite sometime in Ireland when he assisted Linfield. In May 1950 he was transferred to Port Vale for £4,000 and following an injury stayed with the Valiants for just a season, scoring three times in 11 outings. He then moved to Worcester City and died in Stoke-on-Trent on Christmas Day 1992.

PESCHISOLIDO, Paolo Pasquale

Born at Scarborough, Canada on 25 May 1971, striker Paul Peschisolido stands only 5ft 4ins tall and weighs 10st 6lbs. A Canadian international (14 full caps gained, plus two for the 'B' team and others at both Under-16 and Under-17 levels) he's a nippy striker, quick off the mark with a fine goalscoring record. He came over to England in November 1992 to sign for Birmingham City for £100,000 from Toronto Blizzard whom he had served for three seasons following a good spell in University football. He scored 17 goals in 50 appearances for Blues before transferring to Stoke City for £400,000 on 2 August 1994. For the Potters he did a shade better, netting 24 times in 82 games, being top-scorer with 15 goals in his first season at The Vic. After getting engaged to Karren Brady, the managing director at St Andrew's (whom he subsequently married) 'Pesch' returned to Blues for a second spell on 28 March 1996, the fee again being put at £400,000. He added one goal in nine League outings to his tally before moving to West Bromwich Albion, this time for £550,000 on 24 July 1996. Peschisolido was voted Canada's Footballer of the Year in 1996 after he had helped his country qualify for the 1996 World Cup Finals in France.

PETERBOROUGH UNITED

Stoke's playing record against Posh is:
Football League

Venue	P	W	D	L	F	A
Home	2	1	1	0	6	3
Away	2	0	2	0	2	2
Totals	4	1	3	0	8	5

League Cup

Home	1	0	1	0	0	0
Away	1	1	0	0	2	1
Totals	2	1	1	0	2	1

Autoglass Trophy

Home	1	0	1	0	3	3
Away	1	1	0	0	1	0
Totals	2	1	1	0	4	3

The first two League meetings between the two clubs took place in season 1991-92 (Division Three) – and they both finished level: 1-1 at London Road and 3-3 at Stoke, where the attendance was 14,733.

Stoke registered their best League win over Posh in April 1994 when beating them 3-0 at The Victoria Ground in a First Division match which was seen by 10,181 fans. Wayne Biggins, Mark Walters and Dave Regis (against his future club) scored the goals.

In the League Cup in season 1983-84 Stoke went through to the third round on aggregate after holding Posh to a goalless draw away and then taking them out 2-1 at The Victoria Ground when Ray Hankin (United) and City's Mickey Thomas were both sent-off for fighting.

Players with both clubs: George Berry, Eddie Clamp, Harry Connor, Des Farrow, David Gregory, Mickey Gynn, Gary Hackett, Herby Hales, Eric McManus, Dave Regis, Kevin Russell and Tony Spearing. Richie Barker was a player with Peterborough and manager of Stoke City.

PHILLIPS, Hugh

Phillips, normally a centre-half, kept goal for Stoke in a Football Alliance game against Crewe Alexandra at The Victoria Cricket Ground in November 1890 when regular goalkeepers Billy Rowley and Wilf Merrett were unavailable. A Scotsman, born in Lanark in 1864, had arrived at the club from St Bernard's five months earlier as deputy to Hughie Clifford. He appeared in a total of seven games (all in the Alliance) before he was forced into an early retirement through injury (1892).

PHILLIPS, Wilfred John

Inside-forward Wilf 'Peanuts' Phillips had a nomadic career which spanned 20 years during which time he appeared in well over 300 games for eight different clubs. He joined Stoke for the first season after World War One and stayed with the club until transferring to Ebbw Vale in May 1920. Born in the Black Country town of Brierley Hill on 9 August 1895, he starred for Bilston United prior to moving to the Potteries in May 1919 and after scoring three times in 14 League and Cup games, he became surplus to requirements. After Ebbw Vale his route-march around England took him to Darlaston (1921), Bilston United (1922), Bristol Rovers (May 1923 to November 1925: where he scored 35 goals in 95 games), Millwall (November 1925 – signed for £500, he scored 72 goals in 134 outings for the Lions), Thames Association (June 1930), West Ham United (June 1931 – signed for £500, he netted four goals in 24 appearances for the Hammers), Clapton Orient (June 1932) and Stourbridge (August 1933). Phillips was a player who took on defenders, choosing to dribble past them if possible. He won a Third Division South championship medal and London Cup winners' medal with Millwall. On retiring he became a publican in Stourbridge and later chose to live in Cornwall. He died in Penzance on 25 February 1973.

PHILPOTT, Alan

Philpott came up through the junior ranks at The Victoria Ground to give Stoke City eight years service as a utility player, occupying every outfield position except centre-half. Born in Stoke-on-Trent on 8 November 1942, he turned professional at The Victoria Ground in on his 17th birthday and went on to score twice in 52 senior appearances up to November 1967 when he was transferred to Oldham Athletic (managed by former Stokie Jimmy McIlroy) for £7,500. He later assisted Stafford Rangers and Eastwood (Hanley), the latter as player-coach, before retiring to become a useful coach to the youngsters of Port Vale. He also managed Leek CSOB and Tittensor FC and was a useful club cricketer with Stoke MO in North Staffs League.

PHOTOGRAPHERS

Stoke City have had three official club photographers over the past 20 years or so. Prior to that the pictures used in the matchday programmes were supplied by freelance photographers, established agencies and/or local and national newspapers.

Stoke's first photographer was Chris Doorber whose excellent portraits and action shots started to appear in club publications when Alan Durban was manager at The Victoria Ground.

His place was taken by Kevin Tatton, who came to the fore when Cristal Tiles were sponsoring the Potters.

And since 1988 the club's number one picture-man has been ardent Stoke City supporter Paul Bradbury. His splendid action shots and individual player portraits have even made the national press and in various soccer magazines up and down the country as well as Stoke City's official programme. 'Bradders' also assists in the club shop. He has kindly supplied several pictures from the 1988-97 period which appear in the book.

PHYSIOTHERAPISTS

The title physiotherapist did not come into a football club's directory until the 1950s. Prior to that the man with the responsible of keeping and getting players fit was the senior (or first team) trainer.

The trainers/physiotherapists who have held office at the club include: ex-players Jack Eccles (early 1900s), Jack Benton (1908-18), Harry Pearson (1930s), Harry Ware (1930s) and Robert Liddle (late 1940s/early '50s). Then there have been Mike Allen (in office during 1984-86), W.Allen (1890s), Doug Brown (1963-64 – he was the brother of former Stoke player Roy), Gilbert Swinbourne Glidden (1952 – whose brother, Tommy, skippered West Bromwich Albion in the 1931 FA Cup Final), Richard Gray (1990- 96), Peter Henderson (1990s), Ian Liversedge (from 1996), Harry Nuttall (1930s), W.Pope (1890s), Keith Rowley (1980s), Frederick George Streete (1968-71 – who was also the Arsenal and England trainer) and Norman Tapken (1952-60). Liversedge was in charge during the final campaign at The Victoria Ground.

NB: Occasionally assistant managers and coaches acted as trainers/physiotherapists when required.

PICKERING, Albert Gary

Right-back Ally Pickering was signed by Stoke City manager Lou Macari from Coventry City in August 1996 to replace Ian Clarkson who had left the club to join Northampton Town. Born in Manchester on 22 June 1967, Pickering adds attacking flair to his defensive game. He is quick in recovery and always seems to choose the right time to get forward. He played non-League football with Buxton before becoming a full-time professional with Rotherham United in February 1990 (signed for £18,500). He played over 100 games for the Millermen who then sold him to Coventry City for £80,000 in October 1993. In just under three years in Premiership company, Pickering added a further 76 appearances to his overall tally. His record with the Potters (at May 1997) stood at 45 senior outings.

PICKUP, Reginald John

Inside-left Pickup joined Stoke as an amateur in 1946. He played for Staffordshire Boys in 1946 and 1947 before being called up for National Service with the RAF, whom he played for regularly in various challenge matches. On leaving the forces he signed professional forms at The Victoria Ground (August 1949) and made his only first team appearance for the Potters v Huddersfield Town at home in a First Division match in three months later. A knee injury, suffered while in action against Blackpool Reserves later that season, seriously hampered Pickup's career and after 18 months of playing and breaking down he was forced to have a cartilage removed. The operation was not a complete success and although he remained at Stoke for quite awhile, he eventually retired from competitive football in 1954, joining Stafford Rangers on a part-time basis. He still struggled on for 12 months, but was forced to quit the game altogether in May 1955. Pickup was born in Stoke on 6 September 1929.

PITT, Albert Edward Shardlow

One of the few players who had three separate spells with Stoke, Bert Pitt was a local find (born in nearby Stone c.1880) whose terms of employment at the club were as follows: from Stone Town in August 1903 to Birmingham University in March 1905; from Canterbury Provinces (New Zealand) in August 1908 to Canadian football in May 1909 and from Trentham in September 1912 to Chebsey & Norton Bridge FC in January 1913. A capable half-back, he remained an amateur throughout his career, and scored five goals in a total of 52 appearances during those three seasons at The Victoria Ground.

PLAYERS

Local born players

Stoke's splendid record of producing local talent is second to none and goes back to the club's formative years in the 1860s, early '70s. Indeed, during the late 1800s there were at least a dozen players registered with the club per season who came from within 10 mile radius round the Potteries.

This went on on for a number of years, right through to the 1920s. It wasn't so prominent during the 1930s, but came strong again after the World War Two.

On 4 December 1948 the following Stoke City team played against Blackpool in a First Division match and ten of the players named were born locally. The odd man out was right-half Frank Mountford who was born in Askearn, near Doncaster. The others (in positional order) were: goalkeeper Denis Herod (from Basford); full-backs Billy Mould (Great Chell) and John McCue (Longton); centre-half Neil Franklin (Shelton); left-half Johnny Sellars (Trent Vale) and a forward-line of Johnny Malkin (Longton), Frank Bowyer (Chesterton), Freddie Steele (Hanley), Syd Peppitt (Hanley) and Alex Ormston (Hanley). Each player cost just a £10 signing-on fee.

Most and least used in a season

The fewest total of players utilised by Stoke in a full Football League season is 19 – in 1935-36.
The most called upon in one single League campaign is 34 – in 1925-26.

Goalkeepers:

● Since becoming an established club in the early 1880s (first entering the FA Cup in 1883 and playing League Football in 1888) Stoke have called upon almost 90 goalkeepers for first-team duty in the various competitions they have competed in.

● Peter Fox has appeared in more first-team matches for Stoke than any other goalkeeper, totalling 477 over a period of 15 years (1978-93).

● Stoke used four different goalkeepers in five games during March and April 1967: Paul Shardlow, John Farmer, Harry Gregg and Gordon Banks.

● The club also had three different goalkeepers in successive games in September 1946: Dennis Herod v Middlesbrough, Manny Foster v Bolton Wanderers and Arthur Jepson v Derby County.

● Stuart Roberts (at 18 years, 258 days) is the youngest goalkeeper to play for the Potters at senior level. Bob Doxon made his debut at the age of 18 years, 145 days, John Farmer at 18 years, 157 days, Paul Reece at 18 years, 296 days and Roy John 18 years, 299 days.

● A total of 17 Stoke goalkeepers have represented their country at full international level, either before or after joining the club, or while serving at The Victoria Ground. They are: Tom Baddeley, Horace Bailey, Gordon Banks, Joe Corrigan, Jack Robinson, Billy Rowley and Peter Shilton, (England), Harry Gregg and Bobby Irvine (Northern Ireland), Jimmy O'Neill (Republic of Ireland), Kenny Campbell,

Lawrie Leslie, Gordon Marshall, Tommy Younger (Scotland), Roy John and Dickie Roose (Wales) and Bruce Grobbelaar (Zimbabwe). Doug Jones was a Welsh amateur international goalkeeper.

Utility Players

● Bob Ramsey, scorer of Stoke's first-ever Football League hat-trick, turned out for the club at left-back, wing-half, centre-forward and outside-left.

● Johnny Sellars could play as a wing-half or centre-forward, while Bill Asprey could appear at full-back, centre-half and centre-forward.

● Although both defenders, long-serving Eric Skeels donned every outfield shirt for the Potters except number-five, while Alan Dodd, in his two spells with the club, wore everyone except the number-nine.

● Striker Carl Saunders and midfielder Paul Ware each wore all 10 outfield shirts while with the Potters and both pulled on subs jerseys as well.

A crop of Stoke's locally-produced youngsters in 1935. From left to right are Sale, Matthews, Turner, Mayer, Ware, Peppitt and Steele.

● In recent years, with managers and coaches adopting all sorts of permutations out on the field, several players have lined up in a set position yet have still worn a different numbered shirt from one game to the next.

Four Decades

Three footballers with Stoke City connections have played League football over four decades: Tom Holford from 1898-99 to 1923-24; Stanley Matthews from 1931-32 to 1964-65 and Peter Shilton from 1965-66 to 1996-97.

Players who have played in European soccer leagues and also for Stoke City's senior side:
Austria
Sammy McIlroy (FC Moedling)

Belgium
John Tudor (Ghent), John Woodward (VS Ostende)
Cyprus
Steve Ford (AEL Limasol), Ian Moores (Apoel Tel Aviv)
France
Alan Biley (Brest), Lee Chapman (Niort), Simon Stainrod (Racing Club Strasbourg, FC Rouen),
Germany
Gerry McMahon (Eintracht Frankfurt on trial), Dave Watson (Werder Bremen)
Greece
Alan Biley (Panionios)
Holland
Gary Brooke (Groningen), Louie Donowa (Willem II, Tilburg), Terry Lees (Roda JC, Sparta Rotterdam), Nicky Morgan (Den Haag), Hans Segers (PSV Eindhoven), Loek Ursem (AZ '67 Alkmaar, FC Haarlem)
Iceland
Toddy Orlygsson (KA Akureyri), Larus Sigurdsson (KA Akureyri)
Italy
Gerry McMahon (Udinese on trial)
Norway
John Devine (FK Start)
Portugal
Jose Andrade (Academica Coimbra), Hugo Da Costa (Benfica), Ernest Tapai (Estoril).
Spain
Louie Donowa (La Coruna), Ashley Grimes (Osasuna), Adrian Heath (Espanol)
Sweden
David Bright (Stromsnasbruk), Gary Brooke (GAIS Gothenburg), Alan Dodd (GAIS Gothenburg, Elfsburg, Landskrona Bols), Nyrere 'Tony' Kelly (Gimonas Cycles), Ian Moores (Landskrona Bols).

Longest name (surname)
The two players with the longest surnames ever to represent Stoke (City) are goalkeeper Crossthwaite (Harry) and striker Peschisolido (Paolo) each with 12 letters in their name. The Chamberlain brothers, Mark and Neville, have 11 letters in their surname along with Whittingham (Bob) and a few others.

Shortest name (surname)
The Stoke City players with the shortest surnames have been goalkeeper Box (Arthur) from the early 1900s, Cox (Walter) from the 1880s, goalkeeper Fox (Peter) from the 1980s/90s, centre-forward Gee (Freddie) from 1889-90, full-back Hay (Jimmy) from 1909-11, goalkeeper Lee (Jimmy) from 1921-22 and half-back Soo (Frank) from the 1930s.

● Potters' goalkeeper John Farmer guested for West Bromwich Albion in a pre-season friendly in Holland in 1972.

Most-travelled players
(Not including wartime guest appearances)
Goalkeeper Barry Siddall and striker Billy Whitehurst have both been connected with at least 19 different football clubs during their lengthy careers. Siddall assisted, in turn: Bolton Wanderers, Sunderland, Darlington, Port Vale, Blackpool, Stoke City, Tranmere Rovers, Manchester City, Hartlepool, Stockport County, West Brom, Carlisle United, Chester City, Preston North End, Horwich RMI, Bury, Lincoln City, Burnley and Birmingham City. He was a trialist and/or non-contract player with three clubs. Whitehurst played for Mexborough Town, Hull City, Newcastle United, Oxford United, Reading, Sunderland, Sheffield United, Stoke City, Doncaster Rovers, Crewe Alexandra, Hatfield Main, Kettering Town, Goole Town, Preston Macedonia, Stalybridge Celtic, Stafford Rangers, Mossley, Glentoran and South China.

Jimmy Broad was associated with 15 clubs during his playing days: St Mark's (West Gorton), Stalybridge Celtic, Manchester City, Oldham Athletic, Blackburn Rovers (guest), Greenock Morton (guest), Millwall, Stoke, Sittingbourne, Everton, New Brighton, Watford, Caernarvon Town, Taunton United and Fleetwood. Broad was later groundsman at Chelmsford City (1931) and he also coached ten teams when touring Europe (1920s) including Barcelona, Coruna and Las Palmas. During his playing career, defender Sam Ashworth also served with 15 different clubs at various levels – Stoke Alliance, Fenton Town, Stafford Wednesday, Stafford Rangers, Stoke Nomads, Stoke (1901), Manchester City, Everton, Burslem Port Vale, North Staffs Nomads, Reading, Oxford City, Sheffield FC, Richmond Association and Northern Nomads. He became a director of Stoke in 1920.

Verdi Godwin assisted 14 clubs during his varied career; striker Lee Chapman served with 12 Football League clubs, plus Stafford Rangers and Niort (France); Tommy Broad (Jimmy's brother) represented 13 football clubs between 1901 and 1927; Joe Clennell also turned out for 13 different soccer clubs; amateur goalkeeper Bert Miller served with at least 14 different clubs, mainly based in local non-League soccer, between 1896 and 1912; Welsh international midfielder Mickey Thomas served with 12 clubs; goalkeeper Mark Prudhoe played for 11 League sides between 1981 and 1997 and was also on loan to Liverpool without getting a game, and both Dave Bamber and Kenny Lowe were associated with at least 11 different teams. Goalkeeper Fred Wain was another nomadic footballer who represented at least 12 local clubs during the early 1900s. And goalkeeper Mark Prudhoe was associated with 13 different Football League clubs between 1981 and 1997) having two spells with Hartlepool United.

Change of Name
Stoke City's centre-half Roy Shufflebottom changed his name to Roy Jones by deed poll in 1948. George Antonio was once called George Rowlands and Charlie Wilson used the pseudonyms of C.Williams and C.Forshaw while playing for Spurs in 1918-19.

Scottish-born Players
Over 100 Scottish-born players have served with Stoke City over the years. Bob McSkimming (born in Kilmarnock) was the first to be recruited, joining the club in 1888.

PLASTIC SURFACES

Stoke City have played on all four Football League grounds which had artificial (plastic) surfaces during the 1980/90s. Luton Town (Kenilworth Road), Oldham Athletic (Boundary Park), Queen's Park Rangers (Loftus Road) and Preston North End (Deepdale) and their overall record was pretty abysmal with only one victory to their credit in 10 starts.

Their first game on plastic was in the Football League (Division One) at Queen's Park Rangers on 17 January 1984, and it ended in disaster when they lost 6-0.

The following season, the Potters returned to the same ground and went down this time by 2-0.

Graham Shaw had the pleasure of netting Stoke's first goal on a plastic surface – against Luton Town at Kenilworth Road on 1 March 1988 when the Hatters won a Full Members' Cup-tie with ease by 4-1.

Stoke had no luck whatsoever when they played on Oldham's plastic pitch, drawing one (2-2) and losing three (0-2, 1-5 and 0-2) of their four League matches there, while their three League trips to Deepdale, resulted in a 2-1 victory on 17 October 1992 when defenders John Butler and Lee Sandford found the net. They lost their first game there by 2-0 and drew the other 2-2.

Stoke's full League record on plastic:

P	W	D	L	F	A
10	1	2	7	8	28

PLAY-OFFS

At the end of the 1991-92 season Stoke played Stockport County over two legs in the Third Division Play-off semi-final. The Potters lost 1-0 at Edgeley Park and only managed a 1-1 draw at The Victoria Ground, thus missing out on a Wembley appearance in the Final.

Four years later Stoke again reached the end-of-season Play-offs – this time in the First Division against Leicester City. After battling out a 0-0 draw at Filbert Street, Stoke were confident of taking the home leg, but they again missed out when Gary Parker scored the only goal of the game to send the Foxes through to Wembley from where they reached the Premiership.

There were ugly scenes at the end of the game at The Victoria Ground when Stoke fans poured on to the pitch as the Leicester players celebrated with their fans. It took nine police horses, scores of stewards and beat constables a good ten minutes to get the situation under control.

PLYMOUTH ARGYLE

Stoke's playing record against the Pilgrims is:

Football League

Venue	P	W	D	L	F	A
Home	15	11	4	0	34	10
Away	15	5	3	7	14	25
Totals	30	16	7	7	48	35

Southern League

Venue	P	W	D	L	F	A
Home	2	1	0	1	2	3
Away	2	0	0	2	0	7
Totals	4	1	0	3	2	10

League Cup

Venue	P	W	D	L	F	A
Home	1	0	1	0	1	1
Away	1	0	0	1	1	3
Totals	2	0	1	1	2	4

Watney Cup

Venue	P	W	D	L	F	A
Away	1	1	0	0	1	0

Stoke raced to an emphatic and record-high 9-0 Second Division victory over lack lustre Argyle at The Victoria Ground in December 1960. With defender Bill Asprey in the attack, the Potters torn gaping holes in the visitor's defence and scored at will though Johnny King (3), Gordon Fincham (own-goal), Don Ratcliffe (2), Dennis Wilshaw and Asprey (2). It was 3-0 at half-time and after the break the rampant Potters claimed six more including four in nine minutes late in the game. Before this match Stoke had netted only four goals in their previous six League games.

In five home League games against Argyle, Stoke's Johnny King netted seven goals, while Argyle's striker Tommy Tynam scored six, including a hat-trick in three home matches against the Potters.

Players with both clubs: Paul Barron, Harry Burrows, Neville Chamberlain, Andy Clark, Jeff Cook, Lee Chapman, Cecil Eastwood, Bill Godley, Bruce Grobbelaar, Billy Leech, Arthur Leonard, Dave Regis, Fred Richardson, Peter Shilton, Tony Spearing and Mike Trusson (Potters' reserve). Shilton also managed Argyle. Verdi Godwin was a Stoke City player, who later acted as scout for Argyle, and former Stoke reserve Mike Trusson went on to play 73 League games for the Pilgrims (1977-80).

PONSONBY, Joseph

Irish international right-half Joe Ponsonby, who won eight full caps between 1895 and 1899, was recruited by Stoke from the Belfast club Distillery during the 1897-98 season. He played in only five first-team games for the Potters before returning to his former club. Surprisingly he was born in Dumbarton (of Irish parents) c.1876.

PONTYPRIDD

Stoke's playing record against the Welsh club is:

Southern League

Venue	P	W	D	L	F	A
Home	2	2	0	0	10	1
Away	2	1	0	1	2	4
Totals	4	3	0	1	12	5

These four matches covered two seasons: 1913-14 and 1914-15. All Stoke's ten home League goals were scored past Pontypridd in 1914 when they beat them 5-1 in March and then 5-0 in the December. The Welsh club's solitary victory over the Potters was 4-1 at home in April 1914.

One player associated with both clubs is Freddie Rouse.

POOLE, William E.

Defender Billy Poole played for Kidderminster Harriers and Merthyr Town before joining Stoke (as a reserve) in 1920. Born in West Bromwich c.1902, he made 12 League appearances for the Potters before moving to Watford for £250 in July 1923. Later he assisted Coventry City and thereafter had second spells with both his former clubs, Kidderminster and Merthyr, prior to ending his professional career in the West Midlands with Walsall. He retired in May 1932.

PORTSMOUTH

Stoke's playing record against Pompey is:

Football League

Venue	P	W	D	L	F	A
Home	26	14	4	8	44	31
Away	26	4	8	14	20	43
Totals	52	18	12	22	64	74

Southern League

Venue	P	W	D	L	F	A
Home	1	1	0	0	2	0
Away	1	0	0	1	1	4
Totals	2	1	0	1	3	4

FA Cup

Venue	P	W	D	L	F	A
Home	1	1	0	0	4	1
Away	1	1	0	0	1	0
Totals	2	2	0	0	5	1

League Cup

Venue	P	W	D	L	F	A
Away	1	0	0	1	0	2

Simod Cup

Venue	P	W	D	L	F	A
Away	1	1	0	0	3	0

Stoke's best League win over Pompey is 4-0 – which they achieved at The Victoria Ground on 2 January 1960. Over 16,600 fans were present to see Frank Bowyer score two of the goals.

As reigning League champions, Pompey secured their best League victory over the Potters at Fratton Park in September 1950, beating them 5-1 before 30,000 fans.

Portsmouth also won 4-1 at home in November 1951 and 4-2 at Stoke in February 1937 – nine days after the Potters had put 10 past West Brom – and by the same scoreline in October 1952.

A six-goal thriller in the First Division between the Potters and Pompey in September 1993, finished all square at 3-3. Mark Stein scored twice for Stoke in front of 12,552 sun-drenched spectators.

Stoke's excellent 4-1 FA Cup win over Pompey came about in the third round in January 1964 when almost 29,000 fans saw Dennis Viollet and John Ritchie both score twice.

When winning the Football League title in successive seasons – 1948-49 and 1949-50 – Portsmouth ran up three 1-0 wins in their four games with Stoke.

Stoke's Simod Cup victory came in November 1987 when Philip Heath, Gerry Daly and Graham Shaw found the net at Fratton Park before a meagre crowd of 3,226.

Players with both clubs: Dave Bamber, Mark Chamberlain, Lee Chapman, David Gregory, Fred Groves, Vince Hilaire, Brian Horne, John Love Jones, Mick Kennedy, Jim McAlinden, Ted McDonald, Chris Male, Nicky Morgan, John Ruggiero, Kevin Russell, Lee Sandford and Bob White.

Alan Ball managed both clubs, while Graham Paddon was Ball's assistant at both Fratton Park and The Victoria Ground and later he acted as caretaker manager at Stoke.

PORT VALE (Burslem)

Stoke's playing record against the Valiants is:

Football League

Venue	P	W	D	L	F	A
Home	19	8	5	6	18	14
Away	19	7	6	6	21	20
Totals	38	15	11	12	39	34

FA Cup

Venue	P	W	D	L	F	A
Home	4	2	2	0	4	2
Away	2	1	0	1	5	5
Totals	6	3	2	1	9	7

Autoglass Trophy

Venue	P	W	D	L	F	A
Home	1	0	0	1	0	1

The first meeting between the clubs (at competitive level) was in season 1887-88 when George Lawton scored the winner for Stoke in a 1-0 FA Cup victory over the Vale at The Victoria Ground.

Stoke's best League win over the Vale is 4-0, at The Victoria Ground, in September 1931 when 28,192 fans saw Walter Bussey net a hat-trick.

Vale's best League victory over Stoke is 3-0 – achieved three times, at home and away in 1925-26 and again in February 1932 at Burslem.

A record League crowd of 40,066 at Vale Park saw the Port Vale-Stoke League game in January 1955 when Frank Bowyer's strike gave the Potters a 1-0 victory on a snowbound surface.

The Valiants completed their first League double over Stoke for 70 years when they won both games 1-0 in 1995-96.

The last Potteries League derby at The Victoria Ground saw Stoke beat Vale 2-0 on 19 April 1997.

The Vale Park floodlights were switched on for the first time when Stoke were the visitors in a Second Division League game in October 1956, A crowd of 38,729 saw the Potters win 3-1.

A near capacity crowd of 24,459 saw Stoke held to a 0-0 draw at home by the Vale in a first round FA Cup-tie. Vale won the replay 3-1 in front of 19,810 fans.

Port Vale beat the Potters (the holders) 1-0 in the southern area semi-final of the Autoglass Trophy in 1992-93 in front of more than 22,000 spectators. Dutch midfielder Robin Van Der Laan scored the all-important goal.

Hat-trick heroes for Stoke in games against Vale: Billy Herbert in 9-0 war victory in 1917-18, Bob Whittingham (4 goals) in an 8-1 war win in 1918-19; Arthur Watkin in a 4-2 FA Cup win in January 1922; Walter Bussey in a 4-0 Second Division League triumph in 1931-32; George Mountford (five goals) in another 8-1 war win in 1944-45; Freddie Steele in a 6-2 Regional war victory a week later and George Mountford, again, with four goals in a 6-0 League North triumph in 1944-45.

Former Stoke defender Tom Holford holds the record for being the oldest player ever to appear for Port Vale in a League game – he was 46 years, three months old when he lined up for the last time in April 1924.

Vale celebrated their centenary with a home friendly game against Stoke City in April 1976, which ended in a 1-1 draw.

Players with both clubs (various levels): Elijah Adams, Ron Andrew, Len Armitage, Sam Ashworth, Bill Asprey, Sam Baddeley, Tom Baddeley, Frank Baker, Louis Ballham, George Bateman, Jason Beckford, Harry Benson, Bill Bentley, Brian Bithell, Alan Bloor, Albert Boardman, Lucien Boullimier, Jack Bowman, Arthur Box, Bill Bradbury, Arthur Bridgett, David Brodie, Joe Brough, Jackie Brown, Adrian Capes, Mark Chamberlain, Neville Chamberlain, Tommy Clare, Albert Cook, Billy Cope, Harry Cotton, Tom Coxon, Harry Croxton, Archie Cumberbridge, Dickie Cunliffe, Harry Davies, Alan Dodd, Billy Draycott, Archie Dyke, Billy Eardley, Frank Eardley, Wayne Ebanks, Ted Evans, Arthur Fielding, John Flowers, Peter Ford, Tommy Greaves, Jimmy Greenhoff, Peter Griffiths, Cliff Hallam, Mark Harrison, Arthur Hartshorne, Billy Heames, Geoff Hickson, Teddy Holdcroft, Tom Holford, Vic Horrocks, Sam Howshall, Arthur Jepson, Alf Jones, Tony 'Zico' Kelly, Wilf Kirkham, Tony Lacey, George Lawton

PORTSMOUTH - PORT VALE

Chris Kamara and Robbie Earle lead out their respective teams for a Potteries derby match in September 1989.

(forward), Billy Leech, Terry Lees, Harry Leese, Aaron Lockett (Stoke reserve), Arthur Lockett (Vale reserve), John Lumsdon, Ted McDonald, Bob McSkimming, Arden Maddison, Jack Maddock, Paul Maguire, Alan Martin, Harry Mellor, Bob Milarvie, Bert Miller, Ernie Millward, Ian Moores (trial with Vale), Jackie Mudie, Albert Mullard, Ernie Mullineux, Jimmy O'Neill, Harry Oscroft, Alf S.Owen, Wally Owen, Louis Page, Jack Peart, Syd Peppitt, Ted Proctor, Bob Ramsey, Dr Leigh Richmond Roose, Valentine Rouse, Arthur Rowley, Billy Rowley, Harry Sellars (player-coach at Vale), Kevin Sheldon, George Shutt, Barry Siddall, Eric Skeels, Bob Smith, Sam Spencer (brief spell with Vale), Freddie Steele, Jimmy Swarbrick, Harry Taylor (briefly), Billy Tempest, Billy Twemlow, Steve Waddington, Tom Ward, Cyril Watkin, Frank Watkin, Frank Whitehouse, Bob Whittingham, Louis Williams, Ronnie Wilcox, Ron Wilson, Alf Wood and John Woodward.

Henry Howell and Bob Whittingham guested for both Stoke and Vale during World War One and Stoke's Fred McCarthy guested for Vale. During World War Two, Vale's Harry Griffiths guested for Stoke, while Frank Soo served with the Vale. Also during World War Two, Edwin Blunt, Jack Griffiths, Jimmy Oakes and ex-Potter Charlie Scrimshaw guested for both clubs. Harry Ware guested for Vale in World War two and later became coach with the Valiants, while Dennis Wilshaw (later to join Stoke) was also a World War two guest with Vale.

Harry Wootton played for Stoke during and after World War One of 1914-18 and later became Vale's trainer.

Gordon Banks was a coach at Vale Park for a short while after his retirement.

Robbie (Fitzgerald) Earle was a junior with Stoke before joining Vale as a professional in July 1982 and likewise Andy Shankland, who went on to play 25 League games for the Vale (1981-85).

Five ex-Stoke players – Alan Bloor, Jackie Mudie, Joey Schofield, Freddie Steele and Stanley Matthews – all managed Port Vale after leaving The Victoria Ground. Alan Philpott (ex-Stoke) later became a coach with Vale.

Wilf Kirkham scored 155 goals in 261 League games games for Vale (1923-29 and 1932-34) and 30 in 51 appearances for Stoke (1929-32).

Gilbert Swinburne Glidden made six appearances for the Vale in the 1930s and was later Stoke's physiotherapist for two years: 1952-54. He died in October 1988. Harry Pearson played 175 games for the Vale (1911-1920) who later served as Stoke City's assistant trainer for 15 years: 1936-51. Chris Zoricich was a Stoke City trialist who also played for Vale Reserves.

POSTPONED MATCHES

Stoke, along with most other clubs, had several games postponed during the big freeze of 1962-63 when the League and FA Cup programmes were completely savaged by the atrocious weather. After defeating Rotherham United 2-1 away in a Second Division match on 28 December 1962, the Potters did not play another competitive game for nine weeks, not until 2 March 1963, when they defeated Walsall 3-0 in a League match. The season was extended until 22 May, having started on 18 August.

POTTER, Graham Stephen

Left-sided defender who can also play in midfield, Graham Potter started his League career with Birmingham City, signing professional forms at St Andrew's in July 1992. He made 32 appearances for Blues and also had a loan spell with Wycombe Wanderers before transferring to Stoke City for £75,000 during Christmas week 1993. A good crosser of the ball, the blond-haired Potter, won England youth honours as a teenager, and had 58 outings for Stoke (one goal scored at Wolves) before he was sold to Premiership club Southampton in July 1996 for £300,000 (with more to follow after a set number of appearances). In February 1997 he became manager Ray Harford's first signing for West Bromwich Albion at £300,000 after a disappointing time at The Dell. He was born in Solihull on 20 May 1975 and stands over six feet tall.

POWELL, Edgar Frederick

Inside-forward or outside-left, born in Cardiff on 6 January 1899, Powell joined Stoke on 16 May 1924 from Huddersfield Town. He played in only two senior games for the Potters before signing for Accrington Stanley early in 1925 for whom he scored 17 goals in 65 League games. He represented Barry Schools as a teenager, winning a Welsh schoolboy cap v England in 1913. He played for Barry FC and Denaby United before moving to Huddersfield in May 1923. After leaving Accrington he had a spell with Merthyr Town (from August 1927) and rounded off his career with Barrow (July 1928 to May 1929).

PRESSMAN, Kevin Paul

A competent goalkeeper with excellent left foot, Pressman fancied his chances as a striker after scoring for Sheffield Wednesday in a penalty shoot-out v Wolves in 1995. Born in Fareham on 6 November 1967, he joined the Hillsborough staff as a youngster and turned professional in November 1985. After battling for a first-team place with England's Chris Woods, he finally took over the number-one position with Wednesday in 1993 and has now appeared in over 200 games for the Owls. Capped by England at schoolboy, youth, 'B', Under-19 and Under-21 levels, he had six games on loan with Stoke in March/April 1992.

PRESTON NORTH END

Stoke's playing record against North End is:
Football League

Venue	P	W	D	L	F	A
Home	39	21	8	10	71	42
Away	39	7	8	24	42	93
Totals	78	28	16	34	113	135

FA Cup

	P	W	D	L	F	A
Home	2	1	1	0	4	1
Away	3	0	0	3	3	10
Totals	5	1	1	3	7	11

League Cup
Home	1	1	0	0	4	0
Away	1	0	0	1	1	2
Totals	2	1	0	1	5	2

As founder members of the Football League, Stoke and North End first met in the competition in 1888-89 – and it was the Deepdale side who came out on top, winning both games comfortably, 7-0 at home and 3-0 in the Potteries.

For the game at Preston on 6 October, Stoke had to borrow two North End Reserves – Dempsey and Smalley to make up their team, having reached the ground with only nine men.

The following season North End inflicted upon Stoke the heaviest League defeat in the club's history, whipping them 10-0 at Deepdale on 14 September 1889 when Jimmy Ross scored seven goals.

Stoke's first League victory over Preston came at the seventh attempt – 2-1 at home in November 1892.

The Potters' best League win over North End is 5-0 – achieved twice, both at The Victoria Ground, on Boxing Day 1900 when Willie Maxwell scored a hat-trick, and some 47 years later in February 1947.

Among Preston's other big League wins over Stoke are those of 5-1 at home in successive seasons: September 1929 and September 1930, and they also won 5-2 at Deepdale in April 1935.

On their way to the 1936-37 FA Cup Final, Preston ousted Stoke from competition in round four, beating them 5-1 at Deepdale.

Preston beat Stoke 3-1 at Deepdale in an FA Cup third-round replay in January 1960 in front of almost 35,400 fans.

Two goals by Wayne Biggins helped the Potters to a 4-0 second leg victory over North End in a first round League Cup clash in August 1992. The initial encounter had finished in a 2-1 victory for Preston.

On Martinmas Monday (9 November) 1885, Preston visited Stoke for the first time to play a friendly. Over 5,000 fans (paying record receipts of £114.12s) saw the visitors win 1-0.

Players with both clubs: Jack Bamber, George Berry, Charlie Bishop (Stoke junior), Aaron Callaghan, Archie Dempsey, Cecil Eastwood, Tony Ellis, Lee Fowler, Herby Hales, Sean Haselgrave, Willie Hendry, Frank Hesham, Roy John, Jason Kearton, Howard Kendall, Arthur Lockett, Sammy McIlroy, Willie McIntosh, Jack Palethorpe, George Roche, Les Scott, Graham Shaw, Barry Siddall, Bill Smalley, Billy Smith and Tommy Thompson.

Kendall was the youngest player (at the time) ever to appear in an FA Cup Final when he lined up at right-half (number-four) for Preston v West Ham United in 1964 at the age of 17.

PROCTOR, Edward

Ted Proctor (born in Leek in 1870) was a hard-working, efficient inside-right who played for Leek and the Royal Dublin Fusiliers before signing for Stoke. He scored two goals in three games for the Potters up to October 1896 when he joined Port Vale. He found the net on his debut for the Valiants – the first of four goals in 17 games for Stoke's rivals. He was released in the summer of 1897.

PROCTOR, John

Jack Proctor was a solid centre-half, born in Stoke-on-Trent in 1871, who played for Fenton and Dresden United before joining Stoke as a 20-year-old in August 1891. He quickly gained a place in the first XI and went on to make 52 appearances at senior level (one goal scored).

But then sadly, during the early part of the 1893-94 season, he was became ill and died of pneumonia at Fenton on 8 November 1893, thus Stoke had lost a quality player who was on the threshold of a fine career.

PROFESSIONALISM

Stoke became a professional football club in August 1885 with Abraham Fielding as chairman. The first players signed up as paid pros at The Victoria Ground were: goalkeeper Percy Birch; full-backs Tommy Clare and Edgar Mountford, half-backs Elijah Smith and George Shutt and forwards Alf Edge and Bernard Rhodes. Each player received 2/6d (12p) per match.

At the time a handful of players went on strike as the club attempted to introduce a somewhat differential payment scheme, but in the end all was well as the committee (under chairman Fielding) agreed to increase each players' match wage by 100 per-cent from 2/6d (13p) to 5s (25p).

The FA had been totally against professionalism right up until 1885.

PROGRAMME (Matchday)

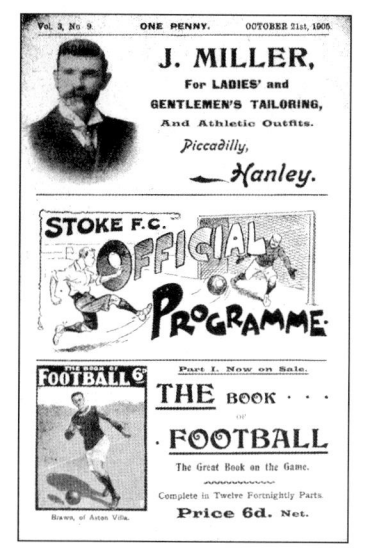

Stoke first produced a full matchday programme for the 1903-04 season which cost the buyer one old penny. The price was then doubled soon afterwards and the 2d (1p) charge remained in force until after World War Two. Come 1952 the cost of the Stoke matchday programme had risen to 3d (2p) and ten years later it was selling for one shilling (5p).

In the 1972-73 season – after winning the League Cup – the Potters' programme went up to 10p and the price rose gradually thereafter until it finally reached the £1 mark in 1989. It then rose slowly until it touched £1.50 in the early 1990s.

PROSSER, Benjamin

Unknown amateur centre-forward who played one League game for Stoke in a 2-0 at Derby in March 1903. Born in Yorkshire in 1878, he came down to the Potteries from Leeds FC and left for Bradford City at the end of the season (May) and went on to score five times in 19 games in his single campaign at Valley Parade.

PRUDHOE, Mark

Well-built goalkeeper, with fine shot-stopping technique, he is one of soccer's wanderers. Born in Washington, County Durham on 8 November 1963, Prudhoe began his career as an apprentice with

Mark Prudhoe

Sunderland, turning professional at Roker Park in September 1981. He made seven League appearances for the Wearsiders before beginning his trek around the country, playing in turn, for Hartlepool United (loan), Birmingham City (£22,000), Walsall (also £22,000), Doncaster Rovers, Grimsby Town, Hartlepool United (again) and Bristol City (all on loan), Carlisle United (£10,000) and Darlington (£10,000) before signing for Stoke City for £120,000 in June 1993. He has since been loaned out to Peterborough United (September 1994), Liverpool (November 1994) and York City (February 1997) and during his four seasons at The Victoria Ground Prudhoe has had to battle for a place with Carl Muggleton and Ronnie Sinclair, and at one stage Gordon Marshall. But he is a fighter and at May 1997 had made 101 appearances for Stoke (and more than 360 in his career).

PUCKETT, David

Southampton, Nottingham Forest (on loan) and AFC Bournemouth were Puckett's three major clubs before he had seven games on loan with Stoke during March-May 1988. A midfield player, with good vision, he was born in Southampton on 29 October 1960, and after his spell at The Victoria Ground he had a brief spell with Swansea City prior to joining Aldershot. He returned to Dean Court and rounded off his career with Woking Town.

PUGH, David Henry

Utility forward 'Dai' Pugh scored once in 20 League and Cup games for Stoke during the 1897-98 season. Born in Wrexham in 1875, he played for Wrexham Grosvenor and Wrexham (from 1895) before moving to The Victoria Ground in May 1897. After leaving the Potters in March 1898 he signed for Lincoln City and quit professional football in May 1902. A Welsh international (seven caps gained between 1896 and 1901, four against Scotland), Pugh had good dribbling qualities and at times was described as 'a brilliant footballer with plenty of pluck even when roughly handled.' He was basically an orthodox outside-right but was played in the inside-right berth by the Potters. He won a Welsh Cup winners' medal with Wrexham in 1897, having gained a runners-up prize 12 months earlier. He died in the village of Waddington, Lincolnshire, on 26 May 1945.

QUEENS PARK

Stoke were drawn away against the Glasgow amateur side in 1st qualifying round of the FA Cup in October 1884, but Stoke withdrew from the competition because they couldn't afford to make the long return trip to Scotland.

QUEENS PARK RANGERS

Stoke's playing record against Rangers is:

Football League

Venue	P	W	D	L	F	A
Home	9	3	3	3	8	7
Away	8	1	3	5	9	18
Totals	18	4	6	8	17	25

Southern League

Home	2	0	1	1	0	2
Away	2	0	0	2	0	2
Totals	4	0	1	3	0	4

FA Cup

Away	1	0	0	1	0	3

Stoke's best win over Rangers is 4-1, achieved at The Victoria Ground in December 1973 (Division One).

Stoke's first game on a plastic pitch was at Loftus Road in January 1984 when they crashed 6-0 – their worst-ever defeat against Rangers.

Geoff Hurst scored the winner in both games as Stoke ran up two 1-0 scorelines over Rangers in their First Division fixtures in 1974-75.

Hurst also netted twice for the Potters in a thrilling 3-3 draw with Rangers in London in September 1973.

Rangers dumped Stoke out of the FA Cup 3-0 in the fourth round in January 1948 before 24,100 fans at Loftus Road.

There was a near riot during the Stoke-Rangers Southern League game in December 1911. In fact the referee abandoned the game with two minutes remaining. Stoke were made to erect fences round the ground at a cost of £4,000 – money they could ill-afford to spend.

Players with both clubs: Neil Adams, Paul Barron, Gary Bannister, Des Farrow, Billy Finney, Robbie James, Percy Knott, George Mountford, Tony Parks, Fred Pentland, Freddie Rouse, Mike Sheron and Mark Stein.

RAISBECK, Alexander Galloway

Alex Raisbeck was a class performer, able to play in a number of positions, including full-back, centre-half, outside-right (where he began his career) and as an inside-forward. One of the few footballers ever to wear spectacles out on the field, he was one of seven brothers born in the Stirlingshire village of Polmont (on 26 December 1878). He played for Blantyre Boys Brigade, Larkhall Thistle and Royal Albert before linking up with Edinburgh Hibernian in 1896. He represented the Scottish League v The Football League the following year and came south to sign for Stoke at the age of 20, in March 1898. Raisbeck played in eight games at the end of that season, claiming one goal. His presence in the Potters' team in the four vital Test Matches certainly went a long way in helping them retain their First Division status. Two months into the summer of 1898 he surprisingly left The Victoria Ground and signed for Liverpool for a bargain fee of £350 and whilst at Anfield won the first of eight full international caps (seven against England) and also collected three more inter League XI caps. He won two League championships with the Merseysiders (in 1901 and 1906) and a Second Division winners' medal in 1905. In all, he scored 21 goals in 340 League and Cup games for the Reds in 11 tremendous seasons at Anfield before retiring to Scotland to play for Partick Thistle and then Hamilton Academical. In 1917 he became a director and team manager of the Accies and between 1921 and 1929 was in charge of Bristol City. In 1930 he took the managerial reins at Halifax Town and after a brief spell with Bath City, he spent two years (1936-38) as boss of Chester. He unfortunately fell out with the board of directors at Chester and left to become scout for Liverpool, a job he held until his death on 12 March 1949. In his book: *Liverpool – A Complete Record* Brian Pead's pen-picture on Raisbeck stated: 'Restless energy marked him as a dedicated professional. He was an aggressive but fair player, a hard tackler, swift to recover.' One contemporary soccer writer described Raisbeck as 'an intelligent automation, pulsating in his finger tips with the joy of life.'

RALPHS, Bertram Victor

Born in Handsworth, Birmingham *c.*November 1896, Bert Ralphs had an interesting career as a 'fast and enterprising' inside-forward or occasional wing-half. After playing initially for Dennisons FC he moved to Reading (May 1914) and thenon toNuneaton Town, and after guesting for Blackpool during the 1917-18 wartime season (13 appearances) he scored six goals in 41 games for Blackburn Rovers (from January 1921) having joining the Lancashire club for £1,500. He switched from Ewood Park to Stoke in July 1922 and netted six times in his 96 senior outings for the Potters before transferring to Chesterfield in July 1926. He later assisted Crewe Alexandra (August 1927 to May 1928). After retiring he ran a tailoring business in Stoke.

RAMSEY, David Robert

Born in the Potteries late 1864, Bob Ramsey joined Burslem Port Vale as a 21-year-old in April 1886 and moved to Stoke in August 1888, just in time to start the first season of League football. Indeed, Ramsey who had earlier been a versatile full-back, lined up at right-half in Stoke's first game in the new competition v West Bromwich Albion and the following season had the pleasure of scoring the Potters' first-ever League hat-trick in a 7-1 home win over Accrington on 1 March 1890. He left The Victoria Ground for Newton Heath, later assisting West Manchester and Northwich Victoria. He then returned to Port Vale for a second spell in October 1893, but was released in May 1894 because of a niggling knee injury. For Stoke his record was five goals in 47 appearances and for the Vale he hit just one goal in 90 outings.

RANDALL, Paul

Utility forward Randall hit eight goals in 51 appearances for Stoke between December 1978 and January 1981. Born in Liverpool on 16 December 1958, he played originally in Somerset with Frome Town before moving to Bristol Rovers from where he joined the Potters for £150,000. He returned to Eastville for £55,000 and later assisted Yeovil Town and Bath City.

RANDLES, Thomas

Stoke City manager Tony Waddington paid £1,500 for inside-forward Randles from non-League Ellesmere Port in February 1960. He remained in the Reserves for practically all of his stay at The Victoria Ground, appearing in just two senior games, both in April 1962, one of them away at Liverpool in front of 41,000 fans. Randles left The Victoria Ground at the end of that season when he went down under to play in New South Wales and Canterbury in New Zealand. Randles was born in Blackpool on 13 October 1940.

RATCLIFFE, Donald

Ratcliffe had an excellent career with Stoke City, playing in all five forward-line positions while scoring 19 goals in 260 outings in League and Cup competitions. Born in Newcastle (Staffs) on 13 November 1934, he joined the club in 1950, turned professional at the age of 17 and became a regular in the first team in 1957. A member of Stoke's 1963 Second Division championship winning team, he gave the fans an enormous amount of pleasure with his performances both at home and away. Ratcliffe left the club for Middlesbrough in a £30,000 deal in September 1963 and later assisted Crewe Alexandra and Northwich Victoria.

RATHBONE, Frederick

Goalkeeper Fred Rathbone had two spells with Stoke and all told played in 32 League games. Born in Meir, Stoke-on-Trent on 3 August 1885, he joined the club initially from Newcastle Rangers in August 1906, having earlier played church football with May Bank Sunday School (like so many other players around this time). He had to contest the number-one spot initially with Welshman Dicky Roose and Ike Turner, and then with the likes of Arthur Box, Bert Miller, Fred Wain, Harry Cotton, Jack Robinson, Tom Baddeley, Jack Baxter and Horace Bailey. And when Dick Herron was introduced between the sticks in 1910-11, Rathbone's career at Stoke was over. Indeed, he never got much activity in the first XI until the second half of the 1908-09 campaign when he made 18 appearances – this after having had a brief sojourn away from the Potters with Whitchurch in October/November 1908. He finally left The Victoria Ground on a permanent transfer in May 1912 when he joined Winsford United.

RAYNOR, Albert Victor

Inside-forward Raynor made just four appearances for the Potters in a five-year stay at the club (1955-60). Born in Salford on 18 August 1932 he was signed from Northwich Victoria and left The Victoria Ground for Chelmsford Town.

READING

Stoke's playing record against Reading is:

Football League

Venue	P	W	D	L	F	A
Home	12	7	3	2	27	10
Away	12	4	4	4	14	20
Totals	24	11	7	6	41	30

Southern League

Venue	P	W	D	L	F	A
Home	3	2	1	0	5	0
Away	3	0	1	2	3	9
Totals	6	2	2	2	8	9

FA Cup

Venue	P	W	D	L	F	A
Home	1	0	1	0	2	2
Away	1	0	0	1	0	3
Totals	2	0	1	1	2	5

Stoke's best League win over the Royals is 5-0, achieved at The Victoria Ground in a Second Division match on 16 March 1929. That day both Josh Williams and Charlie Wilson scored two goals apiece and the attendance was under 9,500.

The Potters had recorded a 4-1 home victory 13 months earlier when Harry Davies netted twice in front of an 11,800 crowd.

A 4-2 Stoke win at The Victoria Ground in a Second Division game in December 1987 was seen by a meagre pre-Christmas crowd of just 6,968. The Potters' goals came from Brian Talbot, Tony Henry, Nicky Morgan and Tony Ford.

Reading thrashed Stoke 7-3 at Elm Park in a Second Division fixture on 3 April 1931. Arthur Bacon netted a double hat-trick (a club record six goals) for the Biscuitmen (as they were then called).

Stoke suffered their second biggest League defeat at the hands of Reading on 30 August 1994, going down 4-0 also at Elm Park. They had both Vince Overson and Wayne Biggins sent-off and all four goals were scored in the last 28 minutes.

The six Southern League matches were played over three seasons: 1910-13. Stoke's best win was 4-0 at home in April 1913 (when Tommy Revill scored twice) while Reading's best victory was a 6-2 triumph at Elm Park in December 1912.

Players with both clubs: Sam Ashworth, Paul Barron, Jimmy Bradley, Gary Brooke, Bill Capewell, Lloyd Davies, Bill Godley, George Harris, Sam Higginson, Fred Houldsworth, Joe Hutton, Frank Jordan, Billy Leech, Arthur Leonard, Jim Martin, Jack Palethorpe, Bert Ralphs, Fred Richardson, Bill S.Robertson, Walter Rogers, Herby Smith, Mark Smith, Ray Wallace, Billy Whitehurst and Dick Williams.

Gilbert Glidden was associated with Reading as a player and trainer for 13 years (1933-50). he later became Stoke City's physiotherapist: 1952-54.

REAL MADRID

In 1993 it was ascertained that Stoke City FC was formed in 1868 and not in 1863 as was previously thought. Consequently the club's centenary was celebrated five years earlier that it should have been. Nevertheless, that's history now and on 24 April 1963, during the club's 100th year (so it was thought) mighty Real Madrid of Spain, one of the greatest teams in the world, came over to England to play Stoke City at The Victoria Ground to bring the curtain down on the Potters' centenary year.

A crowd of 44,914 assembled to witness a magnificent game of football when these two teams fought out a splendid 2-2 draw:

Stoke City: O'Neill; Asprey, Allen; Clamp, Stuart, Skeels; Matthews, Viollet, Mudie, McIlroy, Ratcliffe. Sub. Andrew.

Ream Madrid: Vicente; Casado, Meira; Muller, Santamaria, Pochin; Amancio, Ruiz, Di Stefano, Puskas, Bueno.

The raven-haired Ruiz put Real in front on 16 minutes, firing home a powerful right-footer from outside the penalty area.

Three minutes into the second-half and Stoke were level through Dennis Viollet, who drifted into space, rounded Vicente and scored with ease from eight yards.

On 53 minutes, Jimmy McIlroy finished off a fine run by outside-left Don Ratcliffe to edge Stoke ahead at 2-1, but it was fitting that Real should earn a share of the spoils and they did just that when Stoke substitute Ron Andrew conceded a penalty by bringing down the 'galloping Major' Ferenc Puskas. The chubby Hungarian international, picked himself up and duly fired a bullet past Jimmy O'Neill from the spot.

Real twice hit the woodwork late on through Ruiz and Puskas and at the final whistle both teams received a standing ovation from the packed crowd after a superb evening of football.

REECE, Paul John

A relatively small goalkeeper, standing a fraction under 5ft 10ins, Paul Reece was born in Nottingham on 16 July 1968 and joined the apprentice staff at The Victoria Ground in the summer of 1984, turning professional two years later. He played in just two League games for the Potters, replacing Peter Fox both times in April 1987 against Shrewsbury Town and Barnsley, saving a penalty against the Tykes. At the end of the season he left the club for Kettering Town, but returned to League action with Grimsby Town in July 1988 (£10,000), later spending four weeks with Doncaster Rovers (in September 1992) and then assisting Oxford United (from October 1992), Notts County (from August 1994) and West Bromwich Albion (from August 1995). In March 1996, Reece went on loan to Ilkeston Town before signing permanently for the non-League club four months later. In February 1997 he switched to Woking where he teamed up with Hans Segers.

REEVES, Arthur

Reeves took over as Stoke's secretary-manager in January 1892 from Joe Bradshaw. He got the team playing reasonably well, especially after introducing several local-born players to join the more experienced professionals already in the team. But in May 1895 he was replaced by former player Billy Rowley after seeing the Potters win 35 League games (out of 97) under his control. A Staffordshire man, born in 1837, Reeves died in 1915 at the age of 78 (See MANAGERS).

REGIS, David

Cousin of the former England international Cyrille Regis, Dave was born in Paddington, London on 3 March 1964. Also a well-built striker, 6ft 3ins tall with good speed and strong shot, he started his career with Fisher Athletic, then had spells with Dunstable Town and Windsor & Eton before joining Barnet. He moved into League football with Notts County in September 1990 for a fee of £25,000 and in November 1991 switched to Plymouth Argyle for £200,000. After a

Dave Regis

loan spell with AFC Bournemouth, he was transferred to Stoke City for £100,000 in October 1992, being manager Macari's record buy at that time. Regis netted 20 goals in 78 first-team appearances for the Potters, helping them win the Second Division championship before moving to Birmingham City for £200,000 in August 1994. He never settled at St Andrew's and spent only a month with Blues, moving to Southend United where he was sidelined for 12 weeks after a cartilage operation. He then moved on to Barnsley in February 1996, but when failing to hold down a regular place in the side at Oakwell he was loaned out by manager Danny Wilson to Peterborough United in October 1996 and then to his former club Notts County in February 1997.

RENNIE, Paul

Full-back or centre-half, born in Nantwich on 9 May 1970, Rennie completed a Youth Training Scheme at Crewe Alexandra and after 21 games he went for trails with Stoke City. He did well and was taken on as a full-time professional at The Victoria Ground in 1988, with £2,000 going to the Alex, and an agreement made for more cash to be paid to the Gresty Road club in respect of appearances and a percentage of any subsequent sale. Restricted to just six first-team outings, owing to the presence, in the main of John Butler, Rennie left Stoke for Wigan Athletic on a free transfer in March 1992.

RESERVE TEAM FOOTBALL

(Central League & Pontins League Details)
Stoke first entered the Central League for season 1921-22 and six years later they took their first championship with this record:

P	W	D	L	F	A	Pts
42	24	8	10	104	62	56

From 1982-83 there were two Divisions and at the end of the 1984-85 campaign Stoke were relegated from the First to the Second section. They stayed down until 1991-92 when they were promoted as Second Division champions with this record:

P	W	D	L	F	A	Pts
34	25	5	4	93	30	80

Unfortunately the following term Stoke were relegated again but quickly returned to the top flight in 1993-94 by finishing third in the table.

REVILL, Thomas Frederick

One of the few cricketer-footballers to play for Stoke, Revill served with Derbyshire CCC as a middle-order batsman and occasional leg-break and googly bowler from 1913 to 1920, scoring 231 runs in 20 innings for an average of 14.43. He was a useful footballer, too, and after joining the Potters from the Midland League side Chesterfield in January 1912, he proceeded to net 24 goals in 74 games for the Potters up to April 1914 when he returned to the Crooked Spire club. Born in Bolsover, Derbyshire on 9 May 1892, Revill was only 5ft 6ins tall and he had a good 'innings', for he died in Mansfield on 29 March 1979, aged 86.

RHYL

Stoke's playing record against Rhyl is:

FA Cup

Venue	P	W	D	L	F	A
Home	1	0	1	0	1	1
Away	2	0	1	1	2	3
Totals	3	0	2	1	3	4

These three games took place in the first round of the competition in season 1926-27 and after two 1-1 draws the non-League side beat Stoke 2-1 in a second replay at neutral Old Trafford.

Players with both clubs: Paul Crooks, Fred Groves, Horace Viner and Dennis Wilson.

RICE, Brian

Red-headed midfielder who preferred to occupy the left-hand side of the park, Rice made 18 League appearances for the Potters on a three month loan from Nottingham Forest at the end of the 1990-91 season. Born in Belshill (Glasgow) on 11 October 1963, and a junior with Whitburn Central, he was signed by Forest boss Brian Clough from Hibernian in August 1985. He took time to settle in at The City Ground and featured only occasionally in Forest's first team in his early years, although he did gain a Scottish Under-21 cap and was loaned out to both Grimsby Town and West Bromwich Albion. He went on to play over 50 games for Forest and then returned home to play for Dundee, Falkirk and Dunfermline Athletic.

RICHARDSON, Frank

Centre or inside-forward Richardson had a fine scoring record as a professional, netting 132 goals in 271 League games while serving with five major clubs – Plymouth Argyle (May 1921 to March 1923), Stoke (March 1923 to March 1924), West Ham United (March 1924 to summer 1925), Swindon Town (1925), Reading and Swindon (again) before retiring in 1931. He made a terrific start to League football, hitting a hat-trick on his debut for Argyle and then claiming 31 goals in his first season. Born in Barking in 1897, Richardson played for his home-town club before joining the Pilgrims. He scored three goals in 14 League games for the Potters and died on 19 May 1987 at the age of 90.

RICHARDSON, Paul

Born at Shirebrook near Selson (Notts) on 25 October 1949, Richardson was splendid midfielder, tall and stylish who could score goals as well as make them. After serving his apprenticeship, he started his professional career with Nottingham Forest in August 1967 and spent 10 years at The City Ground before having one with Chester City (from October 1976). Stoke manager George Eastham moved in and brought him to The Victoria Ground for £50,00 in June 1977 – and that was certainly money well spent as Richardson went on to net 11 goals in 142 appearances for the Potters, including a vital promotion-clinching winner at Notts County on the last day of the 1978-79 season. From Stoke he was transferred to Sheffield United for £25,000 in August 1981 and after a loan spell with Blackpool (January 1983) he assisted both Swindon Town (1983-84 season) and Swansea City (as a non-contract player September-December 1984) prior to entering non-League soccer as player-manager of Gloucester City. He later took charge of Fairford FC while also working for British Telecom. Winner of England youth caps as a teenager, Richardson amassed a League record of 435 appearances and 32 goals, scoring 18 in 221 outings for Forest.

RIPLEY, Stanley

Sadly Ripley, a keen tackling half-back, was killed in action while serving in France in 1916. Born in Seaham, County Durham *c*.1893, he joined Stoke from Seaham Harbour FC for the 1914-15 season and played in one League game v Brentford in the December.

RITCHIE, John

Stoke City's champion marksman of all-time, Ritchie scored a total of 176 goals in 343 first-team games for the Potters during two spells with the club: June 1962 to November 1966 and July 1969 to May 1975. Born in Kettering on 12 July 1941, Ritchie played for his hometown club before transferring to The Victoria Ground for just £2,500, Potters' boss Tony Waddington gambling on a footballer he had never seen play. That gamble paid off in a big way. He made only five senior appearances in his first season at The Vic as Stoke won the Second Division title. But from then on, after hours of hard work on the training ground, he blossomed and became a regular in the side during the following campaign when he scored 30 goals in 42 games as Stoke reached the League Cup Final. Playing alongside Dennis Viollet, Jimmy McIlroy and Peter Dobing was of great benefit to Ritchie and it came as a massive shock to everyone associated with the club when in November 1966 Sheffield Wednesday came in with a £70,000 bid and took Ritchie away to Hillsborough – without there being a ready replacement in the Potters' camp. Manager Waddington publicly admitted that he had made a big mistake and in August 1969, he went out and brought Ritchie back home, paying £25,000 for the fans' favourite striker who had actually done well at Hillsborough, gaining Football League representative honours v The League of Ireland in Dublin in November 1967 when he scored twice in a 7-2 win. Ritchie responded superbly and immediately began to hit the net once again for Stoke, securing 16 goals in his first season 'back in the fold'. Wearing the number-nine shirt, he was a constant threat for defenders up and down the country and in 1972 was as proud as anyone when he helped the Potters win the League Cup at Wembley. A complicated double fracture of the leg ended his League career, although after leaving Stoke he did have a handful of games for Stafford Rangers. On retiring Ritchie concentrated on his pottery business based near to The Victoria Ground. His son, David, was on Stoke's books for a short time (under manager Alan Ball) but was transferred to Stockport County for £10,000 without making the Potters' first XI.

NB: Coming on as a substitute for Stoke in their away UEFA Cup game with Kaiserslautern in Germany in 1972, Ritchie was sent-off after just 29 seconds for throwing a punch at an opponent. He never touched the ball. (This is one of the fastest dismissals in football history).

ROBERTS, Arthur

Inside-forward, born in Newcastle (Staffs) c.1876 who had a brief spell with Stoke at the end of the last century, playing in two League games in March 1900 against Derby County and West Bromwich Albion. He joined the club from Newcastle Casuals and left The Victoria Ground for Tunstall Rangers.

ROBERTS, Stuart W.

After developing through the intermediate and reserve-team ranks at The Victoria Ground, 6ft 2ins goalkeeper Roberts went on to appear in three First Division matches and two FA Cup-ties for Stoke City in season 1984-85, being the youngest-ever goalkeeper (at 17 years) to play in the senior side when making his debut v Ipswich Town on 8 December 1984. As a teenager, he had played for Newtown and Oswestry Town, and also won youth international honours for Wales. Roberts was born in Chirk on 25 March 1967 and he left Stoke at the end of the 1985-86 campaign to sign for Derry City where he stayed for only a short time.

ROBERTSON, James

Scottish utility forward Jimmy Robertson joined Stoke in August 1892 from Dundee United. Born in Dundee c.1868, he was a useful marksman who netted 20 goals in 78 League and Cup games for the Potters before signing for Ashton North End in May 1895. He later returned to Scotland to play for Dundee Wanderers.

ROBERTSON, James Glen

A fast-raiding, skilful and highly effected outside-right, Jimmy Robertson had been a junior with Middlesbrough and a part-time player with Celtic before signing amateur forms for Cowdenbeath in 1959. He made his Scottish League debut as a 16-year-old and won both youth and amateur caps for his country before being taken on as a professional by St Mirren in 1962. Three months after winning the first of four Under-23 caps (v Wales), he moved to Tottenham Hotspur for £25,000 in May 1964, and became a big favourite at White Hart Lane, scoring 43 goals in 215 appearances for Spurs in four and a half years with the club as well as winning his only full cap (also v Wales in 1964) and gaining an FA Cup winners' medal (v Chelsea in 1967). In October 1968, Robertson made the short trip across North London to Highbury, joining Arsenal for £55,000, a deal which saw David Jenkins travel in the opposite direction. It was not one of Bill Nicholson's best decisions as Spurs' boss for Robertson still had plenty of football left in him. He spent two years with the Gunners (hitting seven goals in 46 League games); netted ten goals in 87 First Division outings for Ipswich Town (March 1970 to June 1972); scored 14 times in 139 matches for Stoke City in five years (up to September 1977); made 16 League appearances for Walsall (1977-78) and ended up with 33 outings for Crewe Alexandra. Born at Cardonald, Glasgow on 17 December 1944, Robertson retired from competitive football in May 1979 to become involved with a computer insurance company of which he later was made a director.

ROBERTSON, John Thomas

Stoke imported several Scottish players during the late 1890s/early 1900s, and rugged defender Jack Robertson was one of them. Born in Newton Mearns, Renfrewshire in 1877, he served with Newton Thistle and Edinburgh St Bernard's before joining the Potters in May 1894 for less than £100. He could play at right-back or centre-half and in his first season at The Victoria Ground he scored once in 13 League games. In the summer of 1895 he returned north to Edinburgh to play for Hibernian with whom he won a Scottish Cup runners-up medal. Two years after leaving Stoke, he returned to the camp (May 1897) and spent another three seasons with the Potters, taking his overall appearance record to 113 games (three goals). In April 1900 Robertson went to Liverpool and in his first season at Anfield helped the Merseysiders win the Football League championship. From there he switched to Southampton (May 1902) and assisted the Saints to two Southern League titles (in 1903 and 1904) before rounding off an interesting career with Brighton & Hove Albion (June 1904-May 1906). He stayed in Hove after retiring and ran a pub for many years.

ROBERTSON, William Harold

Bill Robertson started out as a centre-forward in junior football with

Crowthorne Boys club. and carried on the same line off attack with Camberley ATC for whom he was top scorer, and in fact gained his only soccer medal at any level with that club – for winning the Aldershot Minor League in 1938. Born in Crowthorne on 25 March 1923, Robertson eventually turned to goalkeeping when serving with RAF Lossiemouth during the first half of the war. He was spotted by Chelsea and became a professional at Stamford Bridge in October 1945. From there he transferred to Birmingham City in December 1948 and in June 1952 became manager Frank Taylor's first signing for Stoke at £8,100. He spent eight splendid seasons at The Victoria Ground, accumulating a fine record of exactly 250 senior appearances (58 clean sheets) for the Potters – this after recovering from a broken leg. His tally of games stood as a club record for a goalkeeper until Peter Fox beat it in the 1980s. Robertson retired in May 1960 and kept a newsagents shop in Bucknall for three years before moving back to his roots in the South of England.

ROBERTSON, William S.

Billy Robertson was a tenacious, quick-tackling right-half who worked for a bath manufacturer in his native Scotland while also playing for Third Lanark and Ayr United (from 1926), helping the latter club win the Scottish League 'B' Division by a margin of nine points over his former club. He was signed by Stoke for what was described as a 'substantial fee' in October 1929 and at the time was regarded as one of the best half-backs North of the Border. He helped the Potters win the Second Division title in 1932-33 and scored three goals in 126 games for Stoke before transferring to Manchester United in March 1934. He was a success at Old Trafford and made 50 appearances for the Reds before winding down his career with Reading (January 1936 to May 1937). Robertson was born in Falkirk on 20 April (possibly in 1904).

ROBINSON, Jack

Outside-right, born in Birmingham *c.*1887, Robinson was a reserve with Aston Villa before spending a season with Stoke, playing in eight first-team games between September and November 1911. He later joined Kings Heath.

ROBINSON, John Wilkes

Considered to be the country's top goalkeeper around the turn of the century, Jack Robinson had a fine career between the posts, serving with a dozen clubs at various levels. Born in Derby in April 1870, he started off with Derby St Neots, Midland before joining Lincoln City in 1889. From there he switched to Derby County (June 1891) and played over 160 League games for the Rams in six years up to August 1897, receiving a First Division runners-up medal in his penultimate season at The Baseball Ground. He signed for New Brighton Tower next and stayed there until May 1898 when he was acquired by Southampton for £400. Robinson appeared in 137 games for Saints in the next five years, collecting four Southern League championship medals, playing in two FA Cup Finals (those of 1900 and 1902) and winning six full England caps (out of a total of 11 he gained in all). In May 1903 he travelled along the south coast to sign for Plymouth Argyle. A little over two years later he was transferred to Exeter City (October 1905) and two months after that joined Millwall. He stayed with the London club until May 1907 when he returned to South Devon to play for the Plymouth side, Green Waves FC, representing the Devon County Select XI in 1907-08 before going back to Exeter (September 1908). He finally found his way to Stoke in May 1909 at the age of 39 and made 67 appearances for the Potters in the next two years (his debut coming in an 11-0 Southern League win over Merthyr Town) before choosing to go over to America in October 1912 where he played for Rochester (New York). In 1915 he returned to England to take over a pub in Southampton and later became an insurance agent in Turnditch near Derby. In December 1922 he was seriously injured when falling from an upstairs window of a house and as a result suffered from epilepsy. He died in Derby on 28 October 1931. It must be said that Robinson was a rather wayward character who was involved in many unsavoury incidents during his enterprising career. In 1900 he was reported to the FA for allegedly trying to poach Steve Bloomer from Derby (for Southampton). Two years later, in October 1902, he was suspended for attacking a supporter during a game at New Brompton and two months after that was severely cautioned by the FA for an article he wrote in the local press about that same incident. And when at Stoke (in November 1910) he was again suspended, this time by the club's directors for allegedly insubordination after a Birmingham & District League match.

ROBSON, Harold Robert

Full-back from the North-East of England, born in Gateshead on 15 April 1897, Robson joined Stoke from Usworth Colliery for the 1923-24 season and played in one League game for the club – a 5-1 defeat away at Wolverhampton Wanderers in the February 1926. He left the Potters to sign for Southport for £50. Robson died in Gateshead on 22 September 1962.

NB: Robson won the Military Medal in 1916 as a 19-year-old in the Battle of the Somme for attending to the injured whilst badly wounded himself.

ROBSON, William Paisley

Centre-forward, born in Newcastle on 14 January 1908, Billy Robson had unsuccessful trials with Huddersfield Town and played for Washington Colliery before moving down to the Potteries to score six goals in 14 games for Stoke City over a four-year period from August 1933. He then moved back north to Burnley (October 1937) where he stayed for a season, netting three times in 12 outings. In May 1938, after being released from Turf Moor, he returned to his native North-East.

ROCHDALE

Stoke's playing record against Rochdale is:
Football League

Venue	P	W	D	L	F	A
Home	1	1	0	0	3	1
Away	1	0	0	1	0	4
Totals	2	1	0	1	3	5

These two League games took place in the Third Division North in 1926-27. The Potters' 3-1 home win in mid-November was seen by 11,144 fans, while the return fixture in Lancashire, saw Dale completely outplay championship-chasing Stoke, in front of just 3,388 hardy supporters.

Players with both clubs: Joe Clennell, Mick Doyle, Bill Finney, Tom Flannigan, Dave Goodwin, Ellis Hall, Doug Jones, Tony Lacey, Tom Kay, Jim McClelland, Leigh Palin, David Parkes, Jack Peart, William Tompkinson, Don Whiston and Albert Whitehurst. Jimmy Greenhoff played for Stoke and later managed Rochdale. Alan Ball senior was a player with Rochdale and later coach at Stoke City.

ROCHE, George

A Liverpool University graduate, Roche was a wing-half who appeared in three Southern League games for Stoke (in March 1913) having joined the club almost two years earlier. Born in Birkenhead c.1889, he also assisted Preston North End (before Stoke) and prior to World War One played for Lancaster Town.

RODGER, Simon Lee

Left-sided midfielder who was taken on loan by Stoke manager Lou Macari in February 1997, Rodger made his debut for the Potters in a 2-1 defeat at Southend. Born at Shoreham on 3 October 1971, he started his career, in earnest, with Bognor Regis Town before transferring to Crystal Palace for £1,000 in July 1990. Prior to his arrival at The Victoria Ground, Rodger had amassed over 140 appearances for the Eagles whom he helped win the First Division championship in 1993-94. He missed most of the following season with a back injury but regained full fitness in 1995-96 when Palace reached the Play-off Final at Wembley (beaten by Leicester). In 1997, however, he starred in Palace's Play-off triumph over Sheffield United at Wembley. Rodger made five appearances for Stoke.

ROGERS, Walter

Short, stocky half-back who had trials with Burslem Port Vale before joining Stoke with five other players from the Vale. He appeared in one League game for Potters, in February 1908 against Glossop North End. Born in Stoke c.1883, Rogers later assisted Reading (after Stoke had gone bust), returning to the Potteries area prior to World War One.

ROOSE, Dr Leigh Richmond

Born at Holt in Denbighshire on 27 November 1877, goalkeeper Dickie Roose was capped 24 times by Wales over a period of 11 years: 1900-11. He played for UCW Aberystwyth, Aberystwyth Juniors, Aberswyth Town, Druids and London Welsh before having the first of two spells with Stoke (1901 to April 1904). He then served with Everton, Sunderland, Stoke again (September 1905 to September 1907), Celtic (on loan) and Port Vale, as a guest in a vital North Staffordshire District League match against Stoke Reserves away on 3 April 1910. However, with time fast running out and Vale leading 2-0, the home fans swarmed onto the pitch. They surrounded Roose, jostling him around before carrying him off towards the River Trent. Thankfully, stewards and police prevented a serious incident. The match itself was abandoned. Later Roose agreed to turn out for the Vale if required but alas he was never called into action. He continued his career by playing for Sunderland (again), Huddersfield Town, Aston Villa, Woolwich Arsenal, Aberystwyth Town, Llandudno Town and the 9th Royal Fusiliers. He was killed in action while serving with the latter in France on 7 October 1916.

ROTHERHAM UNITED (County & Town)

Stoke's playing record against United is:
Football League

Venue	P	W	D	L	F	A
Home	16	10	2	4	38	17
Away	16	6	7	3	18	14
Totals	32	16	9	7	56	31

League Cup

Venue	P	W	D	L	F	A
Home	2	1	0	1	4	4
Away	1	0	1	0	1	1
Totals	3	1	1	1	5	5

Stoke's biggest League win over the Millermen is 6-0, achieved at The Victoria Ground on 6 October 1956 (Division Two) when a crowd of 21,589 saw Tim Coleman (2), Johnny King (2), Frank Bowyer and Harry Oscroft hit the net for the in-form Potters who had registered 13 goals in their previous two matches at The Victoria Ground.

George Kelly scored a hat-trick in Stoke's 4-1 home League win over Rotherham the following season – and when the Second Division title was won in 1962-63, the Potters doubled-up over United, winning 2-1 away and 3-1 at home, The latter game was seen by over 31,200 fans.

Rotherham's best win over Stoke is 4-1 at The Victoria Ground on April Fool's Day 1961 (Division Two). They had earlier beaten the Potters 3-0 at Millmoor, also in a Second Division match, on 2 April 1960.

Of the three League Cup games played, the best was perhaps Stoke's 3-2 quarter-final home win in December 1963 when 13,000 fans saw John Ritchie net twice for the Potters.

Players with both clubs: Phil Bonnyman, Bill Burns, Joe Depledge, Gareth Evans, Carl Muggleton, Dave Watson and Josh Williams. Former Stoke reserve Mike Trusson played over 120 games for Rotherham (1983-87).

ROUSE, Frederick William

Centre-forward Fred Rouse was born in Bracknell, Berkshire, on 28

November 1881, and after playing schoolboy football, he began his senior playing career with the Middlesex club, Southall. He then had spells with both High Wycombe and Wycombe Wanderers and also served with Queen's Park Rangers, prior to joining Grimsby Town as a professional in February 1903. After scoring five goals in 37 games for the Mariners Rouse moved to Stoke in April 1904 for £150. He did well at The Victoria Ground, scoring 26 goals in 73 appearances for the Potters, up to November 1906 when he was transferred to Everton for £750. Chelsea paid £850 for his signature in October 1907 and kept him at Stamford Bridge until May 1909 when he signed for West Bromwich Albion for £250. He ended his career with spells at Croydon Common (September 1910-May 1911), Brentford (1911-12) and Slough Town, retiring in May 1915. Described as a 'hefty attacker, who had lots of wit' Rouse had his best days at Grimsby and Stoke and he twice represented the Football League whilst a Stokie. He died in 1953.

ROUSE, Valentine Alfred

Although born at Hoddesdon (near Harlow) on 14 February 1898 (St Valentine's Day – hence his Christian name) left-half Rouse started his playing career in South Wales with Pontypridd, where, in 1921, he was discovered by Wolverhampton Wanderers. He made only five senior appearances during his brief stay a Molineux before transferring to Stoke for £1,000 in 1922. A gentleman on the field (and off it) Vic Rouse quickly settled into the side as a hard-working left-half and he scored twice in 94 outings for the Potters, up to May 1925, when he returned to South Wales to sign for Swansea Town. He returned to the Potteries in June 1926 and joined Port Vale for whom he made 103 appearances in three seasons. He then assisted Crewe Alexandra, Connah's Quay and Shotton, retiring in 1933. Rouse died in Hereford in 1961.

ROWLANDS, Walter

Born in Hanley c.1888, centre-forward Rowlands played in one Southern League game for the Potters versus Pontypridd (away) in April 1914. He also served with Munton Juniors (1912) and after leaving Stoke, he assisted Stafford Rangers.

ROWLEY, Arthur

Born in Leek in 1870, Rowley was a competent right-half or left-back who played for Leek, Distillery and the North Staffordshire Regiment before joining Stoke in September 1895. He left The Victoria Ground for Bristol Rovers in 1899 and later signed for Port Vale (September 1904), staying with the Valiants for two seasons, during which time he scored four goals in 69 games. He had 62 outings for Stoke.

ROWLEY, William Spencer

Rowley was born in Hanley c.1865 and started his career as a centre-forward with Hanley Orion. He joined Stoke in August 1883, but stayed with the club for barely a season before moving to neighbours Port Vale in April 1884. By now he was a goalkeeper and, in fact, scored a goal for the Valiants in a 12-0 demolition of Ironbridge in the Final of the Burslem Charity Cup in March 1885 when he got bored with having nothing to do and went up field to try his luck at shooting. In the midst of controversy, he was transferred back to Stoke in August 1886, but there followed a legal hearing at Burslem County Court in the November where it was claimed that Rowley (and George Bateman) had both joined the Potters despite having signed binding contracts with the Vale. Vale's claim, that he (Rowley) was their man, was upheld and Stoke were made to pay £20 to a Burslem Charity. They released Rowley and Bateman back to the Vale, yet both players stayed at The Victoria Ground for all that, and Rowley duly made his Potters' senior debut on 30 October 1896 in the home FA Cup-tie against Caernarvon, which resulted in a 10-1 win. A fine and fearless goalkeeper, Rowley had an enormous kick, he handled the ball well, and was never afraid to go in where it hurts (when the legs and boots were flying). Consequently he suffered a lot of injuries and although he remained with the Potters until 1897, he made only 143 first-team appearances. He represented Staffordshire in several county matches and on the international scene he played for the Football League and finally won the first of two England caps in 1889, in a 6-1 win over Ireland. His other appearance, also v Ireland, came in 1892 when his full-backs were also Stoke players – Clare and Underwood. He also helped Stoke win the Football Alliance title in 1891. Four years later, and now registered as an amateur player, Rowley was appointed secretary-manager of Stoke, a position he held until August 1897 when he stepped down to the secretary's office in favour of Horace Austerberry. In August 1898, Rowley was involved in an unusual incident when he transferred himself from Stoke to Leicester Fosse for a small signing on fee. He had made only one appearance for the Foxes when the FA stepped in and cancelled the transaction. The Leicester club was fined £10 (for their part in the deal) and both Rowley and the Leicester secretary, William Clark, were duly suspended by the FA Commission, each for 12 months. A postman by by trade, Rowley later became a publican, taking over the Cock Inn in John Street (off Liverpool Road) in Stoke-on-Trent. He then emigrated to America where it is believed he died c.1939.

NB: Rowley had over 60 games for Vale and once broke a rib playing in a friendly against Stoke, an injury which sidelined him for four months. As manager, he saw the Potters win 26 of the 60 League games played during his reign: May 1895 to August 1897 (See MANAGERS).

ROXBURGH, John A.

Born at Granton, Edinburgh on 10 November 1901, Roxburgh was actually selected for an England amateur international before it was agreed that his birthplace was in Scotland and not in Rugby, Warwickshire. An inside or wing forward, he played his early football with Rugby Town and in June 1920 joined Leicester City. He went on to appear in 50 League and Cup games for the Foxes (three goals scored) before signing for Aston Villa in October 1922. He didn't achieve a great deal at Villa Park, making only 12 senior appearances, up to February 1924, when he was transferred to Stoke City. Similarly he struggled to establish himself in the Potters first XI, and after netting once in 14 starts, he was sold to Sheffield United in August 1925, later assisting Sheffield FC before retiring in 1928.

NB: Roxburgh's elder brother, Andrew, also played for Rugby Town and Leicester City. And a third Roxburgh sibling, Walter, also played for Leicester City in pre-season trials in 1921.

RUGGIERO, John Salvatore

Despite his Italian-sounding name, Ruggiero was born in Blurton, Stoke-on-Trent on 26 November 1954. He joined the Potters as a youngster, turned professional in 1972 and went on to score twice in nine senior outings for the club as an inside-forward before transferring to Brighton & Hove Albion in June 1977 for £30,000 after a loan spell with Workington. He later assisted Portsmouth (on loan), Chester, Telford United, Ndoila United and Cape Town City (in South Africa).

RUSSELL, Colin

Something of a soccer nomad, Russell, who was born in Liverpool on 21 January 1961, played for Liverpool, Huddersfield Town, Stoke City (on loan), AFC Bournemouth, Doncaster Rovers, Scarborough (on loan), Wigan Athletic, Colne Dynamos, Bangor City, Morecambe, Droylesden and Warrington Town between 1978 and 1994. An orthodox centre-forward, he scored twice in 11 appearances for the Potters during March-May 1984.

RUSSELL, Kevin John

'Rooster' Russell, born in Brighton on 6 December 1966, was easily recognisable by his bald head, A midfielder grafter, he began his career in 1982 with Brighton & Hove Albion and thereafter toured England, playing in turn, for Portsmouth, Wrexham (first time round: 1987-89), Leiester City, Peterborough United (on loan), Cardiff City (on loan), Hereford United (on loan), Stoke City (on loan in January 1992, signed for £95,000 in July 1992), Burnley (June 1993 from Stoke for £150,000), AFC Bournemouth, Notts County and Wrexham (again – he returned there in July 1995). Come 1997, Russell had amassed well over 400 senior appearances at club level with almost 100 goals scored. His record for the Potters was 55 outings and seven goals. He won England six youth caps as a teenager and helped Stoke win the Second Division title in 1993.

SALE, Mark David

Lanky 6ft 5ins striker from Burton upon Trent (born 27 February 1972) Mark Sale made two substitute appearances for Stoke. He joined the club as a youngster and turned pro at the age of 18 in 1990. Whilst at the club he went on loan to Yeovil Town before signing for Cambridge United in the summer of 1991. A trial with Stafford Rangers preceded a move to Rocester and he returned to Football League action with Birmingham City, later playing for Torquay United, Preston North End, Mansfield Town and Colchester United whom he joined in March 1997.

SALE, Thomas

Centre-forward or inside-left Tommy Sale accumulated a superb scoring record with Stoke City. In 483 first-team appearances (in two spells with the club) he netted 282 goals – 98 in 204 League games, five in 19 FA Cup matches and 179 in 260 wartime fixtures. Born in Stoke-on-Trent on 30 April 1910, he worked in a pottery factory as a 14-year-old, playing junior football for Stoke St Peter's (a nursery side to Stoke City FC). In August 1929 he was taken on at The Victoria Ground, initially as an amateur, but turned professional in May 1930, making his senior debut on Christmas Day v Bradford City later that same year. He soon established himself in the first team and helped the Potters win the Second Division championship in 1932-33, when he netted 11 goals in 21 matches. The following season he topped the club's scoring list with 17 goals and repeated that feat in 1934-35 with a total of 24 strikes and in 1935-36. Then, perhaps surprisingly, Stoke manager Bob McGrory, knowing that Freddie Steele was about to hit the headlines as a marksman, transferred Sale to Blackburn Rovers for £6,000 in March 1936. He spent two years at Ewood Park, returning to The Victoria Ground (to the delight of the supporters) in March 1938 as cover for Steele who was injured. Sale responded magnificently, scoring five goals (including a hat-trick) in three games. He held his place, bagged 18 more goals in the 1938-39 campaign and then went goal-crazy during the hostilities, when he gave defenders up and down the country heart failure. In 1941-42 he weighed in with 56 goals and hit a total of 64 over two seasons: 1943-44 and 1944-45. He netted hat-tricks galore and secured a six-timer in an 8-0 Cup win over Walsall. A penalty specialist, he hardly ever missed from the spot, and, indeed, it is believed he only fluffed one 12-yard kick in his entire professional career. By the time the war was over Sale was coming to the end of a terrific career and his last appearance for the Potters was on 8 April 1946 in a transitional League (North) game against Sheffield United at The Victoria Ground. In 1947 he joined Northwich Victoria and his swan song came with Hednesford Town in 1949. Sale died in Stafford on 10 November 1990.

SALISBURY CITY

Stoke's playing record against City is:
Southern League

Venue	P	W	D	L	F	A
Home	2	2	0	0	8	0
Away	2	1	1	0	5	4
Totals	4	3	1	0	13	4

These four games were played in seasons 1909-10 and 1910-11. In the former campaign, the Potters won 3-2 away and 2-0 at home, while the following term they drew 2-2 at Salisbury after racing to a 6-0 win at The Victoria Ground on 2 January when Alf Smith scored a hat-trick.

SALMON, Henry

Born in Fenton on 14 March 1910, former electrician Salmon was a versatile player who lined up at both centre-forward as well as centre-half, and once netted five goals for the Potters in a reserve-team game before turning professional. He started out with Stoke St Peter's in 1925 and after a spell with Macclesfield he joined Stoke in May 1932. Two years later after playing in three League games for the Potters, he was transferred to Millwall (May 1934) and later assisted Wellington Town, Southport and Shrewsbury Town up to World War Two. Sadly he was killed in action while serving as a sergeant with the Royal Warwickshire regiment in Caen, France, on 30 July 1944. He is buried in Fonteney-le-Pesnel Cemetery, Tesnel, France.

SALMONS, Geoffrey

Midfielder Salmons was predominantly left-footed. He had been a constant threat to Stoke before finally joining the Potters from Sheffield United for £160,000 in July 1974. He was a vital piece to manager Tony Waddington's jigsaw, and indeed Salmons – and Stoke – had a fine 1974-75 season when fourth place was attained in the First Division. Salmons, who had a great sense of humour, the joker in the pack, scored eight goals and was an ever-present in the League side. Born in Mexborough on 14 January 1948, Salmons joined the staff at Bramall Lane as a teenager, turning professional in 1966. He netted eight times in 180 League games for the Blades and added 16 more goals in 134 senior outings for Stoke before transferring back to Sheffield United in September 1977. A month later he moved to Leicester City for £45,000 and after 26 League outings for the Foxes he wound down his senior career at Chesterfield (August 1978 to May 1981), ending up with a total of 449 League appearances in his locker (41 goals). Salmons then combined playing for Gainsborough Trinity with the running of a pub in his native Yorkshire.

SALT, Herbert A.

Goalkeeper Herby Salt played in one League game for Stoke a 3-0 home win over West Bromwich Albion in April 1903 when he deputised for Tom Wilkes. Not the tallest of men, Salt, who was born in Stoke c.1880, was only a reserve during his short spell at The Victoria Ground which lasted half a season. He came to the club from Newcastle St Peter's and left to join Stafford Rangers.

SANDFORD, Lee Robert

Left-sided defender, able to play at full-back or centre-half, Lee Sandford gave Stoke City excellent service for six and a half years – from December 1989 – during which time he amassed 324 appearances and scored 14 goals. Born in Basingstoke on 22 April 1968, he gained England youth honours as a teenager with his first club Portsmouth. He had 90 outings for the Fratton Park club before transferring to The Victoria Ground for £140,000. On leaving the Potters in August 1996, he moved north to join Sheffield United, managed by former Stokie Howard Kendall. The fee was £500,000. He helped United reach the First Division Play-off Final in 1997, where they lost to Crystal Palace in the dying seconds of the game.

SANDLAND, Edward T.

Bustling inside-forward Teddy Sandland scored three goals in 13 League appearances for Stoke during a two-and-a-half year spell with the club. Born locally at Hanley c.1870, he joined the Potters from

Newcastle Swifts in the summer of 1894 and and left The Vic for Congleton early in 1897.

SAUNDERS, Carl S.

Born near the the old Birmingham Airport, at Marston Green, Warwickshire on 28 December 1964, Saunders was a fine goalscorer who always looked likely to breach even the soundest of defences. He graduated through the junior and youth ranks at The Victoria Ground and turned professional in March 1983. He took time to establish himself in the first team, having made his debut as a sub against Everton at Goodison Park a month after signing pro. But in 1984-85 he finally made it on a regular basis and scored three goals for a struggling team. An adaptable performer, who lined up as a full-back, in midfield and on the wing, as well as an out and out striker, Saunders formed a fine partnership in attack with Nicky Morgan and he went on to register 31 goals in 165 first-team appearances for the Potters before transferring to Bristol Rovers for £70,000 in February 1990. Ironically at the end of that season, Rovers took Stoke's place in the Second Division. He left Rovers for Oxford United in 1994 and five months later quit the big-time to enter non-League soccer.

NB: Members of his family played for the Birmingham basketball team.

SAVAGE, Albert

Scorer of four goals from the centre-forward position in April 1911, Bert Savage came from Warwick (born c.1888). He played for Nuneaton before and Bulkington after his short spell at The Victoria Ground.

SAVAGE, Robert J.

Robbie Savage's career ended in 1990 after breaking his leg. Prior to that he had done well as a full-back or midfielder in competitive football, playing, in turn for Liverpool, Wrexham (on loan), Stoke City (season 1983-84 – when he made seven appearances), AFC Bournemouth, Bradford City and finally Bolton Wanderers (from September 1987). Born in Liverpool on 8 January 1960, he accumulated around 250 League and Cup appearances for his six clubs.

SAWERS, William

Inside-forward Bill Sawyers was born in Bridgton, Glasgow on 13 June 1871. After playing for Clyde and then Blackburn Rovers (from May 1892) he left Ewood Park for Stoke in August 1893, but at the end of that season returned to Scotland to play for Dundee. He came south to The Victoria Ground for the second time in August 1895, yet on this occasion stayed barely a month before going back to Dundee. His record for the Potters was five goals in 20 appearances. Sawers hit top form during that 1895-96 season and represented his country against Wales at Wrexham. He later played for Glasgow Rangers, Kilmarnock, Abercorn and Clyde (again). After retiring from football, Sawers ran a sports shop in Eglington Street, Glasgow for many years.

SAYER, James B.

Sayer's outstanding virtue was his blistering pace over 30-40 yards. An England international outside-right, he was known as 'greyhound Sayer' by the fans who appreciated his speed and aggression down the flank. Born at Mexborough, Yorkshire in 1862, he played for Heeley FC (Sheffield), Sheffield Wednesday and the Sheffield FA, before joining the Potters for the 1883-84 season. He remained at The Victoria Ground until May 1890 when he joined his home-town club, Mexborough. Capped once in a 7-0 win over Ireland in February 1887, Sayer scored three times in 24 senior games for the Potters. On retiring from football he became a director of Fielding Ltd., makers of Devon pottery at Stoke. He died on 1 February 1922.

SCARBOROUGH

As yet Stoke City have not opposed Scarborough in a competitive match, but some players have been associated with both clubs and they include: Kenny Lowe and Colin Russell while Frank Taylor managed both Stoke City and Scarborough.

SCATTERGOOD, Kenneth

Scattergood's father, Ernald, won one England cap v Wales in March 1913. Both father and son were goalkeepers, but unfortunately Ken never quite reached the high standards of his father, although during his career he did reasonably well, making over 50 senior appearances. A Yorkshireman, born in Bradford c.1910, Scattergood was released by Wolverhampton Wanderers as a teenager and joined Bristol City. From there he switched to The Victoria Ground for £50 in May 1934 for £500. He was mainly a reserve at Stoke, playing in just four League games prior to his transfer to Derby County in June 1935. He conceded seven goals on his debut for the Rams versus Everton yet still went on to play in 25 games for that club. He quit competitive football in 1939.

SCHOFIELD, Joseph Alfred

Joey Schofield had the distinction of being secretary-manager of both Stoke and Port Vale. He was also a director of Stoke. Born at Hanley on 1 January 1871, he was a very clever, enterprising outside-left, who won three full England caps (the first in March 1892 v Wales at Wrexham) and twice represented the Football League whilst at The Victoria Ground. A schoolmaster by profession, teaching at Broom Street School, Hanley, Schofield joined the Potters directly from Hanley Hope Sunday School but was plagued by ill-health during his career which finally resulted in him quitting the game (as a player) after he had netted 94 goals for the Potters in 230 competitive games between October 1891 when he made his senior debut v Sunderland, and April 1899, after scoring in his final game v Wolverhampton Wanderers. At this juncture Schofield entered the administration side of the club and when Stoke hit financial trouble he was one of the men who helped pull things round. He duly became a director in 1908 when the club was reformed and entered the Birmingham & District League after losing Football League status. During World War One Schofield took over the secretarial and managerial duties at The Victoria Ground. He chose to leave Stoke for Port Vale in January 1919, immediately taking over responsibility for internal office duties as well as team selection in conjunction with the club captain and vice-skipper. It is said that he was a man with 'well-balanced judgement' when it came to discovering talent and he was also a player's friend, confidant and counsellor. He helped guide Vale to victories in the Staffordshire Infirmary Cup Finals of 1920 and 1921, but was then fined £25 in June 1925 for being involved in the illegal payment of bonuses to 17 players. In March 1927 he was upgraded to full-time team-manager of Vale, but two years later on 29 September 1929, after becoming a Poor Law official, he sadly passed away at Hartshill when the Vale were sitting on top of the Third Division North table.

SCOTT, Geoffrey Samuel

Blond defender Geoff Scott had a long and interesting career. Born in Birmingham on 31 October 1956, he played for Solihull Borough and Highgate United before joining Stoke City as a professional in April 1977. After three years at The Victoria Ground during which time he scored three goals in 88 appearances, he was transferred to Leicester City (February 1980). Two years later he moved to Birmingham City, but stayed only six months at St Andrew's before teaming up with Charlton Athletic. From The Valley he went to Middlesbrough (June 1984) and then served, in turn, with Northampton Town, Cambridge United, Solihull Borough (again) and Moor Green before becoming manager of another of former clubs Highgate United, a position he held from July 1988 to August 1989.

SCOTT, Ian

Full-back/midfielder Scott scored twice in 38 games for Stoke City whom he served from July 1989 until November 1991. Born at Radcliffe on 20 September 1967, and an England schoolboy international (five caps won), he played for Manchester City before moving to The Victoria Ground for a fee of £175,000 (he signed the appropriate transfer forms on his return from holiday at Manchester airport after being met by Stoke boss Mick Mills). Unfortunately he could never hold down a regular place in the first team and left the Potteries on a free transfer to Bury after a loan spell at Gigg Lane when he scored on his debut. He also played for Crewe Alexandra on loan in season 1990-91 but did not impress boss Dario Gradi.

SCOTT, Keith

Striker Scott left The Victoria Ground in December 1994 for Norwich City in a £450,000 transaction which saw goal ace Mike Sheron join the Potters. Scott was valued at £300,000, Sheron at £150,000 – and it was Stoke who got the better deal. Born in London on 9 June 1967, Scott, 6ft 3ins tall and weighing over 14st, started his career in the East Midlands with Leicester United. He moved into League football with Lincoln City in March 1990 and then switched to Wycombe Wanderers for £30,000 in July 1991. From Adams Park he went to Swindon Town, for £300,000 (November 1993) and scored 16 goals in 59 appearances for the Robins before joining Stoke City, also for £300,000, in December 1994. His record at The Victoria Ground was four goals in 28 outings. In February/March 1996 he went on loan from Carrow Road to AFC Bournemouth and a year later was loaned out to Watford, before joining Wycombe Wanderers (on loan) in March 1997.

SCOTT, Leslie

Goalkeeper Scott played in 20 League games for the Potters in season 1922-23 after the club had utilised five different men between the posts since August 1920. Born in Sunderland c.1898, Scott played around 100 games for his home-town club (from 1913) having been signed from Fulwell FC. He left Roker Park for The Victoria Ground in July 1922 and in the summer of 1923, following the introduction of Kenny Campbell and the arrival of Bob Dixon, he departed for Preston North End.

SCOTTISH OPPOSITION

Stoke were due to meet Scottish opposition at competitive level for the first time in the FA Cup of 1884-85, but the 1st qualifying round tie against Queen's Park never took place as Stoke withdrew from the competition thus handing the Glasgow amateurs a walk over.

Earlier, in season 1877-78, the Potters had been beaten 1-0 at home by Queen's Park in a friendly match. The following season Stoke visited Glasgow and lost a 'return friendly' against Queen's by 4-1, but then invited them back to the Potteries and achieved an identical scoreline in another friendly.

In 1879-90 Queen's ran up a 7-1 win over Stoke in Glasgow.

Over the years a number of other Scottish sides have played Stoke in friendly matches, including Aberdeen (drew 4-4 in 1953-54), Airdrieonians, Brechin City, Celtic (won 5-0 at home in 1892-93), Dundee, Dundee East End, East Fife, Dundee United, Dunfermline Athletic, East Stirling, Edinburgh Hibernians, Forfar Athletic, Glasgow Rangers (drew 0-0 at home in 1937-38 and won 3-1, also at home, in 1966-67), Hamilton Academical, Heart of Midlothian, Hibernian, Morton, Motherwell, Partick Thistle, St Bernard's, Third Lanark, Third Lanark Rifle Volunteers and Wishaw Thistle.

The Potters have also played Motherwell four times in the Anglo-Scottish Cup (1970s).

SCRIMSHAW, Charles Thomas

Born at Heanor, Derbyshire on 3 April 1909, Charlie Scrimshaw was a very reliable full-back, always steady in his play and extremely dedicated to the game. He played his intermediate football with Hebden Bridge before signing for Stoke City in May 1929, initially as an amateur, turning professional within two months. It took him quite some time before he became a regular in the senior side owing to the presence of McGrory, Spencer and Beachill, but he battled on and eventually amassed 130 appearances for the Potters. He moved from The Victoria Ground to Middlesbrough in October 1938 for £3,000 and during the wartime period came back to the Potteries to guest for both Stoke and Port Vale, as well as assisting Portsmouth, playing eight games for the Valiants in the first part of the 1939-40 season. A bricklayer by trade, he skippered Stoke's reserve team during his early years at the club. Scrimshaw died at Smallthorne on 4 June 1973.

Charlie Scrimshaw

SCUNTHORPE UNITED

Stoke's playing record against the Iron is:

Football League

Venue	P	W	D	L	F	A
Home	5	3	0	2	10	9
Away	5	0	5	0	5	5
Totals	10	3	5	2	15	14

League Cup

	P	W	D	L	F	A
Home	2	1	1	0	4	3
Away	1	0	1	0	2	2
Totals	3	1	2	0	6	5

All 10 League games took place in the Second Division between 1958 and 1963 and amazingly each of Stoke's away games at The Old Show Ground ended in draws, three of them by 1-1. Stoke's best win (in terms of goals scored) is 4-3 at home in September 1958 when almost 18,000 fans saw Dennis Wilshaw score twice for the Potters.

The Iron beat Stoke at The Victoria Ground by 3-2 in May 1963 before a crowd of 25,530 when the Potters were getting ready to celebrate winning the championship.

The three clashes in the League Cup took place in 1963-64 when Stoke won a second round, second replay by 1-0 at Hillsborough after 2-2 and 3-3 draws at Scunthorpe at The Victoria Ground respectively.

Players with both clubs: Tony Ford, Joe Johnson, Paul Reece and John Woodward. Frank Soo played for Stoke and later became manager of Scunthorpe United.

SECRETARIES

The first officially appointed secretary of Stoke Football Club was John Whitta Thomas, who presumably took office in 1868-69 when the team started to play friendly matches under the name of Stoke Ramblers.

Then, four years after the name Ramblers had been dropped to leave plain Stoke, Tom Slaney was appointed secretary-manager of the club in August 1874, and thereafter, until the summer of 1935, the team manager who was in office also held the joint position as club secretary (i.e. secretary-manager).

The first man to hold the official title of Stoke City Football Club secretary was Tom Hancock, who took up the position following the departure of secretary-manager Tom Mather and the appointment of former player Bob McGrory as team boss in June 1935.

William C. (Bill) Williams was next in line (from the 1950s) and he was followed by Mike Potts, who was upgraded from assistant secretary to club secretary in the summer of 1977.

By May 1997 Potts had completed 38 years' service at The Victoria Ground, starting off on a part-time basis in 1959.

SEGERS, Johannes

Dutch goalkeeper Hans Segers left PSV Eindhoven to sign for

Nottingham Forest for £50,000 in August 1984. He made 67 appearances under Brian Clough's management and during his time at The City Ground went on loan to Stoke, playing in one League game – a 4-1 defeat at West Bromwich Albion in February 1987. He also assisted both Sheffield United (November/December 1987) and Dunfermline Athletic (March 1988) before transferring to Wimbledon for £180,000 in September 1988, replacing Dave Beasant. Born in Eindhoven on 30 October 1961, Segers remained with the Dons until the summer of 1996 when he moved to Wolverhampton Wanderers (as cover for Mike Stowell) after more than 300 appearances for the London club. Then, in February 1997, he left Molineux to join non-League Woking.

NB: In January 1997 Segers, along with goalkeeper Bruce Grobbelaar, who also played on loan with Stoke, former Wimbledon and Aston Villa striker John Fashanu and a Malaysian businessman, Heng Suan Lim, appeared at Winchester Crown Court, charged with match-rigging. The jury failed to reach a verdict and the judge ordered a re-trial, scheduled for later in the year.

SELLARS, Harold

Born in the village of Beamish, County Durham on 9 April 1902, Harry Sellars was brought to The Victoria Ground from Ledgate Park in December 1923. It was the start of a long association for the Sellars family with Stoke City FC for later Harry's son, John, joined the Potters and remained at The Victoria Ground until 1959. Sellars senior was a miner who could play at left-half or inside-forward. His great strength was his passing and he was also a fine defender under pressure. A 100 per-cent performer every time he took the field, Sellars went on to score 21 goals in 394 League and FA Cup appearances for Stoke, up to July 1937, when he was transferred to neighbours Port Vale. He won a Second Division championship medal in 1933 and was assistant manager to Bob McGrory for a while before leaving The Vic. Later in his career Sellars had a spell in Dublin with Drumcondra. He died in Stoke-on-Trent on 30 December 1978.

SELLARS, John

Born at Trent Vale, Stoke-on-Trent on 28 April 1924, Johnny Sellars was a formidable athlete who often competed in the famous Powderhall Sprint events in the 1950s. He was brought to The Victoria Ground by his father in the 1930s and vowed that he would eventually wear the famous red and white striped shirt. And he did just that. With the war in Europe, Sellars bided his time and finally signed as a part-time professional for Stoke during the 1942-43 season. Never a full-time pro he became a regular member of the side in 1947-48, and as a hard-working left-half, who occasionally lined up at centre-forward and even full-back, he gave Stoke City FC great service, accumulating 413 League and FA Cup appearances and scoring 15 goals up until the end of the 1958-59 campaign when a serious eye injury forced him to quit sport altogether. Sellars divided his time between soccer and that of being a quality shoe designer working for the Lotus Shoe Company in Stone.

SENDINGS-OFF

● Ted 'Jammer' Evans was the first Stoke player to be sent off in a Football League game – receiving his marching orders in an away game against Everton on 12 November 1892. The match ended in a 2-2 draw.

● Centre-forward John Ritchie came on a substitute for the injured Alan Bloor during Stoke's UEFA Cup game against FC Kaiserslauten in Germany in September 1972 and was sent off after just 29 seconds for striking an opponent. He never touched the ball – and this is recorded as one of the quickest dismissals in football history.

● England's World Cup hero Geoff Hurst, perhaps one of the mild-mannered of footballers, was sent-off for the first time in his career playing for Stoke against Ipswich Town in a League game on 17 September 1972.

● Mickey Thomas was sent-off twice while playing for Stoke in season 1983-84.

● Goalkeeper Peter Fox was dismissed by referee Napthine for handling the ball outside his penalty area during a home League game with Luton Town on 25 September 1982. The Potters, with Paul Bracewell in goal, fought back three times to earn a 4-4 draw in front of the TV cameras. Luton's Dave Moss missed a last-minute penalty.

● Three players – Martin Bennett and Jimmy Nicholl of West Bromwich Albion and Keith Bertschin of Stoke City – were all sent-off during a League game between the two clubs at The Victoria Ground on 12 March 1985.

● Wayne Biggins and Vince Overson were both sent-off during Stoke's 4-0 League defeat at Reading in August 1994.

● Bob Whittingham and George Smart were both sent-off playing for Stoke against Derby County in a Lancashire Section War game on 1 April 1916.

● The following Manchester United players, all of whom later served with Stoke City in some capacity, were sent-off during their time at Old Trafford: Maurice Setters (1962), Harry Gregg (1965), Lou Macari (1973) and Joe Jordan (1978).

SETTERS, Maurice Edgar

With his bandy legs, crew-cut hair and forceful approach to the game, Maurice Setters looked what he was on the field of play – a real terrier. As hard as nails, determined and fearless in the tackle, he loved to get involved in the action. Standing only 5ft 6ins tall, he was a match for anyone, even the burly six foot strikers. Born in Honiton, Devon, on 16 December 1936, he represented Honiton & Collumpton Schools and England Boys as an inside-forward before joining Exeter City in January 1954. From St James' Park (where he won England Youth caps) he moved to West Bromwich Albion for £3,000 in January 1955 and went on to appear in 132 games for the Baggies up to January 1960 when he was transferred to Manchester United for £30,000. Whilst at The Hawthorns Setters was converted into a full-back and he added 16 Under-23 caps to his collection as well as s playing twice for the FA XI and for Young England in 1958. He did exceedingly well at Old Trafford, appearing in 186 first-team matches and helping United win the FA Cup in 1963. From there he went to Stoke City (November 1964) also for £30,000 and netted five goals in his 97 outings for the Potters before switching to Coventry City for £10,000 in November 1967. After helping the Sky Blues establish themselves in the First Division he moved on to Charlton Athletic (January 1970) and finally retired as a player at the end of that season with around 500 senior games under his belt (434 at League level). He managed Doncaster Rovers (May 1971 to November 1974) before taking a coaching position with Sheffield Wednesday. He was then assistant to manager George Kerr at Rotherham United (1983-84) and was chief scout for Newcastle United (1984-86) before spending 10 years as Jack Charlton's right-hand man with the Republic of Ireland national team (to 1996). Setters now lives in Bawtry near Doncaster.

SHALLCROSS, Arthur

Shallcross played for his native Leek and was also a match referee before taking over as secretary-manager of Stoke in February 1919. He never really hit it off with the supporters, especially after transferring star player Charlie Parker to Sunderland, but he did secure the services of Bob McGrory from Burnley. Under his control, the team had one or two good spells, yet only avoided relegation by the skin of their teeth in 1921. Twelve months later, however, things had turned completely round as he led the Potters to promotion to the First Division. Sadly, from his point of view, results then started to go wrong once more and relegation was suffered immediately. This eventually led to Shallcross resigning in March 1923. He was in charge of team affairs for 162 League games of which only 56 were won. He died in Stoke in 1950, aged 74.

SHAFFERY, Jack

Outside-right Shaffrey was born in Hanley c.1874. He played for Northwood Mission before joining Stoke for the 1897-98 season. After five first-team appearances he left the club to join Hanley Swifts in May 1898.

SHARDLOW, Paul

Sadly, promising young goalkeeper Paul Shardlow collapsed and died during a training session after suffering a heart attack on 14th October 1968. He was just 25 years of age. Born in Stone on 29 April 1943, he joined the Potters from Northwich Victoria in May 1966 and played in four senior games for the club before tragedy struck when least expected.

SHAW, Graham Paul

Striker Graham Shaw developed through the junior ranks at The Victoria Ground to sign professional forms for the Potters in June 1985. Four years later, after scoring 23 goals in 117 games for the Potters, he was transferred to Preston North End for £70,000. He did well at Deepdale, netting 42 goals in less than 150 outings before returning to Stoke for a second spell in August 1992 when Tony Ellis

Graham Shaw

went in the opposite direction plus a cash adjustment of £70,000. This time Shaw did not do as well, although he did help the Potters win the Second Division title. After a loan spell with Plymouth Argyle (August/September 1994) and adding another six goals in 50 games to his Potters' record, he left for Rochdale on a free transfer in August 1995.

SHEFFIELD UNITED

Stoke's playing record against United is:
Football League

Venue	P	W	D	L	F	A
Home	23	20	9	14	82	56
Away	23	9	13	21	45	68
Totals	46	29	22	35	127	124

FA Cup

Home	3	2	0	1	5	3
Away	2	0	1	1	2	3
Totals	5	2	1	2	7	6

Full Members' Cup

Home	1	0	0	1	1	2

The first League meeting between the clubs took place in November 1895 win the Potters won 4-0 in front of 8,000 fans. Tom Hyslop scored twice.

Stoke's best League win over the Blades was achieved at The Victoria Ground in December 1893 when 5,000 fans saw the Blades well and truly blunted to the tune of 5-0. Willie Naughton played a blinder for the Potters that day, scoring twice and having a hand in two more of the goals.

They also beat the Sheffield side 5-2 at home in December 1986 when Carl Saunders netted a hat-trick. Freddie Steele also scored a hat-trick in Stoke's 3-0 home win over United in October 1946.

Three other big Stoke wins were all by 4-0 – at Sheffield in January 1901 when Willie Maxwell scored twice, at The Vic in October 1922 when Harry Davies netted a couple and in the Potteries again in September 1977.

United's best League triumph over the Potters is 5-2 – at Bramall Lane on Boxing Day 1904.

The Blades also carved Stoke apart (from corner-kicks) when winning 4-0 at The Vic in a First Division match in October 1996. Thirty-five years earlier they had won 4-1 at home in a Second Division match and repeated that scoreline on the same Yorkshire ground in September 1963.

Two seven-goal League thrillers both ended in favour of United who won by the same scoreline of 4-3 at Sheffield in September 1897 when Maxwell again scored twice for Stoke and at The Victoria Ground in September 1903.

Stoke had to beat Sheffield United at Bramall Lane on the last day of the 1946-47 season to win the Football League championship. Unfortunately in front of a 30,000 crowd (10,000 supporting the Potters) they lost 2-1 and had to settle for third spot in the table, collecting £110 in talent money.

Stoke were beaten 3-2 at Bramall Lane in a fourth-round FA Cup game by United in season 1945-46, but remained in the competition. This was when each tie (up the the semi-finals) was played over two legs. Stoke had won the first leg 2-0 of that tie and went through 4-3 on aggregate.

Players with both clubs: Peter Beagrie, George Brown, Viv Busby, Tom Cowan, John Evans, Steve Foley, George Gallimore, Fred Groves, Adrian Heath, Willie Hendry, Bobby Howitt, Roy John, Carl Muggleton, John Nibloe, Jack Peart, Paul Richardson, John Roxburgh, Geoff Salmons, Lee Sandford, Hans Segers, Ronnie Sinclair, Simon Stainrod, Albert Sturgess, John Tudor and Billy Whitehurst.

Howard Kendall was a player with Stoke and later manager at Bramall Lane with Adrian Heath his assistant and later ex-Stokie, Viv Busby. Walter Gould played for United and was later coach and then assistant manager at Stoke. Mike Trusson was a Stoke reserve who later played 126 League games for United (1980-83).

SHEFFIELD WEDNESDAY

Stoke's playing record against Wednesday is:
Football League

Venue	P	W	D	L	F	A
Home	35	17	8	10	58	37
Away	35	9	5	21	36	68
Totals	70	26	13	31	94	105

Football Alliance

Home	1	1	0	0	5	1
Away	1	1	0	0	4	2
Totals	2	2	0	0	9	3

FA Cup

Home	2	2	0	0	4	0
Away	5	0	2	3	2	8
Totals	7	2	2	3	6	8

League Cup

Home	2	1	0	1	2	2
Away	1	0	1	0	0	0
Totals	3	1	1	1	2	2

Simod Cup

Away	1	1	0	0	1	0

Stoke recorded their best League win over Wednesday in December 1895, beating them 5-1 at home in the First Division. Tom Hyslop scored a hat-trick that day in front of 4,000 fans.

In Stoke's 4-0 home League win over the Owls in November 1902, Jimmy Bradley almost burst the ball with his penalty kick.

Wednesday's best League victory over Stoke is 4-0, achieved on three occasions, each time at Hillsborough: on Christmas Day 1897 when the crowd was 6,000; on 2 March 1900 when the turnout was just 3,000 and in December 1955 (Division Two) when the attendance topped 23,500.

The points were shared in a cracking 4-4 draw before more than 30,000 fans at The Victoria Ground in November 1963. John Ritchie scored a hat-trick for the Potters against the team he was later to join. And in April 1965, Ritchie was again the thorn in Wednesday's side, when he scored all Stoke's goals in their emphatic 4-1 home win over the Owls. And it was Ritchie again who put one over on Wednesday by netting both goals in Stoke's 2-1 home victory in April 1970 – a defeat which helped send the Owls into the Second Division.

Stoke were dumped out of the FA Cup by Wednesday in 1908-09, losing 5-0 at Hillsborough in the second round.

The Simod Cup-tie was played at Hillsborough in 1987-88.

Players with both clubs: Len Armitage, Gary Bannister, Tom Brittleton, Mark Chamberlain, Lee Chapman, Ian Cranson, Peter Fox, Jack Palethorpe, Dave Parkes, Kevin Pressmen, John Ritchie, Jimmy Sayer, Simon Stainrod and Harry Ware.

Former Stoke boss Richie Barker was assistant manager (to Ron Atkinson) at Wednesday (1990s).

SHELDON, Frederick L.

With Fred Latham not in the best of form and Billy Rowley edging towards retirement, Stoke called up amateur goalkeeper Fred Sheldon to play in the first team during the mid-1890s. A local lad, born in Tunstall c.1871, he served with Stoke St Peter's before joining the playing staff at The Victoria Ground in the summer of 1896. Unfortunately he didn't perform too well for the Potters, conceding 15 goals in his first five outings and was quickly pushed back into the Reserves. He was called upon three more times during the next campaign, but again failed to keep a clean sheet and was eventually released by the club in May 1897, when he signed for Eccleshall.

SHELDON, Kevin John

A outside-right 'Bomber' Sheldon was born at Cheddleton on 14 June 1956, and made 15 appearances in Stoke's first team during his his brief stay at The Victoria Ground. He left the Potters for Wigan Athletic in July 1981 and later played for Port Vale (on loan), Crewe Alexandra and Rocester. He helped Wigan win promotion from the Fourth Division in 1982.

SHERIDAN, James

Paddy Sheridan, although Irish by birth, started playing football in Glasgow for Cambuslang Hibernians. From there he went to Everton who recruited him at the 11th hour when they were a man short. From Goodison Park he moved to Stoke in September 1904 and went on to score once in 12 games for the Potters before transferring to New Brompton in 1905. Sheridan, who was born in April 1884, won six caps for Ireland, one whilst a Stoke player (v England in 1904).

SHERON, Michael Nigel

Mike Sheron came to The Victoria Ground from Norwich City on 13 November 1995 in a deal which sent fellow striker Keith Scott to Carrow Road. Scott was valued at £300,000 and Sheron at £150,000, and it was the latter who turned out to be the better goalscorer as far as the Potters were concerned. Sheron certainly proved his worth by scoring 24 goals in League and Cup appearances for Stoke in 1996-97. A purposeful footballer, direct in his approach and always looking for an opening, he gives defenders nightmares at times and is a big favourite with the fans. Born in Liverpool on 11 January 1972, and a former England Under-21 international (16 caps gained) he was nurtured by Manchester City and signed professional; forms at Maine Road in July 1990. After a loan spell with Bury, he joined Norwich City for £1 million in August 1994, but never settled in Norfolk and subsequently moved to Stoke where he became an instant success. In July 1997 Sheron left Stoke for Queens Park Rangers in a £2.5 million transfer deal. His record for the Potters was 39 goals in 76 first XI appearances.

SHERRATT, Brian

Sherratt kept goal in one League game for Stoke City, lining up against Middlesbrough at The Victoria Ground in the Second Division on 21 April 1962 in place of Irish international Jimmy O'Neill. He did well and helped City to a 2-0 win in front of 9,000 fans. Born in Stoke on 29 March 1944, he had joined the Potters as a professional in April

1961, but owing to the form of other goalkeepers in the camp, he left the club for Oxford United in August 1965. A loan spell with Nottingham Forest preceded his move from The Manor Ground to Barnsley in June 1989 and he ended his senior career with a spell at Colchester United (1970). All told Sherratt appeared in 70 League games for his five major clubs.

SHILTON, Peter Leslie, MBE, OBE

There is no doubt that Peter Shilton was a superb goalkeeper, perhaps the best in the World during a period in the 1980s. He was a great shot-stopper, could gauge crosses to perfection, was alert and watchful in tight situations and above all, was seemingly always in command of his penalty area. Born in Leicester on 18 September 1949, 'Shilts' (as he was to be called) joined the groundstaff at Filbert Street in 1964 and turned professional in September 1966. He went on to play in over 300 games for the Foxes scoring one goal – a long punt downfield against his future club Southampton in a First Division game in October 1967. In November 1974, a fee of £300,000 took him to Stoke City, who two years earlier had lost the services of another former Leicester goalkeeper, Gordon Banks. 'Shilts' assembled a record of 120 appearances for the Potters before transferring to Nottingham Forest for £270,000 in September 1977 and whilst under Brian Clough at The City Ground gained winners' medals in the Football League championship in 1978, the FA Charity Shield also in 1978, two European Cup Finals in 1979 and 1980, the European Super Cup in 1979 and the Football League Cup also in 1979, having earlier gained a Second Division championship prize with Leicester in 1971. After 272 outings for Forest, he switched his allegiance to Southampton, joining the Saints for £325,000 in August 1982. He had 242 outings whilst at The Dell and then returned to the East Midlands to sign for Derby County for £90,000 in July 1987. Six and a half years and 211 games later he left The Baseball Ground for Plymouth Argyle where he later became player-manager. But financial difficulties resulted in him leaving Home Park and after brief non-contract spells with Wimbledon, Bolton Wanderers (two games), Coventry City and West Ham United, Shilton joined Leyton Orient in November 1996. A month later, on 22 December, he became the first footballer in history to appear in 1,000 Football League games when he kept a clean sheet in the O's 2-0 home win over struggling Brighton & Hove Albion at Brisbane Road. In fact, at the end of the 1996-97 season, Shilton had been playing League football for a total of 31 years, having made his debut on 4 May 1966. In his 125 appearances for England at full international level, Shilton skippered his country on 15 occasions and had a 60% success rate in terms of victories. He was also capped three times by the Under-23s and also represented his country at both schoolboy and youth team levels. Besides his two titles which he received from HRH the Queen, he was voted PFA Player of the Year in 1978 and received the PFA Merit Award for services to football in 1990. Shilton's son, Sam, joined Plymouth Argyle as a trainee at the age of 16 in 1994.

SHIRLEY, John A.

Inside-forward Jack Shirley scored 11 goals (two on his debut v Fulham) in 30 League and FA Cup games for Stoke City during the period 1927-30. Born in Crewe c.1903, he played for Whitchurch before moving to The Victoria Ground in April 1927 for £500. Shirley was suspended by the club in 1929-30 for breach of club rules and he left the Potters at the end of that season, signing for non-League Hednesford Town.

SHORE, Victor E.A.

Another inside-forward who began his career in Birmingham minor football with the Dean's Works team. On 29 March 1920 he went 220 miles north to sign for Sunderland, but failed to settle in the North-East and after just five games he returned back to the Midlands to join Stoke in May 1921. Born in Handsworth, Birmingham c.1897, Shore (now deceased) was troubled by a leg injury and poor form during his days at The Victoria Ground and managed only three appearances before leaving enter non-League football after a disagreement with the club's directors when he refused to live in the Potteries. Stoke, in fact, demanded a fee for his transfer having incurred a hefty medical bill in their efforts to get him match fit.

SHORT, John

Yorkshireman Jack Short was born in Barnsley on 18 February 1928. He moved to the Midlands as a youngster and played for Wath Wanderers (a Molineux nursery side) during the latter stages of the war before joining Wolverhampton Wanderers as a professional in May 1948. A steady, competent full-back, he waited patiently in the wings under Stan Cullis' control and behind a posse of good defenders, before breaking into Wolves' first team in 1950-51. He went on to make 107 senior appearances for the club (two goals scored – both from the centre-forward position v Manchester City in an FA Cup-tie). But with so much talent at Molineux, Short, who helped

Peter Shilton

Wolves win their first-ever League championship in 1954, was allowed to leave the club to sign for Stoke City in June of that same year. manager Frank Taylor acquiring him to 'bolster up his defence'. He played in 55 matches for the Potters and then chose to see out the remainder his professional career with his home-town club Barnsley (signed for £3,000 in October 1956) for whom he made 109 League appearances up to his retirement in 1960. Short died after a brief illness in 1976.

SHREWSBURY TOWN

Stoke's playing record against Town is:
Football League

Venue	P	W	D	L	F	A
Home	6	2	3	1	6	6
Away	6	2	0	4	6	9
Totals	12	4	3	5	12	15

Birmingham & District League

	P	W	D	L	F	A
Home	3	2	0	1	6	3
Away	3	2	0	1	3	3
Totals	6	4	0	2	9	6

FA Cup

	P	W	D	L	F	A
Home	1	1	0	0	2	0

League Cup

	P	W	D	L	F	A
Home	2	0	2	0	1	1
Away	2	1	0	1	2	2
Totals	4	1	2	1	3	3

Stoke's best League victory over Shrewsbury is 3-0 at Gay Meadow on 28 November 1987 when Lee Dixon, Carl Saunders and Tony Ford found the net before 5,158 fans.

In reply, the Shrews best League win over the Potters is 4-1 at home earlier in that same year (18 April). The Shrews also won 3-1 at The Victoria Ground in September 1990.

Shrewsbury achieved the double over Stoke in the Birmingham & District League in 1908-09, but the Potters gained revenge by doing likewise in the same competition the following season and again in 1910-11.

Carl Saunders scored in three successive Football League games for Stoke against the Shrews in the 1980s.

Players with both clubs: John Almond, Len Benbow, Noel Blake, Ian Bowers, Gerry Bridgwood, Gilbert Brookes, Cliff Carr, Wayne Clarke, John Clowes, Ernie Cull, Gerry Daly, Billy Davies, John Evans, Tom Flannigan, Gary Hackett, Asa Hartford, Tony Henry, Geoff Hickson, Dave Hockaday, Sammy Irvine, Paul Johnson, Les Johnston, Tony 'Zico' Kelly, Bob Lister, Paul Maguire, John Moore, Leigh Palin, Henry Salmon, Terry Smith, Tim Steele, Mickey Thomas and Charlie Wilson.

Richie Barker and Alan Durban managed both clubs (they worked together at one stage at Gay Meadow); Chic Bates was a player at Gay Meadow who later became assistant manager-coach with Stoke, while goalkeeper Harry Gregg has also been associated with the Potters and the Shrews. Asa Hartford was initially player-coach with Shrewsbury Town and later manager before becoming assistant manager to Joe Jordan at Stoke. Dudley Kernick was a Shrewsbury player who later became commercial manager of Stoke City.

SHUTT, George

Born Stoke-on-Trent in 1861, centre-half Shutt left Stoke Priory to join the Potters in 1880. After scoring two goals in 30 senior games for Stoke, and winning one England cap v Ireland in March 1886 as well as representing Staffordshire on at least 12 occasions, playing for the Birmingham FA, The Players XI and The North of England, he left The Victoria Ground for Hanley in May 1899. In August 1891, he signed for Burslem Port Vale and later returned to Hanley Town. Shutt then retired from soccer to go into the licensing trade, keeping pubs in both Burslem and Hanley. He also became a Football League referee (1891) yet surprisingly he never talked football after hanging up his boots. Described as an intelligent, sure-tackling defender, he died in Hanley on 6 August 1936.

SIDDALL, Alfred Brian

Born in Northwich on 2 May 1930, Siddall challenged Johnny Malkin for the right-wing berth in Stoke's first team for four seasons and had some success, scoring ten goals in 59 League and Cup games. He left the club for Bournemouth in January 1954, and later played for Ipswich Town (1957-61). Siddall, who started out playing for Witton Albion, turned professional with Wolverhampton Wanderers in 1947-48, but a troublesome knee prevented him from making the grade at Molineux. He had a second spell with Witton Albion before joining his home-town club, Northwich Victoria, signing for Stoke City in February 1951 when manager Frank Taylor pipped Arsenal for his signature. Siddall, who could occupy all any forward position, was badly injured playing for Ipswich against West Ham United. He never started a League game again and played only occasionally for Haverhill Rovers. After retiring he became a fully qualified FA coach, living in Ipswich.

SIDDALL, Barry

Former England youth international goalkeeper Siddall, standing over six feet tall and weighing 14st 4lbs travelled all over England playing League football. Born in Ellesmere Port on 12 September 1954, he started off as a professional with Bolton Wanderers (January 1972) and thereafter served, in turn, with Sunderland (from September 1976), Darlington (on loan, October 1980), Port Vale (August 1982), Blackpool (on loan, October 1983), Stoke City (initially on loan, December 1984, January 1985), Tranmere Rovers (on loan, October 1985), Manchester City (on loan, March-April 1986), Blackpool (August 1986), Hartlepool United (1989), Stockport County (1989-90), West Bromwich Albion (month trial, August 1990), Carlisle United (November 1990), Chester City (June 1991), Preston North End (December 1993). Horwich RMI, Bury (loan), Lincoln City (loan), Burnley (December 1994), Birmingham City (non-contract, March 1995). He retired from competitive football in 1995 after amassing more than 700 senior appearances, 606 at League level alone of which 20 were with the Potters.

SIGURDSSON, Larus Orri

Blond Icelandic defender Sigurdsson had already won caps at both youth and Under-21 levels for his country before joining Stoke City – and inevitably full international caps followed as a Stokie. A quality player, he attracted the attentions of several Premiership clubs during 1996 when he was in outstanding form. Born in Akureyri, Iceland on

4 June 1973, 'Ziggy' joined professional staff at The Victoria Ground for a bargain £150,000 from his hometown club FC Akureyri in October 1994. He made an impressive start to his career with Stoke and was an ever present in 1995-96, helping the Potters reach the First Division Play-offs. Strong and controlled in the tackle, he's fast in recovery and reads the game exceedingly well. His playing record for Stoke at May 1997 was 130 appearances (1 goal).

SIMOD CUP

Stoke City entered this short-lived competition on two occasions and their record reads:

Venue	P	W	D	L	F	A
Away	5	2	1	2	5	7

Match details
1987-88

v Portsmouth	(a)	won	3-0
v Sheffield Wednesday	(a)	won	1-0
v Leicester City	(a)	draw	0-0*
v Luton Town	(a)	lost	1-4

* Stoke won 5-3 on penalties

1988-89

v Southampton	(a)	lost	0-3

Only 3,226 fans saw that 3-0 win against Portsmouth in November 1987. And Stoke's penalty heroes against Leicester at Filbert Street were George Berry, Lee Dixon, Carl Caunders, Cliff Carr and Graham Shaw.

SIMPSON, Harry

An inside-forward, born in Scotland *c*.1864, Simpson played for East Stirlingshire before scoring three goals in 12 League and FA Cup games for Stoke in season 1889-90. He returned to his homeland to sign for Forfar Athletic.

SIMPSON, Henry

Another short-term player with Stoke, Simpson was a sturdy centre-half who had eight League outings for the club over a period of two years from 1895. Born in Tunstall *c*.1875, he played for Crewe Alexandra before joining the Potters and went to New Brighton Tower on leaving The Victoria Ground (1897).

SINCLAIR, Ronald McDonald

After making 96 first-team appearances for Stoke City (from November 1991 to September 1995) goalkeeper Ronnie Sinclair dropped out of favour with manager Lou Macari and thereafter was third choice behind Mark Prudhoe and Carl Muggleton. A fine shot-stopper, he was born in Stirling on 19 November 1964, and began his League career with Nottingham Forest, signing professional forms at The City Ground in October 1982. Loan spells with Wrexham, Derby County and Sheffield United preceded his transfer to Leeds United for £10,000 in June 1986, and after two separate loan periods with Halifax Town, he switched to Bristol City on a free (September 1989). A further loan spell, this time with Walsall (September 1991) was followed by a £25,000 move to Stoke City. And before his transfer to Chester City in July 1996, Sinclair also had a loan spell with Bradford City. A Scottish schoolboy and youth international, Sinclair helped the Potters win the Second Divsion title in 1993.

SKEELS, Eric Thomas

Eric Skeels took the liberty of writing to Stoke boss Frank Taylor asking for a trial. He got one, and after being an amateur with Stockport County one week, he was signed by Stoke City the next, becoming a professional at The Victoria Ground in December 1958. He progressed through the intermediate and reserve teams and after 15 months hard work finally made his senior debut, claiming a regular place in the first XI in 1959-60. In the next 17 years or so – up to September 1976 – he gave the Potters tremendous service, appearing in a club record 606 competitive games, 507 in the Football League, 44 in the FA Cup, 38 in the League Cup and 17 others. A very consistent performer in the full-back or left-half positions, and known appropriately as Mr Dependable, he helped Stoke win the Second Division title in 1963, gained a League Cup runners-up medal in 1964, but was out of the side when the League Cup was won in 1972. A short spell on loan in the NASL with Seattle Sounders preceded his departure from Stoke to neighbours Port Vale. And after leaving Vale Park in May 1977, he teamed up with Leek Town. Skeels later kept a pub in the Potteries area and still visits The Victoria Ground when time allows.

SLANEY, Thomas Charles

Secretary-manager of Stoke from August 1874 to May 1883, Slaney was born in the Potteries in 1852 and died in Stoke in 1935. He trained as a schoolteacher and was a leading light both at The Victoria Ground and to local football in general for a number of years. He played for Stoke while in office and, in fact, skippered the side for seven seasons from 1875-82. It is said that he scored nine goals when the Potters beat Mow Cop 26-0 in a Staffordshire Cup-tie in 1877-78. Along with Harry Allen, he helped form the Staffordshire County FA of which he was also secretary. Slaney became a referee when his playing days were over.

SLATER, George

Inside-forward Slater scored one goal in two Football League games for Stoke during the first season of the competition (1888-89). Born in Walsall in 1864, he played briefly for Hanley United before joining the Potters and surprisingly retired at the age of 27 and emigrated to America.

SLATER, John

In the summer of 1919, thirty-year-old John Slater, a former player and owner of both the Berryhill and New Haven collieries, joined the board of directors at The Victoria Ground, bringing his knowledge of the game and business expertise to the club. An immediate move was made to promote Slater to chairman, but this never materialised with Mr E.B.Reynish remaining in office until the summer of 1924.

SLOANE, James

Glaswegian centre-forward Jimmy Sloane scored one goal (in a 4-3 home win over Burnley) in 11 games for Stoke during the first season of League football (1888-89). Born in 1864, he came south from Glasgow Rangers and return to the Ibrox club after less than a year in the Potteries.

SMALLEY, William

When Stoke visited Preston North End for a League game in October 1888 they arrived minus two players and asked the home club to loan them a couple to make up the team. One of them was utility forward Smalley (the other Archie Dempsey). Stoke lost the game 7-0. Smalley was born in Lancaster c.1864 and never appeared in North End's first team. His brother kept goal for Everton.

SMART, George W.

A well-built, impetuous full-back, born in Bristol in 1889, who played for Treharris before joining Stoke in July 1911 along with Joseph Jones. Previously with Lodge Hill (Bristol) and Kingswood Rovers, Smart appeared in 52 senior games for the Potters, up to February 1920. The next month he was transferred to Stafford Rangers. Smart was sent off playing against Derby in a wartime game in 1916.
NB: During the war Smart was wounded but recovered sufficiently to re-sign for the Potters after the hostilities.

SMITH, Alfred

A teacher by profession, inside-forward Alf Smith had two spells at The Victoria Ground, and all told assembled a fine scoring record of 72 goals in 149 senior games for the Potters. Born at Longton c.1880, he first moved to Stoke in 1904 from Burton United, making his League debut against Aston Villa in November 1905. Unfortunately he failed to impress early on and left for Wrexham in May 1906, only to return via Crewe Alexandra in August 1910, a much more experienced footballer and an England Junior international. By now he had been transformed into a fine, studious marksman, a 'dazzling dribbler', adept at getting into scoring positions. He became a firm favourite with the supporters and in 1910-11 rattled in 35 goals in 44 first-team appearances, including a five-timer in a 10-0 drubbing of Halesowen (Birmingham League) and hat-tricks in successive games v Wellington and Salisbury City round the turn of the year. He left The Victoria Ground at the end of the 1914-15 campaign. Outside football he was a very fine all-round cricketer and was vice-captain of Longton CC for a number of seasons.

SMITH, A. Richard

Born in Newcastle-under-Lyme c.1890, wing-half Dicky Smith came to the fore with Newcastle Town and during signed for Stoke in wartime football, making an initial impact in the 1917-18 campaign when he appeared in 32 games, adding another 28 to his tally the following term. When peacetime football returned in 1919, he was a key member of the team and went on to appear in another 110 League and FA Cup games for the Potters before retiring through injury. He played his last game in August 1922.

SMITH, Andrew Walter

A strong, well-built inside or centre-forward (who could play at centre-half) Andy Smith won a First Division championship medal with West Bromwich Albion in 1920 and scored both goals when the Baggies beat Tottenham to win the Charity Shield before leaving The Hawthorns for Stoke in March 1923 for £1,500. He never really settled down at The Victoria Ground, and appeared in only five League games, transferring to Wigan Borough six months after joining the Potters. He later played for Bournemouth (1924) and retired in May 1925. Born in Camberwell, London in April 1896, Smith represented Camberwell & Southwark Schools before moving to the Black Country with his family. He played for Langley Green Juniors in 1912 and then Crosswells Brewery prior to becoming an amateur with Birmingham in August 1912, turning professional two years later. He netted 36 goals in 59 outings for Blues and 22 in 81 starts for Albion. He died in March 1968.

SMITH, Clement

Inside-forward Clem Smith cost Stoke £2,000 when bought from Chester in March 1938. Manager Bob McGrory certainly gambled on Smith whose lack of height (he was only 5ft 7ins tall) went against him in the long run. Born in Wath-on-Deane in 1912, he played his early football with South Kirby and Halifax Town, and scored seven goals in 25 League appearances for the Potters up to 1939 when he returned to Halifax where he played most of his wartime football with

SMITH, Denis

One of the greatest defenders ever to wear the red and white shirt of Stoke City, Smith was terrific servant to the club for some 17 years, amassing almost 500 senior appearances. He overcame countless injuries and was a totally committed footballer, never shirking a challenge, boldly going where every defender should – firmly into a tackle – and was as dedicated as any man to Stoke City Football Club. Born in Meir, Stoke-on-Trent on 19 November 1947, he was a pupil at Queensbury Road School and joined the Potters an apprentice in 1965, turning professional in September 1966. It was not until he was almost 21 that he made his senior debut, lining up against Arsenal at Highbury in a First Division match in September 1968. He made four League appearances that season, but thereafter became a permanent fixture in the side, forming a fine defensive partnership with Alan Bloor. He won Football League honours, but unfortunately England at any level recognition eluded him. He did play at Wembley, helping Stoke win the League Cup in 1972, and all told Smith scored 41 goals in 493 senior games for the Potters, up to the summer of 1982 when he retired. He had also been on the coaching staff at The Victoria Ground since at the start of his last season. On leaving the Potters he became manager of York City, holding office at Bootham Crescent until 1987 when he took a similar position with Sunderland, staying at Roker Park for four years. In 1992 he took charge of Bristol City and after only a short time at Ashton Gate he was given the manager's job at Oxford United (September 1993).

NB: Only three players – teammate Eric Skeels (606) and full-backs John McCue (542) and Bob McGrory (511) – have appeared in more first-class games for Stoke than Denis Smith.

SMITH, Elijah M.

Known as 'Father' Smith during his footballing career, this tough tackling wing-half who was born in Stoke c.1860, played in 31 League and FA Cup-ties for the Potters over a period of five seasons 1885 to 1890. He represented Staffordshire and joined the Potters from Tunstall, leaving The Victoria Ground for Stafford Road FC.

SMITH, Harold G.

Full-back Harry Smith played in one League game for Stoke against West Bromwich Albion in March 1908. Born in Cannock c.1885, he had earlier lined up in 38 senior matches for Walsall (from 1905) and on leaving The Victoria Ground in 1909, he returned to Fellows Park. Unfortunately injury prevented him from making any more first-team appearances for the Saddlers.

SMITH, Herbert

An England international, capped 17 times at amateur level and four times by the seniors, full-back Herby Smith also won a soccer gold medal for Great Britain in the 1908 Olympics. Born in Witney on 22 November 1897, he was a major capture by Stoke in November 1902, after being strongly recommended to the club. One of the finest amateur footballers in the game, Smith played for the losing side, Oxford City, in the 1903 FA Amateur Cup Final and in the same year represented The South v The North in an international trial. Well built, weighing over 13st, he had a trusty left foot and was a very mobile player who could volley a ball supremely well. He played in three League games for Stoke in season 1902-03 after earlier assisting Oxford Schools, Witney, Reading, Oxford City and Richmond. On leaving The Victoria Ground he served with Derby County and Clapton Orient, also Oxfordshire and Beccles College. as well as having a second spell with Richmond. Smith died in Oxford on 6 January 1951.

SMITH, Mark Alexander

Tidy outside-left who played twice for Stoke City (on loan from Dunfermline Athletic) in February 1990. Born in Bellshill (Glasgow) on 16 December 1964, Smith was with Gairdoch United, St Mirren, Queen's Park and Celtic before joining Dunfermline, and he also assisted Hamilton Academical, Nottingham Forest, Reading, Mansfield Town and Shrewsbury Town (up to 1995). He won a Scottish Division One championship medal with Dunfermline.

SMITH, Richard

Centre-forward Dick Smith did well in local junior football with Newcastle PSA and Newcastle Town before doing even better with Leek United. From there he joined Stoke in June 1913 and went on to score 20 goals in 33 competitive games for the Potters, up to April 1915, and added another seven in 23 outings during the first two wartime seasons. Born in Stoke c.1892, he was only 5ft 7ins tall, but was a match for any defender and always looked likely to score when he had the ball inside the area.

SMITH, Robert

Half-back Bob Smith appeared in just one League game for the Potters against Wolverhampton Wanderers in September 1891. Born locally in Newcastle (Staffs) c.1870, he assisted Newcastle Swifts before joining Stoke and left The Victoria Ground for Burslem Port Vale in May 1892.

SMITH, Terence Peter

A centre-forward who was with Stoke for four seasons (1968-72) at Smith scored once in four outings for the Potters. And after a loan spell with Shrewsbury Town he chose to go and play his football in Australia. He was born in Cheltenham on 10 June 1951.

SMITH, William Ernest

Billy Smith was a fine goalscoring inside-forward who netted 62 times in 141 senior games in five and a half years with the Potters – from May 1909 to December 1914. Born at Lostock Hall (near Preston) c.1886, he served with Leyland FC Darwen, Nelson and Bradford City (from May 1908, scoring 50 goals in 88 League games for the Bantams) before moving to Stoke (May 1909) being one of the club's first full-time professionals after the club had been reformed (1908). He made a terrific start to his career at The Victoria Ground, hitting over 50 goals in his first three seasons. Unfortunately after that he was plagued by injuries and managed only nine League outings in his last 30 months with the club. He was subsequently transferred to Preston North End at Christmas 1914 and never played competitive football after World War One.

SMYTH, Samuel

For five years, from 1942, inside-forward Sammy Smyth had played only amateur football in his native Northern Ireland, serving in the main with Distillery and Linfield, along with a handful of junior clubs. In the summer of 1947, after agreeing to sign professional forms for Dundella, which allowed him to be transferred for a fee, he moved to England to join Wolverhampton Wanderers for £1,100. A schoolboy international trialist, he had gained several amateur caps for Ireland (with Distillery) and also represented the Irish League, and once at Molineux he quickly made an impact, netting eight goals in 30 games in his first season there. He was immediately upgraded to senior international football (going on to win nine full caps) and at the same time continued to impress at Wolves, taking his tally to 43 goals in 116 senior appearances, collecting an FA Cup winners' medal in 1949 when he scored twice in a 3-1 Final win over Leicester City, including a real classic – one of the best seen at the stadium.
He left Wolves for Stoke for £25,000 in September 1951 and netted a further 19 goals in 44 games for the Potters before switching to Liverpool for £12,000 in January 1954. He spent just five months at Anfield, quitting competitive League football at the age of 29 to return home to Belfast where he got married and took a full-time job, later working for a bookmaker prior to running his own sports shop. Born in Belfast on 25 February 1915, Smyth scored 72 goals in 187 League games in England.

SOO, Hong Yi (Frank)

One of the finest wing-halves in the country during the late 1930s, Soo, despite his name, was born in Buston, Liverpool on 8 March 1914. A former Liverpool schoolboy, he was working as an office clerk while also assisting Derby Boys Club and Prescot Cables, when Stoke City manager Frank Taylor came along and signed him in January 1933. Soo became the first player of Chinese descent ever to appear in the Football League when making his Potters' debut at inside-left (number-ten) against Middlesbrough at Ayresome Park in November 1933. This was the first of 185 competitive games for Stoke (nine goals scored). Soo also played in 81 wartime matches, adding a further 17 goals. Strong and resilient, he was a very fair player, a crowd-pleaser who hardly ever put in a rash tackle. Rarely spoken to by the referee, he was part of that tremendous Stoke middle-line which read: Tutin-Turner-Soo. During the hostilities Soo won eight England wartime caps, figuring in the same side as fellow Stokies Neil Franklin and Stan Matthews, as well as playing for the FA XI and the RAF and guesting for a number of clubs including Brentford, Chelsea and Everton. In September 1945 Soo moved to Leicester City (managed at the time by former Stoke boss Tom Mather) for £4,600 and from Filbert Street he switched to Luton Town (July 1946) for £5,000. He ended his playing career with Chelmsford City (May 1950) and after retirement went into coaching, taking charge briefly of both the Israeli and Swedish National teams, as well as coaching four teams in Sweden, namely IF City of Eskiltuna (1952), Orebo 1952-53, Djurgaardens IF (1954 – leading them to the Swedish League title in 1955), Oddevold (from 1956) and SC Padua in Italy (April 1950-June 1952). On his return to England Soo managed Scunthorpe United for a season (June 1959 to May 1960) and then took charge of St Albans City before returning to Scandinavia to coach again in Scandinavia, mainly with Koping IS (1962), IFK Stockholm (1963) and AB Copenhagen (1965) as well as seven other junior clubs around Copenhagen and Malmo (1966-71), finally ending his association over there with Hoganas BKin in 1972-73. Soo died at Liverpool in January 1991.

SOUTH SHIELDS (Gateshead)

Stoke's playing record against the North-East club is:
Football League

Venue	P	W	D	L	F	A
Home	7	2	4	1	5	3
Away	7	1	3	3	8	16
Totals	14	3	7	4	13	19

Stoke first met South Shields in season 1919-20 (Division Two) when both games ended in draws: 0-0 at The Victoria Ground and 2-2 in the North-East.

In fact the first five League meetings all ended level.

Stoke's best win of the three against Shields came in December 1927 when in a Second Division match they beat Shields 3-1 at home with Walter Bussey scoring twice in front of a near 14,000 crowd.

The Potters' two heaviest defeats have been those of 4-0 and 5-1, both away, in December 1924 and January 1926 respectively.

Players with both clubs: Arthur Cartlidge, Ernie Cull, Tom Dawson, Jock Grieve, Ellis Hall, Kenny Lowe, Peter McArdle and John Tudor.

SOUTHAMPTON

Stoke's playing record against Saints is:
Football League

Venue	P	W	D	L	F	A
Home	27	15	6	6	52	33
Away	27	7	3	17	28	48
Totals	54	22	9	23	80	81

Southern League

Venue	P	W	D	L	F	A
Home	2	1	0	1	3	4
Away	2	0	0	2	1	3
Totals	4	1	0	3	4	7

FA Cup

Venue	P	W	D	L	F	A
Home	1	1	0	0	1	0

Simod Cup

Venue	P	W	D	L	F	A
Away	1	0	0	1	0	3

Following four meetings in the Southern League before World War One, the first encounter between the Potters and the Saints in the Football League took place on 15 October 1923 (Division Two) when Charlie Kelly scored to give Stoke a 1-0 victory at The Dell in front of 14,000 fans.

Stoke began their 1927-28 Second Division programme by beating Saints 6-3 at The Dell on 27 August. A crowd of 12,000 in brilliant sunshine saw Harry Davies (2), Charlie Wilson, Johnny Eyres, Tom Williamson and Bobby Archibald net for the Potters. This is Stoke's best League win over Saints.

In contrast, Stoke's heaviest League reverse against Southampton is 5-1 at The Dell on the last day of the 1961-62 Second Division campaign (28 April). Under 9,600 fans were present to see Dennis Viollet net for the Potters, while Derek Reeves and George O'Brien both scored twice for Saints.

The first time Stoke and Southampton met in the top flight was in season 1966-67 when 25,554 fans saw the Potters win 3-2 at The Victoria Ground while 23,270 witnessed Saints' 3-2 victory at The Dell.

Stoke beat Saints 4-0 at home in October 1928 and earlier in the year Harry Davies hit a hat-trick in Stoke's 3-0 League triumph over Saints at The Victoria Ground in April 1929.

The last time the teams met in League action was in 1984-85 (Division One) when Stoke lost 3-1 at home and drew 0-0 away.

Stoke's only Southern League win over Saints was 3-1 at home in April 1913 when Billy Holmes netted twice.

Harry Davies scored Stoke's winner in their third round FA Cup victory over Saints at The Victoria ground in

The Simod Cup-tie was played at The Dell in 1988-89.

Players with both clubs: Micky Adams, Tommy Broad, Tom Cain, George Clawley, Alan Curtis, Jimmy Dale, Peter Durber, Jack Farrell, Bruce Grobbelaar, George Harris, Mark Harrison (Saints reserve),

Steve Bould heads goalwards against Southampton in 1984. The Saints' goalkeeper is former Stoke star Peter Shilton.

Arthur Hartshorne, Bran Horne, Wilf Mayer, Sam Meston, Mick Mills, Willie Naughton, Graham Potter, Dave Puckett, Tom Robertson, Jack Robinson, Peter Shilton, Derek Statham, Dave (W.C.) Thomson, Joe Turner, Mark Walters, Dave Watson and Ray Wallace. Joe Jordan played for Saints and later became team manager of Stoke City. Mick Mills also managed Stoke City while full-back Dennis Rofe was a player and later youth-team coach at Southampton, while in 1993-94 he was reserve-team coach at The Victoria Ground.

SOUTHEND UNITED

Stoke's playing record against the Shrimpers is:
Football League

Venue	P	W	D	L	F	A
Home	5	3	0	2	10	4
Away	5	1	1	3	7	9
Totals	10	4	1	5	17	13

League Cup

Home	1	1	0	0	3	1
Away	1	1	0	0	1	0
Totals	2	2	0	0	4	1

Stoke first took on Southend in a League game on 22 September 1990 (Division Three). That day a crowd of 11,901 at The Victoria Ground witnessed an emphatic 4-0 victory by the Potters whose goals came from Paul Ware, Wayne Biggins (2) and John Cornwell (own-goal).

Stoke have also beaten the Shrimpers 4-1 (h) in September 1994 and 4-2 at Roots Hall in November 1995 when Simon Sturridge scored a fine hat-trick in front of 5,967 fans.

Southend's best win over the Potters is 4-2 (h) in March 1995 when 4,240 fans saw six different players figure on the short and both sides net a penalty.

Stoke's first ever League Cup victory came away at Southend in round one on 13 September 1961, when future Shrimper Peter Bullock scored to give them a 1-0 triumph.

Players with both clubs: Charlie Axcell, Tony Bentley, Sidney Blackie, Peter Bullock, Wilber 'Peter' Jackson, Lawrie Leslie, Tommy Little, Jimmy McAlinden, Mark McNally, Jim Martin and Dave Regis and Billy Wootton (Stoke amateur).

Tom Mather managed both clubs: Southend in 1920-21 and Stoke from 1923 to 1935.

SOUTHERN LEAGUE

Stoke spent six seasons playing Southern League football. In 1909-10 they were in the Division Two (Western Division – Section A), occupied Second Division status in 1910-11, 1913-14 and 1914-15

and were in Division One in 1911-12 and 1912-13.
Stoke's full record in the competition was:

Venue	P	W	D	L	F	A	Pts
Home	81	58	9	14	220	64	125
Away	81	29	14	38	123	152	72
Totals	162	87	23	52	343	216	197

Stoke's best seasons were in 1909-10 and 1914-15 when they were declared champions of their Division each time. They were runners-up on 1910-11, losing out on goal-average to Reading: 55-21 to 72-21.

When finishing at the foot of the table in 1912-13, the Potters were three points adrift of next-to-bottom Brentford and five behind Norwich City.

As champions of the Western Division (Section A) in 1909-10, Stoke played Hastings St Leonard's (winners of the Eastern Division) in what was called a championship decider on 25 April. The venue was The Victoria Ground and 3,000 fans saw Stoke win 6-0 with three of the goals coming from Billy Smith.

In fact, Stoke remained unbeaten in they 10 games they fulfilled in 1909-10 and won each of their 11 home matches in season 1910-11.

Stoke's best-ever Southern League win was achieved in their first game in the competition, an 11-0 scoreline v Merthyr Town (home) on 1 September 1909. Billy Smith (4), Arthur Griffiths (3) and Fred Tomlinson led the goal-rush in front of 4,000 fans.

Ebbw Vale were beaten 10-0 in April 1915 and Mid Rhondda 8-0 on 28 November 1914, both games at home. Other big wins were recorded over Barry (7-1) in November 1913 and Millwall Athletic (7-1) in April 1912. Jack Lenghan scored a hat-trick in the latter game.

The Potters' best away win in the Southern League came at Burton United on Christmas Day 1909 when they triumphed by 7-1, Amos Baddeley netting five times. United were beaten 5-0 at Stoke 48 hours later when in-form Baddeley again figured on the scoresheet.

Stoke's first defeat at Southern League level came in their 14th match when they went down 2-1 at Croydon Common on 12 October 1910.

Stoke lost 9-0 at Northampton in a Division One game in January 1913, their heaviest defeat at this level.

SOUTHPORT

Stoke's playing record against Southport is:
Football League

Venue	P	W	D	L	F	A
Home	1	1	0	0	4	0
Away	1	1	0	0	3	0
Totals	2	2	0	0	7	0

League Cup

	P	W	D	L	F	A
Away	1	1	0	0	2	1

The two League games between the clubs were played in season 1926-27 in Division Three North. A crowd of 7,826 witnessed Stoke's 4-0 home win while 3,500 were present at Haig Avenue. Harry Davies scored in each game.

Stoke's 2-1 League Cup triumph over Southport was achieved on 8 September 1971 when goals by Denis Smith and Jimmy Greenhoff earned that 2-1 scoreline in front of 10,225 fans.

Players with both clubs: Bill Dickie, Verdi Geoff Hickson, Sam Johnson, John McGallivaray, Bert Mitchell, Billy Robson, Henry Salmon and Alan Suddick.

Alan Ball senior was a player and manager of Southport and coach at Stoke City.

SPEARING, Anthony

Left-back Tony Spearing played in nine League games whilst on loan to Stoke City from Norwich City in November and December 1984. Born in Romford, Essex on 7 October 1964, he started his career as an apprentice at Carrow Road in 1980, turning professional two years later. Before leaving the Canaries for Leicester City in a £100,000 deal in July 1988, he also went on loan to Oxford United. From Filbert Street he joined Plymouth Argyle (July 1991), and in January 1993 was taken on a free transfer by Peterborough United. An enthusiastic player, he passed the milestone of 350 senior appearances as a pro in the 1996-97 season.

SPENCER, John Samuel

Outside-right Sam Spencer played in 17 League games for the Potters who he served from January 1921 to July 1923. Brought into the first team to replace Harry Crossthwaite, he was a useful competitor, born in Middlesbrough on 18 January 1902 who played initially for the amateur side Crook Town. On leaving Stoke, he signed for New Brighton and thereafter assisted Mid Rhondda (from June 1925), Aberdare (November 1925), Bristol Rovers (June 1928), Newry Town in Ireland (1929) and New Brighton again (August 1931 to June 1932). For two years, from September 1933, he acted as player-coach to Winsford United. A past president of the Wirral Youth Football League, Spencer died in Wallasey on 3 January 1987.

SPENCER, William

Defender Billy Spencer (deceased) had a fine career at The Victoria Ground. A Lancastrian, born in Nelson on 15 May 1903, he moved to The Victoria Ground from Hebden Bridge as an amateur in December 1924, turning professional four months later. An ex-mill worker, he was 'cool, calm and calculated' as they say, and could occupy either full-back role. Very conscious of how the game was being played, he and Bob McGrory formed a fine partnership, playing together for close on 10 seasons and helping the Potters win the Second Division title in 1933. Spencer made his debut in February 1926 v Portsmouth (when Alex Milne moved over to right-back) and he played his last and 354th competitive game for the Potters against Wolverhampton Wanderers in December 1935, handing over the right-back jersey to Bill Winstanley. He remained at The Victoria Ground for two more seasons, playing reserve-team football when required, and in June 1938 was transferred to Crewe Alexandra for £750. He retired in 1940, aged 36.

SPENNYMOOR UNITED

Stoke City have yet to play United at competitive level, but over the years a handful of players have been associated with both clubs, and they include: Jimmy Adam, Sam Davis and Arthur Tutin.

SPONSORSHIP

The first company to sponsor Stoke City FC and indeed, have their official logo on the front of the players' shirts, was Ricoh, in season

1981-82. They later had a second term of sponsorship (from October 1983).

H & R Johnson Tiles (Cristal Tiles) were Stoke's next main sponsors and this company was followed by Fradley Homes (1990-91), who, in turn were succeeded by Ansells (1991-93). Carling came next (1993-95), followed by, Broxap and Corby Ltd. (1995-96) and in the last season at The Victoria Ground, Stoke's shirts featured the name of the club's seventh different sponsor in 15 years, Asics.

In January 1997, The Britannia Building Society – one of the country's biggest mutuals – agreed to put £1.3 million into Stoke City Football Club – and The Potters' new ground was officially named after the company – The Britannia Stadium.

SPROSON, Archibald

One of the many one-match wonders to appear in Stoke's senior side, Sproson had his moment of glory when he lined up at inside-left in a 1-0 defeat by Coventry City in a Southern League game in January 1913. Born c.1890 in Stafford, he played for Stafford Rangers prior to Stoke and on leaving The Victoria Ground he joined forces with nearby Cannock.

STAFFORD RANGERS

Stoke's playing record against Rangers is:
Birmingham & District League

Venue	P	W	D	L	F	A
Home	3	2	1	0	10	4
Away	3	1	2	0	4	1
Totals	6	3	3	0	14	5

Unbeaten in their six Birmingham & District League games against local rivals Rangers, Stoke's best win of the three they registered was a 4-0 home success in April 1911, when 12,000 fans saw Billy Smith score twice.

Players with both clubs: Tony Allen, Sam Ashworth, Bill Bentley, George Berry, Darren Boughey, Albert Bullock, Lee Chapman, John Giblin, Wilf Hall, Charlie Hallam, Gerry Jones, Kevin Lewis, Aaron Lockett, Eric Lowell, Bert Miller, Bert Mitchell, Herbert Myatt, Alan Philpott, Alec Ormston, Reg Pickup, John Ritchie, Wally Rowland, Herby Salt, George Smart, Archie Sproson, George Tooth, Mart Watkins and Billy Whitehurst.

Mick Cullerton became Stoke's commercial manager after playing for Stafford Rangers. Harry Pearson played for Rangers during the 1920s and was Stoke's assistant trainer from 1936 to 1951. Harry Pearson played for Stafford Rangers (1920s) and later was Stoke's trainer for 15 years (to 1951).

STAFFORDSHIRE (SENIOR) CUP

Stoke first entered the Staffordshire Senior Cup in 1877-78 and they went on to win the trophy, beating Talke Rangers 1-0 in the final, having ousted Mow Cop 26-0 on the way.

The Potters retained the trophy the following season (defeating Cobridge 2-1 in the final) but it was not until 1913-14 that they again took the star prize in local football, overcoming Walsall 4-3 at Hanley in a terrific final.

Prior to this the Potters had appeared in seven semi-finals and were beaten by West Bromwich Albion 3-2 in the 1883 final which attracted a crowd of 6,500 to The Victoria Ground.

After the 1914-15 campaign, the Staffordshire Senior Cup was mainly competed for by the reserve teams of all major League clubs: Stoke, Port Vale, Walsall, West Bromwich Albion and Wolverhampton Wanderers etc.) with the Potters occasionally fielding their youth side.

STAINROD, Simon Allan

Goalscorer Stainrod had a useful playing career before going into management north of the border. Born in Sheffield on 1 February 1959, he began his scoring exploits with Sheffield United in 1977 and then served with Oldham Athletic, QPR, Sheffield Wednesday, Aston Villa, Stoke City (he cost £90,000 in December 1987 and stayed at The Victoria Ground until June 1989), Racing Club Strasbourg (on loan), Rouen, Falkirk and Dundee, the latter two as player-manager, and then Ayr United, also as manager (to September 1995). He netted seven times in 30 appearances for the Potters before his £70,000 transfer to Rouen. All told, in English League football, his record was a useful one – 107 goals scored in 387 appearances. He won England youth caps and played in the 1982 FA Cup Final for QPR. He also gained a Second Division championship medal with the same club the following year.

STALYBRIDGE CELTIC

Stoke's playing record against Celtic is:
Southern League

Home	1	0	1	0	1	1
Away	1	0	0	1	0	1
Totals	2	0	1	1	1	2

The two Southern League games took place in season 1914-15, and one player who has been associated with both clubs is Albert Ellis.

STANFORD, Thomas

Local-born defender Tom Stanford played in one FA Cup-tie for Stoke, lining up at right-back against Manchester at The Victoria Ground in the qualifying round in November 1883. He played for Tunstall Park and Congleton either side his time with Stoke and is said to have born in Tunstall c.1860.

STANLEY, Jesse

Another full-back who was given three first-team outings by Stoke in

March 1892 when he came into the side in place of the indisposed Tom Clare. Stoke lost all three games including a 5-3 reverse against Blackburn Rovers. A steady player, he was born in the Potteries c.1870 and had a few games with Northwich Victoria before and after his brief association with Stoke.

STATHAM, Derek James

During the late 1970s and early '80s, Derek Statham was regarded as the second left-back in country – behind Kenny Sansom. And it was Sansom who denied him a regular place in the England team. Born in Whitmore Reans, Wolverhampton on 24 March 1959, and a pupil at St Mary's Primary and St Edmund's Junior Schools, Statham played as a junior with West Bromwich Albion from 1974 and made his League debut for the Baggies against Stoke City at The Victoria Ground in December 1975, scoring in a 2-0 win. He turned professional in April of the following year and as a fine attacking player, went on to appear in 378 games during his time at The Hawthorns, gaining an FA Youth Cup winners' medal and starring in two FA Cup semi-finals as well as a League Cup semi-final. He also won three full England caps in 1982-83 to go with two he collected with the 'B' team, six he won at Under-21 level and seven he gained as a youth player. After a proposed £250,000 transfer to Liverpool had fallen through, Statham left West Brom for Southampton in August 1987 for £100,000. Two years later he moved to The Victoria Ground for £75,000 (a fee paid in full after a set number of appearances) and although he was now past his best, he still gave Stoke fans good value in 49 games (one goal). In August 1991 he left Stoke for Walsall on a free transfer and wound down his career with a spell at Telford United before retiring in 1995.

STATON, Frank

Centre-forward Staton played in each of Stoke's first four League games at the start of the initial campaign of 1888-89 (scoring two goals). Born in Hanley c.1864, he had been with the club the previous season, joining from Goldenhill Wanderers. Staton left The Victoria Ground in 1889 for the Wolverhampton railway works side, Stafford Road.

STEEL, Frederick

Amateur right-half Steel spent two months with Stoke, playing in the opening three games of the 1909-10 season. Born locally c.1884, he assisted Ashwood Villa before serving the Potters and later served with non-League Lancaster Town among others.

STEELE, Edwin

Steele was brought into the side at left-back for the vital end-of-season Test Match v Manchester United at Burslem on 27 April 1895, replacing Jack Eccles. Born in Stoke c.1870 he did not figure at the club the following season.

STEELE, Frederick Charles

Born at Hanley on 6 May 1916, Freddie Steele did splendidly in schoolboy football signing for Stoke City in the summer of 1931, being told by manager Tom Mather that he would work in the offices and play for the club's nursery side, Downings Collieries, until he was old enough to turn professional. That's how confident Mather was that

Mark Stein

Steele would make the grade. Come June 1933 and the appropriate signing on forms were produced, Steele put pen to paper and after that he became a goalscoring supremo in the eyes of the Potters' supporters. Nicknamed Nobby he made his senior debut v Huddersfield Town in December 1934 and scored his first goal in a 3-0 home win over West Bromwich Albion on the Boxing Day (helping his side win 3-0). Thereafter the goals flowed – and up to June 1949, he netted a grand total of 220 for Stoke City – 140 in the Football League, 19 in the FA Cup and a further 81 in wartime competitions. He appeared in 346 first-team matches (95 in the war) and figured in a terrific forward-line which also included Stan Matthews, Tommy Sale and Joe Johnson. In September 1936 Steele played for the Football League XI v The Irish League in Belfast, scoring in a 3-2 defeat. Three weeks later he won the first of his six full England caps and in April 1937 was one of three Stoke City players who lined up against Scotland at Hampden Park in front of 135,000 fans. Steele did well in that 3-1 reverse and went on the end-of-season tour to Scandinavia, scoring twice in big wins over Sweden and Finland. When Europe went to war in 1939, Steele was only 23 years of age. Unfortunately he played very little competitive football during the first part of the hostilities, and when peacetime soccer returned he was 30 – but still eager to play in the First Division. Indeed, during the 1945-46 transitional campaign, he scored 49 goals in 43 League and FA Cup appearances. Three years later, after having given Stoke City magnificent service, and by now suffering with a nagging knee injury, Steele left The Victoria Ground to become player-manager of Mansfield Town (June 1949). He later went to assist Port Vale (again as player-manager) and led them to the Third Division North championship and FA Cup semi-finals in 1953-54. He also spent a short time in South Africa. Earlier, in 1939, Steele shocked a few people by announcing his retirement, stating that he was suffering from depression. After being treated by a psychiatrist he subsequently made a successful return to football, scoring ten goals in his next five matches. Steele died on 23 April 1976.

NB: When at the peak of fitness Steele also hurdled for Staffordshire as well as competing in the men's 4 x 100 yards sprint relay.

STEELE, Timothy Wesley.

Tim Steele played over 60 games on the wing (as a wide midfielder) for Shrewsbury Town (from December 1985) before transferring to Wolverhampton Wanderers in February 1989 for a fee of £80,000. He was taken on loan by the Potters in February/March 1992, scoring once in seven League games. After leaving Molineux he signed for Bradford City on a free transfer in July 1993, and later assisted Hereford United (from January 1994) and Exeter City (1996-97). Steele was born in Coventry on 1 December 1967.

STEIN, Mark Earl Sean

During his first spell at The Victoria Ground (September 1991 to October 1993) Mark Stein established himself as a fine goalscorer, idolised by the Boothen End and a player who became a Wembley hero when he netted the winning goal in the Autoglass Trophy Final against Stockport County. Born in Cape Town, South Africa, on 28 January 1966, he was a junior at Kenilworth Road before turning professional with Luton Town in January 1984. An

England Under-19 international (three caps) and a League Cup winner in 1988, Stein scored 23 goals in 71 games for Luton, and after a loan spell with Aldershot, was transferred to Queen's Park Rangers for £300,000 in August 1988. He never really made his mark at Loftus Road and in September 1989 moved to Oxford United, for whom he claimed 18 goals in 92 appearances before switching to The Victoria Ground for a fee of £100,000. In 133 League and Cup outings for the Potters 'Steino' averaged a goal every two games, scoring 68 times, collecting a Third Division championship medal in 1993 to go with his AGT prize won the previous season. In October 1993 Stein left Stoke to sign for Premiership side Chelsea for £1.4 million. But after a reasonable first season in the top flight, he was plagued by injuries and then found himself out in the cold following the arrival of player-manager Ruud Gullit, and in November 1996 Stein returned to The Victoria Ground, this time on a two-month loan, when he added a further four goals in 11 appearances to his Potters' record. As a teenager Stein won England youth and Under-19 honours.

STENTIFORD, George Robert

Half-back Stentiford was born in Brentford, London on 7 May 1900. After serving with Old Kingstonians, he played next for Huddersfield Town (from May 1920) and joined Stoke in March 1923 after failing to make the first XI at Leeds Road. He played in just 11 League games for the Potters up to October 1924 when he moved to Stockport County. He then spent two seasons at Edgeley Park, making 45 first-team appearances before re-entering non-League soccer with Guildford United (August 1926), retiring in 1932. Stentiford died at Guildford on 1 February 1976.

STEVENSON, William

Stevenson was a stylish wing-half, exceedingly good on the ball, a fine passer and one of the few players sold by the legendary Bill Shankly to another First Division club. Born in Leith on 26 October 1939, Stevenson cost Stoke £48,000 when he moved from Anfield in December 1967, having appeared in over 200 games for the Reds helping them twice win the First Division title (1964 and 1966) and the FA Cup (1965) as well as gaining a runners-up medal in the European Cup-winners' Cup (1966). He commenced his career in his native Scotland with Edna Hearts and after a spell with Dalkeith Thistle he signed for Rangers. He quickly claimed a first-team place at Ibrox and went on to win both League championship and Scottish FA Cup winners' medals with the Glasgow club as well as Schoolboy international honours besides representing the Scottish League. He moved to Liverpool in October 1962. Scorer of seven goals in 107 senior appearances for the Potters, Stevenson missed the team's great FA Cup runs in the early 1970s, and he also sat out the 1972 League Cup Final win over Chelsea. A fractured leg disrupted his final year at The Victoria Ground and in July 1973, he left the club, moving on a free transfer to Tranmere Rovers, later serving in the NASL with Vancouver Whitecaps. On retiring Stevenson went into business with his Stoke colleague, Eric Skeels, in Newcastle (Staffs).

STEVENTON, Thomas William

Amateur goalkeeper Ted Steventon (now deceased) made just three League appearances for Stoke at the end of the 1920-21 season when he replaced Percy Knott, keeping a clean sheet on his debut against Bristol City. Born in Bunbury on 8 September 1898, he joined the Potters as an amateur from Aston Villa in March 1921 and remained with the club until May 1922 when he transferred to Molineux, as part cover for Noel George. He rounded off his career with Tettenhall. Steventon died on 5 March 1971.
NB: There have been references in the past made to an Edwin or Herbert H.Steventon.

STIRLING, John

Outside-right Jock Stirling had an interesting career which spanned 15 years. Born in Glasgow c.1886, he played for Clyde, Middlesbrough (1911-14), Bradford City (briefly) and Bradford Park Avenue (1914-15) before signing for Stoke in July 1919. He scored once in 21 League and FA Cup outings for the Potters, up to March 1930, when he was transferred to Coventry City. He then returned home to see out his playing days with Alloa Athletic (1920-21). Stirling made over 100 appearances whilst at Ayresome Park and 34 for Park Avenue.

STOCKPORT COUNTY

Stoke's playing record against County is:
Football League

Venue	P	W	D	L	F	A
Home	9	6	2	1	14	5
Away	9	2	3	4	8	13
Totals	18	8	5	5	22	18

FA Cup

Home	1	0	0	1	0	2

Autoglass Trophy

Away	1	1	0	0	1	0

The clubs first met at League level in season 1907-08 (Division Two) when Stoke completed the double over County, winning 1-0 at home and 2-1 away.

Stoke's best League win over Stockport is 3-0, achieved twice, each time at The Victoria Ground, on 27 December 1924 (Division Two) and on 29 August 1925. George Clennell scored twice in the second game which started off Stoke's League programme for that season.

County's best win (goal difference) over the Potters in the same competition is 3-1 in October 1919. They have also claimed two 2-0 wins, in March 1921 and August 1924.

Under 10,000 fans witnessed County's shock 2-0 FA Cup Third Round win at Stoke in January 1997.

Stoke beat County 1-0 in the Final of the Autoglass Trophy at Wembley in 1992, striker Mark Stein scoring the all-important goal (See AUTOGLASS TROPHY).

Players with both clubs: Scott Barrett, Tom Brittleton, Billy Burns, Albert Cook, Harry Crossthwaite, Cecil Eastwood, Neil Franklin, Herby Hales, David Herd, Dennis Herod, Darren Hope (Stoke reserve), George Kelly, Peter McArdle, Joey Mawson, Carl Muggleton, John Nibloe, Alf Owen, Barry Siddall, George Stentiford, Eric Skeels (County trialist), Eddie Stuart, Bill Tompkinson, Derek Ward, and Brett Williams.

Brian Doyle was a Stoke player who later managed County while Asa Hartford played for Stockport and later became assistant manager at Stoke.

STOKE RAMBLERS

When the club was formed in 1868 the first name used was that of Stoke Ramblers and it was two old Carthusians, Henry John Almond and William Macdonald Matthews, who suggested the title. They were, at the time, apprentices at the local railway depot and were instrumental in getting football established in a competitive form in Stoke itself.

Stoke Ramblers played their first friendly game against Mr E.W.May's 15 on the Stoke Victoria Cricket ground on 17 October 1868, It was a 15-a-side contest with varying rules and finished in a 1-1 draw.

The cricket club's secretary was Mr J.W.Thomas who was also honorary secretary of the Stoke Ramblers. In 1870 the name Ramblers was dropped from the club's title, and until 1925, it was simply Stoke FC.

STOKOE, Graham

A six-foot midfield player, born in Newcastle-on-Tyne on 17 December 1975, Stokoe, after representing Durham County Schools, and Northumberland FA, had a brief spell with Newcastle United as a junior before graduating through the ranks at The Victoria Ground. He made his senior debut for the Potters in season 1996-97, although he did break into League football while on loan with Hartlepool United in February 1996, and finished the season with two outings for Stoke.

STOURBRIDGE

Stoke's playing record against Stourbridge is:
Birmingham & District League

Venue	P	W	D	L	F	A
Home	3	3	0	0	10	2
Away	3	0	1	2	3	9
Totals	6	3	1	2	13	11

FA Cup

Home	1	1	0	0	11	0

In their third Birmingham & District League game with the Potters, Stourbridge raced to a convincing 5-0 home win in October 1909, but Stoke quickly gained revenge, winning their home fixture 6-1 (February 1910) – this being the best of their three League wins over the Glassboys.

Stoke's 11-0 romp in the preliminary round of the FA Cup in September 1914 was a personal triumph for Arty Watkin who netted a five-timer. Fred McCarthy weighed in with a hat-trick and the crowd was given as 1,500.

Players with both clubs: Gary Hackett, Wilf 'Winkie' Phillips, goalkeeper Ike Turner and Jack Whitehouse, while 'Chic' Bates also played for Stourbridge (where he was a champion goalscorer) and later became assistant manager at Stoke.

STUART, Edward Albert

South African full-back Eddie Stuart was a fine footballer. As hard as they come, he was quick, competitive (when required) and a battler to the end. He tackled hard and fair, and always gave 100 per cent out on the park. Born in Johannesburg on 12 May 1931, he played intermediate football in his homeland for Rangers FC before joining Wolverhampton Wanderers as a professional in January 1951. He went on to appear in well over 300 games for Wolves, and surprisingly made his League debut in the centre-forward position against West Bromwich Albion in April 1952, scoring a goal to celebrate the occasion, his only one for the Black Country club. He helped Wolves win the First Division championship in 1954, 1958 and 1959 and then added an FA Cup winners' medal to his tally in 1960. In July 1962 he was transferred to Stoke City for £8,000, and in his first season at The Victoria Ground skippered the Potters to the Second Division title. He netted twice in 71 games for Stoke up to August 1964 when he moved across country to Tranmere Rovers for £4,000. In July 1966 he signed for Stockport County and with along with several other seasoned professionals at Edgeley Park, helped County take the Fourth Division crown in 1967. On retiring from competitive football with 510 League appearances under his belt, Stuart had an excellent spell with Worcester City (1968-70) making 110 appearances. Thereafter, he managed the the non-League club and in the late 1970s/early '80s while living in Tettenhall, he played in various charity matches around the Midlands as well as running a successful hairdressing business with shops in Wolverhampton, Codsall and Newcastle-under-Lyme. He returned to South Africa in 1996, leaving his daughter to continue to live and work in Wolverhampton.

NB: In 1952, Stuart had to return to South Africa after being infected by a mystery illness. Thankfully he responded to treatment and came back to England to continue his footballing career.

STURGESS, Albert

Born in Etruria on 21 October 1882, Sturgess was 42 years, 116 days old when he played his last senior match for Norwich City in February 1925. A determined full-back with a strong kick, superb anticipation and reliability, he was nicknamed 'hairpin' by his colleagues and arrived at Stoke from Tunstall Cresswells in July 1900. He did well in the Reserves and gained a first-team place in 1905, going from strength to strength to amass a fine record of four goals in 135 first-team appearances before transferring to Sheffield United in June 1908, playing in every position, including goalkeeper, for the Blades with whom he gained an FA Cup winners' medal with in 1915. After World War One he signed for Norwich City (aged 43), for whom he played until 1925, and on retiring returned to Sheffield where he opened a crockery shop in Eccleshall Road. Sturgess, who was also a fine crown green bowler, died in Sheffield on 16 July 1957.

STURRIDGE, Simon Andrew

Fast-raiding striker, with good technique and goalscoring ability, Sturridge was one of several Birmingham City players who subsequently found their way to The Victoria Ground under Lou Macari's management. Born in Birmingham on 9 December 1969, Sturridge joined the junior ranks at St Andrew's in June 1985, after attending William Cowper, Duddeston Manor and St George's schools. He turned professional in three years later (July 1988). He went on to score 38 goals in 186 appearances for the Blues, gaining a winners' medal at Wembley in the 1991 Leyland DAF Cup Final. His move to Stoke cost £75,000 in September 1993 and in his first three campaigns at The Victoria Ground, 'Studger' did well, netting 15 goals in 80 appearances, including an excellent hat-trick in a 4-2 win over Southend in November 1995. He was injured early on in 1996-97 (after five games) and was out of action after that.

NB: Sturridge's brother, Dean, plays for Derby County (1991-97)

SUBSTITUTES

Substitutes were introduced to the Football League in August 1965, and the first number-12 to be used by Stoke was forward Keith Bebbington who replaced Dennis Viollet in the club's opening Division One fixture at Arsenal.

Stoke's first goalscoring substitute at League level was Welsh international John Mahoney, who as on target against Leicester City at The Victoria Ground on 24 August 1965 – his strike proving to be the winner.

Under the single substitute rule, Stoke utilised a record 29 number-12s during season 1982-83; the most used by the Potters since the two subs law was introduced in 1986 has been 65 in 1994-95.

Striker Carl Saunders holds the Stoke record for most substitute appearances for the club – he made a total of 41 (34 in the League) during his time at The Victoria Ground: 1983-90. Forward Martin Carruthers had 37 outings as sub over three years: 1993-96.

Defender John Dreyer holds the record of most substitute appearances for the Potters in one season. He made a total of 17 (16 in the League and one in the Anglo-Italian Cup) in 1995-96.

Nyrere 'Tony' Kelly came off the bench 15 times in 1990-91 (13 in the League and two in Cup-ties) while Carruthers made 13 sub appearances in 1993-94 and 14 in 1995-96.

Ian Gibbons holds the record for the shortest career as a Stoke City player. He came on as a substitute against Crystal Palace three minutes from the end of a Second Division League game in April 1988 – his only outing for the club. Shaun Wade also had made just one substitute appearance for the Potters v Sheffield United in 1994.

SUDDICK, Alan

Born in Chester-le-Street on 2 May 1944, Suddick was a very cultured inside-forward who was certainly unlucky not to have won a full England cap, particularly when he was playing for Blackpool. Stoke fans never saw the best of his talents as manager Tony Waddington cast his net far and wide in an attempt to bring in quality players at a relatively low cost when the club was raising cash in a bold effort to fend off the bank manager. All told Suddick, who also played for Newcastle United (his first club), Southport (on loan) and Bury, scored 108 goals in a total of 503 League games between 1961 and 1978, including 64 strikes in 310 outings with the Seasiders of Bloomfield Road. He was at The Victoria Ground from December

1976 to August 1977, appearing in just nine senior games, netting one goal, in a 3-1 defeat at West Bromwich Albion. He won two England Under-23 caps and also played for his country at youth team level.

SUNDAY FOOTBALL

The first time Stoke played a competitive game on a Sunday was 20 January 1974 when they met Bolton Wanderers in a third round FA Cup-tie at Burnden Park. The Trotters won 3-2, John Byron scoring a hat-trick, with John Ritchie and Sean Haslegrave replying for the Potters. The gate was 39,138.

A week later, on 27 January, Stoke played their first League match on the Sabbath, taking on, and beating Chelsea 1-0 at The Victoria Ground. Geoff Hurst hit the all-important goal from the penalty spot just nine minutes from time in front of a near 32,000 crowd.

SUNDERLAND

Stoke's playing record against the Wearsiders is:

Football League

Venue	P	W	D	L	F	A
Home	56	27	13	16	81	55
Away	56	7	13	36	38	110
Totals	112	34	26	52	119	165

FA Cup

Venue	P	W	D	L	F	A
Home	4	1	3	0	6	4
Away	5	1	2	2	4	8
Totals	9	2	5	2	10	12

League Cup

Venue	P	W	D	L	F	A
Home	1	1	0	0	3	0
Away	1	1	0	0	2	0
Totals	2	2	0	0	5	0

Stoke and Sunderland first met at Football League level in season 1891-92. The Wearsiders won 3-1 at The Victoria Ground and 4-1 at Roker Park.

Tom Hyslop scored Stoke's first-ever penalty against Sunderland in a 5-0 League win in March 1896 – this being the Potters' best-ever victory over the Wearsiders.

Freddie Steele scored a hat-trick in Stoke's 5-3 home League win over Sunderland in March 1937 – two months later the Wearsiders went to Wembley and beat Preston 3-1 in the FA Cup Final.

Sunderland's best League triumph over Stoke is 6-1 – at Roker park in a First Division match in November 1900. That day Alec Raisbeck score one of the Wearsiders' goals. He later joined Stoke.

Other big Sunderland wins include those of 4-0 at home in October 1893; 4-0 again at Roker Park in December 1897 and 5-2 at Stoke in January 1895.

The two First Division games between Stoke and Sunderland over Christmas 1949 were seen by a combined total of 91,881 spectators. There were 50,246 at Roker Park when the Wearsiders won 3-0 and then 41,635 at The Victoria Ground to see the Potters gain revenge with a 2-1 victory.

Sunderland were elected to the Football League in place of Stoke for season 1890-91.

Stoke and Sunderland were involved in a promotion battle from Division Two in 1962-63. In the end Stoke went up as champions, but Sunderland finished third, beaten into second spot by Chelsea on goal-average. The crucial games between the two teams took place over Easter. Stoke drew 0-0 at Roker Park in front of 62,138 fans and then three days later won 2-1 at The Victoria Ground on 15 April 1963 when the turn-out was 42,366.

In the late 1970s (after the Wearsiders had returned to the First Division) there were three successive 0-0 League draws between the clubs and there followed three successive 1-0 scorelines, two in favour of Sunderland.

In the four League games played between the teams in seasons 1994-95 and 1995-96, Stoke scored only one goal.

The first two FA Cup meetings were played in 1891-92 when Sunderland won a third qualifying round replay by 4-0 after a 2-2 draw at Stoke.

It took Stoke three goes to knock Sunderland out of the FA Cup in 1931-32. They eventually won a fourth-round tie after a second replay at Maine Road by 2-1.

The first League Cup-tie was won 3-0 by Stoke at home in September 1972 (Jimmy Greenhoff scored twice) while the Potters also won the second clash by 2-0 at Roker Park in August 1978.

Players with both clubs: Keith Bertschin, Paul Bracewell, Lee Chapman, Jimmy Dale, Tony Ford, Patsy Gallacher, Howard Gayle, Jimmy Gemmill, Ernie Hodkin, Brian Horne, Tom Hyslop, George Kinnell, Willie Maxwell, Iain Munro, Calvin Palmer, Charlie Parker, Mark Prudhoe, Dr Leigh Richmond Roose, Tommy Sale, Bill Sawyers, Les Scott, Vic Shore, Barry Siddall, Dennis Tueart, Loek Ursem, Mart Watkins, Dave Watson and Billy Whitehurst.

Alan Durban managed both clubs and later became Sunderland's chief scout (1995-97) while Denis Smith was a player with Stoke and later boss at Roker Park when he had former Stokie Viv Busby as his assistant. Gilbert Swinburne Glidden was a 1930s player with Sunderland who later became physiotherapist-trainer of Stoke City (1952-54).

SUNDERLAND ALBION

Stoke's playing record against Albion is:

Football Alliance

Venue	P	W	D	L	F	A
Home	1	0	1	0	1	1
Away	1	0	1	0	1	1
Totals	2	0	2	0	2	2

Albion finished runners-up to Stoke in the Football Alliance in season 1890-91 – the only campaign Stoke played in this League.

SWANSEA TOWN (CITY)

Stoke's playing record against the Swans is:

Football League

Venue	P	W	D	L	F	A
Home	22	14	5	3	59	19
Away	22	4	10	8	28	34
Totals	44	18	15	11	87	53

Southern League

Venue	P	W	D	L	F	A
Home	2	1	0	1	1	1
Away	2	1	0	1	3	3
Totals	4	2	0	2	4	4

FA Cup

Venue	P	W	D	L	F	A
Home	1	0	1	0	2	2
Away	4	0	0	4	5	15
Totals	5	0	1	4	7	17

League Cup
Home	2	0	2	0	1	1
Away	2	2	0	0	4	1
Totals	4	2	2	0	5	2

Stoke's best League win over Swansea (goals scored) is 6-2 at The Victoria Ground in a Second Division match on 9 December 1957 when George Kelly (3) and Johnny King (2) led the goal-charge in front of 24,113 fans. The Potters also claimed four 5-0 home victories – in 1928, 1930, 1953 and 1955.

Swansea's best League triumph over the Potters is 4-1, achieved at The Vetch Field on 19 April 1958 when the crowd topped 23,300.

In season 1954-55, the Potters scored nine goals against Swansea, beating them 4-1 at home and 5-3 away.

Stoke were beaten 6-3 by Swansea in a third round FA Cup-tie in Wales in January 1926, and in the same round by 4-1 in January 1935.

After their mammoth fourth round FA Cup-tie with Bury in January 1955, the Potters went out at the next stage, beaten 3-1 by Swansea at The Vetch Field.

Goals from Garth Crooks (2) and Paul Randall gave Stoke a 3-1 home win over the Swans in a second round, second leg League Cup game at The Victoria Ground in September 1979 (Stoke went through 4-2 on aggregate).

Players with both clubs: Gilbert Brookes, Walter Bussey, Alan Curtis, Frank Elliott, Robbie James, Roy John, Bob Jones, John Mahoney, John Moore, Dai Nicholas, David Puckett, Paul Richardson, Valentine Rouse, Jimmy Swarbrick, Ray Wallace and John Williams.

Goalkeeper Harry Gregg was a player with Stoke and later manager at Swansea.

SWARBRICK, James

Born Lytham St Anne's in 1881, outside-left Swarbrick played for Blackpool Red Star, Marton Combination and Blackpool Etrurians before entering League football with Blackburn Rovers in November 1901. He then served with Brentford (June 1903), Grimsby Town (August 1905), Oldham Athletic (May 1907) and Southport Central (November 1909) before joining Stoke on 19 May 1910. He left the Potters for Port Vale in August 1911 and rounded off his career with Swansea Town – December 1912 to May 1916 – when he retired. He won a Welsh Cup winners' medal in 1913. Swarbrick, who on his day was an exceptionally good ball-player, suffered a compound fracture of the leg playing for Oldham against Bradford City at Valley Parade in September 1907. The injury kept him out of action for over a year. He had made his Latics' debut against Stoke earlier that month, scoring in a 3-1 win. Swarbrick netted four times in 28 games for Vale and made only three appearances for Stoke.

SWEETINGS FIELD

Sweetings Field, owned by Alderman R.Sweeting, the Lord Mayor of Stoke, was where the Potters played their home matches from the summer of 1875 until early March 1878. On average up to 250 fans attended each game with the admission price set at one old penny, raising to 2d (1p) after the first year. Stoke's biggest win at The Sweetings was their 26-0 thrashing of luckless Mow Cop in a Staffordshire Cup-tie in 1877.

SWINDON TOWN

Stoke's playing record against Town is:
Football League
Venue	P	W	D	L	F	A
Home	5	3	2	0	6	2
Away	5	1	0	4	1	13
Totals	10	4	2	4	7	15

Southern League
Home	2	0	1	1	2	5
Away	2	0	0	2	2	6
Totals	4	0	1	3	4	11

FA Cup
Home	1	0	0	1	0	1
Away	2	1	1	0	4	2
Totals	3	1	1	1	4	3

League Cup
Home	1	0	1	0	2	2
Away	1	0	0	1	1	2
Totals	2	0	1	1	3	4

The Potters' biggest Football League win over the Robins is 2-0 – achieved at The Victoria Ground in December 1996. Mark Stein scored both goals in front of 10,102 spectators.

Stoke's only League win at Swindon came in April 1995 when they were victors by 1-0, Toddy Orlygsson scoring in the 36th minute before a 10,549 crowd.

The Robins hammered Stoke 6-0 at The County Ground in a Second Division match on 4 November 1989 with Stoke's Dave Bamber (ex-Swindon) scoring an own-goal.

Playing in the Southern League in 1911-12, Stoke were beaten 3-0 at Swindon on Christmas Day and 4-1 at The County Ground 24 hours later.

Two goals by George Mountford helped Stoke to a 3-1 FA Cup win over Swindon in 1948-49.

Players with both clubs: Paul Allen, Dave Bamber, Percy Brooke, Arthur 'Sailor' Capes, Lloyd Davies, Steve Foley, Tom Godfrey, Dave Hockaday, Fred Houldsworth, Sam Johnson, Chris Kamara, John McClelland, Frank Richardson, Paul Richardson, Keith Scott and Mark Walters.

Lou Macari managed Swindon Town before his first spell in charge at The Victoria Ground, while Louis Page played for Stoke and later managed Swindon. 'Chic' Bates played for Swindon and later joined Macari as his assistant at both Stoke and The County Ground.

TALBOT, Brian Ernest

Talbot was a very competitive midfielder who was born in Norwich on 21 July 1953. On leaving school he became an apprentice with Ipswich Town, signing professional forms for the Portman Road club in July 1970. He spent the next eight-and-a-half years with Ipswich, amassing a fine record of 32 goals in 227 senior appearances, gaining an FA Cup winners' medal in 1978. In January 1979, he was transferred to Arsenal for £450,000 and within six months had collected his second FA Cup winners' prize, but it was third time unlucky when he ended up a beaten finalist with the Gunners in 1980. Talbot played in 316 games for Arsenal (45 goals) before moving to Watford in June 1985 for £150,000. He made 60 appearances for the Hornets (8 goals) and in October 1986 switched to Stoke for £25,000. He did well at The Victoria Ground, claiming seven goals in 64 senior outings, up to January 1988, when he joined West Bromwich Albion, also for £25,000. He later became player-manager at The Hawthorns, a position he held until January 1991 when he was sacked following a 4-2 FA Cup defeat against non-League Woking. After leaving Albion, Talbot worked briefly for Capital Radio, assisted Fulham (early March 1991), Aldershot (as player-manager from late March to November 1991)) and Sudbury Town (1992-93). He then got involved in a syndicate which bought Kettering Town (March 1993) and was associated with that club for a short time before becoming player-coach/manager of Hibernians (Malta). But after leading them to their domestic League title in 1995, he resigned his position in the following spring. After a spell out of the game he returned as coach of Rushden & Diamonds in February 1997 taking over as manager a month later. Capped six times by England at senior level, Talbot also played in one Under-21 and eight 'B' internationals and accumulated more than 750 League and Cup appearances in his career, scoring over 100 goals. He was chairman of the PFA in the late 1980s.

NB: *Talbot is only one of a dozen footballers to play for and against the same club in a Wembley FA Cup Final (Ipswich and Arsenal).*

TALKE RANGERS

The North Staffordshire team were the first visitors to The Victoria Athletic Ground when they were defeated by Stoke 1-0 in a friendly in March 1878.

The very next month, Stoke again defeated Talke Rangers by the same scoreline in the Final of the Staffordshire Cup – their first trophy success.

England international full-back Tommy Clare, one of Stoke star performers in their early years, also played for Talke Rangers.

TAPAI, Ernest

Born in Subotica, Yugoslavia on 14 February 1967, Tapei became a naturalised Australian and went on to win over 30 full caps for his adopted country where he played in turn, for Melbourne Hungaria, South Melbourne Hellas, Melbourne Hungaria (again), Footscray, Sunshine George Cross and Adelaide City from where he joined Stoke City for £40,000 in October 1992. He only made one substitute appearance for the Potters – coming on as a forward against Crewe Alexandra in an Autoglass trophy match in January 1993. He left The Victoria Ground for the Portuguese side, Estoril, two months later on a free transfer.

TAYLOR, Frank

Barnsley-born Taylor was manager of Stoke City for eight years – from June 1952 to June 1960. During his time in charge, the Potters played 336 League games of which they won 138 and drew 69. He was a pre-war full-back with Wolverhampton Wanderers, making 54 senior appearances, one coming in the 1939 FA Cup Final defeat by Portsmouth. He also won an England cap during the war, playing against Scotland at Hampden Park in April 1944 before 133,000 fans. Forced to retire through injury at the age of 28, he was taken on the training/coaching staff at Molineux before taking over as manager of Scarborough in 1948. From there he became Major Frank Buckley's managerial assistant at Hull City and did a similar job at Leeds United prior to his move to The Victoria Ground. Taylor was a track-suit manager who loved to be out on the field training with the players and he was so keen that he placed a sign in the dressing room which read 'Are you 90 minutes fit? It's the last 20 minutes that count – train for it.' After suffering relegation at the end of his first season in charge, the Potters spent the rest of Taylor's reign in the Second Division before he was sacked by the club's chairman Albert Henshall in 1960.

NB: *Taylor's brother, Jack, played with him at Molineux (See MANAGERS).*

TAYLOR, Henry

Right or outside-left Harry Taylor had a fine goalscoring record with Stoke, netting 11 times in 26 games during his time with the club – which lasted from February 1929 (first as an amateur, then as a professional from June 1929) to July 1932. Born in Hanley in 1912, he joined the Potters from Stoke St Mary's, initially as a reserve to the two Bobbys, Archibald and Liddle. He left The Victoria Ground for Liverpool where he spent four years, scoring six goals in 69 appearances for the Reds while occupying every forward position.

TAYLOR, Henry George

Utility inside-forward Harry Taylor joined Stoke in the summer of 1909. He scored four times in 10 League games during his only campaign with the club before transferring to Huddersfield Town in May 1910. Born in Fegg Hayes August 1892 and a former North Staffordshire Schoolboy representative, Taylor was a hefty player, who started out with Chell Heath. He then served with his local club, Fegg Hayes, from where he moved to The Victoria Ground. He had 16 games for Huddersfield (5 goals scored) before Port Vale paid £30 for his services in May 1912. He never kicked a ball in earnest for the Valiants who quickly transferred him to Manchester City for £300 four weeks after signing him. He remained there until 1921.

TELEVISION

The first time Stoke City had a game televised live was in April 1965 when a World XI came to The Victoria Ground to play a Potters XI in Stanley Matthews' farewell match. That evening Eurovision beamed the night's action (a 10 goal thriller which ended 6-4 to Matthews' Stoke side) to an estimated 112 million viewers.

At the end of that 1964-65 season, while on tour, Stoke were shown live on Russian television when they opposed Spartak Moscow.

The Potters were featured in a live match on English TV for the first time via BSkyB Sports Channel on 21 November 1990. That night they took on non-League Telford United in an FA Cup first round replay at The Victoria Ground when Lee Sandford netted the game's only goal to send Stoke through to the next stage.

TELFORD UNITED (Wellington Town)

Stoke's playing record against United is:

Birmingham & District League

Venue	P	W	D	L	F	A
Home	3	3	0	0	18	2
Away	3	0	2	1	2	3
Totals	6	3	2	1	20	5

FA Cup

	P	W	D	L	F	A
Home	2	1	1	0	1	0
Away	2	0	1	1	1	2
Totals	4	1	2	1	2	2

Stoke beat Wellington (Telford) 7-0 in the first meeting between the two clubs in the Birmingham & District League on 10 October 1908. Vic Horrocks netted a hat-trick for the Potters in front of 5,000 fans. The following season (on 19 March 1910) Stoke won their home game 5-1 and later that year, on 31 December 1910, Wellington were crushed 6-1 at The Victoria Ground, when Alf Smith weighed in with a treble.

Wellington's only League win over the Potters was 1-0 success at home in November 1909.

After the sides had drawn 0-0 in the first game, Lee Sandford scored Stoke's dramatic winner against non-League Telford in the FA Cup third-round replay at The Victoria Ground in November 1990 when BSkyB Sports beamed the pictures live round the country. And then battling Telford came to Stoke again the following year and held the Potters 0-0 in front of 11,880 fans before landing the knockout punch with a shock 2-1 victory on their own soil before a crowd of 3,709.

Stoke met Telford three times in friendly matches in the 1908s, winning 3-1 in front of 684 spectators in 1980, by 3-0 in 1987 (behind closed doors) and then drawing 3-3 in 1988 before 1,300 fans. All the encounters were staged at Bucks Head.

Players with both clubs: Arthur Beachill, Cliff Carr, Paul Dyson, Lee Fowler, Mark Harrison, Kevin Lewis, John Lumsdon, Wilf Mayer, Bert Mitchell, Ernie Mullineux, Steve Nelson (Stoke reserve), John Ruggiero and Derek Statham. The following ex-Stokies all later managed Telford (Wellington Town): George Antonio, Gordon Banks, Wayne Clarke, Gerry Daly, Neil Franklin and Geoff Hurst, the last five being full internationals for their respective country.

TEMPEST, William

Billy Tempest was born in Stoke-on-Trent on 8 January 1893 and after a brief, but successful spell, with Trentham, he joined Stoke as an amateur in 1912. Standing only 5ft 5ins tall, he was a courageous footballer, who occupied the left-wing with great desire. A positive, attacking player, he was a huge favourite with the Stoke supporters and made 38 appearances in the Southern League prior to the outbreak of World War One. After the hostilities had ended he once more established himself on the left-wing and played on for another five seasons, finally leaving The Victoria ground for neighbouring Port Vale for £1,000 in June 1924. All told he scored 30 goals in 217 senior games for the Potters and had 45 outing for the Vale before retiring in May 1926 through injury.

NB: When Tempest was sold to the Vale, there was a dispute regarding the transfer fee and in the end the League stepped in and it was mutually agreed that £1,000 would be paid to Stoke.

TENNANT, John Willie

Jack Tennant was born in Washington, County Durham, on 3 December 1907 and began as a centre-forward with Washington Colliery FC (where he worked as a pit boy). He did well and was successfully converted into a full-back. He was recruited by Stoke in September 1930 and spent two years at The Victoria Ground, making just one League appearance before moving south to join Torquay United in the summer of 1932. A year later he signed for Liverpool (May 1933) and his next move took him to Bolton Wanderers, who paid £2,750 for his services in December 1935. 'Speedy and tactically aware' Tennant had excellent three years with the Trotters before returning to Stoke for £2,500 in November 1938. He added a further 28 senior appearances to his tally with the Potters in that last pre-war season. He guested for Liverpool, Southport and Wrexham during the war and finally retired in May 1946 after struggling with injury throughout the hostilities. Tennant played in 105 matches for Bolton. He died c.1978.

TEST MATCHES

At the end of the 1894-95 season Stoke had to play Manchester United at Burslem Port Vale's ground in a vital Test Match. The Potters had finished third from bottom of the First Division while United had taken third spot in the Second Division. The two teams were paired together to see who would be playing at what level in 1895-96 and Stoke duly won the game 3-0 to retain their top Division status.

Stoke were involved in four more vital Test Matches at the end of the 1897-98 season – playing two games against Newcastle United and two against Burnley. On this occasion Stoke had ended up in last place in Division One and were forced to compete against the other teams in order to retain their top-billing. They played well and came through with flying colours, heading the mini League table with this record:

Venue	P	W	D	L	F	A	Pts
Home	2	1	1	0	1	0	3
Away	2	1	0	1	3	2	2
Totals	4	2	1	1	4	2	5

Stoke beat Newcastle 1-0 at home but lost 2-0 away, and defeated Burnley 2-0 away and drew 0-0 at home.

TEXACO CUP

Stoke played in this short-lived competition in season 1973-74. The competing clubs were split into two separate groups and the Potters came up against Birmingham City in a tie split over two legs. The first was staged at The Victoria Ground on 19 September 1973 and resulted in a 0-0 draw in front of 9,530 fans. The return fixture played at St Andrew's a fortnight later, on 2 October before a crowd of 13,433, was also drawn 0-0 after extra-time. There followed a penalty shoot-out which Blues eventually won 3-1. Terry Conroy was Stoke's scorer.

THAMES FC

Stoke never met Thames (who played briefly in the Third Division South between the wars) at competitive level, but one player who was associated with both clubs was Wilf Phillips.

THOMAS, Michael Reginald

Thomas was one of only a handful of players who had three separate spells with Stoke City, and each time he was a firm favourite with the fans. An enthusiastic, sometimes tempestuous midfielder, he always gave a good account of himself every time he took the field, no matter what the circumstances were. A very competitive performer, he was born in Mochdre, North Wales on 7 July 1954 and started his career in his homeland with Wrexham as a junior at the age of 16, turning professional at The Racecourse Ground in May 1972. He scored 33 goals in 230 League games for the Welsh club, up to November 1978 when he was transferred to Manchester United for £300,000. He continued his aggressive midfield play at Old Trafford and in almost three complete seasons there netted 15 goals in 120 League and Cup games, including the 1979 FA Cup Final defeat by Arsenal. In August 1981 he switched to Everton in a player exchange deal which took future Stokie John Gidman to United. Unfortunately he failed to bed in at Goodison Park and three months later he was sold to Brighton & Hove Albion for £400,000. His wife found it increasingly difficult to settle so far south from her North Wales home and in August 1982 Thomas was on the move again, this time from Hove to Stoke City for a fee of £200,000. He quickly got into his rhythm at The Victoria Ground and played over 60 games for the Potters before surprising a lot of people (including his wife) by signing for Chelsea in January 1984 for just £75,000. In September 1985, he was on the road again, this time to struggling West Bromwich Albion – and while at The Hawthorns he won his 51st and final cap for Wales, having already collected two at Under-23 level. But when Ron Saunders took over as manager of the Baggies, Thomas was on his way once more, and after a loan spell with Third Division promotion-chasing Derby County, he tried his luck in North America with Wichita Wings. On his return to Britain in August 1988 he signed for Shrewsbury Town and from Gay Meadow he went to Leeds United (June 1989). His second spell at Stoke was a loan period in March/April 1990, and after returning to Elland Road he was eventually signed full-time by the Potters on a free transfer three months later. Leaving The Victoria Ground after his third stint in August 1991, Thomas joined Wrexham for whom he scored a spectacular goal in a marvellous FA Cup win over Arsenal in January 1992. Sadly for the likeable Welshman, a jail sentence followed and on release he quit senior football and played briefly for Inter Cardiff. In his senior career Thomas amassed more than 450 appearances and scored over 50 goals. His full record for Stoke (all competitions) was 22 goals in 122 senior games.

NB: Wrexham played Wolverhampton Wanderers at The Recreation Ground in a benefit match for Thomas on 30 July 1997.

THOMPSON, Thomas

A keen and thrustful goalscoring inside-right, Thompson had a long and varied footballing career which saw him play, in turn, for Lumley YMCA (1944), Newcastle United (August 1946), Aston Villa (£12,000, September 1950), Preston North End (£28,000, June 1955), Stoke City (£2,500, July 1961) and Barrow (free, March 1963). He retired in June 1965 and became a carpenter in Preston. Born in Fencehouses, County Durham on 10 November 1928 and brought up at Houghton-le-Spring, Thompson was capped twice by England (v Wales in 1951 and Scotland in 1957). He also represented his country's 'B' team and the Football League, and was one of the few players to appear at both club level and full international as partner to two of the greatest wingers of all-time, Tom Finney and Stanley Matthews, doing so with the former when at Deepdale and with the latter during his two years at The Victoria Ground when he helped the Potters win the Second Division title. Thommo scored 18 goals in 46 games for Stoke, 117 in 188 League games for Preston and 67 in 148 for Aston Villa, and in his entire League career his full record was a superb one of 224 goals in 442 appearances.

THOMSON, Kenneth Gordon

One of the finest centre-halves ever to don a Stoke City shirt, certainly this century, Ken Thomson scored seven goals in 302 League and FA Cup appearances for the club over a period of seven years during the 1950s. A craggy Scotsman, born in Aberdeen on 25 February 1930, he was watched by Stoke scouts playing for the Caledonian Thistle and Banks o'Dee clubs but was overlooked. He then joined the RAF (on National Service) and on demob signed for Aberdeen (1950). At the time he was considered one of the finest pivots north of the border and in September 1952 Stoke boss Frank Taylor paid £22,500 for his services. Whilst at Pittodrie Park, Thomson came mighty close to gaining full international honours for his country (he was named reserve for Scotland on three occasions and once by the Scottish League). A strong, commanding defender, he made an immediate impact at The Victoria Ground, although his first season was marred by relegation to the Second Division. Indeed, it was Thomson who decided to take a vital penalty-kick against Derby County in the last game of that campaign. He missed from the spot, Stoke lost the match and went down in place of Manchester City, with only a point separating the two teams. Nevertheless, he was a born leader, who skippered the side from the word go and it is said that he hardly ever had a bad game. At the age of 28 Thomson's eyesight started to fade and, in fact, he had to wear contact lenses which failed to cure the problem. Consequently in December 1959, Tony Waddington reluctantly transferred him to Middlesbrough for £8,500. His stay at Ayresome Park was not without controversy and after making over 80 appearances for 'Boro he wound down his career with Hartlepool United, retiring in 1963 with 390 League appearances under his belt. Thomson died tragically young, of a heart attack on a golf course in 1969 at the age of 39.

THOMSON, W. (David) J.G.

Full-back or centre-half who played in nine League games for Stoke. Born in Scotland c.1866, and known as Lauchie he joined Stoke from Strathmore FC in July 1892 and left The Victoria Ground for Southampton St Mary's in March 1894, being one of the forerunners of the Stoke invasion to The Dell. A very popular player with the fans, he was strong with plenty of pluck and made 37 appearances for Saints up to the summer of 1896, when he joined Cowes FC on the Isle of Wight. Thomson appeared in Southampton's first ever Southern League game v Chatham on 6 October 1894. He retired in 1900.

THORLEY, Dennis

Born in Stoke-on-Trent on 7 November 1956, defender Thorley played for Roebuck FC before having six seasons at The Victoria Ground (1976-82) during which time he appeared in 15 first-team games. During his time at Stoke, he also played in the NASL with California Surf, and Howard Kendall took him to Blackburn Rovers on loan as his side went for promotion from the Third Division. He was plagued by injury during his last season with the Potters and announced his retirement at the age of 25.

THORNTON, Thomas

When he was playing for Crewe Alexandra in season 1909-10 Thornton was regarded as one of the best defenders in the Birmingham & District League. So much so that Stoke went out and secured his services in the summer of 1910. He went on to score once in 20 games for the Potters, mainly as a centre-half, before leaving The Victoria Ground for Newport County. Thornton was born in Birmingham c.1885.

TILBURY

Stoke defeated non-League Tilbury 4-0 at home in a third-round FA Cup-tie in January 1978. Jeff Cook (2), David Gregory and Steve Waddington netted the goals before a 16,301 crowd.

TOMLINSON, Frederick

Born in South Shields c.1886, wing-half Tomlinson netted three goals in 22 senior games for Stoke City whom he served for one season: 1909-10. He started his football in the North-East with South Shields Primitive Methodists, and after spells with Workington United and West Stanley he joined Barnsley from where he moved to The Victoria Ground (May 1909). He scored twice on his debut for the Potters in an 11-0 win over Merthyr Town. On leaving Stoke he returned home to play for Washington Sentinel.

TOMPKINSON, William Vincent

An industrious outside-right with a lot of ability, Tompkinson was born in Stone on 18 June 1895 and played for Wolverhampton Wanderers Reserves immediately before joining Stoke in November 1914. Owing to World War One, he only made two first-team appearances for the Potters v Mid Rhondda in April 1915 and against Bury in February 1920 before transferring to Aberdare Athletic at the end of that campaign (June 1920). Tompkinson, who represented the Welsh League while with Athletic, then spent five seasons with Rochdale (from June 1923), making well over 170 senior appearances for the Lancashire club (50 goals scored). And he ended his senior career by having two years with Stockport County (from May 1928), netting another 27 goals in 82 League outings, including a fine hat-trick v Barrow in 1928-29. He rounded off his career with Connah's Quay & Shotton FC (August 1930) and Macclesfield Town (December 1930-May 1931). Tompkinson died at Bamford, near Rochdale, on 26 July 1968.

Bill Tompkinson

TON PENTRE

Stoke's playing record against the Welsh club is:
Southern League

Venue	P	W	D	L	F	A
Home	4	4	0	0	17	2
Away	4	4	0	0	9	4
Totals	8	8	0	0	26	6

Stoke had a 100 per-cent playing record against the Welsh club, beating them in all eight Southern League fixtures over a period of four seasons between 1909 and 1915. Their biggest victory was an 8-1 scoreline at The Victoria Ground on 30 September 1909 when Arthur Griffiths (3), Amos Baddeley (2), Billy Smith (2) and Dai Jones (own-goal) found the net in front of 2,500 fans.

Arty Watkin scored twice in Stoke's 4-1 home win in October 1914.

TOOTH, George

Outside-left Tooth scored two goals in five League games for Stoke during his two years with the club: 1899-1901. Born in Cheshire c.1872, he joined the Potters from Congleton Hornets and left The Victoria Ground for Stafford Rangers.

TORQUAY UNITED

Stoke's playing record against United is:
Football League

Venue	P	W	D	L	F	A
Home	1	1	0	0	3	0
Away	1	0	0	1	0	1
Totals	2	1	0	1	3	1

The first time Stoke met Torquay United at competitive was on 23 November 1991 in a Third Division match at The Victoria Ground. A crowd of 9,124 saw the Potters win 3-0 with goals by Mark Stein (2) and Wayne Biggins.

In a pre-season friendly in the west country in 1978, Stoke beat United 2-1. Defender Denis Smith and Garth Crooks with a penalty were on target.

Players with both clubs: Steve Bould, George Daniels, John Dreyer, Arthur Griffiths, Jimmy Harbot, Sean Haslegrave, Steve Lennox, Gary Pick (Stoke reserve), Mark Sale and Jack Tennant.

Irish international Len Graham played for Torquay United and later became assistant manager at Stoke. Dudley Kernick was a player with Torquay, who later became Stoke's second commercial manager.

TOTTENHAM HOTSPUR

Stoke's playing record against Spurs is:
Football League

Venue	P	W	D	L	F	A
Home	33	15	9	9	45	35
Away	33	1	6	26	26	74
Totals	66	16	15	35	71	109

FA Cup

Venue	P	W	D	L	F	A
Home	5	4	0	1	12	3
Away	2	0	2	0	3	3
Totals	7	4	2	1	15	6

Stoke's best League triumph over Spurs is 4-1 at The Victoria Ground in April 1935 (Division One) when Tommy Sale netted a superb hat-trick.

The Potters suffered their two heaviest League defeats at the hands of Spurs in successive seasons: in October 1950 they crashed 6-1 at White Hart Lane in a First Division match which was seen by over 54,000 fans and on 15 September 1951 they succumbed to the same scoreline at The Victoria Ground – this being Spurs' best ever away win at League level.

Spurs also beat Stoke 4-1 at home in May 1983; 4-0 at White Hart Lane in October 1984

Stoke have a very poor record at White Hart Lane. They have registered only one League victory there – beating Spurs 2-0 in February 1975 when almost 23,000 spectators saw Jimmy Greenhoff and Alan Hudson breach the Londoners' defence.

Joey Mawson scored a hat-trick to earn the Potters a useful Second Division point from a 3-3 draw with the Londoners in the capital in March 1932.

A seven-goal thriller on Spurs' soil ended in a 4-3 victory for the London club in October 1972. John Ritchie scored twice for Stoke.

Stoke lost both League games by 3-1 to Spurs in their Second Division season of 1977-78 – and both Potters' goals were scored by Garth Crooks who later joined Spurs.

Stoke City (the champions) and Tottenham were promoted together from the Second Division at the end of the 1932-33 season and at the end of the 1976-77 campaign both teams were relegated from the top flight, Spurs finishing bottom.

Of their four FA Cup wins over Spurs, Stoke's best has been a 5-0 scoreline in a first-round tie at The Vic in February 1896, when Willie Maxwell stole the limelight with a sparkling hat-trick in front of 6,000 fans.

Stoke's excellent 4-1 victory over Spurs in the quarter-finals of the same competition in February 1899, was seen by a crowd of 22,000 at The Victoria Ground. Joey Schofield, Fred Johnson, Jack Kennedy and Fred Molyneux scored the goals which saw off the Londoners' challenge.

Players with both clubs: Gary Brooke, Joe Brough, Garth Crooks, George Clawley, Ray Evans, Archie Heggarty, Ian Moores, Billy Leech, Tony Parks, Jimmy Robertson and Charlie Wilson.

TRANMERE ROVERS

Stoke's playing record against Rovers is:
Football League

Venue	P	W	D	L	F	A
Home	6	3	2	1	7	3
Away	6	2	3	1	4	4
Totals	12	5	5	2	11	7

FA Cup

Venue	P	W	D	L	F	A
Home	1	1	0	0	2	0
Away	1	0	1	0	2	2
Totals	2	1	1	0	4	2

Stoke's best League victory over Rovers is 2-0 – a scoreline registered twice: in April 1929 (on their way to the Third Division North title) and in December 1996. Both games were played at The Victoria Ground.

Rovers' best win over the Potters is also by 2-0, at Prenton Park in March 1994 (Division One).

Mick Kennedy scored Stoke's winner in their 2-1 League win at Rovers on a balmy Friday night in August 1990.

A record crowd of 24,426 saw Stoke earn a replay from a 2-2 draw with Tranmere in an FA Cup fourth-round tie at Prenton Park in February 1972 The replay saw the Potters' ease through by 2-0 with goals from Terry Conroy and John Ritchie.

Players with both clubs: John Almond, Charlie Bishop (Stoke junior), Sam Davis, Verdi Godwin, Fred Groves, Charlie Kelly, Arthur Lewis, Dick McCarthy, Eric McManus, Barry Siddall, Willie Stevenson, Eddie Stuart, Bob White and Albert Whitehurst. Alan A'Court was caretaker manager of Stoke and a player with Tranmere.

TRANSFERS

Stoke's biggest signings:

Ian Cranson	from Sheffield Wed	£450,000	July	1989
Paul Peschisolido	from Birmingham C	£400,000	Aug	1994
Sammy McIlroy	from Manchester U	£350,000	Feb	1982
Peter Shilton	from Leicester City	£325,000	Nov	1974
Martin Carruthers	from Aston Villa	£300,000	July	1990
Kevin Keen	from West Ham U	£300,000	Oct	1994
Keith Scott	from Swindon T	£300,000	Dec	1994
Paul Maguire	from Shrewsbury T	£262,000	Sep	1980
Tony Ellis	from Preston NE	£250,000	Dec	1989
Alan Hudson	from Chelsea	£240,000	Jan	1974
Wayne Biggins	from Manchester C	£240,000	Aug	1989

Stoke's top 12 sales:

Mike Sheron	to Queens Park R	£2.5m	July	1997
Mark Stein	to Chelsea	£1.5 m	Oct	1993
Peter Beagrie	to Everton	£750,000	Oct	1989
Adrian Heath	to Everton	£700,000	Jan	1982
Garth Crooks	to Tottenham H	£650,000	July	1980
Lee Chapman	to Arsenal	£500,000	Aug	1982
Lee Sandford	to Sheffield Utd	£500,000	Aug	1996
Lee Dixon	to Arsenal	£400,000	Jan	1988
Paul Peschisolido	to Birmingham C	£400,000	Mar	1996
Steve Bould	to Arsenal	£390,000	June	1988
Mark Chamberlain	to Sheffield Wed	£300,000	Sep	1985
Graham Potter	to Southampton	£300,000	Aug	1996*
Keith Scott	to Norwich City	£300,000	Nov	1995†
Paul Bracewell	to Sunderland	£250,000	July	1983

* More money to follow depending on appearances.
† Deal also involved Mike Sheron moving to Stoke for £150,000.

How Stoke's transfers records have been broken since 1966

Sales

£70,000	John Ritchie to Sheffield Wednesday, November 1966
£70,000	Calvin Palmer to Sunderland, February 1968
£125,000	Mike Bernard to Everton, May 1972
£225,000	Alan Hudson to Arsenal, December 1975
£250,000	Peter Shilton to Nottingham Forest, September 1977
£600,000	Garth Crooks to Tottenham Hotspur, July 1980
£700,000	Adrian Heath to Everton, July 1982
£750,000	Peter Beagrie to Everton, October 1989
£1.5m	Mark Stein to Chelsea, November 1993
£2.5m	Mike Sheron to Queens Park Rangers, July 1997

Buys

£100,000	Jimmy Greenhoff from Birmingham City, August 1969
£240,000	Alan Hudson from Chelsea, January 1974
£325,000	Peter Shilton from Leicester City, November 1974
£350,000	Sammy McIlroy from Manchester Utd, February 1982

£450,000   Ian Cranson from Sheffield Wednesday, July 1989
* In November 1995, Mike Sheron was involved in a £450,000 deal which saw Keith Scott move to Carrow Road in part-exchange.

Loan transfers

Over the years – mainly since 1975 – Stoke City have acquired the services of several players on loan from other clubs, and they include the following (listed in A-Z order): Paul Allen (Southampton), Zay Andrade (Academica Coimbra), Paul Barron (WBA), Junior Bent (Bristol City), Alan Biley (Everton), Phil Bonnyman (Grimsby Town), David Brightwell (Manchester City), Gary Brooke (Wimbledon), Wayne Clarke (Manchester City), Joe Corrigan (Brighton & Hove Albion), Tom Cowan (Sheffield United), Alan Curtis (Southampton), Archie Dempsey* (Preston North End), Louie Donowa (Norwich City), Harry Dowd (Manchester City), Wayne Ebanks (WBA), Gareth Evans (Hibernian), Bruce Grobbelaar (Liverpool), Len Hales (Crewe Alexandra), Vic Hall (Mansfield Town), Dave Hockaday (Hull City), Brian Horne (Millwall), Graham Kavanagh (Middlesbrough – later signed on full contract), Gordon Marshall (Celtic), Carl Muggleton (Leicester City), Leigh Palin (Bradford City – signed permanently two weeks later), Tony Parks (Brentford), Kevin Pressman (Sheffield Wednesday), Dave Puckett (Bournemouth), Brian Rice (Nottingham Forest), Simon Rodger (Crystal Palace), Colin Russell (Huddersfield Town), Kevin Russell (Leicester City), Hans Segers (Nottingham Forest), Bill Smalley* (Preston North End), Mark Smith (Dunfermline Athletic), Tony Spearing (Norwich City), Tim Steele (Wolverhampton Wanderers), Mark Stein (Chelsea), Mickey Thomas (Leeds United – signed permanently later), Mark Walters (Liverpool), Billy Whitehurst (Sheffield United), Tom Wilkes (Aston Villa), Brett Williams (Nottingham Forest) and John Williams (Coventry City).
* Dempsey and Smalley were loaned by Preston when Stoke arrived at Deepdale for a League game in October 1888 with only nine players. Clearly these are regarded as being the first loan players to assist the Potters in a competitive game.

Transfer Dealings

● In 1896 Stoke signed Allan Maxwell from Darwen in exchange for a set of wrought-iron gates which were to be erected at the Lancashire cotton town club's ground.

● In April 1932, Stoke travelled south to play Bristol City at Ashton Gate in a Second Division match. So hard up were the West Country club that after the game they offered Potters' manager Tom Mather any player in their side for just £250. Mather moved in quickly and snapped up outside-left Joe Johnson who later won five caps for England.

● After drawing 1-1 at home with Preston North End on 14 October 1961 in front of just 8,409 fans, Stoke manager Tony Waddington contacted Blackpool to ask about the availability of a certain outside-right by the name of Stanley Matthews. A fee of £2,800 was agreed and the great man himself returned home to The Victoria Ground, making his second debut for the Potters, against Huddersfield Town on 28 October in front of a massive 35,974 crowd – 28,500 up on the previous home gate.

● Jimmy Greenhoff was Stoke's first £100,000 signing in the summer of 1969 when he moved from Birmingham City to The Victoria Ground.

● When Stoke secured the services of Peter Shilton from Leicester City in November 1974, the fee paid (£325,000) was the highest in Britain at that time. Ten months earlier Alan Hudson had moved from Chelsea to Stoke for £240,000.

TRAVELLING

Stoke City have travelled all over the world to play their football, visiting scores of countries including as far a field as Australia and Hong Kong (See FOREIGN OPPOSITION).

TREHARRIS

Stoke's playing record against the Welsh club is:
Southern League

Venue	P	W	D	L	F	A
Home	2	2	0	0	7	1
Away	2	2	0	0	9	1
Totals	4	4	0	0	16	2

Four wins from four starts for Stoke in Southern League games against the Welsh club. These matches were played during the seasons 1910-11 when the Potters ran up victories of 2-0 at home victory and 4-1 away, and in 1913-14 when Stoke were easy winners by 5-1 at home and 5-0 away. Billy Herbert hit a hat-trick in the latter game.

Full-back George Smart played for both clubs during the early part of the 20th century.

TRENTHAM LAKES

The sight of Stoke City's new ground, officially opened in August 1997 (See THE BRITANNIA STADIUM).

TUDOR, John A.

Born in Ilkeston on 25 June 1946, blond striker Tudor started off his

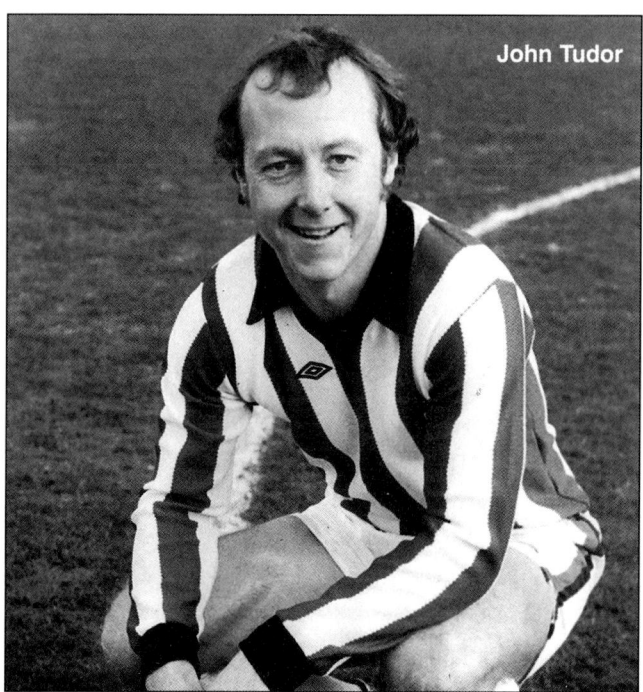

League career with Coventry City in 1966, having moved to Highfield Road from Ilkeston Town. He spent almost three years with the Sky Blues before moving to Sheffield United. He then switched his allegiance to Newcastle (January 1971) and found his way to Stoke in September 1976. He scored three times in 31 outings for the Potters and in August 1977 was sold to the Belgium club, Ghent for £10,000. In his League career in England, Tudor hit 99 goals in 334 games.

TUEART, Dennis

Tueart played on both wings and as an inside-forward during a fine career which spanned 17 years (1967-84) In that time he starred for Sunderland, Manchester City (two spells), New York Cosmos, Stoke City (July-December 1983) and Burnley, He appeared in just four games for the Potters, but all told he netted 137 goals in his tally of 417 League games. An FA Cup winner with Sunderland and a League Cup winner with Manchester City, Tueart won six full England caps plus one at Under-23 level and he also played for the Football League XI. He was born in Newcastle-upon-Tyne on 27 November 1949.

TUNNICLIFFE, John

Half-back Jack Tunnicliffe, younger brother of Billy (below) was born in Hanley in 1866 and played three games in Stoke's first team during the 1888-89 season. Before joining the club he had served with Longton Atlas and after leaving the Potters he assisted Audlam FC.

TUNNICLIFFE, William

Billy Tunnicliffe (born in Hanley in 1864) was with his brother at The Victoria Ground. He joined the Potters from Hanley Town before League Football was introduced and made nine appearances in the senior side, all in the first half of the 1888-89 season (4 goals scored) before moving to Middlewich.

TURLEY, Patrick

Well-built Irish bred half-back from Newry, Turley had five League outings with the Potters over a three year period (1929-31 inclusive). Born c.1908, he came over to England from his home-town club, Newry Town in March 1929, but his opportunities were few and far between at The Victoria Ground and he left Stoke on a free transfer to join St Patrick's (Dublin).

TURNER, A.Wilmot

Born in Cheshire in 1866, Turner arrived at The Victoria Ground practically unnoticed in August 1890, joining the Potters from Chester. A useful forward, he helped Stoke win the Football Alliance championship in his first season and went on to score 22 goals in 59 senior games before transferring to the Manchester club, Ardwick, in December 1892.

TURNER, Arthur Owen

Born at Chesterton on 1 April 1909, centre-half Arthur Turner was no fool when it came to defending. He was rock solid, feared no one and gave his all every time he took the field of play. He began his footballing career with Wolstanton PSA and Downings Collieries while working as an upholsterer. He then signed amateur forms for West Bromwich Albion (1927) but failed to breakthrough at The Hawthorns. When he lost his day job he wrote to Stoke asking for a trial. He succeeded in getting one, and signed for the Potters on amateur forms in November 1930, quickly moving up to the professional ranks. He made rapid progress and established himself in the first XI in 1931 when he made 40 appearances. The following season, as the cornerstone of the Potters' defence, he guided the team to the Second Division championship, being an ever-present in the side. Between 1935 and 1938 he played in 118 consecutive League games for Stoke and remained a regular in the team until February 1939. He was then transferred to Birmingham after scoring 17 goals in 317 appearances for the Potters. Just over six months into his association with Blues War broke out and Turner had to be content, along with scores of other players, of playing regional football for the next seven years. He came through well guesting for Crewe Alexandra, Wrexham and Stoke City during the hostilities as well as amassing 186 wartime appearances for Blues. When peacetime football resumed he again starred in defence for Birmingham City. But in February 1948, after 53 senior outings for Blues, whom he helped win the League South title in 1945-46, he signed for Southport. He retired the following May and was manager at Gresty Road from August 1949 to 1950. A three-year spell as assistant manager at The Victoria Ground followed (1950-53) before he took over as team manager at St Andrew's, a position he held from November 1954 until September 1958 during which time Blues gained promotion from the Second Division and also reached the FA Cup Final. For ten years – from January 1959 to 1969 – he was manager of Oxford United, leading the U's into the Football League and to the Third Division championship (1968). Afterwards he acted as chief scout for Rotherham United before quitting football in 1975. Turner, was also a useful cricketer, playing for Silverdale CC for whom he scored five centuries. He died in Sheffield in January 1994.

TURNER, George

Born in Halmerend c.1887, Turner had a fine career at The Victoria Ground. A speedy player with a fine tackle, he joined Stoke from Hamerend Gymnastics FC in the summer of 1908 and went on to score 17 goals and 190 first-team appearances for the Potters up to April 1915 when League football was suspended due to war in Europe. During the early part of the hostilities Turner had 72 more outings for Stoke before joining the Army in October 1917, being transferred to the battle front in April 1918. Within a matter of weeks he was shot in the leg and sadly had to have the limb amputated. On returning to England he became secretary of Podmore Hall FC.

TURNER, Isaiah

Goalkeeper Ike Turner played in one League game for West Bromwich Albion in 1898 before leaving the Baggies to join Stourbridge, later assisting Dudley Town (1902-03) and then Kidderminster Harriers from where he moved to Stoke in the summer of 1906. He appeared in eight first-team games for the Potters, but left the club in May 1907 for Old Hill Wanderers, retiring in May 1911. Born in Netherton, Dudley in July 1876, Turner attended Blower Green School (Dudley) and played junior football for Dudley St James' before spending a season with Albion. He died in Dudley in February 1935.

TURNER, James

Jim Turner was born at Black Bull (Staffs) in January 1866, brought up in Lancashire and played his early football as an outside-right for Black Lane Rovers (Radcliffe). In July 1888, just two months before the start of League football in Britain, he was signed as a professional by Bolton Wanderers. He had a long stint at Burnden Park and scored 12 goals in 108 games for the Trotters. In 1893 he was involved in a fracas with fans during a Lancashire Cup-tie at Bury and the following year was forced to miss the FA Cup Final through injury. Capped three times by England (while playing for three different clubs) Turner won his first cap against Wales at Stoke in 1893 and it was to The Victoria Ground where he moved in the summer of 1894. After 18 months with the Potters, Turner was sold to Derby County for £750 where he was converted into a dominant half-back, playing in the 1898 FA Cup Final (v Nottingham Forest). Four months after that Final Turner returned to Stoke, but retired from active football at the end of that season owing to ill-health. Turner, who scored once in 63 games for the Potters, died in Stoke in April 1904.

TURNER, James Albert

Jim Turner was a competent right-half, wholehearted, a real fighter and very reliable. Born in Black Bull (Staffs) in 1866, he started his footballing career in Lancashire with the Radcliffe club, Black Lane Rovers. He then joined Bolton Wanderers in July 1888, teaming up with his brother Dick in the Reserves. He did well at Burnden Park, being desperately unlucky to miss the 1894 FA Cup Final through injury. In September of that year – after 108 appearances for the Trotters – he moved to Stoke and spent two seasons at The Victoria Ground, having 56 outings before he was sold to Derby County for £70 in June 1896. Capped three times by England during the mid-1890s, Turner also represented the Football League, and in 1898 he made up for that earlier disappointment by gaining an FA Cup winners' medal with Derby. Four months later he returned to Stoke but made only seven more appearances for the Potters before suffering a serious leg injury in the December which ended his career. He died in Stoke-on-Trent on 9 April 1904 after a short illness.

TURNER, Joseph

An outside-left, with good pace, Turner (born in Burslem in 1873) played locally for Newcastle Swifts and Dresden United before joining Southampton St Mary's in 1896. He moved back to the Potteries to sign for Stoke in May 1898 and went on to score 15 goals in 60 first-team appearances in a two-year spell at The Victoria Ground when he also represented the Football League (1899). In April 1900 he switched to to Merseyside to sign for Everton and soon afterwards returned to The Dell (Southampton having by now dropped their title St Mary's). In his second spell with Saints he picked up a loser's medal in the 1902 FA Cup Final. Later in his career he played for New Brompton (Gillingham), and Northampton Town before ending his soccer days with Eastleigh Athletic in Hampshire. Turner died in Southampton in November 1950, aged 77.

TURNER, Josuah

Left-half Turner made one appearance for Stoke, lining up against Aston Villa Reserves in a Birmingham League game in January 1909, taking over from the injured Albert Pitt. Born in Stoke c.1884, he played amateur football throughout his career, mainly for Tunstall for whom he appeared before and after assisting the Potters.

TUTIN, Arthur

Tutin was a short, stocky wing-half, strong in the tackle, who formed part of that exceptionally well organised and reliable middle-line of Tutin, Turner and Soo. Born in Coundon, County Durham in 1907, he served with a string of northern-based clubs including Bishop Auckland, Consett, Chilton Colliery, Spennymoor United and Crook Town before having unsuccessful trials with Sheffield Wednesday and Bradford Park Avenue. In 1932 he signed for Aldershot, and switched to Stoke the following year – and when Bill Robertson left The Victoria Ground for Manchester United in March 1934, Stoke boss Bob McGrory introduced the diminutive figure of Tutin to the first XI. A fine footballer, neat and tidy, he went on to score three goals in 198 League and FA Cup games for the Potters up to the outbreak of the war. During the hostilities he had nine outings for Stoke and also assisted Crewe Alexandra (near his place of work). He retired from the game in 1945.

TWEMLOW, Charles V.

Outside-right who scored in his only game for Stoke against Derby County in February 1922 (won 4-2). No relation to Bill (below) he was born in Macclesfield c.1900 and played as an amateur throughout his career, serving with Congleton prior to joining Stoke and after leaving the Potters he assisted Macclesfield Town.

TWEMLOW, William T.

Born in Hanley c.1893, Bill Twemlow joined Stoke from Audley in the summer of 1915 after having recovered from a broken leg suffered playing at Cheddleton. That injury occurred shortly before he was due to go for a trial with Aston Villa, and owing to him being sidelined, Villa withdrew their interest. One of the many talented local footballers around at the time, Twemlow played in 70 games for the Stoke during World War One, and followed up with 37 senior outings after the hostilities (two goals scored). In April 1921, he left The Victoria Ground for neighbours Port Vale, but after a cartilage operation the following year, he was released in May 1923. Twemlow later played for Macclesfield and Oswestry and he died in Hanley on 1 June 1933, aged 40.

UEFA CUP

Stoke played four games in this competition – two in season 1972-73 against the German side FC Kaiserslautern, and two in 1974-75 against the Dutch team Ajax Amsterdam.

A crowd of over 22,000 witnessed the first leg of Stoke's tie with Kaiserslautern on 13 September 1972 – and goals by Terry Conroy, Geoff Hurst and John Ritchie gave the Potters a 3-1 advantage to take to Germany. Alas, in front of 18,000, the second leg a fortnight later, belonged entirely to Kaiserslautern who raced to a 4-0 victory to go through 5-3 on aggregate.

The first leg against Ajax took place at Stoke on 18 September 1974, and before a near 37,400 crowd the Potters were held to a 1-1 draw, Denis Smith their scorer. Two weeks later in Amsterdam, some 29,000 fans saw Stoke put up a dogged fight to force a 0-0 draw only to go out of the competition on the away goal rule.

Stoke's full record in this competition is:

Venue	P	W	D	L	F	A
Home	2	1	1	0	4	2
Away	2	0	1	1	0	4
Totals	4	1	2	1	4	6

UNDERWOOD, Alfred

Underwood was a formidable full-back who joined the Potters in the summer of 1887, having previously played for the Hanley Tabernacle and Etruria clubs. Born in Hanley in 1869, he was a prodigious kicker, who occasionally tackled 'far too rashly'. Nevertheless he was still a fine player who gave Stoke excellent service, appearing in 131 senior games up to May 1893 when he retired prematurely at the age of 24, although he was called upon to assist the club from time to time later on. A member of the Stoke side which won the Football Alliance title in 1891, he also gained two full England caps, both against Ireland in March 1891 and March 1892, lining up with his Stoke colleagues Billy Rowley and Tommy Clare in the second international in Belfast. A potter by trade, Underwood suffered with his health over a number of years during the early 1900s and was practically an invalid. In July 1908, he was struck down with a serious illness and at the time was said to be destitute. A group of local notables led by Denny Austerberry, the Stoke secretary, established a fund to support him. Chronically ill, Underwood battled on for 20 years until the 8 October 1928, when died in Stoke-on-Trent, aged 59.

UNITED COUNTIES LEAGUE

Stoke participated in this purely Midland-based competition in season 1893-94, along with seven other teams. There were two sections (A and B) with four teams in each one, but Stoke failed to make progress into the Final, finishing second to West Bromwich Albion who lost to Derby County (winners of section A) in the Final. Here are details of Stoke's six games in group B:

Opponents	Venue	Result
v Small Heath	Home	Won 2-1
v Small Heath	Away	Lost 0-3
v West Brom A	Home	Won 5-2
v West Brom A	Away	Lost 0-5
v Wolves	Home	Won 3-0
v Wolves	Away	Won 2-1

Summary of matches:

Venue	P	W	D	L	F	A	Pts
Home	3	3	0	0	10	3	6
Away	3	1	0	2	2	9	2
Totals	6	4	0	2	12	12	8

Only 5,500 fans witnessed Stoke's three home games, but generally speaking the short-lived competition was poorly supported. Billy Dickson top-scored for Stoke with five goals out of a total of 12.

URSEM, Loek A.J.M.

The first Dutchman to play for Stoke City, Ursem, a midfielder, was born in Amsterdam on 7 January 1958 and scored seven goals in 44 appearances for the club over a four-year period (1979-83). Capped by Holland at Under-23 level, he was signed from AZ '67 Alkmaar for £58,000 and after a loan spell with Sunderland, left The Victoria Ground for FC Haarlem (July 1983), later playing for the now defunct Wageningen club and OSV Velsen.

USHERWOOD, Arthur

Outside-left Usherwood was born in Congleton c.1884. He played for his local team Congleton Excelsior before teaming up with Stoke for the 1904-05 season. He scored once in six outings during that campaign and then left The Victoria Ground for Ashton Town. He remained an amateur throughout his career.

VERNON, Thomas Royston

Vernon was a fine ball-playing inside forward who scored goals as well as making them. He had an excellent career which spanned 20 years during which time he served with four major clubs. Born in Ffynngroew near Holywell, Flintshire, North Wales on 14 April 1937, he joined Blackburn Rovers as a junior, turning professional at Ewood Park in March 1955. He scored 49 goals in 131 League games in the next five years before moving to Everton in February 1960 at a time when Rovers were on their way to the FA Cup Final. He did very well at Goodison Park, netting 110 goals in 199 appearances for the Merseysiders and helping them win the First Division title in 1963. Then, on transfer deadline day in March 1965, Stoke boss Tony Waddington bid £40,000 for Vernon and the Welsh international (32 caps won at senior level and two at Under-23) came to the Potteries to fill

Roy Vernon

the inside-forward berth vacated by Jimmy McIlroy. In his four-and-a-half years with Stoke Vernon scored 24 goals in 100 first-team games – and in January 1969 he also played four times on loan with Halifax Town. At the end of that 1968-69 season he was given a free transfer by the club and signed for Great Harwood. Vernon hit 172 goals in 398 Football League games. Vernon died on 4 December 1993 after a long illness.

VICTORIA GROUND (The)

● Stoke played at The Victoria Ground for more than 119 years – from March 1878 to May 1997 – and by doing so, established a record of staying the longest period of time at one ground in English football history.

● Prior to 1875 Stoke had played on Sweetings Field, a strip of land owned by Alderman Sweeting (The Lord Mayor of Stoke). Then the club merged with the Stoke Victoria Athletic Club (probably in late summer or winter of 1877) and home matches thereafter were played on the Athletic Club's ground which occupied an enormous piece of land which was frequently used for local athletics meetings.

● Part of this large expanse of land later became known as The Victoria Ground, which, when Stoke first started playing there, was, in fact, described as an 'enclosure of the Victoria Athletic club'.

● The Vic was initially oval-shaped, comprising a large running track round with a fair-sized playing-area in the centre (where cricket was the prime sport). There was uncovered banking at either end and along one side, with just one wooden, rather flimsy-looking, stand on the east side (Boothen Road).

● Stoke's first officially organised game of football at The Victoria Athletic Club ground was a friendly against local neighbours Talke Rangers on 28 March 1878, which the Potters won 1-0 in front of an estimated crowd of 2,500.

● Stoke's first match, after the name The Victoria Ground had been adopted, was played on 24 September 1883 when, wearing 'red and white striped flannel shirts and white knickerbockers' they drew 1-1 with the Great Lever club from Manchester in front of 3,000 spectators.

● For the next ten years or so only limited improvements were carried out on the ground, and even after the club had gained Football League status, as founder members in 1888, not too much work was done until the turn of the century, simply because of the lack of money.

● On 8 September 1888, Stoke played their first ever Football League game – at home to West Bromwich Albion. A good sized crowd of 4,524 attended The Victoria Ground to see Albion win 2-0 and in doing so became the first team to head the new League table (on goal-average).

● Coincidentally, it was West Bromwich Albion who were Stoke City's last League visitors to The Victoria Ground, the Nationwide First Division fixture taking place on 4 May 1997 before a crowd of 22,500. The outcome was 2-1 victory for Stoke.

The old Boothen End terracing at the Victoria Ground.

● When Stoke dropped out of the Football League in 1908, The Victoria Ground was regarded as one of the poorest professional club grounds in the country.

● General work was carried out, to a certain degree, and some slight improvements took place before the outbreak of World War One, but not a lot, owing to limited cash resources.

● By the time competitive League football recommenced after the hostilities in 1919, and with Stoke back in the Football League, The Vic was looking a lot better. There were two respectable covered stands along with a wooden one, which could seat 1,000 spectators. This was situated opposite the main stand. At the corner of the Boothen End and Boothen Stand, a small, but adequate hut was erected as a players' dressing room.

● The main feature in this hut was an old stove, around which the home players would assemble after winter training sessions to warm their hands, drink their Bovril and talk about the next match (or the last one). Indeed, this same stove was still being used in the late 1950s.

● During the early 1920s, a new, mainly wooden main stand was erected alongside the dressing room hut. It could seat 2,000 fans and was one of the better ones in the League at that time.

● The freehold of The Victoria Ground was purchased in the summer of 1928 after the club announced record season ticket sales.

● Three years later the Boothen End had been completely terraced and was soon covered to give the supporters some comfort against the elements.

● At this juncture (c.1932) the original oval-shape of The Victoria Ground had gone.

● In 1935, the Butler Street stand was built. This had seating for some 5,000 supporters with a small paddock in front and at each end. The barrel-roof curled round the corners.

● Two years later, on 29 March 1937, a record crowd (never to be bettered) of 51,373 squeezed into The Victoria Ground to watch Stoke City's First Division League game against mighty Arsenal. The result was a 0-0 draw.

● As time progressed, the ground itself was gradually improved, albeit only slightly, and during World War Two the Butler Street stand was actually used as an army camp.

● In 1956, floodlights were installed for the first time – Stoke meeting rivals Port Vale in a Second Division game in October of that year to officially declare them switched on. Stoke won 3-1 and the crowd was 38,729.

● Seven years on, another new Main stand was built in three separate stages, with the final nuts and bolts being screwed down in 1963 to coincide with the team regaining its First Division status and with the club's assumed centenary celebrations.

● Eager to save money, during that year (1963) the directors of Stoke City Football Club ordered that the players should be paid one shilling (5p) an hour to lay concrete on the terracing of the newly refurbished main stand.

● Over the weekend of third and fourth January 1976, a terrific gale hit the city of Stoke-on-Trent, and it was so strong that the roof of the Butler Street stand was blown off. The next home League game, scheduled for The Victoria Ground (Stoke v Middlesbrough) was subsequently switched to nearby Vale Park.

● The roof was replaced with a smart new white cover.

● Three years later, in October 1979, a brand new two-tier stand was opened at the Stoke End of the ground. It contained 4,000 seats above the paddock.

● A floodlight change was made soon afterwards with a pair of new pylons replacing an older set at one end of the ground – and consequently Stoke City became unique inasmuch that it was the only professional football club in the land to have two pairs of completely different floodlights overlooking the playing area.

● In the summer of 1983 the surviving corner of the Butler Street stand was demolished and four years later, the (Sir) Stanley Matthews Suite was officially opened in honour of the famous English international outside-right.

● A new club shop and promotions/commercial office complex was built on the side of the City End stand – this was completed in July 1992.

● Two years later, in the summer of 1994, the Stoke City Board announced plans for a new 9,000 all-seater stand as part of a proposed £5 million ground redevelopment scheme with work commencing in May 1995. (This of course was shelved).

● During the 1994-95 campaign, the interior of the main stand was refurbished along with the official Stoke City souvenir shop.

● Then it was officially announced that Stoke City Football Club would be playing their last season at The Victoria Ground in 1996-97 before it would move to its new home, the Britannia Stadium, at Trentham Lakes, just a mile down the road.

● England have played three full internationals at The Victoria Ground: in February 1889 v Wales (won 4-1 before a crowd of 3,500); in March 1893 v Wales (won 6-0 in front of 6,520 fans) and in November 1936 v Ireland (won 3-1, watched by an audience of 47,882).

● England met Wales in a Victory International in October 1919 (won 2-0 before a 19,765 turnout) and there have also been two Inter League matches at The Victoria Ground – The Football League v Irish League in November 1895 (a 2-2 draw with the crowd 3,160) and Southern League v Football League in October 1911 (2-1 win – attendance of 10,154).

VINER, Horace

Goalkeeper Viner played once for Stoke in a home First Division League game against Nottingham Forest in March 1904 when the visitors won 3-2 in front of 7,000 fans. Born in Wales c.1880, he was recruited to The Victoria Ground from Birkenhead in the summer of 1903 (from under the noses of both Everton and Liverpool) and came as cover for fellow Welshman Dickie Roose and Jack Benton, but was released after one season at The Victoria Ground, moving nearer home to join Rhyl.

VIOLLET, Dennis S.

Dennis Viollet was signed by Stoke City boss Tony Waddington from Manchester United for £22,000 in January 1962, almost four years after surviving the Munich air crash. He was brought into the camp as part of 'Waddo's' rebuilding plan to get the Potters out of the Second Division. And his presence went a long way in achieving that goal, for Voillet did a splendid job in a forward-line which also comprised Stan Matthews, Jackie Mudie, Keith Bebbington and Don Ratcliffe, and later Jimmy McIlroy. A smart goalscorer, able to take the half-chance, Viollett was born in Manchester on 20 September 1933 and joined the Old Trafford club as a junior in 1948, turning professional (as part of the Busby Babes) in September 1950. He gained a regular place in the United side in season 1953-54 (after making his debut at Newcastle in April 1953) and in 1959-60 he created a new club record by scoring 32 times in 39 senior games. Viollet gained two League championship medals and both FA Cup winners and losers' medals during his 13 years with United, and he also netted a total 178 goals in 291 senior appearances, as well as gaining two full England caps to go with schoolboy honours he received as a teenager. His record with Stoke was a sound one – 66 goals in 207 senior outings. He helped the Potters win the Second Division title in 1963 and also played in the League Cup Final the following year.

WADDINGTON, Anthony

Tony Waddington was born in Openshaw, Manchester on 9 November 1924. Educated at St Gregory's School, Openshaw, he played his early football as an amateur with Manchester United prior to joining Crewe Alexandra. He made 179 post-war League appearances for the Alex but a painful knee injury, received during his service in the Navy, forced him into an early retirement.

In 1952 he was taken on at Stoke as a coach, and five years later was upgraded to assistant manager to Frank Taylor. When Taylor left in June 1966, Waddington took over as team boss and immediately set about rejigging the side in order to put in a stern challenge at gaining promotion back to the First Division. He got together a disciplined defence – known affectionately around Stoke as the Waddington Wall, and then he concentrated on the midfield department and the attack. By recruiting the likes of 46-year-old Stan Matthews, Jackie Mudie, Eddie Stuart, Eddie Clamp, Dennis Viollet and Jimmy McIlroy among others, he eventually assembled a very competent side, one full of experience and the Second Division championship duly came to The Victoria Ground in 1962-63.

He worked well with his coaches and at one stage called in the local Fire Brigade to water the pitch just to suit his style of play. Not the most fashionable side in the land, Stoke, under Waddington's guidance, certainly in the late 1960s, were a workmanlike outfit which got results. There was very little money to spend on new recruits (hence the signing of aged players) but Waddington did wonders in the transfer market and among his later acquisitions were players like Alex Elder, Roy Vernon, Jimmy Greenhoff, Peter Dobing, David Herd, John Ritchie, Harry Burrows, George Eastham and a certain Gordon Banks, who cost just £52,000. Several local-born players were also brought into the team, among them defenders Eric Skeels, Denis Smith and Alan Bloor who went on to amass a combined total of almost 1,600 senior appearances for the Potters.

In 1971 and 1972 Waddington's side reached successive FA Cup Finals; the teams also qualified for the UEFA Cup and also in 1972, the first ever major trophy was won, Stoke beating Chelsea 2-1 in the League Cup Final at Wembley. In 1974 Waddington captured the services of one of the most talented footballers in the game – Alan Hudson from Chelsea – and when goalkeeper Banks was badly hurt in a car crash he replaced him with Peter Shilton who, as we know, went

Tony Waddington

on to become a legend and the first footballer ever to appear in 1,000 League games. Stoke finished fifth in the First Division in 1973-74 and again in 1974-75, and at this juncture Waddington believed he'd got the right bunch of players, was using the correct formula and had got the backing of both the board of directors and the supporters.

Unfortunately for all concerned, a financial cloud fell upon the club around 1976 after a freak storm caused thousands of pounds worth of damage to the Butler Street Stand. Quality players left and as relegation loomed, amazingly chants began to ring out round The Victoria Ground seeking Waddington's resignation – and in May 1977 (after Stoke had lost their First Division status) Waddo quit as Potters' manager after serving the club for 25 years. He was out of football for two years yet still remained in contact with Stoke City. Between June 1979 and July 1981 he returned to the game as manager of his former club, Crewe Alexandra, and 12 years later was appointed associate director at The Victoria Ground (summer 1993), a position he held until his death in Crewe on 29 January 1994. Tens of thousands of supporters, young and old, turned out for his funeral to say RIP Tony Waddington, Mr Stoke City, the club's best-ever manager.

Under Waddington's management, the Potters played 701 League games. They were undefeated 438 of them, winning 241 and drawing 197.

WADDINGTON, Steven

Son of Stoke manager Tony, Waddington junior was a outside-right with good skills, who netted six times in 56 senior appearances for the club whom he served from 1972 until September 1978 when he joined Walsall for £40,000. Born in Crewe on 5 February 1956, he later assisted Port Vale (two games), Chesterfield (July 1983), Cape Town City (South Africa), Macclesfield Town (two spells), Northwich Victoria, Winsford United, Leek Town and Rocester. He underwent a cartilage operation when a Vale player and early in 1986-87 he was involved in a car crash with other players on their way to a friendly at Macclesfield.

WADE, Shaun Peter

Wade was signed by Stoke on a non-contract basis from Newcastle Town on 28 October 1994. Looking a useful striker, he appeared just once in the first team, coming on as a sub in the 1-1 home draw with Sheffield United five days after joining the club. Soon afterwards he badly damaged his cruciate knee ligaments in a reserve-team game. The injury required surgery and this unfortunately resulted in his departure from the scene. A bricklayer by trade, Wade was born in Stoke-on-Trent on 22 September 1969.

WAIN, Frederick

Goalkeeper Wain played in two Birmingham & District League games for Stoke in October 1908 while nursing a broken finger which was only diagnosed afterwards. A tall man, standing over six feet tall, he was born in Hanley c.1887, and played his early football with Smallthorne United before joining Stoke from Stone Town, initially as deputy to Bert Miller. After recovering from his hand injury, he became surplus to requirements and like so many other players around this time he left The Victoria ground to return to his former club early in 1909. An amateur throughout his career, it is said that Wain assisted at least a dozen non-League clubs in the Potteries area over a period of 20 years.

WAINWRIGHT, Thomas

Wainwright made one appearance at first-team level for Stoke, lining up at inside-left in a 5-1 away League defeat by Aston Villa in September 1888. Born locally c.1864, he played for Stoke St Jude's before his spell at The Victoria Ground and after leaving the Potters he assisted Stoke Priory.

WALKER, John D.

Cannock Town sold wing-half Jack Walker to Stoke in October 1924. He did well for a couple of seasons, scoring once in 36 appearances for the Potters. But after relegation at the end of the 1925-26 campaign he slipped into the Reserves and was later transferred to Walsall as the Stoke management attempted to rebuild the team in an effort to gain rapid promotion. Born at Great Wyrley c.1900, Walker later assisted Walsall Wood.

WALKER, Thomas J.

Inside-forward Walker made two appearances for Stoke in April 1972 (away at Chelsea and Manchester United) before leaving the club for Burnley. Born in the North-East of England at Gosforth near Newcastle on 20 February 1952, he was a junior at The Victoria Ground, turning professional in 1970, and after an unsuccessful spell at Turf Moor, he joined non-League Yeovil Town.

WALLACE, Benjamin

Amateur outside-left Wallace was given one first-team outing by Stoke in November 1901 against Sheffield Wednesday (away) when the Owls won 3-1. He was reserve to Aaron Lockett during his brief association with the Potters which lasted barely a year. Born in Stoke-on-Trent c.1880, Wallace also played for Stoke St Jude's (two spells) and Stoke Town.

WALLACE, James

One goal in eight senior games was Wallace's record as an inside-forward with Stoke City with whom he spent five years (1955-60). Born in Bebbington on 13 December 1937, he later assisted Northwich Victoria, Doncaster Rovers, Stafford Rangers and Ball Haye Green YC before taking to management with Eastwood Hanley, Nantwich Town and Leek Town, among others.

WALLACE, Raymond George

One of three footballing brothers, all of whom played for Southampton (Rod and Danny were the others) Ray Wallace is perhaps the least known of the trio. Born in Greenwich (London) on

2 October 1969, and an England Under-21 international (4 caps) he joined the junior ranks at The Dell in 1986 and turned professional there in April 1988. He had 47 outings for Saints before transferring to Leeds United for £100,000 in July 1991. Unfortunately he failed to establish himself at Elland Road and after loan spells with Swansea City (March 1992) and Reading (March 1994), he was transferred on a free to Stoke City in five months after returning from Elm Park. At first he took time to settle in at The Victoria Ground and was actually loaned out to lowly Hull City (December 1994) but he returned in a much better frame of mind and when the 1996-97 season ended had amassed a fine record of 10 goals in 132 senior games for the Potters.

WALSALL

Stoke's playing record against the Saddlers is:

Football League

Venue	P	W	D	L	F	A
Home	4	3	0	1	6	4
Away	4	2	1	1	4	4
Totals	8	5	1	2	10	8

Football Alliance

Venue	P	W	D	L	F	A
Home	1	1	0	0	3	1
Away	1	1	0	0	3	1
Totals	2	2	0	0	4	1

Southern League

Venue	P	W	D	L	F	A
Home	1	1	0	0	4	0
Away	1	0	0	1	0	1
Totals	2	1	0	1	4	1

Birmingham & District League

Venue	P	W	D	L	F	A
Home	3	2	0	1	13	5
Away	3	1	1	1	6	7
Totals	6	3	1	2	19	12

FA Cup

Venue	P	W	D	L	F	A
Home	1	0	0	1	0	2
Away	2	0	0	2	1	3
Totals	3	0	0	3	1	5

League Cup

Venue	P	W	D	L	F	A
Away	2	1	0	1	3	3

Autoglass Trophy

Venue	P	W	D	L	F	A
Home	1	1	0	0	3	1
Away	1	1	0	0	2	0
Totals	2	2	0	0	5	1

The first time the teams met in the Football League was in season 1926-27 (Division Three North). Stoke doubled up, winning 4-1 at home and 1-0 away and Harry Davies scored in both matches.

In 1961-62 (Division Two) Stoke won 2-1 at home, but lost 3-0 at Fellows Park when Tony Allen conceded an own-goal. And the following season, when the Potters were promoted to the top flight as champions, they were held 0-0 by the Saddlers at Walsall, but won 3-0 at The Victoria Ground, thanks to a smart hat-trick from Man of the Match Jackie Mudie. Stoke last met Walsall in 1988-89 (Division Two), winning 2-1 away and losing 3-0 at The Victoria Ground.

Much earlier, in the Football Alliance of 1890-91, Stoke again did the double over Walsall, winning 1-0 at home and 3-1, when Alf Edge netted twice.

Stoke ran up a 5-0 home victory over the Saddlers in a Birmingham & District League game in January 1909 and later that same year they cruised to a 5-1 home victory (September).

Walsall won a seven-goal Birmingham League thriller by 4-3 at Stoke in October 1910 and in a Southern League fixture two months later, Stoke gained sweet revenge by winning 4-0 at home with Billy Smith scoring twice.

The Saddlers caused a major shock when beating the Potters 2-0 in the third round of the FA Cup at The Victoria Ground in January 1966. Howard Riley and Allan Clarke were the goalscorers. This was not a happy game for Stoke's goalkeeper Bobby Irvine.

The following season Walsall ousted Stoke from the League Cup, beating them 2-1 at Fellows Park.

In season 1991-92, Stoke and Walsall met each other twice in the same Cup competition, the Autoglass Trophy, and the Potters won each time: 2-0 away (Lee Sandford scored twice) and 3-1 at home.

Players with both clubs: Amos Baddeley, Dave Bamber, Keith Bertschin, Dave Beswick, Noel Blake, Peter Bullock, Wayne Clarke, Louie Donowa, John Eyres, Tom Godfrey, Roy John, Alex McClure, Willie McIntosh, Graham Matthews, Albert Mullard, Billy Poole, Mark Prudhoe, Jimmy Robertson, Ronnie Sinclair, Alex Smith, Harry Smith, Derek Statham, Steve Waddington, Johnny Walker, Dennis Wilshaw and John Woodward.

Bill Moore played for Stoke and later managed Walsall while Brian Caswell was a player with the Saddlers and later reserve-team coach with Stoke City. Former Stoke goalkeeper Eric McManus was appointed Youth Development Officer-coach at Walsall in 1990.

WALTERS, Mark Everton

Forward Mark Walters occupied either flank. A tricky player with pace and telling shot, he could cross a ball with great precision (on the run or otherwise) and had one marvellous feature whereby he dragged his foot over the ball before swaying past a defender. Born in Birmingham

Mark Walters

on 2 June 1964, he joined Aston Villa as a teenager (from Holte Grammar School, Lozells) and remained with the Midlands club until moving to Scotland to sign for Glasgow Rangers for £500,000 in December 1987. From Ibrox Park he moved to Liverpool for £1.25 million in August 1981 and after loan spells with Stoke City (March/April 1994 when he scored twice in 11 League games) and Wolves (September/October 1994) he moved to Southampton in January 1996 on a free transfer and was with Swindon Town in 1996-97. Winner of one full, one 'B' and nine Under-21 caps for England, he gained a European Super Cup winners' medal with Villa (1982) and Scottish three Premier Division and two Scottish League Cup winners medals while at Ibrox, plus an FA Cup winners' medal with Liverpool in 1992. Walters passed the milestone of 550 senior appearances at club level during the 1996-97 season – and he's also scored more than 125 goals.

WARD, Derek

Brother of Terry (below) Derek Ward was an outside-right with some good skills. Born in Stoke-on-Trent on 23 December 1934, he spent ten years at the club, mainly as a reserve, before leaving for Stockport County in July 1961 for £2,000. He appeared in 61 games for the Potters and scored eight goals. For County he netted 21 times in his 81 League appearances.

WARD, Terence

A full-back who had 45 League and Cup games for Stoke City between August 1959 and December 1962. Born in Stoke-on-Trent on 10 December 1939, he graduated through the junior ranks at The Victoria Ground to make his mark in the first XI. Ward was forced to retire at the end of the 1959-60 season through ill-health and died in 1963, aged 23

WARD, Thomas Edward George

Born in Chatham, Kent, on 28 April 1913, Ward was a rugged right-half who was successfully converted into an inside-forward. He served with Chatham, Crystal Palace, Grimsby Town and Port Vale (from June 1936) before joining Stoke in February 1938 in a deal which saw Harry Davies move to the Valiants. He spent just 12 months at The Victoria Ground, making just five senior appearances (four goals scored) before retiring to the Vale in February 1939. Five months later he switched to Mansfield Town and retired during the war. Ward top-scored for Vale in season 1936-37 and in all netted 29 goals in 61 appearances during his two spells with the Valiants.

WARE, Harold

Although born into a Potteries family in Birmingham on 22 October 1911, Ware was educated at Stoke St Peter's School and played for Hanley St Luke's before joining Stoke City, first as an amateur in December 1927, signing as a professional two years later. Encouraged all the way in various sporting activities by his father, who was a British champion boxer in the 1920s, Ware himself took to the ring as well as being a fine swimmer and table tennis star. A burly footballer, physically strong with a powerful shot, he played on the left-wing or as an inside-forward, but early on his his Stoke career his opportunities were restricted owing to the form of Tommy Sale and Harry Davies. Ware though battled on and he spent six years at The Victoria Ground, scoring 15 goals inn 57 senior appearances before transferring to Newcastle United for £2,400 in September 1935. Later he assisted Sheffield Wednesday (from May 1937 for £1,700) and Norwich City (from November 1937). After suffering a chest wound on a Normandy battlefield during the hostilities he was forced to retire from competitive football and became player-manager of Northwich Victoria during the war, taking over as team manager in 1947-48. There followed a spell in Holland as trainer-coach with FC Haarlem (from August 1948), after which he took a coaching position at Vale Park (1956). Ware managed Crewe Alexandra for two years: 1958-60, being in charge at Gresty Road when Spurs beat Alex 13-2 in an FA Cup-tie. He returned to The Victoria Ground to become assistant trainer and later acted as scout for Stoke City, a job he held until his sudden death on 28 October 1970.

WARE, Paul

Hard-working, efficient and competitive midfield player who did a good job in the centre of the park for the Potters, appearing in 142 League and Cup games and netting 14 goals, one a vital winner against Peterborough in the Autoglass Semi-final of 1992 which took the Potters through to Wembley. Born in Congleton on 7 November 1970, he signed for Stoke on YTS forms in 1985 and turned professional in November 1988 (on his 18th birthday). A

WARTIME FOOTBALL

1915-19

For the duration of World War One period (1915-19) Stoke participated in the Lancashire section, comprising each season of a primary competition which preceded a secondary competition.

The Potters finished in mid-table after a rather disappointing 1915-16 campaign when their best win (out of 14 recorded from 36 matches) was a 7-1 demolition of luckless Chesterfield Town in April when Billy Herbert scored a hat-trick. Derby County were beaten 6-1. Stoke's heaviest defeat of 15 suffered) was 4-1 at Everton in January. In their game at Derby (on 1 April 1916 – lost 4-2) Stoke had two players – Bob Whittingham and George Smart – sent-off. Both players were suspended for one game and Whittingham went on to top the scoring list this season with 26 goals.

In 1916-17 the Potters' form-rate improved a great deal out on the park and they ended up in third place after registering a total of 19 wins from 36 starts. The two games against Bolton yielded 18 goals – the Wanderers won 9-2 at Burnden Park while Stoke gained revenge by winning 7-0 at The Victoria Ground. Stoke also ran in two 6-0 home wins over Burnley and Blackpool. Whittingham scored a four-timer against the Clarets and twice against the Seasiders to finish up as leading marksman once more with 22 goals. A crowd of under 400 saw the Oldham-Stoke game on 7 October 1916.

The following season Stoke won the Lancs championship with a terrific record of 24 wins and six draws from their 36 matches. They also scored 119 goals against just 32. Herbert (32) and Henry Howell (28) were the top scorers.

Stoke's best win was an emphatic 16-0 drubbing of Blackburn Rovers at The Victoria Ground on 10 November. Around 8,000 fans saw two players, Whittingham and Ted Turner (playing in his only game of the season) net four goals apiece, while Herbert scored a hat-trick. Other big wins saw Burnley beaten 9-0, Blackburn 8-1 (away), Oldham Athletic 7-0 and neighbours Port Vale 6-0.

By taking the championship Stoke qualified to meet Leeds United (winners of the Midland section) in what was billed the Lancashire League Championship Cup Final.

The contest was over two legs and Leeds came out on top winning 2-1 on aggregate (2-0 to Leeds at Elland Road and 1-0 to Stoke at The Vic).

The last season of First World War football (1918-19) saw Stoke battle hard and long to hold on to their crown, but in the end they had to settle for the runners-up spot behind Everton after claiming 22 wins and five draws from their 36 fixtures. An 8-1 away victory over rivals Port Vale was Stoke's best of the bunch, while their heaviest reverse (1-4) came in the second away clash with their neighbours the Vale. Whittingham again topped the scoring charts with 23 goals.

Stoke's full record of games played: 1915-19

Season	P	W	D	L	F	A
1915-16	36	14	7	15	64	64
1916-17	36	19	7	10	75	42
1917-18	38	25	6	7	120	34
1918-19	36	22	55	9	93	46
Totals	146	80	25	41	352	186

Herbert played 135 of the games, Joey Jones in 133 and Charlie Parker 120. Whittingham top-scored with 86 goals, Herbert netted 64 and Howell 42.

1939-46

After the three void League games at the start of the 1939-40 there followed a short break when no competitive football was played at all, thus allowing the governing bodies to arrange Regional Leagues (and Cup tournaments) up and down the country.

Stoke started off (again in 1939-40) playing in the Western Regional League, drawing 4-4 with Everton in their opening game at Goodison Park, where Tommy Sale scored a hat-trick. The goals flowed thick and fast and a second 4-4 scoreline soon followed at Wrexham. Stoke played some excellent football throughout this campaign and were subsequently declared champions of their Division with 13 wins and five draws from 22 games played, finishing

Neil Franklin, Stoke's magnificent centre-half of the post-war period, seen here in RAF uniform during World War Two.

two points above Liverpool. They also took part in the League War Cup but went out to Everton.

Their biggest League triumphs were 5-1 scores registered against Stockport County and Port Vale, Syd Peppitt netting four goals in the former game.

Sale headed the scoring list this term with 24 goals; Peppitt netted 15 and Alec Ormston 11. And Neil Franklin made his first appearance for the Potters this season, lining up against Everton in a Cup game on 18 May.

On the opening day of the 1940-41 season of South Regional

League soccer, Frank Mountford, playing in only his second game for Stoke, scored a hat-trick in a 4-1 home win over Notts County. He went on to finish up as top marksman with 23 goals; Sale hit 17 and the up-and-coming Frank Bowyer claimed 10.

Several clubs did not complete a full programme of games this season and consequently League placings became a lottery which ended with Stoke finishing in 25th position (nine wins, nine draws and 18 losses from 36 fixtures). Their best wins were against Mansfield Town and Birmingham, both 5-0, while their heaviest reverse was a 7-0 stuffing at Northampton Town.

A crowd of just 300 witnessed the 2-2 draw with Notts County in January 1941.

In the Midland War Cup this term Stoke failed to get past Leicester City at the first hurdle, and in the wartime League Cup they were dismissed by Mansfield also in the opening round.

A friendly match between Stoke City and a strong RAF XI in November 1940 resulted in a 3-2 win for the Potters.

For season 1941-42, Stoke found themselves based in the Football League North, playing also in the League Cup competition. Their League programme was divided into two halves – they took fifth position behind Blackpool, Lincoln, Preston and Manchester United in the first competition which ended on Christmas Day and then claimed 16th spot in the second competition which terminated on 30 May 1942.

In the League Cup, Stoke won five and drew four of their 10 qualifying matches to go forward to the competition proper where West Bromwich Albion ousted them 9-6 on aggregate after two terrific contests which ended 5-3 to Stoke at home and 6-1 to Albion away.

Stoke's best League win this term was 9-0 v Tranmere, while they crashed 10-0 at Northampton late on in the campaign.

Tommy Sale couldn't do a thing wrong when it came to scoring – for he netted 56 goals this season – a haul which included 12 hat-tricks (13 if you include his double-treble (6 goals) in an 8-0 win over Walsall. He also struck a five-timer in that 9-0 victory over Tranmere.

In 1942-43, Stoke continued in the League North and again played out their main programme in two halves. And they also entered the now established Football League North Cup.

The Potters ended the first half in sixth position and their second in 10th, winning 21 of their 38 League matches played over the entire season.

In the Cup Stoke won six, drew two and lost two of their scheduled 10 matches to go through to the latter stages of the competition where they lost to Aston Villa after overcoming Chester.

Frank Mountford took over the scoring mantle from Sale, hitting 20 goals this term; Bowyer netted 18.

Stoke's best League win was 7-1 over Walsall; their heaviest defeat 4-0 against Aston Villa.

The 1943-44 campaign once more saw a divided fixture list, with Stoke playing through a disappointing first half to their programme, registering only six wins from 18 games to finish 34th in the national list. After Christmas their form improved slightly and they rose to 13th after claiming 10 wins and five draws from 21 starts.

In the League Cup qualifying competition, the Potters qualified for the final stages after finishing third, only a point behind the winners Wrexham. But they failed to make progress, losing out to Aston Villa.

In the Midland Cup, the Potters took care of Derby County (4-2 on aggregate), but then succumbed to West Brom by the same scoreline.

Sale bounced back to hit 30 goals this term while his partner in crime in attack, Freddie Steele, scored 20.

A 9-3 walloping of Wolverhampton Wanderers was Stoke's best League win of the campaign (Steele scored six times in this game). The Potters also beat West Bromwich Albion 8-3 when Steele notched a four-timer. Their heaviest defeat was suffered at the hands of Leicester, who won 5-2 at The Victoria Ground.

It was action in both the Football League North, League Cup and Midland Cup competitions once again for the Potters in 1944-45, and they did reasonably well, taking 11th place overall after the first set of 18 League games had been completed. But then they slipped down to 17th spot after the next set of fixtures when they won 12 out of 23.

Of their 10 Football League North Cup matches, six were won, two drawn and two lost, and Stoke were credited with 9th place in the final table. They lost to Aston Villa in the Midland Cup, going down 2-1 over two legs.

Sale (34), Mountford (15) and Steele (10) all got into double figures in the goals scoring charts. Wins of 8-1 over Port Vale and 7-0 v Chester were Stoke's best League victories, while their heaviest set-back was a 6-1 scoreline against Manchester United.

The 1945-46 campaign was regarded as a transitional season, whereby clubs up and down the country concentrated on getting back together their senior squads in readiness for the resumption of serious League soccer in 1946. Stoke played in the Football League North and they also took part in the FA Cup for the first time in seven years.

Unfortunately they had a poor League season, winning 18 and losing 18 of their 42 matches to finish 13th in the table with 42 points, 18 fewer than the champions Sheffield United.

A 6-0 thrashing of Preston at home was their best win, while their heaviest defeat came at Newcastle where they crashed 9-1 in front of a 45,000 crowd.

In early rounds in the FA Cup (up to the semi-final stage) were played over two legs. Stoke defeated Burnley (4-3 on aggregate), Sheffield United (4-3) and then Sheffield Wednesday (2-0) before losing to Bolton Wanderers in the sixth round, also by 2-0. The second leg of this quarter-final clash with the Trotters at Burnden Park saw two crash barriers and surrounding wall collapse causing 33 people to lose their lives (See BOLTON WANDERERS).

In this last war season, Freddie Steele topped the scoring charts with a total of 43 goals – 36 more than George Antonio (9).

This is Stoke's full playing record (League & Cup) during 1939-46:

Season	P	W	D	L	F	A
1939-40*	30	18	6	6	78	49
1940-41	38	10	9	19	39	102
1941-42	38	21	4	13	116	85
1942-43	38	21	7	10	88	59
1943-44	39	16	8	15	105	80
1944-45	41	21	6	14	104	65
1945-46	50	20	8	22	98	92
Totals	274	127	48	99	629	532

* Including three void First Division games.

Tommy Sale appeared in 261 of Stoke's 274 war games and he also topped the scoring charts with a total of 179 goals. Harry Brigham had 221 outings and Neil Franklin 194, while chasing Sale in the goals-race were Freddie Steele with 88 and Fred Basnett 58.

WARWICK COUNTY

County visited Stoke for a first-round qualifying FA Cup-tie in October 1888 and they caused a minor upset by winning 2-1.

WATFORD

Stoke's playing record against the Hornets is:

Football League

Venue	P	W	D	L	F	A
Home	8	5	1	2	14	9
Away	8	1	2	5	6	13
Totals	16	6	3	7	20	22

Southern League

Venue	P	W	D	L	F	A
Home	2	1	0	1	2	2
Away	2	1	0	1	6	6
Totals	4	2	0	2	8	8

FA Cup

Venue	P	W	D	L	F	A
Away	1	0	0	1	0	1

League Cup

Venue	P	W	D	L	F	A
Home	2	1	1	0	2	0
Away	1	0	0	1	1	3
Totals	3	1	1	1	3	3

Stoke and Watford first met at Football League level in season 1982-83 (Division One). The Potters achieved their best result over the Hornets when winning their home game in style by 4-0. The goals came from Mickey Thomas, Ian Painter, Dave McAughtrie and Mark Chamberlain. At Vicarage Road, a lone strike from future England star John Barnes gave the Hornets all three points.

The following season Watford came to The Victoria Ground and ran up their best win over the Potters, swamping them to the tune of 4-0 with Barnes scoring twice this time.

Each side registered a 4-2 victory over the other during the Southern League days of 1911-13 – and both were at Watford.

Tony Allen and Calvin Palmer scored Stoke's goals in their 2-0 League Cup win over Watford in September 1967.

Players with both clubs: Dave Bamber, Jimmy Broad, Roy Brown, Ephraim Colclough, Jock Grieve, Brian Horne, Jack Maxwell, Billy Poole, Keith Scott, Brian Talbot, Bob White and Fred Wilkinson.

Sammy Chung played for Watford and later became assistant manager-coach at Stoke City.

WATKIN, Arthur E.

'Arty' Watkin had two spells at The Victoria Ground – 1913-23 and 1924-27. All told he scored 77 goals in 177 competitive games for the club, collecting a Southern League Division Two championship medal in 1914-15 when he netted 24 times, including a nap-hand of five in a 10-0 win over Ebbw Vale, in just 20 appearances. Born in Burslem in 1896, Watkin was an alert forward who could, if required, occupy any position in the front-line. He never played serious football before joining Stoke – but within a matter of 12 months he was regarded as one of the best strikers in the game. Watkin served in the forces during World War One, but was back in action in 1919 and he divided his time as a pottery manager with that of playing (and scoring goals) for Stoke. He turned his back on the club in 1923 to go and play for Congleton Town, but after a year away, manager Tom Mather enticed him back to The Victoria Ground, where he was to stay for the next three seasons. In that time he netted a few important goals and appeared in six matches when Stoke won the Second Division title in 1926-27. Watkin, whose brother Frank played five times for Stoke in the mid-1920s, retired after that last campaign, and went full-time in the pottery business. He died c.1965.

Atty Watkin

WATKIN, Cyril

A local find, born in Stoke-on-Trent on 21 July 1926, full-back Watkin played his early football all round the Potteries area with Park Road, Packmoor FC, Sneyd Colliery and Port Vale before joining Stoke City in September 1944. After a dozen or so wartime appearances, he got into the first XI at The Victoria Ground in 1948 and went on to play in 90 senior games for the club before transferring to Bristol City for £8,000 in July 1952. Unfortunately his career was brought to an abrupt end when he broke his leg whilst at Ashton Gate. He retired in May 1953, aged 26.

WATKIN, Frank

Born in Stoke-on-Trent on 30 March 1904, centre-forward Watkin scored three times in five League games for Stoke towards the end of the 1926-27 Third Division North championship-winning season when he came into the side in place of the injured Johnny Eyres. Signed from Congleton Town in the summer of 1925, he left The Victoria Ground and joined Port Vale in June 1929 and scored five goals in Vale's 7-1 win over Rotherham in February 1930. On leaving the Valiants in April 1931, he returned to his former club, Congleton. Watkin died at Hartshill on 26 January 1979.

WATKINS, Walter Martin

Mart Watkins was born in Llanwnnog, Montgomeryshire in 1880 and long with his brother Ernie, was brought up on a farm in mid-Wales. Both men gravitated via Cearsws (1894) to Oswestry United (1896), but progressed and it was Mart who interested Stoke most and he duly signed for the Potteries club in July 1900. An adaptable forward, able to occupy any front-line position, he was leading scorer for the club in 1901-02 with 16 goals and in 1902-03 with 13. Described as a 'smart player' with powerful shot, Watkins marshalled his colleagues splendidly and always used his wingers to good effect. In January 1904 Watkins was approached by Manchester City, who offered Stoke £450 for his signature. The deal fell though and in that same month Watkins moved to Aston Villa. He only had spent nine months there, appearing in five games before switching to Sunderland. He never settled in the North-East and in June 1905 came due south to sign for Crystal Palace. From there he went to Northampton Town (May 1906) and 12 months later returned to Stoke. He spent just one term back in the Potteries before having a good spell with Crewe Alexandra, a full season with Stafford Rangers and a year as coach to Tunstall FC Watkins then returned to The Victoria Ground for the third time in August 1911, staying with Stoke until May 1914 when he retired. His full record with the Potters was 62 goals in 139 appearances. Capped by Wales on 10 occasions, Watkins played in his first international in 1902 v England

and his last in 1908 against Ireland. He died in Stoke on 14 May 1942. NB: Mart's brother Ernie Watkins went on to play for Leicester Fosse, Aston Villa, Grimsby Town, Millwall Athletic and Southend United and he won five Welsh caps.

WATNEY CUP

Stoke played three games in this short-lived competition, in August 1973, and they won them all, including the Final. After beating Plymouth Argyle 1-0 at Home Park (Geoff Hurst the scorer) and disposing of Bristol City 4-1 at The Victoria Ground in the semi-final, when Hurst, Mike Pejic, Terry Conroy and Jimmy Greenhoff found the net, Stoke met Hull City in the Final on 18 August. The Potters had home advantage again, and they made it count, beating the Tigers 2-0 with Greenhoff scoring both goals in front of 18,159 fans.

Stoke's full record in this competition is:

Venue	P	W	D	L	F	A
Home	2	2	0	0	6	1
Away	1	1	0	0	1	0
Totals	3	3	0	0	7	1

WATSON, David Vernon

Making the initial breakthrough as a professional with Notts County in January 1967, Dave Watson quickly became an established defender. He developed briefly under Tommy Docherty's management at Rotherham whom he served from January 1968 to December 1970, and carried on his rise to the top with Sunderland (to June 1975), then Manchester City (to the summer of 1978). the German Bundesliga side Werder Bremen and Southampton, whom he joined in October 1979. Born at Stapleford on 5 October 1946, he was certainly one of Richie Barker's best buys for Stoke City whom he joined the Potters from Southampton in January 1982 for £50,000. He went on to score six times in his 64 senior outings for the Potters whom he left in the summer of 1983 to go on an illegal tour to South Africa which never materialised. Instead he played in the NASL with Vancouver Whitecaps, returning in September 1983 to sign for Derby County. He had a second spell with the Whitecaps, and assisted Fort Lauderdale Sun, before winding down his senior career with Notts County as player-coach. He retiring from League action in May 1985 to join Kettering Town. A determined centre-half with an abundance of skill, Watson gained 65 full England caps and amassed a grand total of 660 League appearances (67 goals scored) for his eight English clubs spread over a period of 18 years. A fine defender.

WATSON, Harold

Centre-half Watson played in just four League games for Stoke during his three seasons at The Victoria Ground. Born in Wath-on-Deane in 1908, he joined the Potters from Wath Wanderers in 1927 and left The Victoria Ground in the summer of 1930 to sign for Brighton & Hove Albion. He was reserve to Tom Williamson.

WEMBLEY STADIUM

Stoke City have played twice at The Empire Stadium. They beat Chelsea 2-1 in the 1972 League Cup Final and then defeated Stockport County 1-0 to win the Autoglass Trophy in 1992.

WEST BROMWICH ALBION

Stoke's playing record against Albion is:

Football League

Venue	P	W	D	L	F	A
Home	56	30	17	9	106	57
Away	56	18	10	28	67	110
Totals	112	48	27	37	173	167

FA Cup

Venue	P	W	D	L	F	A
Home	1	0	1	0	2	2
Away	3	0	1	2	2	7
Totals	4	0	2	2	4	9

Autoglass trophy

Venue	P	W	D	L	F	A
Home	1	1	0	0	2	1

Stoke's first League game was against Albion (h) on 8 September 1888. Over 4,500 fans saw Albion win 2-0 to become the first team to head the new Football League table (on goal-average).

By coincidence, the last Football League game to be staged at The Vic was also against West Bromwich Albion, a Nationwide First Division fixture on Sunday 4 May 1997, when a crowd of 22,500 witnessed a 2-1 win for Stoke (McMahon and Kavanagh their scorers).

Stoke's best ever League victory is 10-3 v Albion at The Victoria Ground in a First Division match on 4 February 1937.

An early injury to the visitors' goalkeeper Billy Light didn't help Albion's cause and Stoke completely dominated the game from the 11th minute onwards. Freddie Steele helped himself to five goals with Joe Johnson (soon to move to The Hawthorns) scoring twice.

Stoke beat Albion 5-0 at home in November 1903, 4-0 in September 1937 (another hat-trick for Steele) and 5-1 in January 1953 – all League games.

Albion's best League wins over Stoke (all at home) have been: 5-1 in October 1933, 5-3 in September 1964 (when Baggies' full-back Bobby Cram scored a hat-trick), 6-2 in September 1965 (a hat-trick this time for John Kaye), 5-2 in August 1970 and 6-0 in December 1988.

Stoke were beaten 3-2 at home by Albion in the Final of the 1883 Staffordshire Cup (See STAFFORDSHIRE CUP).

Between 1989 and 1997, Stoke remained unbeaten against Albion in 15 League games and one Autoglass Trophy Cup-tie, Stoke registered 12 wins with four games drawn.

Garth Crooks scored a hat-trick for Stoke in their 3-2 League win over Albion in December 1979. Crooks later joined Albion.

When the sides were drawn together in the fifth round of the FA Cup in 1888, Stoke offered Albion £40 to switch the tie to The Victoria Ground. They were rebuffed and Albion swept to a 4-1 victory with Jem Bayliss scoring all four goals.

In a wartime League Cup-tie in February 1944, Stoke thrashed Albion 8-2 with both Steele and Tommy Sale netting hat-tricks.

Players with both clubs: George Baddeley, Gary Bannister, Paul Barron, Tommy Broad, Fred Brown, Garth Crooks, Bill Davies, Paul Dyson, Wayne Ebanks, Fred Fenton, Ross Fielding, Tony Ford, Gary Hackett, Graham Harbey, Willie Hendry, Geoff Hurst, Joe Johnson, Tony Kelly, Neil MacKenzie (Albion reserve), Steve Parkin, Paul Peschisolido, Graham Potter, Paul Reece, Brian Rice, Fred Rouse, Maurice Setters, Andy Smith, Andrew 'Scottie' Smith, Derek Statham, Brian Talbot, Mickey Thomas and Isaiah Turner.

Ex-Albion midfielder Asa Hartford was Stoke's assistant manager-coach in 1993-94; Brian Caswell played for Albion's Reserves and later coached at Stoke; Bill Asprey had over 340 games for Stoke (1954-65) and later managed the Potters (1984-85) after coaching at Albion (1972-74); Stoke goalkeeper John Farmer guested for Albion in 1972 and Sid Glidden, an Albion reserve (1925-28) was Stoke's trainer (1952-54). David Powell, an Albion reserve goalkeeper, was on loan at Stoke in 1988 while another goalkeeper, Barry Siddall, on loan to Albion in 1990, earlier played for Stoke (1984-86) and Peter Ford was an amateur with Albion before joining Stoke. Cyril Lea was a coach at Albion (under Brian Talbot) and coach-assistant to manager Alan Durban at Stoke (1979-80).

WEST BROMWICH ALBION RESERVES

Stoke played Albion Reserves six times in the Birmingham & District League between 1908 and 1911. Their full record against the Baggies' second string was:

Venue	P	W	D	L	F	A
Home	3	2	0	1	8	3
Away	3	1	1	1	4	10
Totals	6	3	1	2	12	13

Stoke's best win of the three recorded against Albion was 5-0 at home in April 1909, while the Baggies handed out an 8-1 thrashing to the Potters at The Hawthorns in October 1908.

WEST HAM UNITED

Stoke's playing record against the Hammers is:

Football League

Venue	P	W	D	L	F	A
Home	29	18	5	6	48	28
Away	29	4	10	15	28	55
Totals	58	22	15	21	76	83

Southern League

Venue	P	W	D	L	F	A
Home	2	1	0	1	4	4
Away	2	0	1	1	0	5
Totals	4	1	1	2	4	9

League Cup

Venue	P	W	D	L	F	A
Home	3	0	1	2	3	5
Away	5	2	1	2	5	7
Totals	8	2	2	4	8	12

The Hammers beat Stoke 5-0 in London in a Southern League game on Christmas Day 1912 and 45 years later, on 16 November 1957. They repeated that scoreline in a Second Division match at Upton Park, these being their two best victories over the Potters at senior level.

When the Potters lost their First Division status in 1984-85, West Ham won 4-2 at The Victoria Ground and 5-1 at Upton Park.

They also beat Stoke 4-1 at The Vic in March 1958, on their way to promotion, and that 4-1 win was repeated at Upton Park in March 1964 (Division One).

Stoke's biggest League win over the Hammers is 5-2 in a First Division match at The Victoria Ground in November 1982. Sammy McIlroy scored twice that day in front of a 17,589 crowd.

Stoke have also gained two 4-3 wins over the Londoners, beating them at The Victoria Ground in a Southern League game in December 1911, when Jack Lenaghan scored a hat-trick, and in London in a First Division match in October 1967, when Harry Burrows and Peter Dobing both scored twice.

Back in the Football League, Stoke won their home Second Division game by 3-0 in March 1956 in front of a near 20,000 crowd, and by the same score in the same month in 1964 when 25,000 fans attended.

Defender Denis Smith netted twice in Stoke's 3-3 away League draw with West Ham in October 1969.

The Hammers defeated Stoke, convincingly, by 3-0 at The Victoria Ground in a fourth-round FA Cup-tie in 1967-68.

In season 1971-72, West Ham met Stoke four times in the semi-final of the League Cup before the Potters finally went through to Wembley after winning the second replay 3-2 at Old Trafford. In the final clash (the second replay) Hammers' lost goalkeeper Bobby Ferguson for a short time with a head injury. He was replaced by Bobby Moore who then saved Mike Bernard's penalty only to be beaten by the rebound.

Players with both clubs: Lee Chapman, Billy Cope, Bob Dixon, Jack Farrell, Peter Fox, Geoff Hurst, Kevin Keen, Lawrie Leslie, Bob Lister, Sam McAllister, Mike Macari (Hammers' junior), Nicky Morgan, Tony Parks, Wilf Phillips, Fred Richardson, Frank Robertson and Peter Shilton.

Lou Macari managed West Ham United in 1989-90 (before taking over at Stoke). Graham Paddon was a player with the Hammers who later became assistant and then caretaker manager at Stoke.

WEST MIDLANDS REGIONAL LEAGUE

Stoke entered their reserve team in this League during the period 1900 to 1921, playing a total of 476 games over 14 seasons.

P	W	D	L	F	A	Pts
476	209	89	178	917	765	507

Stoke's A team participated in this same competition from 1959 to 1964, accumulating this record:

P	W	D	L	F	A	Pts
174	45	28	101	281	391	118

WESTLAND, Douglas G.

Doug Westland was born in Aberdeen c.1909 and played in six League games for Stoke over a period of two years (1937-39) making his debut in that record 10-3 League win over West Brom in February 1937. A former junior with the Banks o'Dee club, he joined the Potters from Aberdeen in May 1936 (signed by fellow Scot Bob McGrory) and left The Victoria Ground after a handful of wartime appearances. Then played briefly for Barlaston St Giles before emigrating to Canada (1945), and it is believed Westland is still alive today, living in that country.

WESTLAND, James

A Scotsman, born in Aberdeen in July 1917, Jimmy Westland, brother of goalkeeper Doug (previous) was a useful forward with Inchgarth FC, Banks o'Dee and Aberdeen, he was recruited to The Victoria Ground in July 1935 for a trial and impressed so much that he was signed on a permanent basis the following month. He spent the next 11 years as a registered player with Stoke, accumulating a useful set of statistics – 16 goals in 64 League and Cup outings, plus wartime appearances, although his career was severely disrupted between 1939 and 1945. An under graduate from Aberdeen University, Westland could have become a professional dancer – but he chose the football pitch instead of the ballroom. He died in Newcastle (Staffs) in 1972, aged 55.

Jimmy Westland

WESTON, Thomas

Weston was a tough-tackling Black Country full-back who had a fine career with Aston Villa before joining Stoke in September 1922, as a stand-by for Bob McGrory and Alec Milne. Born in Halesowen in August 1890, Weston played his early football with Red Hill School. From 1905 to 1907 he assisted Quarry Bank and afterwards starred for Old Hill Comrades and Coombes Wood before becoming a professional with Villa (July 1911). He gained two FA Cup winners' medals whilst at Villa Park (1913 and 1920) and was close to full England honours on a number of occasions. During World War One he was wounded in a battle in Ervilliers in France in March 1918, but returned to play three post-war seasons with the Villa, taking his record up to 179
appearances. He remained at The Victoria Ground for just two years, starting only four League games. On his retirement in 1924 Weston went into coaching youngsters at schools inn the Stourbridge and Cradley Heath areas. He died in Stourbridge in 1952.

WHARTON, Tancey C.

Wharton spent one season with Stoke, playing as a left half-back in 19 first-team games in season 1913-14. Born in Dawden c.1890, he joined the Potters from Seaham Harbour FC in March 1913 and left The Victoria Ground for Grantham.

WHISTON, Donald

It is reported that Don Whiston was spotted by an eagle-eyed Stoke City scout playing for a local Boys Brigade team. He was eventually recruited to the club as amateur in 1948 and taken on as a full-time professional in December 1949. Described as a 'genuine all-rounder' Whiston was born in Stoke-on-Trent on 4 April 1930 and it was as a full-back where he played his best soccer. A dedicated clubman, he stayed at The Victoria Ground until February 1957, performing mainly in the Reserves, and having only 36 first-team outings (5 goals scored) in that time. He left Stoke for Crewe Alexandra on a free transfer and after two seasons at Gresty Road he went on to play for Rochdale.

WHITE, Robert Nelson

Outside-right Bob White had a good career in the game, serving a number of clubs, starting off with Prudhoe Castle in 1919, then Huddersfield Town before joining Stoke City (May 1924 to March 1925). He then switched to Tranmere Rovers, had a brief spell with Yeovil & Petters and then netted twice in three League games for Wolves in 1929-30. He later assisted Watford, Portsmouth and Carlisle United. Born in Newburn-on-Tyne c.1903, White appeared in just three League games for the Potters, coming into the forward-line in place of John Evans.

WHITEHOUSE, Frank

Inside or centre-forward 'Tinker' Whitehouse was a willing and purposeful player, born in Newcastle (Staffs) in 1876, who joined Stoke from neighbours Burslem Port Vale in May 1900. After five years at The Vic he was transferred to Glossop North End (June 1905) and following a brief spell with Wolverhampton Wanderers Reserves he quit football in the summer of 1908. He scored 24 goals in 95 League and Cup appearances for the Potters whom he joined in June 1899 from Bucknall.

WHITEHOUSE, Jack

A very stylish yet competitive half-back, the fair-haired Whitehouse was a regular in the Wolverhampton Wanderers League side for five years (from 1901). He made 155 appearances and scored one goal for the Molineux club and always gave 100 per-cent effort on the field of play (he was sent-off at least once during his time with Wolves). Born in Swan Village, West Bromwich in August 1878, Whitehouse, who had four brothers, two of them footballers, played for Wednesbury Town for a couple of years before moving to Wolves in July 1900, acting initially as reserve to Ted Pheasant, before claiming a place in the first XI the following year. He had a brief two-month spell with Stourbridge after being forced to leave Molineux following a flare-up with two colleagues. He signed for Stoke in October 1906 and played in two League games for the Potters, against Everton and Blackburn Rovers the following month, before being released early in 1907. He then went on to play for a number of Black Country sides, among them Bloxwich Strollers, Darlaston, Dudley and Gornal Wood. He retired in 1915.

WHITEHURST, Albert John

Born in Fenton on 22 June 1898, Bert Whitehurst turned out to be a fine centre-forward who played League football from 1921 to 1934. He joined Stoke from New Haden Colliery in June 1920, made his debut for the Potters against Stockport County the following March and went on to score four goals in 18 outings before leaving The Victoria Ground for Rochdale in June 1923. After five excellent years at Spotland when he netted 116 goals in 168 League North appearances, including 44 in 42 matches in 1926-27 when he headed the Division's scoring charts, he moved to Liverpool (May 1928). Sadly, he failed to impress at Anfield (two goals in eight games) and in February 1929 was sold to Bradford City. He helped the Bantams win the Third Division North title at the end of that season by claiming 24 goals in only 15 appearances including seven in an 8-0 drubbing of Tranmere Rovers in March. Ironically, from Valley Parade he went to Tranmere Rovers (June 1931) and played as a centre-half during the latter stages of his time at Prenton Park. He retired in May 1934 with a record of 180 goals in 313 League games. Whitehurst died in 1976.

WHITEHURST, William

Tough, aggressive striker who had five outings for Stoke on loan from Sheffield United in November 1990. Born at Thurnscoe on 10 June 1959, Whitehurst also served with Mexborough Town, Hull City, Newcastle United, Oxford United, Reading, Sunderland, Hull (again), Doncaster Rovers and Crewe Alexandra. He netted 52 goals in 229 League games all told (up to 1994) when he moved down a peg to play, in turn, for Hatfield Main, Kettering Town (two spells), Goole Town, Preston Macedonia (in Australia), Stalybridge Celtic, Stafford Rangers, Mossley, Glentoran (in Ireland) and in South China. He won an Associate Members Cup losers' medal with Hull in 1984.

Billy Whitehurst

WHITLEY, John

When Welsh international goalkeeper Dickie Roose left The Victoria Ground for Everton in the summer of 1904, Stoke went out and recruited Cornishman Jack Whitley from Goodison Park as his replacement. But after playing in 34 games for the Potters in his first season at The Vic, Whitley suddenly found himself in the Reserves as Roose chose to return for a second spell with the Potters. In April 1906, after adding four more appearances to his tally, Whitley was transferred to Leeds City, quickly moving on to Lincoln City before teaming up with Chelsea in July 1907. He spent the next seven years at Stamford Bridge, making 127 League appearances for the Londoners before announcing his retirement in 1914. He immediately took over as trainer at the Bridge, a position he held for 32 years, until 1939 – one of the longest associations anyone has had with Chelsea. Whitley, who was a real gentleman and fine billiards player, acted as guardian to several of the youngsters at the club. He was noted for his immaculate dress-sense, and as he ran onto the pitch to treat an injured player, his coat tails flapped behind him and his bald head glistened. Born in Seacombe in April 1880, Whitley played for Liskeard YMCA before making the long trip north to sign for Darwen (1899). From there he went to Aston Villa (May 1900) and found his way to Everton in 1902. He died in London in 1955.

WHITTAKER, Enos

Lancastrian outside-right from Nelson (born c.1888) Whittaker attempted to make the grade in Devon with Exeter City, but failed to get a first team call-up and joined Stoke in the summer of 1912. He did better at The Victoria Ground and scored once in 18 games for the Potters before having an unsuccessful two-month spell with Clapton Orient (August-September 1913).

WHITTAKER, Harvey

Another outside-right who scored once in four League appearances for Stoke during the 1899-1900 season. Born in Congleton c.1875, Whittaker played for his local team Congleton Hornets prior to joining the Potters and after leaving The Victoria Ground he assisted Newcastle Town.

WHITTINGHAM, Robert

Bob Whittingham was a vigorous, all-action, stocky centre-forward, 5ft 8ins tall and weighing a fraction over 12st, who was renowned for his powerful shooting. He was the scourge of goalkeepers, one saying: "I'd rather face his Satanic Majesty than Whittingham." Born in Goldenhill (Staffs) c.February 1889, he played for Goldenhill Villa, Crewe Alexandra (from August 1906), Burslem Port Vale (May 1907), Blackpool (May 1908), Bradford City (January 1909) and Chelsea (April 1910, signed for £1,300) before signing officially for Stoke in September 1919, having guested for the Potters, Port Vale and South Shields during World War One. He left The Victoria Ground in March 1920, and had a couple of games for Stoke United. He then signed for Wrexham, but did not play a game for the Welsh club's first XI, returning home to sign for Goldenhill Wanderers in 1925. On 9 June 1926 Whittingham collapsed and died at his home in Goldenhill. He was 37. He netted 86 goals in 84 wartime games for the Potters (at least half from outside the penalty area) and he followed up with eight more in 18 League matches in the first peacetime campaign. He appeared in two Victory internationals for England v Scotland in 1919. All told he scored 147 goals in 249 League and FA Cup appearances, plus over 100 more strikes in his wartime exploits.

WHITTLE, Justin

Central defender, 6ft 1ins tall and 12st 12lbs in weight, Whittle was signed by manager Lou Macari from Celtic on a free transfer in October 1994 – after Macari had returned to The Victoria Ground following a spell in charge at Parkhead. Born in Derby on 18 March 1971, Whittle struggled to get a look in at Celtic, although he did perform well in the Reserves. He took time to settle in Stoke, but after

Justin Whittle

Vince Overson had moved on and Ian Cranson was forced to retire, he stepped up and made the number-five slot his own during the 1996-97 campaign, when he took his appearance tally up to 50.

WIGAN ATHLETIC

Stoke's playing record against Athletic is:
Football League

Venue	P	W	D	L	F	A
Home	3	3	0	0	7	1
Away	3	0	1	2	1	6
Totals	6	3	1	2	8	7

It was not until season 1990-91 that Stoke first met Athletic in a League game. The clash in the Potteries saw Stoke win 2-0, but a 4-0 thrashing at Springfield Park saw the end of Alan Ball's reign as manager at The Victoria Ground. The Potters' best win over Athletic is 3-0 at home in December 1991 when only 8,419 fans saw Mark Stein, Tony Kelly and Wayne Biggins hit the net.

Players with both clubs: Charlie Bishop (Stoke junior), Darren Boughey, John Butler, Chris Hemming, Jack Howshall, Tony 'Zico' Kelly, Mick Kennedy, Paul Rennie, Colin Russell and Kevin Sheldon.

WIGAN BOROUGH

Stoke's playing record against Borough is:
Football League

Venue	P	W	D	L	F	A
Home	1	1	0	0	2	0
Away	1	1	0	0	3	0
Totals	2	2	0	0	5	0
FA Cup						
Away	1	1	0	0	5	2

The first League game was played at Stoke on 30 August 1926 and a crowd of 6,778 saw goals from Dick Johnson and Charlie Wilson give the Potters both points from a 2-0 win as they commenced their march towards the Third Division North championship. On target in Stoke's 3-0 win at Wigan a week later, were Walter Bussey, Bobby Archibald and Wilson again.

Stoke's scorers in their emphatic 5-2 FA Cup win in January 1926 were Dick Johnson (3) and Harry Davies (2). The crowd was under 4,000.

Stoke met Borough in a friendly in August 1982 and won 1-0 with a second-half goal from Peter Griffiths. There were just 1,059 fans present on a 'pig of a night'. The Potters beat Wigan 3-0 in another friendly in 1985, but then lost 1-0 in the Isle of Man tournament the following year. Twelve months later, in the same competition, Stoke gained sweet revenge with a 1-0 victory (they went on to win the trophy). And in 1992, the Potters again beat Athletic, this time by 2-0, as they powered on to take the trophy for a second time.

Players with both clubs: Billy Herbert and Andy Smith.

WILKES, Thomas Henry

One of the most popular players in the game, goalkeeper Tom Wilkes, who was born in Alcester, Warwickshire on 19 June 1874, started his career with Congregational Unity of Redditch in 1889. He then had two years with Redditch Town before joining Aston Villa as a professional in April 1893. A tall, hefty man (over six feet tall and weighing almost 13st) he was both agile and brave, had a massive pair of hands and could claw a ball out of the air with ease. In his first five years with the Villa he helped them win the FA Cup in 1895 and the League championship the following year. But after losing his place to Jimmy Whitehouse, he was loaned out to Stoke at a crucial time (January 1898) when the Potters were desperately trying to claw themselves out of trouble at the foot of the First Division. He failed to save Stoke from competing in the end-of-season Test Matches, but in those four vital games he did marvelously well, keeping three clean sheets as the Potters survived to fight another day in the top flight. After this Wilkes returned to Villa Park, but was then signed permanently by Stoke to replace George Clawley in July 1899. He remained at The Victoria Ground for four seasons, taking his appearance tally to 89 before retiring to take over the Wharf Tavern in the town centre. In April 1913, a benefit match was arranged for Wilkes when it was learnt that he had fallen on hard times and was also suffering from ill-health. He died in Stoke-on-Trent in February 1921.

WILKINSON, Frederick

A well-built half-back, born in Hertford c.1897, Fred Wilkinson played in three League games for Stoke during the early part of the 1921-22 season. He had joined the club from Watford and left The Victoria Ground for Bury St Edmunds.

WILKINSON, Norman

Goalkeeper Wilkinson was a Stoke City player from 17 years – from July 1935 to May 1952. During that time he appeared in 186 League games, 12 FA Cup-ties and 14 wartime matches. Born in Tantobie,

County Durham on 8 June 1910, he was manager Bob McGrory's first signing when the former Potters' full-back took over the reins from Tom Mather. He cost a bargain £100 from Huddersfield Town having earlier served with West Stanley FC Tannfield Lea and Tantobie, where he had been a centre-half. He switched to playing between the posts in an emergency and stuck to the job with great effect. Wilkinson became first-choice goalkeeper at The Vic almost immediately and held his position until the outbreak of the war. On his return from active duty, he found that Dennis Herod had taken over the gloves, but in 1949 was called back into the fray and made over 40 extra appearances when he through his career was over. Wilkinson was 42 when he left Stoke for Oswestry Town in 1952.

Norman Wilkinson

WILLIAMS, Brett

Stoke City took full-back Williams on loan from Nottingham Forest in August/September 1993. He made two League appearances. Born in Dudley on 19 March 1968, he also played on loan with Stockport County (1987), Northampton Town (1988), Hereford United (1989) and Oxford United in a relatively short Football League career which ended in 1994. He made exactly 50 appearances for Forest.

WILLIAMS, James

Williams could play as a full-back or wing-half. He was a 'sturdy fellow' born in Tunstall c.1888, who had a brief spell with Blackpool (no first-team appearances) before joining Stoke in March 1909. He played in nine games for the Potters, up to 1911, when he was released to Hanley Swifts.

WILLIAMS, John Nelson

Stoke City boss Lou Macari acquired 6ft 2ins striker John Williams from Coventry City in December 1994. He played in four League (three as sub) before retiring to Highfield Road. Born in Birmingham on 11 May 1968, he was a postman, playing non-League soccer for Cradley Heath when Swansea City signed him for £5,000 in August 1991, this after he had been on trial with the Potters playing in a friendly v Worcester City. He adapted to top-class football very well and scored 11 goals in 46 games for the Welsh club before transferring to Coventry for £250,000 in July 1992. Life wasn't so easy in the Premiership, but Williams battled on and netted another 11 goals in 86 appearances for the Sky Blues, while having loan spells with his old club, Swansea, Notts County and the Potters. In September 1995 he left Highfield Road for Wycombe Wanderers in a £150,000 deal and was with Hereford United in February 1997.

WILLIAMS, Joshua Joseph 'Josh'

One of the smallest players in League football during the 1920s, Williams stood only 5ft 5ins tall and weighed barely 10st but he was a useful player, occupying the right-wing position in 86 League and Cup games for Stoke and scoring 17 goals. Born in Yorkshire on 4 June 1898, he played for his home-town club, Rotherham County before joining Huddersfield Town with whom he gained a League championship medal under manager Herbert Chapman. In March 1926 Williams was transferred to Stoke, arriving far too late to save the club from relegation from the Second Division. But he was a key member of the side which won the Third Division North title at the first time of trying the following season. In September 1929, manager Chapman, who had now moved from Leeds Road to Highbury, recruited Williams for Arsenal, paying Stoke £3,000 for his signature. The winger did reasonably well with the Gunners and he rounded off his interesting career at Middlesbrough and then Ipswich Town. An ex-tool maker, he did c.1986.

WILLIAMS, Lewis (Louis)

Born at Longton late in 1888, Williams was a dogged defender with ferocious tackle and good technique. He played for North Staffordshire Nomads before signing for Stoke in 1906. In July 1908 he left the Potteries for Bradford City and later assisted Bristol Rovers for three years (from May 1909) before teaming up with Port Vale in June 1912, making his debut in a 7-0 win over New Brighton Tower Amateurs in the FA Cup. He made eight first-team appearances for the Vale before leaving the club in 1913.

WILLIAMS, Richard

Goalkeeper Dick Williams played in 62 games for Stoke between April 1927 and April 1930. Born in Newcastle-upon-Tyne c.1905, he served with Jarrow before being spotted by Stoke, who brought down to the Potteries initially as cover for Bob Dixon. After almost a full season in the second team, he finally got his chance in the senior side, making his debut at Lincoln City in the penultimate League game of Stoke's Third Division North championship-winning campaign, and he did well, saving a penalty in a 3-1 win. Williams eventually left The Victoria Ground in the summer of 1930, following the emergence of Norman Lewis, signing for Reading for £250. He later assisted Chester. Williams died on 27 May 1983.

WILLIAMS, Terence J.

Midfielder Terry Williams was forced to quit the game through injury when only 21 years of age. Born in Stoke-on-Trent on 23 October 1966, he joined the Potters as a teenager in 1982, turned professional on his 18th birthday and appeared in 17 first-team games before a spate of aggravating leg injuries halted his career. He played his last game against Brighton in October 1986 before he had turned pro.

WILLIAMSON, Ira William M.

Bill Williamson was an orthodox outside-right, who played for Stoke Nomads, Stoke (summer of 1905 to April 1908), Crewe Alexandra and Leicester Fosse. He appeared in eight first-team games for the Potters, as a stand-in for Ross Fielding.

WILLIAMSON, Thomas Robertson

A ship's plater working on the River Clyde during the week, centre-half Tom Williamson played football at the weekends for Kilbowie Ross Dhu and Kirkintilloch Rob Roy before signing for Blackburn Rovers. Unfortunately he never fitted in at Ewood Park and made an early return to Scotland to sign for Third Lanark. In December 1926, Stoke moved in and persuaded the rugged defender to sign for them – and he went on to become a star performer, scoring 15 goals in 162 games for the Potters, up to July 1931. Born in Dalmuir, Glasgow on 8 February 1901, Williamson was an attack-minded defender, who loved to carry the ball forward, and it was he who led the rest of the Stoke players in asking for improved in wages and conditions. He had five excellent seasons at The Victoria Ground before transferring to Norwich City, whom he skippered prior to leaving Carrow Road to round off his career with Frosts Athletic. On retiring he chose to live in Norwich where he ran the Rose Tavern. Sadly Williamson died in a house fire in Norwich on 1 April 1988, aged 87.

WILSHAW, Dennis James

Wilshaw was a natural goalscorer – a player who, in today's game, would have fitted into any forward-line superbly well. He was strong and determined, two-footed, and could unleash a powerful shot and wasn't bad with his head either. Born in Stoke-on-Trent on 11 March 1926, he was a pupil at Hanley High School and played junior football for the Packmoor Boys Club – and it was from here that he was signed by Wolverhampton Wanderers during the early part of World War Two. With the hostilities in full flow, he was loaned out to nearby Walsall and he also guested for Port Vale v Stoke at The Victoria Ground on 5 May 1946 when the Vale were beaten 6-0. Wilshaw returned to Molineux in 1949 to score a hat-trick on his League debut against Newcastle United, lining up in the number-11 shirt. Indeed, during his long association with Wolves he played in four front-line positions, outside-right being the odd one out. Wilshaw established himself in the Wanderers' first team in 1952 and two years later was a key member of the team which landed the First Division championship. Wilshaw went on to score 117 goals in 232 first-team matches for Wolves – and he also collected two 'B' and 12 full England caps, netting four goals in an emphatic 7-2 win over Scotland at Wembley in April 1955. He moved from Molineux to Stoke in December 1957 and was a vital cog in the forward-line for four years before breaking a leg against Newcastle United in an FA Cup-tie in 1961. It was ironic that he should play his first and last senior game of his career against the Geordies for he was forced to retire after that injury. He scored exactly 50 goals in 108 games for the Potters, and on leaving the club he concentrated on his profession as a schoolteacher, rising to the Head of Service and Community Studies at Crewe and Alsager College. He attended games regularly at The Victoria Ground right up until 1994.

WILSON, Charles

Born Atherstone, Warwickshire on 30 March 1897, Wilson was a prolific marksman, one of the best Stoke have ever signed. He netted 118 goals in 167 League and FA Cup appearances for the club over a period of five years between March 1926 and May 1931. He was initially a reserve-team player with Coventry City before joining Tottenham Hotspur during the latter stages of World War One. He scored 48 goals in 80 first-class games for the Londoners – including a hat-trick against South Shields when making his League debut on 20 September 1919 – before leaving White Hart Lane for Huddersfield Town in 1923. Initially he played under the great Herbert Chapman at Leeds Road and top-scored for the Terriers in 1923-24 and 1925-26, helping them win the First Division championship in successive seasons. After netting 57 goals in 99 League games for Town he left Leeds Road for Stoke, his services being acquired on transfer deadline day in 1926. He hit three precious relegation-saving goals for Stoke at the end of that campaign and thereafter went from strength to strength, rattling in goals from all angles, including a record 37 in 44 games in 1927-28. He helped the Potters win the Third Division North title and was, in fact, leading scorer for the team in four of the five full seasons he spent at The Vic. Very powerful, he was difficult to knock off the ball and when in sight of the goal-frame he always tried a shot. In his League career Wilson struck 194 goals in 310 appearances – a fine record. He left Stoke for Stafford Rangers and at the same time took over as licensee of the Doxey Arms in walking distance of the Rangers' ground. He moved from Stafford to Atherstone, and also assisted Wrexham, Shrewsbury Town and Alfreton Town, before retiring in 1938. He later became mine host of the Noah's Ark (in Stafford) and he died in the town c.1971.

NB: During the 1918-19 wartime season, Wilson played in six games for Spurs. In four he used the name of C.Williams (and described as a 'colt from the Midlands'); in another the pseudonym of C.Forshaw and in only one did he call himself Charlie Wilson.

WILSON, Dennis James

Wilson played in both full-back and centre-half positions for the Potters, and despite being only 5ft 9ins tall he was always a match for the bigger and stronger opponents. Born in Bebbington on 30 April 1936, he was recruited from Rhyl in August 1959, having earlier assisted Wrexham (1954-55). He played in 18 League games for Stoke, up to May 1961 when he left The Victoria Ground to sign for Bangor City on a free transfer.

WILSON, Edward James

Ted Wilson played at inside-left for Stoke in the first-ever FA Cup-tie against Manchester in November 1883, this being his only senior appearance for the club. Born in Fenton in December 1855, he served with Stoke from August 1882 to April 1884 and during that period played in a number of friendly matches.

WILSON, Ronald

Born in Edinburgh on 6 September 1941, 'Chunky' Wilson played for Tynecastle Athletic and Musselburgh Athletic before joining Stoke City as a full-back in August 1959. He spent five years at The Victoria Ground, acting as reserve to Tony Allen, and was given just 11 League outings by the club before moving to neighbours Port Vale in November 1963 for £6,000. He went on to make 264 League appearances for the Valiants and later served in South Africa with Hellenic FC of Cape Town (from 1971).

WIMBLEDON

Stoke's playing record against the Dons is:

Venue	P	W	D	L	F	A
Home	1	0	1	0	0	0
Away	1	0	0	1	0	1
Totals	2	0	1	1	0	1

These two matches were played in 1985-86 (Division Two). Just over 6,700 fans saw the game at Stoke and there were 5,959 present for the return fixture at Plough Lane on the last day of the season.

Players with both clubs: Gary Brooke and goalkeepers Hans Segers and Peter Shilton. Verdi Godwin was a Stoke player who later scouted for the Dons.

Robbie Earle was a junior with Stoke before embarking on his professional career with Port Vale (1982) and then Wimbledon.

WINSTANLEY, Ira William

Full-back Winstanley was at The Victoria Ground for the six seasons leading up to World War Two. Initially understudy to Bob McGrory, he went on to appear in 53 first-team games as well as skippering the Reserves in 1937-38. Winstanley was born in Manchester on 26 October 1906 and was signed (after a trial) from the Cheshire League side, Altrincham in August 1933. He left Stoke and returned home to sign for Trafford Park in the summer of 1939, but did not play football after the war.

WOLVERHAMPTON WANDERERS

Stoke's playing record against fellow founder members of the Football League Wolves is:

Football League

Venue	P	W	D	L	F	A
Home	61	31	11	19	105	75
Away	61	12	14	35	67	123
Totals	122	43	25	54	172	198

FA Cup

Venue	P	W	D	L	F	A
Home	1	0	1	0	2	2
Away	7	0	0	7	3	23
Totals	8	0	1	7	3	25

Anglo Italian Cup

Venue	P	W	D	L	F	A
Away	1	0	1	0	3	3

5-1 is the best League win recorded by either club. Stoke's came in December 1904 at The Victoria Ground when Arthur Capes scored a hat-trick, while Wolves achieved theirs at Molineux in February 1926, when Tom Phillipson netted twice and had two more efforts disallowed.

Scotsman Billy Dickson hit a hat-trick in Stoke's 4-1 League win over Wolves in November 1895 and fellow countryman Willie Maxwell scored all three goals when Wolves were beaten 3-0 in the Potteries in December 1900.

Paul Maguire claimed all Stoke's goals (two of them penalties) in a memorable 4-0 last-match victory over relegated Wolves in a First Division match at The Victoria Ground in May 1984.

In a fine Second Division encounter at Stoke in December 1928, the Potters earned a 4-3 victory before 9,000 fans, Charlie Wilson (2) leading the charge for City. Wilf Chadwick figured on the scoresheet for Wolves and at the end of the season he moved to Stoke.

One of Stoke's best away performances against Wolves saw them win 4-1 at Molineux in an Endsleigh League Division One game in October 1995. A crowd of 26,483 witnessed goals from Nigel Gleghorn, Graham Potter (with his first for the club), Ray Wallace and Martin Carruthers

In 1890 Stoke lost 4-0 to Wolves in an away third qualifying round tie but then protested about the state of the heavy, uneven pitch. Wolves had no complaints, nor did they worry about the enforced replay as they doubled their account and hammered the Potters 8-0 with Jack Brodie scoring five times.

A crowd of over 55,592 saw Wolves beat Stoke 3-0 at Molineux in the first season after World War Two.

Players with both clubs: Arthur Arrowsmith, Tom Baddeley, Charlie Baker, Scott Barrett, George Berry, Wilf Chadwick, Eddie Clamp, Harry Davies, Alan Dodd, Keith Downing, James Gorman, Arthur Hartshorne, Kevin Keen, Norman Lewis, Jim Martin, Jack Miller, Derek Parkin, Valentine Rouse, Ken Scattergood, Jack Short, Brian Siddall, Sammy Smyth, Tim Steele, Ed Steventon, Eddie Stuart, Billy Tompkinson, Mark Walters, Harry Watson (a Wolves junior), Bob White, Jack Whitehouse and Dennis Wilshaw.

Frank Taylor played for Wolves before managing Stoke; Richie Barker managed both clubs as well as being an assistant manager at Molineux, and Sammy Chung was manager at Molineux and assistant manager at Stoke. Brian Caswell was a player with Wolves who later became reserve-team coach with Stoke, while Bill Asprey was a player and later manager of Stoke who coached at Molineux in the late 1970s.

WOLVERHAMPTON WANDERERS RESERVES

Stoke played Wolves' second string in six Birmingham & District League games Between 1908 and 1911 the details of which were:

Venue	P	W	D	L	F	A
Home	3	2	0	1	9	4
Away	3	1	1	1	5	5
Totals	6	3	1	2	14	9

Stoke's best win was 6-0 at home in November 1910 when Jack Peart scored a hat-trick.

WOOD, Alfred Josiah Edward

Born at Smallthorne in June 1876, and a former pupil at Stoke-on-Trent Council School, Wood joined the playing staff at The Victoria Ground in October 1895 at the age of 18 from neighbours Port Vale having started out with his local team, Smallthorne Albion. A very capable half-back with a fair degree of skill, he went on to score ten goals in 134 League and Cup appearances for the Potters before transferring to Aston Villa in March 1901. He added another 111 senior appearances to his tally while at Villa Park and later in his career had spells with Derby County (from May 1905) and Bradford Park Avenue (from May 1907), before retiring through injury in June 1908. Wood helped Villa to runners-up spot in the First Division in 1903. He died in May 1919.

WOODALL, Arthur J.

Stoke signed Woodall from Tunstall Park in 1950. A outside-left with pace and strong shot, his chances were limited at the club and he only managed one League outing before moving to Altrincham in 1954. Woodall was born in the Potteries on 4 June 1930.

WOODS, Samuel B.

Stoke gambled when they brought Scottish inside-forward Woods down from Morton in October 1896. Born in Glasgow in February 1871, he never really fitted into the team's style of play and returned Morton after just one League game for the Potters.

WOODWARD, John

Another player signed from Tunstall Park, utility forward Woodward started his Stoke career in 1964, He struggled to get first-team football and scored once in 11 outings for the club before transferring to Aston Villa for £30,000 in October 1966. He later played for Walsall, Port Vale, Scunthorpe United and VG Ostende (Belgium). In his career Woodward, who was born in Tunstall on 16 October 1947 and suffered his fair share of injuries, including a broken leg, made well over 400 senior appearances and netted over 80 goals

WOOTTON, Harold

Half-back Wootton played in just one League game for Stoke and 133 for Crewe Alexandra. Born in Hanley in July 1896, he had two spells with Stafford Rangers, either side his one season at The Victoria Ground (1919-20). He later became a trainer with Port Vale.

WOOTTON, William

Born at Longton on 27 August 1904, Billy Wootton (now relation to Harry) was a capable full-back who played for Trentham, Stoke (amateur 1922) and Congleton Town before going on to make 59 appearances for Port Vale (June 1925-August 1932). He then assisted Southend United before becoming player-manager of Northwich Victoria and team boss of both Oldham Athletic (1947-50) and Halifax Town.

WORCESTER CITY

Stoke's playing record against Worcester City reads:

Birmingham & District League

Venue	P	W	D	L	F	A
Home	3	3	0	0	8	2
Away	3	0	1	2	3	10
Totals	6	3	1	2	11	12

FA Cup

Home	1	1	0	0	7	0

Stoke's best League win was 3-0 (home) in February 1909, while their heaviest defeat has been 5-1 (away) in October 1908.

The fourth qualifying round FA Cup-tie took place in November 1910 and in-form Amos Baddeley scored a hat-trick.

Striker Keith Bertschin, goalkeeper Wilf Hall and full-back Eddie Stuart are among the handful of players who have served with both clubs. Stuart also managed Worcester (1970-71).

WORKINGTON

Players with both clubs: Dave Goodwin and John Ruggiero. Brian Doyle, a Stoke player later managed Workington.

WORDLEY, Edward Henry

Wordley played in 10 League games as a half-back or inside-left for Stoke during a brief spell at the club immediately after World War Two. Born in Stoke on 17 October 1923, he signed for the club during the hostilities and turned professional on the resumption of competitive football in 1946. He left The Victoria Ground for Bury in June 1950 but failed to make any appearances for the Shakers' slipping into non-League circles in 1951.

WORSDALE, Michael John

Four appearances was all outside-right Worsdale made for Stoke City during an eight-year association with the club (1963-71). Born in Stoke on 29 October 1948, he later netted nine goals in 57 League games for Lincoln City before drifting out of League football to play, in turn, for Worksop Town (from August 1974), Gainsborough Trinity (July 1976) and Skegness Town (June 1977). He later worked in a sports centre in Lincoln.

WORTHINGTON, Nigel

Northern Ireland international left-back who was signed on a free transfer form Leeds United in the summer of 1996 to replace Lee Sandford (sold to Sheffield United). Prior to joining the Potters, Worthington had appeared in 82 games for Notts County (1981-84), 417 for Sheffield Wednesday, with whom he won a League Cup winners' medal in 1991 and 55 for Leeds. He had also been capped 64 times by Northern Ireland and during his first season at The Victoria Ground, he pushed that tally further towards the 70 mark. Besides wearing the number-three shirt, Worthington has also played in midfield and on occasion at the heart of the defence. Born in Ballymena on 4 November 1961, he was an Irish League player with his home-town club before going to Meadow Lane for £100,000. His move to Hillsborough cost the Owls £125,000 and Leeds boss Howard Wilkinson splashed out £325,000 for his services. A steady, no-nonsense player, he has a sweet left foot and always enjoys a flourish down the flank when the opportunity presents itself. Worthington scored once in 15 games for Stoke.

WREXHAM

Stoke's full playing record against Wrexham is:

Football League

Venue	P	W	D	L	F	A
Home	2	2	0	0	5	0
Away	2	2	0	0	7	2
Totals	4	4	0	0	12	2

Birmingham & District League

Venue	P	W	D	L	F	A
Home	3	3	0	0	13	4
Away	3	1	0	2	4	10
Totals	6	4	0	2	17	14

FA Cup

Venue	P	W	D	L	F	A
Home	1	1	0	0	2	1

League Cup

Venue	P	W	D	L	F	A
Home	1	1	0	0	1	0
Away	1	1	0	0	1	0
Totals	2	2	0	0	2	0

Autoglass Trophy

Venue	P	W	D	L	F	A
Away	1	1	0	0	2	0

Stoke's best win of the eight they've recorded over Wrexham to date, is 6-2 at home in a Southern League game in November 1910 when Jack Peart scored twice and made another two. The attendance was 7,500.

Stoke's heaviest defeat is 1-7 (away) also in the Southern League in March 1911.

In fact, all six Southern League meetings between the clubs produced goals with 31 being scored for an average of just over five per 90 minutes of football.

The two League Cup games were played in season 1985-86 and Keith Bertschin was Stoke's scorer in each match.

Kevin Russell and Paul Ware scored for the holders, Stoke, in that 2-0 AGT win at The Racecourse Ground in December 1992.

Players with both clubs: Matt Burton, Billy Cope, Bill Dickie, Peter Fox, David Gregory, Arthur Griffiths, Harry Holt, Harry Hutsby, Jock Kirkby, Sam McAllister, Hugh McMahon, Jack Moorwood, Mel Pejic, Harry Pugh, Colin Russell, Kevin Rooster Russell, Robbie Savage, Ronnie Sinclair, Alf Smith, Mickey Thomas, Bob Whittingham, Charlie Wilson and Dennis Wilson.

Kevin Russell scored a dramatic last minute winner for Wrexham against Premiership side West Ham United in a third-round FA Cup replay at Upton Park in January 1997.

Peter Jackson was a Stoke player who later managed Wrexham. Bobby Roberts managed Wrexham from 1982 to 1985 and was also coach at Stoke City.

WRIGHT, Ian Matthew

Reserve centre-half, well over six feet tall and born in Lichfield on 10 March 1972, Wright was given just nine outings by Stoke during the early 1990s. He joined the club as a junior in 1988, turned professional two years later and after a loan spell with Corby Town, moved to Bristol Rovers for £25,000 in September 1993.

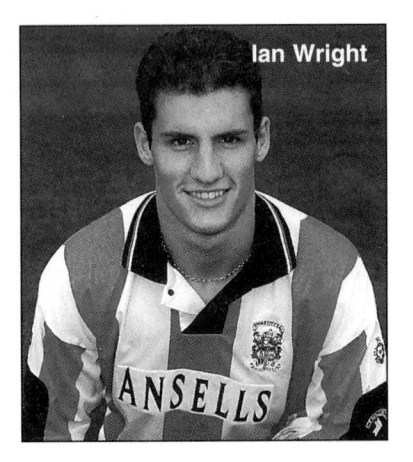

WYCOMBE WANDERERS

Stoke have yet to play the Wanderers in a competitive game, although the sides did meet in a friendly in Wycombe in 1906-07.

Players with both clubs: Viv Busby, Freddie Rouse, Keith Scott and John Williams.

YATES, Jack

Yates made one FA Cup appearance for Stoke, lining up at inside-right in the club's first-ever game in the competition v Manchester in November 1883. He was born in Stoke in July 1896 and joined the Potters from Stone WM in August 1883 and left for Sandbach Ramblers the following May.

YORK CITY

Stoke have yet to play the Minstermen in League Football. However, there has been one FA Cup meeting involving the two clubs, a third-round tie played at Bootham Crescent in January 1969. On a chilly afternoon and in front of an 11,129 crowd, the Potters went through to the next round with a 2-0 scoreline 2-0, winger Harry Burrows hitting both goals.

Players with both clubs: Harry Brough, Viv Busby, Johnny Eyres, Sean Haselgrave, Sam Johnson, Roger Jones, Dave McAughtrie and Mark Prudhoe. Denis Smith played for Stoke and later managed York, having Busby as his assistant at Bootham Crescent. Walter Gould played for York and was later coach and then assistant manager at Stoke.

YOUNGER, Thomas

Born in Edinburgh on 10 April 1930, goalkeeper Younger played his early football for Hutchison Vale FC and during World War Two represented the BAOR XI when serving with the Royal Scots Greys in Germany. After the hostilities he signed for Hibernian, with whom he gained the first of his 24 full caps for Scotland plus two League championship winning medals (1951 and 1952) and a Scottish Cup runners-up medal. He moved to Liverpool in June 1956 for £9,000 and spent almost three years at Anfield, gaining further international honours as well as representing the Football League and appearing in 127 senior matches for the Reds. In June 1959 when he was transferred to Falkirk (in exchange for Bert Slater). He was appointed player-manager by the Scottish club, but in February 1960 Younger retired with a severe back problem. Surprisingly, the following month, he was recruited by Stoke City – ironically after Geoff Hickson had conceded five goals in a League game at Anfield. An agile and dependable goalkeeper, ever alert with good reflexes and a clean pair of hands, Younger played in 10 Second Division games for Stoke, before being replaced by Irishman Jimmy O'Neill for the 1960-61 season, although he remained at The Vic until September 1961 when he signed for Leeds United. He played for the Elland Road club until October 1962, making a further 37 League appearances. On retiring (second time round) he acted as a scout at Elland Road prior to taking a coaching position with Toronto City (Canada). In October 1969 he returned to Scotland to become public relations officer of Hibernian and later joined the board of directors at Easter Road when a successful businessman, working a s a partner in a vending machine firm. At the time of his death on 13 January 1984, Younger was president of the Scottish Football League.

YOUTH CUP

Stoke City first entered the FA Youth Cup in 1952-53 when they were beaten 7-0 in the second round by West Bromwich Albion at The Hawthorns. This is Stoke's heaviest defeat to date in the competition.

They did not compete the following year, but in their second match – at the start of 1954-55 – they crushed Kidderminster Harriers 14-1 at home, still their best-ever win in the tournament. The Potters went on to reach the semi-final stage that term only to lose over two legs to West Brom.

Stoke's youngsters again reached the semi-final stage in 1960-61, beaten by Everton, and in 1983-84 they went one better by claiming their place in the Final. Here they again came face to face with Everton who won the trophy 4-2 on aggregate.

Stoke fielded this team in both legs of the Final: Dawson; Williams, Hemming; Callaghan, Howells, Parkin; Mountford, O'Neill, Chapman, Sutton and Johns. Sub: Shaw.

Howells and Sutton scored the goals in the 2-2 draw at Goodison Park before the Merseysiders won 2-0 at The Victoria Ground in the return leg.

This is Stoke's full record in FA Youth Cup: 1952-97 inclusive:

Venue	P	W	D	L	F	A
	129	67	18	44	252	193

ZENITH DATA SYSTEMS CUP

Venue	P	W	D	L	F	A
Home	2	1	1*	0	4	3

Stoke played Bradford City and Leeds United, both at home in this competition in 1989-90. Goals by George Berry (penalty) and Dave Bamber earned the Potters a 2-1 victory over the Bantams. And after battling out a 2-2 draw with Leeds, Stoke eventually lost 5-4 on penalties*.